# Microeconomics
## for Today

## FIFTH EDITION

 # Irvin B. Tucker
### University of North Carolina
### Charlotte

THOMSON
™
SOUTH-WESTERN

Australia · Brazil · Canada · Mexico · Singapore · Spain · United Kingdom · United States

THOMSON
SOUTH-WESTERN

*Microeconomics for Today,* **Fifth Edition**
Irvin B. Tucker

**VP/Editorial Director:**
Jack W. Calhoun

**Editor-in-Chief:**
Alex von Rosenberg

**Senior Acquisitions Editor:**
Steve Scoble

**Developmental Editor:**
Michael Guendelsberger

**Senior Marketing Manager:**
John Carey

**Marketing Communications Manager:**
Sarah Greber

**Content Project Manager:**
Amy Hackett

**Manager, Editorial Media:**
John Barans

**Technology Project Manager:**
Dana Cowden

**Senior Manufacturing Coordinator:**
Sandee Milewski

**Marketing Coordinator:**
Courtney Wolstoncroft

**Editorial Assistant:**
Jessica Hartman

**Production House:**
Lachina Publishing Services

**Printer:**
R.R. Donnelley
Willard Manufacturing Division

**Art Director:**
Michelle Kunkler

**Cover and Internal Designer:**
Lou Ann Thesing

**Cover Image:**
© Stephanie Carter—Images.com

**Photography Manager:**
Deanna Ettinger

**Photo Researcher:**
Charlotte Goldman

Library of Congress Control
Number: 2006936652

For more information about our
products, contact us at:

Thomson Learning Academic
Resource Center

1-800-423-0563

Thomson Higher Education
5191 Natorp Boulevard
Mason, OH 45040
USA

# Brief Contents

# Contents

© Photodisc/Getty Images

© Photodisc/Getty Images

© Photodisc/Getty Images

## The Three Versions of This Book

| Economics for Today | | Economics for Today | Microconomics for Today | Macroconomics for Today |
|---|---|:---:|:---:|:---:|
| 1 | Introducing the Economic Way of Thinking | X | X | X |
| 2 | Production Possibilities, Opportunity Cost, and Economic Growth | X | X | X |
| 3 | Market Demand and Supply | X | X | X |
| 4 | Markets in Action | X | X | X |
| 5 | Price Elasticity of Demand and Supply | X | X | |
| 6 | Consumer Choice Theory | X | X | |
| 7 | Production Costs | X | X | |
| 8 | Perfect Competition | X | X | |
| 9 | Monopoly | X | X | |
| 10 | Monopolistic Competition and Oligopoly | X | X | |
| 11 | Labor Markets | X | X | |
| 12 | Income Distribution, Poverty, and Discrimination | X | X | |
| 13 | Antitrust and Regulation | X | X | |
| 14 | Environmental Economics | X | X | |
| 15 | Gross Domestic Product | X | | X |
| 16 | Business Cycles and Unemployment | X | | X |
| 17 | Inflation | X | | X |
| 18 | The Keynesian Model | X | | X |
| 19 | The Keynesian Model in Action | X | | X |
| 20 | Aggregate Demand and Supply | X | | X |
| 21 | Fiscal Policy | X | | X |
| 22 | The Public Sector | X | | X |
| 23 | Federal Deficits, Surpluses, and the National Debt | X | | X |
| 24 | Money and the Federal Reserve System | X | | X |
| 25 | Money Creation | X | | X |
| 26 | Monetary Policy | X | | X |
| 27 | The Phillips Curve and Expectations Theory | X | | X |
| 28 | International Trade and Finance | X | X | X |
| 29 | Economies in Transition | X | X | X |
| 30 | Growth and the Less-Developed Countries | X | X | X |

Note: Chapter numbers refer to the complete book, *Economics for Today*

Irvin B. Tucker has over twenty-five years of experience teaching introductory economics at the University of North Carolina Charlotte and the University of South Carolina. He earned his B.S. in Economics at N.C. State University and his M.A. and Ph.D. in economics from the University of South Carolina. Dr. Tucker is former director of the Center for Economic Education at the University of North Carolina Charlotte and longtime member of the National Council on Economic Education. He is recognized for his ability to relate basic principles to economic issues and public policy. His work has received national recognition by being awarded the Meritorious Levy Award for Excellence in Private Enterprise Education, the Federation of Independent Business Award for Postsecondary Educator of the Year in Entrepreneurship and Economic Education, and the Freedom Foundation's George Washing Medal for Excellence in Economic Education. In addition, his research has been published in numerous professional journal articles on a wide range of topics including industrial organization, entrepreneurship, and economics of education. Dr. Tucker is also the author of the highly successful *Survey of Economics*, fifth edition, a text for the one-semester principles of economics courses, published by South-Western Publishing. Also, Dr. Tucker has coauthored, with Professor Allan Layton and Tim Robins of Queensland University of Technology, a one-semester edition of *Economics for Today* for Australia, New Zealand, and Southeast Asia, published by Thomson Learning Australia.

## Text with a Mission

The purpose of *Economics for Today,* fifth edition, is to teach, in an engaging style, the basic operations of the U.S. economy to students who will take a two-term economics course. Rather than taking an encyclopedic approach to economic concepts, *Economics for Today* focuses on the most important tool in economics—supply and demand analysis—and applies it to clearly explain real world economic issues.

Every effort has been made to make *Economics for Today* the most "student friendly" text on the market. This text was written because so many others expose students to a confusing array of economic analyses that force students to simply memorize in order to pass the course. Instead, *Economics for Today* presents a straightforward and unbiased approach that effectively teaches the application of basic economic principles. After reading this text, the student should be able to say "now that economics stuff in the news makes sense."

## How It Fits Together

The text presents the core principles of microeconomics, macroeconomics, and international economics. The first 14 chapters introduce the logic of economic analysis and develop the core of microeconomic analysis. Here students learn the role of demand and supply in determining prices in competitive versus monopolistic markets. This part of the book explores such issues as minimum wage laws, rent control, and pollution. The next 13 chapters develop the macroeconomics part of the text. Using the modern, yet simple, aggregate demand and aggregate supply model, the text explains measurement of and changes in the price level, national output, and employment in the economy. The study of macroeconomics also includes how the supply of money and the demand for money influence the economy. Finally, the text concludes with three chapters devoted entirely to international issues. For example, students will learn how the supply of and demand for currencies determine exchange rates and what the complications of a strong or a weak dollar are.

## Text Flexibility

The full version of *Economics for Today* is easily adapted to an instructor's preference for the sequencing of microeconomics and macroeconomics topics. The text can be used in a macroeconomic-microeconomic sequence by teaching the first four chapters and then Parts 5 through 7. Next, microeconomics is covered in Parts 2 through 4. Finally, the course can be completed with Part 8, consisting of three chapters devoted to international economics.

An important design of this text is that it accommodates the two camps for teaching principles of macroeconomics: (1) those who cover both the Keynesian Cross and *AD/AS* models and (2) those who skip the Keynesian model and cover only the *AD/AS* model. For instructors who prefer the former model sequence, *Economics for Today* moves smoothly in Chapters 18–19 (8–9) from the Keynesian model (based on the Great Depression) to the *AD/AS* model in Chapter 20 (10). For instructors using the latter approach, this text is written so that instructors can skip the Keynesian model in Chapters 18–19 (8–9) and proceed from Chapter 17 (7) to Chapter 20 (10) without losing anything. For example, the spending multiplier is completely covered both in the Keynesian and *AD/AS* model chapters.

For instructors who wish to teach the self-correcting *AD/AS* model, emphasis can be placed on the appendixes to Chapters 20 (10) and 26 (16). Instructors who choose not to cover this model can simply skip these appendixes. In short, *Economics for Today* provides more comprehensive and flexible coverage of macroeconomics models than is available in other texts.

## How Not to Study Economics

To some students, studying economics is a little frightening because many chapters are full of graphs. Students often make the mistake of preparing for tests by trying to memorize the lines of graphs. When their graded tests are returned, the students using this strategy will probably exclaim, "What happened?" The answer to this query is that the students should have learned the economic concepts *first;* then they would understand the graphs as *illustrations* of these underlying concepts. Stated simply, superficial cramming for economics quizzes does not work.

For students who are anxious about using graphs, the appendix to Chapter 1 provides a brief review of graphical analysis. In addition, *The Graphing Workshop* and the *Study Guide* contain step-by-step features on how to interpret graphs. Both are available in ThomsonNOW for Tucker. (www.thomsonedu.com/thomsonnow)

## New to the Fifth Edition

The basic layout of the fifth edition remains the same. The following are major changes:

- Graphs added to summaries of nonprice determinants of demand and supply exhibits in Chapter 3.
- An appendix added to Chapter 3 on consumer and producer surplus.
- An Analyze the Issue titled "European trading in carbon-emissions permits" added to Chapter 14 on environmental economics.

- An exhibit added to the appendix to the aggregate demand and supply chapter that illustrates the changes in macro equilibrium over time.

- The explanation of the multiplier expanded in the chapter on fiscal policy to accommodate those instructors who wish to skip the Keynesian model.

- An exhibit added to the chapter on federal deficits, surpluses, and the national debt showing federal deficits and surpluses as a percentage of GDP over recent years.

- An exhibit added to the appendix to the chapter on monetary policy on the effect of expansionary policy and the graphical relationship between monetary policy and aggregate demand.

- An exhibit added to the chapter on international trade and finance showing the U.S. average tariff rate over time and countries with the largest trade deficits with the United States.

- The practice quiz questions at the end of each chapter were increased and sample study guide questions added. The complete study guide is now available only on ThomsonNOW for Tucker. (www.thomsonedu.com/thomsonnow)

# Motivational Pedagogical Features

*Economics for Today* strives to motivate and advance the boundaries of pedagogy with the following features:

### PART OPENERS

Each part begins with a statement of the overall mission of the chapters in the part. In addition, there is a nutshell introduction of each chapter in relation to the part's learning objective.

### CHAPTER PREVIEWS

Each chapter begins with a preview designed to pique the student's interest and reinforce how the chapter fits into the overall scheme of the book. Each preview appeals to the student's "Sherlock Holmes" impulses by posing several economics puzzles that can be solved by understanding the material presented in the chapter.

### MARGIN DEFINITIONS

Key concepts introduced in the chapter are highlighted in bold type and then defined in the text and again in the margins. This feature therefore serves as a quick reference.

### CONCLUSION STATEMENTS

Throughout the chapters, highlighted conclusion statements of key concepts appear at the ends of sections and tie together the material just presented. Students will be able to see quickly if they have understood the main points of the section. A summary of these conclusion statements is provided at the end of each chapter.

## YOU'RE THE ECONOMIST

Each chapter includes boxed inserts that provide the acid test of "relevance to everyday life." This feature gives the student an opportunity to encounter timely, real-world extensions of economic theory. For example, students read about Fred Smith as he writes an economics term paper explaining his plan to create FedEx. To ensure that the student wastes no time figuring out which concepts apply to the article, applicable concepts are listed after each title. Many of these boxed features include quotes from newspaper articles over a period of years demonstrating that economics concepts remain relevant over time.

**Global Economics**

## INTERNATIONAL ECONOMICS

Today's economic environment is global. *Economics for Today* carefully integrates international topics throughout the text and presents the material using a highly readable and accessible approach designed for students with no training in international economics. All sections of the text that present international economics are identified by a special global icon in the text margin and in the International Economics boxes. In addition, the final three chapters of the book are devoted entirely to international economics.

## ANALYZE THE ISSUE

This feature follows each *You're the Economist* and *International Economics* feature and asks specific questions that require students to test their knowledge of how the material in the boxed insert is relevant to the applicable concept. To allow these questions to be used in classroom discussions or homework assignments, answers are provided in the Instructor's Manual rather than the text.

## CHECKPOINT

Watch for these! Who said learning economics can't be fun? This feature is a unique approach to generating interest and critical thinking. These questions spark students to check their progress by asking challenging economics puzzles in game-like style. Students enjoy thinking through and answering the questions, and then checking the answers at the end of the chapter. Students who answer correctly earn the satisfaction of knowing they have mastered the concepts.

## ILLUSTRATIONS

Attractive large graphical presentations with grid lines and real-world numbers are essential for any successful economics textbook. Each exhibit has been carefully analyzed to ensure that the key concepts being represented stand out clearly. Brief descriptions are included with graphs to provide guidance for students as they study the graph. When actual data are used, the Web site reference is provided so that students can easily locate the data source.

## CAUSATION CHAINS

This will be one of your favorites. The highly successful causation chains are included under many graphs throughout the text. This pedagogical device helps students visualize complex economic relationships in terms of simple box diagrams that illustrate how one change causes another change. The Animated Causation Chains game on ThomsonNOW makes it fun to learn. Arrange the blocks correctly and hear the cheers.

## KEY CONCEPTS

Key concepts introduced in the chapter are listed at the end of each chapter and on the Tucker Web site (www.thomsonedu.com/economics/tucker). As a study aid, you can use the key concepts as flashcards to test your knowledge. First state the definition and then click on the term to check for correctness.

## VISUAL SUMMARIES

Each chapter ends with a brief point-by-point summary of the key concepts. Many of these summarized points include miniaturized versions of the important graphs and causation chains that illustrate many of the key concepts. These are intended to serve as visual reminders for students as they finish the chapters and are also useful in reviewing and studying for quizzes and exams.

## STUDY QUESTIONS AND PROBLEMS

The end-of-chapter questions and problems offer a variety of levels ranging from straightforward recall to deeply thought-provoking applications. The answers to odd questions and problems are in the back of the text. This feature gives students immediate feedback without requiring the instructor to check their work.

## STUDY GUIDE QUESTIONS

A sample of study guide questions illustrates the type of questions in the complete Study Guide available at www.thomsonedu.com/thomsonnow.

## END-OF-CHAPTER PRACTICE QUIZZES

A great help before quizzes. Many instructors test students using multiple-choice questions. For this reason, the final section of each chapter provides the type of multiple-choice questions given in the instructor's Test Bank. The answers to all of these questions are given in the back of the text. In addition, students may visit the Tucker Web site (www.thomsonedu.com/economics/tucker) and then click the tutorial to obtain a visual explanation of each correct answer. Here students can actually see the graphs shift as arrows point to key changes in prices, output and other key variables.

## ONLINE EXERCISES

These exercises are designed to spark students' excitement about researching on the Internet by asking them to access economic data and then answer questions related to the content of the chapter. All Internet exercises are on the Tucker Web site (www.thomsonedu.com/economics/tucker) with direct links to the addresses so that students will not have the tedious and error-prone task of entering long Web site addresses.

### INTERNET LINKS

Visit the Tucker Web site, www.thomsonedu.com/economics/tucker, and find up-to-date links pertaining to relevant topics on the subject matter. These addresses provide students with access to specific content and real-world application. There's no need to type in the links; they're a mere click away!

# A Supplements Package Designed for Success

To learn more about the supplements for *Economics for Today,* visit the Tucker Web site, www.thomsonedu.com/economics/tucker. For additional information, contact your Thomson South-Western sales representative.

# Instructor Resources

### INSTRUCTOR'S MANUAL

This manual, prepared by Douglas Copeland of Johnson County Community College, provides valuable course assistance to instructors. It includes chapter outlines, instructional objectives, critical thinking/group discussion questions, hints for effective teaching, answers to the Analyze the Issue questions, answers to even-numbered questions and problems, and summary quizzes with answers. Instructor's Manual ISBN: 0-324-35952-7.

### TEST BANKS

Prepared by the text author to match the text, the Test Bank (micro and macro versions) includes over 8,000 multiple-choice, true-false, and short essay questions. The questions are arranged by the order presented in the chapter and are grouped with concept headings that make it easy to select questions. Most questions have been thoroughly tested in the classroom by the author and are classified by topic and degree of difficulty. Text page references help locate pages where material related to the question is explained. Microeconomics Test Bank ISBN: 0-324-35941-1. Macroeconomics Test Bank ISBN: 0-324-35963-2.

### EXAMVIEW

ExamView Computerized Testing Software contains all of the questions in the printed *Test Bank*. ExamView is an easy-to-use test creation software compatible with both Microsoft Windows and Apple Macintosh. Instructors can add or edit questions, instructions, and answers; select questions by previewing them on the screen; or you can select them randomly or by number. Instructors can also create and administer quizzes online, whether over the Internet, a local area network

(LAN), or a wide area network (WAN). Available only on the Instructor's Resource CD. Microeconomics ExamView ISBN: 0-324-35944-6. Macroeconomics ExamView ISBN: 0-324-35965-9.

## POWERPOINT LECTURE SLIDES

This state-of-the-art slide presentation provides instructors with visual support in the classroom for each chapter. The package includes two sets of slides: "Lecture Slides," which contain vivid highlights of important concepts; and "Exhibit Slides," which illustrate concepts from the text. Instructors can edit the Power-Point presentations or create their own exciting in-class presentations. These slides are available on the Instructor's Resource CD as well as for downloading from the Tucker Web site at www.thomsonedu.com/economics/tucker.

## INSTRUCTOR'S RESOURCE CD-ROM

Get quick access to all instructor ancillaries from your desktop. This easy-to-use CD lets you review, edit, and copy exactly what you need in the format you want. This supplement contains the Instructor's Manual, Test Bank, Examview Testing software, and the PowerPoint presentation slides. IRCD ISBN: 0-324-54529-3.

## TRANSPARENCY ACETATES

Transparency Acetates are available by request. Please contact your Thomson South-Western sales representative.

# Student Resources

## STUDY GUIDE

The *Study Guide* is recommended for each student using the text. It is perhaps the best way to prepare for quizzes. Too often, study guides are not written by the author, and the material does not really fit the text. Not so here. The *Study Guide* was prepared by the text author to prepare students before they take tests in class. The *Study Guide* contains student-friendly features such as the chapter in a nutshell, key concepts review, learning objectives, fill-in-the-blank questions, step-by-step interpretation of the graph boxes, multiple-choice questions, true-false questions, and crossword puzzles. The Study Guide is available exclusively in ThomsonNOW for Tucker. (www.thomsonedu.com/thomsonnow)

## HOMEWORK SETS

These sets of exercises, prepared by William Weber of Eastern Illinois University, review economic concepts presented in the text. They can be given as homework assignments or used by students to practice for exams. Answers are found in the Instructor's Manual. Available on the Tucker Web site at www.thomsonedu.com/economics/tucker.

## ThomsonNOW for Tucker!

Access to ThomsonNOW for Tucker (www.thomsonedu.com/thomsonnow) is available for purchase with the textbook. This product offers a robust set of multimedia learning tools, including:

- **Integrated Text.** A printable online version of the entire text.
- **Pre- and Post-Assessment Quizzes.** These quizzes automatically generate a personalized learning plan for each student. They can evaluate their knowledge and assess their comprehension once they've learned the subject.
- **Algorithmic Questions.** Select exercises and problems can be algorithmically modified to create unlimited versions for practice or testing.
- **The Graphing Workshop.** The Graphing Workshop is a one-stop learning resource for help in mastering the language of graphs, one of the more difficult aspects of an economics course for many students. It enables students to explore important economic concepts through a unique learning system made up of tutorials, interactive drawing tools, and exercises that teach how to interpret, reproduce, and explain graphs.
- **ABC News Video Segments.** ABC video segments bring the "real world" right to students' desktops. The ABC News videos illustrate how economics is an important part of students' daily lives and help them learn the material by applying it to current events.
- **Ask the Instructor Video Clips.** Via streaming video, difficult concepts are explained and illustrated. These video clips are extremely helpful review and clarification tools if a student has trouble understanding an in-class lecture or is a visual learner.
- **InfoTrac College Edition.** With InfoTrac College Edition, journals like *Business Week, Fortune,* and *Forbes* are just a click away! InfoTrac College Edition provides students with anytime, anywhere access to 20 years' worth of full-text articles (**more than 10 million!**) from nearly **4,000** scholarly and popular sources. In addition to receiving the latest business news as reported in the popular business press, students also have access to many other journals, including those that are particularly valuable to the economic discipline—including the *Economist, U.S. American Economist, Economic Review,* and *Quarterly Journal of Economics.*
- **Economic Applications (EconApps).** EconNews Online, EconDebate Online, and EconData Online features help to deepen students' understanding of the theoretical concepts through hands-on exploration and analysis of the latest economic news stories, policy debates, and data.

# For Students and Instructors

## The Wall Street Journal

*The Wall Street Journal* is synonymous with the latest word on business, economics, and public policy. *Economics for Today* makes it easy for students to apply economic concepts to this authoritative publication, and for you to bring the most up-to-date, real world events into your classroom. For a nominal additional cost, *Economics for Today* can be packaged with a card entitling students to a 15-week subscription to both the print and online versions of *The Wall Street Journal*. Instructors with at least seven students who activate their subscriptions will automatically receive their own free subscription. Contact your Thomson South-Western sales representative for package pricing and ordering information.

## TEXTCHOICE: ECONOMIC ISSUES AND ACTIVITIES

TextChoice is the home of Thomson Learning's online digital content. TextChoice provides the fastest, easiest way for you to create your own learning materials. South-Western's Economic Issues and Activities content database includes a wide variety of high-interest, current event/policy applications as well as classroom activities that are designed specifically to enhance introductory economics courses. Choose just one reading, or many—even add your own material—to create an accompaniment to the textbook that is perfectly customized to your course. Contact your Thomson South-Western sales representative for more information.

## TUCKER WEB SITE

The Tucker Web site at www.thomsonedu.com/economics/tucker provides open access to: PowerPoint chapter review slides, Animated Causation Chains, tutorials for the text's end-of-chapter Practice Quizzes, online quizzing, direct links to the Internet Activities mentioned in the text, updates to the text, the opportunity to communicate with the author, and other downloadable teaching and learning resources.

# Acknowledgments

A deep debt of gratitude is owed to the reviewers for their expert assistance. All comments and suggestions were carefully evaluated and served to improve the final product. To each of the reviewers of all five editions, I give my sincerest thanks.

Jack E. Adams
*University of Arkansas-Little Rock*

John W. Alderson, III
*East Arkansas Community College*

Irma Alonso
*Florida International University*

Hasaan Aly
*The Ohio State University*

James Q. Aylsworth
*Lakeland Community College*

Randy Barnes
*Mirimar College*

Atin Basu
*Virginia Military Institute*

Klaus G. Becker
*Texas Tech University*

Randall W. Bennett
*Gonazaga University*

John P. Blair
*Wright State University*

Orn B. Bodvarsson
*St. Cloud State University*

Tantatape Brahmasrene
*Purdue University North Central*

Joyce Bremer
*Oakton Community College*

Anne Bresnock
*California State University, Pomona*

Stacey Brook
*University of Sioux Falls*

Juan Castro
*ETX Baptist University*

Dell Champlin
*Eastern Illinois University*

Doug Copeland
*Johnson County Community College*

John P. Dahlquist
*College of Alameda*

James P. D'Angelo
*University of Cininnati*

Jan L. Dauve
*University of Missouri*

Gregory J. Delemeester
*Marietta College*

Robert C. Dolan
*University of Richmond*

William Dougherty
*Carroll County Community College*

James W. Eden
*Portland Community College*

Ronald Elkins
*Central Washington University*

Tommy Eshleman
*University of Nebraska, Kearney*

John L. Ewing-Smith
*Burlington County College*

Chris Fawson
*Utah State University*

Arthur A. Fleisher, III
*Metropolitan State College of Denver*

Kaya Ford
*Northern Virginia Community College*

Arthur Friedberg
*Mohawk Valley Community College*

Scott Gabeheart
*Mesa Community College*

Linda Ghent
*Eastern Illinois Univeristy*

Cindy Gibson
*Keuka College*

J.P. Gilbert
*Mira Costa College*

Deborah Goldsmith
*City College of San Francisco*

Sanford D. Gordon
*University of South Florida*

Gary Green
*Manatee Community College*

Serge S. Grushchin
*ASA College of Advanced Technology*

Steven Hackett
*Humbolt State University*

Gail A. Hawks
*Miami Dade Community College*

Michael G. Heslop
*Northern Virginia Community College*

Yu-Mong Hsiao
*Campbell University*

R. Jack Inch
*Oakland Community College*

Hans R. Isakson
*University of Northern Iowa*

Barbara H. John
*University of Dayton*

Petur O. Jonsson
*Fayetteville State University*

Paul Jorgensen
*Linn-Benton Community College*

Louise Keely
*University of Wisconsin*

Randall G. Kesselring
*Arkansas State University*

Harry T. Kolendrianos
*Danville Community College*

William F. Kordsmeier
*University of Central Arkansas*

Margaret Landman
*Bridgewater State College*

David Latzko
*Pennsylvania State University, York*

Ralph F. Lewis
*Orange Coast College*

Stephen E. Lile
*Western Kentucky University*

Dandan Liu
*Bowling Green State University*

Melody Lo
*University of Southern Mississippi*

Thomas Maloy
*Muskegon Community College*

Dayle Mandelson
*University of Wisconsin—Stout*

Robert A. Margo
*Vanderbilt University*

Melanie Marks
*Longwood College*

Michael Marlow
*Cal Polytechnic State U-SLO*

James C. McBrearty
*University of Arizona*

Diana L. McCoy
*Truckee Meadows Community College*

Donald P. McDowell
*Florida Community College*

Fazlul Miah
*Fayetteville State University*

David S. Moewes
*Concordia College*

Margaret Moore
*Franklin University*

Marie Mora
*New Mexico State University*

Kevin J. Murphy
*Oakland University*

Jack Muryn
*University of Wisconsin—Washington County*

Lee Nordgren
*Indiana University*

Peter K. Olson
*Indiana University*

Patrick B. O'Neill
*University of North Dakota*

Jan Palmer
*Ohio University*

Michael L. Palmer
*Maple Woods Community College*

Elliott Parker
*University of Nevada in Reno*

Kathy Parkison
*Indiana University—Kokomo*

Donald W. Pearson
*Eastern Michigan University*

Martin Perline
*Wichita State University*

Maurice Pfannestiel
*Wichita State University*

L. Wayne Plumly, Jr.
*Valdosta State University*

Ray Polchow
*Muskingum Area Technical College*

Elaine Peterson
*California State University, Stanislaus*

Michael J. Pisani
*Texas A&M University*

Renee Prim
*Central Piedmont Community College*

Fernando Quijano
*Dickinson State University*

R. Larry Reynolds
*Boise State University*

Kathryn Roberts
*Chipola Junior College*

Steve Robinson
*University of North Carolina
at Wilmington*

Craig Rogers
*Canisius College*

Lawrence P. Schrenk
*University of Baltimore*

Kurt A. Schwabe
*Ohio University*

Lisa Simon
*California Polytechnic State University*

Larry Singell
*University of Oregon*

Alden W. Smith
*Anne Arundel Community College*

Tricia Snyder
*William Patterson University*

Larry Spizman
*SUNY-Oswego*

Rebecca Summary
*Southeast Missouri State University*

Daniel A. Talley
*Dakota State University*

Daryl Thorne
*Valencia Community College*

Larry Towle
*Eastern Nazarene College*

Greg Trandel
*University of Georgia*

Richard Trieff
*Des Moines Area Community College*

Tracy M. Turner
*Kansas State University*

Roy van Til
*University of Maine—Farmington*

Lee Van Scyok
*University of Wisconsin—Oshkosh*

Darlene Voeltz
*Rochester Community and Technical
College*

Rosemary Walker
*Washburn University*

Harold Warren
*East Tennessee State University*

Robert G. Welch
*Midwestern State University*

Herbert D. Werner
*University of Missouri*

Michael D. White
*St. Cloud State University*

Leo M. Weeks
*Northwestern University*

Gwen Williams
*Alvernia College*

Virginia S. York
*Gulf Coast Community College*

Paul Young
*Dodge City Community College*

Michael J. Youngblood
*Rock Valley College*

## Special Thanks

I especially wish to express my deepest appreciation to Peter Schwarz, my colleague at UNC Charlotte. Many of the ideas in the Checkpoint sections are the result of brainstorming sessions with him. Special thanks also go to Douglas Copeland of Johnson County Community College for preparing the Instructor's Manual.

My appreciation goes to Steve Scoble, Acquisitions Editor for Thomson South-Western. My thanks also to Michael Guendelsberger, Developmental Editor; Amy Hackett, Content Project Manager; Jessica Hartmann, Editorial Assistant; and Courtney Wolstoncroft, Marketing Coordinator, who put all the pieces of the puzzle together and brought their creative talent to this text. Robert Green was superb in his copyediting of the manuscript. I am also grateful to John Carey for his skillful marketing. Finally, I give my sincere thanks for a job well done to the entire team at Thomson South-Western.

# Microeconomics
## for Today

FIFTH EDITION

## Irvin B. Tucker
University of North Carolina
Charlotte

# Introduction to Economics

The first two chapters introduce you to a foundation of economic knowledge vital to understanding the other chapters in the text. In these introductory chapters, you will begin to learn a valuable reasoning approach to solving economics puzzles that economists call "the economic way of thinking." Part 1 develops the cornerstone of this type of logical analysis by presenting basic economic models that explain such important topics as scarcity, opportunity cost, production possibilities, and economic growth.

# Introducing the Economic Way of Thinking

© Photodisc/Getty Images

**W**elcome to an exciting and useful subject economists call "the economic way of thinking." As you learn this reasoning technique, it will become infectious. You will discover that the world is full of economics problems requiring more powerful tools than just common sense. As you master the methods explained in this book, you will appreciate economics as a valuable reasoning approach to solving economics puzzles. Stated differently, the economic way of thinking is important because it provides a logical framework for organizing your thoughts and understanding an economic issue or event. Just to give a sneak preview, in later chapters you will study the perils of government price-fixing for gasoline and health care. You will also find out why colleges and universities charge students different tuitions for the same education. You will investigate whether you should worry if the federal government fails to balance its budget. You will learn that the island of Yap uses large stones with holes in the center as money. In the final chapter, you will study why some countries grow rich while others remain

poor and less developed. And the list of fascinating and relevant topics continues throughout each chapter. As you read these pages, your efforts will be rewarded by an understanding of just how economic theories and policies affect our daily lives—past, present, and future.

Chapter 1 acquaints you with the foundation of the economic way of thinking. The first building blocks joined are the concepts of scarcity and choice. The next building blocks are the steps in the model-building process that economists use to study the choices people make. Then we look at some pitfalls of economic reasoning and explain why econo-

mists might disagree with one another. The chapter concludes with a discussion of why you may wish to be an economics major.

**In this chapter, you will learn to solve these economics puzzles:**

- Can you prove there is no person worth a trillion dollars?
- Why would you purchase more Coca-Cola when the price increases?
- How can we explain the relationship between the Super Bowl winner and changes in the stock market?
- What famous people majored in economics?

# The Problem of Scarcity

Our world is a finite place where people, both individually and collectively, face the problem of **scarcity**. Scarcity is the condition in which human wants are forever greater than the available supply of time, goods, and resources. Because of scarcity, it is impossible to satisfy every desire. Pause for a moment to list some of your unsatisfied wants. Perhaps you would like a big home, gourmet meals, designer clothes, clean air, better health care, shelter for the homeless, more leisure time, and so on. Unfortunately, nature does not offer the Garden of Eden, where every desire is fulfilled. Instead, there are always limits on the economy's ability to satisfy unlimited wants. Alas, scarcity is pervasive, so "You can't have it all."

You may think your scarcity problem would disappear if you were rich, but wealth does not solve the problem. No matter how affluent an individual is, the wish list continues to grow. We are familiar with the "rich and famous" who never seem to have enough. Although they live well, they still desire finer homes, faster planes, and larger yachts. In short, the condition of scarcity means all individuals, whether rich or poor, are dissatisfied with their material well-being and would like more. What is true for individuals also applies to society. Even Uncle Sam can't escape the problem of scarcity because the federal government never has enough money to spend for the poor, education, highways, police, national defense, Social Security, and all the other programs it wishes to fund.

Scarcity is a fact of life throughout the world. In much of South America, Africa, and Asia, the problem of scarcity is often life threatening. On the other hand, North America, Western Europe, and some parts of Asia have achieved substantial economic growth and development. Although life is much less grueling in the more advanced countries, the problem of scarcity still exists because individuals and countries never have as much of all the goods and services as they would like to have.

**Scarcity**
The condition in which human wants are forever greater than the available supply of time, goods, and resources.

# Scarce Resources and Production

Because of the economic problem of scarcity, no society has enough **resources** to produce all the goods and services necessary to satisfy all human wants. Resources are the basic categories of inputs used to produce goods and services. Resources are also called *factors of production*. Economists divide resources into three categories: *land, labor,* and *capital* (see Exhibit 1).

**Resources**
The basic categories of inputs used to produce goods and services. Resources are also called *factors of production*. Economists divide resources into three categories: land, labor, and capital.

## LAND

**Land** is a shorthand expression for any natural resource provided by nature. *Land* includes those resources that are gifts of nature available for use in the production process. Farming, building factories, and constructing oil refineries would be impossible without land. Land includes anything natural above or below the ground, such as forests, gold, diamonds, oil, wildlife, and fish. Other examples are rivers, lakes, seas, air, the sun, and the moon. Two broad categories of natural resources are *renewable resources* and *nonrenewable resources*. Renewable resources are basic inputs that nature can automatically replace. Examples include lakes, crops, and clean air. Nonrenewable resources are basic inputs that nature

**Land**
A shorthand expression for any natural resource provided by nature.

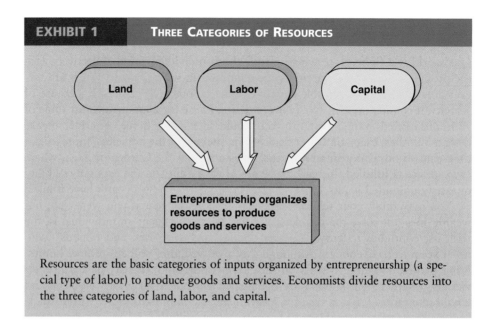

**EXHIBIT 1**     **THREE CATEGORIES OF RESOURCES**

Land       Labor       Capital

Entrepreneurship organizes
resources to produce
goods and services

Resources are the basic categories of inputs organized by entrepreneurship (a special type of labor) to produce goods and services. Economists divide resources into the three categories of land, labor, and capital.

cannot automatically replace. There is only so much coal, oil, and natural gas in the world. If these fossil fuels disappear, we must use substitutes.

## LABOR

**Labor**
The mental and physical capacity of workers to produce goods and services.

**Labor** is the mental and physical capacity of workers to produce goods and services. The services of farmers, assembly-line workers, lawyers, professional football players, and economists are all *labor*. The labor resource is measured both by the number of people available for work and by the skills or quality of workers. One reason nations differ in their ability to produce is that human characteristics, such as the education, experience, health, and motivation of workers, differ among nations.

**Entrepreneurship**
The creative ability of individuals to seek profits by taking risks and combining resources to produce innovative products.

    **Entrepreneurship** is a special type of labor. Entrepreneurship is the creative ability of individuals to seek profits by taking risks and combining resources to produce innovative products. An *entrepreneur* is a motivated person who seeks profits by undertaking such risky activities as starting new businesses, creating new products, or inventing new ways of accomplishing tasks. Entrepreneurship is a scarce human resource because relatively few people are willing or able to innovate and make decisions involving greater-than-normal chances for failure.

    Entrepreneurs are the agents of change who bring material progress to society. The birth of the Levi Strauss Company is a classic entrepreneurial success story. In 1853, at the age of 24, Levi Strauss, who was born in Bavaria, sailed from New York to join the California Gold Rush. His intent was not to dig for gold, but to sell cloth. By the time he arrived in San Francisco, he had sold most of his cloth to other people on the ship. The only cloth he had left was a roll of canvas for tents and covered wagons. On the dock, he met a miner who wanted sturdy pants that would last while digging for gold, so Levi made a pair from the canvas. Later a customer gave Levi the idea of using little copper rivets to strengthen the seams.

Presto! Strauss knew a good thing when he saw it, so he hired workers, built factories, and became one of the largest pants makers in the world. As a reward for taking business risks, organizing production, and introducing a product, the Levi Strauss Company earned profits, and Strauss became rich and famous.

## CAPITAL

**Capital** is the physical plants, machinery, and equipment used to produce other goods. Capital goods are human-made goods that do not directly satisfy human wants. Before the Industrial Revolution, *capital* meant a tool, such as a hoe, an axe, or a bow and arrow. In those days, these items served as capital to build a house or provide food for the dinner table. Today, capital also consists of factories, office buildings, warehouses, robots, trucks, and distribution facilities. College buildings, the printing presses used to produce this textbook, and pencils are also examples of capital.

   The term *capital* as it is used in the study of economics can be confusing. Economists know that capital in everyday conversations means money or the money value of paper assets, such as stocks, bonds, or a deed to a house. This is actually *financial* capital. In the study of economics, capital does not refer to money assets. Instead, capital in economics means a factor of production, such as a factory or machinery. Stated simply, you must pay special attention to this point: money is not capital and is therefore not a resource.

> **CONCLUSION** *Financial capital by itself is not productive; instead, it is only a paper claim on economic capital.*

**Capital**
The physical plants, machinery, and equipment used to produce other goods. Capital goods are human-made goods that do not directly satisfy human wants.

# Economics: The Study of Scarcity and Choice

The perpetual problem of scarcity forcing people to make choices is the basis for the definition of **economics**. Economics is the study of how society chooses to allocate its scarce resources to the production of goods and services in order to satisfy unlimited wants. You may be surprised by this definition. People often think economics means studying supply and demand, the stock market, money, and banking. In fact, there are many ways one could define *economics*, but economists accept the definition given here because it includes the link between *scarcity* and *choices*.

   Society makes two kinds of choices: economywide, or macro choices, and individual, or micro, choices. The prefixes *macro* and *micro* come from the Greek words meaning "large" and "small," respectively. Reflecting the macro and micro perspectives, economics consists of two main branches: *macroeconomics* and *microeconomics*.

**Economics**
The study of how society chooses to allocate its scarce resources to the production of goods and services in order to satisfy unlimited wants.

## MACROECONOMICS

The old saying "Looking at the forest rather than the trees" describes **macroeconomics.** Macroeconomics is the branch of economics that studies decision making for the economy as a whole. Macroeconomics applies an overview perspective to

**Macroeconomics**
The branch of economics that studies decision making for the economy as a whole.

an economy by examining economywide variables, such as inflation, unemployment, growth of the economy, the money supply, and the national incomes of developing countries. Macroeconomic decision making considers such "big picture" policies as the effect that federal tax cuts will have on unemployment and the effect that changing the money supply will have on prices.

## MICROECONOMICS

**Microeconomics**
The branch of economics that studies decision making by a single individual, household, firm, industry, or level of government.

Examining individual trees, leaves, and pieces of bark, rather than surveying the forest, illustrates **microeconomics.** Microeconomics is the branch of economics that studies decision making by a single individual, household, firm, industry, or level of government. Microeconomics applies a microscope to study specific parts of an economy, as one would examine cells in the body. The focus is on small economic units, such as economic decisions of particular groups of consumers and businesses. An example of microeconomic analysis would be to study economic units involved in the market for ostrich eggs. Will suppliers decide to supply more, less, or the same quantity of ostrich eggs to the market in response to price changes? Will individual consumers of these eggs decide to buy more, less, or the same quantity at a new price?

We have described macroeconomics and microeconomics as two separate branches, but they are related. Because the overall economy is the sum, or aggregation, of its parts, micro changes affect the macro economy, and macro changes produce micro changes.

# The Methodology of Economics

As used by other disciplines, such as criminology, biology, chemistry, and physics, economists employ a step-by-step procedure for solving problems by developing a theory, gathering data, and testing whether the data are consistent with the theory. Based on this analysis, economists formulate a conclusion. Exhibit 2 summarizes the model-building process.

## PROBLEM IDENTIFICATION

The first step in applying the economic method is to define the issue. Suppose an economist wishes to investigate the microeconomic problem of why U.S. motorists cut back on gasoline consumption in a given year from, for example, 100 billion gallons per month in September to 80 billion gallons per month in December.

## MODEL DEVELOPMENT

**Model**
A simplified description of reality used to understand and predict the relationship between variables.

The second step in our hypothetical example toward finding an explanation is for the economist to build a **model.** A model is a simplified description of reality used to understand and predict the relationship between variables. The terms *model* and *theory* are interchangeable. A model emphasizes only those variables that are most important to explaining an event. As Albert Einstein said, "Theories should be as simple as possible, but not more so." The purpose of a model is to construct an abstraction from real-world complexities and make events understandable.

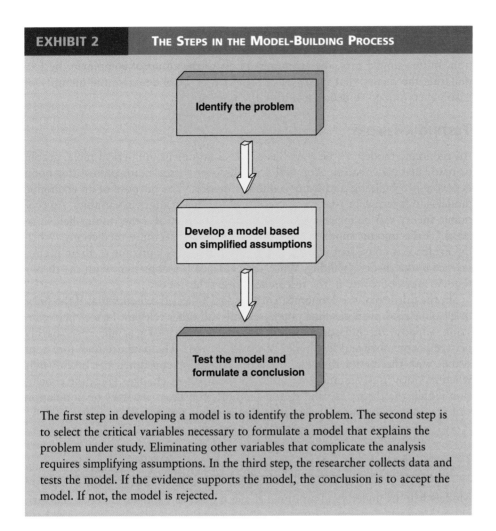

**EXHIBIT 2**          **THE STEPS IN THE MODEL-BUILDING PROCESS**

Identify the problem

Develop a model based on simplified assumptions

Test the model and formulate a conclusion

The first step in developing a model is to identify the problem. The second step is to select the critical variables necessary to formulate a model that explains the problem under study. Eliminating other variables that complicate the analysis requires simplifying assumptions. In the third step, the researcher collects data and tests the model. If the evidence supports the model, the conclusion is to accept the model. If not, the model is rejected.

Consider a model airplane that is placed in a wind tunnel to test the aerodynamics of a new design. For this purpose, the model must represent only the shapes of the wings and fuselage, but it does not need to include tiny seats, electrical wiring, or other interior design details. A highway map is another example. To find the best route to drive between two distant cities, you do not want extraneous information on the location of all roads, streets, potholes, telephone lines, trees, stoplights, schools, hospitals, and firehouses. This would be too much detail, and the complexity would make it difficult to choose the best route.

To be useful, a model requires simplified assumptions. Someone must decide, for example, whether a map will include only symbols for the major highways or the details of hiking trails through mountains. In our gasoline consumption example, several variables might be related to the quantity of gasoline consumed, including consumer incomes, the prices of goods other than gasoline, the price of gasoline, the fuel economy of cars, and weather conditions. Because a theory focuses only on the main or critical variables, the economist must be a Sherlock Holmes and use a keen sense of observation to form a model. Using his or her expertise, the economist must select the variables that are related to gasoline consumption and reject variables that have only slight or no relationship to gasoline consumption. In this simple case, the economist removes the cloud of complexity by formulating the theory that increases in the price of gasoline *cause* the quantity of gasoline consumed to decrease during the time period.

## TESTING A THEORY

An economic model can be stated as a verbal argument, numerical table, graph, or mathematical equation. You will soon discover that a major part of this book is devoted to building and using economic models. The purpose of an economic model is to *forecast*, or *predict*, the results of various changes in variables. An economic theory can be expressed in the form "If *A*, then *B*, other things held constant." An economic model is useful only if it yields accurate predictions. When the evidence is consistent with the theory that *A* causes outcome *B*, there is confidence in the theory's validity. When the evidence is inconsistent with the theory that *A* causes outcome *B*, the researcher rejects this theory.

In the third step, the economist gathers data to test the theory that if the price of gasoline rises, then gasoline purchases fall—all other relevant factors held constant. Suppose the investigation reveals that the price of gasoline rose sharply between September and December of the given year. The data are therefore consistent with the theory that the quantity of gasoline consumed per month falls when its price rises, assuming no other relevant factors change. Thus, the conclusion is that the theory is valid if, for example, consumer incomes or population size does not change at the same time that gasoline prices rise.

# Hazards of the Economic Way of Thinking

Models help us understand and predict the impact of changes in economic variables. A model is an important tool in the economist's toolkit, but it must be handled with care. The economic way of thinking seeks to avoid reasoning mistakes. Two of the most common pitfalls to clear thinking are (1) failing to understand the *ceteris paribus assumption* and (2) confusing *association* and *causation*.

## CHECKPOINT

### Can You Prove There Is No Trillion-Dollar Person?

Suppose a theory says no U.S. citizen is worth $1 trillion. You decide to test this theory and send researchers to all corners of the nation to check financial records to see whether someone qualifies by owning assets valued at $1 trillion or more. After years of checking, the researchers return and report that not a single person is worth at least $1 trillion. Do you conclude that the evidence proves the theory?

## THE CETERIS PARIBUS ASSUMPTION

As you work through a model, try to think of a host of relevant variables assumed to be "standing still," or "held constant." **Ceteris paribus** is a Latin phrase that means while certain variables change, "all other things remain unchanged." In short, the ceteris paribus assumption allows us to isolate or focus attention on selected variables. In the gasoline example discussed earlier, a key simplifying assumption of the model is that changes in consumer incomes and certain other variables do not occur and complicate the analysis. The ceteris paribus assumption holds everything else constant and therefore allows us to concentrate on the relationship between two key variables: changes in the price of gasoline and the quantity of gasoline purchased per month.

**Ceteris paribus**
A Latin phrase that means while certain variables change, "all other things remain unchanged."

Now suppose an economist examines a model explaining the relationship between the price and quantity purchased of Coca-Cola. The theory is "If the price increases, then the quantity of Coca-Cola purchased decreases, ceteris paribus." Now assume you observe that the price of Coca-Cola increased one summer and some people actually bought more, not less. Based on this real-world observation, you declare the theory is incorrect. Think again! The economist responds that this is a reasoning pitfall because the model is valid based on the assumption of ceteris paribus and your observation gives us no reason to reject the model. The reason the model appeared flawed is because another factor, a sharp rise in the temperature, *caused* people to buy more Coca-Cola in spite of its higher price. If the temperature and all other factors are held constant as the price of Coca-Cola rises, then people will indeed buy less Coca-Cola, as the model predicts.

> **CONCLUSION** *A theory cannot be tested legitimately unless its ceteris paribus assumption is satisfied.*

## ASSOCIATION VERSUS CAUSATION

Another common error in reasoning is confusing *association* (or correlation) and *causation* between variables. Stated differently, you err when you read more into a relationship between variables than is actually there. A model is valid only when a cause-and-effect relationship is stable over time, rather than being an association that occurs by chance and eventually disappears. Suppose a witch doctor performs a voodoo dance during three different months and stock market prices skyrocket during each of these months. The voodoo dance is *associated* with the increase in stock prices, but this does not mean the dance *caused* the event. Even though there is a statistical relationship between these two variables in a number of observations, eventually the voodoo dance will be performed, and stock prices will fall or remain unchanged. The reason is that there is no true economic relationship between voodoo dances and stock prices.

Further investigation may reveal that stock prices actually responded to changes in interest rates during the months that the voodoo dances were performed. Changes in interest rates affect borrowing and, in turn, profits and stock prices. In contrast, there is no real economic relationship between voodoo dances and stock prices, and, therefore, the voodoo model is not valid.

> **CONCLUSION** *The fact that one event follows another does not necessarily mean that the first event caused the second event.*

Throughout this book, you will study economic models or theories that include variables linked by stable cause-and-effect relationships. For example, the theory that a change in the price of a good *causes* a change in the quantity purchased is a valid microeconomic model. The theory that a change in the money supply *causes* a change in interest rates is an example of a valid macroeconomic model. The You're the Economist gives some amusing examples of the "association means causation" reasoning pitfall.

# Why Do Economists Disagree?

Why might one economist say a clean environment should be our most important priority and another economist say economic growth should be our most important goal? If economists share the economic way of thinking and carefully avoid reasoning pitfalls, then why do they disagree? Why are economists known for giving advice by saying, "On the one hand, if you do this, then *A* results, and, on the other hand, doing this causes result *B*"? In fact, President Harry Truman once jokingly exclaimed, "Find me an economist with only one hand." George Bernard Shaw offered another famous line in the same vein: "If you took all the economists in the world and laid them end to end, they would never reach a conclusion." These famous quotes imply that economists should agree, but they ignore the fact that physicists, doctors, business executives, lawyers, and other professionals often disagree.

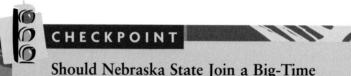

**CHECKPOINT**

## Should Nebraska State Join a Big-Time Athletic Conference?

Nebraska State (a mythical university) stood by while Penn State, Florida State, the University of Miami, and the University of South Carolina joined big-time athletic conferences. Now Nebraska State officials are pondering whether to remain independent or to pursue membership in a conference noted for high-quality football and basketball programs. An editorial in the newspaper advocates joining and cites a study showing that universities belonging to major athletic conferences have higher graduation rates than nonmembers. Because educating its students is the number one goal of Nebraska State, will this evidence persuade Nebraska State officials to join a big-time conference?

## You're the Economist

# Mops and Brooms, the Boston Snow Index, the Super Bowl, and Other Economic Indicators

*Applicable Concept: association versus causation*

Although the Commerce Department, the Wharton School, the Federal Reserve Board, and other organizations publish economic forecasts and data on key economic indicators, they are not without armchair competition. For example, the chief executive of Standex International Corporation, Daniel E. Hogan, reports that his company can predict economic downturns and recoveries from sales reports of its National Metal Industries subsidiary in Springfield, Massachusetts. National makes metal parts for about 300 U.S. manufacturers of mops and brooms. A drop in National's sales always precedes a proportional fall in consumer spending. The company's sales always pick up slightly before consumer spending does.[1]

The Boston Snow Index (BSI) is the brainchild of a vice president of a New York securities firm. It predicts a rising economy for the next year if there is snow on the ground in Boston on Christmas Day. The BSI has predicted correctly about 73 percent of the time over the past 30 years. However, its creator, David L. Upshaw, does not take it too seriously and views it as a spoof of other forecasters' methods.

Greeting card sales are another tried and true indicator, according to a vice president of American Greetings. Before a recession sets in, sales of higher-priced greeting cards rise. It seems that people substitute the cards for gifts, and since there is no gift, the card must be fancier.

A Super Bowl win by an NFC team predicts that in the following December the stock market will be higher than the year before. A win by an old AFL team predicts a dip in the stock market.

Several other less well-known indicators have also been proposed. For example, one economist says that

the surliness of waiters is a countercyclical indicator. If they are nice, expect that bad times are coming, but if they are rude, expect an upturn. Waiters, on the other hand, counter that a fall in the average tip usually precedes a downturn in the economy.

Finally, Anthony Chan, chief economist for Bank One Investment Advisers, studied marriage trends over a 34-year period. He discovered that when the number of marriages increases, the economy rises significantly, and a slowdown in marriages is followed by a decline in the economy. Chan explains that there is usually about a one-year lag between a change in the marriage rate and the economy.[2]

### ANALYZE THE ISSUE

Which of the above indicators are examples of causation? Explain.

[1]"Economic Indicators, Turtles, Butterflies, Monks, and Waiters," *The Wall Street Journal,* Aug. 27, 1979, pp. 1, 16.

[2]Sandra Block, "Worried? Look at Wedding Bell Indicator," *The Charlotte Observer,* Apr. 15, 1995, p. 8A.

Economists may appear to disagree more than other professionals partly because it is more interesting to report disagreements than agreements. Actually, economists agree on a wide range of issues. Many economists, for example, agree on free trade among nations, the elimination of farm subsidies and rent ceilings, government deficit spending to recover from a recession, and many other issues. When disagreements do exist, the reason can often be explained by the difference between *positive economics* and *normative economics*.

## POSITIVE ECONOMICS

**Positive economics**
An analysis limited to statements that are verifiable.

**Positive economics** deals with facts and therefore addresses "what is" or "verifiable" questions. Positive economics is an analysis limited to statements that are verifiable. Positive statements can be proven either true or false. Often a positive statement is expressed, "If *A*, then *B*." For example, if the national unemployment rate rises to 7 percent, then teenage unemployment exceeds 80 percent. This is a positive "if-then" prediction, which may or may not be correct. Accuracy is not the criterion for being a positive statement. The key consideration is whether the statement is *testable* and not whether it is true or false. Suppose the data show that when the nation's overall unemployment rate is close to 7 percent, the unemployment rate for teenagers never reaches 80 percent. For example, the overall unemployment rate was 6.9 percent in 1993, and the rate for teenagers was 19 percent—far short of 80 percent. Based on the facts, we would conclude that this positive statement is false.

Now we can explain one reason why economists' forecasts can diverge. The statement "If event *A* occurs, then event *B* follows" can be thought of as a *conditional* positive statement. For example, two economists may agree that if the federal government cuts spending by 10 percent this year, prices will fall about 2 percent next year. However, their predictions about the fall in prices may differ because one economist assumes Congress will not cut spending, while the other economist assumes Congress will cut spending by 10 percent.

> **CONCLUSION**  *Economists' forecasts can differ because, using the same methodology, economists can agree that event* A *causes event* B *but disagree over the assumption that event* A *will occur.*

## NORMATIVE ECONOMICS

**Normative economics**
An analysis based on value judgment.

Instead of using objective statements, an argument can be phrased subjectively. **Normative economics** attempts to determine "what should be." Normative economics is an analysis based on value judgments. Normative statements express an individual or collective opinion on a subject and cannot be proven by facts to be true or false. Certain words or phrases, such as *good, bad, need, should,* and *ought to,* tell us clearly that we have entered the realm of normative economics.

The point here is that people wearing different-colored glasses see the same facts differently. Each of us has individual subjective preferences that we apply to a particular subject. An animal rights activist says that no one *should* purchase a fur coat. Or one senator argues, "We *ought to* see that every teenager who wants a job has one." Another senator counters by saying, "Maintaining the purchasing power of the dollar is *more important* than teenage unemployment."

> **CONCLUSION**  *When opinions or points of view are not based on facts, they are scientifically untestable.*

When considering a debate, make sure to separate the arguments into their positive and normative components. This distinction allows you to determine if you are choosing a course of action based on factual evidence or on opinion. The material presented in this textbook, like most of economics, takes pains to stay

## You're the Economist

# Does Raising the Minimum Wage Help the Working Poor?
*Applicable Concepts: positive and normative analyses*

In 1938, Congress enacted the federal Fair Labor Standards Act, commonly known as the "minimum-wage law." Today, a minimum-wage worker who works full-time still earns a deplorably low annual income. One approach to help the working poor earn a living wage might be to raise the minimum wage.

The dilemma for Congress is that a higher minimum wage for the employed is enacted at the expense of jobs for unskilled workers. Opponents forecast that the increased labor cost from a large minimum-wage hike would jeopardize hundreds of thousands of unskilled jobs. For example, employers may opt to purchase more capital and less expensive labor. The fear of such sizable job losses forces Congress to perform a difficult balancing act to assure that a minimum-wage increase is large enough to help the working poor but not so large as to threaten their jobs.

Some politicians claim that raising the minimum wage is a way to help the working poor without cost to taxpayers. Others believe the cost is hidden in inflation and lost employment opportunities for marginal workers, such as teenagers, the elderly, and minorities.

Another problem with raising the minimum wage to aid the working poor is that minimum wage is a blunt weapon for redistributing wealth. Studies show that only a small percentage of minimum-wage earners are full-time workers whose family income falls below the poverty line. This means that most increases in the minimum wage go to workers who are not poor. For example, many minimum-wage workers are students living at home or workers whose spouse earns a much higher income. To help only the working poor, some economists argue that the government should target only those who need assistance, rather than using the "shotgun" approach of raising the minimum wage.

Supporters of raising the minimum wage are not convinced by these arguments. They say it is outrageous that a worker can work full-time and still live in poverty. Moreover, people on this side of the debate believe that opponents exaggerate the dangers to the economy from a higher minimum wage. Economist Lester Thurow of the Massachusetts Institute of Technology, for example, argues that a higher minimum wage will force employers to upgrade the skills and productivity of their workers. Increasing the minimum wage may therefore be a win-win proposition, rather than a win-lose proposition. Professor Thurow is supported by the research of David Card and Alan B. Krueger. These economists studied data including the 1992 increase in New Jersey's minimum wage, the 1988 rise in California's minimum wage, and the 1990–1991 increases in the federal minimum wage. In each case, their evidence shows that modest increases in the minimum wage have resulted in little or no loss in jobs.[1] And across the United States, numerous localities have implemented living-wage laws, while dozens more are considering them. Note that we will return to this issue in Chapter 4 as an application of supply and demand analysis.

### ANALYZE THE ISSUE

1. Identify two positive and two normative statements given above concerning raising the minimum wage. List other minimum-wage arguments not discussed in this You're the Economist, and classify them as either positive or normative economics.

2. Give a positive and a normative argument why a business leader would oppose raising the minimum wage. Give a positive and a normative argument why a labor leader would favor raising the minimum wage.

3. Explain your position on this issue. Identify positive and normative reasons for your decision. Are there alternative ways to aid the working poor?

[1] David Card and Alan B. Krueger, *Myth and Measurement: The New Economics of the Minimum Wage* (Princeton, N.J.: Princeton University Press, 1995).

within the boundaries of positive economic analysis. In our everyday lives, however, politicians, business executives, relatives, and friends use mostly normative statements to discuss economic issues. Economists also may associate themselves with a political position and use normative arguments for or against some economic policy. When using value judgments, an economist's normative arguments may have no greater validity than those of others. Biases or preconceptions can cloud an economist's thinking about deficit spending or whether to increase taxes on gasoline. Like beginning economics students, economists are human.

# Careers in Economics

The author of this text entered college more years ago than I would like to admit. In those days, economics was not taught in high school, so I knew nothing of the subject. Like many students taking this course, I was uncertain about which major to pursue, but selected electrical engineering because I was an amateur radio operator and enjoyed building radio receivers and transmitters. My engineering curriculum required a course in economics. I signed up thinking that "econ is boring." Instead, it was an eye-opening experience that inspired me to change my major to economics and pursue an economics teaching career.

The study of economics has attracted a number of well-known people. For example, the Rolling Stones' Mick Jagger attended the London School of Economics, and Tiger Woods studied economics at Stanford. Other famous people who majored in economics include Supreme Court Justice Sandra Day O'Connor, California Governor Arnold Schwarzenegger, and three former presidents—George H. W. Bush, Ronald Reagan, and Gerald Ford.

An economics major can lead to many career paths. Most economics majors work for business firms. Because economists are trained in analyzing financial matters, they find good jobs in management, sales, or as a market analyst interpreting economic conditions relevant to a firm's markets. With an undergraduate degree, private-sector job opportunities exist in banking, securities brokering, management consulting, computer and data processing firms, the power industry, statistical and market research and analysis, finance, health care, and many other industries. Other economics majors work for government agencies and in colleges and universities.

Government economists work for federal, state, and local governments. For example, a government economist might compile and report national statistics for economic growth or work on projects such as how to improve indexes to measure trends in consumer prices. Economists in academe not only enjoy the challenge of teaching economics, but have great freedom in selecting research projects.

Studying economics is also an essential preparation for other careers. Those preparing for law school, for example, find economics an excellent major because of its emphasis on a logical approach to problem solving. Economics is also great preparation for an MBA. In fact, students majoring in any field will benefit throughout their lives from learning how to apply the economic way of thinking to analyze real-world economic issues.

Finally, economics majors shine in salary offers upon graduation. Exhibit 3 shows average yearly salary offers for bachelor's degree candidates for September 2005.

| EXHIBIT 3 | AVERAGE YEARLY SALARY OFFERS FOR SELECTED MAJORS |
|---|---|
| **Undergraduate Major** | **Average Offer, September 2005** |
| Computer engineering | $52,242 |
| Electrical engineering | 51,773 |
| Computer science | 50,664 |
| Management information systems | 43,663 |
| Mathematics | 43,304 |
| Accounting | 42,940 |
| **Economics** | **41,994** |
| Nursing | 41,060 |
| Business administration | 39,480 |
| Chemistry | 38,635 |
| Marketing | 36,409 |
| Foreign language | 33,038 |
| Political science | 32,985 |
| Liberal arts and sciences | 32,725 |
| Secondary education | 31,845 |
| History | 31,739 |
| Sociology | 31,368 |
| Animal science | 30,438 |
| Psychology | 30,073 |
| Journalism | 29,962 |
| Criminal justice | 29,583 |
| Social work | 26,623 |

Source: National Association of Colleges and Employers, Salary Survey, Fall 2005, pp. 4–5.

## Key Concepts

Scarcity
Resources
Land
Labor
Entrepreneurship

Capital
Economics
Macroeconomics
Microeconomics
Model

Ceteris paribus
Positive economics
Normative economics

## Summary

- **Scarcity** is the fundamental economic problem that human wants exceed the availability of time, goods, and resources. Individuals and society therefore can never have everything they desire.

- **Resources** are factors of production classified as land, labor, and capital. Entrepreneurship is a special type of labor. An entrepreneur seeks profits by taking risks and combining resources to produce innovative products.

- **Economics** is the study of how individuals and society choose to allocate scarce resources in order to satisfy unlimited wants. Faced with unlimited wants and scarce resources, we must make choices among alternatives.

- **Macroeconomics** applies an economywide perspective that focuses on such issues as inflation, unemployment, and the growth rate of the economy.

- **Microeconomics** examines individual decision-making units within an economy, such as a consumer's response to changes in the price of coffee and the reasons for changes in the market price of personal computers.

- **Models** are simplified descriptions of reality used to understand and predict economic events. An economic model can be stated verbally or in a table, a graph, or an equation. If the evidence is not consistent with the model, the model is rejected.

- **Ceteris paribus** holds "all other factors unchanged" that might affect a particular relationship. If this assumption is violated, a model cannot be tested. Another reasoning pitfall is to think that *association* means *causation*.

- Use of **positive versus normative economic analysis** is a major reason for disagreements among economists. **Positive economics** uses testable statements. Often a positive argument is expressed as an "*if-then*" statement. **Normative economics** is based on value judgments or opinions and uses words such as *good, bad, ought to,* and *should.*

## Summary of Conclusion Statements

- Financial capital by itself is not productive; instead, it is only a paper claim on economic capital.

- A theory cannot be tested legitimately unless its ceteris paribus assumption is satisfied.

- The fact that one event follows another does not necessarily mean that the first event caused the second event.

- Economists' forecasts can differ because, using the same methodology, economists can agree that event *A* causes event *B* but disagree over the assumption that event *A* will occur.

- When opinions or points of view are not based on facts, they are scientifically untestable.

## Study Questions and Problems

1. Explain why both nations with high living standards and nations with low living standards face the problem of scarcity. If you won $1 million in a lottery, would you escape the scarcity problem?

2. Why isn't money considered capital in economics?

3. Computer software programs are an example of
   a. capital.
   b. labor.

c. a natural resource.

d. none of the above.

4. Explain the difference between macroeconomics and microeconomics. Give examples of the areas of concern to each branch of economics.

5. Which of the following are microeconomic issues? Which are macroeconomic issues?

a. How will an increase in the price of Coca-Cola affect the quantity of Pepsi-Cola sold?

b. What will cause the nation's inflation rate to fall?

c. How does a quota on textile imports affect the textile industry?

d. Does a large federal budget deficit reduce the rate of unemployment in the economy?

6. A model is defined as a

a. value judgment of the relationship between variables.

b. presentation of all relevant aspects of real-world events.

c. simplified description of reality used to understand the way variables are related.

d. data set adjusted for irrational actions of people.

7. Explain why it is important for an economic model to be an abstraction from the real world.

8. Explain the importance of the ceteris paribus assumption for an economic model.

9. Having won the Cold War, Congress cuts spending for the military, and then unemployment rises in the U.S. defense industry. Is there causation in this situation, or are we observing an association between events?

10. Which of the following is an example of a proposition from positive economics?

a. If John Kerry had been elected president, taxpayers would have been treated more fairly than under George W. Bush.

b. The average rate of inflation was higher during George W. Bush's presidency than during Bill Clinton's presidency.

c. In economic terms, George W. Bush is a better president than Bill Clinton.

d. Bill Clinton's policies were more just toward poor people than George W. Bush's.

11. "The government should collect higher taxes from the rich and use the additional revenues to provide greater benefits to the poor." This statement is an illustration of a

a. testable statement.

b. basic principle of economics.

c. statement of positive economics.

d. statement of normative economics.

12. Analyze the positive versus normative arguments in the following case. What statements of positive economics are used to support requiring air bags? What normative reasoning is used?

## Should the Government Require Air Bags?

Air bag advocates say air bags will save lives and the government should require them in all cars. Air bags add an estimated $600 to the cost of a car, compared with $100 for a set of regular seat belts. Opponents argue that air bags are electronic devices subject to failure and have produced injuries and death. For example, air bags have killed both adults and children whose heads were within the inflation zone at the time of deployment. Opponents therefore believe the government should leave the decision of whether to spend an extra $600 or so for an air bag to the consumer. The role of the government should be limited to providing information on the risks of having versus not having air bags.

## Study Guide Questions

1. _____ applies an economywide perspective, which focuses on such issues as inflation, unemployment, and the growth rate of the economy.

2. Select the normative statement that completes the following sentence: If the minimum wage is raised,

a. cost per unit of output will rise.

b. workers will gain their rightful share of total income.

c. the rate of inflation will increase.

d. profits will fall.

3. If a textbook price rises and then students reduce the quantity demanded of textbooks, an economic model can show a cause-and-effect relationship only if which of the following occurs?

a. Students' incomes fall.

b. Tuition decreases.

c. The number of students increases.

d. All other factors are held constant.

e. The bookstore no longer accepts used book trade-ins.

4. Which of the following is *not* a factor of production?
   a. A computer chip
   b. The service of a lawyer
   c. Dollars
   d. All of the above are factors of production.
   e. None of the above

5. T  F  The statement "It would be better to put up with price controls than to have continually higher medical care prices" is an example of normative economic analysis.

**Answers to these questions are in the complete Study Guide at www.thomsonedu.com/thomsonnow.**

For Online Exercises, go to the text Web site at www.thomsonedu.com/economics/tucker.

## Checkpoint Answers

### Can You Prove There Is No Trillion-Dollar Person?

How can researchers ever be certain they have seen all the rich people in the United States? There is always the possibility that somewhere there is a person who qualifies. If the researchers had found one, you could have rejected the theory. Because they did not, you cannot reject the theory. If you said that the evidence can support, but never prove, the theory, **YOU ARE CORRECT.**

### Should Nebraska State Join a Big-Time Athletic Conference?

Suppose universities that belong to big-time athletic conferences do indeed have higher graduation rates than nonmembers. This is not the only possible explanation for the statistical correlation (or association) between the graduation rate and membership in a big-time athletic conference. A more plausible explanation is that improving academic variables, such as tuition, quality of faculty, and student-faculty ratios—and not athletic conference membership—increase the graduation rate. If you said correlation does not mean causation, and therefore Nebraska State officials will not necessarily accept the graduation rate evidence, **YOU ARE CORRECT.**

## Practice Quiz

For an explanation of the correct answers, please visit the tutorial at www.thomsonedu.com/economics/tucker.

1. Scarcity exists
   a. when people consume beyond their needs.
   b. only in rich nations.
   c. in all countries of the world.
   d. only in poor nations.

2. Which of the following would eliminate scarcity as an economic problem?
   a. Moderation of people's competitive instincts
   b. Discovery of sufficiently large new energy reserves
   c. Resumption of steady productivity growth
   d. None of the above because scarcity cannot be eliminated

3. Which of the following is *not* a resource?
   a. Land
   b. Labor
   c. Money
   d. Capital

4. Economics is the study of
   a. how to make money.
   b. how to operate a business.
   c. people making choices because of the problem of scarcity.
   d. the government decision-making process.

5. Microeconomics approaches the study of economics from the viewpoint of
   a. individual or specific markets.
   b. the operation of the Federal Reserve.
   c. economywide effects.
   d. the national economy.

6. A review of the performance of the U.S. economy during the 1990s is primarily the concern of
   a. macroeconomics.
   b. microeconomics.
   c. both macroeconomics and microeconomics.
   d. neither macroeconomics nor microeconomics.

7. An economic theory claims that a rise in gasoline prices will cause gasoline purchases to fall, ceteris paribus. The phrase *ceteris paribus* means that
   a. other relevant factors like consumer incomes must be held constant.
   b. gasoline prices must first be adjusted for inflation.
   c. the theory is widely accepted but cannot be accurately tested.
   d. consumers' need for gasoline remains the same regardless of price.

8. An economist notices that sunspot activity is high just prior to recessions and concludes that sunspots cause recessions. The economist has
   a. confused association and causation.
   b. misunderstood the ceteris paribus assumption.
   c. used normative economics to answer a positive question.
   d. built an untestable model.

9. Which of the following is a statement of positive economics?
   a. The income tax system collects a lower percentage of the incomes of the poor.
   b. A reduction in tax rates of the rich makes the tax system more fair.
   c. Tax rates ought to be raised to finance health care.
   d. All of the above are primarily statements of positive economics.

10. Which of the following is a statement of positive economics?
    a. An unemployment rate greater than 8 percent is good because prices will fall.
    b. An unemployment rate of 7 percent is a serious problem.
    c. If the overall unemployment rate is 7 percent, unemployment rates among African Americans will average 15 percent.
    d. Unemployment is a more severe problem than inflation.

11. Which of the following is a statement of normative economics?
    a. The minimum wage is good because it raises wages for the working poor.
    b. The minimum wage is supported by unions.
    c. The minimum wage reduces the number of jobs for less-skilled workers.
    d. The minimum wage encourages firms to substitute capital for labor.

12. Select the normative statement that completes the following sentence: If the minimum wage is raised rapidly, then
    a. inflation will increase.
    b. workers will gain their rightful share of total income.
    c. profits will fall.
    d. unemployment will rise.

13. Computer programs, or software, are an example of
    a. land.
    b. labor.
    c. capital.
    d. none of the above.

14. Which of the following would *not* be classified as a capital resource?
    a. The Empire State Building.
    b. A Caterpillar bulldozer.
    c. A Macintosh computer.
    d. 100 shares of stock in General Motors.

15. A model (or theory):
    a. is a general statement about the causal relationship between variables based on facts.
    b. helps explain and predict the relationship between variables.
    c. when expressed as a downward (negatively) sloping graph implies an inverse relationship between the variables.
    d. all of the above.

# Applying Graphs to Economics

Economists are famous for their use of graphs. The reason is "a picture is worth a thousand words." Graphs are used throughout this text to present economics models. By drawing a line, you can use a two-dimensional illustration to analyze the effects of a change in one variable on another. You could describe the same information using other model forms, such as verbal statements, tables, or equations, but a graph is the simplest way to present and understand the relationship between economic variables.

Don't be worried that graphs will "throw you for a loop." Relax! This appendix explains all the basic graphical language you will need. The following illustrates the simplest use of graphs for economic analysis.

## A Direct Relationship

Basic economic analysis typically concerns the relationship between two variables, both having positive values. Hence, we can confine our graphs to the upper right (northeast) quadrant of the coordinate number system. In Exhibit A-1, notice that the scales on the horizontal axis (x-axis) and the vertical axis (y-axis) do not necessarily measure the same numerical values.

The horizontal axis in Exhibit A-1 measures annual income, and the vertical axis shows the amount spent per year for a personal computer (PC). In the absence of any established traditions, we could decide to measure income on the vertical axis and expenditure on the horizontal axis. The intersection of the horizontal and vertical axes is the *origin*, the point at which both income and expenditure are zero. In Exhibit A-1, each point is a coordinate that matches the dollar value of income and the corresponding expenditure for a PC. For example, point *A* on the graph shows that people with an annual income of $10,000 spent $1,000 per year for a PC. Other incomes are associated with different expenditure levels. For example, at $30,000 per year (point *C*), $3,000 will be spent annually for a PC.

The straight line in Exhibit A-1 allows us to determine the direction of change in PC expenditure as annual income changes. This relationship is *positive* because PC expenditure, measured along the vertical axis, and annual income, measured along the horizontal axis, move in the same direction. PC expenditure increases as annual income increases. As income declines, so does the amount spent on a PC. Thus, the straight line representing the relationship between income and PC expenditure is a **direct relationship**. A direct relationship is a positive association between two variables. When one variable increases, the other variable increases,

**Direct relationship**
A positive association between two variables. When one variable increases, the other variable increases, and when one variable decreases, the other variable decreases.

| EXHIBIT A-1 | A DIRECT RELATIONSHIP BETWEEN VARIABLES |
|---|---|

**Expenditure for a Personal Computer at Different Annual Incomes**

| Point | Personal computer expenditure (thousands of dollars per year) | Annual income (thousands of dollars) |
|---|---|---|
| A | $1 | $10 |
| B | 2 | 20 |
| C | 3 | 30 |
| D | 4 | 40 |

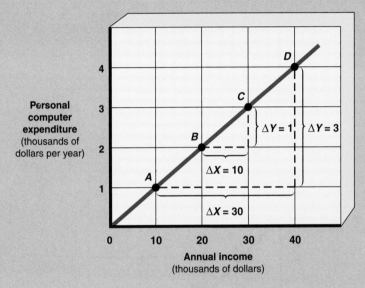

The line with a positive slope shows that the expenditure per year for a personal computer has a direct relationship to annual income, ceteris paribus. As annual income increases along the horizontal axis, the amount spent on a PC also increases, as measured by the vertical axis. Along the line, each 10-unit increase in annual income results in a 1-unit increase in expenditure for a PC. Because the slope is constant along a straight line, we can measure the same slope between any two points. Between points $B$ and $C$ or between points $A$ and $D$, the slope = $\Delta Y/\Delta X = +3/+30 = +1/+10 = 1/10$.

and when one variable decreases, the other variable decreases. In short, both variables change in the *same* direction.

Finally, an important point to remember: a two-variable graph, like any model, isolates the relationship between two variables and holds all other variables constant under the ceteris paribus assumption. In Exhibit A-1, for example, such factors as the prices of PCs and education are held constant by assumption. In Chapter 3, you will learn that allowing variables not shown in the graph to change can shift the position of the curve.

# An Inverse Relationship

Now consider the relationship between the price of compact discs (CDs) and the quantity consumers will buy per year, shown in Exhibit A-2. These data indicate a *negative* relationship between the price and quantity variables. When the price is low, consumers purchase a greater quantity of CDs than when the price is high.

| EXHIBIT A-2 | AN INVERSE RELATIONSHIP BETWEEN VARIABLES |
|---|---|

**The Quantity of Compact Discs Consumers Purchase at Different Prices**

| Point | Price per compact disc | Quantity of compact discs purchased (millions per year) |
|:---:|:---:|:---:|
| A | $25 | 0 |
| B | 20 | 25 |
| C | 15 | 50 |
| D | 10 | 75 |
| E | 5 | 100 |

The line with a negative slope shows an inverse relationship between the price per compact disc and the quantity of CDs consumers purchase, ceteris paribus. As the price of a CD rises, the quantity of CDs purchased falls. A lower price for CDs is associated with more CDs purchased by consumers. Along the line, with each $5 decrease in the price of CDs, consumers increase the quantity purchased by 25 units. The slope $= \Delta Y/\Delta X = -5/+25 = -1/5$.

In Exhibit A-2, there is an **inverse relationship** between the price per CD and the quantity consumers buy. An inverse relationship is a negative association between two variables. When one variable increases, the other variable decreases, and when one variable decreases, the other variable increases. Stated simply, the variables move in *opposite* directions.

The line drawn in Exhibit A-2 is an inverse relationship. By long-established tradition, economists put price on the vertical axis and quantity on the horizontal axis. In Chapter 3, we will study in more detail the relationship between price and quantity called the *law of demand*.

In addition to observing the inverse relationship (slope), you must interpret the *intercept* at point *A* in the exhibit. The intercept in this case means that at a price of $25 no consumer is willing to buy a single CD.

**Inverse relationship**
A negative association between two variables. When one variable increases, the other decreases, and when one variable decreases, the other variable increases.

# The Slope of a Straight Line

Plotting numbers gives a clear visual expression of the relationship between two variables, but it is also important to know how much one variable changes as another variable changes. To find out, we calculate the **slope**. The slope is the ratio of the change in the variable on the vertical axis (the rise or fall) to the change in the variable on the horizontal axis (the run). Algebraically, if *Y* is on the vertical axis and *X* is on the horizontal axis, the slope is expressed as follows (the delta symbol, $\Delta$, means "change in"):

**Slope**
The ratio of the change in the variable on the vertical axis (the rise or fall) to the change in the variable on the horizontal axis (the run).

$$\text{Slope} = \frac{\text{rise}}{\text{run}} = \frac{\text{change in vertical axis}}{\text{change in horizontal axis}} = \frac{\Delta Y}{\Delta X}$$

Consider the slope between points *B* and *C* in Exhibit A-1. The change in expenditure for a PC, *Y*, is equal to $+1$ (from $2,000 up to $3,000 per year), and the change in annual income, *X*, is equal to $+10$ (from $20,000 up to $30,000 per year). The slope is therefore $+1/+10$. The sign is positive because computer expenditure is directly, or positively, related to annual income. The steeper the line, the greater the slope because the ratio of $\Delta Y$ to $\Delta X$ rises. Conversely, the flatter the line, the smaller the slope. Exhibit A-1 also illustrates that the slope of a straight line is constant. That is, the slope between any two points along the line, such as between points *A* and *D*, is equal to $+3/+30 = 1/10$.

What does the slope of 1/10 mean? It tells you that a $1,000 increase (decrease) in PC expenditure each year occurs for each $10,000 increase (decrease) in annual income. The line plotted in Exhibit A-1 has a *positive slope*, and we describe the line as "upward sloping."

On the other hand, the line in Exhibit A-2 has a *negative slope*. The change in *Y* between points *C* and *D* is equal to $-5$ (from $15 down to $10), and the change in *X* is equal to 25 (from 50 million up to 75 million CDs purchased per year). The slope is therefore $-5/+25 = -1/5$, and this line is described as "downward sloping."

What does this slope of $-1/5$ mean? It means that raising (lowering) the price per CD by $1 decreases (increases) the quantity of CDs purchased by 5 million per year.

Suppose we calculate the slope between any two points on a flat line—say, points *B* and *C* in Exhibit A-3. In this case, there is no change in *Y* (expenditure for toothpaste) as *X* (annual income) increases. Consumers spend $20 per year on toothpaste regardless of annual income. It follows that $\Delta Y = 0$ for any $\Delta X$, so the slope is equal to 0. The two variables along a flat line (horizontal or vertical) have an **independent relationship**. An independent relationship is a zero association between two variables. When one variable changes, the other variable remains unchanged.

**Independent relationship**
A zero association between two variables. When one variable changes, the other variable remains unchanged.

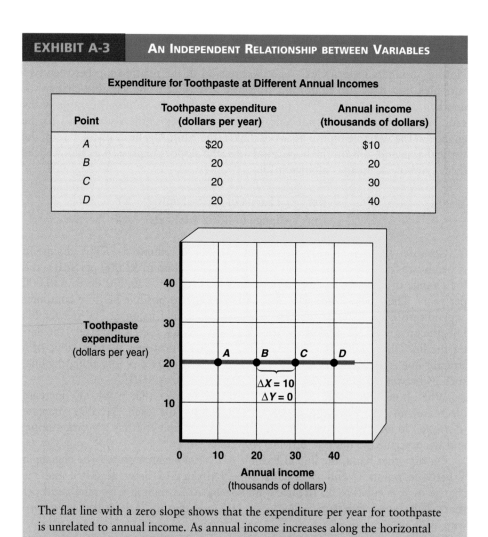

**EXHIBIT A-3          AN INDEPENDENT RELATIONSHIP BETWEEN VARIABLES**

**Expenditure for Toothpaste at Different Annual Incomes**

| Point | Toothpaste expenditure (dollars per year) | Annual income (thousands of dollars) |
|-------|-------------------------------------------|--------------------------------------|
| *A* | $20 | $10 |
| *B* | 20 | 20 |
| *C* | 20 | 30 |
| *D* | 20 | 40 |

The flat line with a zero slope shows that the expenditure per year for toothpaste is unrelated to annual income. As annual income increases along the horizontal axis, the amount spent each year for toothpaste remains unchanged at 20 units. If annual income increases 10 units, the corresponding change in expenditure is zero. The slope = $\Delta Y / \Delta X = 0/+10 = 0$.

# The Slope of a Curve

The slope of a curve changes from one point to another. Suppose the relationship between the expenditure for a PC per year and annual income is not a straight line, but an upward-sloping curve, as drawn in Exhibit A-4. This means the slope of the curve is *positive* as we move along the curve. To calculate the slope of a given point on the curve requires two steps. For example, at point *A*, the first step is to draw a tangent line that just touches the curve at this point without crossing it. The second step is to determine the slope of the tangent line. In Exhibit A-4, the slope of the tangent line, and therefore the slope of the curve at point *A*, is $+2/+30 = +1/+15 = 1/15$. What does this slope of $+1/+15$ mean? It means that at point *A* there will be a $1,000 increase (decrease) in PC expenditure each year for each $15,000 increase (decrease) in annual income.

Now consider that the relationship between the price per CD and the quantity demanded by consumers per year is the downward-sloping curve shown in Exhibit A-5. In this case, the slope of the curve is *negative* as we move along the curve. To calculate the slope at point *A*, draw a line tangent to the curve at point *A*. Thus, the slope of the curve at point *A* is $-10/+50 = -1/+5 = -1/5$.

**EXHIBIT A-4**   **THE SLOPE OF AN UPWARD-SLOPING CURVE**

Personal computer expenditure (thousands of dollars per year)

$\Delta Y = 2$

*A*

$\Delta X = 30$

Annual income (thousands of dollars)

The slope of a curve at any given point, such as point *A*, is equal to the slope of the straight line drawn tangent to the curve at that point. The tangent line just touches the curve at point *A* without crossing it. The slope of the upward-sloping curve at point *A* is $+2/+30 = +1/+15 = 1/15$.

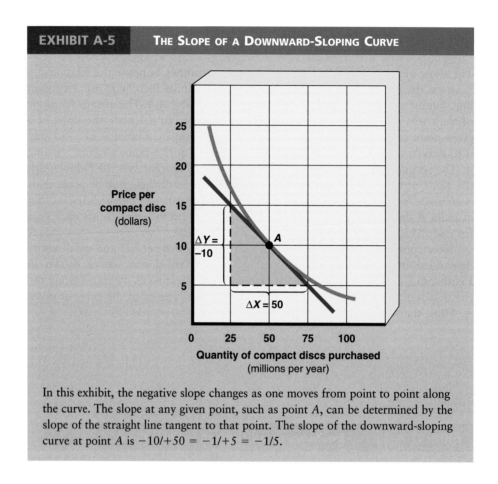

**EXHIBIT A-5          THE SLOPE OF A DOWNWARD-SLOPING CURVE**

In this exhibit, the negative slope changes as one moves from point to point along the curve. The slope at any given point, such as point $A$, can be determined by the slope of the straight line tangent to that point. The slope of the downward-sloping curve at point $A$ is $-10/+50 = -1/+5 = -1/5$.

# A Three-Variable Relationship in One Graph

The two-variable relationships drawn so far conform to a two-dimensional flat piece of paper. For example, the vertical axis measures the price per CD variable, and the horizontal axis measures the quantity of CDs purchased variable. All other factors, such as consumer income, that may affect the relationship between the price and quantity variables are held constant by the ceteris paribus assumption. But reality is frequently not so accommodating. Often a model must take into account the impact of changes in a third variable (consumer income) drawn on a two-dimensional piece of graph paper.

Economists' favorite method of depicting a three-variable relationship is shown in Exhibit A-6. As explained earlier, the cause-and-effect relationship between price and quantity of CDs determines the downward-sloping curve. A change in the price per CD causes a movement downward along either of the two separate curves. As the price falls, consumers increase the quantity of CDs demanded. The location of each curve on the graph, however, depends on the annual income of consumers. As the annual income variable increases from $30,000 to $60,000 and consumers can afford to pay more, the price–quantity-demanded curve shifts rightward. Conversely, as the annual income variable

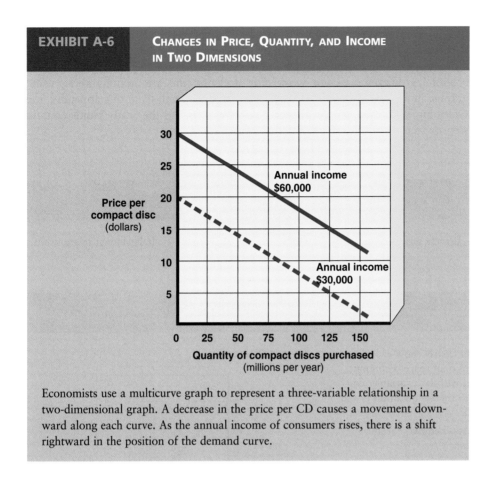

| EXHIBIT A-6 | CHANGES IN PRICE, QUANTITY, AND INCOME IN TWO DIMENSIONS |

Economists use a multicurve graph to represent a three-variable relationship in a two-dimensional graph. A decrease in the price per CD causes a movement downward along each curve. As the annual income of consumers rises, there is a shift rightward in the position of the demand curve.

decreases and consumers have less to spend, the price-quantity demanded curve shifts leftward.

This is an extremely important concept that you must understand: throughout this book, you must distinguish between *movements along* and *shifts in* a curve. Here's how to tell the difference. A change in one of the variables shown on either of the coordinate axes of the graph causes *movement along* a curve. On the other hand, a change in a variable not shown on one of the coordinate axes of the graph causes a *shift in* a curve's position on the graph.

**CONCLUSION** *A shift in a curve occurs only when the ceteris paribus assumption is relaxed and a third variable not shown on either axis of the graph is allowed to change.*

# A Helpful Study Hint for Using Graphs

To some students, studying economics is a little frightening because many chapters are full of graphs. An often-repeated mistake is to prepare for tests by trying to memorize the lines of graphs. When their graded tests are returned, the students using this strategy will probably exclaim, "What happened?" The answer is that if you learn the economic concepts first, then you will understand the graphs as illustrations of these underlying concepts. Stated simply, superficial cramming for economics quizzes does not work. For students who are anxious about using graphs, in addition to the brief review of graphical analysis in this appendix, the Graphing Workshop on the Tucker Xtra! Web site and the Study Guide contain step-by-step features on how to interpret graphs.

## Key Concepts

Direct relationship          Inverse relationship          Slope          Independent relationship

## Summary

■ **Graphs** provide a means to clearly show economic relationships in two-dimensional space. Economic analysis is often concerned with two variables confined to the upper right (northeast) quadrant of the coordinate number system.

■ A **direct relationship** occurs when two variables change in the *same* direction.

**DIRECT RELATIONSHIP**

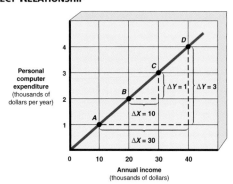

■ An **inverse relationship** occurs when two variables change in *opposite* directions.

**INVERSE RELATIONSHIP**

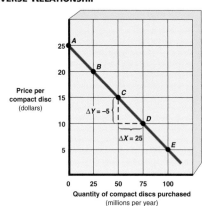

■ An **independent relationship** occurs when two variables are unrelated.

**INDEPEDENT RELATIONSHIP**

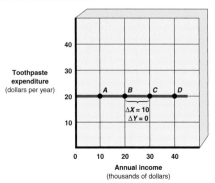

■ **Slope** is the ratio of the vertical change (the rise or fall) to the horizontal change (the run). The slope of an *upward-sloping* line is *positive*, and the slope of a *downward-sloping* line is *negative*.

**POSITIVE SLOPE OF AN UPWARD-SLOPING CURVE**

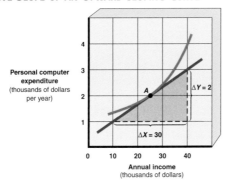

**NEGATIVE SLOPE OF A DOWNWARD-SLOPING CURVE**

■ A **three-variable relationship** is depicted by a graph showing a shift in a curve when the ceteris paribus assumption is relaxed and a third variable (such as annual income) not on either axis of the graph is allowed to change.

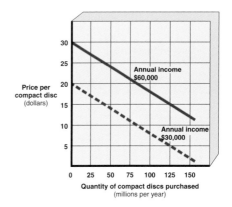

## Summary of Conclusion Statements

■ A shift in a curve occurs only when the ceteris paribus assumption is relaxed and a third variable not shown on either axis of the graph is allowed to change.

## Study Questions and Problems

1. Draw a graph without specific data for the expected relationship between the following variables:
   a. The probability of living and age
   b. Annual income and years of education
   c. Inches of snow and sales of bathing suits
   d. The number of football games won and the athletic budget

   In each case, state whether the expected relationship is *direct* or *inverse*. Explain an additional factor that would be included in the *ceteris paribus* assumption because it might change and influence your theory.

2. Assume a research firm collects survey sales data that reveal the relationship between the possible selling prices of hamburgers and the quantity of

hamburgers consumers would purchase per year at alternative prices. The report states that if the price of a hamburger is $4, 20,000 will be bought. However, at a price of $3, 40,000 hamburgers will be bought. At $2, 60,000 hamburgers will be bought, and at $1, 80,000 hamburgers will be purchased.

Based on these data, describe the relevant relationship between the price of a hamburger and the quantity consumers are willing to purchase, using a verbal statement, a numerical table, and a graph. Which model do you prefer, and why?

## Study Guide Questions

1. The ratio of the vertical change (the rise or fall) to the horizontal change (the run) is called the
   _____.

2. Measured between two points on a curve, the ratio of the change in the variable on the vertical axis to the change in the variable on the horizontal axis is the
   a. axis.
   b. slope.
   c. dependent curve.
   d. independent curve.

3. A line that has a different slope at each point is a
   a. curve.
   b. straight line.
   c. vertical line.
   d. horizontal line.

4. In a graphic relationship, shifts in a curve are caused by a change in
   a. the slope of the curve.
   b. a factor not measured on the axes of the graph.
   c. one of the factors measured on either axis of the graph.
   d. any factor, whether measured on the axes of the graph or not.

5. A change in a third variable *not* on either axis of a graph is illustrated with
   a. a horizontal or vertical line.
   b. a movement along a curve.
   c. a shift of a curve.
   d. a point of intersection.

**Answers to these questions are in the complete Study Guide at www.thomsonedu.com/thomsonnow.**

## Practice Quiz

For an explanation of the correct answers, please visit the tutorial at www.thomsonedu.com/economics/tucker.

**EXHIBIT A-7  STRAIGHT LINE**

1. Straight line CD in Exhibit A-7 shows that
   a. increasing the value of X will increase the value of Y.
   b. decreasing the value of X will decrease the value of Y.
   c. there is a direct relationship between X and Y.
   d. all of the above are true.

2. In Exhibit A-7, the slope of straight line CD is
   a. 3.
   b. 1.
   c. −1.
   d. 1/2.

3. In Exhibit A-7, the slope of straight line CD is
   a. positive.
   b. zero.
   c. negative.
   d. variable.

**EXHIBIT A-8  STRAIGHT LINE**

4. Straight line *AB* in Exhibit A-8 shows that
   a. increasing the value of *X* reduces the value of *Y*.
   b. decreasing the value of *X* increases the value of *Y*.
   c. there is an inverse relationship between *X* and *Y*.
   d. all of the above are true.

5. As shown in Exhibit A-8, the slope of straight line *AB*
   a. decreases with increases in *X*.
   b. increases with increases in *X*.
   c. increases with decreases in *X*.
   d. remains constant with changes in *X*.

6. In Exhibit A-8, the slope of straight line *AB* is
   a. 3.
   b. 1.
   c. −1.
   d. −5.

7. A shift in a curve represents a change in
   a. the variable on the horizontal axis.
   b. the variable on the vertical axis.
   c. a third variable that is not on either axis.
   d. any variable that is relevant to the relationship being graphed.

8. A change in a third variable *not* on either axis of a graph is illustrated by a
   a. horizontal or vertical line.
   b. movement along a curve.
   c. shift of a curve.
   d. point of intersection.

9. What is used to illustrate an independent relationship between two variables?
   a. An upward-sloping curve
   b. A downward-sloping curve
   c. A hill-shaped curve
   d. A horizontal or vertical line

10. When an inverse relationship is graphed, the resulting line or curve is
    a. horizontal.
    b. vertical.
    c. upward sloping.
    d. downward sloping.

11. Which of the following pairs is the *most* likely to exhibit an inverse relationship?
    a. The amount of time you study and your grade point average
    b. People's annual income and their expenditure on personal computers
    c. Baseball players' salaries and their batting averages
    d. The price of a concert and the number of tickets people purchase

12. Which of the following pairs is the *most* likely to exhibit a direct relationship?
    a. The price of gasoline and the amount of gasoline that people purchase
    b. Cholesterol levels and the likelihood of developing heart disease
    c. Outdoor temperature and heating oil sales
    d. Annual income and weekly pawn shop visits

# Production Possibilities, Opportunity Cost, and Economic Growth

© Photodisc/Getty Images

This chapter continues building on the foundation laid in the preceding chapter. Having learned that *scarcity* forces *choices*, here you will study the choices people make in more detail. This chapter begins by examining the three basic choices: *what, how,* and *for whom* to produce. The process of answering these basic questions introduces two other key building blocks in the economic way of thinking: *opportunity cost* and *marginal analysis*. Once you understand these important concepts stated in words, it will be easier to interpret our first formal economic model, the *production possibilities curve*. This model illustrates how economists use graphs as a powerful tool to supplement words and develop an understanding of basic economic principles. You will discover that the production possibilities model teaches many of the most important concepts in eco-

nomics, including scarcity, the law of increasing opportunity costs, efficiency, investment, and economic growth. For example, the chapter concludes by using the production possibilities curve to explain why underdeveloped countries do not achieve economic growth and thereby improve their standard of living.

**In this chapter, you will learn to solve these economics puzzles:**

■ Why do so few rock stars and movie stars go to college?
■ Why would you spend an extra hour reading this text rather than going to a movie or sleeping?
■ Why are investment and economic growth so important?

## Three Fundamental Economic Questions

Whether rich or poor, every nation must answer the same three fundamental economic questions: (1) *What* products will be produced? (2) *How* will they be produced? (3) *For whom* will they be produced? Later, the chapter on economies in transition introduces various types of economic systems and describes how each deals with these three economic choices.

## WHAT TO PRODUCE?

Should society devote its limited resources to producing more military goods and fewer consumer goods and services? Should society produce more CDs and fewer computer software programs? Should more small cars and fewer SUVs be produced, or should more buses be produced instead of cars? The problem of scarcity restricts our ability to produce everything we want during a given period, so the choice to produce "more" of one good requires producing "less" of another good.

## HOW TO PRODUCE?

After deciding which products to make, the second question for society to decide is how to mix technology and scarce resources in order to produce these goods. For instance, a towel can be sewn primarily by hand (labor), partially by hand and partially by machine (labor and capital), or primarily by machine (capital). In short, the *how* question asks whether a production technique will be more or less capital-intensive.

Education plays an important role in answering the *how* question. Education improves the ability of workers to perform their work. Variation in the quality and quantity of education among nations is one reason economies differ in their capacities to apply resources and technology to answer the *how* question. For example, the United States is striving to catch up with Japan in the use of robotics. Answering the question *How do we improve our robotics?* requires engineers and employees with the proper training in the installation and operation of robots.

## FOR WHOM TO PRODUCE?

Once the *what* and *how* questions are resolved, the third question is *for whom*. Among all those desiring the produced goods, who actually receives them? Who is fed well? Who drives a Mercedes? Who receives organ transplants? Should economics professors earn a salary of $1 million a year and others pay higher taxes to support economists? The *for whom* question means that society must have a method to decide who will be "rich and famous" and who will be "poor and unknown."

# Opportunity Cost

Because of scarcity, the three basic questions cannot be answered without sacrifice or cost. But what does the term *cost* really mean? The common response would be to say that the purchase price is the cost. A movie ticket *costs* $8, or a shirt *costs* $50. Applying the economic way of thinking, however, *cost* is defined differently. A well-known phrase from Nobel Prize–winning economist Milton Friedman says, "There is no such thing as a free lunch." This expression captures the links among the concepts of scarcity, choice, and cost. Because of scarcity, people must make choices, and each choice incurs a cost (sacrifice). Once one option is chosen, another option is given up. The money you spend on a movie ticket cannot also buy a DVD. A business may purchase a new textile machine to manufacture towels, but this same money cannot be used to buy a new recreation facility for employees.

**Opportunity cost**
The best alternative
sacrificed for a chosen
alternative.

The DVD and recreation facility examples illustrate that the true cost of these decisions is the **opportunity cost** of a choice, not the purchase price. Opportunity cost is the best alternative sacrificed for a chosen alternative. Stated differently, it is the cost of not choosing the next best alternative. This principle states that some highly valued opportunity must be forgone in all economic decisions. The actual good or use of time given up for the chosen good or use of time measures the opportunity cost. We may omit the word *opportunity* before the word *cost*, but the concept remains the same. Exhibit 1 illustrates the causation chain linking scarcity, choice, and opportunity cost.

Examples are endless, but let's consider a few. Suppose your economics professor decides to become a rock star in the Rolling in Dough band. Now all his or her working hours are devoted to creating hit music, and the opportunity cost is the educational services no longer provided. Now a personal example: the opportunity cost of dating a famous model or movie star (name your favorite) might be the loss of your current girlfriend or boyfriend. Opportunity cost also applies to national economic decisions. Suppose the federal government decides to spend tax revenues on a space station. The opportunity cost depends on the next best program *not* funded. Assume roads and bridges are the highest-valued projects not built as a result of the decision to construct the space station. Then the opportunity cost of the decision to devote resources to the space station is the forgone roads and bridges and not the money actually spent to build the space station.

To personalize the relationship between time and opportunity cost, ask yourself what you would be doing if you were not reading this book. Your answer might be watching television or sleeping. If sleeping is your choice, the opportunity cost of studying this text is the sleep you sacrifice. Rock stars and movie stars, on the other hand, must forfeit a large amount of income to attend college. Now you know why you see so few of these stars in class.

Decisions often involve sacrifice of *both* goods and time. Suppose you decide to see a movie at a theater located 15 minutes from campus. If you had not spent the money at the movie theater, you could have purchased a DVD and watched a movie at home. And the time spent traveling to and from the movie and sitting through it could have been devoted to studying for your economics exam. The opportunity cost of the movie consists of giving up (1) a DVD and (2) study time needed to score higher on the economics exam.

**EXHIBIT 1**     **THE LINKS BETWEEN SCARCITY, CHOICE, AND OPPORTUNITY COST**

Scarcity → Choice → Opportunity cost

Scarcity means no society has enough resources to produce all the goods and services necessary to satisfy all human wants. As a result, society is always confronted with the problem of making choices. This concept is captured in the famous phrase "There is no such thing as a free lunch." This means that each decision has a sacrifice in terms of an alternative not chosen.

# Marginal Analysis

At the heart of many important decision-making techniques used throughout this text is **marginal analysis**. Marginal analysis examines the effects of additions to or subtractions from a current situation. This is a very valuable tool in the economic-way-of-thinking toolkit because it considers the "marginal" effects of change. The rational decision maker decides on an option only if the marginal benefit exceeds the marginal cost. For example, you must decide how to use your scarce time. Should you devote an extra hour to reading this book, going to a movie, watching television, talking on the phone, or sleeping? Which of your many options do you choose? The answer depends on marginal analysis. If you decide the benefit of a higher grade in economics exceeds the opportunity cost of, say, sleep, then you allocate the extra hour to studying economics. Excellent choice!

Businesses use marginal analysis. Hotels, for example, rent space to student groups for dances and other events. Assume you are the hotel manager and a student group offers to pay $400 to use the ballroom for a party. To decide whether to accept the offer requires marginal analysis. The marginal benefit of renting otherwise vacant space is $400, and the marginal cost is $300 for extra electricity and janitorial service. Since the marginal benefit exceeds the marginal cost, the manager sensibly accepts the offer.

Similarly, farmers use marginal analysis. For example, a farmer must decide whether to add fertilizer when planting corn. Using marginal analysis, the farmer estimates that the corn revenue yield will be about $75 per acre without fertilizer and about $100 per acre using fertilizer. If the cost of fertilizer is $20 per acre, marginal analysis tells the farmer to fertilize. The addition of fertilizer will increase profit by $5 per acre because fertilizing adds $25 to the value of each acre at a cost of $20 per acre.

Marginal analysis is an important concept when the government considers changes in various programs. For example, as demonstrated in the next section, it is useful to know that an increase in the production of military goods will result in an opportunity cost of fewer consumer goods produced.

**Marginal analysis**
An examination of the effects of additions to or subtractions from a current situation.

# The Production Possibilities Curve

The economic problem of scarcity means that society's capacity to produce combinations of goods is constrained by its limited resources. This condition can be represented in a model called the **production possibilities curve**. The production possibilities curve shows the maximum combinations of two outputs that an economy can produce in a given period of time with its available resources and technology. Three basic assumptions underlie the production possibilities curve model:

1. **Fixed Resources.** The quantities and qualities of all resource inputs remain unchanged during the time period. But the "rules of the game" do allow an economy to shift any resource from the production of one output to the production of another output. For example, an economy might shift workers from producing consumer goods to producing capital goods. Although the number of workers remains unchanged, this transfer of labor will produce fewer consumer goods and more capital goods.

**Production possibilities curve**
A curve that shows the maximum combinations of two outputs an economy can produce in a given period of time with its available resources and technology.

2. **Fully Employed Resources.** The economy operates with all its factors of production fully employed and producing the greatest output possible without waste or mismanagement.

**Technology**
The body of knowledge
applied to how goods
are produced.

3. **Technology Unchanged.** Holding existing **technology** fixed creates limits, or constraints, on the amounts and types of goods any economy can produce. Technology is the body of knowledge applied to how goods are produced.

Exhibit 2 shows a hypothetical economy that has the capacity to manufacture any combination of military goods ("guns") and consumer goods ("butter") per year along its production possibilities curve (*PPC*), including points *A*, *B*, *C*, and *D*. For example, if this economy uses all its resources to make military goods, it can produce a *maximum* of 160 billion units of military goods and zero units of consumer goods (combination *A*). Another possibility is for the economy to use all its resources to produce a *maximum* of 100 billion units of consumer goods and zero units of military goods (point *D*). Between the extremes of points *A* and *D* lie other production possibilities for combinations of military and consumer goods. If combination *B* is chosen, the economy will produce 140 billion units of military goods and 40 billion units of consumer goods. Another possibility (point *C*) is to produce 80 billion units of military goods and 80 billion units of consumer goods.

What happens if the economy does not use all its resources to their capacity? For example, some workers may not find work, or plants and equipment may be idle for any number of reasons. The result is that our hypothetical economy fails to reach any of the combinations along the *PPC*. In Exhibit 2, point *U* illustrates an *inefficient* output level for any economy operating without all its resources fully employed. At point *U*, our model economy is producing 80 billion units of military goods and 40 billion units of consumer goods per year. Such an economy is underproducing because it could satisfy more of society's wants if it were producing at some point along *PPC*.

Even if an economy fully employs all its resources, it is impossible to produce certain output quantities. Any point outside the production possibilities curve is *unattainable* because it is beyond the economy's present production capabilities. Point Z, for example, represents an unattainable output of 140 billion units of military goods and 80 billion units of consumer goods. Society would prefer this combination to any combination along, or inside, the *PPC*, but the economy cannot reach this point with its existing resources and technology.

> **CONCLUSION** *Scarcity limits an economy to points on or below its production possibilities curve.*

Because all the points along the curve are *maximum* output levels with the given resources and technology, they are all called *efficient* points. A movement between any two efficient points on the curve means that *more* of one product is produced only by producing *less* of the other product. In Exhibit 2, moving from point *A* to point *B* produces 40 billion additional units of consumer goods per year but only at a cost of sacrificing 20 billion units of military goods. Thus, a movement between any two efficient points graphically illustrates that "There is no such thing as a free lunch."

| EXHIBIT 2 | THE PRODUCTION POSSIBILITIES CURVE FOR MILITARY GOODS AND CONSUMER GOODS |
|---|---|

**Production Possibilities Schedule for Military and Consumer Goods per Year**

| Output (billions of units per year) | Production possibilities | | | |
|---|---|---|---|---|
| | *A* | *B* | *C* | *D* |
| Military goods | 160 | 140 | 80 | 0 |
| Consumer goods | 0 | 40 | 80 | 100 |

All points along the production possibilities curve (*PPC*) are maximum possible combinations of military goods and consumer goods. One possibility, point *A*, would be to produce 160 billion units of military goods and zero units of consumer goods each year. At the other extreme, point *D*, the economy uses all its resources to produce 100 billion units of consumer goods and zero units of military goods each year. Points *B* and *C* are obtained by using some resources to produce each of the two outputs. If the economy fails to utilize its resources fully, the result is the inefficient point *U*. Point *Z* lies beyond the economy's present production capabilities and is unattainable.

> **CONCLUSION**  *The production possibilities curve consists of all efficient output combinations at which an economy can produce more of one good only by producing less of the other good.*

# The Law of Increasing Opportunity Costs

Why is the production possibilities curve shaped the way it is? Exhibit 3 will help us answer this question. It presents a production possibilities curve for a hypothetical economy that must choose between producing tanks and producing sailboats. Consider expanding the production of sailboats in 20,000-unit increments. Moving from point *A* to point *B*, the *opportunity cost* is 10,000 tanks; between point *B* and point *C*, the *opportunity cost* is 20,000 tanks; and the *opportunity cost* of producing at point *D* rather than point *C* is 50,000 tanks.

Exhibit 3 illustrates the **law of increasing opportunity costs**, which states that the opportunity cost increases as production of one output expands. Holding the stock of resources and technology constant (ceteris paribus), the law of increasing opportunity costs causes the production possibilities curve to display a *bowed-out* shape.

Why must our hypothetical economy sacrifice larger and larger amounts of tank output in order to produce each additional 20,000 sailboats? The reason is that all workers are not equally suited to producing one good, compared to another good. Expanding the output of sailboats requires the use of workers who are less suited to producing sailboats than producing tanks. Suppose our hypothetical economy produces no sailboats (point *A*) and then decides to produce them. At first, the least-skilled tank workers are transferred to making sailboats, and 10,000 tanks are sacrificed at point *B*. As the economy moves from point *B* to point *C*, more–highly skilled tank makers become sailboat makers, and the opportunity cost rises to 20,000 tanks. Finally, the economy can decide to move from point *C* to point *D*, and the opportunity cost increases even more, to 50,000 tanks. Now the remaining tank workers, who are superb tank makers but poor sailboat makers, must adapt to the techniques of sailboat production.

Finally, it should be noted that the production possibilities curve model could assume that resources can be substituted and the opportunity cost remains constant. In this case, the production possibilities curve would be a straight line, which is the model employed in the chapter on international trade and finance.

**Law of increasing opportunity costs** The principle that the opportunity cost increases as production of one output expands.

# Sources of Economic Growth

The economy's production capacity is not permanently fixed. If either the resource base increases or technology advances, the economy experiences **economic growth,** and the production possibilities curve shifts outward. Economic growth is the ability of an economy to produce greater levels of output, represented by an outward shift of its production possibilities curve. Exhibit 4 illustrates the importance of an outward shift. (Note the causation chain, which is often used in this text to focus on a model's cause-and-effect relationship.) At point *A* on $PPC_1$, a hypothetical

**Economic growth** The ability of an economy to produce greater levels of output, represented by an outward shift of its production possibilities curve.

**EXHIBIT 3**   THE LAW OF INCREASING OPPORTUNITY COSTS

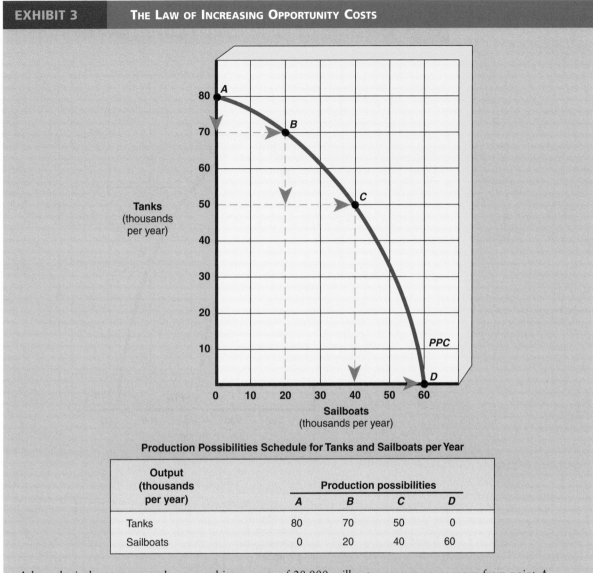

**Production Possibilities Schedule for Tanks and Sailboats per Year**

| Output (thousands per year) | Production possibilities | | | |
|---|---|---|---|---|
| | **A** | **B** | **C** | **D** |
| Tanks | 80 | 70 | 50 | 0 |
| Sailboats | 0 | 20 | 40 | 60 |

A hypothetical economy produces equal increments of 20,000 sailboats per year as we move from point *A* through point *D* on the production possibilities curve (*PPC*). If the economy moves from point *A* to point *B*, the opportunity cost of 20,000 sailboats is a reduction in tank output of 10,000 per year. This opportunity cost rises to 20,000 tanks if the economy moves from point *B* to point *C*. Finally, production at point *D*, rather than point *C*, results in an opportunity cost of 50,000 tanks per year. The opportunity cost rises because workers are not equally suited to making tanks and sailboats.

full-employment economy produces 40,000 computers and 200 million pizzas per year. If the curve shifts outward to the new curve, $PPC_2$, the economy can expand its full-employment output options. One option is to produce at point *B* and increase computer output to 70,000 per year. Another possibility is to increase pizza output to 400 million per year. Yet another choice is to produce more of both at some point between points *B* and *C*.

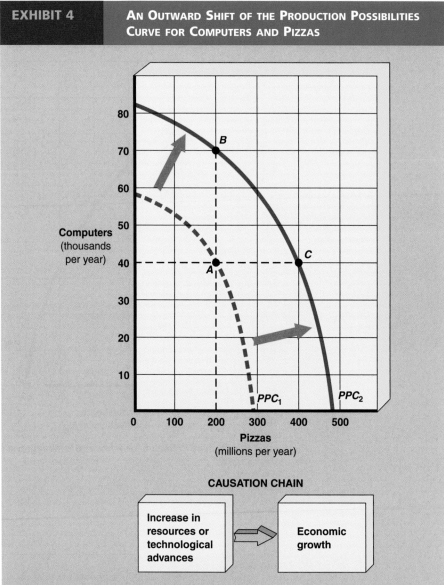

| EXHIBIT 4 | AN OUTWARD SHIFT OF THE PRODUCTION POSSIBILITIES CURVE FOR COMPUTERS AND PIZZAS |
|-----------|---------------------------------------------------------------------------------|

**CAUSATION CHAIN**

Increase in resources or technological advances ⟹ Economic growth

The economy begins with the capacity to produce combinations along the first production possibilities curve, $PPC_1$. Growth in the resource base or technological advances can shift the production possibilities curve outward from $PPC_1$ to $PPC_2$. Points along $PPC_2$ represent new production possibilities that were previously impossible. This outward shift permits the economy to produce greater quantities of output. Instead of producing combination $A$, the economy can produce, for example, more computers at point $B$ or more pizzas at point $C$. If the economy produces at a point between $B$ and $C$, more of both pizzas and computers can be produced, compared to point $A$.

## CHANGES IN RESOURCES

One way to accelerate economic growth is to gain additional resources. Any increase in resources—for example, more natural resources, a "baby boom," or more factories—will shift the production possibilities curve outward. In Exhibit 4, assume curve $PPC_1$ represents Japan's production possibilities for clothing and food in a given year. Suddenly, Japan discovers within its borders new sources of labor and other resources. As a result of the new resources, Japan will have an expanded capacity to produce any combination along an expanded curve, such as $PPC_2$.

Reductions in resources will cause the production possibilities curve to shift inward. Assume curve $PPC_2$ describes Japan's economy before World War II and the destruction of its factors of production during the war caused Japan's curve to shift leftward to $PPC_1$. Over the years, Japan trained its workforce, built new factories and equipment, and used new technology to shift its curve outward and surpass its original production capacity at $PPC_2$.

## TECHNOLOGICAL CHANGE

Another way to achieve economic growth is through research and development of new technologies. The knowledge of how to transform a stone into a wheel vastly improved the prehistoric standard of living. Technological change also makes it possible to shift the production possibilities curve outward by producing more from the same resources base. One source of technological change is *invention*. Light bulbs, transistors, computer chips, satellites, and the Internet are all examples of technological advances resulting from the use of science and engineering knowledge.

Technological change also results from the innovations of entrepreneurship, introduced in the previous chapter. Innovation involves creating and developing new products or productive processes. Seeking profits, entrepreneurs create new, better, or less expensive products. This requires organizing an improved mix of resources, which expands the production possibilities curve.

**CHECKPOINT**

### What Does a War on Terrorism Really Mean?

With the disappearance of the former Soviet Union and the end of the Cold War, the United States is the world's only superpower and is no longer engaged in an intense competition to build up its military. As a result, in the 1990s Congress and the White House had the opportunity to reduce the military's share of the budget and spend more funds for nondefense goods. This situation was referred to as the "peace dividend." Now consider that the need to combat terrorism diverts resources back to military and security output. Does the peace dividend or a reversal to more military spending represent a possible shift of the production possibilities curve or a movement along it?

## You're the Economist

# FedEx Wasn't an Overnight Success
*Applicable Concept: entrepreneurship*

Frederick W. Smith is a classic entrepreneurial success story. Young Fred went to Yale University, had a good new idea, secured venture capital, worked like crazy, made a fortune, and the Smithsonian Institution rendered its ultimate accolade. It snapped up an early Federal Express jet for its collection, displaying it for a time in the Air and Space Museum in Washington, D.C., not far from the Wright brothers' first airplane.

Smith's saga began with a college economics term paper that spelled out a nationwide overnight parcel delivery system that would be guaranteed to "absolutely, positively" beat the pants off the U.S. Postal Service. People, he said, would pay much more if their packages would arrive at their destination the next morning. To accomplish his plan, planes would converge nightly on Memphis, Tennessee, carrying packages accepted at any location throughout the nation. Smith chose this city for its central U.S. location and because its airport has little bad weather to cause landing delays. In the morning hours, all items would be unloaded, sorted, and rerouted to other airports, where vans would battle rush-hour traffic to make deliveries before the noon deadline.

Smith's college term paper got a C grade. Perhaps the professor thought the idea was too risky, and lots of others certainly agreed. In 1969, after college and a tour as a Marine pilot in Vietnam, the 24-year-old Smith began pitching his parcel delivery plan to mostly skeptical financiers. Nevertheless, with $4 million of his family's money, he persuaded a few venture capitalists to put up $80 million. At this time, this was the largest venture capital package ever assembled. In 1973, delivery service began with 33 jets connecting 25 cities, but on the first night only 86 packages showed up.

It was years before Smith looked like a genius. The company posted a $27 million loss the first year, turned the corner in 1976, and then took off, helped by a 1981 decision to add letters to its basic package delivery service. Today, Smith's basic strategy hasn't changed, but the scale of the operation has exploded. FedEx is the world's largest express transportation company, with 3.5 million packages sorted and routed on an average night. The company flies more than 700 planes around the world, painted a distinctive purple, orange, and white. Worldwide there are more than 100,000 computerized delivery vans and a 260,000-person workforce.

The U.S. Postal Service may have been miffed with Smith in the past, but today FedEx is a "cash cow" that helps the Postal Service cut its annual losses. The Postal Service's blue mailboxes have been joined by FedEx's familiar purple, orange, and white drop boxes. Also, the Postal Service ships express and priority mail on FedEx airplanes. This historic alliance means FedEx will pay the Postal Service as much as $230 million over seven years and FedEx will gain revenue because customers will have more–conveniently located FedEx drop boxes. And currently, FedEx is test-driving a new fleet of hybrid electric delivery trucks designed to reduce fuel costs by up to 50 percent.

### ANALYZE THE ISSUE

Draw a production possibilities curve for an economy producing only pizzas and computers. Explain how Fred Smith and other entrepreneurs affect the curve.

One entrepreneur, Henry Ford, changed auto industry technology by pioneering the use of the assembly line for making cars. Another entrepreneur, Chester Carlson, a law student, became so frustrated copying documents that he worked on his own to develop photocopying. After years of disappointment, a small firm named Xerox Corporation accepted Carlson's invention and transformed a good idea into a revolutionary product. These, and a myriad of other business success stories, illustrate that entrepreneurs are important because they transform their new ideas into production and practical use.

The phrase "new economy" refers to economic growth resulting from technological advances that make businesses and workers more productive. Success stories in the new economy are endless. The dizzying array of technological changes

## International Economics

# When Japan Tumbles, Where Is It on the Curve?
### *Applicable Concept: production possibilities curve*

In spite of its recent economic woes, Japan is known for quality products produced by dedicated workers who seek ways to avoid wasting resources—and management listens to them. Although the practice of lifetime employment is changing, workers in large industrial companies still enjoy considerable job security, which diminishes worker resistance to technological change. Japanese industry uses twice as many robots as industry in the United States and Western Europe combined.

One key to Japanese production is a bit of management genius called "just-in-time delivery." The goal is to produce products at precisely the right time with a minimum inventory on hand. This inventory-on-demand system allows the industrial giants to focus on assembling the final product, while smaller firms make and stock parts. For example, Mazda's workers have a small bin of headlights beside the assembly line so that parts can be quickly picked up and installed. A production manager constantly checks the supply of headlights and other parts to make sure there is no surplus of materials. As soon as more headlights are needed to fill the assembly-line bin, Mazda orders a new supply from a small outside subcontractor located in Tokyo. The headlights arrive in a matter of hours.

© Photodisc/GETTY IMAGES

Thus, Mazda's only concern is installing the headlights quickly, and it does not have to invest in large inventories of headlights and other auto parts.

Many subcontractors supplying parts to the industrial giants have businesses located in their homes. Mom, Pop, and children operate a small factory in their apartment on the kitchen table and living room floor. Small children are cared for by a female member of the family who works when the children take naps. Women and children usually deliver orders, allowing men to continue producing parts at home.

Scarcity of housing is an acute problem in Japan. In fact, the average poor American has a third more living space than the average Japanese. In Tokyo, for example, few public parks are built because of the opportunity cost in terms of factories or apartment buildings. The typical Japanese family of four in Tokyo lives in an apartment with a tiny kitchen, two small rooms, and

no yard. One room serves as the living room by day and the bedroom by night. Each morning family members simply roll up their mattress beds and put them in a closet. In addition to limited space, many houses lack central heating, so the Japanese must warm themselves with small electric heaters. Moreover, most areas of Japan do not have sewers, so people must use septic tanks. These deficiencies explain why couples save so much in Japan; it is the only way they can hope to afford better housing. (The last chapter in this book explains in more detail how saving allows a country to invest and thereby create economic growth and development by shifting its production possibilities curve outward.)

### ANALYZE THE ISSUE

Construct a production possibilities curve that represents Japan's goal of producing both cars and housing. Assume the Japanese economy is in a downturn, and indicate with an X the point on your graph where the Japanese are operating. (Hint: compare an inefficient point with an efficient point.) Give examples to explain the location you have chosen for point X. Also, based on the above article, explain how the Japanese can move their production possibilities curve outward.

marches on cutting costs, boosting productivity and profits. Oil companies, for example, use new computer technology to generate three-dimensional maps, and they now hit oil with half as many "dry holes" as they previously drilled. McDonald's now uses computer systems that transfer orders at the counter instantly to the cooks. The system also forecasts supply needs, so restaurants throw away less food. New technology is even saving tropical fish at pet stores. Computer-controlled monitors that track water temperatures, acidity, and chlorine levels are resulting in fewer fish deaths per store. Such widespread technological gains mean real progress in the way we work and live.

It can be argued that there is nothing really "new" in the new economy concept. Throughout history, technological advances have fostered economic growth by increasing our nation's productive power. Today, the Internet and computers are "new" technologies, but railroads, electricity, and automobiles, for example, were also "new" technologies in their time.

**Global Economics**

# Present Investment and the Future Production Possibilities Curve

When the decision for an economy involves choosing between capital goods and consumer goods, the output combination for the present period can determine future production capacity.

Exhibit 5 compares two countries producing different combinations of capital and consumer goods. Part (a) shows the production possibilities curve for the low-investment economy of Alpha. This economy was producing combination $A$ in 2000, which is an output of $C_a$ of consumer goods and an output of $K_a$ of capital goods per year. Let's assume $K_a$ is just enough capital output to replace the capital being worn out each year (depreciation). As a result, Alpha failed to accumulate the net gain of factories and equipment required to expand its production possibilities curve outward in future years.[1] Why wouldn't Alpha simply move up along its production curve by shifting more resources to capital goods production? The problem is that sacrificing consumer goods for capital formation causes the standard of living to fall.

Comparing Alpha to Beta illustrates the importance of being able to do more than just replace worn-out capital. Beta operated in 2000 at point $A$ in part (b), which is an output of $C_b$ of consumer goods and $K_b$ of capital goods. Assuming $K_b$ is more than enough to replenish worn-out capital, Beta is a high-investment economy, adding to its capital stock and creating extra production capacity. This process of accumulating capital (*capital formation*) is **investment**. Investment is the accumulation of capital, such as factories, machines, and inventories, that is used to produce goods and services. Newly built factories and machines in the present provide an economy with the capacity to expand its production options in the future. For example, the outward shift of its curve allows Beta to produce $C_c$ consumer goods at point $B$ in the year 2010. This means Beta will be able to improve its standard of living by producing $C_c - C_b$ extra consumer goods, while Alpha's standard of living remains unchanged because the production of consumer goods remains unchanged.

**Investment**
The accumulation of capital, such as factories, machines, and inventories, that is used to produce goods and services.

> **CONCLUSION** *A nation can accelerate economic growth by increasing its production of capital goods in excess of the capital being worn out in the production process.*

[1]Recall from the Appendix to Chapter 1 that a third variable can affect the variables measured on the vertical and horizontal axes. In this case, the third variable is the quantity of capital worn out per year.

| EXHIBIT 5 | ALPHA'S AND BETA'S PRESENT AND FUTURE PRODUCTION POSSIBILITIES CURVES |
|---|---|

(a) Low-investment country Alpha

(b) High-investment country Beta

In part (a), each year Alpha produces only enough capital ($K_a$) to replace existing capital being worn out. Without greater capital, and assuming other resources remain fixed, Alpha is unable to shift its production possibilities curve outward. In part (b), each year Beta produces $K_b$ capital, which is more than the amount required to replenish its depreciated capital. In the year 2010, this expanded capital provides Beta with the extra production capacity to shift its production possibilities curve outward. If Beta chooses point $B$ on its curve, it has the production capacity to increase the amount of consumer goods from $C_b$ to $C_c$ without producing fewer capital goods.

## Key Concepts

| | | |
|---|---|---|
| *What, how,* and *for whom* questions | Production possibilities curve | Economic growth |
| Opportunity cost | Technology | Investment |
| Marginal analysis | Law of increasing opportunity costs | |

## Summary

■ Three fundamental economic questions facing any economy are *what, how,* and *for whom* to produce goods. The *what* question asks exactly which goods are to be produced and in what quantities. The *how* question requires society to decide the resource mix used to produce goods. The *for whom* problem concerns the division of output among society's citizens.

■ **Opportunity cost** is the best alternative forgone for a chosen option. This means no decision can be made without cost.

■ **Marginal analysis** examines the impact of changes from a current situation and is a technique used extensively in economics. The basic approach is to compare the additional benefits of a change with the additional costs of the change.

■ A **production possibilities curve** illustrates an economy's capacity to produce goods, subject to the constraint of scarcity. The production possibilities curve is a graph of the maximum possible combinations of two outputs that can be produced in a given period of time, subject to three conditions: (1) All resources are fully employed. (2) The resource base is not allowed to vary during the time period. (3) **Technology**, which is the body of knowledge applied to the production of goods, remains constant. **Inefficient** production occurs at any point inside the production possibilities curve. All points along the curve are **efficient** points because each point represents a maximum output possibility.

### PRODUCTION POSSIBILITIES CURVE

■ The **law of increasing opportunity costs** states that the opportunity cost increases as the production of

an output expands. The explanation for this law is that the suitability of resources declines sharply as greater amounts are transferred from producing one output to producing another output.

■ **Economic growth** is represented by the production possibilities curve shifting outward as the result of an increase in resources or an advance in technology. The phrase **new economy** refers to economic growth resulting from technological advances that make businesses and workers more productive.

### ECONOMIC GROWTH

CAUSATION CHAIN

■ **Investment** means that an economy is producing and accumulating capital. Investment consists of factories, machines, and inventories (capital) produced in the present that are used to shift the production possibilities curve outward in the future.

---

## Summary of Conclusion Statements

■ Scarcity limits an economy to points on or below its production possibilities curve.

■ The production possibilities curve consists of all efficient output combinations at which an economy can produce more of one good only by producing less of the other good.

■ A nation can accelerate economic growth by increasing its production of capital goods in excess of the capital being worn out in the production process.

## Study Questions and Problems

1. Explain why scarcity forces individuals and society to incur opportunity costs. Give specific examples.

2. Suppose a retailer promotes its store by advertising a drawing for a "free car." Is this car *free* because the winner pays *zero* for it?

3. Explain verbally the statement "There is no such thing as a free lunch" in relation to scarce resources.

4. Which of the following decisions has the greater opportunity cost? Why?
   a. A decision to use an undeveloped lot in Tokyo's financial district for an apartment building.
   b. A decision to use a square mile in the desert for a gas station.

5. Attending college is expensive, time-consuming, and it requires effort. So why do people decide to attend college?

6. The following is a set of hypothetical production possibilities for a nation.

| Combination | Automobiles (thousands) | Beef (thousands of tons) |
|---|---|---|
| A | 0 | 10 |
| B | 2 | 9 |
| C | 4 | 7 |
| D | 6 | 4 |
| E | 8 | 0 |

   a. Plot these production possibilities data. What is the opportunity cost of the first 2,000 automobiles produced? Between which points is the opportunity cost per thousand automobiles highest? Between which points is the opportunity cost per thousand tons of beef highest?
   b. Label a point *F* inside the curve. Why is this an inefficient point? Label a point *G* outside the curve. Why is this point unattainable? Why are points *A* through *E* all efficient points?
   c. Does this production possibilities curve reflect the law of increasing opportunity costs? Explain.
   d. What assumptions could be changed to shift the production possibilities curve?

7. The following table shows the production possibilities for pies and flowerboxes. Fill in the opportunity cost (pies forgone) of producing the first through the fifth flowerbox.

| Combination | Pies | Flowerboxes | Opportunity cost |
|---|---|---|---|
| A | 30 | 0 | _____ |
| B | 26 | 1 | _____ |
| C | 21 | 2 | _____ |
| D | 15 | 3 | _____ |
| E | 8 | 4 | _____ |
| F | 0 | 5 | _____ |

8. Why does a production possibilities curve have a bowed-out shape?

9. Interpret the phrases "There is no such thing as a free lunch" and "A free lunch is possible" in terms of the production possibilities curve.

10. Suppose, unfortunately, your mathematics and economics professors have decided to give tests two days from now and you can spend a total of only 12 hours studying for both exams. After some thought, you conclude that dividing your study time equally between each subject will give you an expected grade of C in each course. For each additional 3 hours of study time for one of the subjects, your grade will increase one letter for that subject and your grade will fall one letter for the other subject.
   a. Construct a table for the production possibilities and corresponding number of hours of study in this case.
   b. Plot these production possibilities data in a graph.
   c. Does this production possibilities curve reflect the law of increasing opportunity costs? Explain.

11. Draw a production possibilities curve for a hypothetical economy producing capital goods and consumer goods. Suppose a major technological breakthrough occurs in the capital goods industry and the new technology is widely adopted only in this industry. Draw the new production possibilities curve. Now assume that a technological advance occurs in consumer goods production but not in capital goods production. Draw the new production possibilities curve.

12. The present choice between investing in capital goods and producing consumer goods now affects the ability of an economy to produce in the future. Explain.

## Study Guide Questions

1. The _____ problem concerns the division of output among society's citizens. The _____ question asks exactly what goods are to be produced and in what quantities. The _____ question requires society to decide the resource mix used to produce goods.

**EXHIBIT 6  PRODUCTION POSSIBILITIES CURVE**

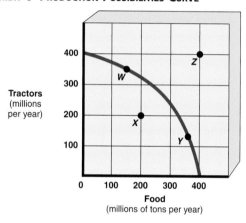

2. If the economy represented in Exhibit 6 is operating at Point *W*,
   a. no tractor production must be forgone to produce more food in the current period.
   b. resources are not fully used.
   c. some tractor production must be forgone to produce more food in the current period.
   d. increased food production would be impossible.

3. Which of the following moves from one point to another in Exhibit 6 would represent an increase in economic efficiency?
   a. *Z* to *W*
   b. *W* to *Y*
   c. *W* to *X*
   d. *X* to *Y*

4. Movement along the production possibilities curve shown in Exhibit 6 indicates
   a. that labor is not equally productive or homogeneous.
   b. declining opportunity costs.
   c. all inputs are homogeneous.
   d. all of the above.

5. T  F  Of all the points on the production possibilities curve, only one point represents an efficient division of labor.

**Answers to these questions are in the complete Study Guide at www.thomsonedu.com/thomsonnow.**

**For Online Exercises, go to the text Web site at www.thomsonedu.com/economics/tucker.**

## Checkpoint Answer

### What Does a War on Terrorism Really Mean?

A "peace dividend" suggests resources are allocated away from military production and used for greater nonmilitary production. The war on terrorism arguably shifts resources in the opposite direction. If you said that this phrase represents a movement along the production possibilities curve, **YOU ARE CORRECT.**

## Practice Quiz

For an explanation of the correct answers, please visit the tutorial at www.thomsonedu.com/economics/tucker.

1. Which of the following decisions must be made by all economies?
   a. How much to produce? When to produce? How much does it cost?
   b. What is the price? Who will produce it? Who will consume it?
   c. What to produce? How to produce it? For whom to produce?
   d. None of the above

2. A student who has one evening to prepare for two exams on the following day has the following two alternatives:

| Possibility | Score in economics | Score in accounting |
|---|---|---|
| A | 95 | 80 |
| B | 80 | 90 |

   The opportunity cost of receiving a 90 rather than an 80 on the accounting exam is represented by how many points on the economics exam?
   a. 15 points
   b. 80 points
   c. 90 points
   d. 10 points

3. Opportunity cost is the
   a. purchase price of a good or service.
   b. value of leisure time plus out-of-pocket costs.
   c. best option given up as a result of choosing an alternative.
   d. undesirable sacrifice required to purchase a good.

4. On a production possibilities curve, the opportunity cost of good X in terms of good Y is represented by
   a. the distance to the curve from the vertical axis.
   b. the distance to the curve from the horizontal axis.
   c. the movement along the curve.
   d. all of the above.

5. If a farmer adds one pound of fertilizer per acre, the value of the resulting crops rises from $80 to $100 per acre. According to marginal analysis, the farmer should add fertilizer if it costs less than
   a. $12.50 per pound.
   b. $20 per pound.

   c. $80 per pound.
   d. $100 per pound.

6. On a production possibilities curve, a change from economic inefficiency to economic efficiency is obtained by
   a. movement along the curve.
   b. movement from a point outside the curve to a point on the curve.
   c. movement from a point inside the curve to a point on the curve.
   d. a change in the slope of the curve.

7. Any point inside the production possibilities curve is a(an)
   a. efficient point.
   b. unfeasible point.
   c. inefficient point.
   d. maximum output combination.

8. Using a production possibilities curve, unemployment is represented by a point located
   a. near the middle of the curve.
   b. at the top corner of the curve.
   c. at the bottom corner of the curve.
   d. outside the curve.
   e. inside the curve.

9. Along a production possibilities curve, an increase in the production of one good can be accomplished only by
   a. decreasing the production of another good.
   b. increasing the production of another good.
   c. holding constant the production of another good.
   d. producing at a point on a corner of the curve.

10. Education and training that improve the skill of the labor force are represented on the production possibilities curve by a(an)
    a. movement along the curve.
    b. inward shift of the curve.
    c. outward shift of the curve.
    d. movement toward the curve from an exterior point.

11. A nation can accelerate its economic growth by
    a. reducing the number of immigrants allowed into the country.
    b. adding to its stock of capital.
    c. printing more money.
    d. imposing tariffs and quotas on imported goods.

**EXHIBIT 7  PRODUCTION POSSIBILITIES CURVE**

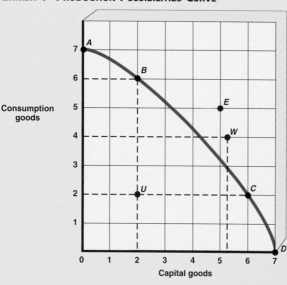

12. From the information in Exhibit 7, which of the following points on the production possibilities curve are attainable with the resources and technology currently available?
    a. *A, B, C, E, U*
    b. *A, B, C, D, W*
    c. *E, U, W*

    d. *B, C, D, U*
    e. *A, B, C, E*

13. In Exhibit 7, which of the following points on the production possibilities curve are efficient production points?
    a. *A, B, C, U*
    b. *A, B, C, D, U*
    c. *E, U, W*
    d. *B, C, D, U*
    e. *A, B, C, D*

14. In Exhibit 7, to move from *U* to *B*, the opportunity cost
    a. would be 4 units of consumption goods.
    b. would be 2 units of capital goods.
    c. would be zero.
    d. would be 5 units of capital goods.
    e. cannot be estimated.

15. In Exhibit 7, which of the following points on the production possibilities curve are full-employment production points?
    a. *A, B, C, D*
    b. *A, B, C, D, U*
    c. *E, U, W*
    d. *B, C, D, U*
    e. *A, B, C, U*

© Photodisc/Getty Images

# part 2

# Microeconomic Fundamentals

In order to study the microeconomy, the chapters in Part 2 build on the basic concepts learned in Part 1. Chapters 3 and 4 explain the market demand and supply model, which has a wide range of real-world applications. Chapter 5 takes a closer look at movements along the demand curve introduced in Chapter 3. Chapter 6 returns to the law of demand and explores in more detail exactly why consumers make their choices among goods and services. Part 2 concludes in Chapter 7 with an extension of the concept of supply that explains how various costs of production change as output varies.

# Market Demand and Supply

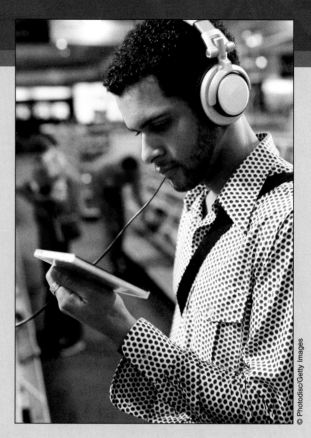

© Photodisc/Getty Images

A cornerstone of the U.S. economy is the use of markets to answer the basic economic questions discussed in the previous chapter. Consider baseball cards, CDs, physical fitness, gasoline, soft drinks, alligators, and tennis shoes. In a *market economy,* each is bought and sold by individuals coming together as buyers and sellers in markets. This chapter is extremely important because it introduces basic supply and demand analysis. This technique will prove to be valuable because it is applicable to a multitude of real-world choices of buyers and sellers facing the problem of scarcity. For example, the International Economics feature asks you to consider the highly controversial issue of international trade in human organs.

Demand represents the choice-making behavior of consumers, while supply represents the choices of producers. The chapter begins by looking closely at demand and then

supply. Finally, it combines these forces to see how prices and quantities are determined in the marketplace. Market demand and supply analysis is the basic tool of microeconomic analysis.

**In this chapter, you will learn to solve these economics puzzles:**

■ What is the difference between a "change in quantity demanded" and a "change in demand"?
■ Can Congress repeal the law of supply to control oil prices?
■ Does the price system eliminate scarcity?

## The Law of Demand

**Law of demand**
The principle that there is an inverse relationship between the price of a good and the quantity buyers are willing to purchase in a defined time period, ceteris paribus.

Economics might be referred to as "graphs and laughs" because economists are so fond of using graphs to illustrate demand, supply, and many other economic concepts. Unfortunately, some students taking economics courses say they miss the laughs.

Exhibit 1 reveals an important "law" in economics called the **law of demand.** The law of demand states there is an inverse relationship between the price of a good and the quantity buyers are willing to purchase in a defined time period,

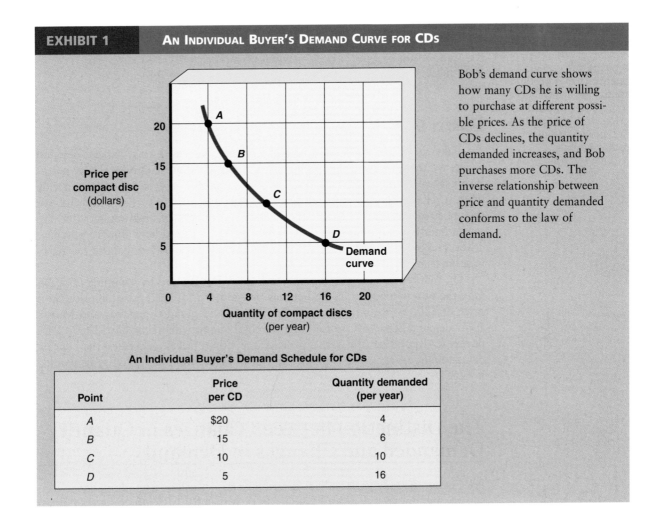

| EXHIBIT 1 | AN INDIVIDUAL BUYER'S DEMAND CURVE FOR CDs |
| --- | --- |

Bob's demand curve shows how many CDs he is willing to purchase at different possible prices. As the price of CDs declines, the quantity demanded increases, and Bob purchases more CDs. The inverse relationship between price and quantity demanded conforms to the law of demand.

**An Individual Buyer's Demand Schedule for CDs**

| Point | Price per CD | Quantity demanded (per year) |
| --- | --- | --- |
| A | $20 | 4 |
| B | 15 | 6 |
| C | 10 | 10 |
| D | 5 | 16 |

ceteris paribus. The law of demand makes good sense. At a "sale," consumers buy more when the price of merchandise is cut.

In Exhibit 1, the *demand curve* is formed by the line connecting the possible price and quantity purchased responses of an individual consumer. The demand curve therefore allows you to find the quantity demanded by a buyer at any possible selling price by moving along the curve. For example, Bob, a sophomore at Marketplace College, loves listening to music on his stereo while studying. Bob's demand curve shows that at a price of $15 per prerecorded compact disc (CD) his quantity demanded is 6 CDs purchased annually (point *B*). At the lower price of $10, Bob's quantity demanded increases to 10 CDs per year (point *C*). Following this procedure, other price and quantity possibilities for Bob are read along the demand curve.

Note that until we know the actual price, we do not know how many CDs Bob will actually purchase annually. The demand curve is simply a summary of Bob's buying intentions. Once we know the market price, a quick look at the demand curve tells us how many CDs Bob will buy.

**Demand**
A curve or schedule showing the various quantities of a product consumers are willing to purchase at possible prices during a speci-fied period of time, ceteris paribus.

> **CONCLUSION** *Demand is a curve or schedule showing the various quantities of a product consumers are willing to purchase at possible prices during a specified period of time, ceteris paribus.*

## MARKET DEMAND

To make the transition from an *individual* demand curve to a *market* demand curve, we total, or sum, the individual demand schedules. Suppose the owner of Rap City, a small chain of retail music stores serving a few states, tries to decide what to charge for CDs and hires a consumer research firm. For simplicity, we assume Fred and Mary are the only two buyers in Rap City's market, and they are sent a questionnaire that asks how many CDs each would be willing to purchase at several possible prices. Exhibit 2 reports their price-quantity demanded responses in tabular and graphical form.

The market demand curve, $D_{total}$, in Exhibit 2 is derived by summing *horizontally* the two individual demand curves, $D_1$ and $D_2$, for each possible price. At a price of $20, for example, we sum Fred's 2 CDs demanded per year and Mary's 1 CD demanded per year to find that the total quantity demanded at $20 is 3 CDs per year. Repeating the same process for other prices generates the market demand curve, $D_{total}$. For example, at a price of $5, the total quantity demanded is 12 CDs.

# The Distinction between Changes in Quantity Demanded and Changes in Demand

Price is not the only variable that determines how much of a good or service con-sumers will buy. Recall from Exhibit A-6 of Appendix 1 that the price and quan-tity variables in our model are subject to the ceteris paribus assumption. If we relax this assumption and allow other variables held constant to change, a variety of fac-tors can influence the position of the demand curve. Because these factors are not the price of the good itself, these variables are called *nonprice determinants*, or sim-ply, *demand shifters*. The major nonprice determinants include (1) the number of buyers; (2) tastes and preferences; (3) income; (4) expectations of future changes in prices, income, and availability of goods; and (5) prices of related goods.

Before discussing these nonprice determinants of demand, we must pause to explain an important and possibly confusing distinction in terminology. We have been referring to a **change in quantity demanded**, which results solely from a change in the price. A change in quantity demanded is a movement between points along a stationary demand curve, ceteris paribus. In Exhibit 3(a), at the price of $15, the quantity demanded is 20 million CDs per year. This is shown as point A on the demand curve, D. At a lower price of, say, $10, the quantity demanded increases to 30 million CDs per year, shown as point B. Verbally, we describe the impact of the price decrease as an increase in the quantity demanded of 10 million CDs per year. We show this relationship on the demand curve as a movement down along the curve from point A to point B.

**Change in quantity demanded**
A movement between points along a station-ary demand curve, ceteris paribus.

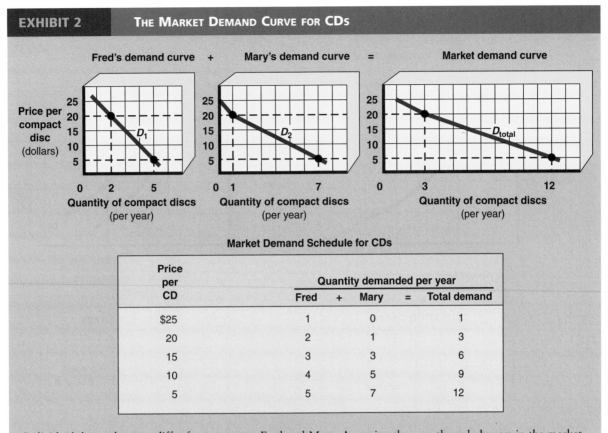

| EXHIBIT 2 | THE MARKET DEMAND CURVE FOR CDs |
|---|---|

**Market Demand Schedule for CDs**

| Price per CD | Quantity demanded per year | | |
|---|---|---|---|
| | Fred + | Mary = | Total demand |
| $25 | 1 | 0 | 1 |
| 20 | 2 | 1 | 3 |
| 15 | 3 | 3 | 6 |
| 10 | 4 | 5 | 9 |
| 5 | 5 | 7 | 12 |

Individual demand curves differ for consumers Fred and Mary. Assuming they are the only buyers in the market, the market demand curve, $D_{total}$, is derived by summing horizontally the individual demand curves, $D_1$ and $D_2$.

**CONCLUSION** *Under the law of demand, any decrease in price along the vertical axis will cause an increase in quantity demanded, measured along the horizontal axis.*

A **change in demand** is an increase (rightward shift) or a decrease (leftward shift) in the quantity demanded at each possible price. If ceteris paribus no longer applies and if one of the five nonprice factors changes, the location of the demand curve shifts.

**Change in demand**
An increase or a decrease in the quantity demanded at each possible price. An increase in demand is a rightward shift in the entire demand curve. A decrease in demand is a leftward shift in the entire demand curve.

**CONCLUSION** *Changes in nonprice determinants can produce only a shift in the demand curve and not a movement along the demand curve, which is caused by a change in the price.*

Comparing parts (a) and (b) of Exhibit 3 is helpful in distinguishing between a change in quantity demanded and a change in demand. In part (b), suppose the market demand curve for CDs is initially at $D_1$ and there is a shift to the right (an

**EXHIBIT 3** — **MOVEMENT ALONG A DEMAND CURVE VERSUS A SHIFT IN DEMAND**

Part (a) shows the demand curve, *D*, for CDs per year. If the price is $15 at point *A*, the quantity demanded by consumers is 20 million CDs. If the price decreases to $10 at point *B*, the quantity demanded increases from 20 million to 30 million CDs.

Part (b) illustrates an increase in demand. A change in some nonprice determinant can cause an increase in demand from $D_1$ to $D_2$. At a price of $15 on $D_1$ (point *A*), 20 million CDs is the quantity demanded per year. At this same price on $D_2$ (point *B*), the quantity demanded increases to 30 million.

increase in demand) from $D_1$ to $D_2$. This means that at *all* possible prices consumers wish to purchase a larger quantity than before the shift occurred. At $15 per CD, for example, 30 million CDs (point *B*) will be purchased each year, rather than 20 million CDs (point *A*).

Now suppose a change in some nonprice factor causes demand curve $D_1$ to shift leftward (a decrease in demand). The interpretation in this case is that at *all* possible prices consumers will buy a smaller quantity than before the shift occurred.

Exhibit 4 summarizes the terminology for the effects of changes in price and nonprice determinants on the demand curve.

## Nonprice Determinants of Demand

Distinguishing between a change in quantity demanded and a change in demand requires some patience and practice. The following discussion of specific changes in nonprice factors will clarify how each nonprice variable affects demand.

| EXHIBIT 4 | TERMINOLOGY FOR CHANGES IN PRICE AND NONPRICE DETERMINANTS OF DEMAND |
|-----------|---------------------------------------------------------------------|

| Change | Effect | Terminology |
|--------|--------|-------------|
| Price increases | Upward movement along the demand curve | Decrease in the quantity demanded |
| Price decreases | Downward movement along the demand curve | Increase in the quantity demanded |
| Nonprice determinant | Leftward or rightward shift in the demand curve | Decrease or increase in demand |

**Quantity of good or service per unit of time**

Caution! It is important to distinguish between a change in quantity demanded, which is a movement along a demand curve ($D_1$) caused by a change in price, and a change in demand, which is a shift in the demand curve. An increase in demand (shift to $D_2$) or decrease in demand (shift to $D_3$) is not caused by a change in price. Instead, a shift is caused by a change in one of the nonprice determinants.

## NUMBER OF BUYERS

Look back at Exhibit 2, and imagine the impact of adding more individual demand curves to the individual demand curves of Fred and Mary. At all possible prices, there is extra quantity demanded by the new customers, and the market demand curve for CDs shifts rightward (an increase in demand). Population growth therefore tends to increase the number of buyers, which shifts the market demand curve for a good or service rightward. Conversely, a population decline shifts most market demand curves leftward (a decrease in demand).

The number of buyers can be specified to include both foreign and domestic buyers. Suppose the market demand curve $D_1$ in Exhibit 3(b) is for CDs purchased in the United States by customers at home and abroad. Also assume Japan restricts the import of CDs into Japan. What would be the effect of Japan removing this trade restriction? The answer is that the demand curve shifts rightward from $D_1$ to $D_2$ when Japanese consumers add their individual demand curves to the U.S. market demand for CDs.

## TASTES AND PREFERENCES

Fads, fashions, advertising, and new products can influence consumer preferences to buy a particular good or service. Beanie Babies became the rage in the 1990s, and the demand curve for these products shifted to the right. When people tire of a product, the demand curve will shift leftward. The physical fitness trend has increased the demand for health clubs and exercise equipment. On the other hand, have you noticed many stores selling hula hoops?

## INCOME

Most students are all too familiar with how changes in income affect demand. There are two possible categories for the relationship between changes in income and changes in demand: (1) **normal goods** and (2) **inferior goods**.

A normal good is any good for which there is a direct relationship between changes in income and its demand curve. For many goods and services, an increase in income causes buyers to purchase more at any possible price. As buyers receive higher incomes, the demand curve shifts rightward for such *normal goods* as cars, steaks, vintage wine, cleaning services, and CDs. A decline in income has the opposite effect, and the demand curve shifts leftward.

An inferior good is any good for which there is an inverse relationship between changes in income and its demand curve. A rise in income can result in reduced purchases of a good or service at any possible price. This might happen with such *inferior* goods as generic brands, Spam, and bus service. Instead of buying these inferior goods, higher incomes allow consumers to buy brand-name products, steaks, or a car. Conversely, a fall in income causes the demand curve for inferior goods to shift rightward.

**Normal good**
Any good for which there is a direct relationship between changes in income and its demand curve.

**Inferior good**
Any good for which there is an inverse relationship between changes in income and its demand curve.

## EXPECTATIONS OF BUYERS

What is the effect on demand in the present when consumers anticipate future changes in prices, incomes, or availability? What happens when a war breaks out in the Middle East? Expectations that there will be a shortage of gasoline induce consumers to say "fill 'er up" at every opportunity, and demand increases. Suppose students learn that the prices of the textbooks for several courses they plan to take next semester will double soon. Their likely response is to buy now, which causes an increase in the demand curve for these textbooks. Another example is a change in the weather, which can indirectly cause expectations to shift demand for some products. Suppose a hailstorm destroys a substantial portion of the peach crop. Consumers reason that the reduction in available supply will soon drive up prices, and they dash to stock up before it is too late. This change in expectations causes the demand curve for peaches to increase.

## PRICES OF RELATED GOODS

Possibly the most confusing nonprice factor is the influence of other prices on the demand for a particular good or service. The term *nonprice* seems to forbid any shift in demand resulting from a change in the price of *any* product. This confusion exists when one fails to distinguish between changes in quantity demanded and changes in demand. Remember that ceteris paribus holds all prices of other goods constant. Therefore, movement along a demand curve occurs solely in response to changes in the price of a product, that is, its "own" price. When we draw the demand curve for Coca-Cola, for example, we assume the prices of Pepsi-Cola and other colas remain unchanged. What happens if we relax the ceteris paribus assumption and the price of Pepsi rises? Many Pepsi buyers switch to Coca-Cola, and the demand curve for Coca-Cola shifts rightward (an increase in demand). Coca-Cola and Pepsi-Cola are one type of related goods called **substitute goods**. A substitute good competes with another good for consumer purchases. As a result, there is a direct relationship between a price change for one good and the demand for its "competitor" good. Other examples of substitutes include margarine and butter, domestic cars and foreign cars, videocassettes and DVDs, e-mail and the U.S. Postal Service, and iTunes versus CDs.

CDs and CD players illustrate a second type of related goods called **complementary goods**. A complementary good is jointly consumed with another good. As a result, there is an inverse relationship between a price change for one good and the demand for its "go together" good. Although buying a CD and buying a CD player can be separate decisions, these two purchases are related. The more CD players consumers buy, the greater the demand for CDs. What happens if the price of CD players falls sharply, say, from $150 to $30? The market demand curve for CDs shifts rightward (an increase in demand) because new owners of players add their individual demand curves to those of persons already owning players and buying CDs. Conversely, a sharp rise in college tuition decreases the demand for textbooks.

Exhibit 5 summarizes the relationship between changes in the nonprice determinants of demand and the demand curve, accompanied by examples for each type of nonprice factor change.

**Substitute good**
A good that competes with another good for consumer purchases. As a result, there is a direct relationship between a price change for one good and the demand for its "competitor" good.

**Complementary good**
A good that is jointly consumed with another good. As a result, there is an inverse relationship between a price change for one good and the demand for its "go together" good.

# The Law of Supply

In everyday conversations, the term *supply* refers to a specific quantity. A "limited supply" of golf clubs at a sporting goods store means there are only so many for sale and that's all. This interpretation of supply is *not* the economist's definition. To economists, supply is the relationship between ranges of possible prices

**CHECKPOINT**

### Can Gasoline Become an Exception to the Law of Demand?

The Iraqi invasion of Kuwait in 1990 was followed by sharply climbing gasoline prices. Consumers feared future oil shortages if war cut off oil supplies, and they rushed to fill up their gas tanks. In this case, as the price of gas increased, consumers bought more, not less. Is this an exception to the law of demand?

| EXHIBIT 5 | SUMMARY OF THE IMPACT OF CHANGES IN NONPRICE DETERMINANTS OF DEMAND ON THE DEMAND CURVE | | |
|---|---|---|---|

| Nonprice determinant of demand | Relationship with the demand curve | Shift in the demand curve | Example |
|---|---|---|---|
| 1. Number of buyers | Direct | | ■ The Japanese remove import restrictions on American CDs, and Japanese consumers increase the demand for American CDs. |
| | | | ■ A decline in the birthrate reduces the demand for baby clothes. |
| 2. Tastes and preferences | Direct | | ■ For no apparent reason, consumers want Beanie Babies, and demand increases. |
| | | | ■ After a while, the fad dies, and demand declines. |
| 3. Income | | | |
|   a. Normal goods | Direct | | ■ Consumers' incomes increase, and the demand for steaks increases. |
| | | | ■ A decline in income decreases the demand for air travel. |
|   b. Inferior goods | Inverse | | ■ Consumers' incomes increase, and the demand for hamburger decreases. |
| | | | ■ A decline in income increases the demand for bus service. |
| 4. Expectations of buyers | Direct | | ■ Consumers expect that gasoline will be in short supply next month and that prices will rise sharply. Consequently, consumers fill the tanks in their cars this month, and there is an increase in demand for gasoline. |
| | | | ■ Months later, consumers expect the price of gasoline to fall soon, and the demand for gasoline decreases. |

*continued on next page*

Continued from previous page

| Nonprice determinant of demand | Relationship with the demand curve | Shift in the demand curve | Example |
|---|---|---|---|
| 5. Prices of related goods | | | |
|   a. Substitute goods | Direct | Price / Quantity ($D_2$ $D_1$) | ■ A reduction in the price of tea decreases the demand for coffee. |
| | | Price / Quantity ($D_1$ $D_2$) | ■ An increase in the price of air fares causes higher demand for bus transportation. |
|   b. Complementary goods | Inverse | Price / Quantity ($D_1$ $D_2$) | ■ A decline in the price of CD burners increases the demand for recordable CDs. |
| | | Price / Quantity ($D_2$ $D_1$) | ■ A higher price for peanut butter decreases the demand for jelly. |

and quantities supplied, which is stated as the **law of supply**. The law of supply states there is a direct relationship between the price of a good and the quantity sellers are willing to offer for sale in a defined time period, ceteris paribus. Interpreting the individual *supply curve* for Rap City shown in Exhibit 6 is basically the same as interpreting Bob's demand curve shown in Exhibit 1. Each point on the curve represents a quantity supplied (measured along the horizontal axis) at a particular price (measured along the vertical axis). For example, at a price of $10 per disc (point *C*), the quantity supplied by the seller, Rap City, is 35,000 CDs per year. At the higher price of $15, the quantity supplied increases to 45,000 CDs per year (point *B*).

> **CONCLUSION** *Supply is a curve or schedule showing the various quantities of a product sellers are willing to produce and offer for sale at possible prices during a specified period of time, ceteris paribus.*

Why are sellers willing to sell more at a higher price? Suppose Farmer Brown is trying to decide whether to devote more of his land, labor, and barn space to the production of soybeans. Recall from Chapter 2 the production possibilities curve and the concept of increasing opportunity cost developed in Exhibit 3. If Farmer Brown devotes few of his resources to producing soybeans, the opportunity cost of, say, producing milk is small. But increasing soybean production means a higher opportunity cost, measured by the quantity of milk not produced. The logical question is: What would induce Farmer Brown to produce more soybeans for sale and overcome the higher opportunity cost of producing less milk?

**Law of supply**
The principle that there is a direct relationship between the price of a good and the quantity sellers are willing to offer for sale in a defined time period, ceteris paribus.

**Supply**
A curve or schedule showing the various quantities of a product sellers are willing to produce and offer for sale at possible prices during a specified period of time, ceteris paribus.

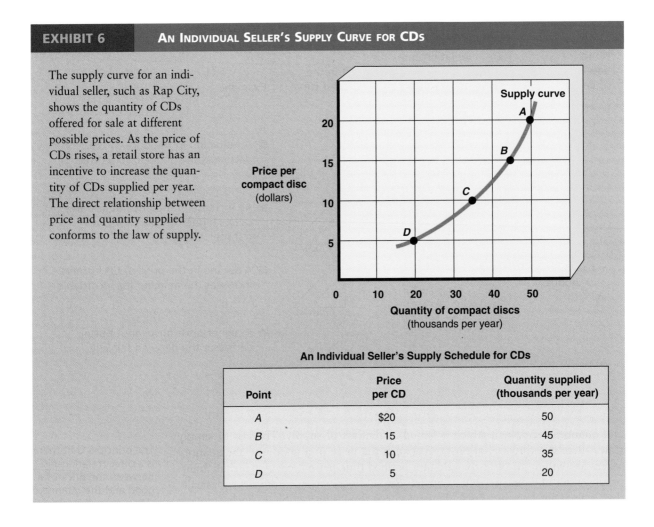

**EXHIBIT 6          AN INDIVIDUAL SELLER'S SUPPLY CURVE FOR CDs**

The supply curve for an individual seller, such as Rap City, shows the quantity of CDs offered for sale at different possible prices. As the price of CDs rises, a retail store has an incentive to increase the quantity of CDs supplied per year. The direct relationship between price and quantity supplied conforms to the law of supply.

**An Individual Seller's Supply Schedule for CDs**

| Point | Price per CD | Quantity supplied (thousands per year) |
|---|---|---|
| A | $20 | 50 |
| B | 15 | 45 |
| C | 10 | 35 |
| D | 5 | 20 |

You guessed it! There must be the *incentive* of a higher price for soybeans.

**CONCLUSION**  *Only at a higher price will it be profitable for sellers to incur the higher opportunity cost associated with producing and supplying a larger quantity.*

## MARKET SUPPLY

To construct a *market* supply curve, we follow the same procedure used to derive a market demand curve. That is, we *horizontally* sum all the quantities supplied at various prices that might prevail in the market.

Let's assume Super Sound Company and High Vibes Company are the only two firms selling CDs in a given market. As you can see in Exhibit 7, the market supply curve, $S_{total}$, slopes upward to the right. At a price of $25, Super Sound will supply 25,000 CDs per year and High Vibes will supply 35,000 CDs per year. Thus, summing the two individual supply curves, $S_1$ and $S_2$, *horizontally*, the total

**EXHIBIT 7**  **THE MARKET SUPPLY CURVE FOR CDS**

Super Sound supply curve  +  High Vibes supply curve  =  Market supply curve

Price per compact disc (dollars)

Quantity of compact discs (thousands per year)

The Market Supply Schedule for CDs

| Price per CD | Quantity supplied per year | | |
|---|---|---|---|
| | Super Sound | + High Vibes = | Total supply |
| $25 | 25 | 35 | 60 |
| 20 | 20 | 30 | 50 |
| 15 | 15 | 25 | 40 |
| 10 | 10 | 20 | 30 |
| 5 | 5 | 15 | 20 |

Super Sound and High Vibes are two individual businesses selling CDs. If these are the only two firms in the CD market, the market supply curve, $S_{total}$, can be derived by summing horizontally the individual supply curves, $S_1$ and $S_2$.

of 60,000 CDs is plotted at this price on the market supply curve, $S_{total}$. Similar calculations at other prices along the price axis generate a market supply curve, telling us the total amount of CDs these businesses offer for sale at different selling prices.

## CHECKPOINT

### Can the Law of Supply Be Repealed?

The United States experienced two oil shocks during the 1970s in the aftermath of Middle East tensions. Congress said no to high oil prices by passing a law prohibiting prices above a legal limit. Supporters of such price controls said this was a way to ensure adequate supply without allowing oil producers to earn excess profits. Did price controls increase, decrease, or have no effect on U.S. oil production during the 1970s?

**Change in quantity supplied**
A movement between points along a stationary supply curve, ceteris paribus.

**Change in supply**
An increase or a decrease in the quantity supplied at each possible price. An increase in supply is a rightward shift in the entire supply curve. A decrease in supply is a leftward shift in the entire supply curve.

# The Distinction between Changes in Quantity Supplied and Changes in Supply

As in demand theory, the price of a product is not the only factor that influences how much sellers offer for sale. Once we relax the ceteris paribus assumption, there are six principal *nonprice determinants* (or simply, *supply shifters*) that can shift the supply curve's position: (1) the number of sellers, (2) technology, (3) resource prices, (4) taxes and subsidies, (5) expectations, and (6) prices of other goods. We will discuss these nonprice determinants in more detail momentarily, but first we must distinguish between a **change in quantity supplied** and a **change in supply**.

A change in quantity supplied is a movement between points along a stationary supply curve, ceteris paribus. In Exhibit 8(a), at the price of $10, the quantity supplied is 30 million CDs per year (point $A$). At the higher price of $15, sellers offer a larger "quantity supplied" of 40 million CDs per year (point $B$). Econo-

**EXHIBIT 8**          **MOVEMENT ALONG A SUPPLY CURVE VERSUS A SHIFT IN SUPPLY**

Part (a) presents the market supply curve, $S$, for CDs per year. If the price is $10 at point $A$, the quantity supplied by firms will be 30 million CDs. If the price increases to $15 at point $B$, the quantity supplied will increase from 30 million to 40 million CDs.

Part (b) illustrates an increase in supply. A change in some nonprice determinant can cause an increase in supply from $S_1$ to $S_2$. At a price of $15 on $S_1$ (point A), the quantity supplied per year is 30 million CDs. At this price on $S_2$ (point $B$), the quantity supplied increases to 40 million.

mists describe the effect of the rise in price as an increase in the quantity supplied of 10 million CDs per year.

> **CONCLUSION** *Under the law of supply, any increase in price along the vertical axis will cause an increase in the quantity supplied, measured along the horizontal axis.*

A change in supply is an increase (rightward shift) or a decrease (leftward shift) in the quantity supplied at each possible price. If ceteris paribus no longer applies and if one of the six nonprice factors changes, the impact is to alter the supply curve's location.

> **CONCLUSION** *Changes in nonprice determinants can produce only a shift in the supply curve and not a movement along the supply curve.*

In Exhibit 8(b), the rightward shift (an increase in supply) from $S_1$ to $S_2$ means that at all possible prices sellers offer a greater quantity for sale. At $15 per CD, for instance, sellers provide 40 million for sale annually (point *B*), rather than 30 million (point *A*).

Another case is that some nonprice factor changes and causes a leftward shift (a decrease in supply) from supply curve $S_1$. As a result, a smaller quantity will be offered for sale at any price.

Exhibit 9 summarizes the terminology for the effects of changes in price and nonprice determinants on the supply curve.

# Nonprice Determinants of Supply

Now we turn to how each of the six basic nonprice factors affects supply.

## NUMBER OF SELLERS

What happens when a severe drought destroys wheat or a frost ruins the orange crop? The damaging effect of the weather may force orange growers out of business, and supply decreases. When the government eases restrictions on hunting alligators, the number of alligator hunters increases, and the supply curve for alligator meat and skins increases. Internationally, the United States may decide to lower trade barriers on textile imports, and this action increases supply by allowing new foreign firms to add their individual supply curves to the U.S. market supply curve for textiles. Conversely, higher U.S. trade barriers on textile imports shift the U.S. market supply curve for textiles leftward.

## TECHNOLOGY

Never have we experienced such an explosion of new production techniques. Throughout the world, new and more efficient technology is making it possible to manufacture more products at any possible selling price. New, more-powerful computers reduce production costs and increase the supply of all sorts of goods and services. For example, computers are now milking cows. Computers admit the cows into the milking area and then activate lasers to guide milking cups into

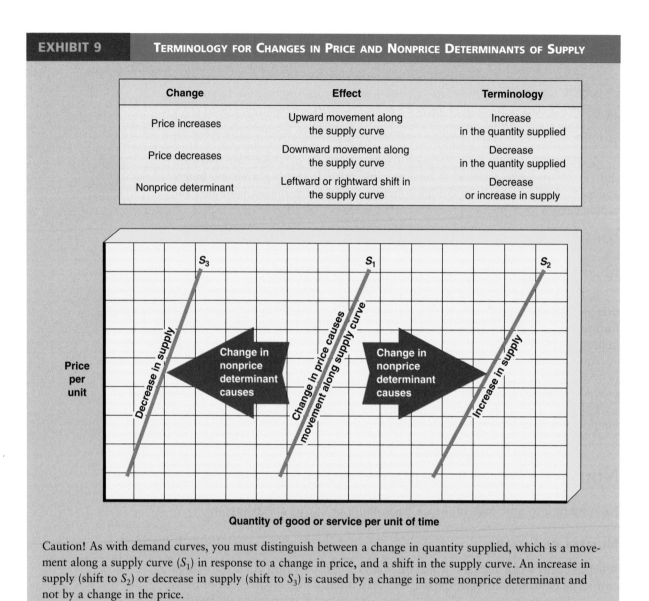

| **EXHIBIT 9** | **TERMINOLOGY FOR CHANGES IN PRICE AND NONPRICE DETERMINANTS OF SUPPLY** |
|---|---|

| Change | Effect | Terminology |
|---|---|---|
| Price increases | Upward movement along the supply curve | Increase in the quantity supplied |
| Price decreases | Downward movement along the supply curve | Decrease in the quantity supplied |
| Nonprice determinant | Leftward or rightward shift in the supply curve | Decrease or increase in supply |

Caution! As with demand curves, you must distinguish between a change in quantity supplied, which is a movement along a supply curve ($S_1$) in response to a change in price, and a shift in the supply curve. An increase in supply (shift to $S_2$) or decrease in supply (shift to $S_3$) is caused by a change in some nonprice determinant and not by a change in the price.

place. Dairy farmers no longer must wake up at 5:30 a.m., and cows get milked whenever they fancy, day or night. As this technology spreads across the United States, it will be possible to offer more milk for sale at each possible price, and the entire supply curve for milk shifts to the right.

## RESOURCE PRICES

Natural resources, labor, capital, and entrepreneurship are all required to produce products, and the prices of these resources affect supply. Suppose many firms are competing for computer programmers to design their software, and the salaries of these highly skilled workers increase. This increase in the price of labor adds to the cost of production. As a result, the supply of computer software decreases because sellers must charge more than before for any quantity supplied. Any

## PC Prices: How Low Can They Go?
*Applicable Concept: nonprice determinants of demand and supply*

Radio was in existence for 38 years before 50 million people tuned in. Television took 13 years to reach that benchmark. Sixteen years after the first PC kit came out, 50 million people were using one. Once opened to the public, the Internet crossed that line in four years.[1]

An Associated Press article reported in 1998:

*Personal computers, which tumbled below the $1,000-price barrier just 18 months ago, now are breaking through the $400-price-mark—putting them within reach of the average U.S. family. The plunge in PC prices reflects declining wholesale prices for computer parts, such as microprocessors, memory chips and hard drives. "We've seen a massive transformation in the PC business," said Andrew Peck, an analyst with Cowen & Co., based in Boston. Today's computers costing below $1,000 are equal or greater in power than PCs costing $1,500 and more just a few years ago— working well for word processing, spreadsheet applications and Internet access, the most popular computer uses.[2]*

In 1999, a *Wall Street Journal* article reported that PC makers and distributors were bypassing their industry's time-honored sales channels. PC makers such as Hewlett-Packard are now using the Internet to sell directly to consumers. In doing so, they are following the successful strategy of Dell, which for years has bypassed storefront retailers and the PC distributors who traditionally keep them stocked, going instead straight to the consumer with catalogs, an 800 number, and Web sites.[3]

In 2001, a *New York Times* article described a computer price war:

*We reached a situation where the market was saturated in 2000. People who needed computers had them. Vendors are living on sales of replacements, at least in the United States. But that doesn't give you the kind of growth these compa-*

*nies were used to. In the past, most price cuts came from falling prices for processors and other components. In addition, manufacturers have been narrowing profit margins for the last couple years. But when demand dried up last fall, the more aggressive manufacturers decided to try to gain market share by cutting prices to the bone. This is an all-out battle for market share.[4]*

In 2006, an analyst in *USA Today* observed that users could pick up good deals on desktop and notebook PCs following computer chip price cuts. Chipmakers Intel and AMD reduced the cost of computer chips in a price war. This article concluded that prices were falling at the right time and users will get good specification for their investment.[5] And in 2005, Dell, Gateway, and CompUSA sold computers for less than $400 that outperformed most middle-of-the-road PCs from only a few years previously.

### ANALYZE THE ISSUE

Identify changes in quantity demanded, changes in demand, changes in quantity supplied, and changes in supply described in the article. For any change in demand or supply, also identify the nonprice determinant causing the change.

[1]The Emerging Digital Economy (U.S. Department of Commerce, 1998), Chap. 1, p. 1 (http://www.ecommerce.gov/chapter1.htm).

[2]David E. Kalish, "PC Prices Fall Below $400, Luring Bargain-Hunters," Associated Press/*Charlotte Observer*, Aug. 25, 1998, p. 3D.

[3]George Anders, "Online Web Seller Asks: How Low Can PC Prices Go?" *The Wall Street Journal*, Jan. 19, 1999, p. B1.

[4]Barnaby J. Feder, "Five Questions for Martin Reynolds: A Computer Price War Leaves Buyers Smiling," *New York Times*, May 13, 2001.

[5]Michelle Kessler, "School Shoppers See PC Prices Fall," *USA Today*, Aug. 14, 2006, P.B.1.

reduction in production cost caused by a decline in the price of resources will have an opposite effect and increase supply.

### TAXES AND SUBSIDIES

Certain taxes, such as sales taxes, have the same effect on supply as an increase in the price of a resource. The impact of an increase in the sales tax is similar to a rise in the salaries of computer programmers. The higher sales tax imposes an additional production cost on, for example, CDs, and the supply curve shifts left-ward. Conversely, a payment from the government for each CD produced (an unlikely subsidy) would have the same effect as lower prices for resources or a technological advance. That is, the supply curve for CDs shifts rightward.

### EXPECTATIONS OF PRODUCERS

Expectations affect both current demand and current supply. Suppose a war in the Middle East causes oil producers to believe that oil prices will rise dramatically. Their initial response could be to hold back a portion of the oil in their storage tanks so they can sell more and make greater profits later when oil prices rise. One approach used by the major oil companies might be to limit the amount of gaso-line delivered to independent distributors. This response by the oil industry shifts the current supply curve to the left. Now suppose farmers anticipate the price of wheat will soon fall sharply. The reaction is to sell their inventories stored in silos today before the price declines tomorrow. Such a response shifts the supply curve for wheat to the right.

### PRICES OF OTHER GOODS THE FIRM COULD PRODUCE

Businesses are always considering shifting resources from producing one good to producing another good. A rise in the price of one product relative to the prices of other products signals to suppliers that switching production to the product with the higher relative price yields higher profit. If the price of tomatoes rises while the price of corn remains the same, many farmers will divert more of their land to tomatoes and less to corn. The result is an increase in the supply of toma-toes and a decrease in the supply of corn. This happens because the opportunity cost of growing corn, measured in forgone tomato profits, increases.

    Exhibit 10 summarizes the relationship between changes in the nonprice deter-minants of supply and the supply curve, accompanied by examples for each type of nonprice factor change.

# A Market Supply and Demand Analysis

**Market**
Any arrangement in which buyers and sell-ers interact to deter-mine the price and quantity of goods and services exchanged.

A drumroll please! Buyer and seller actors are on center stage to perform a bal-ancing act in a **market**. A market is any arrangement in which buyers and sellers interact to determine the price and quantity of goods and services exchanged. Let's consider the retail market for tennis shoes. Exhibit 11 displays hypothetical mar-ket demand and supply data for this product. Notice in column 1 of the exhibit that price serves as a common variable for both supply and demand relationships. Columns 2 and 3 list the quantity demanded and the quantity supplied for pairs of tennis shoes per year.

**Surplus**
A market condition existing at any price where the quantity supplied is greater than the quantity demanded.

    The important question for market supply and demand analysis is: Which sell-ing price and quantity will prevail in the market? Let's start by asking what will happen if retail stores supply 75,000 pairs of tennis shoes and charge $105 a pair. At this relatively high price for tennis shoes, consumers are willing and able to purchase only 25,000 pairs. As a result, 50,000 pairs of tennis shoes remain as unsold inventory on the shelves of sellers (column 4), and the market condition is a **surplus** (column 5). A surplus is a market condition existing at any price where the quantity supplied is greater than the quantity demanded.

| EXHIBIT 10 | SUMMARY OF THE IMPACT OF CHANGES IN NONPRICE DETERMINANTS OF SUPPLY ON THE SUPPLY CURVE | | |
|---|---|---|---|
| **Nonprice determinant of demand** | **Relationship with the supply curve** | **Shift in the supply curve** | **Example** |
| 1. Number of sellers | Direct | Price / Quantity ($S_1$, $S_2$) | ■ The United States lowers trade restrictions on foreign textiles, and the supply of textiles in the United States increases. |
| | | Price / Quantity ($S_2$, $S_1$) | ■ A severe drought destroys the orange crop, and the supply of oranges decreases. |
| 2. Technology | Direct | Price / Quantity ($S_1$, $S_2$) | ■ New methods of producing automobiles reduce production costs, and the supply of automobiles increases. |
| | | Price / Quantity ($S_2$, $S_1$) | ■ Technology is destroyed in war, and production costs increase; the result is a decrease in the supply of good $X$. |
| 3. Resource prices | Inverse | Price / Quantity ($S_1$, $S_2$) | ■ A decline in the price of computer chips increases the supply of computers. |
| | | Price / Quantity ($S_2$, $S_1$) | ■ An increase in the cost of farm equipment decreases the supply of soybeans. |
| 4. Taxes and subsidies | Inverse and direct | Price / Quantity ($S_2$, $S_1$) | ■ An increase in the per-pack tax on cigarettes reduces the supply of cigarettes. |
| | | Price / Quantity ($S_1$, $S_2$) | ■ A government payment to dairy farmers based on the number of gallons produced increases the supply of milk. |
| 5. Expectations | Inverse | Price / Quantity ($S_2$, $S_1$) | ■ Oil companies anticipate a substantial rise in future oil prices, and this expectation causes these companies to decrease their current supply of oil. |
| | | Price / Quantity ($S_1$, $S_2$) | ■ Farmers expect the future price of wheat to decline, so they increase the present supply of wheat. |
| 6. Prices of other goods and services | Inverse | Price / Quantity ($S_2$, $S_1$) | ■ A rise in the price of brand-name drugs causes drug companies to decrease the supply of generic drugs. |
| | | Price / Quantity ($S_1$, $S_2$) | ■ A decline in the price of tomatoes causes farmers to increase the supply of cucumbers. |

| EXHIBIT 11 | | DEMAND, SUPPLY, AND EQUILIBRIUM FOR TENNIS SHOES (PAIRS PER YEAR) | | | |
|---|---|---|---|---|---|
| (1)<br>Price<br>per pair | (2)<br>Quantity<br>demanded | (3)<br>Quantity<br>supplied | (4)<br>Difference<br>(3) − (2) | (5)<br>Market<br>condition | (6)<br>Pressure<br>on price |
| $105 | 25,000 | 75,000 | +50,000 | Surplus | Downward |
| 90 | 30,000 | 70,000 | +40,000 | Surplus | Downward |
| 75 | 40,000 | 60,000 | +20,000 | Surplus | Downward |
| 60 | 50,000 | 50,000 | 0 | Equilibrium | Stationary |
| 45 | 60,000 | 35,000 | −25,000 | Shortage | Upward |
| 30 | 80,000 | 20,000 | −60,000 | Shortage | Upward |
| 15 | 100,000 | 5,000 | −95,000 | Shortage | Upward |

How will retailers react to a surplus? Competition forces sellers to bid down their selling price to attract more sales (column 6). If they cut the selling price to $90, there will still be a surplus of 40,000 pairs of tennis shoes, and pressure on sellers to cut their selling price will continue. If the price falls to $75, there will still be an unwanted surplus of 20,000 pairs of tennis shoes remaining as inventory, and pressure to charge a lower price will persist.

Now let's assume sellers slash the price of tennis shoes to $15 per pair. This price is very attractive to consumers, and the quantity demanded is 100,000 pairs of tennis shoes each year. However, sellers are willing and able to provide only 5,000 pairs at this price. The good news is that some consumers buy these 5,000 pairs of tennis shoes at $15. The bad news is that potential buyers are willing to purchase 95,000 more pairs at that price, but cannot because the shoes are not on the shelves for sale. This out-of-stock condition signals the existence of a **shortage**. A shortage is a market condition existing at any price where the quantity supplied is less than the quantity demanded.

In the case of a shortage, unsatisfied consumers compete to obtain the product by bidding to pay a higher price. Because sellers are seeking the higher profits that higher prices make possible, they gladly respond by setting a higher price of, say, $30 and increasing the quantity supplied to 20,000 pairs annually. At the price of $30, the shortage persists because the quantity demanded still exceeds the quantity supplied. Thus, a price of $30 will also be temporary because the unfulfilled quantity demanded provides an incentive for sellers to raise their selling price further and offer more tennis shoes for sale. Suppose the price of tennis shoes rises to $45 a pair. At this price, the shortage falls to 25,000 pairs, and the market still gives sellers the message to move upward along their market supply curve and sell for a higher price.

**Shortage**
A market condition existing at any price where the quantity supplied is less than the quantity demanded.

## EQUILIBRIUM PRICE AND QUANTITY

Assuming sellers are free to sell their products at any price, trial and error will make all possible price-quantity combinations unstable except at **equilibrium**. Equilibrium occurs at any price and quantity where the quantity demanded and the quantity supplied are equal. Economists also refer to *equilibrium* as *market clearing*.

In Exhibit 11, $60 is the *equilibrium* price, and 50,000 pairs of tennis shoes is the *equilibrium* quantity per year. Equilibrium means that the forces of supply and demand are in balance and there is no reason for price or quantity to change,

**Equilibrium**
A market condition that occurs at any price and quantity where the quantity demanded and the quantity supplied are equal.

ceteris paribus. In short, all prices and quantities except a unique equilibrium price and quantity are temporary. Once the price of tennis shoes is $60, this price will not change unless a nonprice factor changes demand or supply.

English economist Alfred Marshall (1842–1924) compared supply and demand to a pair of scissor blades. He wrote, "We might as reasonably dispute whether it is the upper or the under blade of a pair of scissors that cuts a piece of paper, as whether value is governed by utility [demand] or cost of production [supply]."[1] Joining market supply and market demand in Exhibit 12 allows us to clearly see the "two blades"—that is, the demand curve, $D$, and the supply curve, $S$. We can

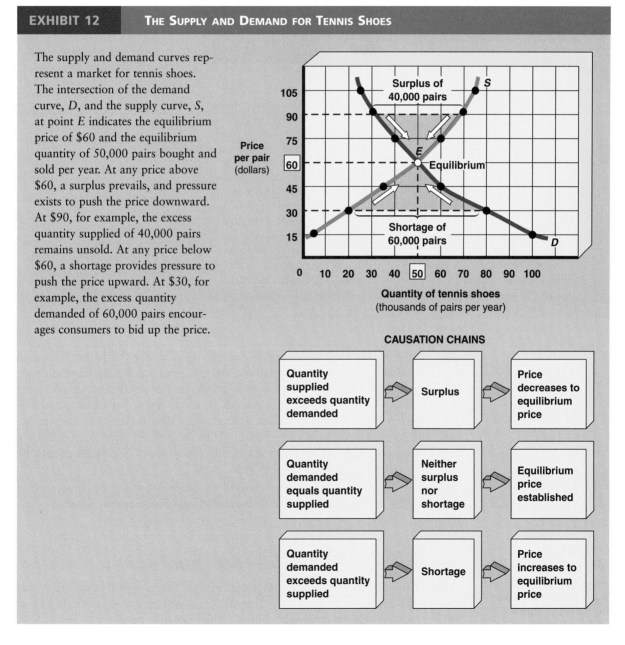

**EXHIBIT 12**     **THE SUPPLY AND DEMAND FOR TENNIS SHOES**

The supply and demand curves represent a market for tennis shoes. The intersection of the demand curve, $D$, and the supply curve, $S$, at point $E$ indicates the equilibrium price of $60 and the equilibrium quantity of 50,000 pairs bought and sold per year. At any price above $60, a surplus prevails, and pressure exists to push the price downward. At $90, for example, the excess quantity supplied of 40,000 pairs remains unsold. At any price below $60, a shortage provides pressure to push the price upward. At $30, for example, the excess quantity demanded of 60,000 pairs encourages consumers to bid up the price.

[1]Alfred Marshall, *Principles of Economics*, 8th ed. (New York: Macmillan, 1982), p. 348.

## International Economics

# The Market Approach to Organ Shortages
*Applicable Concept: price system*

The Chinese government has been charged with selling organs from political and criminal prisoners it puts to death. Witnesses report that when prisoners are executed, surgeons wait in nearby vans to remove the organs. In the Chinese culture, there are few voluntary organ donations because people believe it desecrates the body. However, people from other countries flock to China for cheap transplants.

The National Transplant Organ Act of 1984 made sale of organs illegal in the United States. Economist James R. Rinehart wrote the following on this subject.

*If you were in charge of a kidney transplant program with more potential recipients than donors, how would you allocate the organs under your*

control? Life and death decisions cannot be avoided. Some individuals are not going to get kidneys regardless of how the organs are distributed because there simply are not enough to go around. Persons who run such programs are influenced in a variety of ways. It would be difficult not to favor friends, relatives, influential people, and those who are championed by the press. Dr. John la Puma, at the Center for Clinical Med-

ical Ethics, University of Chicago, suggested recently that we use a lottery system for selecting transplant patients. He feels that the present rationing system is unfair.

The selection process frequently takes the form of having the patient wait at home until a suitable donor is found. What this means is that, at any given point in time, many potential recipients are just waiting for an organ to be made available. In essence, the organs are rationed to those who are able to survive the wait. In many situations, patients are simply screened out because they are not considered to be suitable candidates for a transplant. For instance, patients with

measure the amount of any surplus or shortage by the horizontal distance between the demand and supply curves. At any price *above* equilibrium—say, $90—there is an *excess quantity supplied* (surplus) of 40,000 pairs of tennis shoes. For any price *below* equilibrium—$30, for example—the horizontal distance between the curves tells us there is an *excess quantity demanded* (shortage) of 60,000 pairs. When the price per pair is $60, the market supply curve and the market demand curve intersect at point *E*, and the quantity demanded equals the quantity supplied at 50,000 pairs per year.

> **CONCLUSION** *Graphically, the intersection of the supply curve and the demand curve is the market equilibrium price-quantity point. When all other nonprice factors are held constant, this is the only stable coordinate on the graph.*

**Price system**
A mechanism that uses the forces of supply and demand to create an equilibrium through rising and falling prices.

Our analysis leads to an important conclusion. The predictable or stable outcome in the tennis shoes example is that the price will eventually come to rest at $60 per pair. All other factors held constant, the price may be above or below $60, but the forces of surplus or shortage guarantee that any price other than the equilibrium price is temporary. This is the theory of how the **price system** operates, and *heart disease and overt psychosis often are excluded. Others with end-stage liver disorders are denied new organs on the grounds that the habits that produced the disease may remain to jeopardize recovery. . . .*

*Under the present arrangements, owners receive no monetary compensation; therefore, suppliers are willing to supply fewer organs than potential recipients want. Compensating a supplier monetarily would encourage more people to offer their organs for sale. It also would be an excellent incentive for us to take better care of our organs. After all, who would want an enlarged liver or a weak heart. . . ?*[1]

The following excerpt from a newspaper article illustrates the controversy:

*Mickey Mantle's temporary deliverance from death, thanks to a liver transplant, illustrated how the organ-donations system is heavily weighted against poor potential recipients who cannot pass what University of Pennsylvania medical ethicist Arthur Caplan calls the "wallet biopsy.". . . Thus, affluent patients like Mickey Mantle may get evaluated and listed simultaneously in different regions to increase their odds of finding a donor. The New Yorker found his organ donor in Texas' Region 4. Such a system is not only highly unfair, but it leads to other kinds of abuses.*[2]

Based on altruism, the organ donor distribution system continues to result in shortages. In 2005, the United Network for Organ Sharing (UNOS) reported that there were over 25,000 transplants in the United States while over 80,000 patients waited on the list for organs.

## ANALYZE THE ISSUE

1. Draw supply and demand curves for the U.S. organ market and compare the U.S. market to the market in a country where selling organs is legal.

2. What are some arguments against using the price system to allocate organs?

3. Should foreigners have the right to buy U.S. organs and U.S. citizens have the right to buy foreign organs?

[1] James R. Rinehart, "The Market Approach to Organ Shortages," *Journal of Health Care Marketing* 8, no. 1 (March 1988): 72–75.

[2] Carl Senna, "The Wallet Biopsy," *Providence Journal*, June 13, 1995, p. B-7.

it is the cornerstone of microeconomic analysis. The price system is a mechanism that uses the forces of supply and demand to create an equilibrium through rising and falling prices. Stated simply, price plays a rationing role. The price system is important because it is a mechanism for distributing scarce goods and services. At the equilibrium price of $60, only those consumers willing to pay $60 per pair get tennis shoes, and there are no shoes for buyers unwilling to pay that price.

## CHECKPOINT

### Can the Price System Eliminate Scarcity?

You visit Cuba and observe that at "official" prices there is a constant shortage of consumer goods in government stores. People explain that in Cuba scarcity is caused by low prices combined with low production quotas set by the government. Many Cuban citizens say that the condition of scarcity would be eliminated if the government would allow markets to respond to supply and demand. Can the price system eliminate scarcity?

# Key Concepts

Law of demand
Demand
Change in quantity demanded
Change in demand
Normal good
Inferior good

Substitute good
Complementary good
Law of supply
Supply
Change in quantity supplied
Change in supply

Market
Surplus
Shortage
Equilibrium
Price system

# Summary

■ The **law of demand** states there is an inverse relationship between the price and the quantity
demanded, ceteris paribus. A market demand curve
is the horizontal summation of individual demand
curves.

■ A **change in quantity demanded** is a movement along
a stationary demand curve caused by a change in
price. When any of the nonprice determinants of
demand changes, the demand curve responds by
shifting. An *increase in demand* (rightward shift) or
a *decrease in demand* (leftward shift) is caused by a
change in one of the nonprice determinants.

**CHANGE IN QUANTITY DEMANDED**

**CHANGE IN DEMAND**

■ **Nonprice determinants of demand** are as follows:
 a. Number of buyers
 b. Tastes and preferences
 c. Income (normal and inferior goods)
 d. Expectations of future price and income changes
 e. Prices of related goods (substitutes and
  complements)

■ The **law of supply** states there is a direct relationship
between the price and the quantity supplied, ceteris
paribus. The market supply curve is the horizontal
summation of individual supply curves.

■ A **change in quantity supplied** is a movement along a
stationary supply curve caused by a change in price.
When any of the nonprice determinants of supply
changes, the supply curve responds by shifting. An
*increase in supply* (rightward shift) or a *decrease in
supply* (leftward shift) is caused by a change in one
of the nonprice determinants.

**CHANGE IN QUANTITY SUPPLIED**

## CHANGE IN SUPPLY

- **Nonprice determinants of supply** are as follows:
  a. Number of sellers
  b. Technology
  c. Resource prices
  d. Taxes and subsidies
  e. Expectations of future price changes
  f. Prices of other goods and services

- A **surplus or shortage** exists at any price where the quantity demanded and the quantity supplied are not equal. When the price of a good is higher than the equilibrium price, there is an excess quantity supplied, or a *surplus*. When the price is less than the equilibrium price, there is an excess quantity demanded, or a *shortage*.

- **Equilibrium** is the unique price and quantity established at the intersection of the supply and demand curves. Only at equilibrium does quantity demanded equal quantity supplied.

## EQUILIBRIUM

- The **price system** is the supply and demand mechanism that establishes equilibrium through the ability of prices to rise and fall.

## Summary of Conclusion Statements

- Demand is a curve or schedule showing the various quantities of a product consumers are willing to purchase at possible prices during a specified period of time, ceteris paribus.

- Under the law of demand, any decrease in price along the vertical axis will cause an increase in quantity demanded, measured along the horizontal axis.

- Changes in nonprice determinants can produce only a shift in the demand curve and not a movement along the demand curve, which is caused by a change in price.

- Supply is a curve or schedule showing the various quantities of a product sellers are willing to produce and offer for sale at possible prices during a specified period of time, ceteris paribus.

- Only at a higher price will it be profitable for sellers to incur the higher opportunity cost associated with producing and supplying a larger quantity.

- Under the law of supply, any increase in price along the vertical axis will cause an increase in quantity supplied, measured along the horizontal axis.

- Changes in nonprice determinants can only produce a shift in the supply curve and not a movement along the supply curve.

- Graphically, the intersection of the supply curve and the demand curve is the market equilibrium price-quantity point. When all other nonprice factors are held constant, this is the only stable coordinate on the graph.

## Study Questions and Problems

1. Some people will pay a higher price for brand-name goods. For example, some people buy Rolls Royces and Rolex watches to impress others. Does knowingly paying higher prices for certain items just to be a "snob" violate the law of demand?

2. Draw graphs to illustrate the difference between a decrease in the quantity demanded and a decrease in demand for Mickey Mantle baseball cards. Give a possible reason for change in each graph.

3. Suppose oil prices rise sharply for years as a result of a war in the Persian Gulf region. What happens and why to the demand for
   a. Cars
   b. Home insulation
   c. Coal
   d. Tires

4. Draw graphs to illustrate the difference between a decrease in quantity supplied and a decrease in supply for condominiums. Give a possible reason for change in each graph.

5. Use supply and demand analysis to explain why the quantity of word processing software exchanged increases from one year to the next.

6. Predict the direction of change for either supply or demand in the following situations:
   a. Several new companies enter the home computer industry.
   b. Consumers suddenly decide large cars are unfashionable.
   c. The U.S. Surgeon General issues a report stating that tomatoes prevent colds.
   d. Frost threatens to damage the coffee crop, and consumers expect the price to rise sharply in the future.
   e. The price of tea falls. What is the effect on the coffee market?
   f. The price of sugar rises. What is the effect on the coffee market?
   g. Tobacco lobbyists convince Congress to remove the tax paid by sellers on each carton of cigarettes sold.
   h. A new type of robot is invented that will pick peaches.
   i. A computer game company anticipates that the future price of its games will fall much lower than the current price.

7. Explain and illustrate graphically the effect of the following situations:
   a. Population growth surges rapidly.
   b. The prices of resources used in the production of good X increase.
   c. The government is paying a $1-per-unit subsidy for each unit of a good produced.
   d. The incomes of consumers of normal good X increase.
   e. The incomes of consumers of inferior good Y decrease.
   f. Farmers are deciding what crop to plant and learn that the price of corn has fallen relative to the price of cotton.

8. Explain why the market price may not be the same as the equilibrium price.

9. If a new breakthrough in manufacturing technology reduces the cost of producing CD players by half, what will happen to the
   a. supply of CD players?
   b. demand for CD players?
   c. equilibrium price and quantity of CD players?
   d. demand for CDs?

10. The U.S. Postal Service is facing increased competition from firms providing overnight delivery of packages and letters. Additional competition has emerged because messages can be sent over computers and fax machines. What will be the effect of this competition on the market demand for mail delivered by the post office?

11. There is a shortage of college basketball and football tickets for some games, and a surplus occurs for other games. Why do shortages and surpluses exist for different games?

12. Explain the statement "People respond to incentives and disincentives" in relation to the demand curve and supply curve for good X.

## Study Guide Questions

1. The principle that there is a direct relationship between the price of a good and the quantity sellers are willing to offer for sale in a defined time period, ceteris paribus, is the _____.

2. Which of the following will increase the demand for large automobiles?
   a. A fall in the price of small automobiles
   b. A rise in insurance rates for large automobiles
   c. A fall in the price of large automobiles.
   d. An increase in buyers' incomes (assuming large automobiles to be a normal good)

3. Assume that both oranges and peaches can be grown on the same type of land. A decrease in the price of peaches, other things being equal, will cause a (an)

a. upward movement along the supply curve for oranges.
b. downward movement along the supply curve for oranges.
c. rightward shift of the supply curve for oranges.
d. leftward shift of the supply curve for oranges.

4. Assume Congress passes a new tax of $2.00 per pack on cigarettes. The effect on the supply curve is a (an)
a. decrease in supply.

b. increase in supply.
c. decrease in quantity supplied.
d. increase in quantity supplied.

5. T  F  Suppose the market price of good X is below the equilibrium price. The result is a shortage, and sellers can be expected to decrease the quantity of good X supplied.

**Answers to these questions are in the complete Study Guide at www.thomsonedu.com/thomsonnow.**

 **For Online Exercises, go to the text Web site at www.thomsonedu.com/economics/tucker.**

 Checkpoint Answers

## Can Gasoline Become an Exception to the Law of Demand?

As the price of oil began to rise, the expectation of still higher prices caused buyers to buy more now, and, therefore, demand increased. As shown in Exhibit 13 below, suppose the price per gallon of gasoline was initially at $P_1$ and the quantity demanded was $Q_1$ on demand curve $D_1$ (point $A$). Then the Iraqi invasion of Kuwait caused the demand curve to shift rightward to $D_2$. Along the new demand curve, $D_2$, consumers increased their quantity demanded to $Q_2$ at the higher price of $P_2$ per gallon of gasoline (point $B$).

The expectation of rising gasoline prices in the future caused "an increase in demand" rather than "an increase in quantity demanded" in response to a higher price. If you said there are no exceptions to the law of demand, **YOU ARE CORRECT.**

**EXHIBIT 13**

Quantity of gasoline
(millions of gallons per day)

## Can the Law of Supply Be Repealed?

There is not a single quantity of oil—say, 3 million barrels—for sale in the world on a given day. The supply curve for oil is not vertical. As the law of supply states, higher oil prices will cause greater quantities of oil to be offered for sale. At lower prices, oil producers have less incentive to drill deeper for oil that is more expensive to discover.

The government cannot repeal the law of supply. Price controls discourage producers from oil exploration and production, which causes a reduction in the quantity supplied. If you said U.S. oil production decreased in the 1970s when the government put a lid on oil prices, **YOU ARE CORRECT.**

## Can the Price System Eliminate Scarcity?

Recall from Chapter 1 that scarcity is the condition in which human wants are forever greater than the resources available to satisfy those wants. Using markets free from government interference will not solve the scarcity problem. Scarcity exists at any price for a good or service. This means scarcity occurs at any disequilibrium price at which a shortage or surplus exists, and scarcity remains at any equilibrium price at which no shortage or surplus exists.

Although the price system can eliminate shortages (or surpluses), if you said it cannot eliminate scarcity, **YOU ARE CORRECT.**

## Practice Quiz

For an explanation of the correct answers, please visit the tutorial at www.thomsonedu.com/economics/tucker.

1. If the demand curve for good X is downward sloping, an increase in the price will result in
   a. an increase in the demand for good X.
   b. a decrease in the demand for good X.
   c. no change in the quantity demanded for good X.
   d. a larger quantity demanded for good X.
   e. a smaller quantity demanded for good X.

2. The law of demand states that the quantity demanded of a good changes, other things being equal, when
   a. the price of the good changes.
   b. consumer income changes.
   c. the prices of other goods change.
   d. a change occurs in the quantities of other goods purchased.

3. Which of the following is the result of a decrease in the price of tea, other things being equal?
   a. A leftward shift in the demand curve for tea
   b. A downward movement along the demand curve for tea
   c. A rightward shift in the demand curve for tea
   d. An upward movement along the demand curve for tea

4. Which of the following will cause a movement along the demand curve for good X?
   a. A change in the price of a close substitute
   b. A change in the price of good X
   c. A change in consumer tastes and preferences for good X
   d. A change in consumer income

5. Assuming beef and pork are substitutes, a decrease in the price of pork will cause the demand curve for beef to
   a. shift to the left as consumers switch from beef to pork.
   b. shift to the right as consumers switch from beef to pork.
   c. remain unchanged, because beef and pork are sold in separate markets.
   d. none of the above.

6. Assuming coffee and tea are substitutes, a decrease in the price of coffee, other things being equal, results in a (an)
   a. downward movement along the demand curve for tea.

   b. leftward shift in the demand curve for tea.
   c. upward movement along the demand curve for tea.
   d. rightward shift in the demand curve for tea.

7. Assuming steak and potatoes are complements, a decrease in the price of steak will
   a. decrease the demand for steak.
   b. increase the demand for steak.
   c. increase the demand for potatoes.
   d. decrease the demand for potatoes.

8. Assuming steak is a normal good, a decrease in consumer income, other things being equal, will
   a. cause a downward movement along the demand curve for steak.
   b. shift the demand curve for steak to the left.
   c. cause an upward movement along the demand curve for steak.
   d. shift the demand curve for steak to the right.

9. An increase in consumer income, other things being equal, will
   a. shift the supply curve for a normal good to the right.
   b. cause an upward movement along the demand curve for an inferior good.
   c. shift the demand curve for an inferior good to the left.
   d. cause a downward movement along the supply curve for a normal good.

10. Yesterday seller A supplied 400 units of good X at $10 per unit. Today seller A supplies the same quantity of units at $5 per unit. Based on this evidence, seller A has experienced a (an)
    a. decrease in supply.
    b. increase in supply.
    c. increase in the quantity supplied.
    d. decrease in the quantity supplied.
    e. increase in demand.

11. An improvement in technology causes a (an)
    a. leftward shift of the supply curve.
    b. upward movement along the supply curve.
    c. firm to supply a larger quantity at any given price.
    d. downward movement along the supply curve.

12. Suppose autoworkers receive a substantial wage increase. Other things being equal, the price of autos will rise because of a (an)
    a. increase in the demand for autos.
    b. rightward shift of the supply curve for autos.

c. leftward shift of the supply curve for autos.

d. reduction in the demand for autos.

13. Assuming soybeans and tobacco can be grown on the same land, an increase in the price of tobacco, other things being equal, causes a (an)

    a. upward movement along the supply curve for soybeans.

    b. downward movement along the supply curve for soybeans.

    c. rightward shift in the supply curve for soybeans.

    d. leftward shift in the supply curve for soybeans.

14. If $Q_d$ = quantity demanded and $Q_s$ = quantity supplied at a given price, a shortage in the market results when

    a. $Q_s$ is greater than $Q_d$.

    b. $Q_s$ equals $Q_d$.

    c. $Q_d$ is less than or equal to $Q_s$.

    d. $Q_d$ is greater than $Q_s$.

15. Assume that the equilibrium price for a good is $10. If the market price is $5, a

    a. shortage will cause the price to remain at $5.

    b. surplus will cause the price to remain at $5.

    c. shortage will cause the price to rise toward $10.

    d. surplus will cause the price to rise toward $10.

**Exhibit 14 Supply and Demand Curves**

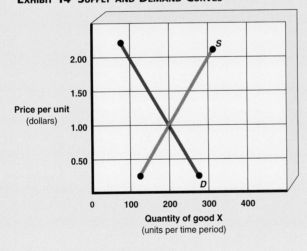

16. In the market shown in Exhibit 14, the equilibrium price and quantity of good X are

    a. $0.50, 200.

    b. $1.50, 300.

    c. $2.00, 100.

    d. $1.00, 200.

17. In Exhibit 14, at a price of $2.00, the market for good X will experience a

    a. shortage of 150 units.

    b. surplus of 100 units.

    c. shortage of 100 units.

    d. surplus of 200 units.

18. In Exhibit 14, if the price of good X moves from $1.00 to $2.00, the new market condition will put

    a. upward pressure on price.

    b. no pressure on price to change.

    c. downward pressure on price.

    d. no pressure on quantity to change.

19. In Exhibit 14, if the market price of good X is initially $.50, a movement toward equilibrium requires

    a. no change, because an equilibrium already exists.

    b. the price to fall below $.50 and both the quantity supplied and the quantity demanded to rise.

    c. the price to remain the same but the supply curve to shift to the left.

    d. the price to rise above $.50, the quantity supplied to rise, and the quantity demanded to fall.

20. In Exhibit 14, if the market price of good X is initially $1.50, a movement toward equilibrium requires

    a. no change, because an equilibrium already exists.

    b. the price to fall below $1.50 and both the quantity supplied and the quantity demanded to fall.

    c. the price to remain the same but the supply curve to shift to the left.

    d. the price to fall below $1.50, the quantity supplied to fall, and the quantity demanded to rise.

# Consumer Surplus, Producer Surplus, and Market Efficiency

This chapter explained how the market forces of demand and supply establish the equilibrium price and output. Here it will be demonstrated that the equilibrium price and quantity determined in a competitive market are desirable because the result is *market efficiency*. To understand this concept, we use the area between the market price and the demand and supply curves to measure gains or losses from market transactions for consumers and producers.

## Consumer Surplus

Consider the market demand curve shown in Exhibit A-1 (a). The height of this demand curve shows the maximum willingness of consumers to purchase ground beef at various prices per pound. At a price of $4.00 (point $X$) no one will purchase ground beef. But if the price drops to $3.50 at point $A$, consumers will purchase one million pounds of ground beef per year. Moving downward along the demand curve to point $B$, consumers will purchase an additional million pounds of ground beef per year at a lower price of $3.00 per pound. If the price continues to drop to $2.50 per pound at point $C$ and lower, consumers are willing to purchase more pounds of ground beef consistent with the law of demand.

Assuming the market equilibrium price for ground beef is $2.00 per pound, we can use the demand curve to measure the net benefit or *consumer surplus* in this market. **Consumer surplus** is the value of the difference between the price consumers are willing to pay for a product on the demand curve and the price actually paid for it. At point $A$, consumers are willing to pay $3.50 per pound, but they actually pay the equilibrium price of $2.00. Thus, consumers earn a surplus of $1.50 ($3.50 − $2.00) per pound multiplied by one million pounds purchased, which is a $15 million consumer surplus. This value is represented by the shaded vertical rectangle formed at point $A$ on the demand curve. At point $B$, consumers who purchase an additional million pounds of ground beef at $3.00 per pound receive a lower extra consumer surplus than at point $A$, represented by a rectangle of lower height. At point $C$, the marginal consumer surplus continues to fall until at equilibrium point $E$, where there is no consumer surplus.

The total value of consumer surplus can be interpreted from the explanation given above. As shown in Exhibit A-1 (b), begin at point $X$ and instead of selected prices, now imagine offering ground beef to consumers at each possible price downward along the demand curve until the equilibrium price of $2.00 is reached at point $E$. The result is that the entire green triangular area between the demand curve and the horizontal line at the equilibrium price represents total consumer

**Consumer surplus**
The value of the difference between the price consumers are willing to pay for a product on the demand curve and the price actually paid for it.

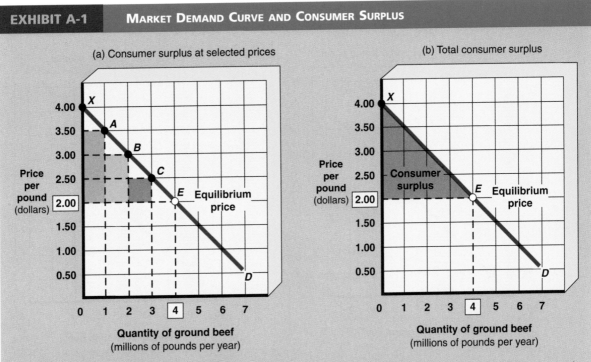

| EXHIBIT A-1 | MARKET DEMAND CURVE AND CONSUMER SURPLUS |

As illustrated in part (a), consumers are willing at point A on the market demand curve to pay $3.50 per pound to purchase one million pounds of ground beef per year. Since the equilibrium price is $2.00, this means they receive a consumer surplus of $1.50 for each pound of ground beef and the vertical shaded rectangular area is the consumer surplus earned only at point A. Others who pay less at points B, C, and E receive less consumer surplus and the height of the corresponding rectangles falls at each of these prices. In part (b), moving downward along all possible prices on the demand curve yields the green-shaded triangle, which is equal to total consumer surplus (net benefit).

surplus. Note that a rise in the equilibrium price decreases total consumer surplus and a fall in the equilibrium price increases total consumer surplus.

**CONCLUSION** *Total consumer surplus measured in dollars is represented by the total area under the market demand curve and above the equilibrium price.*

# Producer Surplus

Similar to the concept of consumer surplus, the height of the market supply curve in Exhibit A-2 (a) shows the producers' minimum willingness to accept payment for ground beef offered for sale at various prices per pound. At point X, firms offer no ground beef for sale at a price of zero and they divert their resources to an alternate use. At a price of $0.50 (50 cents) per pound (point A), the supply

**EXHIBIT A-2         MARKET SUPPLY CURVE AND PRODUCER SURPLUS**

(a) Producer surplus at selected prices

(b) Total producer surplus

Quantity of ground beef
(millions of pounds per year)

Quantity of ground beef
(millions of pounds per year)

In part (a), firms are willing at $0.50 per pound (point A) to supply one million pounds of ground beef per year. Because $2.00 is the equilibrium price, the sellers earn a producer surplus of $1.50 per pound of ground beef sold. The first vertical shaded rectangle is the producer surplus earned only at point A. At points B, C, and E, sellers receive less producer surplus at each of these higher prices and the sizes of the rectangles fall. In part (b), moving upward along all possible selling prices on the supply curve yields the red-shaded triangle that is equal to total producer surplus (net benefit).

**Producer surplus**
The value of the difference between the actual selling price of a product and the price producers are willing to sell it for on the supply curve.

curve tells us that one million pounds will be offered for sale. Moving upward along the supply curve to point B, firms will offer an additional million pounds of ground beef for sale at the higher price of $1.00 per pound. If the price rises to $1.50 at point C and higher, firms allocate more resources to ground beef production and another million pounds will be supplied along the supply curve.

Again we will assume the equilibrium price is $2.00 per pound, and the supply curve can be used to measure the net benefit or *producer surplus*. **Producer surplus** is the value of the difference between the actual selling price of a product and the price producers are willing to sell it for on the supply curve. Now assume the first million pounds of ground beef is sold at point A on the supply curve. In this case, producer surplus is the difference between the equilibrium selling price of $2.00 and the $0.50 price that is the minimum price that producers will accept to supply this quantity of ground beef. Thus producer surplus is equal to $1.50 ($2.00 − $0.50) per pound multiplied by one million pounds sold, which is $1.5 million producer surplus. This value is represented by the vertical shaded rectangle formed at point A on the supply curve. The second million pounds of ground beef offered for sale at point B also generates a producer surplus because the selling price of $2.00 exceeds the $1.00 price at which firms are willing to supply this additional quantity of ground beef. Note that producer surplus is lower at point B compared to point A, and marginal producer surplus continues to fall at point C until it reaches zero at the equilibrium point E.

The total value of producer surplus is represented in Exhibit A-2 (b). Start at point X, where none of the product will be supplied at the price of zero. Now consider the quantities of ground beef producers are willing to offer for sale at each possible price upward along the supply curve until the equilibrium price of $2.00 is reached at point E. The result is that the entire red triangular area between the horizontal line at the equilibrium price and the supply curve represents total producer surplus.

> **CONCLUSION** *Total producer surplus measured in dollars is represented by the total area under the equilibrium price and above the supply curve.*

# Market Efficiency

In this section, the equilibrium price and quantity will be shown to achieve market efficiency because at any other market price the total net benefits to consumers and producers will be less. Stated differently, competitive markets are efficient when they maximize the sum of consumer and producer surplus. The analysis continues in Exhibit A-3 (a), which combines parts (b) from the two previous exhibits. The green triangle represents consumer surplus earned in excess of the $2.00 equilibrium price consumers pay for ground beef. The red triangle represents producer surplus producers receive by selling ground beef at $2.00 per pound in excess of the minimum price at which they are willing to supply it. The total net benefit (total surplus) is therefore the entire triangular area consisting of both the green consumer surplus and red producer surplus triangles.

Now consider in Exhibit A-3(b) the consequences to market efficiency of producers devoting fewer resources to ground beef production and only 2 million pounds being bought and sold per year compared to 4 million pounds at the equilibrium price of $2.00. The result is a deadweight loss. **Deadweight loss** is the net loss of consumer and producer surplus from underproduction or overproduction of a product. In Exhibit A-3(b), the deadweight loss is equal to the gray triangle ABE, which represents the total surplus of green and red triangles in part (a) that is not obtained because the market is operating below equilibrium point E.

Exhibit A-3 (c) illustrates that a deadweight loss of consumer and producer surplus can also result from overproduction. Now suppose more resources are devoted to production and 6 million pounds of ground beef are bought and sold at the equilibrium price. However, from the producers' side of the market, the equilibrium selling price is only $2.00 and below any possible selling price on the supply curve between points E and C. Therefore, firms have a net loss for each pound sold, represented by the area under the supply curve and bounded below by the horizontal equilibrium price line. Similarly, consumers pay the equilibrium price of $2.00, but this price exceeds any price consumers are willing to pay between points E and D on the demand curve. This means consumers experience

**Deadweight loss** The net loss of consumer and producer surplus for underproduction or overproduction of a product.

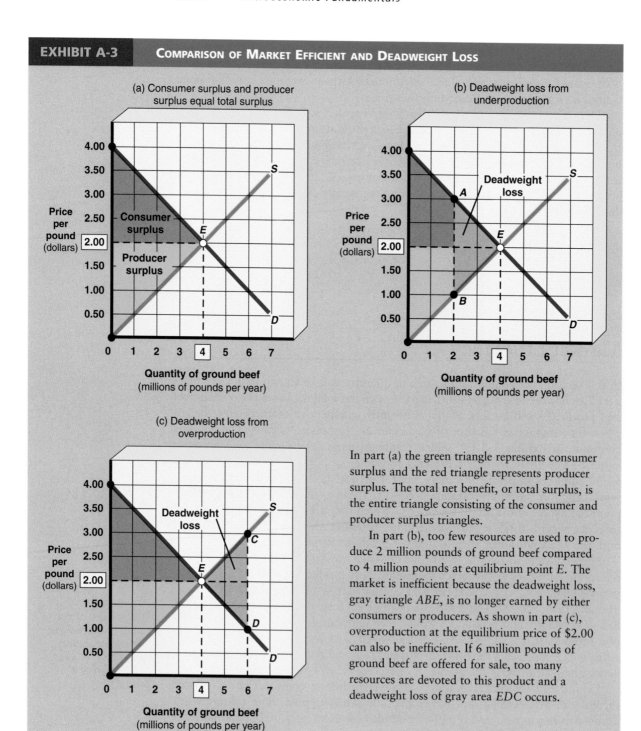

**EXHIBIT A-3    COMPARISON OF MARKET EFFICIENT AND DEADWEIGHT LOSS**

**(a) Consumer surplus and producer surplus equal total surplus**

**(b) Deadweight loss from underproduction**

**(c) Deadweight loss from overproduction**

In part (a) the green triangle represents consumer surplus and the red triangle represents producer surplus. The total net benefit, or total surplus, is the entire triangle consisting of the consumer and producer surplus triangles.

In part (b), too few resources are used to produce 2 million pounds of ground beef compared to 4 million pounds at equilibrium point *E*. The market is inefficient because the deadweight loss, gray triangle *ABE*, is no longer earned by either consumers or producers. As shown in part (c), overproduction at the equilibrium price of $2.00 can also be inefficient. If 6 million pounds of ground beef are offered for sale, too many resources are devoted to this product and a deadweight loss of gray area *EDC* occurs.

a total net benefit loss for each pound purchased, represented by the rectangular area between the horizontal equilibrium price line above and the demand curve below. The total net loss of consumer and producer surplus (deadweight loss) is equal to the gray-shaded area *EDC*.

> **CONCLUSION** *The total dollar value of potential benefits not achieved is the deadweight loss resulting from too few or too many resources used in a given market.*

Looking ahead, the conclusion drawn from this appendix is that market equilibrium is efficient, but this conclusion is not always the case. In the next chapter, the topic of *market failure* will be discussed in which market equilibrium under certain conditions can result in too few or too many resources being used to produce goods and services. For example, the absence of a competitive market, existence of pollution, or vaccinations to prevent a disease can establish equilibrium conditions with misallocations of resources. In these cases, government intervention may be preferable in order to achieve optimal allocation of resources. In other cases, such as the government imposing price ceilings and price floors, the result of government intervention is a market that is no longer efficient.

## Key Concepts

Consumer surplus                Producer surplus                Deadweight loss

## Summary

- **Consumer surplus** measures the value between the price consumers are willing to pay for a product along the demand curve and the price they actually pay.
- **Producer surplus** measures the value between the actual selling price of a product and the price along the supply curve at which sellers are willing to sell

the product. Total surplus is the sum of consumer surplus and producer surplus.

- **Deadweight loss** is the result of a market that operates in disequilibrium. It is the net loss of both consumer and producer surplus resulting from underproduction or overproduction of a product.

## Summary of Conclusion Statements

- Total consumer surplus measured in dollars is represented by the total area under the market demand curve and above the equilibrium price.
- Total producer surplus measured in dollars is represented by the total area under the equilibrium price and above the supply curve.

- The total dollar value of potential benefits not achieved is the deadweight loss resulting from too few or too many resources used in a given market.

## Study Questions and Problems

1. Consider the market for used textbooks. Use Exhibit A-4 to calculate the total consumer surplus.

**EXHIBIT A-4  USED TEXTBOOK MARKET**

| Potential buyer | Willingness to pay | Market price |
|---|---|---|
| Brad | $60 | $30 |
| Juan | 45 | 30 |
| Sue | 35 | 30 |
| Jamie | 25 | 30 |
| Frank | 10 | 30 |

2. Consider the market for used textbooks. Use Exhibit A-5 to calculate the total producer surplus.

**EXHIBIT A-5  USED TEXTBOOK MARKET**

| Potential seller | Willingness to sell | Market price |
|---|---|---|
| Forest | $60 | $30 |
| Betty | 45 | 30 |
| Alpha | 35 | 30 |
| Paul | 25 | 30 |
| Alice | 10 | 30 |

3. Using Exhibits A-4 and A-5 above, calculate the total surplus. Now calculate the effect on consumer surplus, producer surplus, and total surplus of a fall in the equilibrium price of textbooks from $30 to $15 each. Explain the meaning of your calculations.

4. Using Exhibit A-6, and assuming the market is in equilibrium at $Q_E$, identify areas *ACD*, *DCE*, and *ACE*. Now explain the result of underproduction at *Q* in terms of areas *BCG*, *GCF*, and *BCF*.

**EXHIBIT A-6  USED TEXTBOOK MARKET**

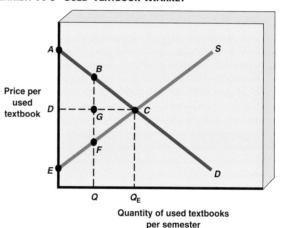

Quantity of used textbooks per semester

## Practice Quiz

For an explanation of the correct answers, please visit the tutorial at www.thomsonedu.com/economics/tucker.

1. If Bill is willing to pay $10 for one good X, $8 for a second, and $6 for a third, and the market price is $5, then Max's consumer surplus is
   a. $24.
   b. $18.
   c. $9.
   d. $6.

2. Suppose Gizmo Inc. is willing to sell one gizmo for $10, a second gizmo for $12, a third for $14, and a fourth for $20, and the market price is $20. What is Gizmo Inc.'s producer surplus?
   a. $56
   b. $24
   c. $20
   d. $10

3. In an efficient market, deadweight loss is _____.
   a. maximum.
   b. minimum.
   c. constant.
   d. zero.

4. Deadweight loss results from
   a. equilibrium.
   b. underproduction.
   c. overproduction.
   d. none of the above are correct.
   e. either b or c.

5. Total surplus equals
   a. consumer surplus + producer surplus − deadweight loss.
   b. consumer surplus − producer surplus − deadweight loss.
   c. consumer surplus − producer surplus + deadweight loss.
   d. consumer surplus + producer surplus.

# Markets in Action

chapter

# 4

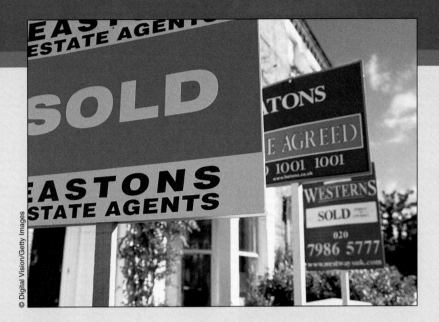

© Digital Vision/Getty Images

Once you understand how buyers and sellers respond to changes in equilibrium prices, you are progressing well in your quest to understand the economic way of thinking. This chapter begins by showing that changes in supply and demand influence the equilibrium price and quantity of goods and services exchanged around you every day. For example, you will study the impact of changes in supply and demand curves on the markets for Caribbean cruises, new homes, and AIDS vaccinations. Then you will see why the laws of supply and demand cannot be repealed. Using market supply and demand analysis, you will learn that government policies to control markets have predictable consequences. For example, you will understand what happens when the government limits the maximum rent landlords can charge and who benefits and who loses from the federal minimum-wage law.

In this chapter, you will also study situations in which the market mechanism fails. Have you visited Los Angeles and lamented the smog that blankets the beautiful surroundings? Or have you ever wanted to swim or fish in a stream, but could not because of industrial waste? These are obvious cases in which market-system magic failed and the government must consider cures to reach socially desirable results.

**In this chapter, you will learn to solve these economics puzzles:**

- How can a spotted owl affect the price of homes?
- Why might government warehouses overflow with cheese and milk?
- What do ticket scalping and rent controls have in common?

## Changes in Market Equilibrium

Using market supply and demand analysis is like putting on glasses if you are nearsighted. Suddenly, the fuzzy world around you comes into clear focus. In the following examples, you will open your eyes and see that economic theory has something important to say about so many things in the real world.

87

## CHANGES IN DEMAND

The Caribbean cruise market shown in Exhibit 1(a) assumes market supply, $S$, is constant and market demand increases from $D_1$ to $D_2$. Why has the demand curve shifted rightward in the figure? We will assume the popularity of cruises to these vacation islands has suddenly risen sharply due to extensive advertising that influenced tastes and preferences. Given supply curve $S$ and demand curve $D_1$, the initial equilibrium price is $600 per cruise, and the initial equilibrium quantity is 8,000 cruises per year, shown as point $E_1$. After the impact of advertising, the new equilibrium point, $E_2$, becomes 12,000 cruises per year at a price of $900 each. Thus, the increase in demand causes both the equilibrium price and the equilibrium quantity to increase.

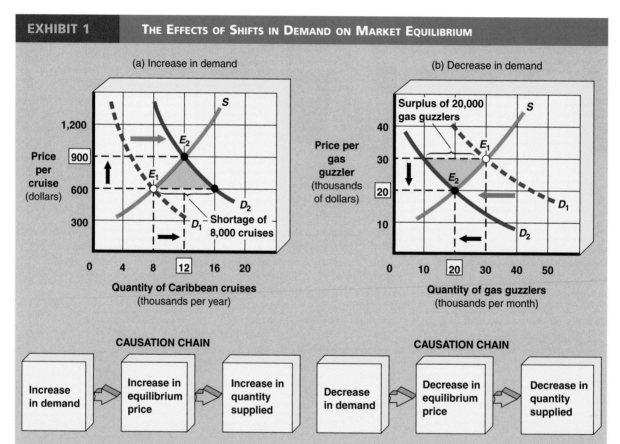

**EXHIBIT 1**     **THE EFFECTS OF SHIFTS IN DEMAND ON MARKET EQUILIBRIUM**

In part (a), demand for Caribbean cruises increases because of extensive advertising, and the demand curve shifts rightward from $D_1$ to $D_2$. This shift in demand causes a temporary shortage of 8,000 cruises per year at the initial equilibrium of $E_1$. This disequilibrium condition encourages firms in the cruise business to move upward along the supply curve to a new equilibrium at $E_2$.

Part (b) illustrates a decrease in the demand for gas-guzzling automobiles (SUVs) caused by a sharp rise in the price of gasoline (a complement). This leftward shift in demand from $D_1$ to $D_2$ results in a temporary surplus of 20,000 gas guzzlers per month at the initial equilibrium of $E_1$. This disequilibrium condition forces sellers of these cars to move downward along the supply curve to a new equilibrium at $E_2$.

It is important to understand the force that caused the equilibrium to shift from $E_1$ to $E_2$. When demand initially increased from $D_1$ to $D_2$, there was a temporary shortage of 8,000 cruises at $600 per cruise. Firms in the cruise business responded to the excess demand by hiring more workers, offering more cruises to the Caribbean, and raising the price. The cruise lines therefore move upward along the supply curve (increasing quantity supplied, but not changing supply). During some period of trial and error, Caribbean cruise sellers increase their price and quantity supplied until a shortage no longer exists at point $E_2$. Therefore, the increase in demand causes both the equilibrium price and the equilibrium quantity to increase.

What will happen to the demand for gas-guzzling automobiles (for example, SUVs) if the price of gasoline triples? Because gasoline and automobiles are complements, a rise in the price of gasoline decreases the demand for gas guzzlers from $D_1$ to $D_2$ in Exhibit 1(b). At the initial equilibrium price of $30,000 per gas guzzler ($E_1$), the quantity supplied now exceeds the quantity demanded by 20,000 automobiles per month. This unwanted inventory forces automakers to reduce the price and quantity supplied. As a result of this movement downward on the supply curve, market equilibrium changes from $E_1$ to $E_2$. The equilibrium price falls from $30,000 to $20,000, and the equilibrium quantity falls from 30,000 to 20,000 gas guzzlers per month.

## CHANGES IN SUPPLY

Now reverse the analysis by assuming demand remains constant and allow some nonprice determinant to shift the supply curve. In Exhibit 2(a), begin at point $E_1$ in the video rental industry with an equilibrium price of $3 per rental and 40 million video rentals per month. Then word spreads to entrepreneurs that the video business is a hot prospect for earning profits. New firms enter the video rental market, and the market supply curve shifts from $S_1$ to $S_2$. This creates a temporary surplus of 40 million video rentals at point $E_1$. Video rental firms respond to stacks of unrented videos on their shelves by reducing the rental price and the number available for rent. As the price falls, buyers move down along their demand curve and rent more videos per month. When the rental price falls to $2, the market is in equilibrium again at point $E_2$, instead of $E_1$, and consumers rent 60 million videos per month.

## CHECKPOINT

### Why the Higher Price for Lower Cholesterol?

A few years ago a number-one best-selling book proclaimed the virtues of oat bran in reducing cholesterol. More and more consumers added oat bran cereal and muffins to their diets. At the same time, producers switched over to oat bran production from other agricultural crops. Within a two-month period, the price of a pound of oat bran shot up from $0.99 to $2.59. During this two-month period, which increased more—demand, supply, or neither?

In part (a), begin at equilibrium $E_1$ in the video rental industry, and assume an increase in the number of video rental firms shifts the supply curve rightward from $S_1$ to $S_2$. This shift in supply causes a temporary surplus of 40 million video rentals per month. This disequilibrium condition causes a movement downward along the demand curve to a new equilibrium at $E_2$. At $E_2$, the equilibrium rental price declines, and the equilibrium quantity rises.

In part (b), steps to protect the environment cause the supply curve for lumber to shift leftward from $S_1$ to $S_2$. This shift in supply results in a temporary shortage of 4 billion board feet per year. Customer bidding for the available lumber raises the price. As a result, the market moves upward along the demand curve to a new equilibrium at $E_2$, and the quantity demanded falls.

Exhibit 2(b) illustrates the market for lumber. Suppose this market is at equilibrium at point $E_1$, where the going price is $400 per thousand board feet, and 8 billion board feet are bought and sold per year. Now suppose a new Endangered Species Act is passed, and the federal government sets aside huge forest resources to protect the spotted owl and other wildlife. This means the market supply curve shifts leftward from $S_1$ to $S_2$ and a temporary shortage of 4 billion board feet of lumber exists at point $E_1$. Suppliers respond by hiking their price from $400 to $600 per thousand board feet, and a new equilibrium is established at $E_2$, where the quantity is 6 billion board feet per year. This higher cost of lumber, in turn, raises the price of a new 1,800-square-foot home by $4,000, compared to the price of an identical home the previous year.

| EXHIBIT 3 | EFFECT OF SHIFTS IN DEMAND OR SUPPLY ON MARKET EQUILIBRIUM | |
|---|---|---|
| **Change** | **Effect on equilibrium price** | **Effect on equilibrium quantity** |
| Demand increases | Increases | Increases |
| Demand decreases | Decreases | Decreases |
| Supply increases | Decreases | Increases |
| Supply decreases | Increases | Decreases |

Exhibit 3 gives a concise summary of the impact of changes in demand or supply on market equilibrium.

## TREND OF EQUILIBRIUM PRICES OVER TIME

Basic demand and supply analysis allows us to explain a trend in prices over a number of years. Exhibit 4 shows the effect of changes in nonprice determinants that increase both the demand and supply curves for good X between 2000, 2005, and 2010. A line connects the equilibrium prices for each year in order to summarize the trend of equilibrium price and quantity changes over this time period. In this case, the observed prices trace an upward-sloping trend line.

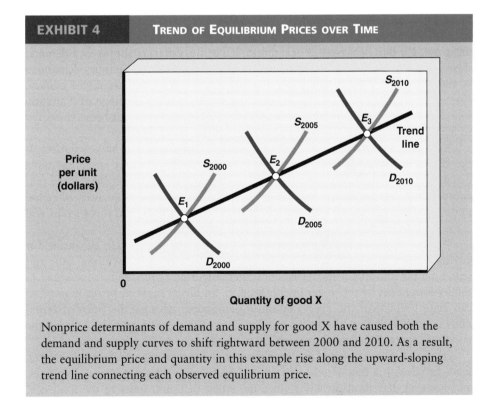

**EXHIBIT 4 — TREND OF EQUILIBRIUM PRICES OVER TIME**

Nonprice determinants of demand and supply for good X have caused both the demand and supply curves to shift rightward between 2000 and 2010. As a result, the equilibrium price and quantity in this example rise along the upward-sloping trend line connecting each observed equilibrium price.

# Can the Laws of Supply and Demand be Repealed?

The government intervenes in some markets with the objective of preventing prices from rising to the equilibrium price. In other markets, the government's goal is to intervene and maintain a price higher than the equilibrium price. Market supply and demand analysis is a valuable tool for understanding what happens when the government fixes prices. There are two types of price controls: *price ceilings* and *price floors*.

## PRICE CEILINGS

**Price ceiling**
A legally established maximum price a seller can charge.

What happens if the government prevents the price system from setting a market price "too high" by mandating a **price ceiling**? A price ceiling is a legally established maximum price a seller can charge. Rent controls are an example of the imposition of a price ceiling in the market for rental units. New York City, Washington, D.C., Los Angeles, San Francisco, and other communities in the United States have some form of rent control. Since World War I, rent controls have been widely used in Europe. The rationale for rent controls is to provide an "essential service" that would otherwise be unaffordable by many people at the equilibrium rental price. Let's see why most economists believe that rent controls are counterproductive.

Exhibit 5 is a supply and demand diagram for the quantity of rental units demanded and supplied per month in a hypothetical city. We begin the analysis by assuming no rent controls exist and equilibrium is at point *E*, with a monthly rent of $600 per month and 6 million units occupied. Next, assume the city council imposes a rent control (ceiling price) that by law forbids any landlord from renting a unit for more than $400 per month. What does market supply and demand theory predict will happen? At the low rent ceiling of $400, the quantity demanded of rental units will be 8 million but the quantity supplied will be only 4 million. Consequently, the price ceiling creates a persistent market shortage of 4 million rental units because suppliers cannot raise the rental price without being subjected to legal penalties.

Note that a rent ceiling at or above $600 per month would have no effect. If the ceiling is set at the equilibrium rent of $600, the quantity of rental units demanded and the quantity of rental units supplied are equal regardless of the rent control. If the rent ceiling is set above the equilibrium rent, the quantity of rental units supplied exceeds the quantity of rental units demanded, and this surplus will cause the market to adjust to the equilibrium rent of $600.

What is the impact of rent controls on consumers? First, as a substitute for paying higher prices, consumers must spend more time on waiting lists and searching for housing. This means consumers incur an *opportunity cost* added to the $400 rent set by the government. Second, an illegal market, or *black market*, can arise because of the excess quantity demanded. Because the price of rental units is artificially low, the profit motive encourages tenants to risk breaking the law by subletting their unit to the highest bidder over $400 per month.

From the seller's perspective, rent control encourages two undesirable effects. First, faced with a mandated low rent, landlords may cut maintenance expenses, and housing deterioration will reduce the stock of rental units in the long run.

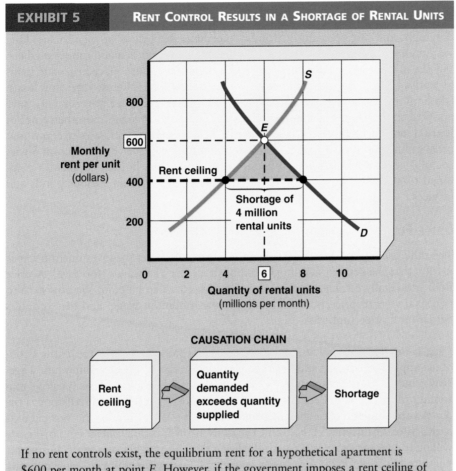

| EXHIBIT 5 | RENT CONTROL RESULTS IN A SHORTAGE OF RENTAL UNITS |

**CAUSATION CHAIN**

Rent ceiling ⇨ Quantity demanded exceeds quantity supplied ⇨ Shortage

If no rent controls exist, the equilibrium rent for a hypothetical apartment is $600 per month at point *E*. However, if the government imposes a rent ceiling of $400 per month, a shortage of 4 million rental units occurs. Because rent cannot rise by law, one outcome is that consumers must search for available units instead of paying a higher rent. Other outcomes include a black market, bribes, discrimination, and other illegal methods of dealing with a shortage of 4 million rental units per month.

Second, landlords may use discriminatory practices to replace the price system. Once owners realize there is an excess quantity demanded for rentals at the controlled price, they may resort to preferences based on pet ownership, family size, or race to determine how to allocate scarce rental space.

The government placed ceilings on most nonfarm prices during World War II and, to a lesser extent, during the Korean War. In 1971, President Nixon "froze" virtually all wages, prices, and rents for 90 days in an attempt to control inflation. As a result of an oil embargo in late 1973, the government imposed a price ceiling of 55 cents per gallon of gasoline. To deal with the shortage, nonprice rationing schemes were introduced in 1974. Some states used a first-come, first-served system, while other states allowed consumers with even-numbered license plates to buy gas on even-numbered days and those with odd-numbered license plates to buy on odd-numbered days. Gas stations were required to close on Friday night and not open until Monday morning. Regardless of the scheme, long waiting lines for gasoline formed, just as the supply and demand model predicts. Finally, in the past, legally imposed price ceilings have been placed on such items as natural gas shipped in interstate commerce and on interest rates for loans. Maximum interest rate laws are called *usury laws*, and state governments have adopted these ceilings in the past to regulate home mortgages and other types of loans. Internationally, as discussed later in the chapter on economies in transition, price ceilings on food and rent were common in the former Soviet Union. Soviet sociologists estimated that members of a typical urban household spent a combined total of 40 hours per week standing in lines to obtain various goods and services.

## PRICE FLOORS

**Price floor**
A legally established minimum price a seller can be paid.

The other side of the price-control coin is a **price floor** set by government because it fears that the price system might establish a price viewed as "too low." A price floor is a legally established minimum price a seller can be paid. We now turn to two examples of price floors. The first is the minimum wage, and the second is agricultural price supports.

**Case 1: The Minimum-Wage Law**   In the first chapter, the second You're the Economist applied *normative* and *positive* reasoning to the issue of the minimum wage. Now you are prepared to apply market supply and demand analysis (positive reasoning) to this debate. Begin by noting that the demand for unskilled labor is the downward-sloping curve shown in Exhibit 6. The wage rate on the vertical axis is the price of unskilled labor, and the amount of unskilled labor employers are willing to hire varies inversely with the wage rate. At a higher wage rate, businesses will hire fewer workers. At a lower wage rate, they will employ a larger quantity of workers.

On the supply side, the wage rate determines the number of unskilled workers willing and able to work per year. At higher wages, workers will give up leisure or schooling to work, and at lower wages, fewer workers will be available for hire. The upward-sloping curve in Exhibit 6 is the supply of labor.

Assuming the freedom to bargain, the price system will establish an equilibrium wage rate of $W_e$ and an equilibrium quantity of labor employed of $Q_e$. But suppose the government enacts a minimum wage, $W_m$, which is a price floor above the equilibrium wage, $W_e$. The intent of the legislation is to "wave a carrot" in front of people who will not work at $W_e$ and to make lower-paid workers better off with a higher wage rate. But consider the undesirable consequences. One result of an artificially high minimum wage is that the number of workers willing to offer their labor increases upward along the supply curve to $Q_s$, but there are fewer jobs because the number of workers firms are willing to hire decreases to $Q_d$ on the demand curve. The predicted outcome is a labor surplus of unskilled workers, $Q_s - Q_d$, who are unemployed. Moreover, employers are encouraged to substitute machines and skilled labor for the unskilled labor previously employed at equilibrium wage $W_e$. The minimum wage is therefore considered counterproductive because employers lay off the lowest-skilled workers, who ironically are the type of workers minimum wage legislation intends to help. Also,

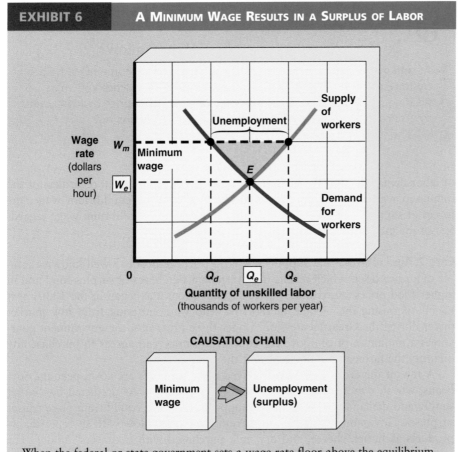

**EXHIBIT 6**    **A MINIMUM WAGE RESULTS IN A SURPLUS OF LABOR**

**CAUSATION CHAIN**

Minimum wage $\Rightarrow$ Unemployment (surplus)

When the federal or state government sets a wage-rate floor above the equilibrium wage, a surplus of unskilled labor develops. The supply curve is the number of workers offering their labor services per year at possible wage rates. The demand curve is the number of workers employers are willing and able to hire at various wage rates. Equilibrium wage, $W_e$, will result if the price system is allowed to operate without government interference. At the minimum wage of $W_m$, there is a surplus of unemployed workers, $Q_s - Q_d$.

loss of minimum wage jobs represents a loss of entry-level jobs to those who seek to enter the workforce.

Supporters of the minimum wage are quick to point out that those employed ($Q_d$) are better off. Even though the minimum wage causes a reduction in employment, some economists argue that a more equal or fairer income distribution is worth the loss of some jobs. Moreover, the shape of the labor demand curve may be much more vertical than shown in Exhibit 6. If this is the case, the unemployment effect of a rise in the minimum wage would be small. In addition, they claim opponents ignore the possibility that unskilled workers lack bargaining power versus employers.

Finally, a minimum wage set at or below the equilibrium wage rate is ineffective. If the minimum wage is set at the equilibrium wage rate of $W_e$, the quantity of labor demanded and the quantity of labor supplied are equal regardless of the minimum wage. If the minimum wage is set below the equilibrium wage, the forces of supply of and demand for labor establish the equilibrium wage regardless of the minimum wage rate.

**Case 2: Agricultural Price Supports**  A farm price support is a well-known example of a price floor, which results in government purchases of surplus food and in higher food prices. Agricultural price support programs began in the 1930s as a means of raising the income of farmers, who were suffering from low market prices during the Great Depression. Under these programs, the government guarantees a minimum price above the equilibrium price and agrees to purchase any quantity the farmer is unable to sell at the legal price.

A few of the crops that have received price supports are corn, peanuts, soybeans, wheat, cotton, rice, tobacco, and dairy products. As predicted by market supply and demand analysis, a price support above the equilibrium price causes surpluses. Government warehouses therefore often overflow with such perishable products as butter, cheese, and dry milk purchased with taxpayers' money. The following You're the Economist on the dairy industry examines one of the best-known examples of U.S. government interference with agricultural market prices.

# Market Failure

In this chapter and the previous chapter, you have gained an understanding of how markets operate. Through the price system, society coordinates economic activity, but markets are not always "Prince Charmings" that achieve *market efficiency* without a misallocation of resources. It is now time to step back with a critical eye and consider markets that become "ugly frogs" by allocating resources inefficiently. **Market failure** occurs when market equilibrium results in too few or too many resources being used in the production of a good or service. In this section, you will study four important cases of market failure: lack of competition, externalities, public goods, and income inequality. Market failure is discussed in more detail in the chapter on environmental economics, except for the macroeconomics version of the text.

**Market failure**
A situation in which market equilibrium results in too few or too many resources used in the production of a good or service. This inefficiency may justify government intervention.

## LACK OF COMPETITION

There must be competition among both producers and consumers for markets to function properly. But what happens if the producers fail to compete? In *The*

## You're the Economist

# Rigging the Market for Milk
*Applicable Concept: price supports*

Each year the milk industry faces an important question: What does the federal government plan to do about its dairy price support program, which has helped boost farmers' income since 1949? Under the price support program, the federal government agrees to buy storable milk products, such as cheese, butter, and dry milk. If the farmers cannot sell all their products to consumers at a price exceeding the price support level, the federal government will purchase any unsold grade A milk production. Although state-run dairy commissions set their own minimum prices for milk, state price supports closely follow federal levels and are kept within 3 percent of levels in bordering states to reduce interstate milk price competition.

Members of Congress who advocate changes in the price support programs worry that milk surpluses are costing taxpayers too much. Each year the federal government pays billions of dollars to dairy farmers for milk products held in storage at a huge cost. Moreover, the problem is getting worse because the federal government encourages dairy farmers to use ultramodern farming techniques to increase the production per cow. Another concern is that the biggest government price support checks go to the largest farmers, while the number of dairy farmers continues to decline.

Congress is constantly seeking a solution to the milk price-support problem. The following are some of the ideas that have been considered:

1. Freeze the current price support level. This prospect dismays farmers, who are subject to increasing expenses for feed, electricity, and other resources.

2. Eliminate the price supports gradually in yearly increments over the next five years. This would subject the milk market to the price fluctuations of the free market, and farmers would suffer some bad years from low milk prices.

3. Have the Department of Agriculture charge dairy farmers a tax of 50 cents for every 100 pounds of milk they produce. The farmers oppose this approach because it would discourage production and run small farmers out of business.

© Photodisc/GETTY IMAGES

4. Have the federal government implement a "whole herd buyout" program. The problem is that using taxpayers' money to get farmers out of the dairy business pushes up milk product prices and rewards dairy farmers who own a lot of cows. Besides, what does the government do with the cows after it purchases them?

Finally, opponents of the dairy price support program argue that the market for milk is inherently a competitive industry and that consumers and taxpayers would be better served without government price supports for milk.

## ANALYZE THE ISSUE

1. Draw a supply and demand graph to illustrate the problem described in the case study, and prescribe your own solution.

2. Which proposal do you think best serves the interests of small dairy farmers? Why?

3. Which proposal do you think best serves the interests of consumers? Why?

4. Which proposal do you think best serves the interests of a member of Congress? Why?

**Adam Smith**
(1723–1790)
Smith, the father of
modern economics,
wrote *The Wealth
of Nations*, published
in 1776.

© Prints & Photographs Division, Library of Congress, LC-USZ62-1740

*Wealth of Nations*, Adam Smith stated, "People of the same trade seldom meet together, even for merriment and diversion, but the conversation ends in a conspiracy against the public, or in some diversion to raise prices."[1] This famous quotation clearly underscores the fact that in the real world businesses seek ways to replace consumer sovereignty with "big business sovereignty." What happens when a few firms rig the market and they become the market's boss? By restricting supply through artificial limits on the output of a good, firms can enjoy higher prices and profits. As a result, firms may waste resources and retard technology and innovation.

Exhibit 7 illustrates how IBM, Apple, Gateway, and other suppliers of personal computers (PCs) could benefit from rigging the market. Without collusive action, the competitive price for PCs is $1,500, the quantity of 200,000 per month is sold, and efficient equilibrium prevails at point $E_1$. It is in the best interest of sell-

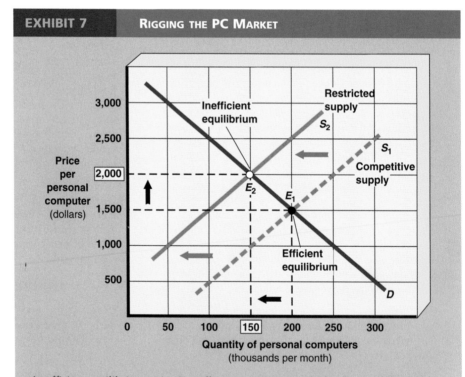

**EXHIBIT 7　　RIGGING THE PC MARKET**

At efficient equilibrium point $E_1$, sellers compete. As a result, the price charged per PC is $1,500, and the quantity of PCs exchanged is 200,000. Suppose suppliers use collusion, government intervention, or other means to restrict the supply of this product. The decrease in supply from $S_1$ to $S_2$ establishes inefficient market equilibrium $E_2$. At $E_2$, firms charge the higher price of $2,000, and the equilibrium quantity of PCs falls to 150,000. Thus, the outcome of restricted supply is that the market fails because firms use too few resources to produce PCs at an artificially higher price.

[1]Adam Smith, *An Inquiry into the Nature and Causes of the Wealth of Nations* (1776; reprint, New York: Random House, The Modern Library, 1937), p. 128.

ers, however, to take steps that would make PCs artificially scarce and raise the price. Graphically, the sellers wish to shift the competitive supply curve, $S_1$, leftward to the restricted supply curve, $S_2$. This could happen for a number of reasons, including an agreement among sellers to restrict supply (collusion) and government action. For example, the sellers could lobby the government to pass a law allowing an association of PC suppliers to set production quotas. The proponents might argue this action raises prices and, in turn, profits. Higher profits enable the industry to invest in new capital and become more competitive in world markets.

Opponents of artificially restricted supply argue that, although the producers benefit, the lack of competition means the economy loses. The result of restricting supply is that the efficient equilibrium point, $E_1$, changes to the inefficient equilibrium point, $E_2$. At point $E_2$, the higher price of $2,000 is charged, and the lower equilibrium quantity means that firms devote too few resources to producing PCs and charge an artificially high price. Note that under U.S. antitrust laws, the Justice Department is responsible for prosecuting firms that collude to restrict supply to force higher prices.

## EXTERNALITIES

Even when markets are competitive, some markets may still fail because they suffer from the presence of side effects economists call **externalities**. An externality is a cost or benefit imposed on people other than the consumers and producers of a good or service. Externalities are also called *spillover effects* or *neighborhood effects*. People other than consumers and producers who are affected by these side effects of market exchanges are called *third parties*. Externalities may be either negative or positive; that is, they may be detrimental or beneficial. Suppose you are trying to study and your roommate is listening to Steel Porcupines at full blast on the stereo. The action of your roommate is imposing an unwanted *external cost* or *negative externality* on you and other third parties who are trying to study or sleep. Externalities can also result in an *external benefit* or *positive externality* to nonparticipating parties. When a community proudly displays its neat lawns, gorgeous flowers, and freshly painted homes, visitors are third parties who did none of the work but enjoy the benefit of the pleasant scenery.

**Externality**
A cost or benefit imposed on people other than the consumers and producers of a good or service.

**A Graphical Analysis of Pollution**  Exhibit 8 provides a graphical analysis of two markets that fail to include externalities in their market prices unless the government takes corrective action. Exhibit 8(a) shows a market for steel in which steel firms burn high-sulfur coal and pollute the environment. Demand curve $D$ and supply curve $S_1$ establish the inefficient equilibrium $E_1$ in the steel market. Not included in $S_1$ are the *external costs* to the public because the steel firms are not paying for the damage from smoke emissions. If steel firms discharge smoke and ash into the atmosphere, foul air reduces property values, raises health care costs, and, in general, erodes the quality of life. Because supply curve $S_1$ does not include these external costs, they are also not included in the price of steel, $P_1$. In short, the absence of the cost of pollution in the price of steel means the firms produce more steel and pollution than is socially desirable.

$S_2$ is the supply curve that would exist if the external costs of respiratory illnesses, dirty homes, and other undesirable side effects were included. Once $S_2$ includes the charges for environmental damage, the equilibrium price rises to $P_2$, and the equilibrium quantity becomes $Q_2$. At the efficient equilibrium point, $E_2$,

**EXHIBIT 8**    **EXTERNALITIES IN THE STEEL AND AIDS VACCINATION MARKETS**

In part (a), resources are overallocated at inefficient market equilibrium $E_1$ because steel firms do not include the cost per ton of pollution in the cost per ton of steel. Supply curve $S_2$ includes the external costs of pollution. If firms are required to purchase equipment to remove the pollution or to pay a tax on pollution, the economy achieves the efficient equilibrium of $E_2$.

Part (b) demonstrates that external benefits cause an underallocation of resources. The efficient output at equilibrium point $E_2$ is obtained if people are required to purchase AIDS shots or if the government pays a subsidy equal to the external benefit per shot.

the steel market achieves allocative efficiency. At $E_2$, steel firms are paying the full cost and using fewer resources to produce the lower quantity of steel at $Q_2$.

> **CONCLUSION** *When the supply curve fails to include external costs, the equilibrium price is artificially low, and the equilibrium quantity is artificially high.*

Regulation and pollution taxes are two ways society can correct the market failure of pollution:

1. **Regulation.** Legislation can set standards that force firms to clean up their emissions as a condition of remaining in business. This means firms must buy,

install, and maintain pollution-control equipment. When the extra cost of the pollution equipment is added to the production cost per ton of steel, the initial supply curve, $S_1$, shifts leftward to supply curve $S_2$. This means regulation has forced the market equilibrium to change from $E_1$ to $E_2$. At point $E_2$, the firms use fewer resources to produce $Q_2$ compared to $Q_1$ output of steel per year, and, therefore, the firms operate efficiently.

2. **Pollution Taxes.** Another approach would be for the government to levy a tax per ton of steel equal to the external cost imposed on society when the firm emits pollution into the air. This action inhibits production by imposing an additional production cost per ton of steel from the pollution taxes and shifts the supply curve leftward from $S_1$ to $S_2$. Again, the objective is to change the equilibrium from $E_1$ to $E_2$ and eliminate the overuse of resources devoted to steel production and its pollution. The tax revenue could be used to compensate those damaged by the pollution.

**A Graphical Analysis of AIDS Vaccinations.**  As explained above, the supply curve can understate the *external costs* of a product. Now you will see that the demand curve can understate the *external benefits* of a product. Suppose a vaccination is discovered that prevents AIDS. Exhibit 8(b) illustrates the market for immunization against AIDS. Demand curve $D_1$ reflects the price consumers would pay for shots to receive the benefit of a reduced probability of infection by AIDS. Supply curve $S$ shows the quantities of shots suppliers offer for sale at different prices. At equilibrium point $E_1$, the market fails to achieve an efficient allocation of resources. The reason is that when buyers are vaccinated, other people who do not purchase AIDS shots (called *free riders*) also benefit because this disease is less likely to spread. Once demand curve $D_2$ includes external benefits to nonconsumers of AIDS vaccinations (increase in the number of buyers), the efficient equilibrium of $E_2$ is established. At $Q_2$, sellers devote greater resources to AIDS vaccinations, and the underallocation of resources is eliminated.

How can society prevent the market failure of AIDS vaccinations? Two approaches follow:

1. **Regulation.** The government can boost consumption and shift the demand curve rightward by requiring all citizens to purchase AIDS shots each year. This approach to capturing external benefits in market demand explains why all school-age children must have polio and other shots before entering school.

2. **Special Subsidies.** Another possible solution would be for the government to increase consumer income by paying consumers for each AIDS vaccination. This would mean the government pays each citizen a dollar payment equal to the amount of external benefits per shot purchased. Since the subsidy amount is payable at any price along the demand curve, the demand curve shifts rightward until the efficient equilibrium price and quantity are reached.

> **CONCLUSION** *When externalities are present, market failure gives incorrect price and quantity signals, and as a result, resources are misallocated. External costs cause the market to overallocate resources, and external benefits cause the market to underallocate resources.*

## PUBLIC GOODS

**Public good**
A good or service with two properties: (1) users collectively consume benefits, and (2) there is no way to bar people who do not pay (free riders) from consuming the good or service.

Private goods are produced through the price system. In contrast, national defense is an example of a **public good** provided by the government because of its special characteristics. A public good is a good or service that, once produced, has two properties: (1) users collectively consume benefits, and (2) there is no way to bar people who do not pay (free riders) from consuming the good or service.

To see why the marketplace fails, imagine that Patriot Missiles Inc. offers to sell missile defense systems to people who want private protection against attacks from incoming missiles. First, once the system is operational, everyone in the defense area benefits from increased safety. Second, the *nonexclusive* nature of a public good means it is impossible or very costly for any owner of a Patriot missile defense system to prevent nonowners, the free riders, from reaping the benefits of its protection.

Given the two properties of a public good, why would any private individual purchase a Patriot missile defense system? Why not take a free ride and wait until someone else buys a missile system? Thus, each person wants a Patriot system, but does not want to bear the cost of the system when everyone shares in the benefits. As a result, the market fails to provide Patriot missile defense systems, and everyone hopes no missile attacks occur before someone finally decides to purchase one. Government can solve this public goods problem by producing Patriot missiles and taxing the public to pay. Unlike a private citizen, the government can use force to collect payments and prevent the free-rider problem. Other examples of public goods include the judicial system, the national emergency warning system, air traffic control, prisons, and traffic lights.

**CONCLUSION** *If public goods are available only in the marketplace, people wait for someone else to pay, and the result is an underproduction or zero production of public goods.*

## INCOME INEQUALITY

In the cases of insufficient competition, externalities, and public goods, the marketplace allocates too few or too many resources to producing output. The market may also result in a very unequal distribution of income, thereby raising a very

**CHECKPOINT**

### Should There Be a War on Drugs?

The U.S. government fights the use of drugs, such as marijuana and cocaine, in a variety of ways, including spraying crops with poisonous chemicals; imposing jail sentences for dealers and users; and confiscating drug-transporting cars, boats, and planes. Which market failure motivates the government to interfere with the market for drugs: lack of competition, externalities, public goods, or income inequality?

# Can Vouchers Fix Our Schools?
*Applicable Concept: public goods versus private goods*

In their book, *Free to Choose*, published in 1980, economists Milton Friedman and his wife Rose Friedman proposed a voucher plan for schools.[1] The objective of their proposal was to retain government financing, but give parents greater freedom to choose the schools their children attend. The Friedmans pointed out that under the current system parents face a strong incentive not to remove their children from the public schools. This is because, if parents decide to withdraw their children from a public school and send them to a private school, they must pay private tuition in addition to the taxes that finance children enrolled in the public schools.

To remove the financial penalty that limits the freedom of parents to choose schools, the government could give parents a voucher, which is a piece of paper redeemable for a sum of money payable to any approved school. For example, if the government spends $8,000 per year to educate a student, then the voucher could be for this amount. The voucher plan embodies exactly the same principle as the GI Bill that provides educational benefits to military veterans. The veteran receives a voucher good only for educational expenses and is completely free to choose the school where it is used, provided the school satisfies certain standards.

The Friedmans argue that parents could, and should, be permitted to use the vouchers not only at private schools but also at other public schools—and not only at schools in their own district, city, or state, but at any school that is willing to accept their child. That would give every parent a greater opportunity to choose and at the same time would require public schools to charge tuition. The tuition would be competitive because public schools must compete for students, both with other public schools and with private schools. It is important to note that this plan relieves no one of the burden of taxation to pay for schooling. It simply gives parents a wider choice as to which competing schools their children attend, given the amount of funding per student that the community has obligated itself to provide. The plan also does not affect the present standards imposed on private schools to ensure that students attending them satisfy the compulsory attendance laws.

In 1990, Milwaukee began an experiment with school vouchers. The program gave selected children from low-income families taxpayer-funded vouchers to allow them to attend private schools. There has been a continuing heated debate among parents,

politicians, and educators over the results. In 1998, Wisconsin's highest court ruled in a 4–2 decision that Milwaukee can use public money for vouchers for students who attend religious schools without violating the constitutional separation of church and state. A 2002 article in *USA Today* reported:

> Opponents of vouchers have repeatedly argued that they would damage the public schools, draining them of resources and better students. A recent study of the Milwaukee voucher program by Caroline Hoxby, a Harvard economist, suggests just the opposite. She wrote that "schools that faced the most potential competition from vouchers had the best productivity response." No doubt, the nation's experience with vouchers is limited, yet the evidence cited in a recent Brookings Institution report shows that they do seem to benefit African-American youngsters.[2]

The controversy continues: In a 2002 landmark case, the U.S. Supreme Court ruled that government vouchers for private or parochial schools is constitutional. In 2003, however, a Denver judge struck down Colorado's new school voucher law, ruling that it violated the state's constitution by stripping local school boards of their control over education.[3] And in 2006, the Florida Supreme Court ruled that Florida's voucher program for students in the lowest-rated public schools was unconstitutional.

## ANALYZE THE ISSUE

1. In recent years, school choice has been a hotly debated issue. Explain whether education is a public good. If education is not a public good, why should the government provide it?

2. The Friedmans present a very one-sided view of the benefits of a voucher system. Other economists disagree about the potential effectiveness of vouchers. Do you support a voucher system for education? Explain your reasoning.

[1]Milton Friedman and Rose Friedman, *Free to Choose: A Personal Statement* (New York: Harcourt Brace Jovanovich, 1980), pp. 160–161.

[2]Robert J. Bresler, "Vouchers and the Constitution," *USA Today*, May 2002, p. 15.

[3]Joseph E. Meyer, "Colorado's New Voucher Law is Struck Down in State Court," *The New York Times*, Dec. 4, 2003, p. A.24.

controversial issue. Under the impersonal price system, movie stars earn huge incomes for acting in movies, while homeless people roam the streets penniless. The controversy is therefore over how equal the distribution of income should be and how much government intervention is required to achieve this goal. Some people wish to remove most inequality of income. Others argue for the government to provide a "safety net" minimum income level for all citizens. Still others see high income as an incentive and a "fair" reward for productive resources.

To create a more equal distribution of income, the government uses various programs to transfer money from people with high incomes to those with low incomes. Unemployment compensation and food stamps are examples of such programs. The federal minimum wage is another example of a government attempt to raise the earnings of low-income workers.

## Key Concepts

Price ceiling
Price floor

Market failure
Externality

Public good

## Summary

- **Price ceilings** and **price floors** are maximum and minimum prices enacted by law, rather than allowing the forces of supply and demand to determine prices. A *price ceiling* is a maximum price mandated by government, and a *price floor,* or *support price* for agricultural products, is a minimum legal price. If a price ceiling is set below the equilibrium price, a shortage will persist. If a price floor is set above the equilibrium price, a surplus will persist.

### PRICE CEILING

### PRICE FLOOR

- **Market failure** occurs when the market mechanism does not achieve an efficient allocation of resources. Sources of market failure include lack of competition, externalities, public goods, and income inequality. Although controversial, government intervention is a possible way to correct market failure.

- An **externality** is a cost or benefit of a good imposed on people who are not buyers or sellers of that good. Pollution is an example of an *external cost*, which means too many resources are used to produce the product responsible for the pollution. Two basic approaches to solve this market failure are regulation and pollution taxes. Vaccinations provide *external* *benefits*, which means sellers devote too few resources to produce this product. Two basic solutions to this type of market failure are laws to require consumption of shots and special subsidies.

## EXTERNALITIES

External costs of pollution

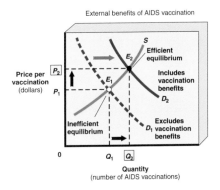

External benefits of AIDS vaccination

■ **Public goods** are goods that are consumed by all people in a society regardless of whether they pay or not. National defense, air traffic control, and other public goods can benefit many individuals simultaneously and are provided by the government.

## Summary of Conclusion Statements

■ When the supply curve fails to include external costs, the equilibrium price is artificially low, and the equilibrium quantity is artificially high.

■ When externalities are present, market failure gives incorrect price and quantity signals, and as a result, resources are misallocated. External costs cause the market to overallocate resources, and external benefits cause the market to underallocate resources.

■ If public goods are available only in the marketplace, people wait for someone else to pay, and the result is an underproduction or zero production of public goods.

## Study Questions and Problems

1. Market researchers have studied the market for milk, and their estimates for the supply of and the demand for milk per month are as follows:

| Price per gallon | Quantity demanded (millions of gallons) | Quantity supplied (millions of gallons) |
|---|---|---|
| $2.50 | 100 | 500 |
| 2.00 | 200 | 400 |
| 1.50 | 300 | 300 |
| 1.00 | 400 | 200 |
| 0.50 | 500 | 100 |

a. Using the above data, graph the demand for and the supply of milk. Identify the equilibrium point as *E*, and use dotted lines to connect *E* to the equilibrium price on the price axis and the equilibrium quantity on the quantity axis.

b. Suppose the government enacts a milk price support of $2 per gallon. Indicate this action on your graph, and explain the effect on the milk market. Why would the government establish such a price support?

c. Now assume the government decides to set a price ceiling of $1 per gallon. Show and explain how this legal price affects your graph of the milk market. What objective could the government be trying to achieve by establishing such a price ceiling?

2. Use a graph to show the impact on the price of Japanese cars sold in the United States if the United States imposes import quotas on Japanese cars. Now draw another graph to show how the change in the price of Japanese cars affects the price of American-made cars in the United States. Explain the market outcome in each graph and the link between the two graphs.

3. Using market supply and demand analysis, explain why labor union leaders are strong advocates of raising the minimum wage above the equilibrium wage.

4. What are the advantages and disadvantages of the price system?

5. Suppose a market is in equilibrium and both demand and supply curves increase. What happens to the equilibrium price if demand increases more than supply?

6. Consider this statement: "Government involvement in markets is inherently inefficient." Do you agree or disagree? Explain.

7. Suppose coal-burning firms are emitting excessive pollution into the air. Suggest two ways the government can deal with this market failure.

8. Explain the impact of external costs and external benefits on resource allocation.

9. Why are public goods not produced in sufficient quantities by private markets?

10. Which of the following are public goods?
   a. Air bags
   b. Pencils
   c. Cycle helmets
   d. Smoking
   e. Contact lenses

## Study Guide Questions

1. Vaccination shots provide _____, which means sellers devote too few resources to produce this product. Two basic solutions to this type of market failure are laws to require consumption of shots and special subsidies.

2. Suppose the government imposes rent control (a price ceiling) below the equilibrium price for rental housing. Which of the following will result?
   a. Black markets
   b. The quality of existing rental housing deteriorates
   c. Shortages
   d. All of the above

3. If the equilibrium price of good X is $5 and a price ceiling is imposed at $4, the eventual result will be a (an)
   a. accumulation of inventories of unsold gas.
   b. shortage.
   c. surplus.
   d. all of the above.

4. Which of the following is a property of a public good?
   a. A public good is free from externalities.
   b. Many individuals benefit simultaneously.
   c. A public good is not subject to free riders.
   d. A public good is established by law.

5. T  F  It's difficult for a private firm to provide a public good because of free riders.

**Answers to these questions are in the complete Study Guide at www.thomsonedu.com/thomsonnow.**

**For online exercises, go to the text Web site at www.thomsonedu.com/economics/tucker.**

## Checkpoint Answers

### Why the Higher Price for Lower Cholesterol?

As shown in Exhibit 9, an increase in demand leads to higher prices, while an increase in supply leads to lower prices. Because the overall direction of price in the oat bran market was up, the demand increase must have been larger than the supply increase. If you said demand increased by more than supply because consumers reacted more quickly than producers, **YOU ARE CORRECT.**

**EXHIBIT 9**

### Is There Price Fixing at the Ticket Window?

Scalpers are evidence of a shortage whereby buyers are unable to find tickets at the official price. As shown in Exhibit 10, scalpers (often illegally) profit from the shortage by selling tickets above the official price. Short-

ages result when prices are restricted below equilibrium, as is the case when there is a price ceiling. If you said scalping occurs when there is a price ceiling because scalpers charge more than the official maximum price, **YOU ARE CORRECT.**

**EXHIBIT 10**

### Should There Be a War on Drugs?

Drug use often affects not only the person using the drugs, but other members of society as well. For example, higher crime rates are largely attributable to increased drug usage, and AIDS is often spread when users inject drugs with nonsterile needles. When one person's actions affect others not involved in the decision to buy or sell, the market fails to operate efficiently. If you said the market failure motivating government intervention in the drug market is externalities because drug users impose costs on nonusers, **YOU ARE CORRECT.**

## Practice Quiz

For an explanation of the correct answers, please visit the tutorial at www.thomsonedu.com/economics/tucker.

1. Suppose prices for new homes have risen, yet the number of new homes sold has also risen. We can conclude that
   a. the demand for new homes has risen.
   b. the law of demand has been violated.
   c. new firms have entered the construction industry.
   d. construction firms must be facing higher costs.

2. Which of the following statements is *true*?
   a. An increase in demand, with no change in supply, will increase the equilibrium price and quantity.
   b. An increase in supply, with no change in demand, will decrease the equilibrium price and the equilibrium quantity.
   c. A decrease in supply, with no change in demand, will decrease the equilibrium price and increase the equilibrium quantity.
   d. All of the above are true.

3. Consider the market for chicken. An increase in the price of beef will
   a. decrease the demand for chicken, resulting in a lower price and a smaller amount of chicken purchased in the market.

b. decrease the supply of chicken, resulting in a higher price and a smaller amount of chicken purchased in the market.

c. increase the demand for chicken, resulting in a higher price and a greater amount of chicken purchased in the market.

d. increase the supply of chicken, resulting in a lower price and a greater amount of chicken purchased in the market.

4. An increase in consumers' incomes increases the demand for oranges. As a result of the adjustment to a new equilibrium, there is a (an)
   a. leftward shift of the supply curve.
   b. downward movement along the supply curve.
   c. rightward shift of the supply curve.
   d. upward movement along the supply curve.

5. An increase in the wage paid to grape pickers will cause the
   a. demand curve for grapes to shift to the right, resulting in higher prices for grapes.
   b. demand curve for grapes to shift to the left, resulting in lower prices for grapes.
   c. supply curve for grapes to shift to the left, resulting in lower prices for grapes.
   d. supply curve for grapes to shift to the left, resulting in higher prices for grapes.

6. If the federal government wants to raise the price of cheese, it will
   a. take cheese from government storage and sell it.
   b. encourage farmers to research ways to produce more cheese.
   c. subsidize purchases of farm equipment.
   d. encourage farmers to produce less cheese.

7. Which of the following is *least* likely to result from rent controls set below the equilibrium price for rental housing?
   a. Shortages and black markets will result.
   b. The existing rental housing will deteriorate.
   c. The supply of rental housing will increase rapidly.
   d. People will demand more apartments than are available.

8. Suppose the equilibrium price set by supply and demand is lower than the price ceiling set by the government. The eventual result will be
   a. a shortage.
   b. that quantity demanded is equal to quantity supplied.
   c. a surplus.
   d. a black market.

9. A good that provides external benefits to society has
   a. too few resources devoted to its production.
   b. too many resources devoted to its production.

c. the optimal resources devoted to its production.
d. not provided profits to producers of the good.

10. Pollution from cars is an example of
    a. a harmful opportunity cost.
    b. a negative externality.
    c. a production dislocation.
    d. none of the above.

11. Which of the following is the *best* example of a public good?
    a. Pencils
    b. Education
    c. Defense
    d. Trucks

12. A public good may be defined as any good or service that
    a. allows users to collectively consume benefits.
    b. must be distributed to all citizens in equal shares.
    c. is never produced by government.
    d. is described by answers (a) and (c) above.

**EXHIBIT 11  SUPPLY AND DEMAND CURVES**

13. In Exhibit 11, which of the following might cause a shift from $S_1$ to $S_2$?
    a. A decrease in input prices
    b. An improvement in technology
    c. An increase in input prices
    d. An increase in consumer income

14. In Exhibit 11, an increase in supply would cause a move from which equilibrium point to another, other things being equal?
    a. $E_1$ to $E_2$
    b. $E_1$ to $E_3$
    c. $E_4$ to $E_1$
    d. $E_3$ to $E_4$

15. Beginning from an equilibrium at point $E_1$ in Exhibit 11, an increase in demand for good X, other things being equal, would move the equilibrium point to
    a. $E_1$ (no change).
    b. $E_2$.
    c. $E_3$.
    d. $E_4$.

# Applying Supply and Demand Analysis to Health Care

One out of every seven dollars spent in the United States is spent for health care services. This is a greater percentage than in any other industrialized country.[1] The topic of health care arouses deep emotions and generates intense media coverage. How can we understand many of the important health care issues? One approach is to listen to the normative statements made by politicians and other concerned citizens. Another approach is to use supply and demand theory to analyze the issue. Here again the objective is to bring textbook theory to life and use it to provide you with a deeper understanding of health service markets.

## The Impact of Health Insurance

There is a downward-sloping demand curve for health care services just as there is for other goods and services. Following the same law of demand that applies to cars, clothing, entertainment, and other goods and services, movements along the demand curve for health care occur because consumers respond to changes in the price of health care. As shown in Exhibit A-1, we assume that health care—including doctor visits, medicine, hospital bills, and other medical services—can be measured in units of health care. Without health insurance, consumers buy $Q_1$ units of health care services per year at a price of $P_1$ per unit. Assuming supply curve $S$ represents the quantity supplied, the market is in equilibrium at point $A$. At this point, the total cost of health care can be computed by the price of health care ($P_1$) times the quantity demanded ($Q_1$) or represented geometrically by the rectangle $0P_1 AQ_1$.

Analysis of the demand curve for health care is complicated by the way health care is financed. About 80 percent of all health care is paid for by *third parties*, including private insurance companies and government programs, such as Medicare and Medicaid. The price of health care services therefore depends on the *copayment rate*, which is the percentage of the cost of services consumers pay out-of-pocket. To understand the impact, it is more realistic to assume consumers are insured and extend the analysis represented in Exhibit A-1. Because patients pay only 20 percent of the bill, the quantity of health care demanded in the figure increases to $Q_2$ at a lower price of $P_2$. At point $B$ on the demand curve, insured consumers pay an amount equal to rectangle $0P_2BQ_2$, and insurers pay an amount represented by rectangle $P_2P_3CB$. Health care providers respond by

[1]U.S. Census Bureau, *Statistical Abstract of the United States*, 2006, Table 1323, http://www.census .gov/prod/www/statistical-abstract.html.

**EXHIBIT A-1**     **THE IMPACT OF INSURANCE ON THE HEALTH CARE MARKET**

Without health insurance, the market is in equilibrium at point $A$, with a price of $P_1$ and a quantity demanded of $Q_1$. Total spending is $0P_1AQ_1$. With copayment health insurance, consumers pay the lower price of $P_2$, and the quantity demanded increases to $Q_2$. Total health care costs rise to $0P_3CQ_2$, with $0P_2BQ_2$ paid by consumers and $P_2P_3CB$ paid by insurers. As a result, the quantity supplied increases from point $A$ to point $C$, where it equals the quantity demanded of $Q_2$

increasing the quantity supplied from point $A$ to point $C$ on the supply curve $S$, where the quantity supplied equals the quantity demanded of $Q_2$. The reason that there is no shortage in the health care market is that the combined payments from the insured consumers and insurers equal the total payment required for the movement upward along the supply curve. Stated in terms of rectangles, the total health care payment of $0P_3CQ_2$ equals $0P_2BQ_2$ paid by consumers plus $P_2P_3CB$ paid by insurers.

> **CONCLUSION** *Compared to a health care market without insurance, the quantity demanded, the quantity supplied, and the total cost of health care are increased by copayment health care insurance.*

Finally, note that Exhibit A-1 represents an overall or general model of the health care market. Individual health care markets are subject to *market failure*. For example, there would be a lack of competition if hospitals, doctors, health maintenance organizations (HMOs), or drug companies conspired to fix prices. Externalities provide another source of market failure, as illustrated for vaccinations in Exhibit 8 of Chapter 4. We are also concerned that health care be distributed in a fair way. This concern explains why the government Medicare and Medicaid programs help the elderly and poor afford health care.

# Shifts in the Demand for Health Care

While changes in the price of health care cause movements along the demand curve, other factors can cause the demand curve to shift. The following are some of the nonprice determinants that can change the demand for health care.

## NUMBER OF BUYERS

As the population increases, the demand for health care increases. In addition to the total number of people, the distribution of older people in the population is important. As more people move into the 65-and-older age group, the demand for health care services becomes greater because older people have more-frequent and prolonged spells of illness. An increase in substance abuse involving alcohol, tobacco, or drugs also increases the demand for health care. For example, if the percentage of babies born into drug-prone families increases, the demand for health care will shift rightward.

## TASTES AND PREFERENCES

Changes in consumer attitudes toward health care can also change demand. For example, television, movies, magazines, and advertising may be responsible for changes in people's preferences for cosmetic surgery. Moreover, medical science has improved so much that we believe there must be a cure for most ailments. As a result, consumers are willing to buy larger quantities of medical services at each possible price.

Doctors also influence consumer preferences by prescribing treatment. It is often argued that some doctors guard against malpractice suits or boost their incomes by ordering more tests or office visits than are really needed. Some estimates suggest that fraud and abuse account for about 10 percent of total health care spending. These studies reveal that as many as one-third of some procedures are inappropriate.

## INCOME

Health care is a normal good. Rising inflation-adjusted incomes of consumers in the United States cause the demand curve for health care services to shift to the right. On the other hand, if real median family income remains unchanged, there is no influence on the demand curve.

## PRICES OF SUBSTITUTES

The prices of medical goods and services that are substitutes can change and, in turn, influence the demand for other medical services. For example, treatment of a back problem by a chiropractor is an alternative for many of the treatments provided by orthopedic doctors. If the price of orthopedic therapy rises, then some people will switch to treatment by a chiropractor. As a result, the demand curve for chiropractic therapy shifts rightward.

# Shifts in the Supply of Health Care

Changes in the following nonprice factors change the supply of health care.

### Number of Sellers

Sellers of health care include hospitals, nursing homes, physicians in private practice, HMOs, drug companies, chiropractors, psychologists, and a host of other suppliers. To ensure the quality and safety of health care, virtually every facet of the industry is regulated and licensed by the government or controlled by the American Medical Association (AMA). The AMA limits the number of persons practicing medicine primarily through medical school accreditation and licensing requirements. The federal Food and Drug Administration (FDA) requires testing that delays the introduction of new drugs. Tighter restrictions on the number of sellers shift the health care supply curve leftward, and reduced restrictions shift the supply curve rightward.

### Resource Prices

An increase in the costs of resources underlying the supply of health care shifts the supply curve leftward. By far the single most important factor behind increasing health care spending has been technological change. New diagnostic, surgical, and therapeutic equipment is used extensively in the health care industry, and the result is higher costs. Wages, salaries, and other costs, such as the costs of malpractice suits, also influence the supply curve. If hospitals, for example, are paying higher prices for inputs used to produce health care, the supply curve shifts to the left because the same quantities may be supplied only at higher prices.

# Price Elasticity of Demand and Supply

© Creatas Images/Jupiterimages

This chapter teaches you to calculate the percentage change in the quantity demanded when the price changes by a given percentage. Then you will see how this relates to total revenue. This knowledge of the sensitivity of demand is vital for pricing and targeting markets for goods and services. Next, you will see how changes in consumer income and the prices of related goods affect percentage changes in the quantity demanded. The chapter concludes by relating the concept of price elasticity to supply and the impact of taxation.

**In this chapter, you will learn to solve these economics puzzles:**

■ Can total revenue from a Steel Porcupines concert remain unchanged regardless of changes in the ticket price?
■ How sensitive is the quantity of cigarettes demanded to changes in the price of cigarettes?
■ What would happen to the sales of Mercedes, BMWs, and Jaguars in the United States if Congress prohibited sales of luxury Japanese cars in this country?

uppose you are the manager of the Steel Porcupines rock group. You are considering raising your ticket price, and you wonder how the fans will react. You have studied economics and know the law of demand. When the price of a ticket rises, the quantity demanded goes down, ceteris paribus. So you really need to know how many tickets fans will purchase if the band boosts the ticket price. If the ticket price for a Steel Porcupines concert is $25, you will sell 20,000 tickets. At $30 per ticket, only 10,000 tickets will be sold.

Thus, a $5 increase per ticket cuts the number of tickets sold in half.

Which ticket price should you choose? Is it better to charge a higher ticket price and sell fewer tickets or to charge a lower ticket price and sell more tickets? The answer depends on changes in *total revenue*, or sales, as we move upward along points on Steel Porcupines' demand curve. At $30 per ticket, sales will be $300,000. If you charge $25, the group will take in $500,000 for a concert. Okay, you say, what happens at $20 per ticket?

## Price Elasticity of Demand

In Chapter 3, when you studied the demand curve, the focus was on the law of demand. This law states there is an inverse relationship between the price and the quantity demanded of a good or service. In this chapter, the emphasis is on measuring the *relative size* of changes in the price and the quantity demanded. Now

113

we ask: By *what percentage* does the quantity demanded rise when the price falls by, say, 10 percent?

## THE PRICE ELASTICITY OF DEMAND MIDPOINTS FORMULA

**Price elasticity of demand**
The ratio of the percentage change in the quantity demanded of a product to a percentage change in its price.

Economists use a **price elasticity of demand** formula to measure the degree of consumer responsiveness, or sensitivity, to a change in price. Price elasticity of demand is the ratio of the percentage change in the quantity demanded of a product to a percentage change in its price. Suppose a university's enrollment drops by 20 percent because tuition rises by 10 percent. Therefore, the price elasticity of demand is 2 ($-20$ percent/$+10$ percent). The number 2 means that the quantity demanded (enrollment) changes 2 percent for each 1 percent change in price (tuition). Note there should be a minus sign in front of the 2 because, under the law of demand, price and quantity move in *opposite* directions. However, economists drop the minus sign because we know from the law of demand that quantity demanded and price are inversely related.

The number 2 is an *elasticity coefficient*, which economists use to measure the degree of elasticity. The elasticity formula is

$$E_d = \frac{\text{percentage change in quantity demanded}}{\text{percentage change in price}}$$

where $E_d$ is the elasticity of demand coefficient. Here you must take care. *There is a problem using this formula.* Let's return to our rock group example from the chapter preview. Suppose Steel Porcupines raises its ticket price from $25 to $30 and the number of seats sold falls from 20,000 to 10,000. We can compute the elasticity coefficient as

$$E_d = \frac{\%\Delta Q}{\%\Delta P} = \frac{\dfrac{10,000 - 20,000}{20,000}}{\dfrac{30 - 25}{25}} = \frac{50\%}{20\%} = 2.5$$

Now consider the elasticity coefficient computed between these same points on Steel Porcupines' demand curve when the price is lowered. Starting at $30 per ticket and lowering the ticket price to $25 cause the number of seats sold to rise from 10,000 to 20,000. In this case, the rock group computes a much different elasticity coefficient, as follows:

$$E_d = \frac{\%\Delta Q}{\%\Delta P} = \frac{\dfrac{20,000 - 10,000}{10,000}}{\dfrac{25 - 30}{30}} = \frac{100\%}{17\%} = 5.9$$

There is a reason for the different elasticity coefficients between the same two points on a demand curve (2.5 if price is raised, 5.9 if price is cut). The natural approach is to select the initial point as the base and then compute a percentage change. But price elasticity of demand involves changes between two possible initial base points ($P_1$, $Q_1$ or $P_2$, $Q_2$). Economists solve this problem of different base points by using the *midpoints* as the base points of changes in prices and quantities demanded. The *midpoints formula* for price elasticity of demand is

$$E_d = \frac{\text{change in quantity}}{\text{sum of quantitites}/2} \div \frac{\text{change in price}}{\text{sum of prices}/2}$$

which can be expressed as

$$E_d = \frac{\%\Delta Q}{\%\Delta P} = \frac{\dfrac{Q_2 - Q_1}{(Q_1 + Q_2)}}{\dfrac{P_2 - P_1}{(P_1 + P_2)}}$$

where $Q_1$ represents the first quantity demanded, $Q_2$ represents the second quantity demanded, and $P_1$ and $P_2$ are the first and second prices. Expressed this way, we divide the change in quantity demanded by the *average* quantity demanded. Then this value is divided by the change in the price divided by the *average* price.[1]

It does not matter if $Q_1$ or $P_1$ is the first or second number in each term because we are finding averages. Also note that you can drop the 2 as a divisor of both the $(Q_1 + Q_2)$ and $(P_1 + P_2)$ terms since the 2s in the numerator and the denominator cancel out. Now we can use the midpoints formula to calculate the price elasticity of demand of 3.7 regardless of whether Steel Porcupines raises the ticket price from $25 to $30 or lowers it from $30 to $25.

$$E_d = \frac{\dfrac{Q_2 - Q_1}{Q_1 + Q_2}}{\dfrac{P_2 - P_1}{P_1 + P_2}} = \frac{\dfrac{10,000 - 20,000}{20,000 + 10,000}}{\dfrac{30 - 25}{25 + 30}} = \frac{33\%}{9\%} = 3.7$$

and

$$E_d = \frac{\dfrac{Q_2 - Q_1}{Q_1 + Q_2}}{\dfrac{P_2 - P_1}{P_1 + P_2}} = \frac{\dfrac{20,000 - 10,000}{10,000 + 20,000}}{\dfrac{25 - 30}{30 + 25}} = \frac{33\%}{9\%} = 3.7$$

## THE TOTAL REVENUE TEST OF PRICE ELASTICITY OF DEMAND

As reflected in the midpoints formula, the *responsiveness* of the quantity demanded to a change in price determines the value of the elasticity coefficient.

[1]The midpoints formula is also commonly called the *arc elasticity formula*.

There are three possibilities: (1) the numerator is greater than the denominator, (2) the numerator is less than the denominator, and (3) the numerator equals the denominator. Exhibit 1 presents three cases that the Steel Porcupines rock band may confront.

## ELASTIC DEMAND ($E_d > 1$)

**Elastic demand**
A condition in which the percentage change in quantity demanded is greater than the percentage change in price.

**Total revenue**
The total number of dollars a firm earns from the sale of a good or service, which is equal to its price multiplied by the quantity demanded.

Suppose Steel Porcupines' demand curve is as depicted in Exhibit 1(a). Using the above midpoints formula, which drops the 2 as a divisor, if the group lowers its ticket price from $30 to $20, the quantity demanded increases from 10,000 to 30,000. Using the midpoints formula, this means that a 20 percent reduction in ticket price brings a 50 percent increase in quantity demanded. Thus, $E_d = 2.5$, and demand is **elastic**. Elastic demand is a condition in which the percentage change in quantity demanded is greater than the percentage change in price. Demand is elastic when the elasticity coefficient is greater than 1. Because the percentage change in quantity demanded is greater than the percentage change in price, the drop in price causes **total revenue** (**TR**) to rise. Total revenue is the total number of dollars a firm earns from the sale of a good or service, which is equal to its price multiplied by the quantity demanded. Perhaps the simplest way to tell whether demand is elastic, unitary elastic, or inelastic is to observe the response of total revenue as the price of a product changes. For example, in Exhibit 1(a), the total revenue at $30 is $300,000. The total revenue at $20 is $600,000. Compare the shaded rectangles under the demand curve, representing total revenue at each price. The gray area is an amount of total revenue unaffected by the price change. Note that the green shaded area gained at $20 per ticket ($400,000) is greater than the red shaded area lost at $30 per ticket ($100,000). This net gain of $300,000 causes the total revenue to increase by this amount when Steel Porcupines lowers the ticket price from $30 to $20.

## INELASTIC DEMAND ($E_d < 1$)

**Inelastic demand**
A condition in which the percentage change in quantity demanded is less than the percentage change in price.

The demand curve in Exhibit 1(b) is inelastic. The quantity demanded is less responsive to a change in price. Here a fall in Steel Porcupines' ticket price from $30 to $20 causes the quantity demanded to increase by just 5,000 tickets (20,000 to 25,000 tickets). Using the midpoints formula, a 20 percent fall in the ticket price causes an 11 percent rise in the quantity demanded. This means $E_d = 0.55$ and demand is **inelastic**. Inelastic demand is a condition in which the percentage change in quantity demanded is less than the percentage change in price. Demand is inelastic when the elasticity coefficient is less than 1. When demand is inelastic, the drop in price causes total revenue to fall from $600,000 to $500,000. Note the net change in the shaded rectangles.

## UNITARY ELASTIC DEMAND ($E_d = 1$)

An interesting case exists when a demand curve is neither elastic nor inelastic. Exhibit 1(c) shows a demand curve for which any percentage change in price along the curve causes an exact proportional change in quantity demanded. When this situation occurs, the total amount of money spent on a good or service does not vary with changes in price. If Steel Porcupines drops the ticket price from $30 to $20, the quantity demanded rises from 20,000 to 30,000. Therefore, using the

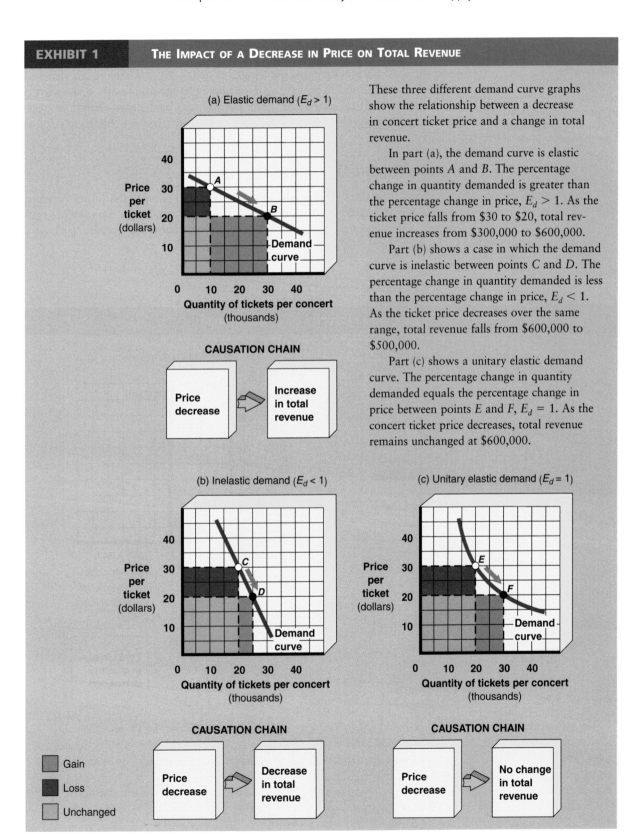

**EXHIBIT 1**    **THE IMPACT OF A DECREASE IN PRICE ON TOTAL REVENUE**

**(a) Elastic demand ($E_d > 1$)**

These three different demand curve graphs show the relationship between a decrease in concert ticket price and a change in total revenue.

In part (a), the demand curve is elastic between points $A$ and $B$. The percentage change in quantity demanded is greater than the percentage change in price, $E_d > 1$. As the ticket price falls from $30 to $20, total revenue increases from $300,000 to $600,000.

Part (b) shows a case in which the demand curve is inelastic between points $C$ and $D$. The percentage change in quantity demanded is less than the percentage change in price, $E_d < 1$. As the ticket price decreases over the same range, total revenue falls from $600,000 to $500,000.

Part (c) shows a unitary elastic demand curve. The percentage change in quantity demanded equals the percentage change in price between points $E$ and $F$, $E_d = 1$. As the concert ticket price decreases, total revenue remains unchanged at $600,000.

**CAUSATION CHAIN**

Price decrease ⇨ Increase in total revenue

**(b) Inelastic demand ($E_d < 1$)**

**(c) Unitary elastic demand ($E_d = 1$)**

Gain
Loss
Unchanged

**CAUSATION CHAIN**

Price decrease ⇨ Decrease in total revenue

**CAUSATION CHAIN**

Price decrease ⇨ No change in total revenue

**Unitary elastic demand**
A condition in which the percentage change in quantity demanded is equal to the percentage change in price.

midpoints formula, a 20 percent decrease in price brings about a 20 percent increase in quantity demanded. If this is the case, demand is **unitary elastic** ($E_d = 1$), and the total revenue remains unchanged at $600,000. Unitary elastic demand is defined as a condition in which the percentage change in quantity demanded is equal to the percentage change in price. Because the percentage change in price equals the percentage change in quantity, total revenue does not change regardless of changes in price.

## PERFECTLY ELASTIC DEMAND ($E_d = \infty$)

Two extreme cases are shown in Exhibit 2. These represent the limits between which the three demand curves explained above fall. Suppose for the sake of argument that a demand curve is perfectly horizontal, as shown in Exhibit 2(a). At a

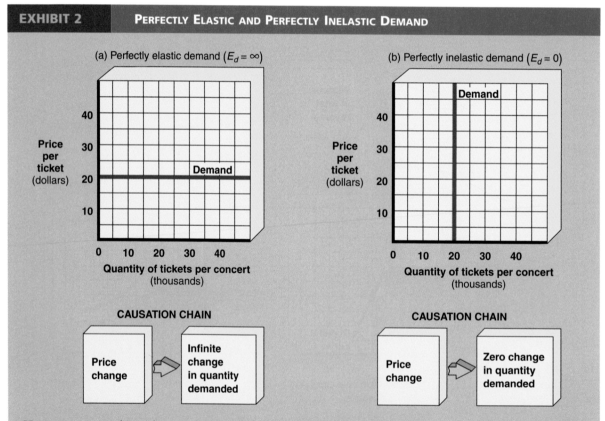

**EXHIBIT 2     PERFECTLY ELASTIC AND PERFECTLY INELASTIC DEMAND**

(a) Perfectly elastic demand ($E_d = \infty$)

(b) Perfectly inelastic demand ($E_d = 0$)

CAUSATION CHAIN

CAUSATION CHAIN

Here two extreme demand curves for Steel Porcupines concert tickets are presented. Part (a) shows a demand curve that is a horizontal line. Such a demand curve is perfectly elastic. At $20 per ticket, the Steel Porcupines can sell as many concert tickets as it wishes. At any price above $20, the quantity demanded falls from an infinite number to zero.

Part (b) shows a demand curve that is a vertical line. This demand curve is perfectly inelastic. No matter what the ticket price, the quantity demanded remains unchanged at 20,000 tickets.

price of $20, buyers are willing to buy as many tickets as the Steel Porcupines band is willing to offer for sale. At higher prices, buyers buy nothing. For example, at $20.01 per ticket or higher, buyers will buy zero tickets. If so, $E_d = \infty$, and demand is **perfectly elastic**. Perfectly elastic demand is a condition in which a small percentage change in price brings about an infinite percentage change in quantity demanded.

## PERFECTLY INELASTIC DEMAND ($E_d = 0$)

Exhibit 2(b) shows the other extreme case, which is a perfectly vertical demand curve. No matter how high or low the Steel Porcupines' ticket price is, the quantity demanded is 20,000 tickets. Such a demand curve is **perfectly inelastic**, and $E_d = 0$. Perfectly inelastic demand is a condition in which the quantity demanded does not change as the price changes.

Exhibit 3 summarizes the ranges for price elasticity of demand.

**Perfectly elastic demand**
A condition in which a small percentage change in price brings about an infinite percentage change in quantity demanded.

**Perfectly inelastic demand**
A condition in which the quantity demanded does not change as the price changes.

| EXHIBIT 3 | PRICE ELASTICITY OF DEMAND TERMINOLOGY | | |
|---|---|---|---|
| **Elasticity coefficient** | **Definition** | **Demand** | **Graph** |
| $E_d > 1$ | Percentage change in quantity demanded is greater than the percentage change in price | Elastic | |
| $E_d < 1$ | Percentage change in quantity demanded is less than the percentage change in price | Inelastic | |
| $E_d = 1$ | Percentage change in quantity demanded is equal to the percentage change in price | Unitary elastic | |
| $E_d = \infty$ | Percentage change in quantity demanded is infinite in relation to the percentage change in price | Perfectly elastic | |
| $E_d = 0$ | Quantity demanded does not change as the price changes | Perfectly inelastic | |

# Price Elasticity of Demand Variations along a Demand Curve

The price elasticity of demand for a downward-sloping straight-line demand curve varies as we move along the curve. Look at Exhibit 4, which shows a linear demand curve in part (a) and the corresponding total revenue curve in part (b). Begin at $40 on the demand curve and move down to $35, to $30, to $25, and so on. The table in Exhibit 4 lists variations in the total revenue and the elasticity coefficient $(E_d)$ at different ticket prices. As we move down the upper segment of the demand curve, price elasticity of demand falls, and total revenue rises. For example, measured over the price range of $35 to $30, the price elasticity of demand is 4.33, so this segment of demand is elastic $(E_d > 1)$. Between these two prices, total revenue increases from $175,000 to $300,000. At $20, price elasticity is unitary elastic $(E_d = 1)$, and total revenue is maximized at $400,000. As we move down the lower segment of the demand curve, price elasticity of demand falls below a value of 1.0, and total revenue falls. Over the price range of $15 to $10, for example, the price elasticity of demand is 0.45, and, therefore, this segment of demand is inelastic $(E_d < 1)$. Between these two prices, total revenue decreases from $375,000 to $300,000.

> **CONCLUSION** *The price elasticity coefficient of demand applies only to a specific range of prices.*

It is no coincidence that the demand curve in Exhibit 4(a) has elastic, unitary elastic, and inelastic segments. In fact, *any downward-sloping straight-line demand curve has ranges of all three of these types of price elasticity of demand.* As we move downward, first, there is an elastic range; second, a unitary elastic range; and, third, an inelastic range. Why? Recall that price elasticity of demand is a ratio of percentage changes. At the upper end of the demand curve, quantities demanded are lower, and prices are higher. A change of 1 unit in quantity demanded is a large percentage change. On the other hand, a $1 price change is a relatively small percentage change. At the lower end of the curve, the situation reverses. A 1-unit change in quantity demanded is a small percentage change. A $1 price change is

## CHECKPOINT

### Will Fliers Flock to Low Summer Fares?

USAirways is concerned over low sales and announces special cuts in its fares this summer. The New York–Los Angeles fare, for example, is reduced from $500 to $420. Does USAirways think demand is elastic, unitary elastic, or inelastic?

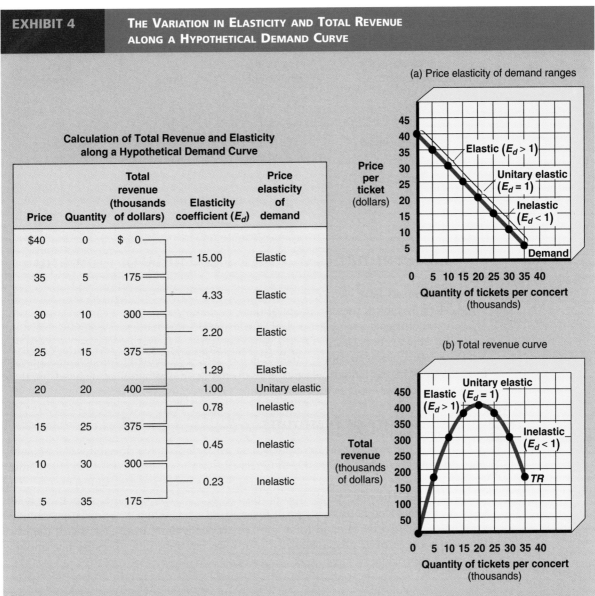

EXHIBIT 4 — THE VARIATION IN ELASTICITY AND TOTAL REVENUE ALONG A HYPOTHETICAL DEMAND CURVE

(a) Price elasticity of demand ranges

(b) Total revenue curve

Calculation of Total Revenue and Elasticity along a Hypothetical Demand Curve

| Price | Quantity | Total revenue (thousands of dollars) | Elasticity coefficient ($E_d$) | Price elasticity of demand |
|---|---|---|---|---|
| $40 | 0 | $ 0 | | |
| | | | 15.00 | Elastic |
| 35 | 5 | 175 | | |
| | | | 4.33 | Elastic |
| 30 | 10 | 300 | | |
| | | | 2.20 | Elastic |
| 25 | 15 | 375 | | |
| | | | 1.29 | Elastic |
| 20 | 20 | 400 | | |
| | | | 1.00 | Unitary elastic |
| | | | 0.78 | Inelastic |
| 15 | 25 | 375 | | |
| | | | 0.45 | Inelastic |
| 10 | 30 | 300 | | |
| | | | 0.23 | Inelastic |
| 5 | 35 | 175 | | |

Part (a) shows a straight-line demand curve and its three elasticity ranges. In the $40–$20 price range, demand is elastic. As price decreases in this range, total revenue increases. At $20, demand is unitary elastic, and total revenue is at its maximum. In the $20–$5 price range, demand is inelastic. As price decreases in this range, total revenue decreases. The total revenue (TR) curve is plotted in part (b) to trace its relationship to price elasticity.

a relatively larger percentage change. Now pause and refer back to parts (a) and (b) of Exhibit 1. If we examine changes in price along the entire length of these demand curves, we will find elastic, unitary elastic, and inelastic segments.

Exhibit 5 summarizes the relationships between elasticity, price change, and total revenue.

| EXHIBIT 5 | RELATIONSHIPS AMONG ELASTICITY, PRICE CHANGE, AND TOTAL REVENUE | | |
|---|---|---|---|
| **Price elasticity of demand** | **Elasticity coefficient** | **Price** | **Total revenue** |
| Elastic | $E_d > 1$ | ↑ | ↓ |
| Elastic | $E_d > 1$ | ↓ | ↑ |
| Unitary elastic | $E_d = 1$ | ↑ ↓ | No change |
| Inelastic | $E_d < 1$ | ↑ | ↑ |
| Inelastic | $E_d < 1$ | ↓ | ↓ |

# Determinants of Price Elasticity of Demand

Economists have estimated price elasticity of demand for various goods and services. Exhibit 6 presents some of these estimates, and as you can see, the elasticity coefficients vary a great deal. For example, the demand for automobiles and for chinaware is elastic. On the other hand, the demand for jewelry and watches and for theater and opera tickets is inelastic. The demand for tires and tubes is approximately unitary elastic. Why do the price elasticities of demand for these products vary so much? The following factors cause these differences.

## AVAILABILITY OF SUBSTITUTES

By far the most important influence on price elasticity of demand is the availability of substitutes. Demand is more elastic for a good or service with close substitutes. If the price of cars rises, consumers can switch to buses, trains, bicycles, and walking. The more public transportation is available, the more responsive quantity demanded is to a change in the price of cars. When consumers have limited alternatives, the demand for a good or service is more price inelastic. If the price of tobacco rises, people addicted to it have few substitutes because not smoking is unappealing to most users.

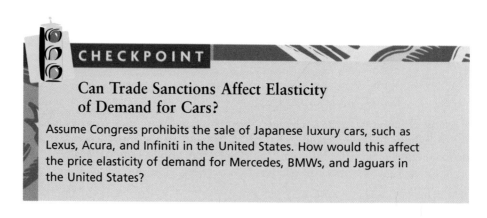

**CHECKPOINT**

### Can Trade Sanctions Affect Elasticity of Demand for Cars?

Assume Congress prohibits the sale of Japanese luxury cars, such as Lexus, Acura, and Infiniti in the United States. How would this affect the price elasticity of demand for Mercedes, BMWs, and Jaguars in the United States?

| EXHIBIT 6 | ESTIMATED PRICE ELASTICITIES OF DEMAND | |
|---|---|---|
| | Elasticity coefficient | |
| Item | Short run | Long run |
| Automobiles | 1.87 | 2.24 |
| Chinaware | 1.54 | 2.55 |
| Movies | 0.87 | 3.67 |
| Tires and tubes | 0.86 | 1.19 |
| Commuter rail fares | 0.62 | 1.59 |
| Jewelry and watches | 0.41 | 0.67 |
| Medical care | 0.31 | 0.92 |
| Housing | 0.30 | 1.88 |
| Gasoline | 0.20 | 0.70 |
| Theater and opera tickets | 0.18 | 0.31 |
| Foreign travel | 0.14 | 1.77 |
| Air travel | 0.10 | 2.40 |

Sources: Robert Archibald and Robert Gillingham, "An Analysis of the Short-Run Consumer Demand for Gasoline Using Household Survey Data," Review of Economics and Statistics 62 (November 1980): 622–628; Hendrik S. Houthakker and Lester D. Taylor, Consumer Demand in the United States: Analyses and Projections (Cambridge, Mass.: Harvard University Press, 1970): pp. 56–149; Richard Voith, "The Long-Run Elasticity of Demand for Commuter Rail Transportation," Journal of Urban Economics 30 (November 1991): 360–372.

**CONCLUSION** *The price elasticity coefficient of demand is directly related to the availability of good substitutes for a product.*

Price elasticity also depends on the market used to measure demand. For example, studies show the price elasticity of Chevrolets is greater than that of automobiles in general. Chevrolets compete with other cars sold by GM, Ford, DaimlerChrysler, Toyota, and other automakers and with buses and trains—all of which are substitutes for Chevrolets. But using the broad class of cars eliminates these specific types of cars as competitors. Instead, substitutes for automobiles include buses and trains, which are also substitutes for Chevrolets. In short, there are more close substitutes for Chevrolets than there are for all cars.

## SHARE OF BUDGET SPENT ON THE PRODUCT

When the price of salt changes, consumers pay little attention. Why should they notice? The price of salt or matches can double, and this purchase will remain a small percentage of one's budget. If, however, college tuition, the price of dinners at restaurants, or housing prices double, people will look for alternatives. These goods and services account for a large part of people's budgets.

**CONCLUSION** *The price elasticity coefficient of demand is directly related to the percentage of one's budget spent for a good or service.*

## ADJUSTMENT TO A PRICE CHANGE OVER TIME

Exhibit 6 separates the elasticity coefficients into short-run and long-run categories. As time passes, buyers can respond fully to a change in the price of a product by finding more substitutes. Consider the demand for gasoline. In the short run, people find it hard to cut back the amount they buy when the price rises sharply. They are accustomed to driving back and forth to work alone in their cars. The typical short-run response is to cut luxury travel and reduce speed on trips. If high prices persist over time, car buyers will find ways to cut back. They can buy cars with better fuel economy (more miles per gallon), form car pools, and ride buses or commuter trains. This explains why the short-run elasticity coefficient of gasoline in the exhibit is more inelastic at 0.2 than the long-run elasticity coefficient of 0.7.

> **CONCLUSION** *In general, the price elasticity coefficient of demand is higher the longer a price change persists.*

# Other Elasticity Measures

The elasticity concept has other applications beyond calculating the price elasticity of demand. Broadly defined, it is a technique for measuring the response of one variable to changes in some other variable.

## INCOME ELASTICITY OF DEMAND

**Income elasticity of demand**
The ratio of the percentage change in the quantity demanded of a good or service to a given percentage change in income.

Recall from Chapter 3 that an increase in income can increase demand (shift the demand curve rightward) for a normal good or service and decrease demand (shift the demand curve leftward) for an inferior good or service. To measure exactly how consumption responds to changes in income, economists calculate the **income elasticity of demand**. Income elasticity of demand is the ratio of the percentage change in the quantity demanded of a good or service to a given percentage change in income. We use a midpoints formula similar to the one we used for calculating price elasticity of demand:

$$E_I = \frac{\text{percentage change in quantity demanded}}{\text{percentage change in income}}$$

$$E_I = \frac{\%\Delta Q}{\%\Delta I} = \frac{\dfrac{Q_2 - Q_1}{Q_1 + Q_2}}{\dfrac{I_2 - I_1}{I_1 + I_2}}$$

Where $E_I$ is the income elasticity of demand coefficient, $Q_1$ and $Q_2$ represent quantities demanded before and after the income change, and $I_1$ and $I_2$ represent income before and after the income change.

For a *normal* good or service, the income elasticity of demand is *positive*, $E_I > 0$. Recall that for this type of good demand and income move in the same direc-

**You're the Economist**

# Cigarette Smoking Price Elasticity of Demand
*Applicable Concept: price elasticity of demand*

Tobacco use is one of the chief preventable causes of death in the world. Since 1964, health warnings have been mandated in the United States on tobacco advertising, including billboards and printed advertising. In 1971, television advertising was prohibited. Most states have banned smoking in state buildings, and the federal government has restricted smoking in federal offices and military facilities. In 1998, the Senate engaged in heated debate over proposed legislation to curb smoking by teenagers. This bill would have raised the price of cigarettes by $1.10 a pack over five years, and the tobacco industry would have paid $369 billion over the next 25 years. Opponents argued that this price increase would be a massive tax on low-income Americans that would generate huge revenues to finance additional government programs and spending. Proponents countered that the bill was not about taxes. Instead, the bill was an attack on the death march of Americans who die early from tobacco-related diseases. Ultimately, the Senate was so divided on the issue that it was impossible, at least for that year, to pass a tobacco bill.

Estimates of the price elasticity of demand for cigarettes in the United States and other high-income countries fall in the inelastic range of 0.62. This means that if prices rise by 10 percent, cigarette consumption will fall by about 6 percent.[1] The price elasticity of demand for cigarettes also appears to vary by education. Less-educated adults are more responsive to price changes than better-educated adults. This finding supports the theory that less-educated people are more present-oriented, or "myopic," than people with more education. Thus, less-educated individuals tend to be more influenced by current changes in the price of a pack of cigarettes.[2] Another study in 2000 confirmed that education has strong negative effects on the quantity of cigarettes smoked, especially for high-income individuals. The presence of young children reduces smoking, with the effect most pronounced for women.[3]

© Photodisc/Getty Images

A study published in *Health Economics* estimated the relationship between cigarette smoking and price for 34,145 respondents, aged 15–29 years. The price elasticity of smoking was inelastic and varied inversely with age: 0.83 for ages 15–17, 0.52 for ages 18–20, 0.37 for ages 21–23, 0.20 for ages 24–26, and 0.09 for ages 27–29. Thus, younger people were more likely to reduce the number of cigarettes smoked in response to increased prices.[4]

### ANALYZE THE ISSUE

According to the above discussion, what factors influence the price elasticity of demand for cigarettes? What other factors not mentioned in the article might also influence the price elasticity of demand for cigarettes?

[1]Jon P. Nelson, "Cigarette Demand, Structural Change, and Advertising Bans: International Evidence, 1970–1995," *Contribution to Economic Analysis and Policy* 2, no. 1 (2003): article 10.

[2]Frank Chaloupka et al., "Tax, Price and Cigarette Smoking," *Tobacco Control* 11, no. 1 (March 2002): 62–73.

[3]Joni Hersch, "Gender, Income Levels, and the Demand for Cigarettes," *Journal of Risk and Uncertainty* 21, no. 2-3 (November 2000): 263–282.

[4]Jeffrey E. Harris and Sandra W. Chan, "The Continuum of Addiction: Cigarette Smoking in Relation to Price among Americans Aged 15–29," *Health Economics* 8, no. 1 (February 1999): 81–86.

tion. Thus, the variables in the numerator and denominator change in the same direction. For an *inferior* good or service, the reverse is true, and the income elasticity of demand is *negative*, $E_I < 0$.

Why is the income elasticity coefficient important? Returning to our rock group example, the Steel Porcupines band needs to know the impact of a recession on ticket sales. During a downturn when consumers' incomes fall, if a rock concert is a *normal good*, the quantity of ticket sales falls. Conversely, if a rock concert is an *inferior good*, the quantity of ticket sales rises. To illustrate, suppose consumers' incomes increase from $1,000 to $1,250 per month. As a result, the quantity of tickets demanded increases from 10,000 to 15,000. Based on these data, is a rock concert a normal or an inferior good? We compute as follows:

$$E_I = \frac{\dfrac{Q_2 - Q_1}{Q_1 + Q_2}}{\dfrac{I_2 - I_1}{I_1 + I_2}} = \frac{\dfrac{15,000 - 10,000}{10,000 + 15,000}}{\dfrac{1,250 - 1,000}{1,250 + 1,000}} = \frac{.20}{.11} = 1.8$$

The computed income elasticity of demand coefficient of 1.8 summarizes the relationship between changes in rock concert ticket purchases and changes in income. First, $E_I$ is a positive number; therefore, a rock concert is a normal good because people buy more when their incomes rise. Second, ticket purchases are very responsive to changes in income. When income rises by 11 percent, ticket sales increase by more (20 percent).

Exhibit 7 lists estimated income elasticity of demand for selected products.

## CROSS-ELASTICITY OF DEMAND

In Chapter 3, we learned that a change in the price of one good—say, Y—can cause the consumption of another good—say, X—to change (see prices of related goods in Exhibit 5 in Chapter 3). In Exhibit 1(b) in Chapter 4, for example, a sharp rise in the price of gasoline (a complement) causes the number of gas guzzlers pur-

| EXHIBIT 7 | ESTIMATED INCOME ELASTICITIES OF DEMAND | |
|---|---|---|
| | **Elasticity coefficient** | |
| **Item** | **Short run** | **Long run** |
| Potatoes | N.A. | 0.81 |
| Furniture | 2.60 | 0.53 |
| Dental services | 0.38 | 1.00 |
| Automobiles | 5.50 | 1.07 |
| Physician services | 0.28 | 1.15 |
| Clothing | 0.95 | 1.17 |
| Shoes | 0.90 | 1.50 |
| Gasoline and oil | 0.55 | 1.36 |
| Jewelry and watches | 1.00 | 1.60 |
| Toilet articles | 0.25 | 3.74 |

*Sources: Hendrik S. Houthakker and Lester D. Taylor,* Consumer Demand in the United States: Analyses and Projections *(Cambridge, Mass.: Harvard University Press, 1970); Dale M. Helen, "The Structure of Food Demand: Interrelatedness and Duality,"* American Journal of Agricultural Economics *64, no. 2 (May 1982): 213–221.*

chased to decline. This responsiveness of the quantity demanded to changes in the price of some other good is estimated by the **cross-elasticity of demand**. Cross-elasticity of demand is the ratio of the percentage change in the quantity demanded of a good or service to a given percentage change in the price of another good or service. Again, we use the midpoints formula as follows to compute the cross-elasticity coefficient of demand:

$$E_c = \frac{\begin{array}{c}\text{percentage change} \\ \text{in quantity demanded of one good}\end{array}}{\begin{array}{c}\text{percentage change in price} \\ \text{of another good}\end{array}}$$

$$E_c = \frac{\%\Delta Q_X}{\%\Delta P_Y} = \frac{\dfrac{Q_{X_2} - Q_{X_1}}{Q_{X_1} + Q_{X_2}}}{\dfrac{P_{Y_2} - P_{Y_1}}{P_{Y_1} + P_{Y_2}}}$$

where $E_c$ is the cross-elasticity coefficient, $Q_1$ and $Q_2$ represent quantities before and after the price of another good or service changes, and $P_1$ and $P_2$ represent the price of another good or service before and after the price change.

The cross-elasticity coefficient reveals whether a good or service is a *substitute* or a *complement*. For example, suppose Coke increases its price 10 percent, which causes consumers to buy 5 percent more Pepsi. The cross-elasticity of demand for Pepsi is a *positive* .50 (+5 percent/+10 percent). Since $E_c > 0$, Coke and Pepsi are *substitutes* because the numerator and denominator variables change in the same direction. The larger the positive coefficient, the greater the substitutability between the two goods.

Now suppose there is a 50 percent increase in the price of motor oil and the quantity demanded of gasoline decreases by 10 percent. The cross-elasticity of demand for gasoline is a *negative* .20 (−10 percent/+50 percent). Since $E_c < 0$, these two goods are *complements*. The larger the negative coefficient, the greater the complementary relationship between the two goods. The variables in the numerator and denominator change in opposite directions.

## PRICE ELASTICITY OF SUPPLY

The **price elasticity of supply** closely follows the price elasticity of demand concept. Price elasticity of supply is the ratio of the percentage change in the quantity supplied of a product to the percentage change in its price. This elasticity coefficient is calculated using the following formula:

$$E_s = \frac{\text{percentage change in quantity supplied}}{\text{percentage change in price}}$$

where $E_s$ is the price elasticity of supply coefficient. Since price and quantity supplied change in the same direction, the elasticity coefficient is a positive value. Economists use terminology corresponding to that for the elasticity of demand. Supply is *elastic* when $E_s > 1$, *unitary elastic* when $E_s = 1$, *inelastic* when $E_s < 1$, *perfectly elastic* when $E_s = \infty$, and *perfectly inelastic* when $E_s = 0$. Exhibit 8 shows three of these cases.

**Cross-elasticity of demand**
The ratio of the percentage change in the quantity demanded of a good or service to a given percentage change in the price of another good or service.

**Price elasticity of supply**
The ratio of the percentage change in the quantity supplied of a product to the percentage change in its price.

**EXHIBIT 8      PRICE ELASTICITY OF SUPPLY**

This figure shows three supply curves. As shown in Part (a), a small change in price changes the quantity supplied by an infinite amount: $E_s = \infty$. Part (b) shows the quantity supplied is unaffected by a change in price: $E_s = 0$, and supply is perfectly inelastic. In Part (c), the percentage change in quantity supplied is equal to the percentage change in price: $E_s = 1$.

In Chapter 8, we will explain why the time period of analysis is a primary determinant of the shape of the supply curve. More specifically, it will be shown that price elasticity of supply is greater in the long run than in the short run. Thus, the long-run supply curve will be flatter.

Exhibit 9 gives a summary of the three elasticity concepts presented in this section.

**EXHIBIT 9      SUMMARY OF OTHER ELASTICITY CONCEPTS**

| Type | Definition | Elasticity coefficient possibilities | Terminology |
|---|---|---|---|
| Income elasticity of demand | $\dfrac{\text{Percentage change in quantity demanded}}{\text{Percentage change in income}}$ | $E_I > 0$<br>$E_I < 0$<br>$E_I > 1$<br>$E_I < 1$<br>$E_I = 1$ | Normal good<br>Inferior good<br>Income elastic<br>Income inelastic<br>Income unitary elastic |
| Cross-elasticity of demand | $\dfrac{\text{Percentage change in quantity demanded of one good}}{\text{Percentage change in price of another good}}$ | $E_c < 0$<br>$E_c > 0$ | Complements<br>Substitutes |
| Price elasticity of supply | $\dfrac{\text{Percentage change in quantity supplied}}{\text{Percentage change in price}}$ | $E_s > 1$<br>$E_s = 1$<br>$E_s < 1$<br>$E_s = \infty$<br>$E_s = 0$ | Elastic<br>Unitary elastic<br>Inelastic<br>Perfectly elastic<br>Perfectly inelastic |

## PRICE ELASTICITY AND THE IMPACT OF TAXATION

Who pays a tax levied on sellers of goods such as gasoline, cigarettes, and alcoholic beverages? One way to answer this question is to say that if the government places a tax on, say, gasoline, the gasoline companies pay the tax. They collect the tax when they sell gas and write the checks to the government for the tax. But this is not the whole story. Instead of looking simply at who writes the checks, economists use the elasticity concept to analyze who "really" pays a tax. **Tax incidence** is the share of a tax ultimately paid by consumers and sellers. In this section, we show that even though taxes are collected from sellers, buyers do not escape a share of the tax burden. The tax incidence depends on the price elasticities of demand and supply. Let's look at two examples.

Suppose the federal government decides to raise the gasoline tax $.50 per gallon. Exhibit 10 shows the impact of the tax on different demand curves. At $E_1$ in Part (a), the equilibrium price before the tax is $2.00 per gallon and the equilibrium quantity is 30 million gallons per day. The effect of the tax is to shift the supply curve leftward from $S_1$ to $S_2$. From the sellers' viewpoint, the cost of each gallon of gasoline increases $.50 per gallon at any possible selling price. The effect is exactly the same as if the price of crude oil or any resource used to produce gasoline increased.

Sellers would like consumers to pay the entire amount of the tax. This would occur if consumers would pay $2.50 per gallon for the same 30 million gallons per day they purchased before the tax. But the leftward shift in supply establishes a new equilibrium at $E_2$. The new equilibrium price is $2.25 per gallon, and the equilibrium quantity falls to 25 million gallons per day. At $E_2$, the entire shaded area represents the tax revenue. The government collects $12.5 million per day, which equals the $.50 per gallon tax times the 25 million gallons sold each day. The vertical line between points $E_2$ and $T$ represents the $.50 tax per gallon. Since consumers now pay $2.25 instead of $2.00 per gallon, they pay one-half of the tax. The sellers pay the remaining half of the tax. Now the sellers send $.50 to Uncle Sam and keep $.75 compared with the $2.00 per gallon they kept before the tax.

**Tax incidence**
The share of a tax ultimately paid by consumers and sellers.

## CHECKPOINT

### Can Honda Compete with Itself?

When Honda introduced the Acura to compete with European luxury cars, there was a danger that the new line would take sales away from Honda's Accord. To make Acura more competitive with other luxury cars, suppose Honda cuts the price of Acura while keeping the price of Accord unchanged. If Honda's fear comes true, will it find a negative cross-elasticity of demand, a negative income elasticity of demand, or a positive cross-elasticity of demand?

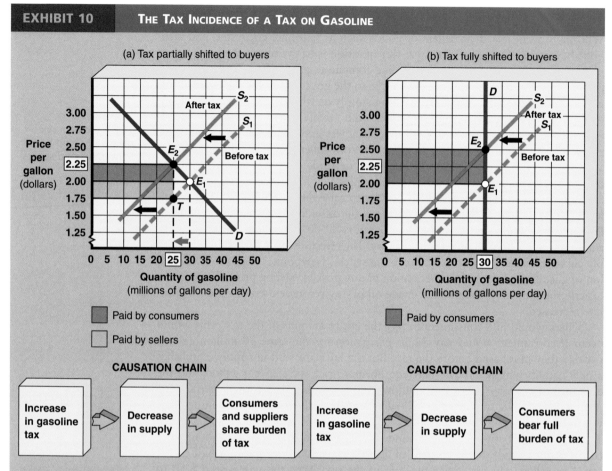

**EXHIBIT 10**   THE TAX INCIDENCE OF A TAX ON GASOLINE

In Parts (a) and (b), $S_1$ is the supply curve before the imposition of a tax of $.50 per gallon on gasoline. The demand curve is not affected by this tax collected from the sellers. The initial equilibrium is $E_1$. Before the tax, the price is $2.00 per gallon, and 30 million gallons are bought and sold.

In Part (a), the equilibrium price rises to $2.25 per gallon at $E_2$ as a result of the tax. After the tax is paid, sellers receive only $1.75 per gallon (point $T$) instead of the $2.00 they received before the tax. Thus, buyers pay $.25 of the tax per gallon, and sellers bear the remaining $.25. The shaded area is the total tax collected.

As shown in Part (b), a tax collected from sellers can be fully shifted to buyers in the unlikely case that demand is perfectly inelastic. Since the quantity of gasoline purchased is unresponsive to a change in price, sellers receive $2.00 per gallon before and after they pay the tax.

**CONCLUSION** *If the demand curve slopes downward and the supply curve slopes upward, sellers cannot raise the price by the full amount of the tax.*

Part (b) of Exhibit 10 is a special case in which the market price increases by the full amount of the tax per gallon. Here the demand for gasoline is perfectly inelastic. In this case, buyers do not decrease the quantity demanded in response to the decrease in supply caused by the tax. The quantity demanded is 30 million gallons per day before and after the tax. The price, however, increases from $E_1$ to $E_2$ by exactly the amount of tax per unit from $2.00 to $2.50 per gallon, and therefore consumers pay the entire burden of the tax. After paying the tax, sellers receive a net price of $2.00 per gallon. The total tax revenue collected by the government is the shaded area. Each day $15 million is collected, which equals the $.50 per gallon tax multiplied by 30 million gallons sold each day.

> **CONCLUSION** *In the case where demand is perfectly inelastic, sellers can raise the price by the full amount of a tax.*

## Key Concepts

| | | |
|---|---|---|
| Price elasticity of demand | Unitary elastic demand | Cross-elasticity of demand |
| Elastic demand | Perfectly elastic demand | Price elasticity of supply |
| Total revenue | Perfectly inelastic demand | Tax incidence |
| Inelastic demand | Income elasticity of demand | |

## Summary

- **Price elasticity of demand** is a measure of the responsiveness of the quantity demanded to a change in price. Specifically, price elasticity of demand is the ratio of the percentage change in quantity demanded to the percentage change in price.

$$E_d = \frac{\%\Delta Q}{\%\Delta P} = \frac{\dfrac{Q_2 - Q_1}{(Q_1 + Q_2)}}{\dfrac{P_2 - P_1}{(P_1 + P_2)}}$$

- **Elastic demand** occurs where there is a change of more than 1 percent in quantity demanded in response to a 1 percent change in price. Demand is elastic when the elasticity coefficient is greater than 1 and *total revenue* (price times quantity) varies inversely with the direction of the price change.

- **Inelastic demand** occurs where there is a change of less than 1 percent in quantity demanded in response to a 1 percent change in price. Demand is inelastic when the elasticity coefficient is less than 1 and total revenue varies directly with the direction of the price change.

- **Unitary elastic demand** occurs where there is a 1 percent change in quantity demanded in response to a 1 percent change in price. Demand is unitary elastic when the elasticity coefficient equals 1 and total revenue remains constant as the price changes.

- **Perfectly elastic demand** occurs when the quantity demanded declines to zero for even the slightest rise or fall in price. This is an extreme case in which the demand curve is horizontal and the elasticity coefficient equals infinity.

- **Perfectly inelastic demand** occurs when the quantity demanded does not change in response to price changes. This is an extreme case in which the demand curve is vertical and the elasticity coefficient equals zero.

- **Determinants of price elasticity of demand** include (a) the availability of substitutes, (b) the percentage of one's budget spent on the product, and (c) the length of time allowed for adjustment. Each of these factors is directly related to the elasticity coefficient.

- **Income elasticity of demand** is the percentage change in quantity demanded divided by the percentage change in income. For a *normal* good or service, income elasticity of demand is positive. For an *inferior* good or service, income elasticity of demand is negative.

- **Cross-elasticity of demand** is the percentage change in the quantity demanded of one product caused by a change in the price of another product. When the cross-elasticity of demand is negative, the two products are complements.

- **Price elasticity of supply** is a measure of the responsiveness of the quantity supplied to a change in price. Price elasticity of supply is the ratio of the percentage change in quantity supplied to the percentage change in price.

- **Tax incidence** is the share of a tax ultimately paid by buyers and sellers. Facing a downward-sloping demand curve and an upward-sloping supply curve, sellers cannot raise the price by the full amount of the tax. If the demand curve is vertical, sellers will raise the price by the full amount of the tax.

### TAX INCIDENCE OF GASOLINE TAX

## Summary of Conclusion Statements

- The price elasticity coefficient of demand applies only to a specific range of prices.

- The price elasticity coefficient of demand is directly related to the availability of good substitutes for a product.

- The price elasticity coefficient of demand is directly related to the percentage of one's budget spent for a good or service.

- In general, the price elasticity coefficient of demand is higher the longer a price change persists.

- If the demand curve slopes downward and the supply curve slopes upward, sellers cannot raise the price by the full amount of the tax.

- In the case where demand is perfectly inelastic, sellers can raise the price by the full amount of a tax.

## Study Questions and Problems

1. If the price of a good or service increases and the total revenue received by the seller declines, is the demand for this good over this segment of the demand curve elastic or inelastic? Explain.

2. Suppose the price elasticity of demand for farm products is inelastic. If the federal government wants to follow a policy of increasing income for farmers, what type of programs will the government enact?

3. Suppose the price elasticity of demand for used cars is estimated to be 3. What does this mean? What will be the effect on the quantity demanded for used cars if the price rises by 10 percent?

4. Consider the following demand schedule:

| Price | Quantity demanded | Elasticity coefficient |
|---|---|---|
| $25 | 20 | |
| 20 | 40 | _____ |
| 15 | 60 | _____ |
| 10 | 80 | _____ |
| 5 | 100 | _____ |

What is the price elasticity of demand between
a. $P = \$25$ and $P = \$20$?
b. $P = \$20$ and $P = \$15$?
c. $P = \$15$ and $P = \$10$?
d. $P = \$10$ and $P = \$5$?

5. Suppose a university raises its tuition from $3,000 to $3,500. As a result, student enrollment falls from 5,000 to 4,500. Calculate the price elasticity of demand. Is demand elastic, unitary elastic, or inelastic?

6. Will each of the following changes in price cause total revenue to increase, decrease, or remain unchanged?
a. Price falls, and demand is elastic.
b. Price rises, and demand is elastic.
c. Price falls, and demand is unitary elastic.
d. Price rises, and demand is unitary elastic.
e. Price falls, and demand is inelastic.
f. Price rises, and demand is inelastic.

7. Suppose a movie theater raises the price of popcorn 10 percent but customers do not buy any less popcorn. What does this tell you about the price elasticity of demand? What will happen to total revenue as a result of the price increase?

8. Charles loves Mello Yello and will spend $10 per week on the product no matter what the price.

What is his price elasticity of demand for Mello Yello?

9. Which of the following pairs of goods has the higher price elasticity of demand?
a. Oranges or Sunkist oranges
b. Cars or salt
c. Foreign travel in the short run or foreign travel in the long run

10. The Energizer Bunny that "keeps going and going" has been a very successful ad campaign for batteries. Explain the relationship between this slogan and the firm's price elasticity of demand and total revenue.

11. Suppose the income elasticity of demand for furniture is 3.0 and the income elasticity of demand for physician services is 0.3. Compare the impact on furniture and physician services of a recession that reduces consumers' incomes by 10 percent.

12. How might you determine whether compact discs and cassettes are in competition with each other?

13. Assume the cross-elasticity of demand for car tires with respect to the price of cars is −2. What does this tell you about the relationship between car tires and cars when the price of cars rises by 10 percent?

14. Consider the following supply schedule:

| Price | Quantity supplied | Elasticity coefficient |
|---|---|---|
| $10 | 50 | |
| 8 | 40 | _____ |
| 6 | 30 | _____ |
| 4 | 20 | _____ |
| 2 | 10 | _____ |
| 0 | 0 | _____ |

What is the price elasticity of supply between
a. $P = \$10$ and $P = \$8$?
b. $P = \$8$ and $P = \$6$?
c. $P = \$6$ and $P = \$4$?
d. $P = \$4$ and $P = \$2$?
e. $P = \$2$ and $P = \$0$?

15. Why would consumers prefer that the government tax products with elastic, rather than inelastic, demand?

16. Opponents of increasing the tax on gasoline argue that the big oil companies just pass the tax along to the consumers. Do you agree or disagree? Explain your answer.

## Study Guide Questions

1. An extreme case in which the demand curve is vertical and the elasticity coefficient equals zero is called _____.

2. If the quantity of tickets to the fair sold decreases by 10 percent when the price increases by 5 percent, the price elasticity of demand over this range of the demand curve is
   a. price elastic.
   b. price inelastic.
   c. perfectly inelastic.
   d. unitary elastic.

3. The number of CDs purchased increased by 50 percent when consumer income increased by 10 percent. Assuming other factors are held constant, CDs would be classified as
   a. social goods.
   b. normal goods.
   c. Giffen goods.
   d. inferior goods.

4. The cross-elasticity of demand between two goods is 2.5. These goods are
   a. perfect complements.
   b. imperfect complements.
   c. unrelated.
   d. substitutes.
   e. inferior.

5. T  F  Suppose an economist found that total revenues increased for the bus system when fares were raised. The conclusion is that the price elasticity demand for subway services over the range of fare increase is inelastic.

**Answers to these questions are in the complete Study Guide at www.thomsonedu.com/thomsonnow.**

**For online exercises, go to the text Web site at www.thomsonedu.com/economics/tucker.**

## Checkpoint Answers

### Will Fliers Flock to Low Summer Fares?

USAirways must believe the quantity of airline tickets demanded during the summer is quite responsive to a price cut. For total revenue to rise with a price cut, the quantity demanded must increase by a larger percentage than the percentage decrease in the price. For this to occur, the price elasticity of demand must exceed 1. If you said USAirways believes demand is elastic, **YOU ARE CORRECT.**

### Can Trade Sanctions Affect Elasticity of Demand for Cars?

Because substitutes (Japanese luxury cars) are no longer available to U.S. consumers, the quantity demanded of Mercedes, BMWs, and Jaguars in the United States would be less responsive to changes in the prices for these cars. If you said the price elasticity of demand for Mercedes, BMWs, and Jaguars would become less elastic, **YOU ARE CORRECT.**

### Can Honda Compete with Itself?

Determining the effect of cutting Acura's price on sales of Accords calls for cross-elasticity. Once the price of Acura is cut, Honda would calculate the change in the quantity of Accords demanded. If Acura's decrease in price causes people to buy fewer Accords, Honda is indeed competing with itself. If you said a positive cross-elasticity of demand indicates the two goods are substitutes, **YOU ARE CORRECT.**

For an explanation of the correct answers, please visit the tutorial at www.thomsonedu.com/economics/tucker.

1. If an increase in bus fares in Charlotte, North Carolina reduces the total revenue of the public transit system, this is evidence that demand is
   a. price elastic.
   b. price inelastic.
   c. unitary elastic.
   d. perfectly elastic.

2. Which of the following will result in an increase in total revenue?
   a. Price increases when demand is elastic.
   b. Price decreases when demand is elastic.
   c. Price increases when demand is unitary elastic.
   d. Price decreases when demand is inelastic.

3. You are on a committee that is considering ways to raise money for your city's symphony program. You would recommend increasing the price of symphony tickets only if you thought the demand curve for these tickets was
   a. inelastic.
   b. elastic.
   c. unitary elastic.
   d. perfectly elastic.

4. The price elasticity of demand for a horizontal demand curve is
   a. perfectly elastic.
   b. perfectly inelastic.
   c. unitary elastic.
   d. inelastic.
   e. elastic.

5. Suppose the quantity of steak purchased by the Jones family is 110 pounds per year when the price is $2.10 per pound and 90 pounds per year when the price is $3.90 per pound. The price elasticity of demand coefficient for this family is
   a. 0.33.
   b. 0.50.
   c. 1.00.
   d. 2.00.

6. If a 5 percent reduction in the price of a good produces a 3 percent increase in the quantity demanded, the price elasticity of demand over this range of the demand curve is
   a. elastic.
   b. perfectly elastic.
   c. unitary elastic.
   d. inelastic.
   e. perfectly inelastic.

7. A manufacturer of Beanie Babies hires an economist to study the price elasticity of demand for this product. The economist estimates that the price elasticity of demand coefficient for a range of prices close to the selling price is greater than 1. The relationship between changes in price and quantity demanded for this segment of the demand curve is
   a. elastic.
   b. inelastic.
   c. perfectly elastic.
   d. perfectly inelastic.
   e. unitary elastic.

8. A downward-sloping straight-line demand curve will have a
   a. higher price elasticity of demand coefficient along the top of the demand curve.
   b. lower price elasticity coefficient along the top of the demand curve.
   c. constant price elasticity of demand coefficient throughout the length of the demand curve.
   d. positive slope.

9. The price elasticity of demand coefficient for a good will be lower
   a. if there are few or no substitutes available.
   b. if a small portion of the budget will be spent on the good.
   c. in the short run than in the long run.
   d. if all of the above are true.

10. The income elasticity of demand for shoes is estimated to be 1.50. We can conclude that shoes
    a. have a relatively steep demand curve.
    b. have a relatively flat demand curve.
    c. are a normal good.
    d. are an inferior good.

11. To determine whether two goods are substitutes or complements, an economist would estimate the
    a. price elasticity of demand.
    b. income elasticity of demand.
    c. cross-elasticity of demand.
    d. price elasticity of supply.

12. If the government wanted to raise tax revenue and shift most of the tax burden to the sellers, it would impose a tax on a good with a
    a. steep (inelastic) demand curve and a steep (inelastic) supply curve.
    b. steep (inelastic) demand curve and a flat (elastic) supply curve.
    c. flat (perfectly elastic) demand curve and a steep (inelastic) supply curve.
    d. flat (perfectly elastic) demand curve and a flat (elastic) supply curve.

13. As shown in Exhibit 11, assume the government places a $1 per pack sales tax on cigarettes. The percentage of the burden of taxation paid by consumers of a pack of cigarettes is
   a. zero.
   b. 25 percent.
   c. 50 percent.
   d. 100 percent.

**EXHIBIT 11  SUPPLY AND DEMAND CURVES FOR CIGARETTES**

14. As shown in Exhibit 11, assume the government places a $1 per pack sales tax on cigarettes. The percentage of the burden of taxation paid by tobacco sellers is
   a. zero.
   b. 50 percent.
   c. 75 percent.
   d. 100 percent.

15. As shown in Exhibit 11, the $1 per pack sales tax on cigarettes raises tax revenue per day totaling
   a. $5 million.
   b. $6 million.
   c. $10 million.
   d. $15 million.

# Consumer Choice Theory

© Comstock/Jupiterimages

Chapter 3, the law of demand rested on a foundation of common sense and everyday observation. When the price of a Big Mac falls, people *do* buy more, and a price rise causes people to buy less. But there is more to the story.

The focus of this chapter is the logic of consumer choice. Why does a consumer buy one bundle of goods rather than another? Suppose someone asked why you bought a milkshake and french fries rather than a Coke and a hot dog. You would probably answer

that, given the money you had to spend, the Coke and hot dog would have given you less satisfaction. In this chapter, you will transform this simple explanation into consumer choice theory and then connect this theory to the law of demand. The chapter ends with another way to explain the demand curve, which involves effects related to income and the prices of other goods.

### In this chapter, you will learn to solve these economics puzzles:

- Under what conditions might you be willing to pay $10,000 for a gallon of water and 1 cent for a one-carat diamond?
- When ordering Big Macs, milkshakes, pizza, and other goods, how can you obtain the highest possible satisfaction?
- Do white rats obey the law of demand?

This chapter expands our understanding of demand by investigating more deeply *why* people buy goods and services. In

## From Utility to the Law of Demand

The basis of the law of demand is self-interested behavior. Consumers spend their limited budget to satisfy some want, such as listening to a compact disc or driving a new car. The motivation to consume goods and services is to gain **utility**. Utility is the satisfaction, or pleasure, that people receive from consuming a good or service. Utility is want-satisfying power "in the eye of the beholder." Just as wants differ among people, utility received from consumption varies from person

**Utility**
The satisfaction, or pleasure, that people receive from consuming a good or service.

137

to person. Fred's utility from consuming a BMW will probably differ from Maria's utility. In spite of the subjective nature of utility, this section develops in steps the derivation of a demand curve based on the utility concept.

## TOTAL UTILITY AND MARGINAL UTILITY

Actual measurement of utility is impossible because only you know the satisfaction from consuming, say, four Big Macs in one day. But suppose we could gauge your **total utility** of consuming four Big Macs in a day. Total utility is the amount of satisfaction received from all the units of a good or service consumed. That is, the utility of the first unit consumed added to that of the second unit, and so on. What units can be used to measure total utility? Economists use a mythical unit called a *util*, which allows us to quantify our thinking about consumer behavior.

No one has invented a "utility meter," but assume we could hook such a meter to your brain. Like taking your temperature, we could read the **marginal utility** each time you eat a Big Mac. Marginal utility is the change in total utility from one additional unit of a good or service. Instead of the total pleasure from eating X number of Big Macs, the question is how much *extra* satisfaction the first, second, or third Big Mac gives you. For example, Exhibit 1(a) shows your marginal utility data for eating four Big Macs in a day. You munch down the first Big Mac. Ah, the util meter hits an 8. You grab another Big Mac and eat it a little more slowly. The util meter hits 4 this time. You're starting to feel full, but you eat a third Big Mac. This one gets a 2. Even though you are pretty full, there is room for one more. You eat the fourth Big Mac very slowly, and it gives you less satisfaction than any of the previous burgers. Your utility meter reads 1. This trend conforms to the **law of diminishing marginal utility**. The law of diminishing marginal utility is the principle that the extra satisfaction provided by a good or service declines as people consume more in a given period. Economists have found that this is a universal principle of human consumption behavior.

Exhibit 1(a) is a marginal utility, *MU*, graph. Consistent with the law of diminishing marginal utility, the *MU* curve slopes downward as you consume more Big Macs. This reflects a steady decline in the utility of each additional Big Mac consumed. If you continued to eat Big Macs, a quantity of Big Macs is eventually reached at which the marginal utility is zero. Here you say to yourself, "If I eat another bite, I'll be sick." Then if you did eat another bite after all, marginal utility would be negative. A rational person never consumes goods when the marginal utility is negative (disutility) unless he or she is paid enough to do so. In our example, we assume you are rational and will not eat a Big Mac that gives you a negative marginal utility and a stomach ache. Also keep in mind that the *MU* curve for a good is different for different circumstances and individuals. Your *MU* curve would be much higher if you had not eaten in days. On the other hand, a vegetarian would receive no positive marginal utility from consuming a Big Mac.

Exhibit 1(b) shows how the shape of the total utility, *TU*, curve varies with marginal utility as you consume more Big Macs each day. The total utility of Big Macs increases steadily because each hamburger provides *additional* satisfaction to the sum of all the Big Macs already consumed. However, the *TU* curve becomes flatter as the marginal utility diminishes. This is because, as you consume more, the positive pleasure per Big Mac declines, and, in turn, each Big Mac adds less to total utility.

**Total utility**
The amount of satisfaction received from all the units of a good or service consumed.

**Marginal utility**
The change in total utility from one additional unit of a good or service.

**Law of diminishing marginal utility**
The principle that the extra satisfaction of a good or service declines as people consume more in a given period.

**EXHIBIT 1**  **DIMINISHING MARGINAL UTILITY AND TOTAL UTILITY CURVES FOR CONSUMING BIG MACS**

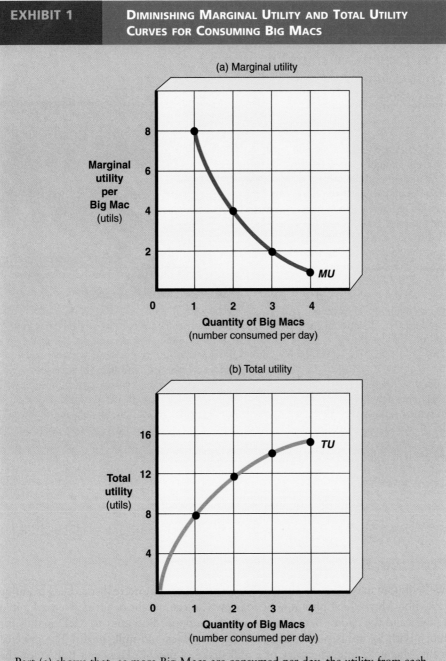

(a) Marginal utility

(b) Total utility

Part (a) shows that, as more Big Macs are consumed per day, the utility from each additional Big Mac declines. The utils are only imaginary because utility cannot be measured. When the marginal utility of each Big Mac consumed is summed, we obtain the total utility curve shown in Part (b).

## You're the Economist

## Why is Water Less Expensive than Diamonds?
*Applicable Concept: total utility and marginal utility*

Adam Smith posed a paradox in *The Wealth of Nations*. Water is essential to life and therefore should be of great value. On the other hand, diamonds are not essential to life, so people should value them less than water. Yet, even though water provides more utility, it is cheaper than diamonds. Smith's puzzle came to be known as the diamond-water paradox. Now you can use marginal utility analysis to explain something that baffled the father of economics.

Early economists failed to find the key to the diamond-water puzzle because they did not distinguish between marginal and total utility. Marginal utility theory was not developed until the late nineteenth century. Water is life-giving and does indeed yield much higher total utility than diamonds. However, marginal utility, and not total utility, determines the price. Water is plentiful in most of the world, so its marginal utility is low. This follows the law of diminishing marginal utility.

Jewelry-quality diamonds, on the other hand, are scarce. Because we have relatively few diamonds, the quantity of diamonds consumed is not large. As a result, the marginal utility of diamonds and the price buyers are willing to pay for them are quite high. Thus, scarcity raises marginal utility and price regardless of the size of total utility.

© Image 100/Jupiterimages

Exhibit 2 presents a graphical analysis that you can use to unravel the alleged paradox. Part (a) shows the marginal utility per carat you receive from each diamond consumed, and Part (b) represents marginal utility per gallon of water consumed. The vertical line, $S$, in each graph is the supply of water or diamonds available per year. Since water is much more plentiful than diamonds, the supply curve for water intersects the marginal utility curve at $MU_w$, which is close to zero. Conversely, the supply curve for diamonds intersects the marginal utility curve at

## CONSUMER EQUILIBRIUM

We will now make our example of consumer choice more realistic. Let's examine how Bob Moore, a sophomore at Seaview College, might behave, given a limited budget and the choice between two goods. Suppose Bob goes to McDonald's for lunch with $8 in his pocket to spend for Big Macs and milkshakes. The price of a Big Mac is $2, and the price of a milkshake is also $2. How can Bob enjoy the maximum total utility with his limited money?

Recall from Chapter 2 the concept of *marginal analysis*. This is the method Bob uses to decide how many Big Macs and milkshakes to order. Exhibit 3 shows Bob's marginal utility for each Big Mac and milkshake consumed. The *marginal utility per dollar* ($MU/P$) is the ratio of the marginal utility of each good to its price. In making purchases, the key consideration is how additional satisfaction relates to price. Using marginal decision making before giving an order, Bob compares the marginal utility of one Big Mac to the marginal utility of one milkshake.

**EXHIBIT 2**  **THE DIAMOND-WATER PARADOX**

(a) Marginal utility of diamonds

Marginal utility per carat (utils)

$MU_d$

$MU$

0

**Quantity of diamonds**
(carats per year)

(b) Marginal utility of water

Marginal utility per gallon (utils)

$MU_w$

$MU$

0

**Quantity of water**
(gallons per year)

a much higher marginal utility, $MU_d$. Because of the relative marginal utilities of water and diamonds, you are willing to pay much more for one more carat of a diamond than for one more gallon of water.

**ANALYZE THE ISSUE**

1. Can you imagine a situation in which water would be more expensive than diamonds?

2. Suppose the price per gallon of water is 1 cent and the price per carat of a diamond is $10,000. Is the total utility of diamonds 10,000 times as great as the total utility received from water?

Being a rational consumer, Bob sees that spending his first $2 on a Big Mac gives more "bang for the buck." The first Big Mac gives him 4 utils per dollar, but the same $2 spent on a milkshake gives him 3 utils per dollar. Next, Bob ponders how to spend his next $2. The best buy now is a milkshake because it gives 3 utils per dollar compared to 2 utils per dollar for a second Big Mac.

Spending Bob's last $4 is a tossup. Both the second Big Mac and the second milkshake give the same 2 utils per dollar. So Bob can spend $2 for a second Big Mac and his last $2 for a second milkshake. Or he can spend $2 for a second milkshake and his last $2 for a second Big Mac. The order does not matter. Now that Bob has spent all his income, the marginal utility per dollar of the last Big Mac is equal to the marginal utility per dollar of the last milkshake.

**CONCLUSION** *If the marginal utility per last dollar spent on each good is equal and the entire budget is spent, total utility is maximized.*

| EXHIBIT 3 | MARGINAL UTILITY FOR BIG MACS AND MILKSHAKES (UTILS PER DAY) | | | | |
|---|---|---|---|---|---|
| | **Big Macs** | | | **Milkshakes** | |
| **Quantity** | *MU* | *MU/P* | | *MU* | *MU/P* |
| 1 | 8 | 4 | | 6 | 3 |
| 2 | 4 | 2 | | 4 | 2 |
| 3 | 2 | 1 | | 1 | 1/2 |
| 4 | 1 | 1/2 | | 0 | 0 |

*Note:* The price per Big Mac and per milkshake is $2.

To convince yourself that two Big Macs and two milkshakes do indeed maximize total utility, consider any other combination Bob could buy with $8. All others yield lower total utility. Suppose Bob were to buy three Big Macs and one milkshake. The third Big Mac adds 2 utils, but giving up the second milkshake subtracts 4 utils. As a result, total utility falls by 2 utils. Or can Bob maximize utility if he were to eat only one Big Mac and drink three milkshakes? The extra utility of the third milkshake is 1 util, but this is less than the 4 utils he would lose by saying no to the second Big Mac. In this case, total utility would fall by 3 utils.

The above example demonstrates the utility-maximizing concept of **consumer equilibrium**. Consumer equilibrium is a condition in which total utility cannot increase by spending more of a given budget on one good and spending less on another good. Suppose Bob knows not only the exact marginal utility of consuming Big Macs and milkshakes, but also the marginal utility of french fries, pizza, and other goods. To obtain the highest possible satisfaction, Bob allocates his budget so the last dollar spent on good A, the last on good B, and so on yield equal *MU/P* ratios. Consumer equilibrium can be restated algebraically as

**Consumer equilibrium**
A condition in which total utility cannot increase by spending more of a given budget on one good and spending less on another good.

$$\frac{MU \text{ of good } A}{\text{Price of good } A} = \frac{MU \text{ of good } B}{\text{Price of good } B} = \frac{MU \text{ of good } Z}{\text{Price of good } Z}$$

The letters A, B, . . . Z indicate all the goods and services purchased by the consumer with a given budget.

## FROM CONSUMER EQUILIBRIUM TO THE LAW OF DEMAND

Understanding the law of diminishing marginal utility and consumer equilibrium provides you with a new set of tools to explore the law of demand. Let's begin with a straightforward link between the law of diminishing marginal utility and the demand curve. Declining marginal utility from consuming more Big Macs and milkshakes means each extra quantity consumed is less important or valuable to the consumer. Therefore, as the quantity consumed increases and the marginal utility falls, Bob is willing to pay less per Big Mac and milkshake. Thus, Bob's individual demand curve conforms to the law of demand and is downward sloping.

A more complete explanation of the law of demand combines diminishing marginal utility and consumer equilibrium. Suppose Bob reaches consumer equilibrium as follows:

$$\frac{MU \text{ of Big Mac}}{\text{Price of Big Mac}} = \frac{MU \text{ of milkshake}}{\text{Price of milkshake}}$$

$$\frac{4 \text{ utils}}{\$2} = \frac{4 \text{ utils}}{\$2}$$

Now suppose the price of a Big Mac falls to $1 and upsets the above equality. This changes the formula to the following:

$$\frac{MU \text{ of Big Mac}}{\text{Price of Big Mac}} > \frac{MU \text{ of milkshake}}{\text{Price of milkshake}}$$

$$\frac{4 \text{ utils}}{\$1} > \frac{4 \text{ utils}}{\$2}$$

Now Bob gains more utility per dollar by buying a Big Mac rather than a milkshake. To restore maximum total utility, he spends more on Big Macs. The marginal utility of a Big Mac must fall as he buys more. At the same time, the marginal utility of a milkshake must rise as Bob buys fewer. A fall in the price of Big Macs therefore causes Bob to buy more Big Macs. Voilà! The law of demand.

# Income and Substitution Effects and the Law of Demand

Since utility is not measurable, it is desirable to have an alternative explanation of demand. Economists offer the following two complementary explanations for the law of demand, which do not rely on utility.

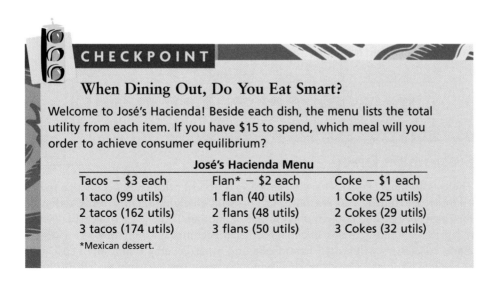

**CHECKPOINT**

## When Dining Out, Do You Eat Smart?

Welcome to José's Hacienda! Beside each dish, the menu lists the total utility from each item. If you have $15 to spend, which meal will you order to achieve consumer equilibrium?

**José's Hacienda Menu**

| Tacos — $3 each | Flan* — $2 each | Coke — $1 each |
|---|---|---|
| 1 taco (99 utils) | 1 flan (40 utils) | 1 Coke (25 utils) |
| 2 tacos (162 utils) | 2 flans (48 utils) | 2 Cokes (29 utils) |
| 3 tacos (174 utils) | 3 flans (50 utils) | 3 Cokes (32 utils) |

*Mexican dessert.

## CHECKPOINT

### Does the Substitution Effect Apply to Buying a Car?

Jenny Tanaka wants to buy a new car, and the annual gasoline expense is a major consideration. Her present car gets 25 miles per gallon (mpg), and she is looking at a new car that gets 40 mpg. Jenny now drives about 12,000 miles per year and pays $2.25 per gallon of gasoline. She therefore calculates an annual gasoline consumption of 480 gallons for her 25-mpg car (12,000 miles/25 mpg) compared to 300 gallons consumed per year for the 40-mpg car (12,000 miles/40 mpg). Since driving the higher-mileage car would use 180 gallons less per year, Jenny estimates the new car will save her $405 in gasoline expense per year (180 gallons × $2.25 per gallon). Suppose Jenny buys the 40-mpg car. Do you predict Jenny will have an annual gasoline savings equal to $405, less than $405, or more than $405?

## INCOME EFFECT

One reason people buy more of a good when the price falls is the effect of a price change on real income. The *nominal*, or *money*, amount of your paycheck is simply the number of dollars you earn. On the other hand, price changes alter your *real* income. A rise in prices decreases purchasing power, and a fall in prices increases purchasing power, ceteris paribus.

Suppose your weekly nominal income is $100 and you decide to stock up on Pepsi-Cola (a normal good). If the price per quart is $1, you can afford to buy 100 quarts this week. If the price is instead $.50 per quart and the prices of other goods remain constant, you are richer because of the rise in purchasing power. As a result, you can buy 200 quarts of Pepsi-Cola without giving up any other goods or less than 200 quarts and more of other goods. As predicted by the law of demand, the lower price for Pepsi-Cola causes real income to rise and, in turn, causes the quantity demanded to rise. This relationship between changes in real income and your ability to buy goods and services is the **income effect**. The income effect is the change in quantity demanded of a good or service caused by a change in real income (purchasing power).

**Income effect**
The change in quantity demanded of a good or service caused by a change in real income (purchasing power).

## SUBSTITUTION EFFECT

There is another reason why the change in a good's price causes a change in the quantity demanded. This reason has to do with changing *relative prices*—that is, the price of one good compared with that of another. If the price of Pepsi falls and the price of Coke remains unchanged, Pepsi becomes a better buy. As a result, many consumers will switch from Coke and other beverages and buy Pepsi. Just as the law of demand predicts, this is an increase in quantity demanded. With the

## You're the Economist

# Testing the Law of Demand with White Rats
*Applicable Concept: substitution effect*

Economists often envy the controlled laboratory experiments of biologists and other scientists. In the real world, the economist is unable to observe consumer behavior without prices of other goods, expectations, and other factors changing. So it is no wonder that the idea of studying the behavior of white rats to test the law of demand was intriguing. The question was whether the consumer choice of a white rat supports the downward-sloping demand curve.

Standard laboratory rats were placed in experimental cages with two levers. If a rat pressed one lever, nonalcoholic Collins mix was the reward. Pressing the second lever rewarded the rat with root beer. It seems rats are fond of these two beverages. Each rat was given a limited "income" of lever presses per day. After, say, 300 presses, a light above the lever went out, signaling the daily budget was gone. The next day the light was turned on, and the rat was given a new income of lever presses. The "price" of each good corresponded to the number of lever pushes required to obtain one milliliter of liquid. For example, if the number of pushes per milliliter for Collins mix released increased by 10 percent, this equaled a 10 percent increase in the price of Collins mix.

The crucial test was to measure the substitution effect resulting from a change in price. As explained in the text, a change in price sets in motion both an income effect and a substitution effect. In the experiment, the price of Collins mix was lowered by decreasing the number of pushes required per milliliter. At the same time, the price of root beer was raised by increasing the number of pushes required per milliliter. To eliminate the income effect, the number of lever presses was raised to compensate for loss of purchasing power. For example, if a rat purchased 4 milliliters of Collins mix per day and 11 milliliters of root beer before the price change, it would be given enough extra pushes after the price change to still purchase these quantities.

In one experiment, a male albino rat was given 300 pushes per day for two weeks, and both liquids were priced at 20 pushes per milliliter. The rat soon settled into a consistent consumption pattern of 4 milliliters of Collins mix and 11 milliliters of root beer per day. Then the experimenters made changes in prices and income. The price (pushes per milliliter) of Collins mix was cut in half, and the price of root beer was doubled. At the same time, the total income of pushes was increased just enough to allow the rat to afford its initial consumption pattern. Stated differently, the income effect was eliminated in order to focus on the substitution effect. After two weeks of decisions under the new conditions, the rat changed its consumption pattern to 17 milliliters of Collins mix and 8 milliliters of root beer per day.

### ANALYZE THE ISSUE

Based on the behavior of the rat described above, what do you conclude about the substitution effect and the slope of the demand curve?

*Source: John H. Kagel, Raymond C. Battalio, Howard Rachlin, and Leonard Green, "Demand Curves for Animal Consumers," Quarterly Journal of Economics 96 (February 1981): 1–16.*

price of Pepsi lower than before, the **substitution effect** causes people to substitute Pepsi for the now relatively more expensive Coke. The substitution effect is the change in quantity demanded of a good or service caused by a change in its price relative to substitutes.

**Substitution effect**
The change in quantity demanded of a good or service caused by a change in its price relative to substitutes.

Above we discussed the income and the substitution effects separately, but they are complementary explanations for the downward-sloping demand curve.

> **CONCLUSION** *When the price of a normal good falls, the income effect and the substitution effect combine to cause the quantity demanded to increase.*

Some students express relief that this conclusion has no reference to the untidy word *utility*.

## Key Concepts

Utility

Total utility

Marginal utility

Law of diminishing marginal utility

Consumer equilibrium

Income effect

Substitution effect

## Summary

- **Utility** is the satisfaction or pleasure derived from consumption of a good or service. Actual measurement of utility is impossible, but economists assume it can be measured by a fictitious unit called a *util*.

- **Total utility** is the total level of satisfaction derived from all units of a good or service consumed. *Marginal utility* is the change in total utility from a 1-unit change in the quantity of a good or service consumed.

**RELATIONSHIP BETWEEN MARGINAL AND TOTAL UTILITY**

(b) Total utility

(a) Marginal utility

- The **law of diminishing marginal utility** states that the marginal utility of a good or service eventually declines as consumption increases.

- **Consumer equilibrium** is the condition of reaching the maximum level of satisfaction, given a budget, when the marginal utility per dollar spent on each good purchased is equal. Consumer equilibrium and the law of diminishing marginal utility can be used to derive a downward-sloping demand curve. When the price of a good falls, consumer equilibrium no longer holds, because the marginal utility per dollar for the good rises. To restore equilibrium, the consumer must increase consumption. As the quantity demanded increases, the marginal utility falls until equilibrium is again achieved. Thus, the price falls, and the quantity demanded rises, as predicted by the law of demand.

$$\frac{MU \text{ of good } A}{\text{Price of good } A} = \frac{MU \text{ of good } B}{\text{Price of good } B} = \frac{MU \text{ of good } Z}{\text{Price of good } Z}$$

■ The **income effect** and **the substitution effect** are complementary explanations for the law of demand. When the price changes, these effects work in combination to change the quantity demanded in the opposite direction. As the price falls, real purchasing power increases, causing an increase in the consumer's willingness and ability to purchase a good or service. This is the *income effect*. Also, as the price falls, the consumer substitutes the cheaper good for other goods that are now relatively more expensive. This is the *substitution effect*.

## Summary of Conclusion Statements

■ If the marginal utility per last dollar spent on each good is equal and the entire budget is spent, total utility is maximized.

■ When the price of a normal good falls, the income effect and the substitution effect combine to cause the quantity demanded to increase.

## Study Questions and Problems

1. Does a dollar given to a rich person raise the rich person's total utility more than a dollar given to a poor person raises the poor person's total utility?

2. Do you agree with the following statement? "If you like tacos, you should consume as many as you can."

3. This week you have gone to two parties. Assume the total utility you gained from these parties is 100 utils. Then you go to a third party, and your total utility rises to 110 utils. What is the marginal utility of the third party attended per week? Given the law of diminishing marginal utility, what will happen to total utility and marginal utility when you go to a fourth party this week?

4. Suppose your marginal utility for meals at the campus cafeteria this week has fallen to zero. Explain what has happened to your total utility curve derived from consuming these meals. Now explain what will happen to total utility if you eat more meals at the cafeteria this week.

5. Suppose you consume three pounds of beef and five pounds of pork per month. The price of beef is $1.50 per pound, and pork is $2.00 per pound.

Assuming you have studied economics and achieved consumer equilibrium, what is the ratio of the marginal utility of beef to the marginal utility of pork?

6. Suppose the marginal utility of a Coke is 15 utils and its price is $1. The marginal utility of a pizza is 20 utils, and its price is $2. If you buy one unit of each good, will you achieve consumer equilibrium? If not, how can greater total utility be obtained?

7. Explain the relationship between the law of diminishing marginal utility and the law of demand.

8. Consider the table below, which lists James's marginal utility schedule for steak and hamburger meals:

| Steak meals per month | Marginal utility of steak meals | Price per steak meal | Hamburger meals per month | Marginal utility of hamburger meals | Price per hamburger meal |
|---|---|---|---|---|---|
| 1 | 20 | $10 | 1 | 15 | $5 |
| 2 | 15 | 10 | 2 | 8 | 5 |
| 3 | 12 | 10 | 3 | 6 | 5 |
| 4 | 10 | 10 | 4 | 4 | 5 |
| 5 | 8 | 10 | 5 | 2 | 5 |

Given a budget of $45, how many steak and hamburger meals will James buy per month to maximize his total utility? What is the total utility realized?

9. Using the marginal utility schedule in question 8, begin in consumer equilibrium, and assume the price per hamburger meal falls from $5 to $2, all other

factors held constant. What is the total utility realized?

10. Suppose the price of a BMW falls. Explain the law of demand based on the income and substitution effects.

## Study Guide Questions

1. A condition in which total utility cannot increase by spending more of a given budget on one good and spending less on another good is called _____.

2. Assume a consumer purchases a combination of goods X and Y such that $MU_xP_x$ = 40 units of utility per dollar and $MU_yP_y$ = 20 units of utility per dollar. To maximize utility, the consumers should buy
   a. more of both X and Y.
   b. less of both X and Y.
   c. neither X nor Y.
   d. more of X and less of Y.
   e. less of X and more of Y.

3. If water is essential for life, while diamonds are not, then why is water cheaper than diamonds?
   a. Because most people would rather die with a big diamond ring than live without one.
   b. Because the total utility generated by diamonds is larger than the total utility generated by water.
   c. Because most people do not understand that they need water to live.
   d. Because water is abundant, the marginal utility of water is low, and price reflects marginal utility, not total utility.

4. Consider a consumer who spends all income on only two goods: bread and wine. An extra loaf of bread would give the consumer 10 extra utils, while an extra bottle of wine would give the consumer 60 extra utils. Bread costs 50 cents per loaf, and wine costs $6 per bottle. In this situation, the consumer
   a. could increase utility by buying more bread and less wine.
   b. could increase utility by purchasing more wine and less bread.
   c. has maximized utility and attained the consumer equilibrium.
   d. is violating the law of diminishing marginal utility.

5. T  F  The substitution effect is the concept that changes in consumption of a good result from changes in the relative price of a jointly consumed good.

**Answers to these questions are in the complete Study Guide at www.thomsonedu.com/thomsonnow.**

**For Online Exercises, go to the text Web site at www.thomsonedu.com/economics/tucker.**

## Checkpoint Answers

### When Dining Out, Do You Eat Smart?

Start with 1 taco (99 marginal utils/$3, or 33 marginal utils/$1). Then order a Coke (25 marginal utils/$1). Next, order another taco (63 marginal utils/$3, or 21

marginal utils/$1). Now treat yourself to a flan (40 marginal utils/$2, or 20 marginal utils/$1). Finish it all with a second flan (4 marginal utils/$1), another Coke (4 marginal utils/$1), and a third taco (4 marginal utils/$1). You have now spent your entire $15 budget. If you said, following the principle of consumer equilibrium, you would order 2 Cokes, 2 flans, and 3 tacos, although not a very nutritious choice, **YOU ARE CORRECT.**

## Does the Substitution Effect Apply to Buying a Car?

Buying a higher-mpg car will reduce the cost per mile of driving relative to substitutes, such as riding a bus, train, or airplane. As the cost of driving falls, the substitution effect predicts Jenny will drive more in the 40-mpg car than the 12,000 miles she now drives per year in the 25-mpg car. The extra cost of gasoline for driving over 12,000 miles per year in the 40-mpg car must be subtracted from the $405 savings that was based on the assumption that Jenny's miles driven per year would remain unchanged when she bought the 40-mpg car. If you said Jenny will save less than $405, **YOU ARE CORRECT.**

## Practice Quiz

For an explanation of the correct answers, please visit the tutorial at www.thomsonedu.com/economics/tucker.

1. As an individual consumes more of a given good, the marginal utility of that good to the consumer
   a. rises at an increasing rate.
   b. rises at a decreasing rate.
   c. falls.
   d. rises.

2. The amount of added utility that a consumer gains from the consumption of one more unit of a good is called
   a. incremental utility.
   b. total utility.
   c. diminishing utility.
   d. marginal utility.

3. A certain consumer buys only food and compact discs. If the quantity of food bought increases, while that of compact discs remains the same, the marginal utility of food will
   a. fall relative to the marginal utility of compact discs.
   b. rise relative to the marginal utility of compact discs.
   c. rise, but not as fast as the marginal utility of compact discs rises.
   d. fall, but not as fast as the marginal utility of compact discs falls.

4. Rational consumers will continue to consume two goods until the
   a. marginal utility per dollar's worth of the two goods is the same for the last dollar spent on each good.
   b. marginal utility is the same for each good for the last dollar spent on each good.

   c. prices of the two goods are equal for the last dollar spent on each good.
   d. prices of the two goods are unequal.

5. Assume that a person's consumption of just the right amounts of pork and chicken is in equilibrium. We can conclude that the
   a. marginal utility of pork must equal the marginal utility of chicken.
   b. price of pork must equal the price of chicken.
   c. ratio of marginal cost to price must be the same in both the pork and the chicken markets.
   d. ratio of marginal utility to price must be the same for pork and chicken.

6. Assume an individual consumes only milk and doughnuts and has arranged consumption so that the last glass of milk yields 12 utils and the last doughnut 6 utils. If the price of milk is $1 per glass and the price of a doughnut is $.50, we can conclude that the
   a. consumer should consume less milk and more doughnuts.
   b. price of milk is too high relative to doughnuts.
   c. consumer should consume more milk and fewer doughnuts.
   d. consumer is in equilibrium.

7. Suppose an individual consumes pizza and cola. To reach consumer equilibrium, the individual must consume pizza and cola so that the
   a. price paid for the two goods is the same.
   b. marginal utility of the two goods is equal.
   c. ratio of marginal utility to price is the same for both goods.
   d. ratio of the marginal utility of cola to the marginal utility of pizza is 1.

8. A state of consumer equilibrium for goods consumed prevails when the
   a. marginal utility of all goods is the same for the last dollar spent for each good.
   b. marginal utility per dollar's worth of two goods is the same for the last dollar spent for each good.
   c. price of two goods is the same for the last dollar spent for each good.
   d. marginal cost per dollar spent on two goods is the same for the last dollar spent for each good.

9. The change in quantity demanded resulting from a change in purchasing power is known as the
   a. income effect.
   b. substitution effect.
   c. law of demand.
   d. consumer equilibrium effect.

**EXHIBIT 4  TOTAL UTILITY FOR MULTIPLEX TICKETS, VIDEO RENTALS, AND POPCORN**

| Total utility from Multiplex tickets | Total utility from video rentals | Total utility from popcorn |
| --- | --- | --- |
| 1 movie (30 utils) | 1 video (14 utils) | 1 bag (8 utils) |
| 2 movies (54 utils) | 2 videos (24 utils) | 2 bags (13 utils) |
| 3 movies (72 utils) | 3 videos (30 utils) | 3 bags (15 utils) |
| 4 movies (84 utils) | 4 videos (32 utils) | 4 bags (16 utils) |

10. In Exhibit 4, assume Multiplex tickets cost $6 each, video rentals cost $2 each, and bags of popcorn cost $1 each. What is the marginal utility of renting a third video?
    a. 6 utils
    b. 8 utils
    c. 10 utils
    d. 30 utils

11. In Exhibit 4, assume Multiplex tickets cost $6 each, video rentals cost $2 each, and bags of popcorn cost $1 each. Suppose the consumer has $12 per week to spend on Multiplex tickets, video rentals, and popcorn. What combination of goods will give the consumer the most utility?
    a. 1 movie, 3 videos, and no popcorn
    b. 1 movie, 2 videos, and 2 bags of popcorn
    c. 1 movie, 1 video, and 4 bags of popcorn
    d. 2 movies, no videos, and no bags of popcorn

**EXHIBIT 5  TOTAL UTILITY FOR MULTIPLEX TICKETS, VIDEO RENTALS, AND POPCORN**

| Total utility from Multiplex tickets | Total utility from video rentals | Total utility from popcorn |
| --- | --- | --- |
| 1 movie (30 utils) | 1 video (14 utils) | 1 bag (8 utils) |
| 2 movies (54 utils) | 2 videos (24 utils) | 2 bags (13 utils) |
| 3 movies (72 utils) | 3 videos (30 utils) | 3 bags (15 utils) |
| 4 movies (84 utils) | 4 videos (32 utils) | 4 bags (16 utils) |

12. In Exhibit 5, assume the Multiplex tickets cost $6 each, video rentals cost $2 each, and bags of popcorn cost $1 each. Suppose the consumer has $12 per week to spend on multiplex tickets, video rentals, and popcorn. In consumer equilibrium, what is the marginal utility per dollar for each of the three goods?
    a. 5 utils per dollar
    b. 9 utils per dollar
    c. 13 utils per dollar
    d. 22 utils per dollar

13. The law of diminishing marginal utility exists for the first four units of a good if they have marginal utilities of
    a. 1, 2, 4, 8.
    b. 8, 4, 1, 2.
    c. 4, 8, 2, 1.
    d. 8, 4, 2, 1.

14. The demand curve is downward sloping because of the law of
    a. diminishing marginal utility.
    b. diminishing consumer equilibrium.
    c. consumer equilibrium.
    d. diminishing utility maximization.

15. The total utilities associated with the first 5 units of consumption of good X are 15, 30, 40, 47, and 50, respectively. What is the marginal utility associated with the third unit?
    a. 15
    b. 70
    c. 85
    d. 10
    e. 45

# Indifference Curve Analysis

This appendix explains another version of consumer choice theory based on indifference curves and budget lines.

## Constructing an Indifference Curve

Let's begin with an experiment to find out a consumer's consumption preferences for quantities of two goods. The consumer samples a number of pairs of servings with various ounces of lobster tail and steak (surf and turf). Each time the same question is asked, "Would you prefer serving *A* or serving *B*?" After numerous trials, suppose the consumer states indifference between eating choices *A–D* shown in Exhibit A-1. This means the consumer is just as satisfied having either 7 ounces of steak and 4 ounces of lobster (*A*), or 3 ounces of steak and 8 ounces of lobster (*D*), or either of the other two combinations of *B* or *C*. Interpretation of the curve connecting these points is that each of these choices yields the same total utility because no choice is preferred to any other choice. Since, as explained in the chapter, there is no such thing as a utility meter, this approach is actually a method for determining equal levels of satisfaction or total utility for different bundles of goods without an exact measure of utils. The curve derived from this experimental data is called an **indifference curve**. Note that not only points *A*, *B*, *C*, and *D* but all other points on the smooth curve connecting them are equally satisfactory combinations to the consumer.

> **Indifference curve**
> A curve showing the different combinations of two goods that provide the same satisfaction or total utility to a consumer.

### Why Indifference Curves Are Downward Sloping and Convex

If total utility is the same at all points along the indifference curve, then consuming more of one good must mean less of the other is consumed. Given this condition, movement along the indifference curve generates a curve with a negative slope. Suppose a consumer moves in marginal increments between any two combination points in Exhibit A-1. For instance, say the consumer decides to move from point *A* to point *B* and consume an extra ounce of lobster. To do so, the consumer increases total utility ($+MU$) by consuming an extra quantity of lobster. However, since by definition total utility is constant everywhere along the curve, the consumer must give up a quantity of steak (2 ounces) in order to reduce total utility ($-MU$) by precisely enough to offset the gain in total utility from the extra lobster.

The inverse relationship between goods along the downward-sloping indifference curve means that the absolute value of the slope of an indifference curve

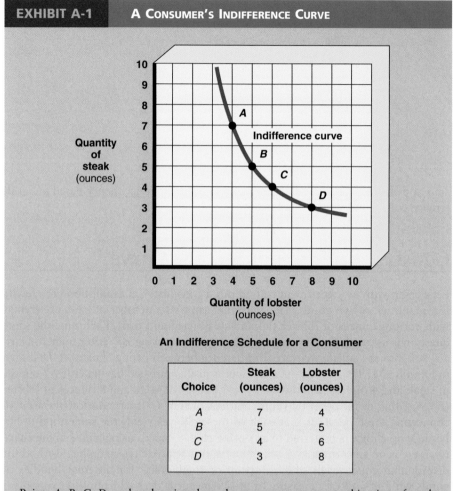

| EXHIBIT A-1 | A CONSUMER'S INDIFFERENCE CURVE |
|---|---|

**An Indifference Schedule for a Consumer**

| Choice | Steak (ounces) | Lobster (ounces) |
|---|---|---|
| A | 7 | 4 |
| B | 5 | 5 |
| C | 4 | 6 |
| D | 3 | 8 |

Points *A, B, C, D,* and each point along the curve represent a combination of steak and lobster that yields equal total utility for a given consumer. Stated differently, the consumer is indifferent between consuming servings having quantities represented by all points composing the indifference curve.

**Marginal rate of substitution (MRS)**
The rate at which a consumer is willing to substitute one good for another good without a change in total utility. The MRS equals the slope of an indifference curve at any point on the curve.

equals what is called the **marginal rate of substitution (MRS)**. The MRS is the rate at which a consumer is willing to substitute one good for another with no change in total utility. Begin at *A* and move to *B* along the curve. The slope and MRS of the curve is −2/1, or simply 2 when the minus sign is removed to give the absolute value. This is the consumer's subjective willingness to substitute *A* for *B*. At point *A*, the consumer has a substantial amount of steak and relatively little lobster. Therefore, the consumer is willing to forgo or "substitute" 2 ounces of steak to get 1 more ounce of lobster. In other words, the marginal utility of losing each ounce of steak between *A* and *B* is low compared to the marginal utility of gaining each ounce of lobster.

Now suppose the consumer moves from *B* to *C*, and the slope changes to 1/1 (MRS = 1). Between these two points, the consumer is willing to substitute 1 ounce of steak for an equal quantity of lobster. This means that between B and C the marginal utility lost per ounce of steak equals the marginal utility gained from each ounce of lobster, while total utility remains constant. Finally, assume the consumer moves from C to D. Here the slope equals 1/2 (MRS = 1/2) because the consumer at point C has a substantial amount of lobster and relatively little steak. Consequently, the marginal utility lost from giving up 1 ounce of steak equals twice the marginal utility gained from an additional ounce of lobster.

As we see in this example, as the quantity of lobster increases along the horizontal axis, the marginal utility of additional ounces of lobster decreases. Correspondingly, as the quantity of steak decreases along the vertical axis, its marginal utility increases. So moving down the curve means the consumer is willing to give up smaller and smaller quantities of steak on the vertical axis to obtain each additional ounce of lobster on the horizontal axis.

> **CONCLUSION** *The slope of the indifference curve is negative and equal to the marginal rate of substitution (MRS), which declines as one moves downward along the curve. The result is a curve with a diminishing slope that is convex (bowed inward) to the origin.*

## THE INDIFFERENCE MAP

As explained above, any point selected along an indifference curve gives the same level of satisfaction or total utility. Actually, there are other indifference curves that can be drawn for a consumer. As shown in Exhibit A-2, indifference curves $I_1$ to $I_6$ also exist to form an **indifference map**, which is a selection of a consumer's indifference curves. In fact, if all possible curves were drawn, they would completely fill the space between the axes because there would be so many. And it is important to note that each curve reflects a different level of total utility. Also, each curve moving from the origin in the northeasterly direction from $I_1$ to $I_6$ and beyond yields higher total utility. This is reasonable because at each higher indifference curve, the consumer is able to select more of both goods and therefore be better off. To verify this concept, select a combination on one indifference curve in Exhibit A-2 and then select a combination of more of both goods on a higher indifference curve.

**Indifference map**
A selection of indifference curves with each curve representing a different level of satisfaction or total utility.

> **CONCLUSION** *Each consumer has a set of indifference curves that form a map. Since consumers wish to achieve the highest possible total utility, they always prefer curves farther from the origin where they can select more quantities of two goods.*

## THE BUDGET LINE

Having considered the consumer's preferences for steak and lobster in the indifference map, the next step is to see what the consumer can afford. The consumer's ability to purchase steak and lobster is limited or constrained by the amount of money (income) that the consumer has to spend and the prices of the two goods. Suppose the consumer likes to go to a fine restaurant and budgets $10 per week

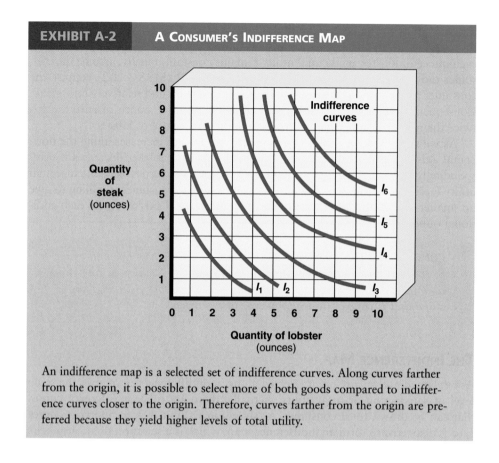

**EXHIBIT A-2**    **A CONSUMER'S INDIFFERENCE MAP**

Quantity of steak (ounces)

Indifference curves

$I_6$
$I_5$
$I_4$
$I_1$  $I_2$  $I_3$

Quantity of lobster (ounces)

An indifference map is a selected set of indifference curves. Along curves farther from the origin, it is possible to select more of both goods compared to indifference curves closer to the origin. Therefore, curves farther from the origin are preferred because they yield higher levels of total utility.

**Budget line**
A line that represents all combinations of two goods that a consumer can purchase with a fixed amount of money given the price of each good.

to dine on surf and turf. The price of steak is $1 per ounce, and the price of lobster is $2 an ounce. If the consumer spends the entire budget on steak, 10 ounces of steak can be purchased. At the other extreme, the whole budget could be spent for lobster, and 5 ounces would be purchased. As shown in Exhibit A-3, and given the consumption possibilities of buying fractions of ounces of steak and lobster, a range of choices can be purchased along the **budget line** ranging from 10 ounces on the steak axis to 5 ounces on the lobster axis. The table in this exhibit computes selected whole-unit combinations that each equal a $10 total expenditure.

**CONCLUSION**  *The budget line represents various combinations of goods that a consumer can purchase at given prices with a given budget.*

Computing the slope of the budget line requires some shorthand mathematical notation. Let $B$ represent the amount of money the consumer has to spend on steak and lobster. Also, let $P_l$ and $P_s$ represent the prices of lobster and steak, respectively, and $L$ and $S$ represent the ounces of lobster and steak, respectively. Given this notation, the budget line may be expressed as

$$P_l L + P_s S = B$$

## EXHIBIT A-3     A CONSUMER'S BUDGET LINE

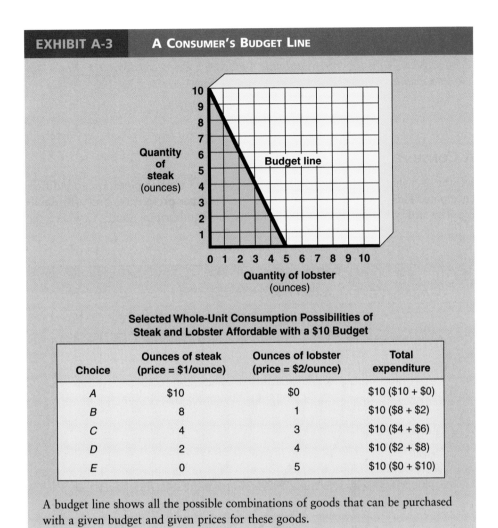

**Selected Whole-Unit Consumption Possibilities of Steak and Lobster Affordable with a $10 Budget**

| Choice | Ounces of steak (price = $1/ounce) | Ounces of lobster (price = $2/ounce) | Total expenditure |
|--------|------------------------------------|--------------------------------------|-------------------|
| A | $10 | $0 | $10 ($10 + $0) |
| B | 8 | 1 | $10 ($8 + $2) |
| C | 4 | 3 | $10 ($4 + $6) |
| D | 2 | 4 | $10 ($2 + $8) |
| E | 0 | 5 | $10 ($0 + $10) |

A budget line shows all the possible combinations of goods that can be purchased with a given budget and given prices for these goods.

In order to express the equation in slope-intercept form, divide both sides by $P_s$ and get

$$\frac{P_l}{P_s}L + S = \frac{B}{P_s}$$

Solving for $S$ yields

$$S = \frac{B}{P_s} - \frac{P_l}{P_s}L$$

Note that $S$ is a linear function of $L$ with a vertical intercept of $B/P_s$ and a slope of $-P_l/P_s$. Since the price of lobster is $2 an ounce and the price of steak is $1 per ounce, the slope of the budget line is $-2$ or 2 as an absolute value.

> **CONCLUSION** *The slope of the budget line equals the ratio of the price of good X on the horizontal axis divided by the price of good Y on the vertical axis. Expressed as a formula:*
>
> **slope of budget line = $P_x/P_y$**

## A CONSUMER EQUILIBRIUM GRAPH

Exhibit A-4 shows the budget line from Exhibit A-3 superimposed on an indifference map. This allows us to easily compare consumer preferences and affordability. The utility-maximizing combination is the equilibrium point X, where the

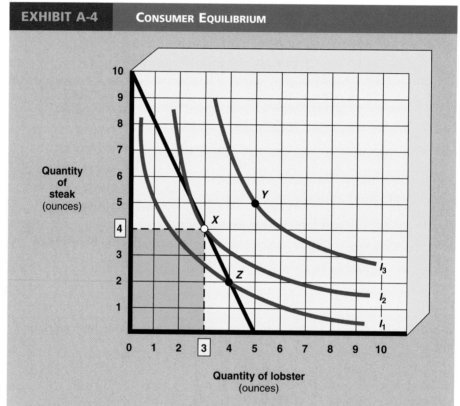

**EXHIBIT A-4     CONSUMER EQUILIBRIUM**

Consumer equilibrium is at point X, where the budget line is tangent to the highest attainable indifference curve, $I_2$. Only at this point does the marginal rate of substitution (MRS) along $I_2$ equal the slope of the budget line, which equals the price ratio $P_l/P_s$. Although point Y is on a higher curve, $I_3$, and would yield a greater total utility than X, point Y is beyond the budget line and therefore is unattainable by the consumer. Point Z is on a lower indifference curve, but it will not be chosen. The consumer can move upward along the budget line by shifting dollars from purchases of lobster to purchases of steak and reach point X on the higher indifference curve $I_2$.

budget line is just tangent to the highest attainable indifference curve $I_2$, and the quantity of steak purchased is 4 ounces and the quantity of lobster is 3 ounces.

As explained in Exhibit A-5 of the appendix to Chapter 1, the slope of a straight line tangent to a curve is equal to the slope of the curve at that point. This mathematical relationship translates into the economic interpretation of the tangency condition in this appendix. At the point of tangency, the MRS equals the slope of the budget line. At point X, the slope is the price ratio $P_l/P_s = 2$ from Exhibit A-3, and, therefore, it follows that MRS = 2 at point X on curve $I_2$ in Exhibit A-4. At any other combination, the MRS will not be equal to the price ratio, and the consumer will reallocate the budget until equilibrium is achieved at point X.

> **CONCLUSION** *Consumer equilibrium occurs where the budget line is tangent to the highest attainable indifference curve. At this unique point, MRS = slope (price ratio of $P_x/P_y$).*

## DERIVATION OF THE DEMAND CURVE

This appendix concludes with Exhibit A-5, which shows how the demand curve for lobster can be derived from a map of two indifference curves. The table in this exhibit reproduces the table from Exhibit A-3 and adds column (4) with the price of lobster equal to $1 per ounce, rather than $2 per ounce. Now compare columns (3) and (4) in the table. Holding the price of steak constant at $1 per ounce and the budget equal to $10, the consumer can afford to purchase more lobster at each choice except A where the entire budget is spent on steak. The top graph is drawn from Exhibit A-4, where at point X the price of lobster is $2 per ounce and the quantity demanded of lobster is 3 ounces. In the bottom graph of Exhibit A-5, this is one point on the demand curve for lobster at X′. To find another point on the demand curve, we decrease the price of lobster to $1 per ounce and trace the new budget line points from column (4) of the table onto the top graph. The budget line swings outward along the horizontal axis, but the original vertical intercept remains unchanged. The reason the vertical axis remains at 10 ounces of steak is because the price of steak is still at $1 per ounce, and if the consumer spends the entire $10 on steak, then the price of lobster is irrelevant to the vertical intercept. However, at a lower price for lobster, the consumer can afford more lobster moving downward along the new budget line with the same $10 budget because lobster is cheaper.

Given the new budget line shown in the top graph in Exhibit A-5, the consumer finds that higher indifference curve $I_3$ is now attainable. As a result, consumer equilibrium moves from point X to point Y, where 7 ounces of lobster are purchased. This gives the corresponding second point Y′ shown in the lower graph. Connecting these two points allows us to draw the consumer's demand curve for lobster. Voilà! Consistent with the law of demand, the demand curve is indeed downward sloping.

| EXHIBIT A-5 | DERIVING THE DEMAND CURVE |

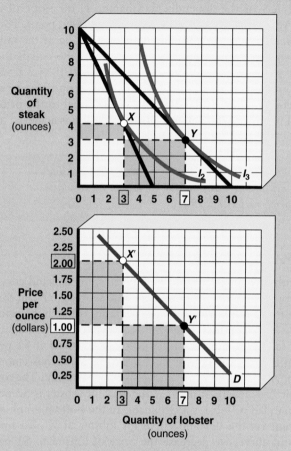

### Selected Whole-Unit Combinations of Steak and Lobster
### Affordable with a $10 Budget

| (1) Choice | (2) Ounces of steak (price = $1/ounce) | (3) Ounces of lobster (price = $2/ounce) | (4) Ounces of lobster (price = $1/ounce) | (5) Total expenditure |
|---|---|---|---|---|
| A | $10 | $0 | $0 | $10 ($10 + $0) |
| B | 8 | 1 | 2 | $10 ($8 + $2) |
| C | 4 | 3 | 6 | $10 ($4 + $6) |
| D | 2 | 4 | 8 | $10 ($2 + $8) |
| E | 0 | 5 | 10 | $10 ($0 + $10) |

In the top part of this exhibit, the initial budget line intersects the highest attainable indifference curve $I_2$ at point $X$ with the price of steak equal to $1 per ounce and the price of lobster equal to $2 per ounce. Holding the budget and the price of steak constant at $10 and $1, respectively, the price of lobsters drops to $1 per ounce. As a result, the budget line shifts to intersect the higher indifference curve $I_3$ at point $Y$.

The bottom part of the exhibit corresponds points $X$ and $Y$ to points $X'$ and $Y'$. At $2 per ounce for lobster, the consumer buys 3 ounces. At $1 per ounce for lobster, the consumer buys 7 ounces. Connecting these two points results in a downward-sloping demand curve.

## Key Concepts

Indifference curve

Marginal rate of
substitution (MRS)

Indifference map

Budget line

## Summary

- An **indifference curve** shows the different quantity combinations of two goods that give the same satisfaction or total utility to a consumer.

### INDIFFERENCE CURVE

- The **marginal rate of substitution (MRS)** is the rate at which a consumer is willing to substitute one good for another with no change in total utility.

- An **indifference map** is a selection of a consumer's indifference curves.

### INDIFFERENCE MAP

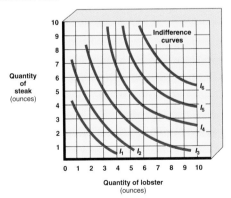

- The **budget line** gives the different combinations of two goods that a consumer can purchase with a given amount of money and relative prices for the goods. The slope of the budget line equals the price

of the good on the horizontal axis divided by the price on the vertical axis.

### BUDGET LINE

- **Consumer equilibrium** occurs where the budget line is tangent to the highest possible indifference curve, as shown originally at point X. If the price of one good falls, then the consumer equilibrium changes to point Y on a higher indifference curve. Connecting the two corresponding price-quantity points X′ and Y′ generates a downward-sloping demand curve.

### CONSUMER EQUILIBRIUM

## Summary of Conclusion Statements

■ The slope of the indifference curve is negative and equal to the marginal rate of substitution (MRS), which declines as one moves downward along the curve. The result is a curve with a diminishing slope that is convex (bowed inward) to the origin.

■ Each consumer has a set of indifference curves that form a map. Since consumers wish to achieve the highest possible total utility, they always prefer curves farther from the origin where they can select more quantities of two goods.

■ The budget line represents various combinations of goods that a consumer can purchase at given prices with a given budget.

■ The slope of the budget line equals the ratio of the price of good X on the horizontal axis divided by the price of good Y on the vertical axis. Expressed as a formula: slope = $P_x/P_y$.

■ Consumer equilibrium occurs where the budget line is tangent to the highest attainable indifference curve. At this unique point, MRS = slope (price ratio of $P_x/P_y$).

## Study Questions and Problems

1. Suppose a consumer's marginal rate of substitution is three slices of pizza for one Coke. If the price of a Coke is $1 and the price of three slices of pizza is $2, would the consumer change his or her consumption combination?

2. Let M represent the quantity of medical services, such as the number of doctor visits, and let O represent the quantity of other goods purchased by a consumer in a given year. Let the budget (B) be in thousands of dollars and the price of medical services and other goods be in terms of dollars per unit, with B = 60, $P_m$ = 6, and $P_o$ = 10.
   a. Graph the budget line and determine the slope.
   b. Show the result if the price of medical services ($P_o$) decreases to $5.
   c. Add two indifference curves to the graph that are tangent to the budget line, and explain the result.

3. Assume that the data in the following table are an indifference curve for a consumer:

| Choice | Units of Y | Units of X |
|---|---|---|
| A | 10 | 2 |
| B | 6 | 4 |
| C | 4 | 6 |
| D | 2 | 12 |

   a. Graph this indifference curve and label "quantity of Y" on the vertical axis and "quantity of X" on the horizontal axis. Label the points A–D.
   b. Assume the consumer's budget is $12 and the prices of X and Y are $1.00 and $1.50, respectively. Draw the budget line in the above graph.
   c. What combination of X and Y will the consumer purchase?
   d. What is the value of the MRS and the slope ($P_x/P_y$) at consumer equilibrium?
   e. Beginning with the graph drawn in (a) above, explain and draw graphs to derive a demand curve for X.

## Study Guide Questions

1. Given the prices of two goods, all quantity combinations inside the budget line are:
   a. indifferent.
   b. efficient.
   c. unattainable.
   d. attainable.

2. Assume the price of good X is $P_x$, price of good Y is $P_y$, and B is the budget. The formula for the budget line for these two goods is
   a. $P_yQ_y/P_xO_x$.
   b. $P_xB + P_yB = B$.
   c. $P_xX + P_xY = B$.
   d. $(1 - P_y/B) P_x$.

3. The ratio of the price of good X on the horizontal axis to the price of good Y on the vertical axis is the _____ of the budget line.
   a. marginal rate
   b. slope
   c. marginal utility
   d. equalization rate

**Answers to these questions are in the complete Study Guide at www.thomsonedu.com/thomsonnow.**

**For Online Exercises, go to the text Web site at www.thomsonedu.com/ecomomics/tucker**

## Practice Quiz

For an explanation of the correct answers, please visit the tutorial at www.thomsonedu.com/economics/tucker.

1. An indifference curve consists of quantity combinations of two goods that yield
   a. equal marginal utilities.
   b. negative marginal utilities.
   c. the same price ratios.
   d. the same total satisfaction.

2. The absolute value of the slope of an indifference curve is called the
   a. marginal rate of transformation.
   b. transitivity slope.
   c. indifference rate of preference.
   d. marginal rate of substitution.

3. The slope of the indifference curve for goods X and Y is called the marginal
   a. product rate.
   b. rate of transformation.
   c. rate of substitution.
   d. rate of utility.

4. Assume $P_x$ is the price of good $X$ on the horizontal axis and $P_y$ is the price of good $Y$ on the vertical axis. The slope of the budget line equals
   a. $P_y/P_x Y$.
   b. $P_y Q_y/P_x Q_x$.
   c. $(1 - P_y/P_x)$.
   d. $P_x/P_y$.

5. Consumer equilibrium occurs where the budget line is tangent to the
   a. lowest possible indifference curve.
   b. highest possible indifference curve.
   c. utility-maximizing indifference curve.
   d. utility-equalization indifference curve.

6. Only at the point of consumer equilibrium does the marginal rate of substitution (MRS) equal the
   a. slope of the budget line.
   b. slope of the indifference curve.
   c. price ratio.
   d. all of the above.

**EXHIBIT A-6  A CONSUMER'S BUDGET LINE AND INDIFFERENCE CURVES**

7. At point $A$ in Exhibit A-6, consumers would be
   a. spending all of their income but not maximizing total utility.
   b. spending all of their income and maximizing total utility.
   c. maximizing total utility without spending all of their income.
   d. none of the above.

8. The consumer equilibrium shown in Exhibit A-6 is located at point
   a. $A$.
   b. $B$.
   c. $C$.
   d. $D$.

9. In Exhibit A-6, point $D$ is
   a. a consumer equilibrium.
   b. unattainable, given the consumer's current budget constraint.
   c. a point that does not exhaust all of the consumer's income.
   d. none of the above.

10. Assume that a consumer's preference is for two goods, $X$ and $Y$ in Exhibit A-6. By holding the price of $Y$ and money income constant while varying the price of $X$, it is possible to derive
    a. the demand curve for $X$.
    b. the demand curve for $Y$.
    c. the demand curve for both $X$ and $Y$.
    d. none of the above.

# Production Costs

Suppose you dream of owning your own company. That's right! You want to be an entrepreneur. You crave the excitement of starting your own firm and making it successful. Instead of working for someone else, you want to be your own boss. You are under no illusions; it is going to take hard work and sacrifice.

You are an electrical engineer who is an expert at designing electronic components for automated teller machines and similar applications. So you quit your job and invest your nest egg in starting Computech (a mythical company). You lease factory space, hire employees, and purchase raw materials, and soon your company's products begin rolling off the assembly line. And then you find production cost considerations influence each decision you make in this new business venture.

The purpose of this chapter is to study production and its relationship to various types of costs. Whether your company is new and small or an international giant, understanding costs is essential for success. In this chapter and the next two chapters, you will follow Computech and learn the basic principles of production and the way various types of costs vary with output.

**In this chapter, you will learn to solve these economics puzzles:**

- Why would an accountant say a firm is making a profit and an economist say it is losing money?
- What is the difference between the short run and the long run?
- Why have multiscreen movie theaters replaced single-screen theaters?

## Costs and Profit

A basic assumption in economics is that the motivation for business decisions is profit maximization. Economists realize that managers of firms sometimes pursue other goals, such as contributing to the United Way or building an empire for the purpose of ego satisfaction. Nevertheless, the profit maximization goal has proved to be the best theory to explain why managers of firms choose a particular level of output or price. To understand profit as a driving force for business firms, we must distinguish between the way economists measure costs and the way accountants measure costs.

## EXPLICIT AND IMPLICIT COSTS

Economists define the total opportunity cost of a business as the sum of *explicit costs* and *implicit costs*. **Explicit costs** are payments to nonowners of a firm for their resources. In our Computech example, explicit costs include the wages paid to labor, the rental charges for a plant, the cost of electricity, the cost of materials, and the cost of medical insurance. These resources are owned outside the firm and must be purchased with actual payments to these "outsiders."

**Implicit costs** are the opportunity costs of using resources owned by the firm. These are opportunity costs of resources because the firm makes no actual payments to outsiders. When you started Computech, you gave up the opportunity to earn a salary as an electrical engineer for someone else's firm. When you invested your nest egg in your own enterprise, you gave up the opportunity to earn interest. You also used a building you own to warehouse Computech products. Although you made no payment to anyone, you gave up the opportunity to earn rental payments.

**Explicit costs**
Payments to nonowners of a firm for their resources.

**Implicit costs**
The opportunity costs of using resources owned by the firm.

## ECONOMIC AND ACCOUNTING PROFIT

In everyday use, the word *profit* is defined as follows:

$$\text{Profit} = \text{total revenue} - \text{total cost}$$

Economists call this concept *accounting profit*. This popular formula is expressed in economics as

$$\text{Accounting profit} = \text{total revenue} - \text{total explicit cost}$$

Because economic decisions include implicit as well as explicit costs, economists use the concept **economic profit** instead of accounting profit. Economic profit is total revenue minus explicit and implicit costs. Economic profit can be positive, zero, or negative (an economic loss). Expressed as an equation:

**Economic profit**
Total revenue minus explicit and implicit costs.

$$\text{Economic profit} = \text{total revenue} - \text{total opportunity costs}$$

or

$$\text{Economic profit} = \text{total revenue} - (\text{explicit costs} + \text{implicit costs})$$

Exhibit 1 illustrates the importance of the difference between accounting profit and economic profit. Computech must know how well it is doing, so you hire an accounting firm to prepare a financial report. The exhibit shows that Computech earned total revenue of $500,000 in its first year of operation. Explicit costs for wages, materials, interest, and other payments totaled $470,000. Based on standard accounting procedures, this left an accounting profit of $30,000.

If the analysis ends with accounting profit, Computech is profitable. But accounting practice overstates profit. Because implicit costs are subjective and therefore difficult to measure, accounting profit ignores implicit costs. A few examples will illustrate the importance of implicit costs. Your $50,000-a-year salary as an electrical engineer was forgone in order to spend all your time as owner of Computech. Also forgone were $10,000 in rental income and $5,000 in interest that you would have earned during the year by renting your building and putting your savings in the bank. Subtracting both explicit and implicit costs from

| EXHIBIT 1 | COMPUTECH'S ACCOUNTING VERSUS ECONOMIC PROFIT | |
|---|---|---|
| Item | Accounting profit | Economic profit |
| Total revenue | $500,000 | $500,000 |
| Less explicit costs: | | |
| Wages and salaries | 400,000 | 400,000 |
| Materials | 50,000 | 50,000 |
| Interest paid | 10,000 | 10,000 |
| Other payments | 10,000 | 10,000 |
| Less implicit costs: | | |
| Forgone salary | 0 | 50,000 |
| Forgone rent | 0 | 10,000 |
| Forgone interest | 0 | 5,000 |
| Equals profit | $30,000 | −$35,000 |

total revenue, Computech had an economic loss of $35,000. The firm is failing to cover the opportunity costs of using its resources in the electronics industry. Thus, the firm's resources would earn a higher return if used for other alternatives.

How would you interpret a zero economic profit? It's not as bad as it sounds. Economists call this condition **normal profit**. Normal profit is the minimum profit necessary to keep a firm in operation. Zero economic profit signifies there is just enough total revenue to pay the owners for all explicit and implicit costs. Stated differently, there is no benefit from reallocating resources to another use. For example, assume an owner earns zero economic profit, including an implicit (forfeited) cost of $50,000 per year that could have been earned working for someone else. This means the owner earned as much as would have been earned in the next best employment opportunity.

**Normal profit**
The minimum profit necessary to keep a firm in operation. A firm that earns normal profits earns total revenue equal to its total opportunity cost.

**CONCLUSION** *Since business decision making is based on economic profit, rather than accounting profit, the word* profit *in this text always means economic profit.*

# Short-Run Production Costs

Having presented the basic definitions of total cost, the next step is to study cost theory. In this section, we explore the relationship between output and cost in the short run. In the next section, the time horizon shifts to the long run.

## SHORT RUN VERSUS LONG RUN

Suppose I asked you, "What is the difference between the short run and the long run?" Your answer might be that the short run is less than a year and the long

## CHECKPOINT

### Should the Professor Go or Stay?

Professor Martin is considering leaving the university and opening a consulting business. For her services as a consultant, she would be paid $75,000 a year. To open this business, Professor Martin must convert a house from which she collects rent of $10,000 per year into an office and hire a secretary at a salary of $15,000 per year. Also, she must withdraw $10,000 from savings for miscellaneous expenses and forgo earning 10 percent interest per year. The university pays Professor Martin $50,000 a year. Based only on economic decision making, do you predict the professor will leave the university to start a new business?

run is over a year. Good guess, but wrong! Economists do not partition production decisions based on any specific number of days, months, or years. Instead, the distinction depends on the ability to vary the quantity of inputs or resources used in production. There are two types of inputs—*fixed inputs* and *variable inputs*. A **fixed input** is any resource for which the quantity cannot change during the period of time under consideration. For example, the physical size of a firm's plant and the production capacity of heavy machines cannot easily change within a short period of time. They must remain as fixed amounts while managers decide to vary output. In addition to fixed inputs, the firm uses *variable inputs* in the production process. A **variable input** is any resource for which the quantity can change during the period of time under consideration. For example, managers can hire fewer or more workers during a given year. They can also change the amount of materials and electricity used in production.

Now we can link the concepts of fixed and variable inputs to the *short run* and the *long run*. The **short run** is a period of time so short that there is at least one fixed input. For example, the short run is a period of time during which a firm can increase output by hiring more workers (variable input), while the size of the firm's plant (fixed input) remains unchanged. The firm's plant is the most difficult input to change quickly. The **long run** is a period of time so long that all inputs are variable. In the long run, the firm can build new factories or purchase new machinery. New firms may enter the industry, and existing firms may leave the industry.

### THE PRODUCTION FUNCTION

Having defined inputs, we can now describe how these inputs are transferred into outputs using a concept called a **production function**. A production function is the relationship between the maximum amounts of output a firm can produce and various quantities of inputs. An assumption of the production function model we are about to develop is that the level of technology is fixed. Technological advances would mean more output is possible from a given quantity of inputs.

Exhibit 2(a) presents a short-run production function for Eaglecrest Vineyard. The variable input is the number of workers employed per day, and each worker is presumed to have equal job skills. The acreage, amount of fertilizer, and all

**Fixed input**
Any resource for which the quantity cannot change during the period of time under consideration.

**Variable input**
Any resource for which the quantity can change during the period of time under consideration.

**Short run**
A period of time so short that there is at least one fixed input.

**Long run**
A period of time so long that all inputs are variable.

**Production function**
The relationship between the maximum amounts of output that a firm can produce and various quantities of inputs.

## EXHIBIT 2          A PRODUCTION FUNCTION AND THE LAW OF DIMINISHING RETURNS

Part (a) shows how the total output of bushels of grapes per day increases as the number of workers increases while all other inputs remain constant. This figure is a short-run production function, which relates outputs to a one-variable input while all other inputs are fixed.

Part (b) illustrates the law of diminishing returns. The first worker adds 10 bushels of grapes per day, and marginal product is 10 bushels per day. Adding a second worker adds another 12 bushels of grapes per day to total output. This is the range of increasing marginal returns. After two workers, diminishing marginal returns set in, and marginal product declines continuously.

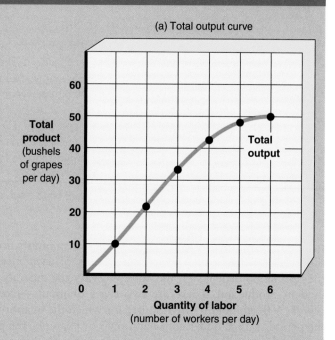

(a) Total output curve

**Short-Run Production Function of Eaglecrest Vineyard**

| (1)<br>Labor input<br>(number of<br>workers<br>per day) | (2)<br>Total output<br>(bushels of<br>grapes<br>per day) | (3)<br>Marginal product<br>(bushels of grapes<br>per day)<br>$[\Delta(2)/\Delta(1)]$ |
|:---:|:---:|:---:|
| 0 | 0 | |
| | | 10 |
| 1 | 10 | |
| | | 12 |
| 2 | 22 | |
| | | 11 |
| 3 | 33 | |
| | | 9 |
| 4 | 42 | |
| | | 6 |
| 5 | 48 | |
| | | 2 |
| 6 | 50 | |

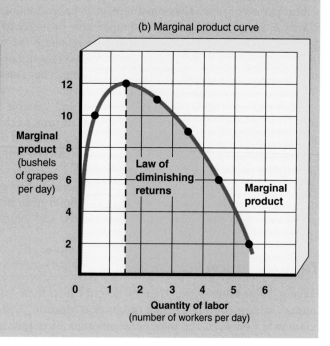

(b) Marginal product curve

other inputs are assumed to be fixed; therefore, our production model is operating in the short run. Employing zero workers produces no bushels of grapes. A single worker can produce 10 bushels per day, but a lot of time is wasted when one worker picks, loads containers, and transports the grapes to the winery. Adding a second worker raises output to 22 bushels per day because the workers divide the tasks and specialize. Adding four more workers raises total product to 50 bushels per day.

## MARGINAL PRODUCT

The relationship between changes in total output and changes in labor is called the **marginal product**. Marginal product is the change in total output produced by adding one unit of a variable input with all other inputs used being held constant. When Eaglecrest increases labor from zero to one worker, output rises from zero to 10 bushels produced per day. This increase is the result of the addition of one more worker. Therefore, the marginal product so far is 10 bushels per worker. Similar marginal product calculations generate the marginal product curve shown in Exhibit 2(b). Note that marginal product is plotted at the midpoints shown in the table because the change in total output occurs between each additional unit of labor used.

**Marginal product**
The change in total output produced by adding one unit of a variable input, with all other inputs used being held constant.

## THE LAW OF DIMINISHING RETURNS

A long-established economic law called the **law of diminishing returns** determines the shape of the marginal product curve. The law of diminishing returns states that beyond some point the marginal product decreases as additional units of a variable factor are added to a fixed factor. Because the law of diminishing returns assumes fixed inputs, this principle is a short-run, rather than a long-run, concept.

This law applies to production of both agricultural and nonagricultural products. Returning to Exhibit 2, we can identify and explain the law of diminishing returns in our Eaglecrest example. Initially, the total output curve rises quite rapidly as this firm hires the first two workers. The marginal product curve reflects the change in the total output curve because marginal product is the slope of the total output curve. As shown in Exhibit 2(b), the range from zero to two workers hired is called *increasing marginal returns*. In this range of output, the last worker hired adds more to total output than the previous worker.

Diminishing returns begin after the second worker is hired and the marginal product reaches its peak. Beyond two workers, diminishing returns occur, and the marginal product declines. The short-run assumption guarantees this condition. Eventually, marginal product falls because the amount of land per worker falls as more workers are added to fixed quantities of land and other inputs used to produce wine. Similar reasoning applies to the Computech example introduced in the chapter preview. Assume Computech operates with a fixed plant size and a fixed number of machines and all other inputs except the number of workers are fixed. Those in the first group of workers hired divide the most important tasks among themselves, specialize, and achieve increasing returns. Then diminishing returns begin and continue as Computech employs each additional worker. The reason is that as more workers are added, they must share fixed inputs, such as machinery. Some workers are underemployed because they are standing around waiting for a machine to become available. Also, as more workers are hired, there are fewer

**Law of diminishing returns**
The principle that beyond some point the marginal product decreases as additional units of a variable factor are added to a fixed factor.

important tasks to perform. As a result, marginal product declines. In the extreme case, marginal product would be negative. At some number of workers, they must work with such limited floor space, machines, and other fixed inputs that they start stepping on each other's toes. No profit-seeking firm would ever hire workers with zero or negative marginal product. Chapter 11 explains the labor market in more detail and shows how Computech decides exactly how many workers to hire.

# Short-Run Cost Formulas

To make production decisions in either the short run or the long run, a business must determine the costs associated with producing various levels of output. Using Computech, you will study the relationship between two "families" of short-run costs and output: first, the total cost curves and, next, the average cost curves.

## TOTAL COST CURVES

### Total Fixed Cost

**Total fixed cost (TFC)**
Costs that do not vary as output varies and that must be paid even if output is zero. These are payments that the firm must make in the short run, regardless of the level of output.

As production expands in the short run, costs are divided into two basic categories—*total fixed cost* and *total variable cost*. **Total fixed cost** (*TFC*) consists of costs that do not vary as output varies and that must be paid even if output is zero. These are payments that the firm must make in the short run, regardless of the level of output. Even if a firm, such as Computech, produces nothing, it must still pay rent, interest on loans, property taxes, and fire insurance. Fixed costs are therefore beyond management's control in the short run. The total fixed cost for Computech is $100, as shown in column 2 of Exhibit 3.

### Total Variable Cost

**Total variable cost (TVC)**
Costs that are zero when output is zero and vary as output varies.

As the firm expands from zero output, total variable cost is added to total fixed cost. **Total variable cost** (*TVC*) consists of costs that are zero when output is zero and vary as output varies. These costs relate to the costs of variable inputs. Examples include wages for hourly workers, electricity, fuel, and raw materials. As a firm uses more input to produce output, its variable costs will increase. Management can control variable costs in the short run by changing the level of output. Exhibit 3 lists the total variable cost for Computech in column 3.

### Total Cost

**Total cost (TC)**
The sum of total fixed cost and total variable cost at each level of output.

Given total fixed cost and total variable cost, the firm can calculate **total cost** (*TC*). Total cost is the sum of total fixed cost and total variable cost at each level of output. As a formula:

$$TC = TFC + TVC$$

Total cost for Computech is shown in column 4 of Exhibit 3. Exhibit 4(a) uses the data in Exhibit 3 to construct graphically the relationships between total cost, total fixed cost, and total variable cost. Note that the *TVC* curve varies with the level of

| EXHIBIT 3 | | | SHORT-RUN COST SCHEDULE FOR COMPUTECH | | | | |
|---|---|---|---|---|---|---|---|
| (1) Total product (Q) | (2) Total fixed cost (TFC) | (3) Total variable cost (TVC) | (4) Total cost (TC) | (5) Marginal cost (MC) | (6) Average fixed cost (AFC) | (7) Average variable cost (AVC) | (8) Average total cost (ATC) |
| 0 | $100 | $ 0 | $100 | | — | — | — |
| | | | | $ 50 | | | |
| 1 | 100 | 50 | 150 | | $100 | $50 | $150 |
| | | | | 34 | | | |
| 2 | 100 | 84 | 184 | | 50 | 42 | 92 |
| | | | | 24 | | | |
| 3 | 100 | 108 | 208 | | 33 | 36 | 69 |
| | | | | 19 | | | |
| 4 | 100 | 127 | 227 | | 25 | 32 | 57 |
| | | | | 23 | | | |
| 5 | 100 | 150 | 250 | | 20 | 30 | 50 |
| | | | | 30 | | | |
| 6 | 100 | 180 | 280 | | 17 | 30 | 47 |
| | | | | 38 | | | |
| 7 | 100 | 218 | 318 | | 14 | 31 | 45 |
| | | | | 48 | | | |
| 8 | 100 | 266 | 366 | | 13 | 33 | 46 |
| | | | | 59 | | | |
| 9 | 100 | 325 | 425 | | 11 | 36 | 47 |
| | | | | 75 | | | |
| 10 | 100 | 400 | 500 | | 10 | 40 | 50 |
| | | | | 95 | | | |
| 11 | 100 | 495 | 595 | | 9 | 45 | 54 |
| | | | | 117 | | | |
| 12 | 100 | 612 | 712 | | 8 | 51 | 59 |

output and the *TFC* curve does not. The *TC* curve is simply the *TVC* curve plus the vertical distance between the *TC* and *TVC* curves, which represents *TFC*.

## AVERAGE COST CURVES

In addition to total cost, firms are interested in the *per-unit cost*, or *average cost*. Average cost, like product price, is stated on a per-unit basis. The last three columns in Exhibit 3 are *average fixed cost* (AFC), *average variable cost* (AVC), and *average total cost* (ATC). These average, or per-unit, curves are also shown in Exhibit 4(b). These three concepts are defined as follows:

## EXHIBIT 4          SHORT-RUN COST CURVES

(a) Relationship of total cost to total variable cost and total fixed cost

(b) Relationship of marginal cost to average total cost, average variable cost, and average fixed cost

The curves in this exhibit are derived by plotting data from Exhibit 3. Part (a) shows that the total cost (*TC*) at each level of output is the sum of total variable cost (*TVC*) and total fixed cost (*TFC*). Because the *TFC* curve does not vary with output, the shape of the *TC* curve is determined by the shape of the *TVC* curve. The vertical distance between the *TC* and the *TVC* curves is *TFC*.

In Part (b), the marginal cost (*MC*) curve decreases at first, then reaches a minimum, and then increases as output increases. The *MC* curve intersects both the average variable cost (*AVC*) curve and the average total cost (*ATC*) curve at the minimum point on each of these cost curves. The average fixed cost (*AFC*) curve declines continuously as output expands. *AFC* is also the difference between the *ATC* and the *AVC* curves at any quantity of output.

### Average Fixed Cost

**Average fixed cost (AFC)**
Total fixed cost divided by the quantity of output produced.

As output increases, **average fixed cost** (*AFC*) falls continuously. Average fixed cost is total fixed cost divided by the quantity of output produced. Written as a formula:

$$AFC = \frac{TFC}{Q}$$

As shown in Exhibit 4(b), the *AFC* curve approaches the horizontal axis as output expands. This is because larger output numbers divide into *TFC* and cause *AFC* to become smaller and smaller.

## Average Variable Cost

The **average variable cost** (*AVC*) in our example forms a U-shaped curve. Average variable cost is total variable cost divided by the quantity of output produced. Written as a formula:

$$AVC = \frac{TVC}{Q}$$

The *AVC* curve is also drawn in Exhibit 4(b). At first, the *AVC* curve falls, and then after an output of 6 units per hour, the *AVC* curve rises. Thus, the *AVC* curve is U-shaped. The explanation for the shape of the *AVC* curve is given in the next section.

**Average variable cost (*AVC*)**
Total variable cost divided by the quantity of output produced.

## Average Total Cost

**Average total cost** (*ATC*) is sometimes referred to as *per-unit cost*. The average total cost is total cost divided by the quantity of output produced. Written as a formula:

$$ATC = AFC + AVC = \frac{TC}{Q}$$

Like the *AVC* curve, the *ATC* curve is U-shaped, as shown in Exhibit 4(b). At first, the *ATC* curve falls because its component parts—*AVC* and *AFC*—are falling. As output continues to rise, the *AVC* curve begins to rise while the *AFC* curve falls continuously. Beyond the output of 7 units per hour, the rise in the *AVC* curve is greater than the fall in the *AFC* curve, which causes the *ATC* curve to rise in a U-shaped pattern.

**Average total cost (*ATC*)**
Total cost divided by the quantity of output produced.

## Marginal Cost

Marginal analysis asks how much it costs to produce an *additional* unit of output. Column 5 in Exhibit 3 is **marginal cost** (*MC*). Marginal cost is the change in total cost when one additional unit of output is produced. Stated differently, marginal cost is the ratio of the change in total cost to a one-unit change in output. Written as a formula:

$$MC = \frac{\text{change in } TC}{\text{change in } Q} = \frac{\text{change in } TVC}{\text{change in } Q}$$

**Marginal cost (*MC*)**
The change in total cost when one additional unit of output is produced.

Note that marginal cost can also be calculated from changes in *TVC*. This is because the only difference between total cost and total variable cost is total fixed cost. Thus, *TC* and *TVC* change by the same amount with each unit change in output. To check this relationship, look at the per-unit changes in *TC*, *TVC*, and *MC* in Exhibit 3.

Changing output by one unit at a time simplifies the marginal cost calculations in our Computech example. The marginal cost data are listed between output levels to show that marginal cost is the change in total cost as the output level changes. Exhibit 4(b) shows this marginal cost schedule graphically. In the short run, a firm's marginal cost initially falls as output expands, eventually reaches a

| EXHIBIT 5 | SHORT-RUN COST FORMULAS | |
|---|---|---|
| Cost concept | Formula | Graph |
| Total cost (TC) | $TC = TFC + TVC$ | |
| Marginal cost (MC) | $\dfrac{\text{change in } TC}{\text{change in } Q} = \dfrac{\text{change in } TVC}{\text{change in } Q}$ | |
| Average fixed cost (AFC) | $AFC = \dfrac{TFC}{Q}$ | |
| Average variable cost (AVC) | $AVC = \dfrac{TVC}{Q}$ | |
| Average total cost (ATC) | $ATC = \dfrac{TC}{Q}$ | |

minimum, and then rises, forming a J-shaped curve. Note that marginal cost is plotted at the midpoints because the change in cost occurs between each additional unit of output.

Exhibit 5 summarizes a firm's short-run cost relationships.

## Marginal Cost Relationships

Part (b) of Exhibit 4 presents two important relationships that require explanation. First, we will explain the rule that links the marginal cost curve to the average cost curves. Second, we will return to the marginal product curve in Exhibit 2(b) and explain its connection to the marginal cost curve.

## CHECKPOINT

### Did Michael Jordan Beat the Marginal-Average Rule?

Michael Jordan, formerly of the Chicago Bulls, is one of the finest players in the history of basketball. Suppose he had an average of 33 points per game over the first 10 games of the season and then scored 20, 25, 40, 50, and 20 points in the next five games. Did Michael Jordan beat the marginal-average rule?

## THE MARGINAL-AVERAGE RULE

Observe that the *MC* curve in Exhibit 4(b) intersects both the *AVC* curve and the *ATC* curve at their minimum points. This is not accidental. It is a result of a relationship called the **marginal-average rule**. The marginal-average rule states that when marginal cost is below average cost, average cost falls. When marginal cost is above average cost, average cost rises. When marginal cost equals average cost, average cost is at its minimum point. The marginal-average rule applies to grades, weights, and any average figure.

Perhaps the best way to understand this rule is to apply it to a noneconomic example. Suppose there are 20 students in your class and each student has a grade point average (GPA) of 4.0. The average GPA of the class is therefore 4.0. Now assume another student who has a GPA of 2.0 joins the class. The new average GPA of 21 students in the class falls to 3.9. The average GPA was pulled down because the *marginal* GPA of the additional student was lower than the *average* GPA of the other students. Now suppose we start with a class of 20 students with a 2.0 GPA and add a student who has a 4.0 GPA. In this case, the new average GPA of the 21 students rises from 2.0 to 2.1. Thus, the *marginal* GPA of the last student was higher than the *average* GPA of all students in class before the addition of the new student.

Now consider the *MC* curve in Part (b) of Exhibit 4. In the range of output from 0 to 6 units per hour, the *MC* curve is below the *AVC* curve, and *AVC* is falling. Beyond 6 units per hour, the *MC* curve is above *AVC*, and *AVC* is rising. Hence, the relationship between *AVC* and *MC* conforms to the marginal-average rule. It follows that the *MC* curve intersects the *AVC* curve at its lowest point. This analysis also applies to the relationship between the *MC* and *ATC* curves. Initially, the *MC* curve is lower than the *ATC* curve until it reaches its minimum, causing the *ATC* curve to fall. Beginning with 8 units of output, the *MC* curve exceeds the *ATC* curve, causing the *ATC* curve to rise.

## MARGINAL COST'S MIRROR IMAGE

Since the *MC* curve determines the U shape of the *AVC* and *ATC* curves, we must explain the J shape of the *MC* curve. Exhibit 6 illustrates that the shape of the *MC* curve is the mirror reflection of the shape of the marginal product (*MP*) curve. Comparing parts (a) and (b) of Exhibit 6 gives the following:

**Marginal-average rule**
The rule that states when marginal cost is below average cost, average cost falls. When marginal cost is above average cost, average cost rises. When marginal cost equals average cost, average cost is at its minimum point.

| EXHIBIT 6 | THE INVERSE RELATIONSHIP BETWEEN MARGINAL PRODUCT AND MARGINAL COST |

| (1) | (2) | (3) | (4) | (5) |
|---|---|---|---|---|
| | | Marginal product | | |
| Labor input | Total output | (bushels of grapes | Total cost | |
| (number of workers | (bushels of grapes | per day) | per day | Marginal cost |
| per day) | per day) | [Δ(2)/Δ(1)] | [$100 × (1)] | [Δ(4)/(3)] |
| 0 | 0 | | $ 0 | |
| | | 10 | | $10.00 |
| 1 | 10 | | 100 | |
| | | 12 | | 8.33 |
| 2 | 22 | | 200 | |
| | | 11 | | 9.09 |
| 3 | 33 | | 300 | |
| | | 9 | | 11.11 |
| 4 | 42 | | 400 | |
| | | 6 | | 16.66 |
| 5 | 48 | | 500 | |
| | | 2 | | 50.00 |
| 6 | 50 | | 600 | |

Part (a) represents the marginal product of labor (*MP*) curve. At first, each additional worker hired adds more to output than does the previously hired worker, and the *MP* curve rises until a maximum is reached at two workers hired. At three workers, the law of diminishing returns sets in, and each additional worker hired adds less output than previously hired workers.

Part (b) shows the marginal cost (*MC*) curve is a J-shaped curve that is inversely related to the *MP* curve. Assuming the wage rate remains constant, as the *MP* curve rises, the *MC* curve falls. When the *MP* curve reaches a maximum at two workers, the *MC* curve is at a minimum. As diminishing returns set in and the *MP* curve falls, the *MC* curve rises.

**CONCLUSION** *The marginal cost declines as the marginal product of a variable input rises if the wage rate is constant. Beginning at the point of diminishing returns, the marginal cost rises as the marginal product of a variable input declines.*

As explained earlier in this chapter, the law of diminishing returns is the declining portion of the *MP* curve that corresponds to the rising portion of the *MC* curve. To understand why this relationship exists, we return to the case of Eaglecrest Vineyard presented earlier in Exhibit 2. Now we again assume that labor is the only variable input and add the new important assumption that the wage rate is constant at $100 per day. When Eaglecrest moves from zero labor to hire one worker, its total output rises from zero to 10 bushels of grapes per day. As explained earlier, the marginal product is also 10 bushels, and the marginal cost is $100/10 = $10 ($\Delta TC/\Delta Q = \Delta TC/MP$). When Eaglecrest hires the second worker, total output rises by 12 bushels per day. Hiring this worker increases the firm's total cost by $100 while the marginal product rises to 12 bushels. The marginal cost of the second worker therefore falls to a minimum at $100/12 = $8.33. At this point, it is noteworthy that the minimum point on the *MC* curve corresponds to the maximum point on the *MP* curve. The third worker hired yields only 11 additional bushels of grapes per day, so marginal cost rises to $9.09. Thus, diminishing returns begin with the third worker, and the marginal cost continues to rise as more workers are hired.

# Long-Run Production Costs

As explained earlier in this chapter, the long run is a time period long enough to change the quantity of all fixed inputs. A firm can, for example, build a larger or smaller factory or vary the capacity of its machinery. In this section, we will discuss how varying factory size and *all* other inputs affects the relationship between production and costs.

## LONG-RUN AVERAGE COST CURVES

Suppose Computech is making its production plans for the future. Taking a long-run view of production means the firm is not locked into a small, medium-sized, or large factory. However, once a factory of any particular size is built, the firm operates in the short run because the plant becomes a fixed input.

**CONCLUSION** *A firm operates in the short run when there is insufficient time to alter some fixed input. The firm plans in the long run when all inputs are variable.*

| EXHIBIT 7 | THE RELATIONSHIP BETWEEN THREE FACTORY SIZES AND THE LONG-RUN AVERAGE COST CURVE |
|---|---|

Each of the three short-run *ATC* curves in the exhibit corresponds to a different plant size. Assuming these are the only three plant-size choices, a firm can choose any one of these plant sizes in the long run. For example, a young firm may operate a small plant represented by the U-shaped short-run average total cost curve $SRATC_s$. As a firm matures and demand for its product expands, it can decide to build a larger factory, corresponding to either $SRATC_m$ or $SRATC_l$. The long-run average cost (*LRAC*) curve is the heavily shaded scalloped curve joining the short-run curves below their intersections.

Exhibit 7 illustrates a situation in which there are only three possible factory sizes Computech might select. Short-run cost curves representing these three possible plant sizes are labeled $SRATC_s$, $SRATC_m$, and $SRATC_l$. *SR* is the abbreviation for short run, and *ATC* stands for *average total cost*. The subscripts *s*, *m*, and *l* represent small, medium, and large plant size, respectively. In the previous sections, there was no need to use *SR* for short run because we were discussing only short-run cost curves and not long-run cost curves.

Suppose Computech estimates that it will be producing an output level of 6 units per hour for the foreseeable future. Which plant size should the company choose? It will build the plant size represented by $SRATC_s$ because this affords a lower cost of $30 per unit (point *A*) than the factory size represented by $SRATC_m$, which has a cost of $40 per unit (point *B*).

What if production is expected to be 12 units per hour? In this case, the firm will choose the plant size represented by $SRATC_l$. At this plant size, the cost is $30 per unit (point *C*), which is lower than $40 per unit (point *D*).

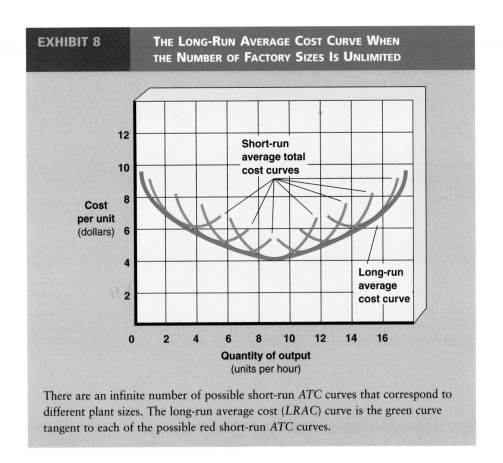

| EXHIBIT 8 | THE LONG-RUN AVERAGE COST CURVE WHEN THE NUMBER OF FACTORY SIZES IS UNLIMITED |

There are an infinite number of possible short-run *ATC* curves that correspond to different plant sizes. The long-run average cost (*LRAC*) curve is the green curve tangent to each of the possible red short-run *ATC* curves.

> **CONCLUSION** *The plant size selected by a firm in the long run depends on the expected level of production.*

Using the three short-run average cost curves shown in Exhibit 7, we can construct the firm's **long-run average cost curve (*LRAC*)**. The long-run average cost curve traces the lowest cost per unit at which a firm can produce any level of output after the firm can build any desired plant size. The *LRAC* curve is often called the firm's planning curve. In Exhibit 7, the heavily shaded curve represents the *LRAC* curve.

Exhibit 8 shows there are actually an infinite number of possible plant sizes from which managers can choose in the long run. As the intersection points of the short-run *ATC* curves move closer and closer together, the lumps in the *LRAC* curve in Exhibit 7 disappear. With a great variety of plant sizes, the corresponding short-run *ATC* curves trace a smooth *LRAC* curve in Exhibit 8. When the *LRAC* curve falls, the tangency points are to the left of the minimum points on the short-run *ATC* curves. As the *LRAC* curve rises, the tangency points are to the right of the minimum points on the short-run *ATC* curves.

**Long-run average cost curve (*LRAC*)** The curve that traces the lowest cost per unit at which a firm can produce any level of output when the firm can build any desired plant size.

# Different Scales of Production

Exhibit 8 depicts long-run average cost as a U-shaped curve. In this section, we will discuss the reasons why the *LRAC* curve first falls and then rises when output expands in the long run. In addition, we will learn that the *LRAC* curve can have a variety of shapes. Note that the law of diminishing returns is not an explanation here because in the long run there are no fixed inputs.

For simplicity, Exhibit 9 excludes possible short-run *ATC* curves that touch points along the *LRAC* curve. Typically, a young firm starts small and builds larger plants as it matures. As the scale of operation expands, the *LRAC* curve can follow three different patterns. Over the lowest range of output from zero to $Q_1$, the firm experiences **economies of scale**. Economies of scale exist when the long-run average cost curve declines as the firm increases output.

There are several reasons for economies of scale. First, a larger firm can increase its *division of labor* and *use of specialization*. Adam Smith noted in *The Wealth of Nations*, published in 1776, that the output of a pin factory is greater when one worker draws the wire, a second straightens it, a third cuts it, a fourth grinds the point, and a fifth makes the head of the pin. As a firm initially expands, having more workers allows managers to break a job into small tasks. Then each worker—including managers—can specialize by mastering narrowly defined tasks

**Economies of scale**
A situation in which the long-run average cost curve declines as the firm increases output.

| EXHIBIT 9 | A LONG-RUN AVERAGE COST CURVE WITH CONSTANT RETURNS TO SCALE |
|---|---|

The long-run average cost (*LRAC*) curve illustrates a firm that experiences economies of scale until output level $Q_1$ is reached. Between output levels $Q_1$ and $Q_2$, the *LRAC* curve is flat, and there are constant returns to scale. Beyond output level $Q_2$, the firm experiences diseconomies of scale, and the *LRAC* curve rises.

## You're the Economist

# Invasion of the Monster Movie Theaters
*Applicable Concept: economies and diseconomies of scale*

A few decades ago most movie theaters had a single screen and offered just one film and few concession stand choices. Now theaters are bigger and better than ever. Megaplexes, defined as cinemas with 16 or more screens, offer several movies at the same time, espresso coffee, gourmet popcorn, Haagen-Daz ice cream, and sometimes valet parking. These megaplexes, with stadium seating providing easier viewing, have become the industry standard.

As movie theaters were transforming into megaplexes in the late 1990s, Kurt Hall, executive vice president of United Artists Entertainment Company, expressed concern that diseconomies of scale would eventually set in:

*When building new theaters, United Artists is limiting its screens per site to about 15, half as many as AMC [American Multi-Cinema, Inc.]. United Artists fears that a larger megaplex won't pull in enough volume and could suffer a fate similar to Tandy Corp.'s Incredible Universe, the "big-box" electronics chain that closed this year. Over 16 screens, the economics start to fall apart.*[1]

Although megaplexes can provide economies of scale, they are not problem free:

*As moviegoers settle down in their comfortable arena seating, it's possible that the focus will be fuzzy, the picture won't be bright enough and the sound will be either too loud or too soft. For all the booming hype, and higher prices, projection at the megaplex is often less than ideal. Putting giant screens in small rooms magnifies focus problems. Projector bulbs are left to grow dim long beyond their rated life spans. And if something goes wrong—with just one projectionist overseeing as many as 20 automated projectors—chances are no one will notice.*[2]

These problems may diminish thanks to technology that may be coming to a theater near you: digital cinema projection. One industry analyst predicts that by the year 2011 nearly half of the nation's theater screens will use this new system. Imagine! No scratches, flutter, magnificent colors, and sharper focus. A satellite signal will beam movies down from space and save the studios the enormous cost of manufacturing and shipping prints around the world. Currently, studios spend more than $1 billion each year to transport heavy reels of film.[3]

Meanwhile, economies of scale in the electronics industry are boosting the invasion of "big rig" home theaters. A 2004 article in *USA Today* stated:

© Brand X Pictures/Getty Images

*The cost of the technology is dropping, the size of components is shrinking, and quality is improving. More homebuilders are including theaters, and more chairs and couches are being made to furnish them. More people are being exposed to the experience in their friends' homes and in stores. And more people just don't want to bother with going out to the movies. Plenty of people are bonding. From 2000 to 2003, Americans tripled their spending on home theater systems to nearly $1 billion a year. An estimated one-fourth of U.S. households have some kind of home theater, 37 percent have a 30-inch or larger TV screen. About 8 percent of new homes are being built with a home theater or media room.*[4]

### ANALYZE THE ISSUE

1. Explain why the long-run average cost curve for movie theaters falls (economies of scale) as movie theaters add screens.

2. Explain why the long-run average cost curve for movie theaters rises (diseconomies of scale) beyond some number of screens.

[1]Kevin Helliker, "Monster Movie Theaters Invade the Cinema Landscape," *The Wall Street Journal*, May 13, 1997, p. B1.

[2]Brian D. Johnson, "Movies Often Look Worse at Megaplex, Thanks to Technology Stretched to the Limit," *Maclean's*, Jan. 22, 2001, p. 30.

[3]Steve Persall, "On the Big Screen, Some Want to Keep It Reel," *St. Petersburg Times*, Apr. 12, 2002, p. 1D.

[4]Maria Puente, "The Multiplex is as Close as the Next Room: For Fans of 'Big Rig' Home Theaters, the Experience Is Worth Every Cent," *USA Today*, Jan. 2, 2004, p. D.08.

rather than trying to be a jack-of-all-trades.[1] The classic example is Henry Ford's assembly line, which greatly reduced the cost of producing automobiles. Today, McDonald's trains its workers at "Hamburger University"; then some workers prepare food, some specialize in taking orders, and a few workers specialize in the drive-through window operation.

Second, economies of scale result from greater *efficiency of capital*. Suppose machine A costs $1,000 and produces 1,000 units per day. Machine B costs $4,000, but it is technologically more efficient and has a capacity of 8,000 units per day. The low-output firm will find it too costly to purchase machine B, so it uses machine A, and its average cost is $1. The large-scale firm can afford to purchase machine B and produce more efficiently at a per-unit cost of only $.50.

The *LRAC* curve may not turn upward and form the U-shaped cost curve in Exhibit 8. Between some levels of output, such as $Q_1$ and $Q_2$ in Exhibit 9, the *LRAC* curve no longer declines. In this range of output, the firm increases its plant size, but the *LRAC* curve remains flat. Economists call this situation **constant returns to scale**. Constant returns to scale exist when the long-run average cost curve does not change as the firm increases output. Economists believe this is the shape of the *LRAC* curve in most real-world industries. The scale of operation is important for competitive reasons. Consider a young firm producing less than output $Q_1$ and competing against a more established firm producing in the constant-returns-to-scale range of output. The *LRAC* curve shows that the older firm has an average cost advantage.

As a firm becomes large and expands output beyond some level, such as $Q_2$ in Exhibit 9, it encounters **diseconomies of scale**. Diseconomies of scale exist when the long-run average cost curve rises as the firm increases output. A very large-scale firm becomes harder to manage. As the firm grows, the chain of command lengthens, and communication becomes more complex. People communicate through forms instead of direct conversation. The firm becomes too bureaucratic, and operations bog down in red tape. Layer upon layer of managers are paid big salaries to shuffle papers that have little or nothing to do with producing output. Consequently, it is no surprise that a firm can become too big, and these management problems can cause the average cost of production to rise.

Steven Jobs, founder of Apple Computer Company, stated:

> When you are growing [too big], you start adding middle management like crazy.... People in the middle have no understanding of the business, and because of that, they screw up communications. To them, it's just a job. The corporation ends up with mediocre people that form a layer of concrete.[2]

**Constant returns to scale**
A situation in which the long-run average cost curve does not change as the firm increases output.

**Diseconomies of scale**
A situation in which the long-run average cost curve rises as the firm increases output.

## Key Concepts

| | | |
|---|---|---|
| Explicit costs | Normal profit | Short run |
| Implicit costs | Fixed input | Long run |
| Economic profit | Variable input | Production function |

---

[1]Adam Smith, *An Inquiry into the Nature and Causes of the Wealth of Nations* (1776; reprint, New York: Random House, 1937), pp. 4–6.
[2]Deborah Wise and Catherine Harris, "Apple's New Crusade," *Business Week*, Nov. 26, 1984, p. 156.

Marginal product
Law of diminishing returns
Total fixed cost (*TFC*)
Total variable cost (*TVC*)
Total cost (*TC*)

Average fixed cost (*AFC*)
Average variable cost (*AVC*)
Average total cost (*ATC*)
Marginal cost (*MC*)
Marginal-average rule

Long-run average cost curve
  (*LRAC*)
Economies of scale
Constant returns to scale
Diseconomies of scale

## Summary

■ **Economic profit** is equal to total revenue minus both *explicit* and *implicit* costs. **Implicit costs** are the opportunity costs of forgone returns to resources owned by the firm. Economic profit is important for decision-making purposes because it includes implicit costs and accounting profit does not. Accounting profit equals total revenue minus explicit costs.

■ The **short run** is a time period during which a firm has at least one fixed input, such as its factory size. The **long run** for a firm is defined as a period during which all inputs are variable.

■ A **production function** is the relationship between output and inputs. Holding all other factors of production constant, the production function shows the total output as the amount of one input, such as labor, varies.

■ **Marginal product** is the change in total output caused by a one-unit change in a variable input, such as the number of workers hired. The **law of diminishing returns** states that after some level of output in the short run, each additional unit of the variable input yields smaller and smaller marginal product. This range of declining marginal product is the region of diminishing returns.

■ **Total fixed cost** (*TFC*) consists of costs that do not vary with the level of output, such as rent for office space. Total fixed cost is the cost of inputs that do not change as the firm changes output in the short run. **Total variable cost** (*TVC*) consists of costs that vary with the level of output, such as wages. Total variable cost is the cost of variable inputs used in production. **Total cost** (*TC*) is the sum of total fixed cost (*TFC*) and total variable cost (*TVC*).

**TOTAL COST CURVES**

■ **Marginal cost** (*MC*) is the change in total cost associated with one additional unit of output. **Average fixed cost** (*AFC*) is the total fixed cost divided by total output. **Average variable cost** (*AVC*) is the total variable cost divided by total output. **Average total cost** (*ATC*) is the total cost, or the sum of average fixed cost and average variable cost, divided by output.

**AVERAGE AND MARGINAL COST CURVES**

- The **marginal-average rule** explains the relationship between marginal cost and average cost. When marginal cost is less than average cost, average cost falls. When marginal cost is greater than average cost, average cost rises. Following this rule, the marginal cost curve intersects the average variable cost curve and the average total cost curve at their minimum points.

- **Marginal cost** (*MC*) and **marginal product** (*MP*) are mirror images of each other. Assuming a constant wage rate, marginal cost equals the wage rate divided by the marginal product. Increasing returns cause marginal cost to fall, and diminishing returns cause marginal cost to rise. This explains the J-shaped marginal cost curve.

**MARGINAL PRODUCT**

**MARGINAL COST**

- The **long-run average cost curve** (*LRAC*) is a curve drawn tangent to all possible short-run average total cost curves. When the *LRAC* curve decreases as output increases, the firm experiences **economies of scale**. If the *LRAC* curve remains unchanged as output increases, the firm experiences **constant returns to scale**. If the LRAC curve increases as output increases, the firm experiences **diseconomies of scale**.

**LONG-RUN AVERAGE COST CURVE**

## Summary of Conclusion Statements

- Since business decision making is based on economic profit, rather than accounting profit, the word *profit* in this text always means economic profit.

- The marginal cost declines as the marginal product of a variable input rises if the wage rate is constant. Beginning at the point of diminishing returns, the marginal cost rises as the marginal product of a variable input declines.

- A firm operates in the short run when there is insufficient time to alter some fixed input. The firm plans in the long run when all inputs are variable.

- The plant size selected by a firm in the long run depends on the expected level of production.

## Study Questions and Problems

1. Indicate whether each of the following is an explicit cost or an implicit cost:
   a. A manager's salary
   b. Payments to IBM for computers
   c. A salary forgone by the owner of a firm by operating his or her own company
   d. Interest forgone on a loan an owner makes to his or her own company
   e. Medical insurance payments a company makes for its employees
   f. Income forgone while going to college

2. Suppose you own a video rental store. List some of the fixed inputs and variable inputs you would use in operating the store.

3. a. Construct the marginal product schedule for the production function data shown in the next column.
   b. Graph the total output and marginal product curves, and identify increasing and diminishing marginal returns.

4. Consider this statement: "Total output starts falling when diminishing returns occur." Do you agree or disagree? Explain.

| Labor | Total output | Marginal product |
|-------|--------------|------------------|
| 0 | 0 | |
| 1 | 8 | |
| 2 | 18 | |
| 3 | 30 | |
| 4 | 43 | |
| 5 | 55 | |
| 6 | 65 | |
| 7 | 73 | |
| 8 | 79 | |
| 9 | 82 | |
| 10 | 80 | |

5. What effect might a decrease in the demand for videotape recorders have on the short-run average total cost curve for this product?

6. a. Construct the cost schedule using the data given below for a firm operating in the short run.
   b. Graph the average variable cost, average total cost, and marginal cost curves.

| Total product (Q) | Total fixed cost (TFC) | Total variable cost (TVC) | Total cost (TC) | Marginal cost (MC) | Average fixed cost (AFC) | Average variable cost (AVC) | Average total cost (ATC) |
|-------------------|------------------------|---------------------------|-----------------|--------------------|--------------------------|-----------------------------|--------------------------|
| 0 | $ 50 | $ ___ | $ 50 | $ ___ | $ ___ | $ ___ | $ ___ |
| 1 | ___ | ___ | $ 70 | ___ | ___ | ___ | ___ |
| 2 | ___ | ___ | $ 85 | ___ | ___ | ___ | ___ |
| 3 | ___ | ___ | $ 95 | ___ | ___ | ___ | ___ |
| 4 | ___ | ___ | $100 | ___ | ___ | ___ | ___ |
| 5 | ___ | ___ | $110 | ___ | ___ | ___ | ___ |
| 6 | ___ | ___ | $130 | ___ | ___ | ___ | ___ |
| 7 | ___ | ___ | $165 | ___ | ___ | ___ | ___ |
| 8 | ___ | ___ | $215 | ___ | ___ | ___ | ___ |
| 9 | ___ | ___ | $275 | ___ | ___ | ___ | ___ |

7. Explain why the average total cost curve and the average variable cost curve move closer together as output expands.

8. Ace Manufacturing produces 1,000 hammers per day. The total fixed cost for the plant is $5,000 per day, and the total variable cost is $15,000 per day. Calculate the average fixed cost, average variable cost, average total cost, and total cost at the current output level.

9. An owner of a firm estimates that the average total cost is $6.71 and the marginal cost is $6.71 at the current level of output. Explain the relationship between these marginal cost and average total cost figures.

10. What short-run effect might a decline in the demand for electronic components for automatic teller machines have on Computech's average total cost curve?

11. For mathematically minded students, what is the algebraic relationship between the equation for output and the equation for marginal product in Exhibit 2? Explain the circumstances under which the long-run supply curve for an industry is a horizontal line. Next, explain the circumstances under which the long-run supply curve for an industry is an upward-sloping line.

## Study Guide Questions

1. After some level of output in the short run, each unit of the variable input yields smaller and smaller marginal product. This principle is called the _____.

2. A farm is able to produce 5,000 bushels of peaches per season on 100 acres. Assume it adds one more acre and is able to produce 6,000 bushels per season. The marginal product of the additional acre of land for this farm is
   a. 6,000 bushels per acre per year.
   b. 5,000 bushels per acre per year.
   c. 1,000 bushels per acre per year.
   d. 11,000 bushels per acre per year.

3. Which of the following statements is *true*?
   a. Economic profit equals accounting profit minus implicit costs.
   b. The short run is any period of time in which there is at least one fixed input.
   c. A fixed input is any resource for which the quantity cannot change during the period under consideration.

   d. In the long run there are not fixed costs.
   e. All of the above.

4. Which of the following statements is *false*?
   a. $TC = TFC + TVC$.
   b. $AVC = ATC - AFC$.
   c. $AFC = TFC/Q$.
   d. $MC$ equals the change in $ATC$ divided by the change in $Q$.
   e. $ATC = TC/Q$.

5. T  F  If the total variable cost of producing 5 units of output is $10 and the total variable cost of producing 6 units is $15, the marginal cost of producing a sixth unit is $5.

**Answers to these questions are in the complete Study Guide at www.thomsonedu.com/thomsonnow.**

 **For Online Exercises, go to the text Web site at www.thomsonedu.com/economics/tucker.**

## Checkpoint Answers

### Should the Professor Go or Stay?

In the consulting business, the accounting profit is $60,000. An accountant would calculate profit as the annual revenue of $75,000 less the explicit cost of $15,000 per year for the secretary's salary. However, the accountant would neglect implicit costs. Professor Martin's business venture would have implicit costs of $10,000 in forgone rent, $50,000 in forgone earnings, and $1,000 in forgone annual interest on the $10,000 taken out of savings. Her economic profit is −$1,000, calculated as the accounting profit of $60,000 less the total implicit costs of $61,000. If you said the professor will pass up the potential accounting profit and stay with the university to avoid an economic loss, **YOU ARE CORRECT.**

### Did Michael Jordan Beat the Marginal-Average Rule?

Since Jordan's marginal points in games 11 and 12 were below his average points per game, his average points per game fell from 33 to 31. Games 13 and 14 lifted his average from 31 to 33 points per game because his marginal points in both of these games exceeded his average points per game. Finally, the 20 points in game 15 again reduced his average back to 32 points per game. Thus, when Jordan's marginal points scored in a game were below his season's average points per game, his average fell. When Jordan's marginal points scored in a game were above his season's average points per game, his average rose. If you said even Michael Jordan cannot beat the marginal-average rule, **YOU ARE CORRECT.**

| Game | Marginal points | Average points |
|------|------|------|
| 10 | | 33 over 10 games |
| 11 | 20 | 32 = (33 × 10 + 20)/11 games |
| 12 | 25 | 31 = (32 × 11 + 25)/12 games |
| 13 | 40 | 32 = (31 × 12 + 40)/13 games |
| 14 | 50 | 33 = (32 × 13 + 50)/14 games |
| 15 | 20 | 32 = (33 × 14 + 20)/15 games |

## Practice Quiz

For an explanation of the correct answers, please visit the tutorial at www.thomsonedu.com/economics/tucker.

1. Explicit costs are payments to
   a. hourly employees.
   b. insurance companies.
   c. utility companies.
   d. all of the above.

2. Implicit costs are the opportunity costs of using the resources of
   a. outsiders.
   b. owners.
   c. banks.
   d. retained earnings.

3. Which of the following equalities is *true*?
   a. Economic profit = total revenue − accounting profit
   b. Economic profit = total revenue − explicit costs − accounting profit
   c. Economic profit = total revenue − implicit costs − explicit costs
   d. Economic profit = opportunity cost + accounting cost

4. Fixed inputs are factors of production that
   a. are determined by a firm's plant size.
   b. can be increased or decreased quickly as output changes.
   c. cannot be increased or decreased as output changes.
   d. are none of the above.

5. An example of a variable input is
   a. raw materials.
   b. energy.
   c. hourly labor.
   d. all of the above.

6. Suppose a car wash has 2 washing stations and 5 workers and is able to wash 100 cars per day. When it adds a third station, but no more workers, it is able to wash 150 cars per day. The marginal product of the third washing station is
    a. 100 cars per day.
    b. 150 cars per day.
    c. 5 cars per day.
    d. 50 cars per day.

7. If the units of variable input in a production process are 1, 2, 3, 4, and 5 and the corresponding total outputs are 10, 22, 33, 42, and 48, respectively, the marginal product of the fourth unit is
    a. 2.
    b. 6.
    c. 9.
    d. 42.

8. The total fixed cost curve is
    a. upward sloping.
    b. downward sloping.
    c. upward sloping, then downward sloping.
    d. unchanged with the level of output.

9. Assuming the marginal cost curve is a smooth J-shaped curve, the corresponding total cost curve has a (an)
    a. linear shape.
    b. S shape.
    c. U shape.
    d. reverse S shape.

10. If both the marginal cost and the average variable cost curves are J shaped, at the point of minimum average variable cost, the marginal cost must be
    a. greater than the average variable cost.
    b. less than the average variable cost.
    c. equal to the average variable cost.
    d. at its minimum.

11. Which of the following is *true* at the point where diminishing returns set in?
    a. Both marginal product and marginal cost are at a maximum.
    b. Both marginal product and marginal cost are at a minimum.
    c. Marginal product is at a maximum, and marginal cost is at a minimum.
    d. Marginal product is at a minimum, and marginal cost is at a maximum.

**EXHIBIT 10  TOTAL COST CURVE**

12. As shown in Exhibit 10, total fixed cost for the firm is
    a. zero.
    b. $250.
    c. $500.
    d. $750.
    e. $1,000.

13. As shown in Exhibit 10, the total cost of producing 100 units of output per day is
    a. zero.
    b. $250.
    c. $500.
    d. $750.
    e. $1,000.

14. In Exhibit 10, if the total cost of producing 99 units of output per day is $475, the marginal cost of producing the 100th unit of output per day is approximately
    a. zero.
    b. $25.
    c. $475.
    d. $500.

15. Each potential short-run average total cost curve is tangent to the long-run average cost curve at
    a. the level of output that minimizes short-run average total cost.
    b. the minimum point of the average total cost curve.

c. the minimum point of the long-run average cost curve.

d. a single point on the short-run average total cost curve.

16. Suppose a typical firm is producing $x$ units of output per day. Using any other plant size, the long-run average cost would increase. The firm is operating at a point at which

a. its long-run average cost curve is at a minimum.

b. its short-run average total cost curve is at a minimum.

c. both (a) and (b) are true.

d. neither (a) nor (b) is true.

17. The downward-sloping segment of the long-run average cost curve corresponds to

a. diseconomies of scale.

b. both economies and diseconomies of scale.

c. the decrease in average variable costs.

d. economies of scale.

18. Long-run diseconomies of scale exist when the

a. short-run average total cost curve falls.

b. long-run marginal cost curve rises.

c. long-run average total cost curve falls.

d. short-run average variable cost curve rises.

e. long-run average cost curve rises.

19. Long-run constant returns to scale exist when the

a. short-run average total cost curve is constant.

b. long-run average cost curve rises.

c. long-run average cost curve is flat.

d. long-run average cost curve falls.

20. Which of the following is *not* a source of economies of scale?

a. Division and specialization of labor

b. Increase in output

c. More-efficient use of capital

d. All of the above

e. Centralized marketing

part
3

© Photodisc/Getty Images

# Market Structures

This part focuses on different types of markets, each defined by a set of characteristics that determine corresponding demand and supply conditions. Chapter 8 describes a highly competitive market consisting of an extremely large number of competing firms, and Chapter 9 explains the theory for a market with only a single seller. Between these extremes, Chapter 10 discusses two markets that have some characteristics of both competition and monopoly. The part concludes by developing labor market theory in Chapter 11.

# Perfect Competition

© Image 100/Jupiterimages

Ostrich farmers in Iowa, Texas, Oklahoma, and other states in the Midwest "stuck their necks out." Many invested millions of dollars converting a portion of their farms into breeding grounds for ostriches. The reason was that mating pairs of ostriches were selling for $75,000. During the late 1980s, ostrich breeders claimed that ostrich meat would become the low-cholesterol, low-fat health treat of the 1990s, and ostrich prices rose. The high prices for ostriches fueled profit expectations, and many cattle ranchers deserted their cattle and went into the ostrich business.

Adam Smith concluded that competitive forces are like an "invisible hand" that leads people who simply pursue their own interests and, in the process, serve the interests of society. In a competitive market, when the profit potential in the ostrich business looked good, firms entered this market and started raising ostriches. Over time more and more ostrich farmers flocked to this market, and the ostrich population exploded. As a result, prices and profits tumbled, and the number of ostrich farms declined in the late 1990s. In 2001,

demand increased unexpectedly because mad cow disease plagued Europe, and people bought alternatives to beef. Profits rose again, causing farmers to increase supply by investing in more ostriches. In 2005, the European Union (EU) banned ostrich imports from South America because of an outbreak of bird flu. The industry feared that consumers will stop buying ostrich meat and this will lead to massive job losses.

This chapter combines the demand, cost of production, and marginal analysis concepts from previous chapters to explain how competitive markets determine

prices, output, and profits. Here firms are small, like an ostrich ranch or an alligator farm, rather than huge, like Sears, Exxon-Mobil, or IBM. Other types of markets in which large and powerful firms operate are discussed in the next two chapters.

**In this chapter, you will learn to solve these economics puzzles:**

■ Why is the demand curve horizontal for a firm in a perfectly competitive market?

■ Why would a firm stay in business while losing money?

■ In the long run, can alligator farms earn an economic profit?

## Perfect Competition

Firms sell goods and services under different market conditions, which economists call market structures. A market structure describes the key traits of a market, including the number of firms, the similarity of the products they sell, and the ease of entry into and exit from the market. Examination of the business sector of our economy reveals firms operating in different **market structures**. In this chapter and the two chapters that follow, we will study four market structures. The first is **perfect competition**, to which this entire chapter is devoted. Perfect, or pure, competition is a market structure characterized by (1) a large number of small firms, (2) a homogeneous product, and (3) very easy entry into or exit from the market. Let's discuss each of these characteristics.

## CHARACTERISTICS OF PERFECT COMPETITION

### Large Number of Small Firms

How many sellers make up a large number? And how small is a small firm? Certainly, one, two, or three firms in a market would not be a large number. In fact, the exact number cannot be stated. This condition is fulfilled when each firm in a market has no significant share of total output and, therefore, no ability to affect the product's price. Each firm acts independently rather than coordinating decisions collectively. For example, there are thousands of independent egg farmers in the United States. If any single egg farmer raises the price, the going market price for eggs is unaffected.

> **CONCLUSION** *The large-number-of-sellers condition is met when each firm is so small relative to the total market that no single firm can influence the market price.*

### Homogeneous Product

In a perfectly competitive market, all firms produce a standardized or homogeneous product. This means the good or service of each firm is identical. Farmer Brown's wheat is identical to Farmer Jones's wheat. Buyers may believe the transportation services of one independent trucker are about the same as another's services. This assumption rules out rivalry among firms in advertising and quality differences.

> **CONCLUSION** *If a product is homogeneous, buyers are indifferent as to which seller's product they buy.*

### Very Easy Entry and Exit

Very easy entry into a market means that a new firm faces no barriers to entry. Barriers can be financial, technical, or government imposed barriers, such as licenses, permits, and patents. Anyone who wants to try his or her hand at raising ostriches needs only a plot of land and feed.

> **CONCLUSION** *Perfect competition requires that resources be completely mobile to freely enter or exit a market.*

No real-world market exactly fits the three assumptions of perfect competition. The perfectly competitive market structure is a theoretical or ideal model, but some

---

**Market structure**
A classification system for the key traits of a market, including the number of firms, the similarity of the products they sell, and the ease of entry into and exit from the market.

**Perfect competition**
A market structure characterized by (1) a large number of small firms, (2) a homogeneous product, and (3) very easy entry into or exit from the market. Perfect competition is also referred to as *pure competition*.

actual markets do approximate the model fairly closely. Examples include farm products markets, the stock market, and the foreign exchange market.

## THE PERFECTLY COMPETITIVE FIRM AS A PRICE TAKER

**Price taker**
A seller that has no control over the price of the product it sells.

For model-building purposes, suppose a firm operates in a market that conforms to all three of the requirements for perfect competition. This means that the perfectly competitive firm is a **price taker**. A price taker is a seller that has no control over the price of the product it sells. From the individual firm's perspective, the price of its products is determined by market supply and demand conditions over which the firm has no influence. Look again at the characteristics of a perfectly competitive firm: A small firm that is one among many firms, sells a homogeneous product, and is exposed to competition from new firms entering the market. These conditions make it impossible for the perfectly competitive firm to have the market power to affect the market price. Instead, the firm must adjust to, or "take," the market price.

Exhibit 1 is a graphical presentation of the relationship between the market supply and demand for electronic components and the demand curve facing a firm in a perfectly competitive market. Here we will assume that the electronic compo-

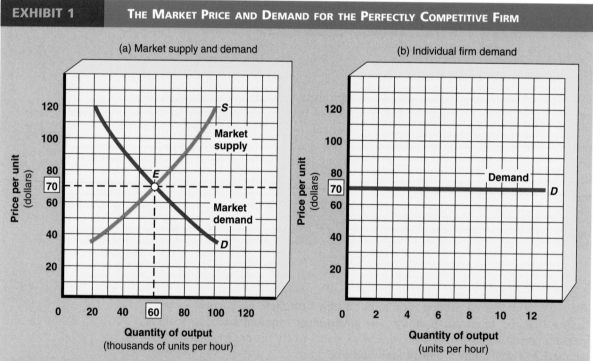

**EXHIBIT 1     THE MARKET PRICE AND DEMAND FOR THE PERFECTLY COMPETITIVE FIRM**

In Part (a), the market equilibrium price is $70 per unit. The perfectly competitive firm in Part (b) is a price taker because it is so small relative to the market. At $70, the individual firm faces a horizontal demand curve, *D*. This means that the firm's demand curve is perfectly elastic. If the firm raises its price even one penny, it will sell zero output.

nents industry is perfectly competitive, keeping in mind that the real-world market does not exactly fit the model. Exhibit 1(a) shows market supply and demand curves for the quantity of output per hour. The theoretical framework for this model was explained in Chapter 4. The equilibrium price is $70 per unit, and the equilibrium quantity is 60,000 units per hour.

Because the perfectly competitive firm "takes" the equilibrium price, the individual firm's demand curve in Exhibit 1(b) is *perfectly elastic* (horizontal) at the $70 market equilibrium price. (Note the difference between the firm's units per hour and the industry's thousands of units per hour.) Recall from Chapter 5 that when a firm facing a perfectly elastic demand curve tries to raise its price one penny higher than $70, no buyer will purchase its product [Exhibit 2(a) in Chapter 5.] The reason is that many other firms are selling the same product at $70 per unit. Hence, the perfectly competitive firm will not set the price above the prevailing market price and risk selling zero output. Nor will the firm set the price below the market price because the firm can sell all it wants to at the going price; therefore, a lower price would reduce the firm's revenue.

# Short-Run Profit Maximization for a Perfectly Competitive Firm

Since the perfectly competitive firm has no control over price, what does the firm control? The firm makes only one decision—what quantity of output to produce that maximizes profit. In this section, we develop two profit maximization methods that determine the output level for a competitive firm. We begin by examining the total revenue–total cost approach for finding the profit-maximizing level of output. Next, we use marginal analysis to show another method for determining the profit-maximizing level of output. The framework for our analysis is the short run with some fixed input, such as factory size.

## THE TOTAL REVENUE–TOTAL COST METHOD

Exhibit 2 provides hypothetical data on output, total revenue, total cost, and profit for our typical electronic components producer—Computech. Using Computech as our example allows us to extend the data and analysis presented in previous chapters. The cost figures are taken from Exhibit 3 in Chapter 7. Total fixed cost at zero output is $100. Total revenue is reported in column 3 of Exhibit 2 and is computed as the product price times the quantity. In this case, we assume the market equilibrium price is $70 per unit, as determined in Exhibit 1. Because Computech is a price taker, the total revenue from selling 1 unit is $70, from selling 2 units is $140, and so on. Subtracting total cost in column 6 from total revenue in column 3 gives the total profit or loss (column 9) that the firm earns at each level of output. From zero to 2 units, the firm incurs losses, and then a *break-even point* (zero economic profit) occurs at about 3 units per hour. If the firm produces 9 units per hour, it earns the maximum profit of $205 per hour. As output expands between 9 and 12 units of output, the firm's profit diminishes. Exhibit 3 illustrates graphically that the maximum profit occurs where the vertical distance between the total revenue and the total cost curves is at a maximum.

| EXHIBIT 2 | | SHORT-RUN PROFIT MAXIMIZATION SCHEDULE FOR COMPUTECH AS A PERFECTLY COMPETITIVE FIRM | | | | | | |

| (1) Output (units per hour) (Q) | (2) Price per unit (P) | (3) Total revenue (TR) | (4) Marginal revenue (MR) | (5) Marginal cost (MC) | (6) Total cost (TC) | (7) Average variable cost (AVC) | (8) Average total cost (ATC) | (9) Profit (+) or Loss (−) [(3) − (6)] |
|---|---|---|---|---|---|---|---|---|
| 0 | $70 | $ 0 | | | $100 | — | — | −$100 |
| | | | $70 | $ 50 | | | | |
| 1 | 70 | 70 | | | 150 | $50 | $150 | −80 |
| | | | 70 | 34 | | | | |
| 2 | 70 | 140 | | | 184 | 42 | 92 | −44 |
| | | | 70 | 24 | | | | |
| 3 | 70 | 210 | | | 208 | 36 | 69 | 2 |
| | | | 70 | 19 | | | | |
| 4 | 70 | 280 | | | 227 | 32 | 57 | 53 |
| | | | 70 | 23 | | | | |
| 5 | 70 | 350 | | | 250 | 30 | 50 | 100 |
| | | | 70 | 30 | | | | |
| 6 | 70 | 420 | | | 280 | 30 | 47 | 140 |
| | | | 70 | 38 | | | | |
| 7 | 70 | 490 | | | 318 | 31 | 45 | 172 |
| | | | 70 | 48 | | | | |
| 8 | 70 | 560 | | | 366 | 33 | 46 | 194 |
| | | | 70 | 59 | | | | |
| 9 | 70 | 630 | | | 425 | 36 | 47 | 205 |
| | | | 70 | 75 | | | | |
| 10 | 70 | 700 | | | 500 | 40 | 50 | 200 |
| | | | 70 | 95 | | | | |
| 11 | 70 | 770 | | | 595 | 45 | 54 | 175 |
| | | | 70 | 117 | | | | |
| 12 | 70 | 840 | | | 712 | 51 | 59 | 128 |

## THE MARGINAL REVENUE EQUALS MARGINAL COST METHOD

A second approach uses *marginal analysis* to determine the profit-maximizing level of output by comparing marginal revenue (marginal benefit) and marginal cost. Recall that marginal cost is the change in total cost as the output level changes one unit. Also recall that these marginal cost data are listed between the quantity of output line entries because the change in total cost occurs between each additional whole unit of output rather than exactly at each listed output level.

**Marginal revenue**
The change in total revenue from the sale of one additional unit of output.

Now we introduce **marginal revenue** (*MR*), a concept similar to marginal cost. Marginal revenue is the change in total revenue from the sale of one additional unit of output. Stated another way, marginal revenue is the ratio of the change in total revenue to a one-unit change in output. Mathematically,

$$MR = \frac{\text{change in total revenue}}{\text{one-unit change in output}}$$

| EXHIBIT 3 | SHORT-RUN PROFIT MAXIMIZATION USING THE TOTAL REVENUE–TOTAL COST METHOD FOR A PERFECTLY COMPETITIVE FIRM |
|---|---|

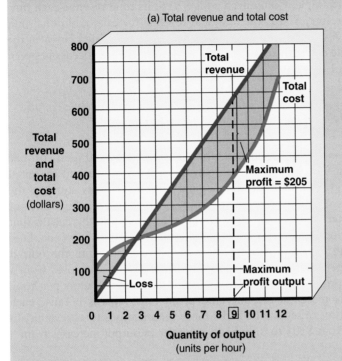

(a) Total revenue and total cost

(b) Profit or loss

This exhibit shows the profit-maximizing level of output chosen by a perfectly competitive firm, Computech. Part (a) shows the relationships between total revenue, total cost, and output, given a market price of $70 per unit. The maximum profit is earned by producing 9 units per hour. At this level of output, the vertical distance between the total revenue and the total cost curves is the greatest. At an output level below 3 units per hour, the firm incurs losses.

Profit maximization is also shown in Part (b). The maximum profit of $205 per hour corresponds to the profit-maximizing output of 9 units per hour, represented in Part (a).

As shown in Exhibit 1(b), the perfectly competitive firm faces a perfectly elastic demand curve. Because the competitive firm is a price taker, the sale of each additional unit adds to total revenue an amount equal to the price (average revenue, $TR/Q$). In our example, Computech adds $70 to its total revenue each time it sells one unit. Therefore, $70 is the marginal revenue for each additional unit of output in column 4 of Exhibit 2. As with $MC$, $MR$ is also listed between the quantity-of-output line entries because the change in total revenue occurs between each additional unit of output.

> **CONCLUSION** *In perfect competition, the firm's marginal revenue equals the price that the firm views as a horizontal demand curve.*

Columns 3 and 6 in Exhibit 2 show that both total revenue and total cost rise as the level of output increases. Now compare marginal revenue and marginal cost in columns 4 and 5. As explained, marginal revenue remains equal to the price, but marginal cost follows the J-shaped pattern introduced in Exhibit 4 of Chapter 7. At first, marginal cost is below marginal revenue, and this means that producing each additional unit adds less to total cost than to total revenue. Economic profit therefore increases as output expands from zero until the output level reaches 9 units per hour. Over this output range, Computech moves from a $100 loss to a $205 profit per hour. Beyond an output level of 9 units per hour, marginal cost exceeds marginal revenue, and profit falls. This is because each additional unit of output raises total cost by more than it raises total revenue. In this case, profit falls from $205 to only $128 per hour as output increases from 9 to 12 units per hour.

Our example leads to this question: How does the firm use its marginal revenue and marginal cost curves to determine the profit-maximizing level of output? The answer is that the firm follows a guideline called the $MR = MC$ rule: *The firm maximizes profit by producing the output where marginal revenue equals marginal cost.* Exhibit 4 relates the marginal revenue curve equals marginal cost curve condition to profit maximization. In Exhibit 4(a), the perfectly elastic demand curve is drawn at the industry-determined price of $70. The average total cost ($ATC$) and average variable cost ($AVC$) curves are traced from Exhibit 2. Using marginal analysis, we can relate the $MR = MC$ rule to the same profit data given in Exhibit 2. Between 8 and 9 units of output, the $MC$ curve is below the $MR$ curve ($59 < $70), and the profit curve rises to its peak at $205. Beyond 9 units of output, the $MC$ curve is above the $MR$ curve, and the profit curve falls. For example, between 9 and 10 units of output, marginal cost is $75, and marginal revenue is $70. Therefore, if the firm produces at 9 units of output rather than, say, 8 or 10 units of output, the $MR$ curve equals the $MC$ curve, and profit is maximized.

You can also calculate profit directly from Exhibit 4(a). At the profit-maximizing level of output of 9 units, the vertical distance between the demand curve and the $ATC$ curve is the *average profit per unit*. Multiplying the average profit per unit times the quantity of output gives the profit ($70 − $47.22) × 9 = $205.02.[1]

---

[1]In Exhibit 3 in Chapter 7, the average total cost figure at 9 units of output was rounded to $47. It also should be noted that there is often no level of output for which marginal revenue exactly equals marginal cost when dealing with whole units of output.

**EXHIBIT 4**    **SHORT-RUN PROFIT MAXIMIZATION USING THE MARGINAL REVENUE EQUALS MARGINAL COST METHOD FOR A PERFECTLY COMPETITIVE FIRM**

(a) Price, marginal revenue, and cost per unit

(b) Profit or loss

In addition to comparing total revenue and total cost, a firm can find the profit-maximizing level of output by comparing marginal revenue (*MR*) and marginal cost (*MC*). As shown in Part (a), profit is at a maximum where marginal revenue equals marginal cost at $70 per unit. The intersection of the marginal revenue and the marginal cost curves establishes the profit-maximizing output at 9 units per hour.

A profit curve is depicted separately in Part (b) to show that the maximum profit occurs when the firm produces at the level of output corresponding to the *MR* = *MC* point. Below 3 units per hour output, the firm incurs losses.

The shaded rectangle also represents the maximum profit of $205 per hour. Note that we have arrived at the same profit maximization amount ($205) derived by comparing the total revenue and the total cost curves.

# Short-Run Loss Minimization for a Perfectly Competitive Firm

Because the perfectly competitive firm must take the price determined by market supply and demand forces, market conditions can change the prevailing price. When the market price drops, the firm can do nothing but adjust its output to make the best of the situation. Here only the marginal approach is used to predict output decisions of firms. Our model therefore assumes that business managers make their output decisions by comparing the *marginal* effect on profit of a *marginal* change in output.

### A PERFECTLY COMPETITIVE FIRM FACING A SHORT-RUN LOSS

Suppose a decrease in the market demand for electronic components causes the market price to fall to $35. As a result, the firm's horizontal demand curve shifts downward to the new position shown in Exhibit 5(a). In this case, there is no level of output at which the firm earns a profit because any price along the demand curve is below the *ATC* curve.

   Since Computech cannot make a profit, what output level should it choose? The logic of the $MR = MC$ rule given in the profit maximization case applies here as well. At a price of $35, $MR = MC$ at 6 units per hour. Comparing Parts (a) and (b) of Exhibit 5 shows that the firm's loss will be minimized at this level of output. The minimum loss of $70 per hour is equal to the shaded area, which is the *average loss per unit* times the quantity of output ($35 − $46.66) × 6 = −$70.

## CHECKPOINT

### Should Motels Offer Rooms at the Beach for Only $50 a Night?

Myrtle Beach, South Carolina, with its famous Grand Strand and Calabash seafood, is lined with virtually identical motels. Summertime rates run about $200 a night. During the winter, one can find rooms for as little as $50 a night. Assume the average fixed cost of a room per night, including insurance, taxes, and depreciation, is $50. The average guest-related cost for a room each night, including cleaning service and linens, is $45. Would these motels be better off renting rooms for $50 in the off-season or shutting down until summer?

| EXHIBIT 5 | SHORT-RUN LOSS MINIMIZATION USING THE MARGINAL REVENUE EQUALS MARGINAL COST METHOD FOR A PERFECTLY COMPETITIVE FIRM |

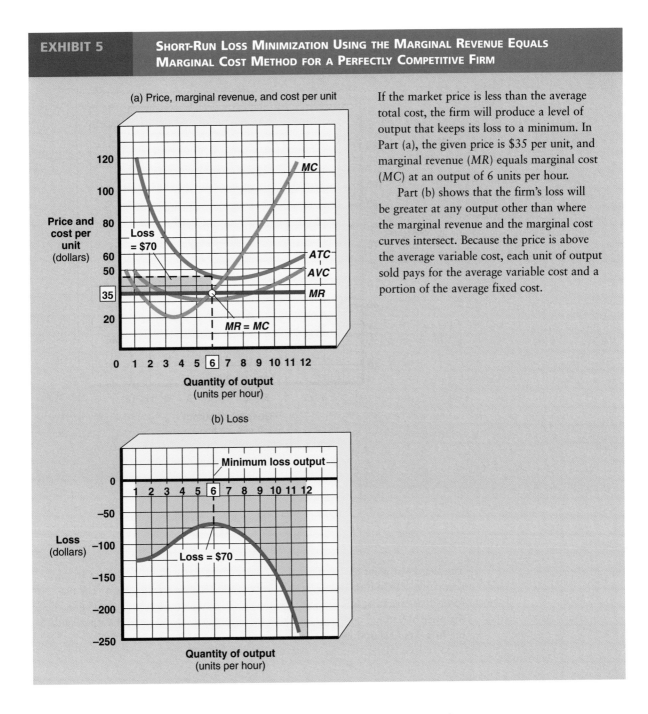

(a) Price, marginal revenue, and cost per unit

(b) Loss

If the market price is less than the average total cost, the firm will produce a level of output that keeps its loss to a minimum. In Part (a), the given price is $35 per unit, and marginal revenue (*MR*) equals marginal cost (*MC*) at an output of 6 units per hour.

Part (b) shows that the firm's loss will be greater at any output other than where the marginal revenue and the marginal cost curves intersect. Because the price is above the average variable cost, each unit of output sold pays for the average variable cost and a portion of the average fixed cost.

Note that although the price is not high enough to pay the average total cost, the price is high enough to pay the average variable cost. Each unit sold also contributes to paying a portion of the average fixed cost, which is the vertical distance between the *ATC* and the *AVC* curves. This analysis leads us to extend the *MR* = *MC* rule: *The firm maximizes profit or minimizes loss by producing the output where marginal revenue equals marginal cost.*

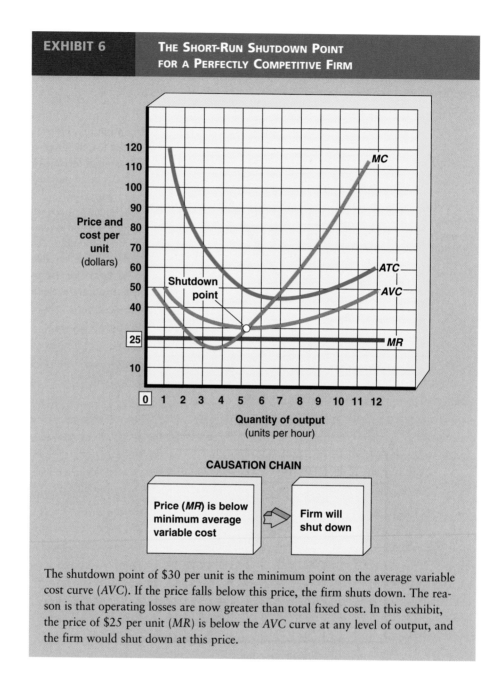

**EXHIBIT 6**   **THE SHORT-RUN SHUTDOWN POINT FOR A PERFECTLY COMPETITIVE FIRM**

**CAUSATION CHAIN**

Price (*MR*) is below minimum average variable cost ⟹ Firm will shut down

The shutdown point of $30 per unit is the minimum point on the average variable cost curve (*AVC*). If the price falls below this price, the firm shuts down. The reason is that operating losses are now greater than total fixed cost. In this exhibit, the price of $25 per unit (*MR*) is below the *AVC* curve at any level of output, and the firm would shut down at this price.

## A PERFECTLY COMPETITIVE FIRM SHUTTING DOWN

What happens if the market price drops below the *AVC* curve, as shown in Exhibit 6? For example, if the price is $25 per unit, should Computech produce some level of output? The answer is no. The best course of action is for the firm to shut down. *If the price is below the minimum point on the AVC curve, each unit produced would not cover the variable cost per unit; therefore, operating would increase losses.* The firm is better off shutting down and producing zero output. While shut down, the firm might keep its factory, pay fixed costs, and hope for higher prices soon. If the firm does not believe market conditions will improve, it will avoid fixed costs by going out of business.

# Short-Run Supply Curves under Perfect Competition

The preceding examples provide a framework for a more complete explanation of the supply curve than was given earlier in Chapter 3. We now develop the short-run supply curve for an individual firm and then derive it for an industry.

### THE PERFECTLY COMPETITIVE FIRM'S SHORT-RUN SUPPLY CURVE

Exhibit 7 reproduces the cost curves from our Computech example. Also represented in the exhibit are three possible demand curves the firm might face—$MR_1$, $MR_2$, and $MR_3$. As the marginal revenue curve moves upward along the marginal cost curve, the $MR = MC$ point changes.

Suppose demand for electronic components begins at a market price close to $30. Point *A* therefore corresponds to a price equal to $MR_1$, which equals $MC$ at the lowest point on the *AVC* curve. At any lower price, the firm cuts its loss by shutting down. At a price of about $30, however, the firm produces 5.5 units per hour. Point *A* is therefore the lowest point on the individual firm's short-run supply curve.

If the price rises to $45, represented in the exhibit by $MR_2$, the firm breaks even and earns a normal profit at point *B* with an output of 7 units per hour. As the marginal revenue curve rises, the firm's supply curve is traced by moving upward along its *MC* curve. At a price of $90, point *C* is reached. Now $MR_3$ intersects the *MC* curve at an output of 10 units per hour, and the firm earns an economic profit. If the price rises higher than $90, the firm will continue to increase the quantity supplied and increase its maximum profit.

We can now define a **perfectly competitive firm's short-run supply curve**. The perfectly competitive firm's short-run supply curve is its marginal cost curve above the minimum point on its average variable cost curve.

### THE PERFECTLY COMPETITIVE INDUSTRY'S SHORT-RUN SUPPLY CURVE

Understanding that the firm's short-run supply curve is the segment of its *MC* curve above its *AVC* curve sets the stage for derivation of the **perfectly competitive industry's short-run supply curve**. The perfectly competitive industry's short-run supply curve is the horizontal summation of the marginal cost curves of all firms in the industry above the minimum point of each firm's average variable cost curve.

In Exhibit 7 in Chapter 3, we drew a market supply curve. Now we will reconstruct this market, or industry, supply curve using more precision. Although in perfect competition there are many firms, we suppose for simplicity that the industry

**Perfectly competitive firm's short-run supply curve**
The firm's marginal cost curve above the minimum point on its average variable cost curve.

**Perfectly competitive industry's short-run supply curve**
The supply curve derived from horizontal summation of the marginal cost curves of all firms in the industry above the minimum point of each firm's average variable cost curve.

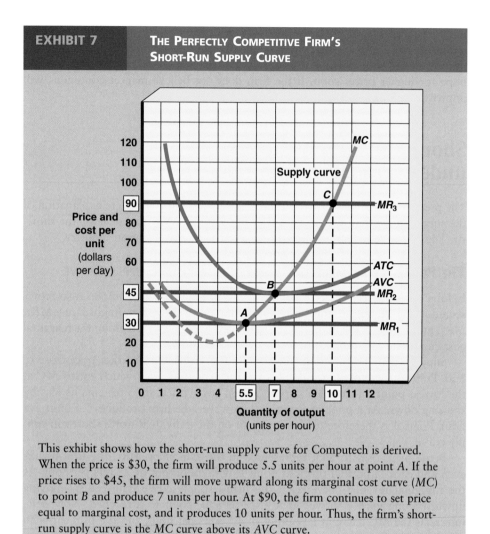

| EXHIBIT 7 | THE PERFECTLY COMPETITIVE FIRM'S SHORT-RUN SUPPLY CURVE |

This exhibit shows how the short-run supply curve for Computech is derived. When the price is $30, the firm will produce 5.5 units per hour at point *A*. If the price rises to $45, the firm will move upward along its marginal cost curve (*MC*) to point *B* and produce 7 units per hour. At $90, the firm continues to set price equal to marginal cost, and it produces 10 units per hour. Thus, the firm's short-run supply curve is the *MC* curve above its *AVC* curve.

has only two firms, Computech and Western Computer Co. Exhibit 8 illustrates the *MC* curves for these two firms. Each firm's *MC* curve is drawn for prices above the minimum point on the *AVC* curve. At a price of $40, the quantity supplied by Computech is 7 units, and the quantity supplied by Western Computer Co. is 11 units. Now we horizontally add these two quantities and obtain one point on the industry supply curve corresponding to a price of $40 and 18 units. Following this procedure for all prices, we generate the short-run industry supply curve.

Note that the industry supply curve derived above is based on the assumption that input prices remain unchanged as output expands. In the next section, we will learn how changes in input prices affect derivation of the supply curve.

## SHORT-RUN EQUILIBRIUM FOR A PERFECTLY COMPETITIVE FIRM

Exhibit 9 illustrates a condition of short-run equilibrium under perfect competition. Exhibit 9(a) represents the equilibrium price and cost situation for one of the

| EXHIBIT 8 | DERIVING THE INDUSTRY SHORT-RUN SUPPLY CURVE |

**Computech *MC* curve  +    Western Computer Co.  =    Industry supply curve**
**                                    *MC* curve**

Assuming input prices remain constant as output expands, the short-run supply curve for an industry is derived by horizontally summing the quantities supplied at each price by all firms in the industry. In this exhibit, we assume there are only two firms in an industry. At $40, Computech supplies 7 units of output, and Western Computer Co. supplies 11 units. The quantity supplied by the industry is therefore 18 units. Other points forming the industry short-run supply curve are obtained similarly.

many firms in an industry. As shown in the exhibit, the firm earns an economic profit in the short run by producing 9 units. Exhibit 9(b) depicts short-run equilibrium for the industry. As explained earlier, the industry supply curve is the aggregate of each firm's *MC* curve above the minimum point on the *AVC* curve. Including industry demand establishes the equilibrium price of $60 that all firms in the industry must take. The industry's equilibrium quantity supplied is 60,000 units. This state of short-run equilibrium will remain until some factor changes and causes a new equilibrium condition in the industry.

# Long-Run Supply Curves under Perfect Competition

Recall from Chapter 7 that *all* inputs are variable in the long run. Existing firms in an industry can react to profit opportunities by building larger or smaller plants, buying or selling land and equipment, or varying other inputs that are fixed in the short run. Profits also attract new firms to an industry, while losses cause some existing firms to leave the industry. As you will now see, the free entry and exit characteristic of perfect competition is a crucial determinant of the shape of the long-run supply curve.

## LONG-RUN EQUILIBRIUM FOR A PERFECTLY COMPETITIVE FIRM

As discussed in Chapter 7, in the long run a firm can change its plant size or any input used to produce a product. This means that an established firm can decide

**EXHIBIT 9**          **SHORT-RUN PERFECTLY COMPETITIVE EQUILIBRIUM**

Short-run equilibrium occurs at point *E*. The intersection of the industry supply and demand curves shown in Part (b) determines the price of $60 facing the firm shown in Part (a). Given this equilibrium price, the firm represented in Part (a) establishes its profit-maximizing output at 9 units per hour and earns an economic profit shown by the shaded area. Note in Part (b) that the short-run industry supply curve is the horizontal summation of the marginal cost (*MC*) curves of all individual firms above their minimum average variable cost points.

to *leave* an industry if it earns below-normal profits (negative economic profits) and that new firms may enter an industry in which earnings of established firms exceed normal profits (positive economic profits). This process of entry and exit of firms is the key to long-run equilibrium. If there are economic profits, new firms enter the industry and shift the short-run supply curve to the right. This increase in short-run supply causes the price to fall until economic profits reach zero in the long run. On the other hand, if there are economic losses in an industry, existing firms leave, causing the short-run supply curve to shift to the left, and the price rises. This adjustment continues until economic losses are eliminated and economic profits equal zero in the long run.

Exhibit 10 shows a typical firm in long-run equilibrium. Supply and demand for the market as a whole set the equilibrium price. Thus, in the long run, the firm faces an equilibrium price of $60. Following the $MR = MC$ rule, the firm produces an equilibrium output of 6 units per hour. At this output level, the firm earns a normal profit (zero economic profit) because marginal revenue (price) equals the minimum point on both the short-run average total cost curve (*SRATC*) and the long-run average cost curve (*LRAC*). Given the U-shaped *LRAC* curve, the firm is producing with the optimal factory size.

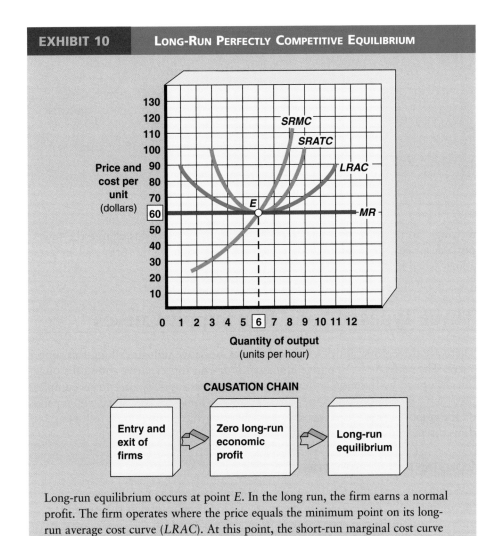

**EXHIBIT 10**        **LONG-RUN PERFECTLY COMPETITIVE EQUILIBRIUM**

**CAUSATION CHAIN**

Entry and exit of firms → Zero long-run economic profit → Long-run equilibrium

Long-run equilibrium occurs at point *E*. In the long run, the firm earns a normal profit. The firm operates where the price equals the minimum point on its long-run average cost curve (*LRAC*). At this point, the short-run marginal cost curve (*SRMC*) intersects both the short-run average total cost curve (*SRATC*) and the long-run average cost curve (*LRAC*) at their minimum points.

With *SRMC* representing short-run marginal cost, the conditions for long-run perfectly competitive equilibrium can also be expressed as an equality:

$$P = MR = SRMC = SRATC = LRAC$$

As long as none of the variables in the above formula changes, there is no reason for a perfectly competitive firm to change its output level, factory size, or any aspect of its operation. Everything is just right! Because the typical firm is in a state of equilibrium, the industry is also at rest. Under long-run equilibrium conditions, there are neither positive economic profits to attract new firms to enter the industry nor negative economic profits to force existing firms to leave. In long-run equilibrium, maximum efficiency is achieved. The adjustment process of firms

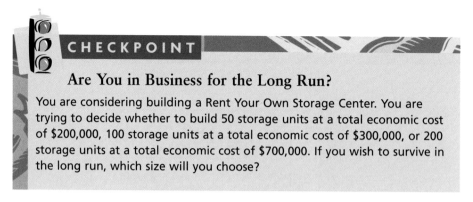

moving into or out of the industry is complete, and the firms charge the lowest possible price to consumers. Next, we will discuss how the firm and industry adjust when market demand changes.

# Three Types of Long-Run Supply Curves

**Perfectly competitive industry's long-run supply curve**
The curve that shows the quantities supplied by the industry at different equilibrium prices after firms complete their entry and exit.

There are three possibilities for a **perfectly competitive industry's long-run supply curve**. The perfectly competitive industry's long-run supply curve shows the quantities supplied by the industry at different equilibrium prices after firms complete their entry and exit. The shape of each of these long-run supply curves depends on the response of input prices as new firms enter the industry. The following sections discuss each of these three cases.

## CONSTANT-COST INDUSTRY

**Constant-cost industry**
An industry in which the expansion of industry output by the entry of new firms has no effect on the individual firm's average total cost curve.

In a **constant-cost industry,** input prices remain constant as new firms enter or exit the industry. A constant-cost industry is an industry in which the expansion of industry output by the entry of new firms has no effect on the firm's cost curves. Exhibit 11(a) reproduces the long-run equilibrium situation from Exhibit 10.

Begin in Part (b) of Exhibit 11 at the initial industry equilibrium point $E_1$ with short-run industry supply curve $S_1$ and industry demand curve $D_1$. Now assume the industry demand curve increases from $D_1$ to $D_2$. As a result, the industry equilibrium moves temporarily to $E_2$. Correspondingly, the equilibrium price rises from $60 to $80, and industry output increases from 50,000 to 70,000 units.

The short-run result for the individual firm in the industry happens this way. As shown in Part (a) of Exhibit 11, the firm takes the increase in price and adjusts its output from 6 to 7 units per hour. At the higher price and output, the firm changes from earning a normal profit to making an economic profit because the new price is above its *SRATC* curve. All the other firms in the industry make the same adjustment by moving upward along their *SRMC* curves.

In perfect competition, new firms are free to enter the industry in response to a profit opportunity, and they will do so. The addition of new firms shifts the short-run supply curve rightward from $S_1$ to $S_2$. Firms will continue to enter the industry until profit is eliminated. This occurs at equilibrium point $E_3$, where short-run industry demand curve $D_2$ intersects short-run supply curve $S_2$. Thus,

## EXHIBIT 11    LONG-RUN SUPPLY IN A CONSTANT-COST INDUSTRY

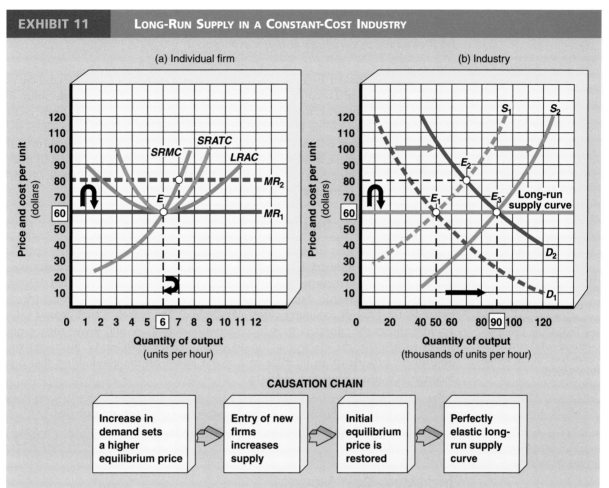

**CAUSATION CHAIN**

| Increase in demand sets a higher equilibrium price | ⇨ | Entry of new firms increases supply | ⇨ | Initial equilibrium price is restored | ⇨ | Perfectly elastic long-run supply curve |

Part (b) shows an industry in equilibrium at point $E_1$, producing 50,000 units per hour and selling them for $60 per unit. In Part (a), the firm is in equilibrium, producing 6 units per hour and earning a normal profit. Then industry demand increases from $D_1$ to $D_2$, and the equilibrium price rises to $80. Industry output rises temporarily to 70,000 units per hour, and the individual firm increases output to 7 units per hour. Firms are now earning an economic profit, which attracts new firms into the industry. In the long run, the entry of these firms causes the short-run supply curve to shift rightward from $S_1$ to $S_2$, the price is reestablished at $60, and a new industry equilibrium point, $E_3$, is established. At $E_3$, industry output rises to 90,000 units per hour, and the firm's output returns to 6 units per hour. Now the typical firm earns a normal profit, and new firms stop entering the industry. Connecting point $E_1$ to point $E_3$ generates the long-run supply curve.

the entry of new firms has restored the initial equilibrium price of $60. The firm responds by moving downward along its *SRMC* curve until it once again produces 6 units and earns a normal profit.

As shown in the exhibit, the path of these changes in industry short-run equilibrium points traces a horizontal line, which is the industry's long-run supply curve.

> **CONCLUSION** *The long-run supply curve in a perfectly competitive constant-cost industry is perfectly elastic.*

Now we reconsider Exhibit 11 and ask what happens when the demand curve shifts leftward from $D_2$ to $D_1$. Beginning in Part (b) at point $E_3$, the decrease in demand causes the price to fall temporarily below $60. As a result, firms incur short-run losses, and some firms leave the industry. The exodus of firms shifts the short-run supply curve leftward from $S_2$ to $S_1$, establishing a new equilibrium at point $E_1$. This decrease in supply restores the equilibrium price to the initial price of $60 per unit. Once equilibrium is reestablished at $E_1$, there is a smaller number of firms, each earning a normal profit.

## DECREASING-COST INDUSTRY

**Decreasing-cost industry**
An industry in which the expansion of industry output by the entry of new firms decreases the individual firm's average total cost curve (cost curve shifts downward).

Input prices fall as new firms enter a **decreasing-cost industry**, and output expands. A decreasing-cost industry is an industry in which the expansion of industry output by the entry of new firms decreases each individual firm's cost curve (cost curve shifts downward). For example, as production of electronic components expands, the price of computer chips may decline. The reason is that greater sales volume allows the suppliers to achieve *economies of scale* and lower their input prices to firms in the electronic components industry. Exhibit 12 illustrates the adjustment process of an increase in demand based on the assumption that our example is a decreasing-cost industry.

> **CONCLUSION** *The long-run supply curve in a perfectly competitive decreasing-cost industry is downward sloping.*

## INCREASING-COST INDUSTRY

**Increasing-cost industry**
An industry in which the expansion of industry output by the entry of new firms increases the individual firm's average total cost curve (cost curve shifts upward).

In an **increasing-cost industry**, input prices rise as new firms enter the industry, and output expands. As this type of industry uses more labor and machines, the demand for greater quantities of these inputs drives up input prices. An increasing-cost industry is an industry in which the expansion of industry output by the entry of new firms increases the individual firm's cost curve (cost curve shifts upward). Suppose the electronic component disc business uses a significant proportion of all electrical engineers in the country. In this case, electrical engineering salaries will rise as firms hire more electrical engineers to expand industry output. In practice, most industries are increasing-cost industries, and, therefore, the long-run supply curve is upward sloping.

Exhibit 13 shows what happens in an increasing-cost industry when an increase in demand causes output to expand. In Part (b), the industry is initially in equilibrium at point $E_1$. As in the previous case, the demand curve shifts rightward from $D_1$ to $D_2$, establishing a new short-run equilibrium at $E_2$. This movement upward along short-run industry supply curve $S_1$ raises the price in the short run from $60 to $80, resulting in profit for the typical firm. Once again, new firms enter the industry, and the short-run supply curve shifts rightward from $S_1$ to $S_2$. Part (a) of Exhibit 13 shows that the response of the firm's *SRATC* curve to

**EXHIBIT 12**    **LONG-RUN SUPPLY IN A DECREASING-COST INDUSTRY**

**CAUSATION CHAIN**

| Increase in demand sets a higher equilibrium price | ⇨ | Entry of new firms increases supply | ⇨ | Equilibrium price and ATC decrease | ⇨ | Downward-sloping long-run supply curve |

The long-run supply curve for a decreasing-cost industry is downward sloping. The increase in industry demand shown in Part (b) causes the price to rise to $80 in the short run. Temporarily, the individual firm illustrated in Part (a) earns an economic profit. Higher profits attract new firms, and supply increases. As the industry expands, the average total cost curve for the firm shifts lower, and the firm reestablishes long-run equilibrium at the lower price of $50.

the industry's expansion differs from the constant-cost industry case. In an increasing-cost industry, the firm's *SRATC* curve shifts upward from $SRATC_1$ to $SRATC_2$, corresponding to the new short-run equilibrium at point $E_3$. At this final equilibrium point, the price of $70 is higher than the initial price of $60. Normal profits are re-established because profits are squeezed from both the price fall and the rise in the *SRATC* curve.

The long-run industry supply curve is drawn by connecting the two long-run equilibrium points of $E_1$ and $E_3$. Equilibrium point $E_2$ is not a long-run equilibrium point because it is not established after the entry of new firms has restored normal profits.

**EXHIBIT 13     LONG-RUN SUPPLY IN AN INCREASING-COST INDUSTRY**

(a) Individual firm

(b) Industry

**CAUSATION CHAIN**

| Increase in demand sets a higher equilibrium price | ⇨ | Entry of new firms increases supply | ⇨ | Equilibrium price and *ATC* increase | ⇨ | Upward-sloping long-run supply curve |

This pair of graphs derives the long-run supply curve based on the assumption that input prices rise as industry output expands. Part (b) shows that an increase in demand from $D_1$ to $D_2$ causes the price to increase in the short run from $60 to $80. The individual firm represented in Part (a) earns an economic profit, and new firms enter the industry, causing an increase in industry supply from $S_1$ to $S_2$. As output expands, input prices rise and push up the firm's short-run average total cost curve from $SRATC_1$, to $SRATC_2$. As a result, a new long-run equilibrium price is established at $70, which is above the initial equilibrium price. The long-run supply curve for an increasing-cost industry is upward sloping.

**CONCLUSION** *The long-run supply curve in a perfectly competitive increasing-cost industry is upward sloping.*

Finally, given the three models presented, you may ask which is the best choice. The answer is that all three versions are possible for any given industry. Only direct observation of the industry can tell which type of industry it is.

## You're the Economist

# Gators Snapping Up Profits
*Applicable Concept: short-run and long-run competitive equilibrium*

In the late 1980s, many farmers who were tired of milking cows, roping steers, and slopping hogs decided to try their hands at a new animal. Anyone feeding this animal, however, could require a gun for protection.

Prior to the late 1970s, alligators were on the endangered species list. Under this protection, their numbers grew so large that wandering alligators became pests in Florida neighborhoods and police were exhausted from chasing them around. Consequently, the ban on hunting was removed, and shrewd entrepreneurs began seeking big profits by turning gators into farm animals. In fact, gator farming became one of Florida's fastest-growing businesses.

The gators spawned several hot industries. The lizard "look" came back into vogue, and the fashionable sported gator-skin purses, shoes, and belts. Chic didn't come cheap. In New York, gator cowboy boots sold for $1,800, and attaché cases retailed for $4,000. And you could order gator meat at trendy restaurants all along the East Coast. "Why not gator?" asked Red Lobster spokesman Dick Monroe. "Today's two-income households are looking for more variety. And they think it's neat to eat an animal that can eat them."

To meet the demand, Florida doubled the number of its licensed alligator farms compared to the previous four years, when they functioned almost entirely as tourist attractions. In 1985, Florida farmers raised 37,000 gators; in 1986, that figure increased by 50 percent. Revenues soared as well. Frank Godwin, owner of Gatorland in Orlando, netted an estimated $270,000 from the 1,000 animals he harvested annually. Improved technology was applied to gator farming in order to boost profits even higher. Lawler Wells, for example, owner of Hilltop Farms in Avon Park, raised 7,000 gators in darkened hothouses that accelerated their growth.[1]

Seven years later, a 1993 article in the *Washington Post* continued the gator tale: "During the late 1980s, gator ranching was booming, and the industry was being compared to a living gold mine. People rushed into the industry. Some farmers became temporarily rich."[2]

In 1995, a *USA Today* interview with a gator hunter provided evidence of long-run equilibrium: "Armed with a pistol barrel attached to the end of an 8-foot wooden pole, alligator hunter Bill Chaplin fires his 'bankstick' and dispatches a six-footer with a single round of .44 magnum ammunition. What's in it for him? Financially, very little. At $3.50 a pound for

the meat and $45 a foot for the hide, an alligator is worth perhaps $100 a foot. After paying for skinning and processing, neither hunter nor landowner gets rich."[3]

A 2000 article in the *Dallas Morning News* provided further evidence: Mark Glass, who began raising gators in 1995 south of Atlanta stated, "I can honestly say I haven't made any money yet, but I hope that's about to change."[4] And a 2003 article from *Knight Ridder/Tribune Business News* gave a pessimistic report for Florida: "Revenue from alligator harvesting has flattened in recent years, despite Florida's efforts to promote the alligator as part of a viable 'aquaculture' industry. It's a tough business."[5] And in 2005, Hurricane Katrina washed away a high percentage of the alligator nests.

### ANALYZE THE ISSUE

1. Draw short-run firm and industry competitive equilibriums for a perfectly competitive gator-farming industry before the number of alligator farms in Florida doubled. For simplicity, assume the gator farm is earning zero economic profit. Now show the short-run effect of an increase in demand for alligators.

2. Assuming gator farming is perfectly competitive, explain the long-run competitive equilibrium condition for the typical gator farmer and the industry as a whole.

[1] Ron Moreau and Penelope Wang, "Gators: Snapping Up Profits," *Newsweek*, Dec. 8, 1986, p. 68.

[2] William Booth, "Bag a Gator and Save the Species," *The Washington Post*, Aug. 25, 1993, p. A1.

[3] J. Taylor Buckley, "S. Carolina Lets Hunters Go for Gators Again," *USA Today*, Sept. 21, 1995, News Section, p. A1.

[4] "More Bite for the Buck," *Dallas Morning News*, Dec. 6, 2000, p. 2A.

[5] Jerry W. Jackson, "Alligators are Growing Part of Florida's Agricultural Landscape," *Knight Ridder/Tribune Business News*, Jan. 26, 2003.

## Key Concepts

Market structure
Perfect competition
Price taker
Marginal revenue (*MR*)
Perfectly competitive firm's
    short-run supply curve

Perfectly competitive industry's
    short-run supply curve
Perfectly competitive industry's
    long-run supply curve

Constant-cost industry
Decreasing-cost industry
Increasing-cost industry

## Summary

■ **Market structure** consists of three market characteristics: (1) the number of sellers, (2) the nature of the product, and (3) the ease of entry into or exit from the market.

■ **Perfect competition** is a market structure in which an individual firm cannot affect the price of the product it produces. Each firm in the industry is very small relative to the market as a whole, all the firms sell a homogeneous product, and firms are free to enter and exit the industry.

■ A **price-taker** firm in perfect competition faces a perfectly elastic demand curve. It can sell all it wishes at the market-determined price, but it will sell nothing above the given market price. This is because so many competitive firms are willing to sell the same product at the going market price.

■ The **total revenue-total cost method** is one way a firm determines the level of output that maximizes profit. Profit reaches a maximum when the vertical difference between the total revenue and the total cost curves is at a maximum.

### TOTAL REVENUE-TOTAL COST METHOD

■ The **marginal revenue equals marginal cost method** is a second approach to finding where a firm maximizes profits. **Marginal revenue (*MR*)** is the change in total revenue from a one-unit change in output. Marginal revenue for a perfectly competitive firm equals the market price. The *MR = MC* rule states that the firm maximizes profit or minimizes loss by producing the output where marginal revenue equals marginal cost. If the price (average revenue) is below the minimum point on the average variable cost curve, the *MR = MC* rule does not apply, and the firm shuts down to minimize its losses.

### MARGINAL REVENUE-MARGINAL COST METHOD

■ The **perfectly competitive firm's short-run supply curve** is a curve showing the relationship between the price of a product and the quantity supplied in the short run. The individual firm always produces along its marginal cost curve above its intersection with the average variable cost curve. The **perfectly competitive industry's short-run supply curve** is the horizontal summation of the short-run supply curves of all firms in the industry.

## SHORT-RUN SUPPLY CURVE

- **Long-run perfectly competitive equilibrium** occurs when a firm earns a normal profit by producing where price equals minimum long-run average cost equals minimum short-run average total cost equals short-run marginal cost.

## LONG-RUN PERFECTLY COMPETITIVE EQUILIBRIUM

- In a **constant-cost industry**, total output can be expanded without an increase in an individual firm's average total cost. Because input prices remain constant, the long-run supply curve in a constant-cost industry is perfectly elastic.

- In a **decreasing-cost industry**, lower input prices result in a downward-sloping industry long-run supply curve. As industry output expands, an individual firm's average total cost curve declines (shifts downward), and the long-run equilibrium market price falls.

- In an **increasing-cost industry**, input prices rise as industry output increases. As a result, an individual firm's average total cost curve rises (shifts upward), and the industry long-run supply curve for an increasing-cost industry is upward sloping.

## Summary of Conclusion Statements

- The large-number-of-sellers condition is met when each firm is so small relative to the total market that no single firm can influence the market price.

- If a product is homogeneous, buyers are indifferent as to which seller's product they buy.

- Perfect competition requires that resources be completely mobile to freely enter or exit a market.

- In perfect competition, the firm's marginal revenue equals the price that the firm views as a horizontal demand curve.

- In perfect competition, the firm maximizes profit or minimizes loss by producing the output where marginal revenue equals marginal cost.

- In perfect competition, if the price is below the minimum point on the *AVC* curve, each unit produced would not cover the variable cost per unit. Therefore, the firm shuts down.

- The long-run supply curve in a perfectly competitive constant-cost industry is perfectly elastic.

- The long-run supply curve in a perfectly competitive decreasing-cost industry is downward sloping.

- The long-run supply curve in a perfectly competitive increasing-cost industry is upward sloping.

## Study Questions and Problems

1. Explain why a perfectly competitive firm would or would not advertise.

2. Does a Kansas wheat farmer fit the perfectly competitive market structure? Explain.

3. Suppose the market equilibrium price of wheat is $2 per bushel in a perfectly competitive industry. Draw the industry supply and demand curves and the demand curve for a single wheat farmer. Explain why the wheat farmer is a price taker.

4. Assuming the market equilibrium price for wheat is $5 per bushel, draw the total revenue and the marginal revenue curves for the typical wheat farmer in the same graph. Explain how marginal revenue and price are related to the total revenue curve.

5. Consider the following cost data for a perfectly competitive firm in the short run:

| Output (Q) | Total fixed cost (TFC) | Total variable cost (TVC) | Total cost (TC) | Total revenue (TR) | Profit |
|---|---|---|---|---|---|
| 1 | $100 | $120 | $____ | $____ | $____ |
| 2 | 100 | 200 | ____ | ____ | ____ |
| 3 | 100 | 290 | ____ | ____ | ____ |
| 4 | 100 | 430 | ____ | ____ | ____ |
| 5 | 100 | 590 | ____ | ____ | ____ |

If the market price is $150, how many units of output will the firm produce in order to maximize profit in the short run? Specify the amount of economic profit or loss. At what level of output does the firm break even?

6. Consider this statement: "A firm should increase output when it makes a profit." Do you agree or disagree? Explain.

7. Consider this statement: "When marginal revenue equals marginal cost, total cost equals total revenue, and the firm makes zero profit." Do you agree or disagree? Explain.

8. Consider Exhibit 14, which shows the graph of a perfectly competitive firm in the short run.

a. If the firm's demand curve is $MR_3$, does the firm earn an economic profit or incur a loss?

b. Which demand curve(s) indicates the firm incurs a loss?

c. Which demand curve(s) indicates the firm would shut down?

d. Identify the firm's short-run supply curve.

**EXHIBIT 14  A PERFECTLY COMPETITIVE FIRM**

9. Consider this statement: "The perfectly competitive firm will sell all the quantity of output consumers will buy at the prevailing market price." Do you agree or disagree? Explain your answer.

10. Suppose a perfectly competitive firm's demand curve is below its average total cost curve. Explain the conditions under which a firm continues to produce in the short run.

11. Suppose the industry equilibrium price of residential housing construction is $100 per square foot and the minimum average variable cost for a residential construction contractor is $110 per square foot. What would you advise the owner of this firm to do? Explain.

12. Suppose independent truckers operate in a perfectly competitive industry. If these firms are earning positive economic profits, what happens in the long run to the following: the price of trucking services, the industry quantity of output, the profits of trucking firms? Given these conditions, is the independent trucking industry a constant-cost, an increasing-cost, or a decreasing-cost industry?

## Study Guide Questions

1. The _____ for a perfectly competitive firm is a curve showing the relationship between the price of a product and the quantity supplied in the short run. The individual firm always produces along its marginal cost curve above its intersection with the average variable cost curve.

2. In the short run, a perfectly competitive firm's *most* profitable level of output is where
   a. marginal cost exceeds marginal revenue.
   b. total revenue is at a maximum.
   c. marginal cost equals marginal revenue.
   d. all of the above.

3. In long-run equilibrium, the typical perfectly competitive firm will:
   a. earn zero economic profit.
   b. change plant size in the long run.
   c. change output in the short run.
   d. do any of the above.

4. Which of the following is *true* of a perfectly competitive firm?
   a. The firm is a price maker.
   b. If the firm wishes to maximize profits it will produce an output level in which total revenue equals total cost.
   c. The firm will not earn an economic profit in the long run.
   d. The firm's short-run supply curve is its *MC* curve below its *AVC* curve.

5. T  F  In long-run equilibrium, a perfectly competitive firm's short-run marginal cost curve crosses the long-run average cost curve at the lowest point on the long-run average cost curve.

**Answers to these questions are in the complete Study Guide at www.thomsonedu.com/thomsonnow.**

**For Online Exercises, go to the text Web site at www.thomsonedu.com/economics/tucker.**

## Checkpoint Answers

### Should Motels Offer Rooms at the Beach for Only $50 a Night?

As long as price exceeds average variable cost, the motel is better off operating than shutting down. Since $50 is more than enough to cover the guest-related variable costs of $45 per room, the firm will operate. The $5 remaining after covering variable costs can be put toward the $50 of fixed costs. Were the motel to shut down, it could make no contribution to these overhead costs. If you said the Myrtle Beach motels should operate during the winter because they can get a price that exceeds their average variable cost, **YOU ARE CORRECT.**

### Are You in Business for the Long Run?

In the long run, surviving firms will operate at the minimum of the long-run average cost curve. The average cost of 50 storage units is $4,000 ($200,000/50), the average cost of 100 storage units is $3,000 ($300,000/100), and the average cost of 200 storage units is $3,500 ($700,000/200). Of the three storage-unit quantities given, the one with the lowest average cost is closest to the minimum point on the *LRAC* curve. If you chose 100 storage units, **YOU ARE CORRECT.**

## Practice Quiz

For an explanation of the correct answers, please visit the tutorial at www.thomsonedu.com/economics/tucker.

1. A perfectly competitive market is *not* characterized by
   a. many small firms.
   b. a great variety of different products.
   c. free entry into and exit from the market.
   d. any of the above.

2. Which of the following is a characteristic of perfect competition?
   a. Entry barriers
   b. Homogeneous products
   c. Expenditures on advertising
   d. Quality of service

3. Which of the following are the same at all levels of output under perfect competition?
   a. Marginal cost and marginal revenue
   b. Price and marginal revenue
   c. Price and marginal cost
   d. All of the above

4. If a perfectly competitive firm sells 100 units of output at a market price of $100 per unit, its marginal revenue per unit is
   a. $1.
   b. $100.
   c. more than $1, but less than $100.
   d. less than $100.

5. Short-run profit maximization for a perfectly competitive firm occurs where the firm's marginal cost equals
   a. average total cost.
   b. average variable cost.
   c. marginal revenue.
   d. all of the above.

6. A perfectly competitive firm sells its output for $100 per unit, and the minimum average variable cost is $150 per unit. The firm should
   a. increase output.
   b. decrease output, but not shut down.
   c. maintain its current rate of output.
   d. shut down.

7. A perfectly competitive firm's supply curve follows the upward-sloping segment of its marginal cost curve above the
   a. average total cost curve.
   b. average variable cost curve.

   c. average fixed cost curve.
   d. average price curve.

### EXHIBIT 15  MARGINAL REVENUE AND COST PER UNIT CURVES

8. Assume the price of the firm's product in Exhibit 15 is $15 per unit. The firm will produce
   a. 500 units per week.
   b. 1,000 units per week.
   c. 1,500 units per week.
   d. 2,000 units per week.
   e. 2,500 units per week.

9. In Exhibit 15, the lowest price at which the firm earns zero economic profit in the short run is
   a. $5 per unit.
   b. $10 per unit.
   c. $20 per unit.
   d. $30 per unit.

10. Assume the price of the firm's product in Exhibit 15 is $6 per unit. The firm should
    a. continue to operate because it is earning an economic profit.
    b. stay in operation for the time being even though it is incurring an economic loss.
    c. shut down temporarily.
    d. shut down permanently.

11. Assume the price of the firm's product in Exhibit 15 is $10 per unit. The maximum profit the firm earns is
    a. zero.
    b. $5,000 per week.
    c. $1,500 per week.
    d. $10,500 per week.

12. In Exhibit 15, the firm's total revenue at a price of $10 per unit pays for
    a. a portion of total variable costs.
    b. a portion of total fixed costs.
    c. none of the total fixed costs.
    d. all of the total fixed costs and total variable costs.

13. As shown in Exhibit 15, the short-run supply curve for this firm corresponds to which segment of its marginal cost curve?
    a. *A* to *D* and all points above
    b. *B* to *D* and all points above
    c. *C* to *D* and all points above
    d. *B* to *C* only

14. In long-run equilibrium, the perfectly competitive firm's price is equal to which of the following?
    a. Short-run marginal cost
    b. Minimum short-run average total cost
    c. Marginal revenue
    d. All of the above

15. In a constant-cost industry, input prices remain constant as
    a. the supply of inputs fluctuates.
    b. firms encounter diseconomies of scale.
    c. workers become more experienced.
    d. firms enter and exit the industry.

16. Suppose that, in the long run, the price of feature films rises as the movie production industry expands. We can conclude that movie production is a (an)
    a. increasing-cost industry.
    b. constant-cost industry.
    c. decreasing-cost industry.
    d. marginal-cost industry.

17. Which of the following is *true* of a perfectly competitive market?
    a. If economic profits are earned, then the price will fall over time.
    b. In long-run equilibrium, $P = MR = SRMC = SRATC = LRAC$.
    c. A constant-cost industry exists when the entry of new firms has no effect on their cost curves.
    d. All of the above are true.

18. Suppose that in a perfectly competitive market, firms are making economic profits. In the long run, we can expect to see
    a. some firms leave.
    b. the market price rise.
    c. market supply shift to the left.
    d. economic profits become zero.
    e. production levels remaining the same as in the short run.

19. Assume the short-run average total cost for a perfectly competitive industry decreases as the output of the industry expands. In the long run, the industry supply curve will
    a. have a positive slope.
    b. have a negative slope.
    c. be perfectly horizontal.
    d. be perfectly vertical.

20. The long-run supply curve for a competitive constant-cost industry is:
    a. horizontal.
    b. vertical.
    c. upward sloping.
    d. downward sloping.

# Monopoly

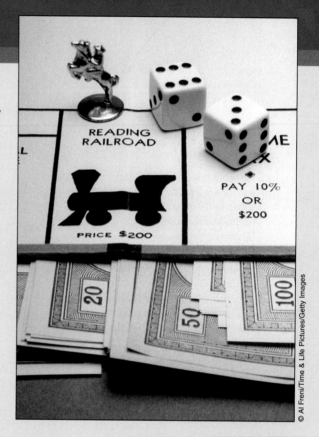

© Al Freni/Time & Life Pictures/Getty Images

Playing the popular board game of Monopoly teaches some of the characteristics of monopoly theory presented in this chapter. In the game version, players win by gaining as much economic power as possible. They strive to own railroads, utilities, Boardwalk, Park Place, and other valuable real estate. Then each player tries to bankrupt opponents by having hotels that charge high prices. A player who rolls the dice and lands on another player's property has no choice—either pay the price or lose the game.

In the last chapter, we studied perfect competition, which may be viewed as the paragon of economic virtue. Why? Under perfect competition, there are many sellers, each lacking any power to influence price. Perfect competition and monopoly are polar extremes. The word *monopoly* is derived from two Greek words meaning "single seller." A monopoly has the market power to set its price and not worry about competitors. Perhaps your college or university has only one bookstore where you can buy textbooks. If so, students are likely to pay higher prices for textbooks than they would if many sellers competed in the campus textbook market.

This chapter explains why firms do not or cannot enter a particular market and compete with a monopolist. Then we explore some of the interesting actual monopolies around the world. We study how a monopolist determines what price to charge and how much to produce. The chapter ends with a discussion of the pros and cons of monopoly. Most of the analytical tools required here have been introduced in previous chapters.

**In this chapter, you will learn to solve these economics puzzles:**

- Why doesn't the monopolist gouge consumers by charging the highest possible price?
- How can price discrimination be fair?
- Are medallion cabs in New York City monopolists?

## The Monopoly Market Structure

The model at the opposite extreme from perfect competition is monopoly. Under monopoly, the consumer has a simple choice—either buy the monopolist's product or do without it. Monopoly is a market structure characterized by (1) a single seller, (2) a unique product, and (3) impossible entry into the market. Unlike perfect competition, there are no close substitutes for the monopolist's product. **Monopoly**, like perfect competition, corresponds only approximately to real-world industries, but it serves as a useful benchmark model. Following are brief descriptions of each monopoly characteristic.

**Monopoly**
A market structure characterized by (1) a single seller, (2) a unique product, and (3) impossible entry into the market.

## SINGLE SELLER

In perfect competition, many firms make up the industry. In contrast, a monopoly means that a single firm *is* the industry. One firm provides the total supply of a product in a given market. Local monopolies are more common real-world approximations of the model than national or world market monopolies. For example, the campus bookstore, local telephone service, cable television company, and electric power company may be local monopolies. The only gas station in Nowhere County, Utah, and a hotdog stand at a football game are also examples of monopolies. Nationally, the U.S. Postal Service monopolizes first-class mail.

## UNIQUE PRODUCT

A unique product means there are *no close substitutes* for the monopolist's product. Thus, the monopolist faces little or no competition. In reality, however, there are few, if any, products that have no close substitutes. For example, students can buy used textbooks from sources other than the campus bookstore, and textbooks can be purchased over the Internet. Natural gas and oil furnaces are good substitutes for electric heat. Similarly, the fax machine and e-mail are substitutes for mail service, and a satellite dish can replace your local cable television service.

## IMPOSSIBLE ENTRY

In perfect competition, there are no constraints to prevent new firms from entering an industry. In the case of monopoly, extremely high barriers make it very difficult or impossible for new firms to enter an industry. Following are the three major barriers that prevent new firms from entering a market and competing with a monopolist.

### Ownership of a Vital Resource

Sole control of the entire supply of a strategic input is one way a monopolist can prevent a newcomer from entering an industry. A famous historical example is Alcoa's monopoly of the U.S. aluminum market from the late 19th century until the end of World War II. The source of Alcoa's monopoly was its control of bauxite ore, which is necessary to produce aluminum. Today, it is very difficult for a new professional sports league to compete with the National Football League (NFL) and the National Basketball Association (NBA). Why? NFL and NBA teams have contracts with the best players and leases for the best stadiums and arenas.

### Legal Barriers

The oldest and most effective barriers protecting a firm from potential competitors are the result of government franchises and licenses. The government permits a single firm to provide a certain product and excludes competing firms by law.

For example, water and sewer service, natural gas, and cable television operate under monopoly franchises established by state and local governments. In many states, the state government runs monopoly liquor stores and lotteries. The U.S. Postal Service has a government franchise to deliver first-class mail.

Government-granted licenses restrict entry into some industries and occupations. For example, the Federal Communications Commission (FCC) must license radio and television stations. In most states, physicians, lawyers, dentists, nurses, teachers, real estate agents, barbers, taxicabs, liquor stores, funeral homes, and other professions and businesses are required to have a license.

Patents and copyrights are another form of government barrier to entry. The government grants patents to inventors, thereby legally prohibiting other firms from selling the patented product for 17 years. Copyrights give creators of literature, art, music, and movies exclusive rights to sell or license their works. The purpose behind granting patents and copyrights is to encourage innovation and new products by guaranteeing exclusive rights to profit from new ideas for a limited period.

## Economies of Scale

Why might competition among firms be unsustainable so that one firm becomes a monopolist? Recall the concept of *economies of scale* from the chapter on production costs. As a result of large-scale production, the long-run average cost (*LRAC*) of production falls. This means a monopoly can emerge in time *naturally* because of the relationship between average cost and the scale of an operation. As a firm becomes larger, its cost per unit of output is lower compared to a smaller competitor. In the long run, this "survival of the fittest" cost advantage forces smaller firms to leave the industry. Because new firms cannot hope to produce and sell output equal or close to that of the monopolist, thereby achieving the monopolist's low costs, they will not enter the industry. Thus, a monopoly can arise over time and remain dominant in an industry even though the monopolist does not own an essential resource or obtain legal barriers.

**Natural monopoly**
An industry in which the long-run average cost of production declines throughout the entire market. As a result, a single firm can supply the entire market demand at a lower cost than two or more smaller firms.

Economists call the situation in which one seller emerges in an industry because of economies of scale a **natural monopoly**. A natural monopoly is an industry in which the long-run average cost of production declines throughout the entire market. As a result, a single firm can supply the entire market demand at a lower cost than two or more smaller firms. Public utilities, such as the natural gas, water, and local telephone companies, are examples of natural monopolies. The government grants these industries an exclusive franchise in a geographic area so consumers can benefit from the cost savings that occur when one firm in an industry with significant economies of scale sells a large output. The government then regulates these monopolies to prevent exploitation.

Exhibit 1 depicts the *LRAC* curve for a natural monopoly. A single firm can produce 100 units at an average cost of $15 and a total cost of $1,500. If two firms each produce 50 units, the total cost rises to $2,500. With five firms producing 20 units each, the total cost rises to $3,500. In the chapter on antitrust and regulation, regulation of a natural monopoly will be explored in greater detail.

**CONCLUSION** *Because of economies of scale, a single firm in an industry will produce output at a lower per-unit cost than two or more firms.*

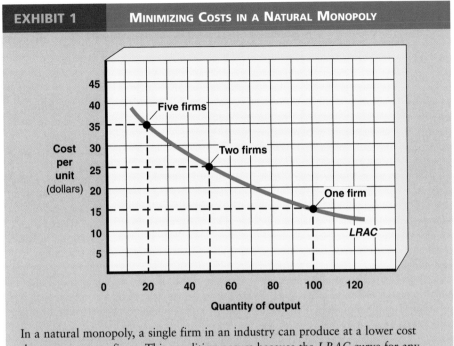

**EXHIBIT 1** | **MINIMIZING COSTS IN A NATURAL MONOPOLY**

In a natural monopoly, a single firm in an industry can produce at a lower cost than two or more firms. This condition occurs because the *LRAC* curve for any firm decreases over the relevant range. For example, one firm can produce 100 units at an average cost of $15 and a total cost of $1,500. Two firms in the industry can produce 100 units of output (50 units each) for a total cost of $2,500, and five firms can produce the same output for a total cost of $3,500.

# Price and Output Decisions for a Monopolist

A major difference between perfect competition and monopoly is the shape of the demand curve, not the shapes of the cost curves. As explained in the previous chapter, a perfectly competitive firm is a *price taker*. In contrast, the next sections explain that a monopolist is a **price maker**. A price maker is a firm that faces a downward-sloping demand curve. This means a monopolist has the ability to select the product's price. In short, a monopolist can set the price with its corresponding level of output, rather than being a helpless pawn at the mercy of the going industry price. To understand the monopolist, we again apply the marginal approach to our hypothetical electronics company—Computech.

**Price maker**
A firm that faces a downward-sloping demand curve and therefore it can choose among price and output combinations along the demand curve.

## MARGINAL REVENUE, TOTAL REVENUE, AND PRICE ELASTICITY OF DEMAND

Suppose engineers at Computech discover an inexpensive miracle electronic device called SAV-U-GAS that anyone can easily attach to a car's engine. Once installed, the device raises gasoline mileage to over 100 miles per gallon. The government grants Computech a patent, and the company becomes a monopolist selling this gas-saver gizmo. Because of this barrier to entry, Computech is the only

## International Economics

# Monopolies around the World
*Applicable Concept: monopoly*

Interesting examples of monopolies can be found in other countries. Let's begin with a historical example. In the sixteenth through eighteenth centuries, monarchs granted monopoly rights for a variety of businesses. For example, in 1600 Queen Elizabeth I chartered the British East India Company and gave it a monopoly over England's trade with India. This company was even given the right to coin money and to make peace or war with non-Christian powers. As a result of its monopoly, the company made substantial profits from the trade in Indian cotton goods, silks, and spices. In the late 1700s, the growing power of the company and huge personal fortunes of its officers provoked more and more government control. Finally, in 1858, the company was abolished, ending its trade monopoly, great power, and patronage.

"Diamonds are forever," and perhaps so is the diamond monopoly. DeBeers, a South African corporation, was close to a world monopoly. Through its Central Selling Organization (CSO) headquartered in London, DeBeers controlled 80 percent of all the diamonds sold in the world. DeBeers controlled the price of jewelry-quality diamonds by requiring suppliers in Russia, Australia, Congo, Botswana, Namibia, and other countries to

© Photodisc/Getty Images

sell their rough diamonds through DeBeers's CSO. Why did suppliers of rough diamonds allow DeBeers to set the price and quantity of diamonds sold throughout the world? The answer was that the CSO could put any uncooperative seller out of business. All the CSO had to do was to reach into its huge stockpile of diamonds and flood the market with the type of diamonds being sold by an independent seller. As a result, the price of diamonds would plummet in the competitor's market, and it ceased to sell diamonds.

In recent years, DeBeers lost some of its control of the market. Mines in Australia became more independent, diamonds were found in Canada, and Russian mines began selling to independents. To deal with the new conditions, DeBeers changed its policy in 2001 by closing the CSO and promoting DeBeers own brand of diamonds rather than trying to control the world diamond supply. DeBeers proclaimed its strategy to be "the diamond

supplier of choice." Will this monopoly continue? It is an interesting question.

Genuine caviar, the salty black delicacy, is naturally scarce because it comes from the eggs of sturgeon harvested by fisheries from the Caspian Sea near the mouth of the Volga River. After the Bolshevik Revolution in Russia in 1917, a caviar monopoly was established under the control of the Soviet Ministry of Fisheries and the Paris-based Petrosian Company. The Petrosian brothers limited exports of caviar and pushed prices up as high as $1,000 a pound for some varieties. As a result of this worldwide monopoly, both the Soviet government and the Petrosian Company earned handsome profits. It is interesting to note that the vast majority of the tons of caviar harvested each year was consumed at government banquets or sold at bargain prices to top Communist Party officials.

With the fall of the Soviet Union, it was impossible for the Ministry of Fisheries to control all exports of caviar. Various former Soviet republics claimed jurisdiction and negotiated independent export contracts. Caviar export prices dropped sharply. But caviar lovers should not be too overjoyed. Today, the supply of caviar is dwindling because of overfishing and pollution of the Volga.

seller in the industry. Although other firms try to compete with this invention, they create poor substitutes. This means the downward-sloping demand curve for the industry and for the monopolist are identical.

Exhibit 2(a) illustrates the demand and the marginal revenue (*MR*) curves for a monopolist such as Computech. As the monopolist lowers its price to increase the quantity demanded, changes in both price and quantity affect the firm's total revenue (price times quantity), as shown graphically in Exhibit 2(b). If Computech charges $150, consumers purchase zero units, and, therefore, total revenue is zero. To sell 1 unit, Computech must lower the price to $138, and total revenue rises from zero to $138. Because the marginal revenue is the increase in total revenue that results from a 1-unit change in output, the *MR* curve at the first unit of output is $138 ($138 − 0). Thus, the price and the marginal revenue from selling 1 unit are equal at $138. To sell 2 units, the monopolist must lower the price to $125, and total revenue rises to $250. The marginal revenue from selling the second unit is $112 ($250 − $138), which is $13 less than the price received.

As shown in Exhibit 2(a), as the monopolist lowers its price, price is greater than marginal revenue after the first unit of output. Like all marginal measurements, marginal revenue is plotted midway between the quantities.

> **CONCLUSION** *The demand and marginal revenue curves of the monopolist are downward sloping, in contrast to the horizontal demand and corresponding marginal revenue curves facing the perfectly competitive firm [compare Exhibit 2(a) with Exhibit 1(b) of the previous chapter].*

Starting from zero output, as the price falls, total revenue rises until it reaches a maximum at 6 units, and then it falls, tracing the "revenue hill" drawn in Part (b). The explanation was presented earlier in the discussion of price elasticity of demand in Chapter 5. Recall that a straight-line demand curve has an elastic ($E_d > 1$) segment along the upper half, a unit elastic ($E_d = 1$) at the midpoint, and an inelastic ($E_d < 1$) segment along the lower half (see Exhibit 4 in Chapter 5). Recall from Chapter 5 that when $E_d > 1$, total revenue rises as the price drops, and total revenue reaches a maximum where $E_d = 1$. When $E_d < 1$, total revenue falls as the price falls.

As shown in Exhibit 2(b), total revenue for a monopolist is related to marginal revenue. When the *MR* curve is above the quantity axis (elastic demand), total revenue is increasing. At the intersection of the *MR* curve and the quantity axis (unit elastic demand), total revenue is at its maximum. When the *MR* curve is below the quantity axis, total revenue is decreasing (inelastic demand). The monopolist will never operate on the inelastic range of its demand curve that corresponds to a negative marginal revenue. The reason is that, in this inelastic range, the monopolist can increase total revenue by cutting output and raising price. In our example, Computech would not charge a price lower than $75 or produce an output greater than 6 units per hour. Now we turn to the question of what price the monopolist will charge to maximize profit.

In Exhibit 2(a), observe that the *MR* curve cuts the quantity axis at 6 units, which is half of 12 units. Following an easy rule helps locate the point along the quantity axis where marginal revenue equals zero: *The marginal revenue curve for a straight-line demand curve intersects the quantity axis halfway between the origin and the quantity axis intercept of the demand curve.*

## EXHIBIT 2          DEMAND, MARGINAL REVENUE, AND TOTAL REVENUE FOR A MONOPOLIST

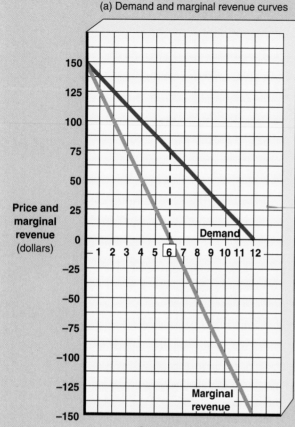

(a) Demand and marginal revenue curves

(b) Total revenue curve

Part (a) shows the relationship between the demand and the marginal revenue curves. The *MR* curve is below the demand curve. Between zero and 6 units of output, *MR* > 0; at 6 units of output, *MR* = 0; beyond 6 units of output, *MR* < 0.

The relationship between demand and total revenue is shown in Part (b). When the price is $150, total revenue is zero. When the price is set at zero, total revenue is also zero. In between these two extreme prices, the price of $75 maximizes total revenue. This price corresponds to 6 units of output, which is where the *MR* curve intersects the quantity axis, halfway between the origin and the intercept of the demand curve.

| Output per hour | Price | Total revenue | Marginal revenue |
|---|---|---|---|
| 0 | $150 | $ 0 | |
| | | | $138 |
| 1 | 138 | 138 | |
| | | | 112 |
| 2 | 125 | 250 | |
| | | | 89 |
| 3 | 113 | 339 | |
| | | | 61 |
| 4 | 100 | 400 | |
| | | | 40 |
| 5 | 88 | 440 | |
| | | | 10 |
| 6 | 75 | 450 | |
| | | | 0 |
| 7 | 63 | 441 | |
| | | | −9 |
| 8 | 50 | 400 | |
| | | | −41 |
| 9 | 38 | 342 | |
| | | | −58 |
| 10 | 25 | 250 | |
| | | | −92 |
| 11 | 13 | 143 | |
| | | | −107 |
| 12 | 0 | 0 | |
| | | | −143 |

## SHORT-RUN PROFIT MAXIMIZATION FOR A MONOPOLIST USING THE TOTAL REVENUE–TOTAL COST METHOD

Exhibit 3 reproduces the demand, total revenue, and marginal revenue data from Exhibit 2 and adds cost data from the previous two chapters. These data illustrate a situation in which Computech can earn monopoly economic profit in the short run. Subtracting total cost in column 6 from total revenue in column 3 gives the total profit or loss in column 8 that the firm earns at each level of output. From zero to 1 unit, the monopolist incurs losses, and then a break-even point occurs before 2 units per hour. If the monopolist produces 5 units per hour, it earns the maximum profit of $190 per hour. As output expands between 5 and 8 units of output, the monopolist's profit diminishes. After 8 units of output, there is a second break-even point, and losses increase as output expands. Exhibit 4 illustrates graphically that the vertical distance between the total revenue and total cost curves corresponds to the profit-maximizing output. Note that the total revenue-maximizing output level of 6 units is greater than the profit-maximizing output at 5 units.

| EXHIBIT 3 | SHORT-RUN PROFIT MAXIMIZATION SCHEDULE FOR COMPUTECH AS A MONOPOLIST | | | | | | |
|---|---|---|---|---|---|---|---|
| (1) Output per hour (Q) | (2) Price per unit (P) | (3) Total revenue (TR) | (4) Marginal revenue (MR) | (5) Marginal cost (MC) | (6) Total cost (TC) | (7) Average total cost (ATC) | (8) Profit (+) or loss (−) |
| 0 | $150 | $ 0 | | | $100 | — | −$100 |
| | | | $138 | $50 | | | |
| 1 | 138 | 138 | | | 150 | $150 | −12 |
| | | | 112 | 34 | | | |
| 2 | 125 | 250 | | | 184 | 92 | 66 |
| | | | 89 | 24 | | | |
| 3 | 113 | 339 | | | 208 | 69 | 131 |
| | | | 61 | 19 | | | |
| 4 | 100 | 400 | | | 227 | 57 | 173 |
| | | | 40 | 23 | | | |
| 5 | 88 | 440 | | | 250 | 50 | 190 |
| | | | 10 | 30 | | | |
| 6 | 75 | 450 | | | 280 | 47 | 170 |
| | | | −9 | 38 | | | |
| 7 | 63 | 441 | | | 318 | 45 | 123 |
| | | | −41 | 48 | | | |
| 8 | 50 | 400 | | | 366 | 46 | 34 |
| | | | −58 | 59 | | | |
| 9 | 38 | 342 | | | 425 | 47 | −83 |
| | | | −92 | 75 | | | |
| 10 | 25 | 250 | | | 500 | 50 | −250 |
| | | | −107 | 95 | | | |
| 11 | 13 | 143 | | | 595 | 54 | −452 |
| | | | −143 | 117 | | | |
| 12 | 0 | 0 | | | 712 | 59 | −712 |

**EXHIBIT 4**    **Short-Run Profit Maximization for a Monopolist Using the Total Revenue–Total Cost Method**

The profit-maximizing level of output for Computech as a monopolist is shown in this exhibit. Part (a) shows that maximum profit is earned by producing 5 units per hour and charging a price of $88 per unit where the vertical distance between the total revenue and total cost curves is the greatest. In Part (b), the maximum profit of $190 per hour corresponds to the profit-maximizing output of 5 units per hour illustrated in Part (a). At output levels below 2 or above 8, the monopolist incurs losses.

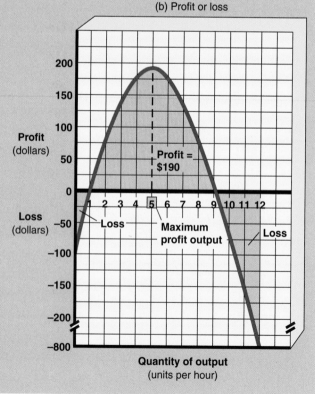

## SHORT-RUN PROFIT MAXIMIZATION FOR A MONOPOLIST USING THE MARGINAL REVENUE EQUALS MARGINAL COST METHOD

Exhibit 5 reproduces the demand and cost curves from the table in Exhibit 3. Like the perfectly competitive firm, a monopolist maximizes profit by producing the quantity of output where $MR = MC$ and charging the corresponding price on its demand curve. In this case, 5 units is the quantity at which $MR = MC$. As represented by point A on the demand curve, the price at 5 units is $88. Point B represents an average total cost (*ATC*) of $50 at 5 units. Because the price of $88 is above the *ATC* curve at the $MR = MC$ output, the monopolist earns a profit of $38 per unit. At the hourly output of 5 units, total profit is $190 per hour, as shown by the shaded area ($38 per unit × 5 units).

Observe that a monopolist charges neither the highest possible price nor the total revenue-maximizing price. In Exhibit 5(a), $88 is not the highest possible price. Because Computech is a *price maker*, it could have set a price above $88 and sold less output than 5 units. However, the monopolist does not maximize profit by charging the highest possible price. Any price above $88 does not correspond to the intersection of the *MR* and *MC* curves. Now note that 5 units is below the output level where *MR* intersects the quantity axis and total revenue reaches its peak. Since $MR = 0$ and $E_d = 1$ when total revenue is maximum at 6 units of output, $MC = 0$ must also hold to maximize revenue and profit at the same time. A monopolist producing with zero marginal cost is an unlikely case. Hence, the price charged to maximize profit is higher on the demand curve than the price that maximizes total revenue.

> **CONCLUSION** *The monopolist always maximizes profit by producing at a price on the elastic segment of its demand curve.*

### A MONOPOLIST FACING A SHORT-RUN LOSS

Having a monopoly does not guarantee profits. A monopolist has no protection against changes in demand or cost conditions. Exhibit 6 shows a situation in which the demand curve is lower at any point than the *ATC* curve, and total cost therefore exceeds total revenue at any price charged. Because the point where $MR = MC$ at a price of $50 (point A) on the demand curve is above the *AVC* curve, but below the *ATC* curve, the best Computech can do is to minimize its loss. This means the monopolist, like the perfectly competitive firm, produces in the short run at a quantity of 5 units per hour where $MR = MC$. At a price of $50 (point A), the *ATC* is $70 (point B), and Computech incurs a loss of $100 per hour, represented by the shaded area ($20 × 5 units).

What if $MR = MC$ at a price on the demand curve that is below the *AVC* for a monopolist? As under perfect competition, the monopolist will shut down. To operate would only add further to its losses.

### MONOPOLY IN THE LONG RUN

In perfect competition, economic profits are impossible in the long run. The entry of new firms into the industry drives the product's price down until profits reach zero. Extremely high barriers to entry, however, protect a monopolist.

**EXHIBIT 5**        **SHORT-RUN PROFIT FOR A MONOPOLIST MAXIMIZATION USING THE MARGINAL REVENUE EQUALS MARGINAL COST METHOD**

Part (a) illustrates a monopolist electronics firm, Computech, maximizing profit by producing 5 units of output where the marginal revenue (*MR*) and the marginal cost (*MC*) curves intersect. The profit-maximizing price the monopolist charges at 5 units of output is $88, which is point *A* on the demand curve. Because $88 is above the average total cost (*ATC*) of $50 at point *B*, the monopolist earns a short-run profit of $190 per hour, represented by the shaded area ($38 profit per unit × 5 units).

At a price of $88 and output of 5 units per hour in Part (a), the shaded area in Part (b) shows that the profit curve is maximized at $190 per hour. At output levels below 2 or above 8, the monopolist incurs losses.

(a) Price, marginal revenue, and cost per unit

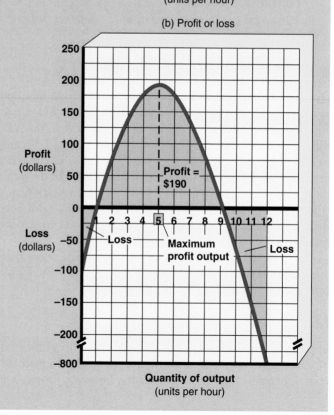

(b) Profit or loss

**EXHIBIT 6**

**SHORT-RUN LOSS MINIMIZATION FOR A MONOPOLIST USING THE MARGINAL REVENUE EQUALS MARGINAL COST METHOD**

In Part (a), all points along the demand curve lie below the *ATC* curve. If the market price charged corresponds to the output where the marginal revenue (*MR*) and marginal cost (*MC*) curves intersect, the firm will keep its loss to a minimum. At point *A*, the loss-minimizing price is $50 per unit, and marginal revenue equals marginal cost at an output of 5 units per hour with *ATC* equal to $70 per unit (point *B*). The short-run loss represented by the shaded area is $100 ($20 loss per unit × 5 units).

Part (b) shows that the firm's short-run loss will be greater at any output other than where the marginal revenue and the marginal cost curves intersect at an output of 5 units per hour. Because the price of $50 is above the average variable cost, each unit of output sold pays for the average variable cost and a portion of the average fixed cost.

(a) Price, marginal revenue, and cost per unit

(b) Loss

## You're the Economist

### The Standard Oil Monopoly
*Applicable Concept: monopoly*

**O**il was discovered in western Pennsylvania by Colonel Edwin L. Drake in 1859, and after the Civil War, oil wells sprang up across the landscape. Because oil was plentiful, there was cutthroat competition, and the result was low prices and profits. At this time, John D. Rockefeller, who had grown up selling eggs, was a young Cleveland produce wholesaler in his early twenties. He was doing well in produce, but realized that greater profits could be made in refining oil, where there was less competition than in drilling for oil. So, in 1869, Rockefeller borrowed all the money he could and began with two small oil refineries.

To boost his market power, Rockefeller's Standard Oil of Ohio negotiated secret agreements with the railroads. In addition to information on his competitors' shipments, Rockefeller negotiated contracts with the railroads to pay rebates not only on Standard Oil's oil shipments, but also on its competitors' shipments. Soon Standard Oil was able to buy 21 of its 26 refining competitors in the Cleveland area. As its

profits grew, Standard Oil expanded its refining empire by acquiring its own oil fields, railroads, pipelines, and ships. The objective was to control oil from the oil well to the consumer. Over time, Rockefeller came to own a major part of the petroleum industry. Competitors found railroads and pipelines closed to their oil shipments. Rivals that could not be forced out of business were merged with Standard Oil.

In 1870, Standard Oil controlled only 10 percent of the oil industry in the United States. By 1880, Standard Oil controlled over 90 percent of the industry, and its oil was being shipped throughout the world. The more Standard Oil monopolized the petroleum industry, the higher its profits rose, and the greater its power to eliminate competition became. As competitors dropped out of the industry, Rockefeller became a price maker. He raised prices, and Standard Oil's profits soared. Finally, in 1911, Standard Oil was broken up under the Sherman Antitrust Act of 1890.

**CONCLUSION** *If the positions of a monopolist's demand and cost curves give it a profit and nothing disturbs these curves, the monopolist will earn profit in the long run.*

In the long run, the monopolist has great flexibility. The monopolist can alter its plant size to lower cost just as a perfectly competitive firm does. But firms such as Computech will not remain in business in the long run when losses persist—regardless of their monopoly status. Facing long-run losses, the monopolist will transfer its resources to a more profitable industry.

In reality, no monopolist can depend on barriers to protect it fully from competition in the long run. One threat is that entrepreneurs will find innovative ways to compete with a monopoly. For example, Computech must fear that firms will use their ingenuity and new electronic discoveries to develop a better and cheaper gasoline-saving device. To dampen the enthusiasm of potential rivals, one alternative for the monopolist is to sacrifice short-run profits to earn greater profits in the long run. Returning to Part (a) of Exhibit 5, the monopolist might wish to charge a price below $88 and produce an output greater than 5 units per hour.

# Price Discrimination

Our discussion so far has assumed the monopolist charges each customer the same price. What if Computech decides to sell identical SAV-U-GAS units for, say, $50 to truckers and $100 to everyone else? Under certain conditions, a monopolist may practice **price discrimination** to maximize profit. Price discrimination occurs when a seller charges different prices for the same product that are not justified by cost differences.

**Price discrimination**
The practice of a seller charging different prices for the same product that are not justified by cost differences.

## CONDITIONS FOR PRICE DISCRIMINATION

All monopolists cannot engage in price discrimination. The following three conditions must exist before a seller can price discriminate:

1. The seller must be a price maker and therefore face a downward-sloping demand curve. This means that monopoly is not the only market structure in which price discrimination may occur.
2. The seller must be able to segment the market by distinguishing between consumers willing to pay different prices. Momentarily, this separation of buyers will be shown to be based on different price elasticities of demand.
3. It must be impossible or too costly for customers to engage in **arbitrage**. Arbitrage is the practice of earning a profit by buying a good at a low price and reselling the good at a higher price. For example, suppose your campus bookstore tried to boost profits by selling textbooks at a 50 percent discount to seniors. It would not take seniors long to cut the bookstore's profits by buying textbooks at the low price, selling these texts under the list price to all students who are not seniors, and pocketing the difference. In so doing, even without knowing the word *arbitrage*, the seniors would destroy the bookstore's price discrimination scheme.

**Arbitrage**
The practice of earning a profit by buying a good at a low price and reselling the good at a higher price.

Although not monopolies, college and university tuition policies meet the conditions for price discrimination. First, lower tuition increases the quantity of openings demanded. Second, applicants' high school grades and SAT scores allow the admissions office to classify "consumers" with different price elasticities of demand. Students with lower grades and SAT scores have fewer substitutes, and their demand curve is less elastic than that of students with higher grades and SAT scores. If the tuition rises at University X, few students with lower grades will be lost because they have few offers of admission from other universities. On the other hand, the loss of students with higher grades and SAT scores is greater because they have more admissions opportunities. Third, the nature of the product prevents arbitrage. A student cannot buy University X admission at one tuition price and sell it to another student for a higher price.

Exhibit 7 illustrates how University X price discriminates. For simplicity, assume the marginal cost of providing education to students is constant and therefore is represented by a horizontal $MC$ curve. To maximize profit, University X follows the $MR = MC$ rule in each market. Given the different price elasticities of demand, the price at which $MR = MC$ differs for average and superior students. As a result, University X sets a higher tuition, $T_1$, in the average-student market, where demand is less responsive to the higher price. In the superior-student market, where demand is more responsive, these students receive scholarships, and their tuition is lower at $T_2$.

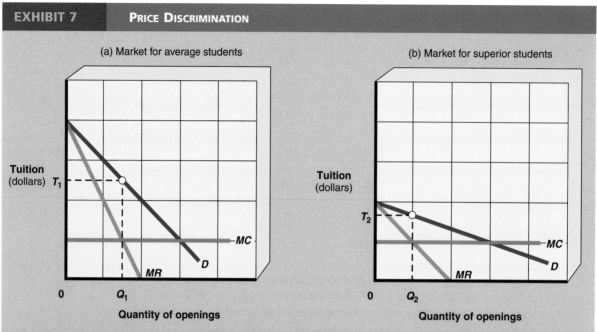

**EXHIBIT 7**  **PRICE DISCRIMINATION**

To maximize profit, University X separates students applying for admission into two markets. The demand curve for admission of average students in Part (a) is less elastic than the demand curve for admission of superior students in Part (b). Profit maximization occurs when $MR = MC$ in each market. Therefore, University X sets a tuition of $T_1$ for average students and gives scholarships to superior students, which lowers their tuition to $T_2$. Using price discrimination, University X earns a greater profit than it would by charging a single tuition to all students.

## IS PRICE DISCRIMINATION UNFAIR?

Examples of price discrimination abound. Movie theaters offer lower prices for children than for adults. Electric utilities, which are monopolies, charge industrial users of electricity lower rates than residential users. Hotels and restaurants often give discounts to senior citizens. Airlines offer lower fares to groups of vacationers.

The typical reaction to price discrimination is that it is unfair. From the viewpoint of buyers who pay the higher prices, it is. But look at the other side of price discrimination. First, the seller is pleased because price discrimination increases profits. Second, many buyers benefit from price discrimination by not being excluded from purchasing the product. In Exhibit 7, price discrimination makes it possible for superior students who could not afford to pay a higher tuition to attend University X. Price discrimination also allows retired persons to enjoy hotels and restaurants they could not otherwise afford and enables more children to attend movies.

## Comparing Monopoly and Perfect Competition

Now that the basics of the two extremes of perfect competition and monopoly have been presented, we can compare and evaluate these market structures. This

## CHECKPOINT

### Why Don't Adults Pay More for Popcorn at the Movies?

At the movies, adults pay a higher ticket price than children, and each group gets a different-colored ticket. However, when adults and children go to the concession stand, both groups pay the same amount for popcorn and other snacks. Which of the following statements best explains why price discrimination stops at the ticket window? (1) The demand curve for popcorn is perfectly elastic. (2) The theater has no way to divide the buyers of popcorn based on different price elasticities of demand. (3) The theater cannot prevent resale.

is an important assessment because the contrast between the disadvantages of monopoly and the advantages of perfect competition is the basis for many government policies, such as antitrust laws. To keep the analysis simple, we assume the monopolist charges a single price, rather than engaging in price discrimination.

## THE MONOPOLIST AS A RESOURCE MISALLOCATOR

Recall the discussion of market efficiency in Chapter 4. This condition exists when a firm charging the equilibrium price uses neither too many nor too few resources to produce a product, so there is no *market failure*. Now you can state this definition of market efficiency in terms of price and marginal cost, as follows: *A perfectly competitive firm that produces the quantity of output at which* $P = MC$ *achieves an efficient allocation of resources*. This means production reaches the level of output when the price of the last unit produced matches the cost of producing it.

Exhibit 8(a) shows that a perfectly competitive firm produces the quantity of output at which $P = MC$. The price, $P_c$ (marginal benefit), of the last unit produced equals the marginal cost of the resources used to produce it. In contrast, the monopolist shown in Exhibit 8(b) charges a price, $P_m$, greater than marginal cost, $P > MC$. Therefore, consumers are shortchanged because the marginal benefit of the last unit produced exceeds the marginal cost of producing it. Consumers want the monopolist to use more resources and produce additional units, but the monopolist restricts output to maximize profit.

> **CONCLUSION** *A monopolist is characterized by inefficiency because resources are underallocated to the production of its product.*

## PERFECT COMPETITION MEANS MORE OUTPUT FOR LESS

Exhibit 9 presents a comparison of perfect competition and monopoly in the same graph. Suppose the industry begins as perfectly competitive. The market demand curve, $D$ (equal to $MR$), and the market supply curve, $S$, establish a perfectly

## EXHIBIT 8        COMPARING A PERFECTLY COMPETITIVE FIRM AND A MONOPOLIST

The perfectly competitive firm in Part (a) sets $P = MC$ and produces $Q_c$ output. Therefore, at the last unit of output, the marginal benefit is equal to the marginal cost of resources used to produce it. This condition means perfect competition achieves efficiency.

Part (b) shows that the monopolist produces output $Q_m$ where $P > MC$. By so doing, consumers are short-changed because the marginal benefit of the last unit produced exceeds the marginal cost of producing it. Under monopoly, inefficiency occurs because the monopolist underallocates resources to the production of its product. As a result, $Q_m$ is less than $Q_c$.

competitive price, $P_c$, and output, $Q_c$. Recall Exhibit 8 in the previous chapter that the competitive industry's supply curve, $S$, is the horizontal sum of the marginal cost ($MC$) curves of all the firms in the industry.

Now let's suppose the market structure changes when one firm buys out all the competing firms and the industry becomes a monopoly. Assume further that the demand and cost curves are unaffected by this dramatic change. In a monopoly, the industry demand curve *is* the monopolist's demand curve. Because the single firm is a price maker, the $MR$ curve lies below the demand curve. The industry supply curve now becomes the $MC$ curve for the monopolist. To maximize profit, the monopolist sets $MR = MC$ by restricting the output to $Q_m$ and raising the price to $P_m$.

**CONCLUSION** *Monopoly harms consumers on two fronts. The monopolist charges a higher price and produces a lower output than would result under a perfectly competitive market structure.*

| EXHIBIT 9 | THE IMPACT OF MONOPOLIZING AN INDUSTRY |
|---|---|

Assume an industry is perfectly competitive, with market demand curve $D$ and market supply curve $S$. The market supply curve is the horizontal summation of all the individual firms' marginal cost curves above their minimum average variable costs. The intersection of market supply and market demand establishes the equilibrium price of $P_c$ and the equilibrium quantity of $Q_c$. Now assume the industry suddenly changes to a monopoly. The monopolist produces the $MR = MC$ output of $Q_m$, which is less than $Q_c$. By restricting output to $Q_m$, the monopolist is able to charge the higher price of $P_m$.

# The Case against and for Monopoly

So far, a strong case has been made against monopoly and in favor of perfect competition. Now it is time to pause and summarize the economist's case against monopoly:

■ A monopolist "gouges" consumers by charging a higher price than would be charged under perfect competition.

■ Because a monopolist restricts output in order to maximize profit, too few resources are used to produce the product. Stated differently, the monopolist misallocates resources by charging a price greater than marginal cost. In perfectly competitive industries, price is set equal to marginal cost, and the result is an optimal allocation of resources.

■ Long-run economic profit for a monopolist exceeds the zero economic profit earned in the long run by a perfectly competitive firm.

## You're the Economist

# New York Taxicabs: Where Have All the Fare Flags Gone?
*Applicable Concept: perfect competition versus monopoly*

In the 1920s, New York taxicabs were competitive. There was no limit on the number of taxis, and hack licenses were only $10. Cabbies could choose among three different flags to attach to their cars. A red flag cab charged a surcharge for extra passengers. A white flag signaled no surcharge for extra passengers. A green flag meant the cabbie was offering a discount fare. Price wars often erupted, and the vast majority of cabbies flew green flags and charged bargain fares. One strategy was to fly the red flag (high rate) during rush hour and the green flag to offer discounts at off-peak times. Taxi companies also offered a variety of cabs—old, new, big, and small.[1]

As years passed, the system changed, and currently the Taxi and Limousine Commission sets rates and imposes regulations. One law created a monopoly by requiring all cabs accepting street hails to be painted yellow and possess a medallion. A 1937 law limits the number of medallions, and today the aluminum badges that give the rights to pick up passengers on the street cost more than $300,000. On the other hand, it is illegal for cabs without medallions to cruise and pick up passengers who hail them, although the law is often ignored. Nonmedallion cabs are authorized to respond only to customers who have ordered the cab in advance by phone or other means. There's no limit on the number of nonmedallion cabs or what the drivers may charge. However, established nonmedallion vehicle owners want the city to make it tougher for new companies to enter the nonmedallion market. "What we want is a little monopoly help from the government," said Robert Mackle, an official of Skyline CreditRide, a cooperative of owner-drivers of nonmedallion black cabs.[2]

In a personal interview with the author, Professor Edward Rogoff (professor of management at Baruch College) estimated that over 12,000 yellow cabs concentrate on Manhattan below 125th Street, while a much larger fleet of radio-dispatched cars handles business in Upper Manhattan and the other boroughs. The outer boroughs generally get better service because there's competition out there. Generally, the nonmedallion cars are better vehicles with more experienced drivers who carry more insurance than the yellow cabs. In general, nonmedallion vehicle owners charge about 25 percent less than medallion cabs.[3]

In 2001, a slowdown in the economy forced nonmedallion taxicabs to become more aggressive in picking up street hails. The medallion taxicabs struck back with radio ads telling consumers not to take nonmedallion taxis because these drivers were not as qualified and trained as medallion taxi drivers. The battle continued in 2002: A group of nonmedallion taxicab drivers called for the resignation of the chairman of the Taxi and Limousine Commission because police constantly gave them tickets when they stopped to pick up clients on the street.[4]

Finally, in 2004, New York City auctioned 3,000 new cab medallions and 600 more were sold over the next two years. This was the biggest increase in new cabs since 1937. The impetus for the new medallion sale was to ease the search for available cabs and earn the city $100 million annually to help balance its budget.[5] And in 2005, a pilot program began to allow customers to hail a cab using their cell phones.

### ANALYZE THE ISSUE

Use a graph to compare the price and output of medallion yellow cabs in New York City before and after the 1920s.

[1] John Tierney, "You'll Wonder Where the Yellow Went," *The New York Times*, July 12, 1998, Section 6, p. 18.

[2] Winston Williams, "Owners Bewail Flood of Cabs in New York," *The New York Times*, Apr. 10, 1989, p. B1.

[3] Personal interview, 2001.

[4] EFE World News Service, Apr. 17, 2002.

[5] "Taken for a Ride? New York Cabs," *The Economist*, April 24, 2004, p. 30.

■ To the extent that the monopolist is a rich John D. Rockefeller, for example, and consumers of oil are poor, monopoly alters the distribution of income in favor of the monopolist.

Not all economists agree that monopoly is bad. Joseph Schumpeter and John Kenneth Galbraith praised monopoly power. They argued that the rate of technological change is likely to be greater under monopoly than under perfect competition. In their view, monopoly profits afford giant monopolies the financial strength to invest in the well-equipped laboratories and skilled labor necessary to create technological change.

The counterargument is that monopolists are slow to innovate. Freedom from direct competition means the monopolist is not motivated and therefore tends to stick to the "conventional wisdom." As Nobel laureate Sir John Hicks put it, "The best of all monopoly profit is a quiet life." In short, monopoly offers the opportunity to relax a bit and not worry about the "rat race" of technological change.

What does research on this issue suggest? Not surprisingly, many attempts have been made to verify or refute the effect of market structure on technological change. Unfortunately, the results to date have been inconclusive. For all we know, a mix of large and small firms in an industry may be the optimal mix to create technological change.

## Key Concepts

Monopoly                    Price maker                    Arbitrage
Natural monopoly            Price discrimination

## Summary

■ **Monopoly** is a single seller facing the entire industry demand curve because it is the industry. The monopolist sells a unique product, and extremely high barriers to entry protect it from competition.

■ **Barriers to entry** that prevent new firms from entering an industry are (1) ownership of an essential resource, (2) legal barriers, and (3) economies of scale. Government franchises, licenses, patents, and copyrights are the most obvious legal barriers to entry.

■ A **natural monopoly** arises because of the existence of economies of scale in which the long-run average cost (*LRAC)* curve falls as production increases. Without government restrictions, economies of scale allow a single firm to produce at a lower cost than any firm producing a smaller output. Thus, smaller firms leave the industry, new firms fear competing

with the monopolist, and the result is that a monopoly emerges *naturally*.

**NATURAL MONOPOLY**

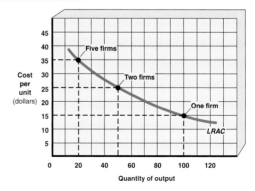

▤ A **price-maker** firm faces a downward-sloping demand curve. It therefore searches its demand curve to find the price-output combination that maximizes its profit and minimizes its loss.

▤ The **marginal revenue** and demand curves are downward sloping for a monopolist. The marginal revenue curve for a monopolist is below the demand curve, and the total revenue curve reaches its maximum where marginal revenue equals zero.

▤ **Price elasticity of demand** corresponds to sections of the marginal revenue curve. When $MR$ is positive, price elasticity of demand is elastic, $E_d > 1$. When $MR$ is equal to zero, price elasticity of demand is unit elastic, $E_d = 1$. When $MR$ is negative, price elasticity of demand is inelastic, $E_d < 1$.

▤ The **short-run profit-maximizing monopolist**, like the perfectly competitive firm, locates the profit-maximizing price by producing the output where the $MR$ and $MC$ curves intersect. If this price is less than the average variable cost ($AVC$) curve, the monopolist shuts down to minimize losses.

▤ The **long-run profit-maximizing monopolist** earns a profit because of barriers to entry. If demand and cost conditions prevent the monopolist from earning a profit, the monopolist will leave the industry.

▤ **Price discrimination** allows the monopolist to increase profits by charging buyers different prices rather than a single price. Three conditions are necessary for price discrimination: (1) the demand curve must be downward sloping, (2) buyers in different markets must have different price elasticities of demand, and (3) buyers must be prevented from reselling the product at a higher price than the purchase price.

**SHORT-RUN MONOPOLIST**

**PRICE DISCRIMINATION**

▤ **Monopoly disadvantages** include the following: (1) a monopolist charges a higher price and produces less output than a perfectly competitive firm, (2) resource allocation is inefficient because the monopolist produces less than if competition existed, (3) monopoly produces higher long-run profits than if competition existed, and (4) monopoly transfers income from consumers to producers to a greater degree than under perfect competition.

## MONOPOLY DISADVANTAGES

Perfectly competitive firm

Monopolist

## Summary of Conclusion Statements

- Because of economies of scale, a single firm in an industry will produce output at a lower per-unit cost than two or more firms.

- The demand and marginal revenue curves of the monopolist are downward sloping in contrast to the horizontal demand and corresponding marginal revenue curves facing the perfectly competitive firm.

- The marginal revenue curve for a straight-line demand curve intersects the quantity axis halfway between the origin and the quantity axis intercepts of the demand curve.

- The monopolist always maximizes profit by producing at a price on the elastic segment of its demand curve.

- If the positions of a monopolist's demand and cost curves give it a profit and nothing disturbs these curves, the monopolist will earn profit in the long run.

- A monopolist is characterized by inefficiency because resources are underallocated to the production of its product.

- Monopoly harms consumers on two fronts. The monopolist charges a higher price and produces a lower output than would result under a perfectly competitive market structure.

## Study Questions and Problems

1. Using the three characteristics of monopoly, explain why each of the following is a monopolist:
   a. Local telephone company
   b. San Francisco 49ers football team
   c. U.S. Postal Service

2. Why is the demand curve facing a monopolist downward sloping while the demand curve facing a perfectly competitive firm is horizontal?

3. Suppose an investigator finds that the prices charged for drugs at a hospital are higher than the prices charged for the same products at drugstores in the area served by the hospital. What might explain this situation?

4. Explain why you agree or disagree with the following statements:
   a. "All monopolies are created by the government."
   b. "The monopolist charges the highest possible price."
   c. "The monopolist never takes a loss."

5. Suppose the average cost of producing a kilowatt-hour of electricity is lower for one firm than for another firm serving the same market. Without the government granting a franchise to one of these competing power companies, explain why a single seller is likely to emerge in the long run.

6. Use the following demand schedule for a monopolist to calculate total revenue and marginal revenue. For each price, indicate whether demand is elastic, unitary elastic, or inelastic. Using the data from the demand schedule, graph the demand curve, the marginal revenue curve, and the total revenue curve. Identify the elastic, unitary elastic, and inelastic segments along the demand curve.

| Price | Quantity demanded (Q) | Total revenue (TR) | Marginal revenue (MR) | Price elasticity of demand ($E_d$) |
|---|---|---|---|---|
| $5.00 | 0 | $_____ | | $_____ |
| 4.50 | 1 | _____ | $_____ | _____ |
| 4.00 | 2 | _____ | _____ | _____ |
| 3.50 | 3 | _____ | _____ | _____ |
| 3.00 | 4 | _____ | _____ | _____ |
| 2.50 | 5 | _____ | _____ | _____ |
| 2.00 | 6 | _____ | _____ | _____ |
| 1.50 | 7 | _____ | _____ | _____ |
| 1.00 | 8 | _____ | _____ | _____ |
| .50 | 9 | _____ | _____ | _____ |
| 0 | 10 | _____ | _____ | _____ |

7. Make the unrealistic assumption that production is costless for the monopolist in question 6. Given the data from the above demand schedule, what price will the monopolist charge, and how much output should the firm produce? How much profit will the firm earn? When marginal cost is above zero, what will be the effect on the price and output of the monopolist?

8. Explain why a monopolist would never produce in the inelastic range of the demand curve.

9. In each of the following cases, state whether the monopolist would increase or decrease output:
   a. Marginal revenue exceeds marginal cost at the output produced.
   b. Marginal cost exceeds marginal revenue at the output produced.

10. Suppose the demand and cost curves for a monopolist are as shown in Exhibit 10 below. Explain what price the monopolist should charge and how much output it should produce.

**EXHIBIT 10  MONOPOLY IN THE SHORT RUN**

11. Which of the following constitute price discrimination?
   a. A department store has a 25 percent-off sale.
   b. A publisher sells economics textbooks at a lower price in North Carolina than in New York.
   c. The Japanese sell cars at higher prices in the United States than in Japan.
   d. The phone company charges higher long-distance rates during the day.

12. Suppose the candy bar industry approximates a perfectly competitive industry. Suppose also that a single firm buys all the assets of the candy bar firms and establishes a monopoly. Contrast these two market structures with respect to price, output, and allocation of resources. Draw a graph of the market demand and market supply for candy bars before and after the takeover.

## Study Guide Questions

1. A (an) _____ arises because of the existence of economies of scale in which the *LRAC* falls as production increases. As a result, smaller firms leave the industry, new firms fear competing with the monopolist, and the result is that a monopoly emerges naturally.

2. Which of the following statements best describes the price, output, and profit conditions of monopoly?
   a. Price will equal marginal cost at the profit-maximizing level of output, and profits will be positive in the long run.

b. Price will always equal average variable cost in the short run, and either profits or losses may result in the long run.

c. In the long run, positive economic profit will be earned.

d. All of the above are true.

3. A monopoly will price its product

a. where total revenue is maximized.

b. where total costs are minimized.

c. at that point on the market demand curve corresponding to an output level in which marginal revenue equals marginal cost.

d. at that point on the market demand curve which intersects the marginal cost curve.

4. A price-discriminating monopoly charges the lowest price to the group that

a. has the most elastic demand.

b. purchases the largest quantity.

c. engages in the most arbitrage.

d. is least responsive to price changes.

5. T  F  Regardless of the demand for its product, a monopolist will be able to earn positive economic profits.

**Answers to these questions are in the complete Study Guide at www.thomsonedu.com/thomsonnow.**

 **For Online Exercises, go to the text Web site at www.thomsonedu.com/economics/tucker.**

## Checkpoint Answers

### Why Don't Adults Pay More for Popcorn at the Movies?

First, there are no other popcorn sellers in the lobby, so the theater is a price maker for popcorn and the demand curve slopes downward. Second, the theater could easily set up different lines for adults and children and charge different prices for popcorn. Third, is there a practical way to prevent resale? Does the theater want to try to stop children who resell popcorn to their parents, friends, and other adults? If you said theaters do not practice price discrimination at the concession counter because resale cannot be prevented, **YOU ARE CORRECT.**

 Practice Quiz

For an explanation of the correct answers, plesae visit the tutorial at www.thomsonedu.com/economics/tucker.

1. A monopolist always faces a demand curve that is

a. perfectly inelastic.

b. perfectly elastic.

c. unitary elastic.

d. the same as the market demand curve.

2. A monopolist sets the

a. price at which marginal revenue equals zero.

b. price that maximizes total revenue.

c. highest possible price on its demand curve.

d. price at which marginal revenue equals marginal cost.

3. A monopolist sets

a. the highest possible price.

b. a price corresponding to minimum average total cost.

c. a price equal to marginal revenue.

d. a price determined by the point on the demand curve corresponding to the level of output at which marginal revenue equals marginal cost.

e. none of the above.

4. Which of the following is *true* for the monopolist?

a. Economic profit is possible in the long run.

b. Marginal revenue is less than the price charged.

c. Profit maximizing or loss minimizing occurs when marginal revenue equals marginal cost.

d. All of the above are true.

**EXHIBIT 11  PROFIT MAXIMIZING FOR A MONOPOLIST**

5. As shown in Exhibit 11, the profit-maximizing or loss-minimizing output for this monopolist is
   a. 100 units per day.
   b. 200 units per day.
   c. 300 units per day.
   d. 400 units per day.

6. As shown in Exhibit 11, this monopolist
   a. should shut down in the short run.
   b. should shut down in the long run.
   c. earns zero economic profit.
   d. earns positive economic profit.

7. To maximize profit or minimize loss, the monopolist in Exhibit 11 should set its price at
   a. $30 per unit.
   b. $25 per unit.
   c. $20 per unit.
   d. $10 per unit.
   e. $40 per unit.

8. If the monopolist in Exhibit 11 operates at the profit-maximizing output, it will earn total revenue to pay about what portion of its total fixed cost?
   a. None
   b. One-half
   c. Two-thirds
   d. All total fixed costs

9. For a monopolist to practice effective price discrimination, one necessary condition is
   a. identical demand curves among groups of buyers.
   b. differences in the price elasticity of demand among groups of buyers.
   c. a homogeneous product.
   d. none of the above.

10. What is the act of buying a commodity at a lower price and selling it at a higher price?
    a. Buying short
    b. Discounting
    c. Tariffing
    d. Arbitrage

11. Under both perfect competition and monopoly, a firm
    a. is a price taker.
    b. is a price maker.
    c. will shut down in the short run if price falls short of average total cost.
    d. always earns a pure economic profit.
    e. sets marginal cost equal to marginal revenue.

12. At any point where a monopolist's marginal revenue is positive, the downward-sloping straight-line demand curve is
    a. perfectly elastic.
    b. elastic, but not perfectly elastic.
    c. unitary elastic.
    d. inelastic.

13. Suppose a monopolist charges a price corresponding to the intersection of the marginal cost and marginal revenue curves. If this price is between its average variable cost and average total cost curves, the firm will
    a. earn an economic profit.
    b. stay in operation in the short-run, but shut down in the long run if demand remains the same.
    c. shut down.
    d. none of the above.

14. In contrast to a perfectly competitive firm, a monopolist operates in the long run at a quantity of output at which
    a. $P = MC$.
    b. $MR = MC$.
    c. $P = ATC$.
    d. $P > MR$.

15. The monopolist, unlike the perfectly competitive firm, can continue to earn an economic profit in the long run because of
    a. collusive agreements with competitors.
    b. price leadership.
    c. cartels.
    d. a dominant firm.
    e. extremely high barriers to entry.

# Monopolistic Competition and Oligopoly

© AbleStock.com/Jupiterimages

firms with which you deal. These firms compete in two market structures: *monopolistic competition* or *oligopoly*. Ivan's operates in the former, and General Motors belongs to the latter. The theories of perfect competition and monopoly from the previous two chapters will help you understand the impact of monopolistic competition and oligopoly market structures on the price and output decisions of real-world firms.

**In this chapter, you will learn to solve these economics puzzles:**

■ Why will Ivan's Oyster Bar make zero economic profit in the long run?

■ Why do OPEC and other cartels tend to break down?

■ Are Cheerios, Rice Krispies, and other brands sold by firms in the breakfast cereal industry produced under monopolistic competition or oligopoly?

■ How does the NCAA Final Four basketball tournament involve imperfect competition?

S uppose your favorite restaurant is Ivan's Oyster Bar. Ivan's does not fit either of the two extreme models studied in the previous two chapters. Instead, Ivan's characteristics are a blend of monopoly and perfect competition. For starters, like a monopolist, Ivan's demand curve is downward sloping. This means Ivan's is a *price maker*, because it can charge a higher price for seafood and lose some customers but many loyal customers will keep coming. The reason is that Ivan's distinguishes its product from the competition by advertising, first-rate service, a great salad bar, and other attributes. In short, like a monopolist, Ivan's has a degree of *market power*, which allows it to restrict output and maximize profit. But like a perfectly competitive firm and unlike a monopolist, Ivan's is not the only place to buy a seafood dinner in town. It must share the market with many other restaurants within an hour's drive.

The small Ivan's Oyster Bars and the gigantic General Motors of the world represent most of the

## The Monopolistic Competition Market Structure

Economists define **monopolistic competition** as a market structure characterized by (1) many small sellers, (2) a differentiated product, and (3) easy market entry and exit. Monopolistic competition fits numerous real-world industries. Following is a brief explanation of each characteristic.

**Monopolistic competition**
A market structure characterized by (1) many small sellers, (2) a differentiated product, and (3) easy market entry and exit.

## MANY SMALL SELLERS

Under monopolistic competition, as under perfect competition, the exact number of firms cannot be stated. Ivan's Oyster Bar, described in the chapter preview, is an example of a monopolistic competitor. Ivan assumes that his restaurant can set prices slightly higher or improve service *independently* without fear that competitors will react by changing their prices or giving better service. Thus, if any single seafood restaurant raises its price, the going market price for seafood dinners increases by a very small amount.

> **CONCLUSION** *The many-sellers condition is met when each firm is so small relative to the total market that its pricing decisions have a negligible effect on the market price.*

## DIFFERENTIATED PRODUCT

**Product differentiation**
The process of creating real or apparent differences between goods and services.

The key feature of monopolistic competition is **product differentiation**. Product differentiation is the process of creating real or apparent differences between goods and services. A differentiated product has close, but not perfect, substitutes. Although the products of each firm are highly similar, the consumer views them as somewhat different or distinct. There may be 25 seafood restaurants in a given city, but they are not all the same. They differ in location, atmosphere, quality of food, quality of service, and so on.

Product differentiation can be real or imagined. It does not matter which is correct so long as consumers believe such differences exist. For example, many customers think Ivan's has the best seafood in town even though other restaurants actually offer a similar product. The importance of this viewpoint is that consumers are willing to pay a slightly higher price for Ivan's seafood. This gives Ivan the incentive to appear on local TV cooking shows and to buy ads showing him personally catching the seafood he serves.

> **CONCLUSION** *When a product is differentiated, buyers are not indifferent as to which seller's product they buy.*

**Nonprice competition**
The situation in which a firm competes using advertising, packaging, product development, better quality, and better service, rather than lower prices.

The example of Ivan's restaurant makes it clear that under monopolistic competition rivalry centers on **nonprice competition** in addition to price competition. With nonprice competition, a firm competes using advertising, packaging, product development, better quality, and better service, rather than lower prices. Nonprice competition is an important characteristic of monopolistic competition that distinguishes it from perfect competition and monopoly. Under perfect competition, there is no nonprice competition because the product is identical for all firms. Likewise, the monopolist has little incentive to engage in nonprice competition because it sells a unique product.

## EASY ENTRY AND EXIT

Unlike a monopoly, firms in a monopolistically competitive market face low barriers to entry. But entry into a monopolistically competitive market is not quite as easy as entry into a perfectly competitive market. Because monopolistically competitive firms sell differentiated products, it is somewhat difficult for new firms to become established. Many persons who want to enter the seafood restaurant business can get loans, lease space, and start serving seafood without too much trouble. However, these new seafood restaurants may at first have difficulty attracting consumers because of Ivan's established reputation as the best seafood restaurant in town.

Monopolistic competition is by far the most common market structure in the United States. Examples include retail firms, such as grocery stores, hair salons, gas stations, video rental stores, diet centers, and restaurants.

# The Monopolistically Competitive Firm as a Price Maker

Given the characteristics of monopolistic competition, you might think the monopolistic competitor is a *price taker*, but it is not. The primary reason is that its product is differentiated. This gives the monopolistically competitive firm, like the monopolist, limited control over its price. When the price is raised, brand loyalty ensures some customers will remain steadfast. As for a monopolist, the demand curve and the corresponding marginal revenue curve for a monopolistically competitive firm are downward sloping. But the existence of close substitutes causes the demand curve for the monopolistically competitive firm to be more elastic than the demand curve for a monopolist. When Ivan's raises its prices 10 percent, the quantity of seafood dinners demanded declines, say, 30 percent. Instead, if Ivan's had a monopoly, no close substitutes would exist, and consumers would be less sensitive to price changes. As a monopolist, the same 10 percent price hike might lose Ivan's only, say, 15 percent of its quantity of seafood dinners demanded.

> **CONCLUSION** *The demand curve for a monopolistically competitive firm is less elastic (steeper) than for a perfectly competitive firm and more elastic (flatter) than for a monopolist.*

## ADVERTISING PROS AND CONS

Before presenting the complete graphical models for monopolistic competition, let's pause to examine the topic of advertising further. As explained at the beginning of this chapter, a distinguishing feature of a monopolistically competitive firm is that it engages in nonprice competition by using expensive ads to differentiate its product. Instead of lowering the price, the firm's goal is to convince customers that its product is really different from its rivals' products. Monopolistically competitive firms are frequently running ads that feature lower prices, a higher quality of service, or new products to win customers. Ads proclaim that products make you smarter, better looking, or nicer to be around. Graphically, the firm hopes advertising will make the demand curve less elastic and shift it rightward by changing consumers' tastes in favor of its product. Profit rises when advertising increases the firm's revenue more than the cost of the advertising.

Exhibit 1 illustrates the effect of advertising on the long-run average cost (*LRAC*) curve for Yummy Frozen Yogurt. Yummy competes with It Can't Be Yogurt and five other stores in the northeastern part of town. Without advertising, the $LRAC_1$ curve represents Yummy's average cost. At the given price charged, the quantity demanded is 6,000 frozen yogurt dishes per month, and the average cost is $2.00 per dish (point *A*).

To increase profits in the short run, Yummy decides to advertise. Yummy knows, however, that in the long run new entrants and rising costs will shrink all yogurt stores' economic profits to zero. Then Yummy must come up with some new product to boost sales. But for now, suppose Yummy's advertising campaign is successful and demand increases. Then two short-run effects occur. One is an upward shift in the average cost curve at any level of output from $LRAC_1$ to $LRAC_2$. The vertical distance between these two curves measures the additional average fixed cost of advertising. Another effect is that the quantity demanded increases to 12,000 frozen yogurt dishes per month. Now the average cost is $1.50 at point *B* on $LRAC_2$.

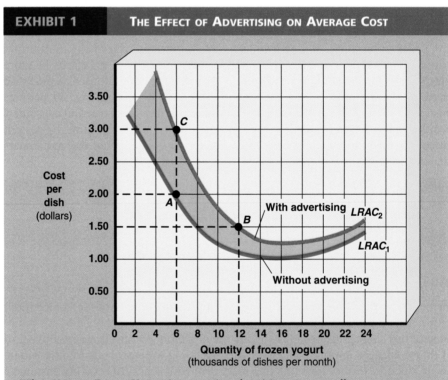

**EXHIBIT 1          THE EFFECT OF ADVERTISING ON AVERAGE COST**

When Yummy Frozen Yogurt increases its advertising costs to sell more yogurt, the firm's average cost curve shifts upward from $LRAC_1$ to $LRAC_2$. If advertising increases the quantity demanded from 6,000 to 12,000 dishes per month, average total cost falls from $2.00 (point *A*) to $1.50 (point *B*). However, if the extra cost of advertising fails to increase the quantity demanded, average total cost rises from $2.00 (point *A*) to $3.00 (point *C*).

## You're the Economist

## The Advertising Game
*Applicable Concepts: advertising and barrier to entry*

Proponents of advertising argue that competition with differentiated products leads to lower prices, more variety, and better-quality products. You are probably familiar with newspaper ads, radio or television commercials, or even Yellow Pages ads that promise legal services at very reasonable rates. Lawyers were not always free to advertise. Not until 1977 did the Supreme Court free lawyers from the disciplinary actions of local bar authorities designed to prohibit lawyers from publicizing themselves. This case involved two young Phoenix lawyers, John Bates and Van O'Steen, who had advertised their legal services in violation of the Arizona Bar's rules. The bar's position was that the "hustle of the marketplace" would "tarnish the dignified public image of the profession." The high court rejected this argument and ruled that lawyers have a constitutional right to advertise their services. In a 1983 study, the Federal Trade Commission (FTC) surveyed 3,200 lawyers in 17 states. The FTC concluded that fees for wills, bankruptcies, uncontested divorces, and uncomplicated accident cases were 5 to 13 percent lower in cities with the least restrictions on advertising.[1] And a 1998 study by Richard J. Cebula using Gallup poll data indicated that the percentage who rate lawyers as honest found that advertising by lawyers raises the public's esteem for the legal profession.[2]

Critics of advertising claim that it provides little informational content and serves as a barrier to entry against new firms. Brand loyalty allows firms to raise their prices and profits without losing many cus-

tomers. For example, a research firm asked 300 computer buyers what factors were most important in the purchase of a personal computer. Performance ranked first and brand name ranked second, while price ranked fifth. Another question on the survey asked for a dollar value buyers would be willing to pay over the average for a brand name. IBM, Apple, and Dell were at the top of the list and lower-tier brand names would not be purchased unless they were discounted. The survey concluded that smaller players in the computer industry would have trouble surviving because price is less important than brand-name image.[3]

Proponents claim that advertising is not a barrier to entry. Instead, advertising allows new entrants to penetrate markets dominated by long-established firms. Advertising gives new competitors a chance to introduce their products and win customers from their entrenched rivals.

### ANALYZE THE ISSUE

Advertising is tasteless, offensive, and a waste of resources; therefore, all advertising should be banned. Give three arguments against this idea.

[1]Ruth Marcus, "Practicing Law in the Advertising Age," *The Washington Post*, June 30, 1987, p. A6.

[2]Richard J. Cebula, "Does Advertising Adversely Influence the Image of Lawyers in the United States?" *Journal of Legal Studies* 27 Part 1 (June 1998): 503–516.

[3]Kyle Pope, "Computers: They're No Commodity," *The Wall Street Journal*, Oct. 15, 1993, p. A6.

So far, our story illustrates a social benefit of advertising. Look again at Exhibit 1. The increased volume of sales caused by advertising leads to *economies of scale*, explained in Chapter 7. Without advertising, Yummy operated with a lower output and a higher average cost. With advertising, the benefit to consumers from the reduction in average total cost from A to B outweighs the boost in cost per unit from advertising.

On the other hand, suppose Yummy's advertising campaign is not successful and demand remains unchanged. In this case, the quantity demanded remains at the original 6,000 frozen yogurt dishes per month, but the average total cost rises to $3.00 (point C). Critics of advertising argue this is the typical case and not the reduction from A to B. Instead of economies of scale, advertising is self-canceling.

Yummy, It Can't Be Yogurt, and other firms spend large outlays on advertising just to keep their present market share. And in the process, the cost, and therefore the price, of yogurt is increased. Moreover, the additional cost of advertising does not improve the yogurt at all. The only purpose is to persuade or mislead consumers into buying something they do not need. From society's viewpoint, the resources used in advertising could be used for schools, software, or other useful products.

Proponents of advertising counter the argument that advertising is valueless. They argue that ads provide information. Advertising informs consumers of sales, the availability of products, and the advantages of products. Although the product costs a little more, this information saves consumers money and time. Ads also increase price competition among sellers. When Yummy offers discount coupons, other yogurt stores see these ads and respond with lower prices. Finally, consumers are rational and cannot be fooled by advertising. If a product is undesirable, customers will not buy it.

Does monopolistic competition lead to lower prices, greater output, and better-informed consumers? Or does this market structure simply raise prices and annoy customers with useless and often misleading information? This fascinating and ongoing debate is perhaps best analyzed on a case-by-case basis. In a later section, you will learn that advertising to differentiate a product is also a key characteristic of oligopoly.

# Price and Output Decisions for a Monopolistically Competitive Firm

Now we are prepared to develop the short-run and long-run graphical models for monopolistic competition. In the short run, you will see that monopolistic competition resembles monopoly. In the long run, however, entry by new firms leads to a more competitive market structure. This section presents a graphical analysis that shows why a monopolistically competitive firm is part perfectly competitive and part monopolistic.

## MONOPOLISTIC COMPETITION IN THE SHORT RUN

Exhibit 2 shows the short-run equilibrium position for Ivan's Oyster Bar—a typical firm under monopolistic competition. As explained earlier, the demand curve slopes downward because customers believe, rightly or wrongly, that Ivan's product is a little better than its competitors' products. Customers like Ivan's family atmosphere, location, and quality of service. These nonprice factors differentiate Ivan's product and allow the restaurant to raise the price of sauteed alligator, shrimp, and oysters at least slightly without losing many sales.

Like the monopolist, the monopolistically competitive firm maximizes short-run profit by following the $MR = MC$ rule. In this case, the marginal cost ($MC$) and marginal revenue ($MR$) curves intersect at an output of 600 seafood meals per week. The price per meal of $18 is the point on the demand curve corresponding to this level of output. Because the price exceeds the average total cost ($ATC$) of $15 per meal, Ivan's earns a short-run economic profit of $1,800 per week. As under monopoly, if the price equals the $ATC$ curve, the firm earns a short-run normal profit. If the price is below the $ATC$ curve, the firm suffers a short-run loss, and if the price is below the average variable cost ($AVC$) curve, the firm shuts down.

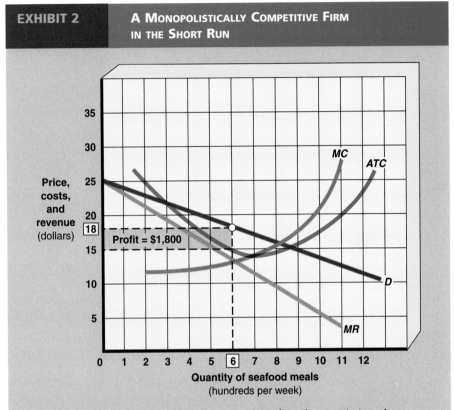

**EXHIBIT 2** | **A MONOPOLISTICALLY COMPETITIVE FIRM IN THE SHORT RUN**

Ivan's Oyster Bar is a monopolistically competitive firm that maximizes short-run profit by producing the output where marginal revenue equals marginal cost. At an output of 600 seafood dinners per week, the price of $18 per dinner is dictated by the firm's demand curve. Given the firm's costs, output, and prices, Ivan's will earn a short-run profit of $1,800 per week.

## MONOPOLISTIC COMPETITION IN THE LONG RUN

The monopolistically competitive firm, unlike a monopolist, will not earn an economic profit in the long run. Rather, like a perfect competitor, the monopolistically competitive firm earns only a normal profit (that is, zero economic profit) in the long run. The reason is that short-run profits and easy entry attract new firms into the industry. When Ivan's Oyster Bar earns a short-run profit, as shown in Exhibit 2, two things happen. First, Ivan's demand curve shifts downward as some of each seafood restaurant's market share is taken away by new firms seeking profit. Second, Ivan's, and other seafood restaurants as well, tries to recapture market share by advertising, improving its decor, and utilizing other forms of nonprice competition. As a result, long-run average costs increase, and the firm's *LRAC* curve shifts upward.

The combination of the leftward shift in the firm's demand curve and the upward shift in its *LRAC* curve continues in the long run until the monopolistic competitive firm earns zero or normal economic profit. The result is the long-run equilibrium condition shown in Exhibit 3. At a price of $17 per meal, the demand

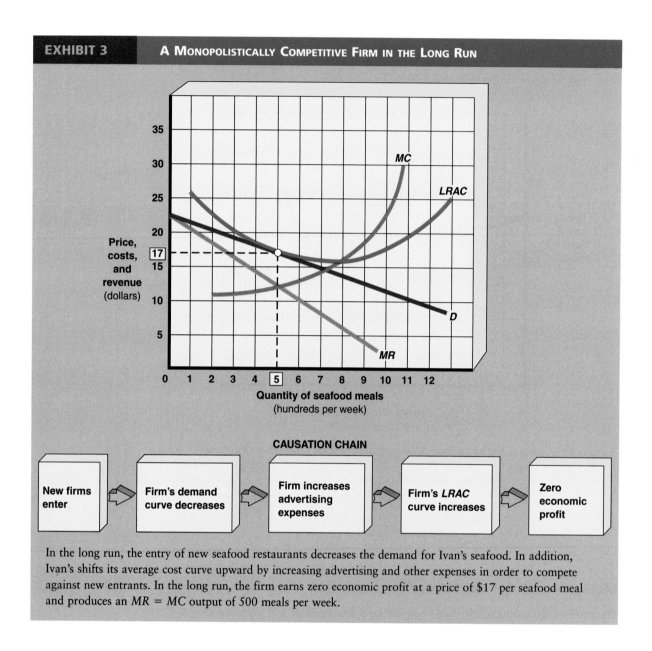

**EXHIBIT 3**    **A MONOPOLISTICALLY COMPETITIVE FIRM IN THE LONG RUN**

**CAUSATION CHAIN**

New firms enter ⇒ Firm's demand curve decreases ⇒ Firm increases advertising expenses ⇒ Firm's *LRAC* curve increases ⇒ Zero economic profit

In the long run, the entry of new seafood restaurants decreases the demand for Ivan's seafood. In addition, Ivan's shifts its average cost curve upward by increasing advertising and other expenses in order to compete against new entrants. In the long run, the firm earns zero economic profit at a price of $17 per seafood meal and produces an $MR = MC$ output of 500 meals per week.

curve is tangent to the *LRAC* curve at the $MR = MC$ output of 500 meals per week. Once long-run equilibrium is achieved in a monopolistically competitive industry, there is no incentive for new firms to enter or established firms to leave.

# Comparing Monopolistic Competition and Perfect Competition

Some economists argue that the long-run equilibrium condition for a monopolistically competitive firm, as shown in Exhibit 3, results in poor economic performance. Other economists contend that the benefits of a monopolistically competitive industry outweigh the costs. In this section, we again use the standard of perfect competition to understand both sides of this debate.

## THE MONOPOLISTIC COMPETITOR AS A RESOURCE MISALLOCATOR

Like a monopolist, the monopolistically competitive firm fails the efficiency test. As shown in Exhibit 3, under monopolistic competition, Ivan's charges a price that exceeds the marginal cost. Thus, the value to consumers of the last meal produced is greater than the cost of producing it. Ivan's could devote more resources and produce more seafood dinners. To sell this additional output, Ivan's must move downward along its demand curve by reducing the $17 price per meal. As a result, customers would purchase the additional benefits of consuming more seafood meals. However, Ivan's uses less resources and restricts output to 500 seafood meals per week in order to maximize profits where $MR = MC$.

## MONOPOLISTIC COMPETITION MEANS LESS OUTPUT FOR MORE

Exhibit 4(a) reproduces the long-run condition from Exhibit 3. Exhibit 4(b) assumes that the seafood restaurant market is perfectly competitive. Recall from Chapter 8 that the characteristics of perfect competition include the condition that customers perceive seafood meals as *homogeneous* and, as a result, no firms engage in advertising. Because we now assume for the sake of argument that Ivan's product is identical to all other seafood restaurants, Ivan's becomes a *price taker*. In this case, the industry's long-run supply and demand curves set an equilibrium price of $16 per meal. Consequently, Ivan's faces a horizontal demand curve with the price equal to marginal revenue. Also recall from Chapter 8 that long-run equilibrium for a perfectly competitive firm is established by the entry of new firms until the minimum point of $16 per meal on the firm's *LRAC* curve equals the price, *MR* and *MC*. Stated as a formula:

$$P = MR = MC = LRAC$$

A comparison of Parts (a) and (b) of Exhibit 4 reveals two important points. First, both the monopolistic competitor and the perfect competitor earn zero economic profit in the long run. Second, the long-run equilibrium output of the monopolistically competitive firm is to the left of the minimum point on the *LRAC* curve and the price exceeds *MC*. Like a monopolist, the monopolistically competitive firm therefore charges a higher price and produces less output than a perfectly competitive firm.

In our example, Ivan's would charge $1 less per meal and produce 300 more seafood meals per week in a perfectly competitive market. The extra 300 meals not produced are *excess capacity*, which represents underutilized resources. The criticism of monopolistic competition, then, is that there are too many firms producing too little output at inflated prices and wasting society's resources in the process. For example, on many nights, there are not enough customers for all the restaurants in town. Servers, cooks, tables, and other resources are therefore underutilized. With fewer firms, each would produce a greater output at a lower price and with a lower average cost.

Opinions vary concerning whether the benefits of monopolistic competition exceed the costs. Having many seafood restaurants offers consumers more choice

| EXHIBIT 4 | COMPARISON OF MONOPOLISTIC COMPETITION AND PERFECT COMPETITION IN THE LONG RUN |

In Part (a), Ivan's Oyster Bar is a monopolistically competitive firm that sets its price at $17 per seafood meal and produces 500 meals per week. As a monopolistic competitor, Ivan's earns zero economic profit in the long run and does not produce at the lowest point on its *LRAC* curve.

Under conditions of perfect competition in Part (b), Ivan's becomes a price taker, rather than a price maker. Here the firm faces a flat demand curve at a price of $16 per seafood meal. The output is 800 meals per week, which corresponds to the lowest point on the *LRAC* curve. Therefore, the price is lower, and the excess capacity of 300 meals per week is utilized when Ivan's operates as a perfectly competitive firm, rather than as a monopolistically competitive firm.

and variety of output. Having Ivan's Oyster Bar and many similar competitors gives consumers extra quality and service options. If you do not like Ivan's sauteed alligator, you may be able to find another restaurant that serves this dish. Also, having many restaurants in a market saves consumers valuable time. Chances are that you will not shed crocodile tears because the travel time required to enjoy an alligator meal is lower.

## The Oligopoly Market Structure

Now we turn to oligopoly, an imperfectly competitive market structure in which a few large firms dominate the market. Many manufacturing industries, such as steel, aluminum, automobiles, aircraft, drugs, and tobacco, are best described as oligopolistic. This is the "big business" market structure, in which firms aggressively compete by bombarding us with advertising on television and filling our mailboxes with junk mail.

Economists define an **oligopoly** as a market structure characterized by (1) few sellers, (2) either a homogeneous or a differentiated product, and (3) difficult market entry. Like monopolistic competition, oligopoly is found in real-world industries. Let's examine each characteristic.

## FEW SELLERS

Oligopoly is competition "among the few." Here we refer to the "Big Three" or "Big Four" to mean that three or four firms dominate an industry. But what does "a few" firms really mean? Does this mean at least two, but less than ten? As with other market structures, the answer is there is no specific number of firms that must dominate an industry before it is an oligopoly. Basically, an oligopoly is a consequence of **mutual interdependence**. Mutual interdependence is a condition in which an action by one firm may cause a reaction from other firms. Stated another way, a market structure with a few powerful firms makes it easier for oligopolists to collude. The large number of firms under perfect competition or monopolistic competition and the absence of other firms in monopoly rule out mutual interdependence and collusion in these market structures.

When General Motors (GM) considers a price hike or a style change, it must predict how Ford and DaimlerChrysler will change their prices and styling in response. Therefore, the decisions under oligopoly are more complex than under perfect competition, monopoly, and monopolistic competition.

> **CONCLUSION** *The few-sellers condition is met when these few firms are so large relative to the total market that they can affect the market price.*

## HOMOGENEOUS OR DIFFERENTIATED PRODUCT

Under oligopoly, firms can produce either a homogeneous or a differentiated product. The steel produced by USX is identical to the steel from Republic Steel. The oil sold by Saudi Arabia is identical to the oil from Iran. Similarly, zinc, copper, and aluminum are standardized products. But cars produced by the major automakers are differentiated products. Tires, detergents, and breakfast cereals are also differentiated products sold in oligopolies.

> **CONCLUSION** *Buyers in an oligopoly may or may not be indifferent as to which seller's product they buy.*

## DIFFICULT ENTRY

Similar to monopoly, formidable barriers to entry in an oligopoly protect firms from new entrants. These barriers include exclusive financial requirements, control over an essential resource, patent rights, and other legal barriers. But the most significant barrier to entry in an oligopoly is *economies of scale*. For example, larger automakers achieve lower average total costs than those incurred by smaller automakers. Consequently, the U.S. auto industry has moved over time from more than 60 firms to only two major U.S. owned firms.

**Oligopoly**
A market structure characterized by (1) few sellers, (2) either a homogeneous or a differentiated product, and (3) difficult market entry.

**Mutual interdependence**
A condition in which an action by one firm may cause a reaction from other firms.

# Price and Output Decisions for an Oligopolist

Mutual interdependence among firms in an oligopoly makes this market structure more difficult to analyze than perfect competition, monopoly, or monopolistic competition. The price-output decision of an oligopolist is not simply a matter of charging the price where $MR = MC$. Making price and output decisions in an oligopoly is like playing a game of chess. One player's move depends on the anticipated reactions of the opposing player. One player thinks, "If I move my rook here, my opponent might move her knight there." Likewise, a firm in an oligopoly can make many different possible reactions to the price, nonprice, and output changes of another firm. Consequently, there are different oligopoly models because no single model can cover all cases. The following is a discussion of five well-known oligopoly models: (1) nonprice competition, (2) the kinked demand curve, (3) price leadership, (4) the cartel, and (5) game theory.

## NONPRICE COMPETITION

Major oligopolists often compete using advertising and product differentiation. Instead of "slugging it out" with price cuts, oligopolists may try to capture business away from their rivals through better advertising campaigns and improved products. This model of behavior explains why advertising expenditures often are large in the cigarette, soft drink, athletic shoe, and automobile industries. It also explains why the research and development (R&D) function is so important to oligopolists. For example, much engineering effort is aimed largely at developing new products and improving existing products.

Why might oligopolists compete through nonprice competition, rather than price competition? The answer is that each oligopolist perceives that its rival will easily and quickly match any price reduction. In contrast, it is much more difficult to combat a clever and/or important product improvement.

## THE KINKED DEMAND CURVE

**Kinked demand curve**
A demand curve facing an oligopolist that assumes rivals will match a price decrease, but ignore a price increase.

Unlike other market structures, different assumptions define different models for any given oligopolistic industry. Over time, the "rules of the game" change, and a new model becomes the best predictor of the behavior of oligopolists. We begin with the **kinked demand curve**. The strange shape of this curve explains why prices in an oligopolistic market selling cars change far less often than prices in a perfectly competitive market selling wheat.

The kinked demand curve is a demand curve facing an oligopolist that assumes rivals will match a price decrease, but ignore a price increase. Without collusion, the kinked demand curve exists because management tacitly believes that the competition will not be "undersold." On the other hand, a price hike by one firm allows competitors to capture its share of the market. Oligopolistic firms must make pricing decisions, so they are *price makers*, rather than price takers. But as we will soon see in the kinked demand model, the high degree of interdependence among oligopolists restricts their pricing discretion.

In Exhibit 5, a kinked demand curve is drawn for Tucker Motor Company, which we assume competes with GM, Ford, and DaimlerChrysler in the automobile market. (I suggest you check out the movie titled *Tucker* at your video rental

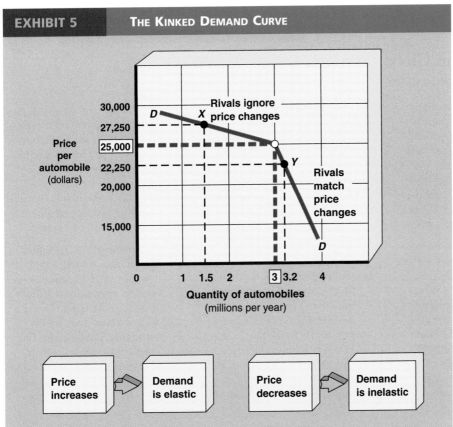

| EXHIBIT 5 | THE KINKED DEMAND CURVE |

An oligopolist's demand curve may be kinked. In this graph, an automobile producer believes it faces two demand curves. A price hike from $25,000 to $27,250
per auto causes a sizable reduction in the quantity demanded from 3 million to 1.5
million autos (point *X*). Demand above the kink is elastic because rivals ignore the
firm when it raises the price. Below the kink, the demand curve is less elastic. A
price reduction from $25,000 to $22,250 per auto attracts very few new customers,
and the quantity demanded increases from 3 million to only 3.2 million autos per
year (point *Y*). Under the kinked demand curve theory, prices will be rigid.

store.) The current price per Tucker car is $25,000, and the quantity demanded
at this price is 3 million cars per year. Tucker's management assumes that if it
raises its price even slightly above $25,000, the other automakers *will not follow*
with higher prices. This price gap between the Tucker and other cars would drive
many of Tucker's customers over to its rivals. The segment of the demand curve
above $25,000 is therefore relatively flat. Stated differently, above the "kink" in
the demand curve, demand is relatively elastic. If Tucker raises the price to, say,
$27,250 at point *X*, this price hike cuts Tucker's quantity demanded to 1.5 mil-
lion cars per year. Since raising its price is ill-advised, management can consider a
price reduction strategy. Suppose Tucker cuts the price of its cars from $25,000 to
$22,250 at point *Y*. The model shows that Tucker gains few customers and the

## International Economics

### Major Cartels in Global Markets
*Applicable Concept: cartel*

Cartels flourished in Germany and other European countries in the first half of the twentieth century. Many had international memberships. After World War II, European countries passed laws against such restrictive trade practices. The following are some of the most important cartels today:

■ **Organization of Petroleum Exporting Countries (OPEC).** OPEC was created by Iran, Iraq, Kuwait, Saudi Arabia, and Venezuela in Baghdad in 1960. Today, OPEC's membership consists of 11 countries that control about 80 percent of the world's oil reserves. Cartels are anticonsumer. OPEC's objective is to set oil production quotas for its members and, in turn, influence global prices of oil and gasoline. In the future, OPEC may become weaker if Russia competes with it. Russia possesses the world's largest oil reserves and may soon obtain Western technology necessary for efficient oil production.

■ **International Telecommunications Union (ITU).** Perhaps the world's least-known and most effective cartel is based in Geneva, Switzerland. The ITU was founded in 1865 and became an agency of the United Nations in 1947. It is responsible for international regulations and standards governing telecommunications. The ITU sets the minimum price you pay for an international telephone call. As a result, rates for international calls are higher than competitive long-distance telephone rates in the United States.

■ **International Air Transport Association (IATA).** Originally founded in 1919, most of the world's international airlines belong to the IATA. This cartel sets safety and security standards for passenger and cargo shipping. It controls access to airports, fixes airline rates, and promotes mutual objectives for its members.

quantity demanded rises only slightly from 3 million to 3.2 million cars per year. The reason for such a small sales boost is that other automakers also cut their prices so that each firm can keep its initial market share. However, the lower price does attract some new buyers who could not afford a car at the higher price. The segment of the demand curve below the kink is therefore relatively steep. Here demand is less elastic, meaning the quantity demanded is not very responsive to a price drop.

Given the kinked demand curve facing the oligopolist, management fears the worst and is afraid to raise or lower the price of its product. Under this model of oligopoly, the price established at the kink changes very infrequently. Price rigidity is eliminated only after large cost increases or decreases force a new kinked demand curve with a new higher or lower price at the kink.

Economists continue to debate the importance of the kinked demand model. Critics challenge the theory on theoretical and empirical grounds. On a theoretical level, there is no explanation for how the original price at the kink was determined. On empirical grounds, studies of certain oligopolistic industries fail to find price stickiness. On the other hand, widespread use of price lists in catalogs that remain fixed for a long time is consistent with kinked demand theory. In any case, the kinked demand theory does not provide a complete explanation of price and output decisions.

## PRICE LEADERSHIP

Without formal agreement, firms can play a game of follow the leader that economists call **price leadership**. Price leadership is a pricing strategy in which a dominant firm sets the price for an industry and the other firms follow. Following this tactic, firms in an industry simply match the price of perhaps, but not necessarily, the biggest firm. Price leadership is not uncommon. In addition to GM, USX Corporation (steel), Alcoa (aluminum), DuPont (nylon), R. J. Reynolds, Goodyear Tire and Rubber (tires), and American Tobacco (cigarettes) are examples of price leaders in U.S. industries.

**Price leadership**
A pricing strategy in which a dominant firm sets the price for an industry and the other firms follow.

## THE CARTEL

The price leadership model assumes that firms do not collude to avoid price competition. Instead, firms avoid price wars by informally playing by the established pricing rules. Another way to avoid price wars is for oligopolists to agree to a peace treaty. Instead of allowing mutual interdependence to lead to rivalry, firms openly or secretly conspire to form a monopoly called a **cartel**. A cartel is a group of firms that formally agree to control the price and the output of a product. The goal of a cartel is to reap monopoly profits by replacing competition with cooperation. Cartels are illegal in the United States, but not in other nations. The best-known cartel is the Organization of Petroleum Exporting Countries (OPEC). The members of OPEC divide crude oil output among themselves according to quotas openly agreed upon at meetings of the OPEC oil ministries. Saudi Arabia is the largest producer and has the largest quota. The International Economics feature provides a brief summary of some of today's major global cartels.

**Cartel**
A group of firms that formally agree to control the price and the output of a product.

Using Exhibit 6, we can demonstrate how a cartel works and why keeping members from cheating is a problem. Our analysis begins before oil-producing firms have formed a cartel. Assume each firm has the same cost curve shown in the exhibit. Price wars have driven each firm to charge $30 a barrel, which is equal to the minimum point on its *LRAC* curve. Because oil is a standardized product, as under perfect competition, each firm fears raising its price because it will lose all its customers. Thus, the typical firm is in long-run competitive equilibrium at a price of $30 per barrel ($MR_1$), producing 6 million barrels per day. In this condition, economic profits are zero, and the firms decide to organize a meeting of all oil producers to establish a cartel.

Now assume the cartel is formed and each firm agrees to reduce its output to 4 million barrels per day and charge $45 per barrel. If no firms cheat, each firm faces a higher horizontal demand curve, represented by $MR_2$. At the cartel price, each firm earns an economic profit of $40 million, rather than a normal profit. But what if one firm decides to cheat on the cartel agreement by stepping up its output while other firms stick to their quotas? Output corresponding to the point at which $MR_2 = MC$ is 8 million barrels per day. If a cheating firm expands its output to this level, it can double its profit by earning an extra $40 million. Of course, if all firms cheat and the cartel breaks up, the price and output of each firm returns to the initial levels, and economic profit again falls to zero.

## GAME THEORY

**Game theory** is a model of the strategic moves and countermoves of rivals. To illustrate, let's use a noncollusive example of USAirways competing with American

**Game Theory**
A model of the strategic moves and countermoves of rivals.

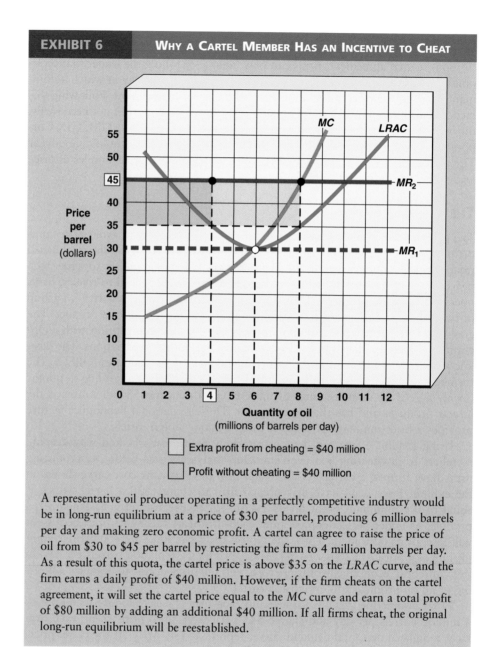

**EXHIBIT 6        WHY A CARTEL MEMBER HAS AN INCENTIVE TO CHEAT**

□ Extra profit from cheating = $40 million

□ Profit without cheating = $40 million

A representative oil producer operating in a perfectly competitive industry would be in long-run equilibrium at a price of $30 per barrel, producing 6 million barrels per day and making zero economic profit. A cartel can agree to raise the price of oil from $30 to $45 per barrel by restricting the firm to 4 million barrels per day. As a result of this quota, the cartel price is above $35 on the *LRAC* curve, and the firm earns a daily profit of $40 million. However, if the firm cheats on the cartel agreement, it will set the cartel price equal to the *MC* curve and earn a total profit of $80 million by adding an additional $40 million. If all firms cheat, the original long-run equilibrium will be reestablished.

Airlines. Each airline independently sets its fare, and Exhibit 7 is a *payoff matrix* that shows profit outcomes for the two airlines resulting from charging either a high fare or a low fare. If both charge the high fare in cell A, they split the market, and each makes a profit of $8 billion. If both decide to charge the low fare in cell D, they also split the market, and the profit for each falls to $5 billion. If one charges the high fare and the other the low fare in cell B or cell C, then the low-fare airline attracts most of the customers and earns the maximum possible profit of $10 billion, while the high-fare airline loses $2 billion.

| EXHIBIT 7 | A TWO-FIRM PAYOFF MATRIX |
|---|---|

<table>
<tr><td rowspan="2" colspan="2"></td><td colspan="2">USAirways' options</td></tr>
<tr><td>High fare</td><td>Low fare</td></tr>
<tr><td rowspan="4">American Airlines' options</td><td>High fare</td><td>A<br>USAirways' profit = $8 billion<br>American Airlines' profit = $8 billion</td><td>B<br>USAirways' profit = $10 billion<br>American Airlines' loss = −$2 billion</td></tr>
<tr><td>Low fare</td><td>C<br>USAirways' loss = −$2 billion<br>American Airlines' profit = $10 billion</td><td>D<br>USAirways' profit = $5 billion<br>American Airlines' profit = $5 billion</td></tr>
</table>

Game theory is a method of analyzing the oligopoly puzzle. Two fare options of charging either a high fare or a low fare are given for USAirways and American Airlines. The profit or loss that each earns in cells A–D depends on the pricing decisions of these two rivals. Their collective interest is best served in cell A where each charges the high fare and each makes the maximum profit of $8 billion. But once either airline independently seeks the higher profit of $10 billion by using a low-fare strategy in cell B or C, the other airline counters with a low fare, and both end up charging the low fare in cell D. As a result, mutual profits are $5 billion, rather than $8 billion in cell A. Cell D is the equilibrium outcome because both fear changing the price and causing the other to counter.

Both rivals in our example are clearly *mutually interdependent* because an action by one firm may cause a reaction from the other firm. Suppose both airlines initially select the most mutually profitable solution and both charge the high fare in cell A. This outcome creates an incentive for either airline to charge a lower fare in cell B or cell C and earn the highest possible profit by pulling customers away from its rival. Consequently, assume the next day one airline cuts its fare to gain higher profits. In order to avoid losing customers, this action causes the other airline to counter with an equally low fare. Price competition has therefore forced both airlines to charge the low fare in cell D and earn less than maximum joint profits. Once cell D is reached, neither airline has an incentive to alter the fare either higher or lower because both fear their rival's countermoves. Note that when both firms charge the low fare in equilibrium at cell D, consumers benefit from not paying high fares in the other cells.

**CONCLUSION** *The payoff matrix demonstrates why a competitive oligopoly tends to result in both rivals using a low-price strategy that does not maximize mutual profits.*

How can these oligopolists avoid the low-fare outcome in cell D and instead stabilize the more jointly profitable high-fare payoffs in cell A? One possible strategy is called *tit for tat*. Under this approach, a player will do whatever the other player did the last time. If one airline defects from cell A by cutting its fare to gain a profit advantage, the other competitor will also cut its fare. After repeated trials, these price cutting responses serve as a signal that says, "You are not going to get the best of me, so move your fare up!" Once the defector responds by moving back to the high fare, the other airline cooperates and also moves to the high fare. The result is that both players return to cell A without a formal agreement.

Another informal approach is for rivals to coordinate their pricing decisions based on price leadership, as discussed earlier in this chapter. For example, one airline may be much more established or dominant, and the other airline follows whatever price the leader sets. Another approach would be to informally rotate the leadership. Thus, without a formal agreement, the leader sets the profit-maximizing high price in cell A and the other competitor follows. However, this system does not eliminate the threat that the price follower will cheat.

Finally, if cartels were legal in the United States, the airlines could collude and make a formal agreement that each will charge the high fare. However, as explained in the previous section, there is always the incentive for one firm to cheat by moving from cell A to either cell B or cell C, and therefore cartels tend to break down. A remedy might be for the rivals to agree on a penalty for any party that reneges by lowering its fare.

> **CONCLUSION** *As long as the benefits exceed the costs, cheating can threaten formal or informal agreements among oligopolists to maximize joint profits.*

# An Evaluation of Oligopoly

Oligopoly is much more difficult to evaluate than other market structures. None of the models just presented gives a definite answer to the question of efficiency under oligopoly. Depending on the assumptions made, an oligopolist can behave much like a perfectly competitive firm or more like a monopoly. Nevertheless, let's assume some likely changes that occur if a perfectly competitive industry is suddenly turned into an oligopoly selling a differentiated product.

### CHECKPOINT

## Which Model Fits the Cereal Aisle?

As you walk along the cereal aisle, notice the many different cereals on the shelves. For example, you will probably see General Mills' Wheaties, Total, and Cheerios; Kellogg's Corn Flakes, Cracklin' Oat Bran, Frosted Flakes, and Rice Krispies; Quaker Oats' Cap'n Crunch and 100% Natural; and Post's Super Golden Crisp, to name only a few. There are many different brands of the same product-cereal on the shelves. Each brand is slightly different from the others. Is the breakfast cereal industry's market structure monopolistic competition or oligopoly?

## An Economist Goes to the Final Four
*Applicable Concepts: oligopoly and cartel*

Many fascinating markets functioned during the Men's Final Four basketball tournament, and as an industrial organization economist, I observed them with great interest.

The competition began shortly after we got off the plane at the Minneapolis airport. A group of high school students was giving away huge inflatable plastic hands with index fingers sticking up in the air. They were imprinted with the Pepsi-Cola slogan and logo and your choice of a Final Four team. And the group was giving away free cans of Pepsi. Uh huh! The latest battle in the Great Cola Wars was on, but this was just the beginning.

Giant inflatable "cans" of Coke and Pepsi appeared all over downtown Minneapolis—on the sidewalks, on top of gas stations—not to mention that entire sides of three-story buildings were painted Coca-Cola red and white with the 64 NCAA basketball finalists and all the winners listed, bracket by bracket, just as they appeared in the newspaper. And on Sunday, following the first-round games, painters were three stories up on scaffolding, filling in the Coke sign's brackets for the final two teams, Duke and Michigan—in school colors no less. This was competition between showboating industry giants—a spectacular example of differentiated oligopoly.

Then there were the hotels, which by joining a centralized booking service became a cartel. The first hotel that I booked had raised its normal price by 75 percent for the weekend. Others did the same. I later found a national chain motel that had not joined in the feeding frenzy. It charged a modest price, but it

was well out into the suburbs. Still, by Saturday afternoon it was filled with Final Four fans.

© Photodisc/Getty Images

Fortunately, I did not have the same problem with the airline, rental car company, or restaurants. Normal rates for transportation prevailed. National market–oriented companies either do not want to bother with adjusting prices for local high-demand special events, or they do not wish to alienate their regular customers by taking advantage of the situation.

### ANALYZE THE ISSUE

1. The author says that the Coke-Pepsi competition was an example of "differentiated oligopoly." What does he mean? In what ways were the soda giants differentiating their products?

2. Why didn't national companies adjust their prices in the face of increased Final Four demand?

*Source: Michael Stoller, "An Economist Goes to the Final Four," Margin 8 (Spring 1993): 48–49.*

First, the price charged for the product will be higher than under perfect competition. The smaller the number of firms in an oligopoly and the more difficult it is to enter the industry, the higher the oligopoly price will be in comparison to the perfectly competitive price.

Second, an oligopoly is likely to spend money on advertising, product differentiation, and other forms of nonprice competition. These expenditures can shift the demand curve to the right. As a result, both price and output may be higher under oligopoly than under perfect competition.

| EXHIBIT 8 | COMPARISON OF MARKET STRUCTURES | | | |
|---|---|---|---|---|
| Market structure | Number of sellers | Type of product | Entry condition | Examples |
| Perfect competition | Large | Homogeneous | Very easy | Agriculture* |
| Monopoly | One | Unique | Impossible | Public utilities |
| Monopolistic competition | Many | Differentiated | Easy | Retail trade |
| Oligopoly | Few | Homogeneous or differentiated | Difficult | Auto, steel, oil |

*In the absence of government intervention.

Third, in the long run, a perfectly competitive firm earns zero economic profit. The oligopolist, however, can earn a higher profit because it is more difficult for competitors to enter the industry.

# Review of the Four Market Structures

Now that we have completed the discussion of perfect competition, monopoly, monopolistic competition, and oligopoly, you are prepared to compare these four market structures. Exhibit 8 summarizes the characteristics and gives examples of each market structure.

## Key Concepts

| | | |
|---|---|---|
| Monopolistic competition | Oligopoly | Price leadership |
| Product differentiation | Mutual interdependence | Cartel |
| Nonprice competition | Kinked demand curve | Game theory |

## Summary

- **Monopolistic competition** is a market structure characterized by (1) many small sellers, (2) a differentiated product, and (3) easy market entry and exit. Given these characteristics, firms in monopolistic competition have a negligible effect on the market price.

- **Product differentiation** is a key characteristic of monopolistic competition. It is the process of creating real or apparent differences between products.

- **Nonprice competition** includes advertising, packaging, product development, better quality, and better service. Under monopolistic competition and oligopoly, firms may compete using nonprice competition rather than price competition.

- **Short-run equilibrium for a monopolistic competitor** can yield economic losses, zero economic profits, or economic profits. In the long run, monopolistic competitors make zero economic profits.

## SHORT-RUN EQUILIBRIUM FOR A MONOPOLISTIC COMPETITOR

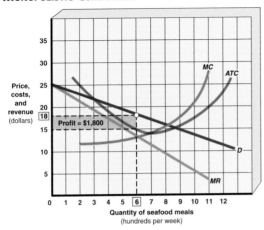

■ Comparing monopolistic competition with perfect competition, we find that in the long run the monopolistically competitive firm does not achieve allocative efficiency, charges a higher price, restricts output, and does not produce where average costs are at a minimum.

## COMPARISON OF MONOPOLISTIC AND PERFECT COMPETITION

■ **Oligopoly** is a market structure characterized by (1) few sellers, (2) either a homogeneous or a differentiated product, and (3) difficult market entry. Oligopolies are **mutually interdependent** because an action by one firm may cause a reaction from other firms.

■ The **nonprice competition model** is a theory that might explain oligopolistic behavior. Under this theory, firms use advertising and product differentiation, rather than price reductions, to compete.

■ The **kinked demand curve** model explains why prices may be rigid in an oligopoly. The kink occurs because an oligopolist assumes that rivals will match a price decrease, but ignore a price increase.

## KINKED DEMAND CURVE

■ **Price leadership** is another theory of pricing behavior under oligopoly. When a dominant firm in an industry raises or lowers its price, other firms follow suit.

■ A **cartel** is a formal agreement among firms to set prices and output quotas. The goal is to maximize profits, but firms have an incentive to cheat, which is a constant threat to a cartel.

## CARTEL

Extra profit from cheating = $40 million

Profit without cheating = $40 million

- **Game theory** reveals that (1) oligopolies are mutually interdependent in their pricing policies; (2) without collusion oligopoly prices and mutual profits are lower; and (3) oligopolists have a temptation to cheat on any collusive agreement.

- **Comparing oligopoly with perfect competition,** we find that the oligopolist allocates resources inefficiently, charges a higher price, and restricts output so that price may exceed average cost.

## Summary of Conclusion Statements

- The many-sellers condition is met when each firm is so small relative to the total market that its pricing decisions have a negligible effect on the market price.

- When a product is differentiated, buyers are not indifferent as to which seller's product they buy.

- The demand curve for a monopolistically competitive firm is less elastic (steeper) than for a perfectly competitive firm and more elastic (flatter) than for a monopolist.

- The few-sellers condition is met when these few firms are so large relative to the total market that they can affect the market price.

- Buyers in an oligopoly may or may not be indifferent as to which seller's product they buy.

- The payoff matrix demonstrates why a competitive oligopoly tends to result in both rivals using a low-price strategy that does not maximize mutual profits.

- As long as the benefits exceed the costs, cheating can threaten formal or informal agreements among oligopolists to maximize joint profits.

## Study Questions and Problems

1. Compare the monopolistically competitive firm's demand curve to those of a perfect competitor and a monopolist.

2. Suppose the minimum point on the *LRAC* curve of a soft-drink firm's cola is $1 per liter. Under conditions of monopolistic competition, will the price of a liter bottle of cola in the long run be above $1, equal to $1, less than $1, or impossible to determine?

3. Exhibit 9 represents a monopolistically competitive firm in long-run equilibrium.

**EXHIBIT 9**

a. Which price represents the long-run equilibrium price?

b. Which quantity represents the long-run equilibrium output?

c. At which quantity is the *LRAC* curve at its minimum?

d. Is the long-run equilibrium price greater than, less than, or equal to the marginal cost of producing the equilibrium output?

4. Consider this statement: "Because price equals long-run average cost and profits are zero, a monopolistically competitive firm is efficient." Do you agree or disagree? Explain.

5. Assuming identical long-run cost curves, draw two graphs, and indicate the price and output that result in the long run under monopolistic competition and perfect competition. Evaluate the differences between these two market structures.

6. Draw a graph that shows how advertising affects a firm's *ATC* curve. Explain how advertising can lead to lower prices in a monopolistically competitive industry.

7. List four goods or services that you have purchased that were produced by an oligopolist. Why are these industries oligopolistic, rather than monopolistically competitive?

8. Why is mutual interdependence important under oligopoly, but not so important under perfect competition, monopoly, or monopolistic competition?

9. Suppose the jeans industry is an oligopoly in which each firm sells its own distinctive brand of jeans. Each firm believes its rivals will not follow its price increases, but will follow its price cuts. Explain the demand curve facing each firm. Does this demand curve mean that firms in the jeans industry do or do not compete against one another?

10. What might be a general distinction between oligopolists that advertise and those that do not?

11. Suppose IBM raised the price of its printers, but Hewlett-Packard (the largest seller) refused to follow. Two years later IBM cut its price, and Hewlett-Packard retaliated with an even deeper price cut, which IBM was forced to match. For the next five years, Hewlett-Packard raised its prices five times, and each time IBM followed suit within 24 hours. Does the pricing behavior of these computer industry firms follow the cartel model or the price leadership model? Why?

12. Evaluate the following statement: "A cartel will put an end to price war, which is a barbaric form of competition that benefits no one."

13. Assume the payoff matrix in Exhibit 7 applies to spending for advertising rather than airline fares. Substitute "Don't Advertise" for "High fare" and "Advertise" for "Low fare." Assume the same profit and loss figures in each cell, but substitute "Marlboro" for "US Airways" and "Camel" for "American Airlines." Explain the dynamics of the model and why cigarette companies might be pleased with a government ban on all cigarette advertising.

## Study Guide Questions

1. _____ means an action by one firm may cause a reaction on the part of other firms.

2. The theory of monopolistic competition predicts that in long-run equilibrium a monopolistically competitive firm will
   a. produce the output level at which price equals long-run marginal cost.
   b. operate at minimum long-run average cost.
   c. overutilize its insufficient capacity.
   d. produce the output level at which price equals long-run average cost.

3. Which of the following is *true* about an oligopoly equilibrium in comparison with equilibrium under similar circumstances but with perfect competition?
   a. Output is larger and price is lower than under perfect competition.
   b. Output is larger but price is higher than under perfect competition.
   c. Output is smaller and price is higher than under perfect competition.
   d. Output is smaller and price is lower than under perfect competition.

4. A game theory strategy for oligopolists to avoid a low-price outcome is _____.
   a. tit for tat
   b. price leadership
   c. second best
   d. win-win

5. T F In the long run, marginal cost must equal marginal revenue for a monopolistic competitive firm, but *not* at the minimum point of the long-run average cost curve.

**Answers to these questions are in the complete Study Guide at www.thomsonedu.com/thomsonnow.**

 **For Online Exercises, go to the text Web site at www.thomsonedu.com/economics/tucker.**

## Checkpoint Answers

### Which Model Fits the Cereal Aisle?

The fact that there is a differentiated product does not necessarily mean that many firms are competing along the cereal aisle. The different cereals listed in this example are produced by only four companies: General Mills, Kellogg's, Quaker Oats, and Post. In fact, there are relatively few firms in the cereal industry, so even though they sell a differentiated product, the market structure cannot be monopolistic competition. If you said the cereal industry is an oligopoly, **YOU ARE CORRECT.**

## Practice Quiz

For an explanation of the correct answers, please visit the tutorial at www.thomsonedu.com/economics/tucker.

1. An industry with many small sellers, a differentiated product, and easy entry would *best* be described as which of the following?
   a. Oligopoly
   b. Monopolistic competition
   c. Perfect competition
   d. Monopoly

2. Which of the following industries is the *best* example of monopolistic competition?
   a. Wheat
   b. Restaurant
   c. Automobile
   d. Water service

3. Which of the following is *not* a characteristic of monopolistic competition?
   a. A large number of small firms
   b. A differentiated product
   c. Easy market entry
   d. A homogeneous product

4. A monopolistically competitive firm will
   a. maximize profits by producing where $MR = MC$.
   b. not earn an economic profit in the long run.
   c. shut down if price is less than average variable cost.
   d. do all of the above.

5. The theory of monopolistic competition predicts that in long-run equilibrium a monopolistically competitive firm will
   a. produce the output level at which price equals long-run marginal cost.
   b. operate at minimum long-run average cost.
   c. overutilize its insufficient capacity.
   d. produce the output level at which price equals long-run average cost.

6. A monopolistically competitive firm is inefficient because the firm
   a. earns positive economic profit in the long run.
   b. is producing at an output where marginal cost equals price.
   c. is not maximizing its profit.
   d. produces an output where average total cost is not minimum.

7. A monopolistically competitive firm in the long run earns the same economic profit as
   a. a perfectly competitive firm.
   b. a monopolist.
   c. a cartel.
   d. none of the above.

8. One possible effect of advertising on a firm's long-run average cost curve is to
   a. raise the curve.
   b. lower the curve.
   c. shift the curve rightward.
   d. shift the curve leftward.

9. Monopolistic competition is an inefficient market structure because
   a. firms earn zero profit in the long run.
   b. marginal cost is less than price in the long run.
   c. a wider variety of products is available compared to perfect competition.
   d. of all of the above.

10. The "Big Three" U.S. automobile industry is described as
    a. a monopoly.
    b. perfect competition.
    c. monopolistic competition.
    d. an oligopoly.

11. The cigarette industry in the United States is described as
    a. a monopoly.
    b. perfect competition.

c. monopolistic competition.

d. an oligopoly.

12. A characteristic of an oligopoly is
    a. mutual interdependence in pricing decisions.
    b. easy market entry.
    c. both (a) and (b).
    d. neither (a) nor (b).

13. The kinked demand curve theory attempts to explain why an oligopolistic firm
    a. has relatively large advertising expenditures.
    b. fails to invest in research and development (R&D).
    c. infrequently changes its price.
    d. engages in excessive brand proliferation.

14. According to the kinked demand curve theory, when one firm raises its price, other firms will
    a. also raise their prices.
    b. refuse to follow.
    c. increase their advertising expenditures.
    d. exit the industry.

15. Which of the following is evidence that OPEC is a cartel?
    a. Agreement on price and output quotas by oil ministries
    b. Ability to raise prices regardless of demand
    c. Mutual interdependence in pricing and output decisions
    d. Ability to completely control entry

**EXHIBIT 10  A TWO-FIRM PAYOFF MATRIX**

| | Tucker Oil Company | |
|---|---|---|
| | **$100** | **$50** |
| Zeba Oil Company **$100** | A $25 billion / $25 billion | B $15 billion / $5 billion |
| Zeba Oil Company **$50** | C $5 billion / $15 billion | D $10 billion / $10 billion |

16. Assume costs are identical for the two firms in Exhibit 10. If both firms were allowed to form a cartel and agree on their prices, equilibrium would be established by
    a. Zeba Oil charging $100 and Tucker Oil charging $100.

    b. Zeba Oil charging $100 and Tucker Oil charging $50.
    c. Zeba Oil charging $50 and Tucker Oil charging $50.
    d. Zeba Oil charging $50 and Tucker Oil charging $100.

17. Suppose costs are identical for the two firms in Exhibit 10. If both firms assume the other will compete and charge a lower price, equilibrium will be established by
    a. Zeba Oil charging $100 and Tucker Oil charging $100.
    b. Zeba Oil charging $100 and Tucker Oil charging $50.
    c. Zeba Oil charging $50 and Tucker Oil charging $100.
    d. Zeba Oil charging $50 and Tucker Oil charging $50.

18. Suppose costs are identical for the two firms in Exhibit 10. Each firm assumes without formal agreement that if it sets the high price, its rival will not charge a lower price. Under these tit-for-tat conditions, equilibrium will be established by
    a. Zeba Oil charging $100 and Tucker Oil charging $100.
    b. Zeba Oil charging $100 and Tucker Oil charging $50.
    c. Zeba Oil charging $50 and Tucker Oil charging $50.
    d. Zeba Oil charging $50 and Tucker Oil charging $100.

19. Which of the following is a game theory strategy for oligopolists to avoid a low-price outcome?
    a. Tit for tat
    b. Win-win
    c. Last-in first-out
    d. Second best

20. Which of the following is a game theory strategy for oligopolists to avoid a low-price outcome?
    a. Tit-for-tat
    b. Price leadership
    c. Cartel
    d. All of the above

# Labor Markets

© Digital Vision/Getty Images

I n 2005, champion golfer Tiger Woods earned the impressive figure of $87 million, but talk show host Oprah Winfrey did even better. She earned $225 million. While one headline reports a sports team signed their star player to a contract paying $10 million annually, another cites a recent survey showing chief executive officers (CEOs) of America's biggest corporations are paid millions of dollars in compensation. The president of the United States is paid $400,000 per year. The worker with a bachelor's degree or higher earns an average of about $55,000. The average high school graduate earns less than $30,000, while many others, including college students, toil for the minimum wage.

How are earnings determined? What accounts for the wide differences in earnings? This chapter provides answers by explaining different types of labor markets that determine workers' compensation and the quantity of workers firms hire. Understanding hiring decisions is indeed a key to understanding

why some become rich and famous by playing baseball—a kid's game— while other workers might be exploited by firms with labor market power.

The chapter begins with the development of a competitive labor market in which no single buyer or seller can influence the price (wage rate) of labor. The chapter concludes with a discussion of power. As in the product markets, labor market determinations are affected by market power. Power on the side of either unions or employers can

alter wage and employment outcomes. For example, the chapter explains how unions affect wages and examines trends in union membership around the world.

**In this chapter, you will learn to solve these economics puzzles:**

- What determines the wage rate an employer pays?
- How do labor unions influence wages and employment?
- Does the NCAA exploit college athletes?

## The Labor Market under Perfect Competition

In Chapters 8–10, you studied the price and quantity determinations of goods and services produced by firms operating under different market structures—perfect competition, monopoly, oligopoly, and monopolistic competition. As you have learned, market structure affects the price and the quantity of a good or service sold by firms to consumers. Similarly, as this chapter will demonstrate, the price (wage rate) paid to labor and the quantity of labor hired by firms are influenced by whether or not the labor market is competitive.

Recall from Chapter 8 that we assumed the hypothetical firm called Computech produces and sells electronic units for automated teller machines in a perfectly competitive market. Here we also assume Computech hires workers in a perfectly competitive labor market. In a perfectly competitive labor market, there are many sellers and buyers of labor services. Consequently, wages and salaries are determined by the intersection of the demand for labor and the supply of labor.

## THE DEMAND FOR LABOR

How many workers should Computech hire? To answer this question, Computech must know how much workers contribute to its output. Column 1 of Exhibit 1 lists possible numbers of workers Computech might hire per day, and as discussed earlier in Chapter 7 on production costs, column 2 shows the total output per day. One worker would produce 5 units per day, 2 workers together would produce 9 units per day, and so on. Note that columns 1 and 2 constitute a *production function*, as represented earlier in Exhibit 2(a) in Chapter 7. Column 3 lists the additional output from hiring each worker. The first worker hired would add 5 units of output per day, the second would produce an additional 4 units (total product of 9–5 units produced), and so on. Recall from Chapter 7 that the additional output from hiring another unit of labor is defined as the *marginal product of labor* [see Exhibit 2(b) in Chapter 7]. Consistent with the *law of diminishing returns*, the marginal product falls as the firm hires more workers.[1]

The next step in Computech's hiring decision is to convert marginal product into dollars by calculating the **marginal revenue product (*MRP*)**, which is the increase in a firm's total revenue resulting from hiring an additional unit of labor or other variable resource. Stated simply, *MRP* is the dollar value of worker productivity. It is the extra revenue a firm earns from selling the output of an extra worker. Returning to Exhibit 1 in Chapter 8 on perfect competition, suppose the market equilibrium price per unit is $70. Because Computech operates in a perfectly competitive market, the firm can sell any quantity of its product at the $70 market-determined price. Given this situation, the first unit of labor contributes an *MRP* of $350 per day to revenue ($70 per unit times the 5 units of output). Column 5 of Exhibit 1 lists the *MRP* of each additional worker hired.

**Marginal revenue product (*MRP*)**
The increase in firm's total revenue resulting from hiring an additional unit of labor or other variable resource.

> **CONCLUSION** *A perfectly competitive firm's marginal revenue product is equal to the marginal product of its labor times the price of its product. Expressed as a formula:*
>
> $$MRP = P \times MP$$

Now assuming all other inputs are fixed, Computech can derive its **demand curve for labor**, which conforms to the law of demand explained in Chapter 3. The demand curve for labor is a curve showing the different quantities of labor

**Demand curve for labor**
A curve showing the different quantities of labor employers are willing to hire at different wage rates in a given time period, ceteris paribus. It is equal to the marginal revenue product of labor.

[1] Recall from Chapter 7 that at low rates of output marginal product may increase with the addition of more labor due to specialization and division of labor. Then, as output expands in the short run, the law of diminishing returns will cause marginal product to decrease.

| EXHIBIT 1 | COMPUTECH'S DEMAND FOR LABOR | | | | |
|---|---|---|---|---|---|
| Points | (1) Labor input (workers per day) | (2) Total output (units per day) | (3) Marginal product (units per day) | (4) Product Price | (5) Marginal revenue product [(3) × (4)] |
|   | 0 | 0 |   | $70 |   |
|   |   |   | 5 |   | $350 |
| A | 1 | 5 |   | 70 |   |
|   |   |   | 4 |   | 280 |
| B | 2 | 9 |   | 70 |   |
|   |   |   | 3 |   | 210 |
| C | 3 | 12 |   | 70 |   |
|   |   |   | 2 |   | 140 |
| D | 4 | 14 |   | 70 |   |
|   |   |   | 1 |   | 70 |
| E | 5 | 15 |   | 70 |   |

employers are willing to hire at different wage rates. It is equal to the *MRP* of labor. The *MRP* numbers from Exhibit 1 are duplicated in Exhibit 2. As shown in the exhibit, the price of labor in terms of daily wages is measured on the vertical axis. The quantity of workers Computech will hire per day at each wage rate is measured on the horizontal axis. The demand curve for labor is downward sloping: As the wage rate falls, Computech will hire more workers per day. If the wage rate is above $350 (point *A*), Computech will hire no workers because the cost of a worker is more than the dollar value of any worker's contribution to total revenue (*MRP*). But what happens if Computech pays each worker $280 per day? At point *B*, Computech finds it profitable to hire 2 workers because the *MRP* of the first worker is greater than the wage rate (extra cost) and the second worker's *MRP* equals the wage rate. If the wage rate is $140 per day at point *D*, Computech will find it profitable to hire 4 workers. In this case, Computech will not hire the fifth worker. Why? The fifth worker contributes an *MRP* of $70 to total revenue (point *E*), but this amount is below the wage rate paid of $140. Consequently, Computech cannot maximize profits by hiring the fifth worker because it would be adding more to costs than to revenue. Specifically, Computech would lose $70 per day by hiring the fifth worker. At a wage rate of $70, however, the fifth worker would be hired.

**CONCLUSION** *A firm hires additional workers up to the point where the* MRP *equals the wage rate.*

**Derived demand**
The demand for labor and other factors of production that depends on the consumer demand for the final goods and services the factors produce.

Each firm in the market has a demand for labor based on its *MRP* data. Summing these individual demand curves for labor provides the market demand curve for labor in the electronic components industry. Another important point must be made. The demand for labor is called **derived demand**. The derived demand for labor and other factors of production depends on the consumer demand for the

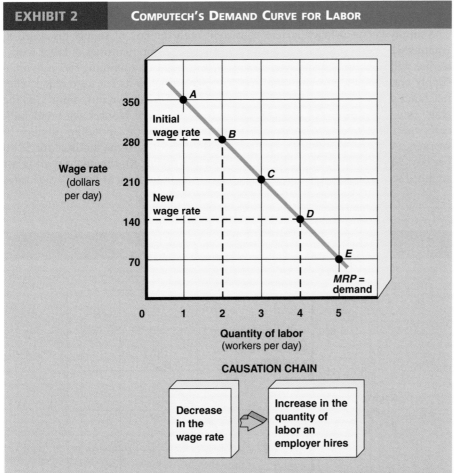

| EXHIBIT 2 | COMPUTECH'S DEMAND CURVE FOR LABOR |
| --- | --- |

**CAUSATION CHAIN**

Decrease in the wage rate ⇨ Increase in the quantity of labor an employer hires

Computech's downward-sloping demand curve for labor is derived from the marginal revenue product (*MRP*) of labor, which declines as additional workers are hired. The *MRP* is the change in total revenue that results from hiring one more worker (see Exhibit 1). At point *B*, Computech pays $280 per day and finds it profitable to pay this wage to 2 workers because each worker's *MRP* equals or exceeds the wage rate. If Computech pays a lower wage rate of $140 per day at point *D*, it is not profitable for the firm to hire the fifth worker because this worker's *MRP* of $70 is below the wage rate of $140 per day. At a wage rate of $70, the fifth worker would be hired.

final goods and services the factors produce. If consumers are not willing to purchase products requiring electronic components, such as bank teller machines, there is no *MRP*, and firms will hire no workers to make electronic components for them. On the other hand, if customer demand for bank teller machines soars, the price of units rises, and the *MRP* of firms in the electronic components industry also rises. The result is a rightward shift in the market demand curve for labor.

## THE SUPPLY OF LABOR

**Supply curve of labor**
A curve showing the different quantities of labor workers are willing to offer employers at different wage rates in a given time period, ceteris paribus.

The **supply curve of labor** is also consistent with the law of supply discussed in Chapter 3. The supply curve of labor shows the different quantities of labor workers are willing to offer employers at different wage rates. Summing the individual supply curves of labor for firms producing electronic units for automated teller machines provides the market supply curve of labor. As shown in Exhibit 3, as the wage rate rises, more workers are willing to supply their labor. Each point indicates the wage rate that must be paid to attract the corresponding number of workers. At point *A*, 20,000 workers offer their services to the industry for $140 per day. At the higher wage rate of $280 per day (point *B*), the quantity of labor supplied is 40,000 workers. More people are willing to work at higher wage rates

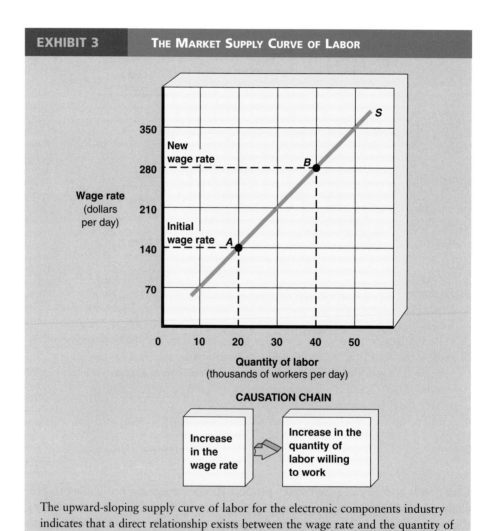

| EXHIBIT 3 | THE MARKET SUPPLY CURVE OF LABOR |

**CAUSATION CHAIN**

Increase in the wage rate ⇨ Increase in the quantity of labor willing to work

The upward-sloping supply curve of labor for the electronic components industry indicates that a direct relationship exists between the wage rate and the quantity of labor supplied. At point *A*, 20,000 workers are willing to work for $140 per day in this market. If the wage rate rises to $280 per day, 40,000 workers will supply their services to the electronic components labor market.

because the incentive of earning more compensates for the opportunity cost of leisure time. Higher wages also attract workers from other industries that require similar skills but have lower wage rates.

Ignoring differences in wage scales, why might the supply of less-skilled workers (carpenters) be greater than that of more skilled workers (physicians)? The explanation for this difference is the **human capital** required to perform various occupations. Human capital is the accumulation of education, training, experience, and health that enables a worker to enter an occupation and be productive. Less human capital is required to be a carpenter than a physician. Therefore, many people are qualified, and the supply of carpenters is larger than the supply of physicians.

**Human capital**
The accumulation of education, training, experience, and health that enables a worker to enter an occupation and be productive.

## THE EQUILIBRIUM WAGE RATE

Wage rates are determined in perfectly competitive markets by the interaction of labor supply and demand. The equilibrium wage rate for the entire electronic components market, shown in Exhibit 4(a), is $210 per day. This wage rate clears the market because the quantity of 30,000 workers demanded equals the quantity of 30,000 workers who are willing to supply their labor services at that wage rate. In a competitive labor market, no single worker can set his or her wage above the equilibrium wage. Such a worker fears not being hired because there are so many

**EXHIBIT 4** — **A COMPETITIVE LABOR MARKET DETERMINES THE FIRM'S EQUILIBRIUM WAGE**

(a) Electronic components labor market

(b) Computech

In Part (a), the intersection of the supply of labor and the demand for labor curves determines the equilibrium wage rate of $210 per day in the electronic components industry. Part (b) illustrates that a single firm, such as Computech, is a "wage taker." The firm can hire all the workers it wants at this equilibrium wage, so its supply curve, $S$, is a horizontal line. Computech chooses to hire 3 workers, where the firm's demand curve for labor intersects its supply curve of labor.

workers who will work for $210 per day. Similarly, so many firms are hiring labor that a single firm cannot influence the wage by paying workers more or less than the prevailing wage. Hence, a wage rate above $210 per day would create a surplus of workers seeking employment (unemployment) in the electronic components market, and a wage rate below $210 per day would cause a shortage.

Why do cardiologists make a much higher hourly wage than a server in a restaurant? As demonstrated in Exhibit 4(a), wage differentials are determined by the demand and supply curves in labor markets for these two occupations. In this case, the equilibrium wage rate for cardiologists greatly exceeds the equilibrium wage rate for servers. In the next chapter, this labor market model is used to explain differences in wages resulting from racial discrimination.

Although the supply curve of labor is upward sloping for the electronic components market, this is not the case for an individual firm, such as Computech, shown in Exhibit 4(b). Because a competitive labor market assumes that each firm is too small to influence the wage rate, Computech is a "wage taker" and therefore pays the market-determined wage rate of $210 per day, regardless of the quantity of labor it employs. For this reason, the labor supply to Computech is represented by a horizontal line at the equilibrium wage rate. Given this wage rate of $210 per day, Computech then hires labor up to the equilibrium point, *E*, where the wage rate equals the third worker's marginal revenue product.

# Labor Unions

The perfectly competitive model does not apply to workers who belong to unions. Unions arose because workers recognized that acting together gave them more bargaining power than acting individually and being at the mercy of their employers. Some of the biggest unions are the Teamsters, United Auto Workers, National Education Association, and American Federation of Government Employees. Two primary objectives of unions are to improve working conditions and to raise the wages of union members above the level that would exist in a competitive labor market. To raise wages, unions use three basic strategies: (1) increase the demand for labor, (2) decrease the supply of labor, and (3) exert power to force employers to pay a wage rate above the equilibrium wage rate.

### UNIONS INCREASE THE DEMAND FOR LABOR

Now suppose the workers form a union. One way to increase wages is to use a method called *featherbedding*. This means the union forces firms to hire more workers than are required or to impose work rules that reduce output per worker. For example, contract provisions may prohibit any workers but carpenters from doing even the simplest carpentry work. Another approach is to boost domestic demand for labor by decreasing competition from other nations. For example, the union might lobby Congress to protect the U.S. electronic parts industry against competition from China. Another approach might be to advertise and try to convince the public to "Look for the Union Label." Effective advertising would boost the demand for electronic products with union-made components and, in turn, the demand for union labor because it is *derived demand*.

Exhibit 5 shows how union power can be used to increase the demand curve for labor. This exhibit reproduces the labor market for electronic components

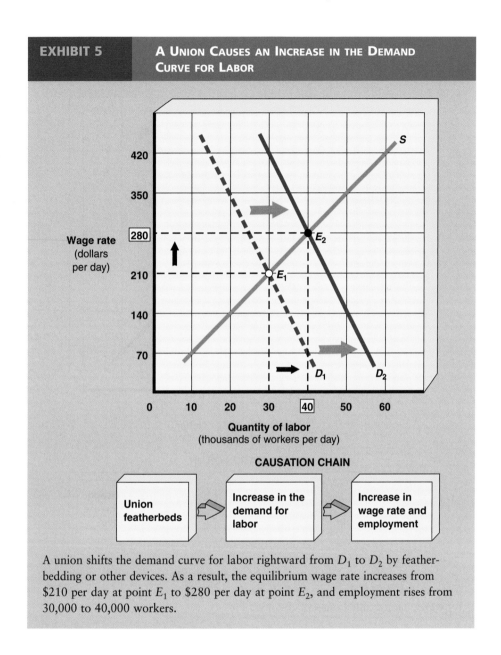

**EXHIBIT 5**     **A UNION CAUSES AN INCREASE IN THE DEMAND CURVE FOR LABOR**

A union shifts the demand curve for labor rightward from $D_1$ to $D_2$ by feather-bedding or other devices. As a result, the equilibrium wage rate increases from $210 per day at point $E_1$ to $280 per day at point $E_2$, and employment rises from 30,000 to 40,000 workers.

workers from Exhibit 4(a). Begin at equilibrium point $E_1$, with the wage rate of $210 per day paid to each of 30,000 workers. Then the union causes the demand curve for labor to increase from $D_1$ to $D_2$. At the new equilibrium point, $E_2$, firms hire an additional 10,000 workers and pay each worker an extra $70 per day.

## UNIONS DECREASE THE SUPPLY OF LABOR

Exhibit 6 shows another way unions can use their power to increase the wage rate of their members by restricting the supply of labor. Now suppose the labor market is in equilibrium at point $E_1$, with 40,000 workers making electronic units and

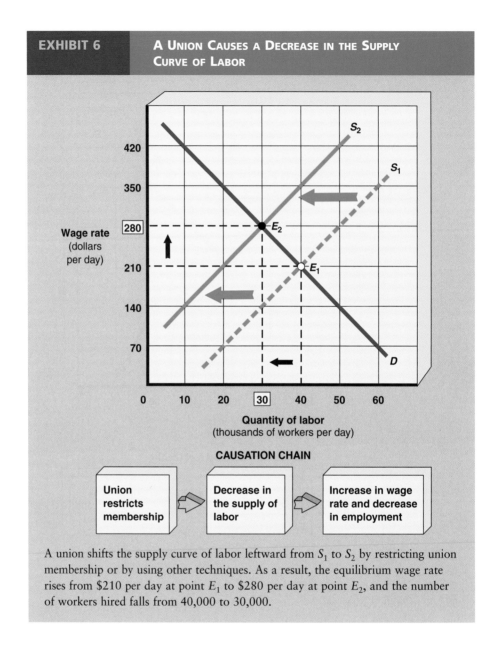

**EXHIBIT 6**

**A UNION CAUSES A DECREASE IN THE SUPPLY CURVE OF LABOR**

**CAUSATION CHAIN**

| Union restricts membership | ⇨ | Decrease in the supply of labor | ⇨ | Increase in wage rate and decrease in employment |

A union shifts the supply curve of labor leftward from $S_1$ to $S_2$ by restricting union membership or by using other techniques. As a result, the equilibrium wage rate rises from $210 per day at point $E_1$ to $280 per day at point $E_2$, and the number of workers hired falls from 40,000 to 30,000.

earning $210 per day. Then the union uses its power to shift the supply curve of labor leftward from $S_1$ to $S_2$ by, say, requiring a longer apprenticeship, charging higher fees, or using some other device designed to reduce union membership. For example, the union might lobby for legislation to reduce immigration or to shorten working hours. As a result of these union actions, the equilibrium wage rate rises to $280 per day at point $E_2$, and employment is artificially reduced to 30,000 workers. It should be noted that self-serving practices of unions to limit the labor supply and raise wages can be disguised as standards of professionalism, such as those required by the American Medical Association and the American Bar Association, teacher certification requirements, Ph.D. requirements for university faculty, and so on.

## Unions Use Collective Bargaining to Boost Wages

A third way to raise the wage rate above the equilibrium level is to use **collective bargaining**. Collective bargaining is the process of negotiating labor contracts between the union and management concerning wages and working conditions. By law, once a union has been certified as the representative of a majority of the workers, employers must deal with the union. If employers deny union demands, the union can strike and reduce profits until the firms agree to a higher wage rate.

The result of collective bargaining is shown in Exhibit 7. Again, we return to the situation depicted for the electronic components market in Exhibit 4(a). At the equilibrium wage rate of $210 per day (point E), there is no surplus or shortage of workers. Then the industry is unionized, and a collective bargaining agreement takes effect in which firms agree to pay the union wage rate of $280 per day. At the higher wage rate, employment falls from 30,000 to 20,000 workers. However, 40,000 workers wish to work for $280 per day, so there is a surplus of 20,000 unemployed workers in the industry. How might firms react to a situation in which they hire fewer workers and pay higher wages? Employers might respond by substituting capital for labor or by transferring operations overseas, where labor costs are lower than in the United States.

**Collective bargaining**
The process of negotiating labor contracts between the union and management concerning wages and working conditions.

| EXHIBIT 7 | UNION COLLECTIVE BARGAINING CAUSES A WAGE RATE INCREASE |
| --- | --- |

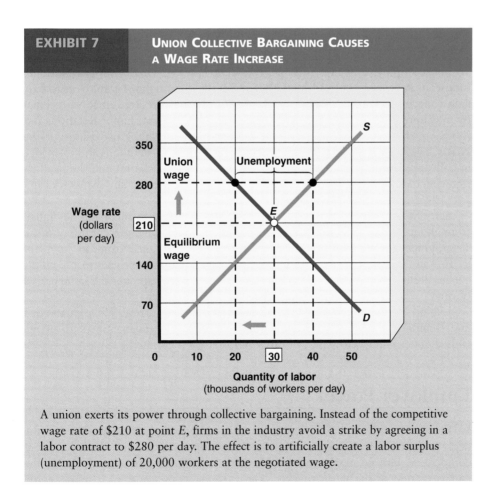

A union exerts its power through collective bargaining. Instead of the competitive wage rate of $210 at point E, firms in the industry avoid a strike by agreeing in a labor contract to $280 per day. The effect is to artificially create a labor surplus (unemployment) of 20,000 workers at the negotiated wage.

| EXHIBIT 8 | FACTORS CAUSING CHANGES IN LABOR DEMAND AND LABOR SUPPLY |
|---|---|
| **Changes in labor demand** | **Changes in labor supply** |
| 1. Unions | 1. Unions |
| 2. Prices of substitute inputs | 2. Demographic trends |
| 3. Technology | 3. Expectations of future income |
| 4. Demand for final products | 4. Changes in immigration laws |
| 5. Marginal product of labor | 5. Education and training |

Finally, several factors can cause either the demand curve for labor or the supply curve of labor to shift. Exhibit 8 provides a list of these factors.

**Global Economics**

# Union Membership Around the World

How important are unions as measured by the percentage of the labor force that belongs to a union? Let's start during the Great Depression, when millions of people were out of work and union membership was relatively low (see Exhibit 9). To boost employment and earnings, President Franklin D. Roosevelt's National Industrial Recovery Act (NIRA) of 1933 established the right of employees to bargain collectively with their employers, but the act was declared unconstitutional by the Supreme Court in 1935. However, the 1935 National Labor Relations Act (NLRA), known as the Wagner Act, incorporated the labor provisions of the NIRA. The Wagner Act guaranteed workers the right to form unions and to engage in collective bargaining. The combined impact of this legislation and the production demands of World War II created a surge in union membership between 1935 and 1945.

Since World War II, union power has declined. Union membership has fallen from about 35 percent of the labor force in 1945 to about 12 percent today. Since 1983, union membership of public sector workers fell slightly from 36.7 percent to 36.4 in 2004. On the other hand, union membership for private sector workers has declined significantly from 16.5 percent to 7.9 percent over the same period of time.

Exhibit 10 shows the unionization rates in other countries. While in Sweden and Denmark nearly all workers belong to a union, union membership in the United States is far below that of other industrialized countries.

# Employer Power

**Monopsony**
A labor market in which a single firm hires labor.

So far, labor markets have been explained with employees possessing varying degrees of power to influence wage rates and employment while employers were competitive with no market power. However, significant power can exist on the employer side of the labor market. The extreme case occurs in a **monopsony**.

| EXHIBIT 9 | U.S. UNION MEMBERSHIP, 1930–2004 |

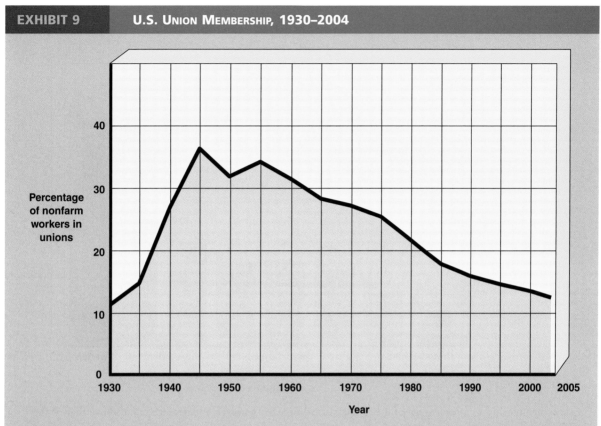

As a percentage of nonfarm workers, union membership in the United States grew most rapidly during the decade 1935–1945. Since its peak in 1945, union membership as a percentage of the labor force has fallen to about the level in 1935.

*Source:* Statistical Abstract of the United States, *2006, http://www.census.gov/prod/www/statistical-abstract.html, Table 647.*

Monopsony is a labor market in which a single firm hires labor. For example, a single textile mill, mining company, or housing contractor might be the only buyer of labor in a particular market. The classical phrase for this situation is the "company town," where for miles around a small town everyone's livelihood depends on a single employer. The reason for the monopsony is the absence of other firms in the area competing for relatively immobile labor because workers must acquire new skills to find work outside the company town market. Even if a firm doesn't dominate a local labor market, it may have monopsony power over certain types of labor. A hospital, for example, may be the only large employer of nurses in a local market; therefore, it has monopsony power.

## MARGINAL FACTOR COST

This chapter began by assuming Computech operated in a competitive labor market in which no single employer in the electronic components market had any direct influence on the market wage rate. Recall from Exhibit 4 that Computech

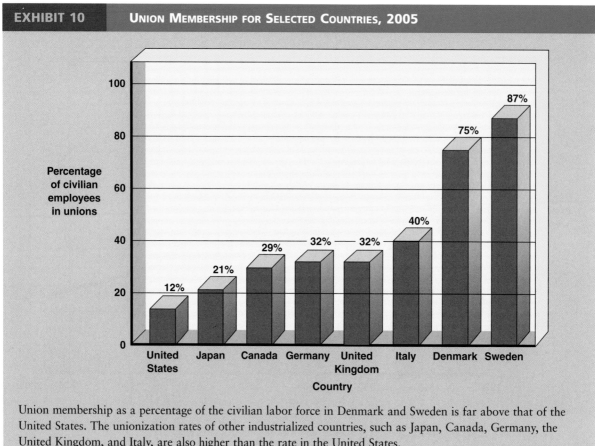

**EXHIBIT 10      UNION MEMBERSHIP FOR SELECTED COUNTRIES, 2005**

Union membership as a percentage of the civilian labor force in Denmark and Sweden is far above that of the United States. The unionization rates of other industrialized countries, such as Japan, Canada, Germany, the United Kingdom, and Italy, are also higher than the rate in the United States.

*Source: U.S. Department of Labor, Bureau of International Labor Affairs,* Foreign Labor Trends, *http://www.dol.gov/ILAB/media/ reports/flt/main.htm.*

---

is a wage taker. More precisely, Computech hires the quantity of labor at the prevailing labor market equilibrium wage rate, which is determined by the point where the firm's downward-sloping *MRP* curve (demand curve for labor) intersects the horizontal supply curve of labor. The equilibrium wage rate is established by a competitive labor market beyond Computech's power to control.

Now we visit the isolated small town of Plainsville and find General Griffin's, which is a monopsonist producing turkeys. As shown in Exhibit 11, the supply of labor curve facing the monopsonist is upward sloping rather than horizontal. The reason is that General Griffin's is the only firm hiring workers in Plainsville, so it faces the industry, or entire, supply curve of labor in the Plainsville labor market. This situation compares with that of the monopolist, which faces the industry demand curve for a particular product. As a result, the monopolist in a product market cannot sell an additional unit of a good without lowering the price, and the marginal revenue curve falls below the demand curve. For the monopsonist, a distinction exists between the supply curve of labor and the **marginal factor cost** (*MFC*) curve. Marginal factor cost is the additional total cost resulting from a

**Marginal factor cost (*MFC*)**
The additional total cost resulting from a one-unit increase in the quantity of a factor.

| EXHIBIT 11 | A MONOPSONIST DETERMINES ITS WAGE RATE |
|---|---|

| Points | (1)<br>Wage rate<br>(per hour) | (2)<br>Labor input<br>(workers<br>per hour) | (3)<br>Total<br>wage cost<br>(per hour)<br>[(1) × (2)] | (4)<br>Marginal<br>factor cost<br>(MFC)<br>[Δ(3)/Δ(2)] |
|---|---|---|---|---|
|  | $ 0 | 0 | $ 0 | |
|  |  |  |  | $ 3 |
| A | 3 | 1 | 3 | |
|  |  |  |  | 9 |
| B | 6 | 2 | 12 | |
|  |  |  |  | 15 |
| C | 9 | 3 | 27 | |
|  |  |  |  | 21 |
| D | 12 | 4 | 48 | |

The monopsonist, General Griffin's, faces the industry upward-sloping supply curve of labor in the small town of Plainsville. As the wage rate rises, all workers must be paid the same higher wage. As a result, the change in total wage cost (marginal factor cost in column 4) exceeds the wage paid to the last worker (column 1). The MFC curve therefore lies above the supply curve of labor.

The demand curve for labor is the marginal revenue product (MRP) or the worth to the monopsonist of each worker it hires. The intersection of the MFC and MRP curves at point E determines that General Griffin's hires 2 workers per hour. Because this firm has a monopsony in the Plainsville labor market, it can pay $6 per hour at point B on the supply curve of labor, which is enough to attract 2 workers. However, the worker is exploited because the MRP at point E for the second worker is $12 per hour and the wage rate is only $6. In a competitive labor market, the equilibrium would be point C, and General Griffin's would pay a higher wage and employ more workers.

## CHECKPOINT

### Can the Minimum Wage Create Jobs?

In Chapter 4, Exhibit 5 explained that the effect of the minimum wage in a competitive labor market is to decrease the number of unskilled workers employed. Assume the minimum wage is $9, and consider the effect on the monopsonist represented in Exhibit 11. This means by law the monopsonist cannot hire a worker for a lower wage. In the case of monopsony, contrary to the case of perfect competition, can the minimum wage increase the number of persons working? Explain your answer using Exhibit 11.

one-unit increase in the quantity of a factor. Note that the *MFC* curve starts above the bottom of the supply curve of labor and then rises above it. The *MFC* points are plotted at the midpoints because the change in total wage cost occurs between additional units of labor. Having made this observation, relax and take a deep breath; then we will proceed to the nuts and bolts of monopsonist theory.

If General Griffin's pays $3 per hour at point *A* on the upward-sloping supply curve of labor in Plainsville, only 1 worker will be willing to be hired. If the monopsonist wants to hire more labor, it must offer higher wages. If the firm raises its wage offer to $6 per hour for each worker (point *B*), the quantity of labor supplied increases to 2 workers per hour. In the exhibit, the total wage cost per hour in column 3 is computed by multiplying the wage rate per hour in column 1 times the number of workers per hour in column 2. At point *A*, the total wage cost per hour is $3, which equals the wage rate. At point *B*, the total wage cost per hour rises to $12, and *MFC* is greater than the wage rate of $6 per hour. The explanation is that all workers are assumed to perform the same job. Consequently, the first worker will demand to be paid the same wage rate as the second

## CHECKPOINT

### If You Don't Like It, Mickey, Take Your Bat and Go Home

Mickey Mantle described his salary negotiations with the Yankees in his autobiography *The Mick*. After winning baseball's Triple Crown in 1955, his salary increased from about $85,000 to $100,000. The next season, he raised his batting average even higher, and the Yankee team owner offered him a pay cut. What is the most likely explanation for the owner's behavior—an increase in the supply of star baseball players, owner monopsony power, or the owner's desire that Mantle find another team?

## You're the Economist

## Should College Athletes Be Paid?
*Applicable Concept: monopsony*

It was perfect football weather on a beautiful autumn Saturday at Nebraska State's stadium. There was a hush in the crowd of 80,000 as the clock showed 5 seconds left in the game and the scoreboard read Home 26 Visitor 30. The Screaming Eagles were playing the Fighting Irish, and the season was on the line. With time running out, the Eagles' All-American quarterback, Joe Wyoming, launched a desperation pass from his 45-yard line. The pass hit the extended fingers of a wide receiver who leaped over three defenders at the Irish 25-yard line and then ran into the end zone all alone. The home crowd roared with the joy of ecstasy after staring defeat in the face.

So the season had been in the hands of Joe Wyoming, who received a full scholarship, which cost the university more than $40,000 over four years. Because Joe led the Eagles to victory over Notre Dame, the team played in the Sugar Bowl, which paid Nebraska State $5 million for the appearance. In addition, the next year's ticket sales, alumni contributions, and trademark licensing boosted revenues $10 million, while applications for admission to the university increased sharply.

Economist John Leonard argues that college athletes are clearly underpaid, because players cannot be paid salaries under National Collegiate Athletic Association (NCAA) rules. His study estimated that a star college football player who is named to an All-American team generates a marginal revenue product of $100,000 per year for the university. Yet that athlete is paid only a $10,000 scholarship per year.

In Chapter 10, a cartel was explained as a group of firms that use a collusive agreement to act as a monopoly. NCAA regulations serve as a collusive agreement among colleges and universities to act as a monopsony and hire the services of college-bound

© Photodisc/Getty Images

athletes. Just like an output or sellers' cartel, such as the Organization of Petroleum Exporting Countries (OPEC), the NCAA must enforce the rules against cheaters.

Because this agreement holds players' wages far below their marginal revenue product, the gap creates an incentive for schools to offer "illegal" inducements of cars, money, clothes, and trips to attract good players. Such cheating benefits the college athletes, whose wages are raised closer to their marginal revenue products. A school that is not caught benefits by recruiting better players, achieving athletic success, and receiving greater sports revenue. Schools that follow the rules must depend on the NCAA to punish cheaters by taking away TV appearances, tournament play, bowl invitations, and scholarships.

### ANALYZE THE ISSUE

Do you favor paying college athletes salaries determined by a competitive labor market rather than by an NCAA agreement? Explain.

worker hired at the higher wage rate. Stated differently, General Griffin's must pay a higher wage not only to each additional worker but also to all previously hired workers. If General Griffin's attempts to pay different wage rates for the same job, worker morale will deteriorate causing labor unrest. Comparing points *A* through *D* confirms that *MFC* is greater than the wage rate for a monopsonist, much like the monopolist's price, which is greater than the marginal revenue.

> **CONCLUSION** *Because the monopsonist can hire additional workers only by raising the wage rate for all workers, the marginal factor cost exceeds the wage rate.*

## MONOPSONISTIC EQUILIBRIUM

How many workers will General Griffin's hire? To answer this question requires the demand curve for labor that traces labor's marginal revenue product ($MRP$), explained earlier in this chapter. Recall that $MRP$ reflects the value or contribution of each additional worker because $MRP$ is the increase in total revenue produced by hiring each additional worker. Also, as explained in Chapter 8, the profit-maximizing producer selects the level of output where marginal revenue equals marginal cost. Similarly, *the monopsonist in the labor market hires the quantity of labor at which the marginal revenue product of labor equals its marginal factor cost.*

In Exhibit 11, General Griffin's will follow the $MRP = MFC$ rule by hiring 2 workers, determined by the intersection of the $MRP$ and $MFC$ curves at point $E$. But pay special attention to this point: The monopsonist is a "wage maker." It has labor market power and does not have to pay $12 per hour, which equals the contribution of the second worker measured by his or her $MRP$. Instead of paying workers what their services are worth, the monopsonist follows the supply curve of labor, selects point $B$, and pays $6 per hour rather than $12 per hour. Since $6 per hour is all the firm must pay to attract and hire 2 workers, the monopsonist can exploit labor by paying less than its marginal revenue product.

One alternative for labor facing a powerful employer is to organize a powerful union and engage in collective bargaining. Totally successful collective bargaining by a labor union could raise the wage rate from $6 per hour at point $B$ to $12 per hour at point $E$. General Griffin's will resist the union's demands and offer a lower wage closer to point $B$. Thus, points $B$ and $E$ represent the boundaries of a potential final settlement. What the negotiated final equilibrium wage rate will be depends on the tactics and resources of the negotiating parties.

Finally, suppose the monopsony is broken up into a large number of small firms. Recall from earlier in this chapter that in competitive labor markets additional workers are hired to the point where the wage rate is equal to $MRP$. In this case, the supply curve of labor intersects the $MRP$ (demand) curve at point $C$, and more workers would be hired with $9 per hour paid to each worker.

> **CONCLUSION** *A monopsonist hires fewer workers and pays a lower wage than a firm in a competitive labor market.*

## Key Concepts

| | | |
|---|---|---|
| Marginal revenue product (*MRP*) | Supply curve of labor | Monopsony |
| Demand curve for labor | Human capital | Marginal factor cost (*MFC*) |
| Derived demand | Collective bargaining | |

# Summary

- **Marginal revenue product** (*MRP*) is determined by a worker's contribution to a firm's total revenue. Algebraically, the marginal revenue product equals the price of the product times the worker's marginal product: $MRP = P \times MP$.

- The **demand curve for labor** shows the quantities of labor a firm is willing to hire at different prices of labor. The marginal revenue product (*MRP*) of labor curve is the firm's demand curve for labor. Summing individual demand for labor curves gives the market demand curve for labor.

### DEMAND CURVE FOR LABOR

- **Derived demand** means that a firm demands labor because labor is productive. Changes in consumer demand for a product cause changes in the demand for labor and for other resources used to make the product.

- The **supply curve of labor** shows the quantities of workers willing to work at different prices of labor. The market supply curve of labor is derived by adding the individual supply curves of labor.

### SUPPLY CURVE OF LABOR

- **Human capital** is the accumulated investment people make in education, training, experience, and health in order to make themselves more productive. One explanation for earnings differences is differences in human capital.

- **Collective bargaining** is the process through which a union and management negotiate a labor contract.

- **Monopsony** is a labor market in which a single firm hires labor. Because the monopsonist faces the industry supply curve of labor and each worker is paid the same wage, changes in total wage cost exceed the wage rate necessary to hire each additional worker. As a result, the **marginal factor cost** (*MFC*) of labor curve, which measures changes in total wage cost per worker, lies above the supply curve of labor. The monopsonist's wage rate and quantity of labor are determined where the *MFC* equals *MRP*. Since at this point the worker's *MRP* is greater than the wage paid, the monopsonist exploits workers.

### MONOPSONY

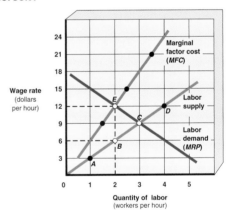

## Summary of Conclusion Statements

- A perfectly competitive firm's marginal revenue product is equal to the marginal product of its labor times the price of its product. Expressed as a formula: $MRP = P \times MP$.

- A firm hires additional workers up to the point where the $MRP$ equals the wage rate.

- Because the monopsonist can hire additional workers only by raising the wage rate for all workers, the marginal factor cost exceeds the wage rate.

- A monopsonist hires fewer workers and pays a lower wage than a firm in a competitive labor market.

## Study Questions and Problems

1. Consider this statement: "Workers demand jobs, and employers supply jobs." Do you agree or disagree? Explain.

2. The Zippy Paper Company has no control over either the price of paper or the wage it pays its workers. The following table shows the relationship between the number of workers Zippy hires and total output:

| Labor input (workers per day) | Total output (boxes of paper per day) |
| --- | --- |
| 0 | 0 |
| 1 | 15 |
| 2 | 27 |
| 3 | 36 |
| 4 | 43 |
| 5 | 48 |
| 6 | 51 |

If the selling price is $10 per box, answer the following questions:
   a. What is the marginal revenue product ($MRP$) of each worker?
   b. How many workers will Zippy hire if the wage rate is $100 per day?
   c. How many workers will Zippy hire if the wage rate is $75 per day?
   d. Assume the wage rate is $75 per day and the price of a box of paper is $20. How many workers will Zippy hire?

3. Assume the Grand Slam Baseball Store sells $100 worth of baseball cards each day, with 1 employee operating the store. The owner decides to hire a second worker, and the 2 workers together sell $150 worth of baseball cards. What is the second worker's marginal revenue product ($MRP$)? If the price per card sold is $5, what is the second worker's marginal product ($MP$)?

4. What is the relationship between the marginal revenue product ($MRP$) and the demand curve for labor?

5. The market supply curve of labor is upward sloping, but the supply curve of labor for a single firm is horizontal. Explain why.

6. Assume the labor market for loggers is perfectly competitive. How would each of the following events influence the wage rate loggers are paid?
   a. Consumers boycott products made with wood.
   b. Loggers form a union that requires longer apprenticeships, charges high fees, and uses other devices designed to reduce union membership.

7. How does a human capital investment in education increase your lifetime earnings?

8. Suppose states pass laws requiring public school teachers to have a master's degree in order to retain their teaching certificates. What effect would this legislation have on the labor market for teachers?

9. Use the data in question 2, and assume the equilibrium wage rate is $90 per day, determined in a perfectly competitive labor market. Now explain the impact of a union-negotiated collective bargaining agreement that changes the wage rate to $100 per day.

10. Some economists argue that the American Medical Association and the American Bar Association create an effect on labor markets similar to that of a labor union. Do you agree?

11. The Jacksonville Jaguars was an expansion professional football team in the National Football League (NFL). NFL draft and employment rules create monopsony power for each member club. In 1995, the Jaguars were in the process of hiring players. Using the following hypothetical table of data, construct a graph to determine the number of quarterbacks the Jaguars hired and the salary paid to each quarterback. Assuming the labor market was competitive, what would be the number of quarterbacks hired and the salary paid each?

| (1)<br>Salary<br>(thousands<br>of dollars) | (2)<br>Number of<br>quarterbacks | (3)<br>Total cost of<br>quarterbacks<br>(thousands<br>of dollars) | (4)<br>Marginal<br>factor cost<br>(MFC)<br>(thousands<br>of dollars) | (5)<br>Marginal<br>revenue<br>product<br>(MRP)<br>(thousands<br>of dollars) |
|---|---|---|---|---|
| $ 0 | 0 | $ 0 | — | — |
| 100 | 1 | 100 | $100 | $700 |
| 200 | 2 | 400 | 300 | 600 |
| 300 | 3 | 900 | 500 | 500 |
| 400 | 4 | 1,600 | 700 | 400 |
| 500 | 5 | 2,500 | 900 | 300 |

## Study Guide Questions

1. The _____ is the curve showing the different quantities of labor a firm is willing to hire at different prices of labor.

2. Assume Ajax Company employs 100 workers and total revenue is $400,000. When Ajax Company employs 101 workers, total revenue is $405,000. The marginal revenue product of the 101st workers is
   a. $40,000.
   b. $5,000.
   c. $405,000.
   d. none of the above.

3. A firm's demand for labor depends, in part, on the demand for the firm's product. To summarize this idea, economists say that the demand for labor is
   a. derived demand.
   b. marginal demand.
   c. secondary demand.
   d. monopsonistic demand.

4. Which of the following statements is *true*?
   a. A monoposony is the only employer of a factor of production.
   b. A monoposony will pay workers a higher wage and employ fewer workers than a competitive labor market.
   c. A monoposony has a marginal factor cost curve which lies below its supply curve of labor.
   d. Unions are becoming a greater influence in American labor markets.
   e. All of the above.

5. T F In a competitive labor market, marginal revenue product equals marginal product times the product price.

**Answers to these questions are in the complete Study Guide at www.thomsonedu.com/thomsonnow.**

**For Online Exercises, go to the text Web site at www.thomsonedu.com/economics/tucker.**

## Checkpoint Answers

### Can the Minimum Wage Create Jobs?

The minimum wage of $9 corresponds to point C in Exhibit 11. At this point, the labor supply and labor demand (*MRP*) curves intersect. Thus, the effect of the minimum wage is to force the monopsonist to operate at the equilibrium that would be established in a competitive labor market. If you said that under monopsony the minimum wage could raise the wage rate and create additional employment, **YOU ARE CORRECT.**

### If You Don't Like It, Mickey, Take Your Bat and Go Home

Baseball players had no free-agent rights in the 1950s. If Mantle did not like the salary offer, his only choice was to go back to his home in Oklahoma. Faced with that alternative, he accepted the salary cut. If you said each team owner achieved monopsony power by prohibiting players from going to another team, **YOU ARE CORRECT.**

## Practice Quiz

For an explanation of the correct answers, please visit the tutorial at www.thomsonedu.com/economics/tucker.

1. Marginal revenue product measures the increase in
   a. output resulting from one more unit of labor.
   b. total revenue resulting from one more unit of output.
   c. revenue per unit from one more unit of output.
   d. total revenue resulting from one more unit of labor.

2. Troll Corporation sells dolls for $10 each in a market that is perfectly competitive. Increasing the number of workers from 100 to 101 would cause output to rise from 500 to 510 dolls per day. Troll should hire the 101st worker only when the wage is
   a. $100 or less per day.
   b. more than $100 per day.
   c. $5.10 or less per day.
   d. none of the above.

3. Derived demand for labor depends on the
   a. cost of factors of production used in the product.
   b. market supply curve of labor.
   c. consumer demand for the final goods produced by labor.
   d. firm's total revenue less economic profit.

4. If demand for a product falls, the demand curve for labor used to produce the product will
   a. shift leftward.
   b. shift rightward.
   c. shift upward.
   d. remain unchanged.

5. The owner of a restaurant will hire waiters if the
   a. additional labor's pay is close to the minimum wage.
   b. marginal product is at the maximum.
   c. additional work of the employees adds more to total revenue than to costs.
   d. waiters do not belong to a union.

6. In a perfectly competitive market, the demand curve for labor
   a. slopes upward.
   b. slopes downward because of diminishing marginal productivity.
   c. is perfectly elastic at the equilibrium wage rate.
   d. is described by all of the above.

7. A union can influence the equilibrium wage rate by
   a. featherbedding.
   b. requiring longer apprenticeships.
   c. favoring trade restrictions on foreign products.
   d. all of the above.
   e. none of the above.

8. In which of the following market structures is the firm *not* a price taker in the factor market?
   a. Oligopoly
   b. Monopsony
   c. Monopoly
   d. Perfect competition

9. The extra cost of obtaining each additional unit of a factor of production is called the marginal
   a. physical product.
   b. revenue product.
   c. factor cost.
   d. implicit cost.

10. A monopsonist's marginal factor cost (MFC) curve lies above its supply curve because the firm must
    a. increase the price of its product to sell more.
    b. lower the price of its product to sell more.
    c. increase the wage rate to hire more labor.
    d. lower the wage rate to hire more labor.

11. To maximize profits, a monopsonist will hire the quantity of labor to the point where the marginal factor cost is equal to
    a. marginal physical product.
    b. marginal revenue product.
    c. total revenue product.
    d. any of the above.

12. BigBiz, a local monopsonist, currently hires 50 workers and pays them $6 per hour. To attract an additional worker to its labor force, BigBiz would have to raise the wage rate to $6.25 per hour. What is BigBiz's marginal factor cost?
    a. $6.25 per hour
    b. $12.50 per hour
    c. $18.75 per hour
    d. $20.00 per hour

13. Suppose a firm can hire 100 workers at $8.00 per hour, but must pay $8.05 per hour to hire 101 workers. Marginal factor cost (MFC) for the 101st worker is approximately equal to
    a. $8.00.
    b. $8.05.
    c. $13.05.
    d. $13.00.

14. A monopsonist in equilibrium has a marginal revenue product of $10 per worker hour. Its equilibrium wage rate must be
    a. less than $10.
    b. equal to $10.
    c. greater than $10.
    d. equal to $5.

**EXHIBIT 12  A LABOR MARKET**

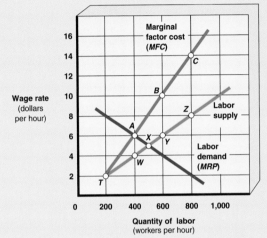

15. If the labor market shown in Exhibit 12 is a monopsony, the wage rate and number of workers employed will be determined at point
    a. A.
    b. W.
    c. C.
    d. Y.
    e. Z.

# Microeconomic Policy Issues

These three chapters apply micro principles learned in previous chapters to explore policy issues concerning some important economic topics. The first chapter in this part extends the theory of labor markets into an examination of actual data on income and poverty. The second chapter mixes politics and economic theory to discuss such interesting topics as the Microsoft case and the deregulation of energy. The third chapter takes a closer look at ways to deal with externalities, such as pollution permits, which are actually traded on the Chicago Board of Trade.

# Income Distribution, Poverty, and Discrimination

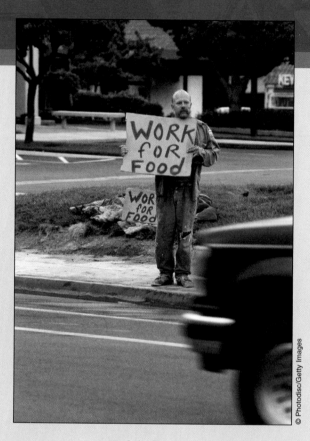

© Photodisc/Getty Images

The previous chapter examined how variations in wages are determined in competitive and monopsonistic labor markets. These labor supply and demand models do not give the complete picture of labor markets. In this chapter, we turn our attention to the distribution of income, poverty, and discrimination, which are important topics related to labor market wage decisions. The chapter begins by exploring the controversial issue of how the total family income "pie" is cut into various size "slices" or shares for different groups of families. You will examine government data that indicate the trend over the years in the share of income for the richest fifth of the population and the poorest fifth. Here the hotly contested issue of whether the "rich got richer" at the expense of the poor is addressed. In addition, the inequality of income in the United States is compared with that in other countries.

Poverty is an unhappy consequence of an unequal income distribution. Eighteenth-century English poet and essayist Samuel Johnson stated, "A decent provision for the poor is the true test of civilization." Former President Bill Clinton campaigned in 1992 on a pledge to "end welfare as we know it," and in 1996 the president signed a landmark bipartisan bill to reform welfare. The consequences of this law are still being felt throughout the nation. Another purpose of this chapter is to define poverty and ask what can be done about it.

The chapter concludes with the subject of discrimination, which is one possible explanation for unequal income distribution and poverty. Here you will apply the supply and demand model to explain why women earn less on average than men and African Americans earn less than whites.

**In this chapter, you will learn to solve these economics puzzles:**

- Could the rich become richer and other income groups also become better off?
- How can a negative income tax solve the welfare controversy?
- What is the effect on labor markets of laws that protect women from jobs deemed too strenuous or too dangerous?

# Distribution of Income

One function of labor markets is to determine the *distribution of income*—that is, how wages and salaries are divided among members of society. Recall from Chapter 2 that the *for whom* question is one of the three basic questions that any economic system must answer. Here we study the *for whom* question in more detail.

## TRENDS IN INCOME DISTRIBUTION

One way to analyze the distribution of income in the United States is illustrated in Exhibit 1. In column 1 of this exhibit, families are divided into six groups, according to the percentage of the total annual money income they received. The remaining columns of the table give the percentages of the total money income for each of the six groups in selected years since 1929. These data reveal changes in the distribution of income among families over time. For example, families with income in the top 5 percent in 1929 earned about 10 percent more of the total income pie than they did in 2005. Otherwise, the distribution of income has not fluctuated greatly since 1947. Nonetheless, there is concern that since 1970 the percentage of income received by families in the lowest 20 percent group has fallen while the income percentages received by the families in the highest fifth and the highest 5 percent have risen.

As shown in Exhibit 1, there is an unequal distribution of income among families. Why didn't each fifth of the families receive 20 percent of the total income? There are many reasons. For example, Exhibit 2 reveals that families headed by a college graduate fare better than those headed by an individual with less education. Recall from the previous chapter that human capital refers to education and skills that increase a worker's productivity. Workers with a greater investment in human capital are likely to be worth more to an employer. Data in this exhibit also indicate that families headed by a male generally earn more than those headed by a female.

| EXHIBIT 1 | THE DIVISION OF TOTAL ANNUAL MONEY INCOME AMONG FAMILIES, 1929–2005 | | | | | |
|---|---|---|---|---|---|---|
| **Percentage of families** | **1929** | **1947** | **1970** | **1980** | **1990** | **2005** |
| Lowest fifth | 4% | 5% | 5% | 5% | 5% | 4% |
| Second-lowest fifth | 9 | 12 | 12 | 12 | 11 | 10 |
| Middle fifth | 14 | 17 | 18 | 18 | 12 | 15 |
| Second-highest fifth | 19 | 23 | 24 | 24 | 23 | 23 |
| Highest fifth | 54 | 43 | 41 | 41 | 44 | 48 |
| Highest 5% | 30 | 17 | 16 | 15 | 17 | 21 |

*Source: U.S. Bureau of the Census, Historical Income Tables, http://www.census.gov/hhes/www/income/histinc/incfamdet.html, Table F-2.*

| EXHIBIT 2 | MEDIAN MONEY INCOME OF FAMILIES, 2004 |
|---|---|
| **Characteristic** | **Median income*** |
| All families | $54,061 |
| Families headed by a male | 40,293 |
| Families headed by a female | 26,964 |
| Families with head aged 25–34 years | 46,878 |
| Families with head aged 65 years and over | 35,825 |
| Families headed by person with less than 9th–grade education | 24,840 |
| Families with head high school graduate | 46,383 |
| Families with head attaining at least a bachelor's degree | 81,406 |

*Fifty percent of families earn less than the median income, and 50 percent earn more.

*Source: U.S. Bureau of the Census, Historical Income Tables, http://www.census.gov/hhes/www/income/histinc/incfamdet.html, Tables F-7, F-11, and F-18.*

## EQUALITY VERSUS EFFICIENCY

Because the data presented in Exhibits 1 and 2 show that an unequal distribution of income exists in the United States, the normative question to be debated concerns the pros and cons of a more equal income distribution. Those who favor greater equality fear the link between the rich and political power. The wealthy may well use their money to influence national policies that benefit the rich. It is also argued that income inequality results in unequal opportunities for various groups. For example, children of the poor have difficulty obtaining a college education. Consequently, their underutilized productive capacity is a waste of human capital. The poor are also unable to afford health care, and this is a national concern.

Advocates of income inequality pose this question. Suppose you had your choice of living in egalitarian society *A*, where every person earns $40,000 a year, or society *B*, where 20 percent earn $100,000 and 80 percent earn $30,000. You would likely choose society *B* because the incentive to earn more and live better is worth the risk of earning less and living worse. After all, why is the average income higher in society *B*? The answer is that income inequality gives people an incentive to be productive. In contrast, people in society *A* lack such motivation because everyone earns the same income. Those who favor equality of income believe that critics ignore the nonmonetary incentives, such as pride in one's work and nation, that can motivate people.

A frequently debated topic concerning income inequality is whether the "rich are getting richer." As we observed earlier, the data in Exhibit 1 reveal that the percentages of total income received by the highest 5 percent and the highest fifth have increased in recent decades, while the percentages received by each of the fifths below the highest decreased slightly.

**CONCLUSION** *Measured by distribution of family money income, the richest families have become a little richer and the rest of the family groups a little poorer in recent decades.*

**EXHIBIT 3**      **REAL MEDIAN FAMILY INCOME, 1980–2004**

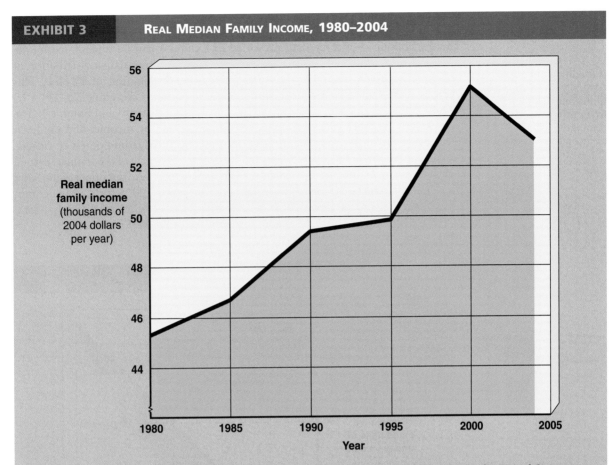

Real median income measures the income adjusted for inflation received by all families in the United States. Fifty percent of families earn less and 50 percent earn more than the median income. The trend of this measure was generally upward until 2000. In 2000, real median income reached a new high before falling during the recession of 2001 and subsequent years.

*Source: U.S. Bureau of the Census, Historical Income Tables, http://www.census.gov/hhes/www/income/histinc/indfamdet.html, Table F-7.*

It is important to note that simply observing changes in income distribution over time does not tell the whole story. Exhibit 3 traces real median family income, adjusted for rising prices, for the period 1980–2004. This measure indicates the trend of the average level of income received by all groups. Generally, the trend for real median income since the 1980s has been upward. This means the size of the income "pie" grew, and, therefore, all of the slices grew larger. However, consistent with the distribution data in Exhibit 1, the relative share of the pie for those with the biggest slice grew slightly larger. In 2000, real median income reached a new high before falling during the recession of 2001 and subsequent years.

## THE LORENZ CURVE

**Lorenz curve**
A graph of the actual cumulative distribution of income compared to a perfectly equal cumulative distribution of income.

The distribution of income data presented in Exhibit 1 can be represented by the **Lorenz curve**. The Lorenz curve is a graph of the actual cumulative distribution of income compared to a perfectly equal cumulative distribution of income. This curve is a primary tool for measuring income distribution developed in 1905 by statistician M. O. Lorenz. Look at the hypothetical Lorenz curve in Exhibit 4. The vertical axis measures the *cumulative* percentage of family income, and the horizontal axis measures the *cumulative* percentage of families from poorest to richest. Starting at the lower left-hand corner on the graph, 0 percent of the families earned 0 percent of the cumulative percentage of money income. At the upper right-hand corner on the graph, 100 percent of the families earned 100 percent of the cumulative percentage of money income. The combination of other total family—total money income points between 0 and 100 percent forms the Lorenz curve.

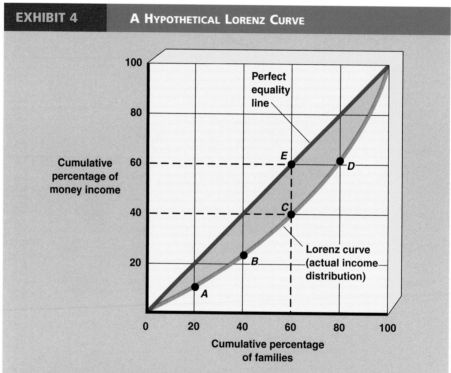

**EXHIBIT 4          A HYPOTHETICAL LORENZ CURVE**

The Lorenz curve shows the cumulative percentage of money income earned from 0 to 100 percent by the cumulative percentage of families, also from 0 to 100 percent. If the income distribution followed the 45-degree perfect equality line, 20 percent of the families earn 20 percent of total money income, 40 percent receive 40 percent of total money income, and so on. The shaded area between the perfect equality line and the Lorenz curve measures the degree of inequality in the distribution of income. The more the Lorenz curve is bowed outward, the more unequal the distribution of income is.

Reading along the horizontal axis, each fifth (20 percent) of the cumulative percentage of families corresponds to its cumulative share of income earned measured along the curve. At point *A*, the lowest 20 percent of families receive 10 percent of total or cumulative income. To read this, go from the 20 percent point on the horizontal axis up to point *A* on the Lorenz curve. Then draw a horizontal line to the vertical axis, and read that it intersects this axis at 10 percent. Point *B* is interpreted as the lowest 40 percent of families earn 10 percent plus 15 percent, which equals a cumulative share of 25 percent. Similarly, point *C* is the cumulative share earned by the lowest 60 percent of families, which equals 40 percent. Finally, point *D* is a bit tricky to interpret. At this point, the lowest 80 percent of families receive about 62 percent of total income. And here is the twist. You must interpret that the richest 20 percent of families earn 38 percent of income (100 percent − 62 percent).

We now turn to the 45-degree line above the Lorenz curve that cuts the box in half. This line represents perfect equality: 20 percent of the families receive 20 percent of total income, 40 percent of the families receive 40 percent of total income, and so on. The distance of the Lorenz curve from the perfect equality line is therefore a measure of unequal income distribution. The gap between points *C* and *E*, for example, indicates that 60 percent of families earn 20 percent less of total income than required for perfect equality. Similar measurements generate the shaded area between the Lorenz curve and the perfect equality line. Thus, the shaded area is a measure of the degree of income inequality for our hypothetical data. A larger shaded area would mean greater income inequality, and the shape of the Lorenz curve would become more bowed outward. A smaller shaded area would represent a more equal income distribution, and the Lorenz curve would be a flatter curve.

It is very important to note that there are limitations associated with using money income statistics. Such data are not adjusted for government-provided food stamps, medical care, housing, or other goods and services. Money income also reflects income before taxes and does not measure unreported income or wealth. Still, used carefully, the Lorenz curve is a convenient tool for visualizing the degree of income inequality.

## INCOME DISTRIBUTION TREND IN THE UNITED STATES

In Exhibit 1, we looked at income distributions for selected years between 1929 and 2005. What can we conclude from these data, using the Lorenz curve? Has the overall income distribution become more or less equal? The table in Exhibit 5 restates the income share data for 1929 and 2005 from Exhibit 1, and the cumulative percentage shares of families of quintiles are calculated from the percentage shares.

Exhibit 5 suggests that overall money income distribution has changed little over the period. In the exhibit, there is only a small shaded area between the 1929 and 2005 Lorenz curves. However, the share of income received by the highest fifth of families fell from 54 percent in 1929 to 48 percent in 2005.

> **CONCLUSION** *The Lorenz curve has shifted only slightly inward, and therefore closer to the perfect equality line between 1929 and 2005.*

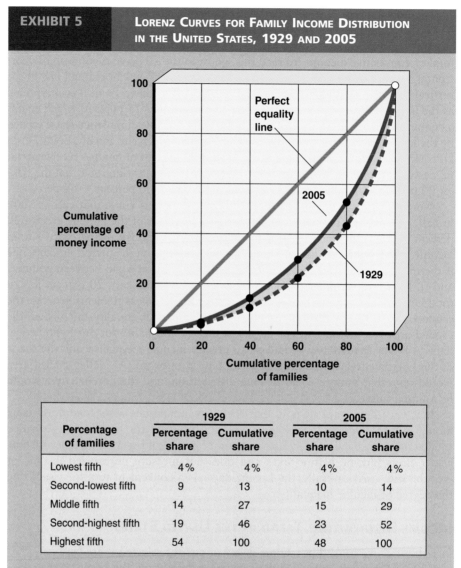

| EXHIBIT 5 | LORENZ CURVES FOR FAMILY INCOME DISTRIBUTION IN THE UNITED STATES, 1929 AND 2005 |
| --- | --- |

| Percentage of families | 1929 | | 2005 | |
| --- | --- | --- | --- | --- |
| | Percentage share | Cumulative share | Percentage share | Cumulative share |
| Lowest fifth | 4% | 4% | 4% | 4% |
| Second-lowest fifth | 9 | 13 | 10 | 14 |
| Middle fifth | 14 | 27 | 15 | 29 |
| Second-highest fifth | 19 | 46 | 23 | 52 |
| Highest fifth | 54 | 100 | 48 | 100 |

Since 1929, the Lorenz curve has shifted somewhat inward toward the perfect equality line. Thus, there has been a reduction in the inequality of distribution of family money income since 1929.

# International Comparisons of Income Distribution

**Global Economics**

How does the distribution of income in the United States compare with that of other countries? Exhibit 6 presents separate Lorenz curves for the United States, the Czech Republic, and Brazil. This exhibit indicates that the degree of income inequality in the United States exceeds that of the Czech Republic. On the other

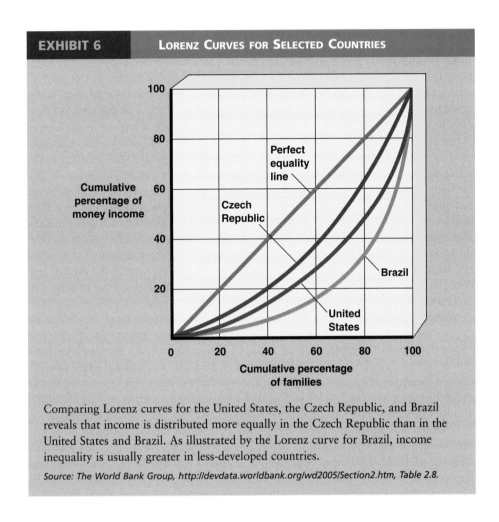

**EXHIBIT 6    LORENZ CURVES FOR SELECTED COUNTRIES**

Comparing Lorenz curves for the United States, the Czech Republic, and Brazil reveals that income is distributed more equally in the Czech Republic than in the United States and Brazil. As illustrated by the Lorenz curve for Brazil, income inequality is usually greater in less-developed countries.

*Source: The World Bank Group, http://devdata.worldbank.org/wd2005/Section2.htm, Table 2.8.*

hand, income distribution is more equal in the United States than in Brazil. In general, the distribution of income in developed nations, such as the United States, Germany, Italy, and Sweden, is more equal than in developing nations, such as Brazil, Mexico, and Zimbabwe.

# Poverty

Having discussed the broader question of how the degree of income distribution inequality is measured, we now turn the spotlight on the fiercely debated issue of poverty. We are all disturbed by homelessness and hungry children. How can poverty exist in a nation of abundance such as the United States? Can economists offer useful ideas to reform and improve our current welfare system? Most of the nation agrees that the welfare system must undergo reforms to reduce poverty, cut welfare dependency, and save taxpayers money. The first step to understanding the problem is to ask this question: Who is poor?

## DEFINING POVERTY

What is poverty? Is it eating pork and beans when others are eating steak? Or is poverty a family having one car when others have two or more? Is the poverty standard only a matter of normative arguments? Indeed, the term *poverty* is difficult to define. A person whose income is comparatively low in the United States may be viewed as well-off in a less-developed country. Or what we in the United States regard as poverty today might have seemed a life of luxury 200 years ago.

There are two views of poverty. One defines poverty in *absolute* terms, and the other defines poverty in *relative* terms. Absolute poverty can be defined as a dollar figure that represents some level of income per year required to purchase some minimum amount of goods and services essential to meeting a person's or a family's basic needs. In contrast, relative poverty might be defined as a level of income that places a person or family in the lowest, say, 20 percent of all persons or families receiving incomes. An unequal distribution of income guarantees that some persons or families will occupy in relative terms the bottom rung of the income ladder. The U.S. government first established an official definition of the **poverty line** in 1964. The poverty line is the level of income below which a person or a family is considered poor. The poverty line is defined in absolute terms: It is based on the cost of a minimal diet multiplied by three, because low-income families spend about one-third of their income on food. In 1964, the poverty income level for a family of four was $3,000 ($1,000 for food × 3). Since 1969, the poverty line figure has been adjusted upward each year for inflation. In 1988, for example, the official poverty income level was $12,092 or below for a family of four. In 2005, a family of four needed an income of $20,144 to clear the poverty threshold.

Exhibit 7(a) shows the percentage of all persons in the U.S. population below the poverty level, beginning with 1959. The poverty rate for all persons was on a downward trend until the early 1980s. From 1980 to 1995, the percentage remained between 13 and 14 percent until the rate dropped to 11 percent in 2000. This was the lowest level in more than a quarter-century. After the recession in 2001, the poverty rate rose to 13 percent in 2005. The exhibit also gives an idea of poverty levels by race for selected years. As shown by comparing Parts (b) and (c), the percentage of blacks below the poverty line remained almost three times the percentage of whites between 1970 and 1995. In 2005, the ratio was 2.3 times as great.

The poverty rate shown in Exhibit 7 has two major problems. First, this percentage gives no indication of how poor the people included are. A person with an income $1 below the poverty line counts, and so does a person whose income is $5,000 below the threshold. Second, the poverty rate is computed by comparing a family's census cash income from all sources to the poverty line. Cash income includes cash payments from Social Security, unemployment compensation, and Temporary Assistance to Needy Families (TANF). Cash income for the poor does not include noncash transfers, called **in-kind transfers**. In-kind transfers are government payments in the form of goods and services, rather than cash, including such government programs as food stamps, Medicaid, and housing. These antipoverty programs will be discussed in more detail in the next section.

## WHO ARE THE POOR?

Exhibit 8 lists selected characteristics of families below the poverty level in 2005. Geographically, poor families are most likely to live in the South. An important

**Poverty line**
The level of income below which a person or a family is considered to be poor.

**In-kind transfers**
Government payments in the form of goods and services, rather than cash, including such government programs as food stamps, Medicaid, and housing.

| EXHIBIT 7 | PERSONS BELOW THE POVERTY LEVEL AS A PERCENTAGE OF THE U.S. POPULATION, 1959–2005 |
|---|---|

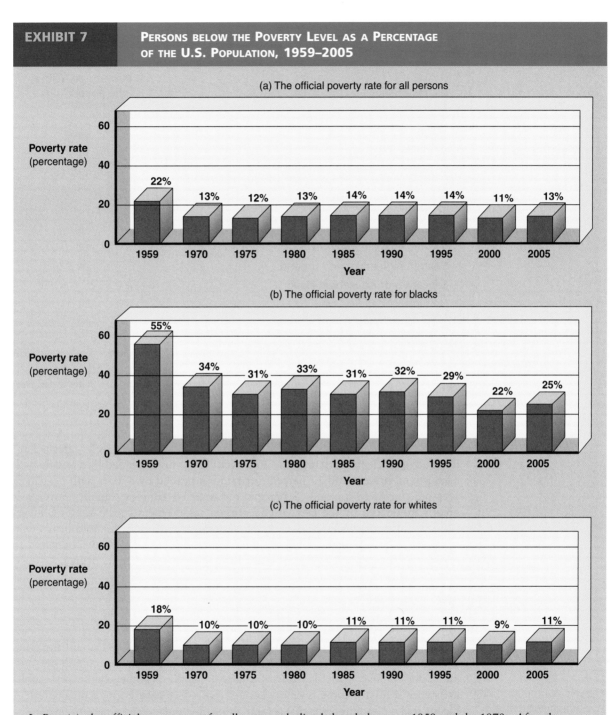

(a) The official poverty rate for all persons

(b) The official poverty rate for blacks

(c) The official poverty rate for whites

In Part (a), the official poverty rate for all persons declined sharply between 1959 and the 1970s. After the recession in 2001, the poverty rate rose. Comparison of Parts (b) and (c) reveals that the poverty rate for blacks fell sharply between 1959 and 1970, but since then it remained almost three times the poverty rate of whites until 1995. In 2005, the ratio was 2.3 times as great.

*Source: U.S. Bureau of the Census,* Income, Poverty, and Health Insurance in the United States: 2006, *http://www.census.gov/hhes/www/poverty.html, p. 4; Table A-1, pp. 22–25.*

| EXHIBIT 8 | CHARACTERISTICS OF U.S. PERSONS AND FAMILIES BELOW THE 2005 POVERTY LEVEL | |
| --- | --- | --- |
| **Characteristic** | | **Percentage below the poverty line** |
| **Region** | | |
| South | | 14% |
| West | | 13 |
| Northeast | | 12 |
| Midwest | | 12 |
| **Type of Family** | | |
| Headed by married couple | | 6 |
| Headed by male, no wife | | 14 |
| Headed by female, no husband | | 28 |
| **Education of Household Head** | | |
| No high school diploma | | 20 |
| High school diploma, no college | | 10 |
| Bachelor's degree or more | | 2 |

Source: *U.S. Bureau of the Census,* Income, Poverty, and Health Insurance in the United States: 2006, *http://www.census.gov/hhes/www/poverty.html, Table 2; and* Statistical Abstract of the United States, *2006, http://www.census.gov/prod/www/statistical-abstract-us.html, Table 707, p. 468.*

characteristic of families living below the poverty line in the United States is family structure. The poverty rate was 26 percent for families headed by a female with no husband present and 12 percent for families headed by a male with no female present, compared to only 5 percent for married couples. Finally, poverty is greatly influenced by the lack of educational achievement of the head of household. As shown in the exhibit, 20 percent of families with household heads who have not received a high school diploma are below the poverty line compared to only 2 percent of families whose heads have at least a bachelor's degree.

# Antipoverty Programs

The government has a number of programs specifically designed to aid the poor. The groups eligible for such assistance include disabled persons, elderly persons, and poor families with dependent children. People become eligible for public assistance if their income is below certain levels as measured by a **means test**. A means test is a requirement that a family's income not exceed a certain level to be eligible for public assistance. People who pass the means test may be *entitled* to government assistance. Thus, government welfare programs are often called *entitlement programs.*

Federal programs to assist the poor in the United States are classified into two broad types of programs: *cash* assistance and *in-kind transfers.* As explained pre-

**Means test**
A requirement that a family's income not exceed a certain level to be eligible for public assistance.

viously, the current definition of the poverty threshold excludes in-kind transfers because these programs did not exist when the poverty rate measure was adopted decades ago.

## CASH TRANSFER PROGRAMS

The following are major government programs that alleviate poverty by providing eligible persons with cash payments needed to purchase food, shelter, clothing, and other basic needs.

**Social Security (OASDHI)** The technical name for our gigantic social insurance program is Old Age, Survivors, and Disability Health Insurance, or OASDHI. Under the Social Security Act passed in 1935, each worker must pay a payroll tax matched in equal amount by his or her employer. Look at your paycheck, and you will find this deduction under FICA, which stands for Federal Insurance Contribution Act. Most of this money is used to pay current benefit recipients, and the remainder goes into the Social Security Trust Fund. Workers may retire between the ages 65 and 67, depending on year of birth, with full benefits, or at age 62, with reduced benefits. If a wage earner dies, Social Security provides payments to survivors, including spouse and children, until about 18 years of age (age 21 if they are in school). In addition, payments are made to disabled workers.

Radical changes in policy are being debated. Since the creation of Social Security in 1935, money paid into the program has been invested exclusively in interest-bearing government securities, mainly long-term bonds. Although the Social Security Trust Fund now takes in more money in taxes and interest than it pays out in benefits, the program will not be able to pay future generations all the benefits received by the baby boom generation because, according to the latest estimates, the trust fund will be depleted in 2041. The debated issue is whether the United States should try to obtain a higher return on investment and increase retirement savings by channeling some of the money into the stock market because stocks generally outperform bonds by a significant margin. Unanswered questions of a partial privatization system include: (1) How much money workers could divert from Social Security into their private investment, (2) The precise transition costs for new government debt required to pay benefits to current retirees not financed by payroll taxes because of money diverted to private accounts, and (3) How workers should be protected if their investments lose money.

Another reform idea is to create an investment account for each person covered by Social Security. The government would require workers to contribute a small amount each year beyond their current level of payroll taxes. These accounts would be held by the Social Security system, but individuals would be free to choose stock index funds, bond index funds, or some combination of these options. When a person retires, money accumulated in the account would be paid out in the form of an annuity, supplementing regular Social Security benefits.

**Unemployment Compensation** **Unemployment compensation** is a government insurance program that pays income for a short time period to unemployed workers. This unemployment insurance is financed by a payroll tax on employers, which varies by state and according to the size of the firm's payroll. This means nothing is deducted from employees' paychecks for unemployment compensation.

**Unemployment compensation**
The government insurance program that pays income for a short time period to unemployed workers.

Although the federal government largely collects the taxes and funds this program, it is administered by the states. Any insured worker who becomes unemployed, and did not just quit his or her job, can become eligible for benefit payments after a short waiting period of usually one week.

**Temporary Assistance to Needy Families (TANF)**   TANF gives states broad discretion to determine eligibility and benefit levels. However, families may not receive benefits for longer than 60 months. Unwed teenage parents must stay in school and live at home, and people convicted of drug-related felonies are banned from receiving TANF or food stamp benefits. In addition, nonworking adults must participate in community service within two months of receiving benefits, and must find work within two years. Parents with children under age one are exempt from the work requirements (under age six if child care is not available).

## IN-KIND TRANSFERS

The following are important government in-kind transfer programs that raise the standard of living for the poor.

**Food Stamps**   The food stamp program began in 1964 as a federally financed program that is administered by state governments. The government issues coupons to the poor, who use them like money at the grocery store. The grocer cashes the stamps at a local bank, which redeems them at face value from the government. The cash value of stamps issued varies with the eligible recipient's income and family size. The food stamp program has become a major part of the welfare system in the United States.

**Medicaid**   This is the largest in-kind transfer program. Medicaid provides medical services to eligible poor under age 65 who pass a means test. TANF families qualify for Medicaid in all states.

**Medicare**   This federal health care program is available to Social Security beneficiaries and persons with disabilities. Coverage is provided for hospital care and post-hospital nursing services.

**Housing Assistance**   Federal and state governments have a number of different programs to provide affordable housing for poor people. The federal agency overseeing most of these programs is the Department of Housing and Urban Development (HUD). These programs include housing projects owned and operated by the government and subsidies to assist people who rent private housing. In both cases, recipients pay less than the market value for apartments and therefore receive an in-kind transfer.

## WELFARE CRITICISMS

The majority of objections to welfare can be classified into the following major criticisms:

- **Work Disincentives.** Critics have argued that because welfare provides income that is easier to obtain than by working, the poor are often induced to reduce their work effort. In fact, the more a recipient earns from a job, the fewer the

### CHECKPOINT

## Does a Negative Income Tax Discourage Work?

Under a negative income system, people who work receive reduced payments from the government. Even worse, beyond the break-even income, workers must pay taxes. This means there is no basis in an NIT system to argue that the poor will have an incentive to work. Explain why you agree or disagree. (Hint: Construct a table using Exhibit 9, and consider after-tax income.)

benefits he or she receives. Moreover, the taxes to finance welfare payments have some disincentive effects on the work effort of taxpayers. Taxes reduce take-home pay and thus reduce the reward for work.

- **Inefficiencies.** Critics have charged that the huge welfare bureaucracy in Washington, D.C., and throughout the nation results in more money in the pockets of bureaucrats than in the pockets of the poor. This major criticism was expressed by economics professor Thomas Sowell as follows:

  *The amount necessary to lift every man, woman, and child in America above the poverty line has been calculated, and it is* one-third *of what is in fact spent on poverty programs. Clearly, much of the transfer ends up in the pockets of highly paid administrators, consultants, and staff as well as higher income recipients of benefits from programs advertised as antipoverty efforts.*[1]

- **Inequities.** Today, many critics argue that poor persons with equal needs receive different benefits. For example, a needy family in California might receive welfare benefits twice as great as those received by a needy family of the same size in South Carolina. The reason is that benefits under TANF and Medicaid are essentially controlled by the states.

As we will see in the next section of this chapter, Congress attempted to meet some of these criticisms when it passed the Welfare Reform Act of 1996.

# Reform Proposals

Although there have been numerous proposals for reforming welfare, the various ideas can be classified into two broad approaches. First, the negative income tax offers a major transformation of the entire patchwork of welfare programs. Second, workfare, which was included in the 1996 welfare bill, is a piecemeal approach, rather than a radical transformation.

---

[1]Thomas Sowell, *Markets and Minorities* (New York: Basic Books, 1981), p. 122.

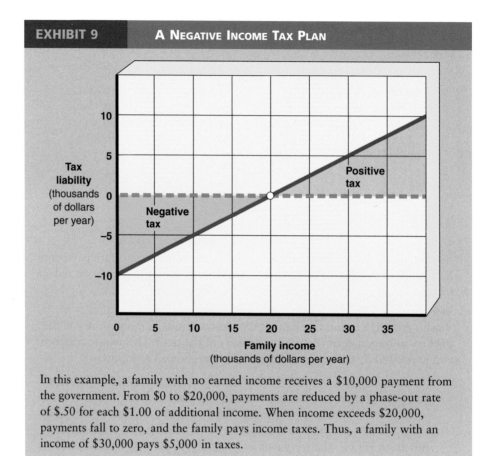

**EXHIBIT 9**          **A NEGATIVE INCOME TAX PLAN**

In this example, a family with no earned income receives a $10,000 payment from the government. From $0 to $20,000, payments are reduced by a phase-out rate of $.50 for each $1.00 of additional income. When income exceeds $20,000, payments fall to zero, and the family pays income taxes. Thus, a family with an income of $30,000 pays $5,000 in taxes.

## NEGATIVE INCOME TAX

**Negative income tax (NIT)**
A plan under which families below a certain break-even level of income would receive cash payments that decrease as their incomes increase.

The idea of **negative income tax** (**NIT**) was first advanced by the prominent economist Milton Friedman in the early 1960s to reduce work disincentives and welfare bureaucracy while providing for the poor. NIT is a plan under which families below a certain break-even level of income would receive cash payments that decrease as their incomes increase. A NIT system would combine all cash and in-kind transfer welfare programs into a single program administered by a single agency.

Exhibit 9 illustrates how a negative income tax might work. A low-income family of four receives a cash payment until it reaches a *break-even income* at $20,000 per year, where the family neither receives a payment nor pays income taxes. Above $20,000, the family pays income taxes. For example, a family with an income of $30,000 pays $5,000 in taxes, while a family with an income of $10,000 is paid an NIT subsidy of $5,000. A family with zero income receives an NIT payment of $10,000. Thus, the government pays families an amount that varies inversely (negatively) with income.

**You're the Economist**

# Pulling on the Strings of the Welfare Safety Net
## *Applicable Concept: welfare reform*

Welfare reform appears to be a success: The number of families on welfare has fallen sharply from 4.4 million in 1996 to 1.9 million in 2005.[1] The following is a sampling of articles describing results of the welfare scheme under the Personal Responsibility and Work Opportunity Act of 1996.

As reported in the *Washington Post*, Los Angeles County provides a striking contrast of welfare prior to and after reform in 1996. In the 1980s, Los Angeles County tested a welfare overhaul aimed at providing education and job training so recipients could qualify for better jobs. At the end of the first year, there was no significant impact. After the welfare reform act of 1996, independent researchers found that 43 percent of poor families who were required to participate in the city's new welfare reform program with work requirements got jobs, while only 32 percent of families randomly selected to remain in the traditional welfare program did. This represented an increase of one-third over the old welfare program. The typical welfare family subject to the new reform initiatives earned $1,286 in the first six months of the program, while "control group" families earned $879, a difference of 46 percent. The study covered the period from 1996 to 1997.[2]

A 2002 article in the *Los Angeles Times* concerns the new approach of the federal government providing block grants to states and mandating that the needy find jobs rather than just handing them welfare checks:

*Before 1996, when the nation's welfare laws were radically altered, welfare families might have gotten a monthly welfare check for the rest of their lives. Martha Soria's job would have been mostly to shuffle their paperwork. But with welfare reform came time limits on such benefits and strict new work requirements. And while Soria still shuffles a lot of paperwork, her job as well as the jobs of welfare caseworkers across the state and nation have changed. They have had to master hundreds of new rules and regulations under welfare reform and take on new responsibilities as guidance counselor, job finder, cheerleader, and taskmaster.[3]*

The following article argues that the states must do more to avoid racial bias:

*Under the 1996 law, states have the option to enforce time limits of their choosing. Because of this flexibility, states are left open to discriminate freely. Across the board, race was the determining factor affecting time limit lengths and their application. Observation of the enforcement of time limits shows that states with a higher proportion of African Americans or Latinos possess shorter time limits than the five-year guideline of the law. Over 20 states have opted to not allow exemptions to these time limits. Over 50 percent of African American families under welfare are subject to time limits shorter than the federal cutoff, as opposed to 30 percent of whites under welfare.[4]*

In 2004, the Cato Institute issued a report card on how well states have performed in moving people from dependence to independence since welfare reform. The report suggested states have a long way to go in implementing "essential reforms," including enforcing stronger sanctions for unemployed welfare recipients, setting stricter definitions of work-related activity, and discouraging teen pregnancy.[5]

### ANALYZE THE ISSUE

The current approach to welfare reform is to cut the growth of welfare by shifting control from the federal government to the states. The idea is that because state and local officials are closer to the people, welfare programs will improve. Analyze the results presented above based on work disincentives, inefficiencies, and inequities.

[1]U.S. Department of Health and Human Services, http://www.acf.dhhs.gov/news/stats/index.htm; under Welfare click caseload figures.

[2]Judith Havemann, "Welfare Reform Success Cited in L.A.," *The Washington Post*, Aug. 20, 1998, p. A1.

[3]Carla Rivera, "Welfare Reform's Enforcers," *The Los Angeles Times*, May 28, 2002, p. A1.

[4]Gordon Hurd, "Safety Net Sinking," *Colorline Magazine*, Summer 2002, p. 17.

[5]"Eight States Get Failing Grade on Welfare Reform Policy," *Economic Opportunity Report*, Oct. 25, 2004, p. 205.

> **CONCLUSION** *The negative income tax is the reverse of a positive income tax system, in which people pay the government an amount that varies directly with their income.*

The basic idea behind the NIT system is simple: Families with incomes above the break-even income finance payments to families with incomes below the break-even income. Begin at zero income in the exhibit, and assume the income guarantee is set at the poverty income threshold of $10,000. Beyond the guaranteed minimum income of $10,000, government payments are reduced by, say, $.50 for each $1.00 earned. This rate, called the *phase-out rate*, determines the cash transfers to low-income families until the break-even income is reached.

The NIT system offers several potential advantages. First, bureaucratic costs would be cut because an NIT program could be administered by a single agency. Second, poor people would not suffer the stigma of repeatedly standing in lines at the welfare office or using food stamps in the grocery store. Third, many economists argue that individuals are rational and know best how to spend their money. Thus, a cash subsidy is preferable to an in-kind transfer.

After years of discussion and study, the NIT has not gained wide support except among many economists. The NIT system is perceived as a political liability because voters perceive it as a "giveaway" of taxpayers' money. These critics believe in-kind welfare is preferable to cash assistance. When a recipient is given food stamps or a housing subsidy, he or she acquires food and housing, rather than, say, buying drugs and gambling. NIT proponents point out, however, it is known that some food stamps are sold illegally for cash, which is used to buy drugs, alcohol, or whatever. Finally, some critics argue that a generous guaranteed minimum income paid in cash might create a disincentive to work rather than an incentive to work.

## WORKFARE

The 1996 welfare reform bill titled the Personal Responsibility and Work Opportunity Act set a lifetime limit of five years of welfare benefits per family and gave the states block grants to run welfare programs. To overcome the disincentive to work characteristic of earlier welfare programs, the current approach is to increase the work performed by welfare recipients and encourage their participation in job-training programs. To keep their benefits, welfare recipients must perform some work activities within two years of receiving welfare or risk losing benefits. This idea is called workfare. Workfare programs require able-bodied adults to work for the local government or any available private-sector employer in order to be eligible for welfare benefits. The paramount question thus becomes how to create jobs for welfare recipients. A large public job plan would be costly and politically unpopular, especially among public employees who fear losing their jobs. Another option is for the government to pay employers to hire welfare recipients. A variation on this idea is for the government to hire personnel firms that would earn a fee for each person placed in a job.

There are potential problems with providing subsidies for companies that hire welfare recipients. One problem is that subsidies can stigmatize welfare recipients and reduce their long-term employment prospects. Another potential problem is that subsidies could be a windfall payment to employers for hiring people who would have been hired without the subsidies. Finally, there is a displacement problem because a subsidized welfare-recipient worker can take the job of an unsubsidized worker who has never received welfare benefits.

# Discrimination

Poverty and discrimination in the workplace are related. Nonwhites and females earn less income when employer prejudice prevents them from receiving job opportunities. Discrimination also occurs when nonwhites and females earn less, but do basically the same work as whites and males. Exhibit 10 uses labor market theory to explain how discrimination can cause the equilibrium wage to be lower for nonwhites than for whites.

Exhibit 10(a) assumes that employers do not discriminate. This means employers hire workers regardless of race—that is, on the basis of their contribution to revenue (their marginal revenue products, *MRPs*). Hence, the intersection of the market demand curve, *D*, and the market supply curve, *S*, determines the equilibrium wage rate of $245 per day paid by nondiscriminating employers. The total number of black and white workers hired is 14,000 workers.

**EXHIBIT 10**  **LABOR MARKETS WITHOUT AND WITH RACIAL DISCRIMINATION**

In Part (a), there is no labor market discrimination against blacks. In this case, the equilibrium wage for all labor is $245 per day. Under discrimination in Part (b), the labor demand and labor supply curves for white and black workers differ. As a result, the equilibrium wage rate for whites, $280, is higher than that for blacks, $210.

# Is a Librarian Worth the Same Wage as an Electrician?
*Applicable Concept: comparable worth*

Few women are typically listed in *Forbes*'s ranking of the nation's top 100 chief executive officers by compensation. On average, women earn only about 75 percent as much as men in spite of laws against pay discrimination. Discrimination in wages and employment on the basis of sex was made illegal by two federal laws. In 1963, Congress passed the Equal Pay Act (EPA), which outlawed pay discrimination between men and women doing substantially the same job. This does not mean that unequal pay for the same work cannot exist, but if it does, the differential must be due to factors other than gender. These factors might include a seniority system, a merit system, or a system that measures earnings by quantity or quality of production.

Comparable worth laws have been passed in several states, Canada, Great Britain, and Australia. Proponents of comparable worth argue that the equal-pay-for-equal-work idea has failed. They observe that the pay is lower in female-dominated occupations and argue that female productivity and experience receive less reward in these jobs than do male productivity and experience in male-dominated jobs. In short, they maintain that women crowd into secretarial work, nursing, and retail sales because of discrimination against women. The increased supply of female labor in these crowded professions lowers the prevailing wage.

Comparable worth advocates urge the courts to interpret such labor market inequalities as a violation of the sex-discrimination provisions of Title VII of the Civil Rights Act of 1964. This law defines discriminatory practices more broadly than does the EPA. Title VII makes it unlawful to discriminate on the basis of race, sex, or national origin in classifying, assigning, or promoting employees; in extending or assigning facilities; in providing training, retraining, or appren-

Now assume for the sake of argument that employers do practice job discrimination against black workers. The result, shown in Exhibit 10(b), is two different labor markets—one for whites and one for blacks. Because discrimination exists, the demand curve for labor for blacks is to the left of the demand curve for labor for whites, reflecting unjustified restricted employment practices. The supply curve of labor for blacks is also to the left of the supply curve of labor for whites because there are fewer blacks seeking employment than whites.

Given the differences in the labor market demand and supply curves, the equilibrium wage rate for whites of $280 is higher than the $210 paid to blacks. Comparison of these wage rates with the labor market equilibrium wage rate of $245 reveals that the effect of discrimination is to change the relative wages of white and black workers. Whites earn a higher wage rate than they would earn in a labor market that did not favor hiring them. Conversely, the black wage rate is lower as a result of discrimination.

ticeships; or in implementing any other terms, conditions, or privileges of employment.

If the courts accept comparable worth and expand the scope of Title VII, they will not consider whether employers intentionally pay less for "women's jobs," but only whether the employers are in compliance with an established rating scheme. The best-known case occurred in 1983, when the American Federation of State, County, and Municipal Employees won the first federal court case against the state of Washington. The state was found guilty of wage discrimination against women because it had not followed its comparable worth point system. To comply with Title VII, the court ordered Washington to upgrade nearly 15,000 female employees and award back pay estimated at $377 million. The decision was appealed to higher courts, and the union ultimately lost the case.

Quantitative job evaluations are not new, although their use is the cornerstone of the comparable worth movement. In the Washington case, independent consultants gave a registered nurse more points than a computer systems analyst, and truck drivers received fewer points than clerks. In another case, job consultants studied the Minnesota job classification system and assigned point values to 762 state job classes. According to the point system, male-dominated jobs often paid more than female-dominated jobs even though the female jobs had greater "worth." The Minnesota Task Force on Pay Equity then recommended to the legislature that it raise the "underpaid" female job classes rather than lower the "overpaid" male job classes.

In 2002, a *New York Times* article reported that the salary gap between men and women managers had widened. A General Accounting Office report, supported by other studies, showed that overall managerial salaries for women slipped from 73 cents for every dollar made by a male manager in 1995 to 71.3 cents in 2000.[1] And a 2003 article studied salaries for female-dominated professions and concluded that the male-female gap continued unabated.[2]

## ANALYZE THE ISSUE

Suppose consultants use a job-scoring system and determine that the wage rate for a secretary is $50 per hour, while the competitive labor market wage rate is $10 per hour. What would be the effect of such a comparable worth law?

[1]Jeffrey L. Seglin, "The Right Thing: How to Get a Company's Attention on Women's Pay," *New York Times*, March 17, 2002, p. C4.

[2]Margaret Gibelman, "So How Far Have We Come: Pestilent and Persistent Gender Gap in Pay," *Social Work*, January 2003, pp. 22–33.

## COMPARABLE WORTH

A controversial public policy aimed at eliminating labor market pay inequities is a concept called **comparable worth**. Comparable worth is the principle that employees who work for the same employer must be paid the same wages when their jobs, even if different, require similar levels of education, training, experience, and responsibility. Comparable worth is a nonmarket wage-setting remedy to the situation where jobs dominated by women pay less than jobs dominated by men. Because women's work is alleged to be undervalued, the solution is equal pay for jobs evaluated as having "comparable worth" according to point scores assigned to different jobs. In essence, comparable worth replaces labor-market–determined wages with bureaucratic judgments about the valuation of different jobs. For example, compensation paid to an elevator inspector and a nurse can be computed based on quantitative scores in a job-rating scheme. If the jobs' point totals are equal, the average elevator inspector and nurse must be paid equally by law.

**Comparable worth**
The principle that employees who work for the same employer must be paid the same wage when their jobs, even if different, require similar levels of education, training, experience, and responsibility. A nonmarket wage-setting process is used to evaluate and compensate jobs according to point scores assigned to different jobs.

## CHECKPOINT

### Should the Law Protect Women?

Do you want women serving in combat, mining coal, and building sky-scrapers? Some states have enacted laws that protect women by keeping them out of jobs deemed "too strenuous" or "too dangerous." Would the likely effect of such laws be to decrease wages in male-dominated occupa-tions, increase wages in female-intensive occupations, or decrease wages in female-intensive occupations?

## Key Concepts

| | | |
|---|---|---|
| Lorenz curve | Means test | Comparable worth |
| Poverty line | Unemployment compensation | |
| In-kind transfers | Negative income tax (NIT) | |

## Summary

■  The **Lorenz curve** is a measure of inequality of income. Since 1947, the share of money income for each fifth of families ranked according to their income has been quite stable. Also, the degree of income inequality among families in the United States has changed little since 1929. In recent decades, the richest families have become richer; however, the median income of all groups has increased.

**LORENZ CURVE**

The **poverty line** is a level of cash income below which a family is classified as poor. The poverty income threshold is three times the cost of a minimal diet for a family. Today, about 11 percent of the U.S. population is officially classified as poor.

**In-kind transfers** are payments to the poor in the form of goods and services, rather than cash. Calculation of the poverty line counts only cash income. In-kind transfers, such as food stamps, Medicaid, and housing, do not count as income for families classified as officially poor. Government cash transfers counted in calculating the poverty line include payments from Social Security, unemployment compensation, and Temporary Assistance to Needy Families.

**Welfare criticisms** include three major arguments: (1) Welfare reduces the incentive to work for the poor and taxpayers. (2) Welfare is inefficient because much of the money covers administrative costs, rather than providing benefits for the poor. (3) Because many antipoverty programs are controlled by the state, welfare benefits vary widely.

The **negative income tax** is a plan to guarantee a certain amount of income for all families. As a low-income family earns income, government payments (negative income tax) are phased out. After reaching a break-even income, families become taxpayers instead of being on the welfare rolls.

**NEGATIVE INCOME TAX**

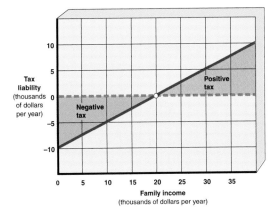

**Comparable worth** is the theory that workers in jobs determined to be of equal value by means of point totals should be paid equally. Instead of allowing labor markets to set wages, independent consultants award points to different jobs on the basis of such criteria as knowledge, experience, and working conditions.

## Summary of Conclusion Statements

Measured by distribution of family money income, the richest families have become a little richer and the rest of the family groups a little poorer in recent decades.

The Lorenz curve has shifted only slightly inward, and therefore closer to the perfect equality line between 1929 and 2005.

The negative income tax is the reverse of a positive income tax system, in which people pay the government an amount that varies directly with their income.

1. The following table contains data on the distribution of income in the countries of Alpha and Beta:

| Percentage of families | Alpha | | Beta | |
|---|---|---|---|---|
| | Percentage share | Cumulative share | Percentage share | Cumulative share |
| Lowest fifth | 17.7% | _____ | 9.0% | _____ |
| Second-lowest fifth | 19.9 | _____ | 14.2 | _____ |
| Middle fifth | 20.4 | _____ | 17.5 | _____ |
| Second-highest fifth | 20.7 | _____ | 21.9 | _____ |
| Highest fifth | 21.3 | _____ | 37.4 | _____ |

a. Compute the cumulative distribution of income for each country.
b. Construct the Lorenz curve for each country.
c. For which country is the distribution of income more equal?

2. Suppose each family in the United States earned an equal money income. What would be the effect?

3. Explain the difference between poverty defined absolutely and poverty defined relatively. Which definition is the basis of the poverty line?

4. Calculate the official poverty threshold annual income for a family of four. Assume the minimally acceptable diet is estimated to be $5 per person per day and the minimum wage is $5 per hour. Will a head of a family of four earn the poverty threshold you have calculated?

5. What are in-kind transfers? Give examples. How are in-kind transfers considered in determining whether a family is below the poverty income threshold?

6. Would free health care reduce poverty, as measured by the government? Would free public housing, day care, and job training for the poor reduce the poverty rate? Explain.

7. What percentage of families in the United States was classified as poor in the 1990s? Which demographic groups have higher poverty rates?

8. List the major government cash assistance and in-kind transfer programs to assist the poor. Which of the programs are not exclusively for the poor?

9. What are three major criticisms of welfare?

10. Assume the government implements a negative income tax plan with a guaranteed minimum income of $5,000 and a phase-out rate for payments of 50 percent. Provide the missing data in the following table:

**A NEGATIVE INCOME TAX PLAN**

| Family income | Negative tax | Total after-tax income |
|---|---|---|
| $      0 | _____ | _____ |
| 2,000 | _____ | _____ |
| 4,000 | _____ | _____ |
| 6,000 | _____ | _____ |
| 8,000 | _____ | _____ |
| 10,000 | _____ | _____ |

11. Critics of welfare argue that the role of government should be to break down legal barriers to employment rather than using programs that directly provide cash or goods and services. For example, advocates of this approach would remove laws mandating minimum wages, comparable worth, union power, professional licensing, and other restrictive practices. Do you agree or disagree? Why?

## Study Guide Questions

1. Government payments in the form of goods and services, rather than cash, including such government programs as food stamps, Medicaid, and housing are called _____ .

2. Which of the following statements is *true*?
   a. Income distribution in the United States has gotten progressively more unequal since 1929.
   b. The Lorenz curve indicates the degree of discrimination in an economy.
   c. The Lorenz curve indicates the degree of income inequality in an economy.
   d. The richest 5 percent of Americans earn approximately half of the nation's income.
   e. All of the above.

3. Which of the following statements is *true*?
   a. All people in poverty are on welfare.
   b. Unemployment compensation is an in-kind transfer.
   c. Temporary Assistance to Needy Families (TANF) is an example of a cash payment made by government to the impoverished.

   d. After cash assistance and in-kind transfers are considered, the distribution of income in the United States is more unequal.
   e. All of the above.

4. Which of the following statements is *true*?
   a. Discrimination against women and blacks reduces the demand for these workers, resulting in lower wages paid these workers.
   b. Discrimination is no longer a problem in the United States.
   c. A negative income tax system is a plan in which everyone pays the same percentage of their income as taxes.
   d. A negative income tax system is a plan in which those below a certain income receive a cash payment from the government.

5. T  F  When determining whether a family's income is below the official poverty line, noncash benefits from the government, such as food, housing, and medical benefits, are not included.

**Answers to these questions are in the complete Study Guide at www.thomsonedu.com/thomsonnow.**

  **For Online Exercises, go to the text Web site at www.thomsonedu.com/economics/tucker.**

## Checkpoint Answers

### Does a Negative Income Tax Discourage Work?

The following table is interpreted from Exhibit 9. Even though payments from the government decrease, total after-tax income increases from the combination of the income earned and the negative tax. After the break-even income of $20,000, total after-tax income continues to rise. If you said the NIT system assumes the poor are rational people who are motivated to earn more total after-tax income by working, **YOU ARE CORRECT.**

| Family income | Negative tax | Positive tax | Total after-tax income |
|---|---|---|---|
| $     0 | $10,000 | $     0 | $10,000 |
| 5,000 | 7,000 | 0 | 12,000 |
| 10,000 | 5,000 | 0 | 15,000 |
| 15,000 | 2,500 | 0 | 17,500 |
| 20,000 | 0 | 0 | 20,000 |
| 25,000 | 0 | −2,500 | 22,500 |
| 30,000 | 0 | −5,000 | 25,000 |
| 35,000 | 0 | −7,500 | 27,500 |

### Should the Law Protect Women?

A law that limits women's access to certain occupations results in their crowding into the remaining occupations. The obstacles facing women in male-dominated occupations artificially restrict competition with men. If you said the increased labor supply in female-intensive occupations decreases their wages, while the decreased labor supply in male-intensive occupations increases wages for males, **YOU ARE CORRECT.**

## Practice Quiz

For an explanation of the correct answers, please visit the tutorial at www.thomsonedu.com/economics/tucker.

1. Currently, the wealthiest 5 percent of all U.S. families earned what percentage of total annual money income among families?
   a. More than 20 percent
   b. Less than 10 percent
   c. More than 25 percent
   d. More than 50 percent

2. A figure that measures the relationship between the cumulative percentage of money income on the vertical axis and the cumulative percentage of families on the horizontal axis is called the
   a. family-income curve.
   b. Washington curve.
   c. Lorenz curve.
   d. Gini curve.

**EXHIBIT 11 LORENZ CURVE**

3. As shown in Exhibit 11, the perfect equality line is drawn between points
   a. W and Y along the curve.
   b. X and Z.
   c. W and Y along the straight line.
   d. W and X.

4. As shown in Exhibit 11, 20 percent of families earned a cumulative share of about _____ percent of income.
   a. 5
   b. 10
   c. 30
   d. 50

5. As shown in Exhibit 11, 40 percent of families earned a cumulative share of about _____ percent of income.
   a. 5
   b. 15
   c. 30
   d. 50

6. Since 1929, the overall family income distribution in the United States has become
   a. much more unequal.
   b. much less unequal.
   c. slightly more unequal.
   d. slightly more equal.

7. Comparing the family income distributions of the United States, the Czech Republic, and Brazil, the conclusion is that income is distributed

a. most equally in Brazil.
b. most equally in the United States.
c. about the same in all three countries.
d. most equally in the Czech Republic.

8. To establish the poverty line that divides poor and nonpoor families, the government
   a. multiplies the cost of a minimal diet by three.
   b. multiplies the cost of a minimal diet by five.
   c. adds 50 percent to the cost of a minimal diet.
   d. adds 100 percent to the cost of a minimal diet.

9. The poverty line
   a. is defined as one-half average family income.
   b. includes in-kind transfers.
   c. includes Medicaid benefits.
   d. has been attacked for overstating poverty.

10. Which of the following is an in-kind transfer?
    a. Social Security payments
    b. Unemployment compensation
    c. Food stamps
    d. Welfare payments

11. Which of the following is a cash assistance (not an in-kind transfer) program?
    a. Temporary Assistance to Needy Families (TANF)
    b. Medicare
    c. Medicaid
    d. Food stamps

12. The negative income tax (NIT) is a plan under which families
    a. above a level of income pay no tax.
    b. pay the same tax rate except for the poor.
    c. below a level of income pay no tax.
    d. below a level of income receive a cash payment.

13. Which of the following might decrease the supply curve of labor?
    a. Discrimination against blacks
    b. Discrimination against women
    c. Difficult licensing requirements
    d. All of the above

14. As shown in Exhibit 12, a family of four pays income taxes at
    a. an income of $5,000.
    b. any income between zero and $40,000.
    c. all levels of income.
    d. any income above $40,000.

15. As shown in Exhibit 12, a family of four with no earned income receives _____ from the government.
    a. zero payment
    b. the break-even income of $40,000
    c. a $20,000 payment
    d. a $20,000 tax deferment

**EXHIBIT 12  NEGATIVE INCOME TAX**

# Antitrust and Regulation

AP Images/Bill Haber

*People of the same trade seldom meet together, even for merriment and diversion, but the conversation ends in a conspiracy against the public, or in some contrivance to raise prices.*[1]

**—Adam Smith**

Once Microsoft dominated the personal computer software industry, the U.S. government charged the firm and Bill Gates, its founder, with anticompetitive business practices, and the media compared the case to John D. Rockefeller's Standard Oil monopoly and the robber barons of the 1890s. In the past, antitrust laws have been successfully used against the nation's largest corporations. This threat of the high legal costs of defending against an antitrust suit serves as a powerful deterrent, discouraging monopolies from engaging in unfair actions intended to eliminate rivals. Here you will explore and form opinions on the Microsoft case, the Standard Oil case, and other major antitrust cases. In addition, this chapter compares antitrust laws in the United States to antitrust laws of other countries.

When antitrust policy is successful, consumers benefit from lower prices and more output. As you study antitrust policy in this chapter, you will learn that antitrust is somewhat of an art form that blends economic theory and politics—perhaps more politics than economic theory. Interestingly, certain industries and organizations are exempt from antitrust legislation: labor unions, professional baseball teams, public utilities, public transit companies, schools, hospitals, and suppliers of military equipment.

The second half of this chapter turns to government regulation, which affects virtually every business and consumer. Our food is regulated, toys are regulated, airline safety is regulated, and most industries must deal with some form of regulation. What are the reasons for regulation, and what are its consequences? The explanation begins with a brief survey of regulation in the United States. Although government regulation remains pervasive, a deregulation movement began in the late 1970s to reduce regulation in industries such as transportation and telecommunications.

Deregulation in the electricity industry began in 1992. In 2001, power shortages in California provoked debate on the issue of regulation versus deregulation in this industry. In the last section, we discuss the rationale for three different types of regulation justified on the basis of market failure.

## In this chapter, you will learn to solve these economics puzzles:

- Can universities and colleges improve education by engaging in price-fixing?
- Why doesn't the water company or electric company compete?
- Why is market failure an economic rationale for regulation?

[1]Adam Smith, *An Inquiry into the Nature and Causes of the Wealth of Nations* (1776, reprint, New York: Random House, The Modern Library, 1937), p. 128.

**319**

# Antitrust

Before the Civil War, industries were populated by small firms, and few economic problems were caused by monopoly. After the Civil War, during the rapid industrialization of the 1870s and 1880s, the railroads and telegraph linked diverse regions of the country and enabled firms to expand into national markets. To gain more control of expanding industries, many competing companies merged or formed a **trust**. A trust is a combination or cartel consisting of firms that place their assets in the custody of a board of trustees. The trust allows firms that have not actually merged to form a cartel, or a cohesive group of firms that controls an industry in order to charge monopoly prices and earn higher profits. The long list of trusts formed during this period included the iron trust, sugar trust, copper trust, steel trust, coal trust, oil trust, tobacco trust, and even the paper-bag trust. The organizers of many of these trusts became widely known as *robber barons* because they exploited and bullied anyone in their way.

During the last decades of the nineteenth century, many trusts used various tactics to avoid competition. Recall from Chapter 9 on monopoly that Standard Oil acquired oil fields, railroads, pipelines, and ships and then denied access to rivals. Thus, competing firms had to merge with Standard Oil or go out of business. With the competition eliminated, John D. Rockefeller, the best-known so-called robber baron, raised Standard Oil's prices and limited production, and consumers suffered along with Standard Oil's competitors.

Another anticompetitive strategy used by the industrial giants was **predatory pricing**. Predatory pricing is the practice of one or more firms temporarily reducing prices in order to eliminate competition and then raising prices. Often trusts would sell a product below cost until their weaker competitors were unable to withstand mounting losses and were forced from the industry. Perhaps even more alarming, some trusts resorted to political corruption. For example, the railroad and petroleum trusts employed corrupt legislators and judges to gain a competitive edge.

By the end of the nineteenth century, the threat of continuing economic and political abuses created a public opinion quite hostile to big business. Newspapers regularly printed news of the trusts' questionable business practices. The numerous and politically influential farmers blamed the trusts for the high railroad charges that were making farming unprofitable. Consumers and labor unions also raised their voices against monopoly power. The influence of the trusts was discussed constantly in the halls of Congress. In 1888, both major political parties added antimonopoly planks to their campaign platforms. Hatred and distrust of the centralization of economic and political power originated in the Jeffersonian tradition of the United States. Against this background of populist (pro-people) fear of big business and its political power, Congress passed laws aimed at preventing firms from engaging in anticompetitive activities.

The following is a brief description of the major antitrust legislation that constitutes basic antitrust law.

## THE SHERMAN ACT

The first antitrust law was the **Sherman Act**. The Sherman Act of 1890 is the federal antitrust law that prohibits monopolization and conspiracies to restrain

**Trust**
A combination or cartel consisting of firms that place their assets in the custody of a board of trustees.

**Predatory pricing**
The practice of one or more firms temporarily reducing prices in order to eliminate competition and then raising prices.

**Sherman Act**
The federal antitrust law enacted in 1890 that prohibits monopolization and conspiracies to restrain trade.

trade. Today, this act remains the cornerstone of antitrust policy in the United States. It has two main provisions:

*Section 1: Every contract, combination in the form of trust or otherwise, or conspiracy in restraint of trade or commerce among the several States, or with foreign nations, is hereby declared to be illegal. . . .*

*Section 2: Every person who shall monopolize, or attempt to monopolize, or combine or conspire with any other person or persons, to monopolize any part of the trade or commerce among the several States, or with foreign nations, shall be deemed guilty of a misdemeanor, and, on conviction thereof, shall be punished by a fine not exceeding five thousand dollars, or by imprisonment not exceeding one year, or by both said punishments, in the discretion of the court.*[2]

In response to the public outcry, Congress intended to craft this law with sweeping language against the trusts. But what does the Sherman Act really say? It is unclear exactly which business practices constitute a "restraint of trade" and therefore a violation of the law. As a result of the extremely vague language, there were numerous court battles, and the act was ineffective for years. For example, the federal government did not win its first notable cases against Standard Oil and American Tobacco until 1911.

The serious consequences of violating the Sherman Act are reflected in the more recent case of Archer Daniels Midland Company (ADM). In 1995, this agribusiness giant pleaded guilty to price-fixing involving lysine and citric acid. It paid a $100 million fine. In 1998, a federal jury convicted three past and present executives of conspiring with competitors to fix the prices of these products. They were sentenced to serve two years in prison and to pay fines of $350,000 each.

## THE CLAYTON ACT

As explained above, the Sherman Act initially proved to be little more than a legislative mandate for the courts to spell out the meaning of antitrust laws. To define anticompetitive acts more precisely, Congress passed the **Clayton Act**. The Clayton Act of 1914 is an amendment that strengthened the Sherman Act by making it illegal for firms to engage in certain anticompetitive business practices. Under this act, the following business practices are illegal with the important controversial condition that the effect must be to "substantially lessen competition or tend to create a monopoly":

1. **Price Discrimination.** A firm charges different customers different prices for the same product with the price differences not related to cost differences. (Recall the discussion of this topic in the chapter on monopoly.)

2. **Exclusive Dealing.** A manufacturer requires a retailer to sign an agreement stipulating the condition that the retailer will not carry any rival products of the manufacturer.

3. **Tying Contracts.** The seller of one product requires the buyer to purchase some other product(s). For example, movie distributors cannot force theaters

**Clayton Act**
A 1914 amendment that strengthens the Sherman Act by making it illegal for firms to engage in anti-competitive business practices.

---

[2]In 1974, the act was amended so that violations would be treated as felonies.

to purchase projection rights to a blockbuster movie only on the condition that they pay for a bundle of films with much less box office potential.

4. **Stock Acquisition of Competing Companies.** One firm buys the stock of a competing firm.

5. **Interlocking Directorates.** The directors of one company serve on the board of directors of another company in the same industry. Interlocking directorates are illegal, whether or not the effect may be to "substantially lessen competition."

Although more specific than the Sherman Act, the Clayton Act is also vague and leaves a key question unanswered: Exactly when does a situation or action "substantially lessen competition"? To this day, the task of interpreting this ambiguous phrase remains with the courts, and the interpretation changes over time.

## THE FEDERAL TRADE COMMISSION ACT

**Federal Trade Commission Act**
The federal act that in 1914 established the Federal Trade Commission (FTC) to investigate unfair competitive practices of firms.

Since the federal government faced a growing antitrust responsibility in the early 1900s, an agency was needed to investigate alleged anticompetitive practices and reach judgments. The **Federal Trade Commission Act** was enacted for this purpose. The Federal Trade Commission Act of 1914 established the Federal Trade Commission (FTC) to investigate unfair competitive practices of firms. This act contains perhaps the most general language of any antitrust act. It declares illegal "unfair methods of competition in commerce." The act established a five-member commission appointed by the president to determine the exact meaning of "unfair methods." Today, the FTC is concerned primarily with (1) enforcing consumer protection legislation, (2) prohibiting deceptive advertising, and (3) preventing collusion. When a complaint is filed with the FTC, the commission investigates. If there is a violation, the FTC can negotiate a settlement, issue a cease-and-desist order, or initiate a lawsuit.

## THE ROBINSON-PATMAN ACT

**Robinson-Patman Act**
A 1936 amendment to the Clayton Act that strengthens the Clayton Act against price discrimination.

The Clayton Act has been amended twice. Although price discrimination became illegal under the Clayton Act, that section was not widely enforced at first. This situation changed with the passage of the **Robinson-Patman Act**. The Robinson-Patman Act of 1936 is an amendment to the Clayton Act that strengthens the Clayton Act's provisions against price discrimination. The Robinson-Patman Act is complex and controversial. Its basic purpose is to prevent large sellers from offering different prices to different buyers where the effect is to harm even a single small firm. In fact, the Robinson-Patman Act is often called the "Chain Store Act" because it was an outgrowth of the competition between small independent sellers and chain stores that developed after World War I.

The Robinson-Patman Act encourages lawsuits by small independent firms because it broadens the list of illegal price discrimination practices. This act, for example, makes it illegal for a firm to offer quantity discounts, free advertising, or promotional allowances to one buyer if the firm does not offer the same concessions to all buyers. Be careful to note that the prohibition on price discrimination in the Robinson-Patman Act is limited to situations where the effect is to "substantially lessen competition or tend to create a monopoly." The first You're the Economist offers the opportunity to debate issues concerning this act.

### THE CELLER-KEFAUVER ACT

Prior to 1950, the U.S. Supreme Court interpreted the Sherman Act as prohibiting mergers between competing firms by stock acquisition, but not prohibiting mergers by the sale of physical assets (plant, equipment, and so on). The **Celler-Kefauver Act** was the second amendment to the Clayton Act, and it was enacted to address this problem. The Celler-Kefauver Act of 1950 is an amendment to the Clayton Act that prohibits one firm from merging with a competitor by purchasing its physical assets if the effect is to substantially lessen competition. Consequently, this act is sometimes called the "Antimerger Act" because it closed the loophole in the Clayton Act and thereby prohibited anticompetitive mergers, which were the target of the original Clayton Act.

The five major antitrust laws are summarized in Exhibit 1.

**Celler-Kefauver Act**
A 1950 amendment to the Clayton Act that prohibits one firm from merging with a competitor by purchasing its physical assets if the effect is to substantially lessen competition.

# Key Antitrust Cases

Antitrust policy can be compared to the rules of baseball or other sports. The House and Senate of the U.S. Congress set the "rules of the game" for antitrust cases, just as the American and National Leagues set the rules of baseball. For example, the rules of baseball say that a player hitting a homer must run from first

| EXHIBIT 1 | SUMMARY OF MAJOR ANTITRUST LAWS |
|---|---|
| **Law (date enacted)** | **Key provisions** |
| Sherman Act (1890) | ■ Prohibits interstate price fixing and other conspiracies and combinations that restrain trade and attempt to monopolize. |
| Clayton Act (1914) | ■ Bolsters and clarifies the Sherman Act by prohibiting specific business practices, including exclusive dealing, tying contracts, stock acquisition of competitors, and interlocking directorates. |
| Federal Trade Commission Act (1914) | ■ Established an agency (the FTC) to help enforce antitrust laws by investigating unfair and deceptive business practices. |
| Robinson-Patman Act (1936) | ■ Amends the Clayton Act by broadening the list of illegal price discrimination practices to include quantity discounts, free advertising, and promotional allowances offered to large buyers and not to small buyers. The Robinson-Patman Act is often called the "Chain Store Act." |
| Celler-Kefauver Act (1950) | ■ Amends the Clayton Act by closing the loophole that permitted a firm to merge by buying assets of a rival, rather than by acquisition of stocks, as outlawed in the original Clayton Act. The Celler-Kefauver Act is often called the "Antimerger Act." |

## You're the Economist

# Is Utah Pie's Slice of the Pie Too Small?
### Applicable Concept: Robinson-Patman Act

In the 1950s, the market for frozen dessert pies was small, but growing. The Salt Lake City market was supplied by distant plants in California that were owned by Carnation, Continental Baking, and Pet Milk. Until 1957, these three firms accounted for almost all the frozen fruit pies sold in the Salt Lake City market.

The Utah Pie Company had been baking dessert pies in Salt Lake City and selling them fresh for 30 years. This family-owned-and-operated business entered the frozen pie market in 1957. It was immediately successful and grabbed a huge share of the Salt Lake City market. During the relevant years, the market shares of the various competitors were as follows:

|             | 1958 | 1959 | 1960 | 1961 |
|-------------|------|------|------|------|
| Utah Pie    | 67%  | 34%  | 46%  | 45%  |
| Pet         | 16   | 36   | 28   | 29   |
| Carnation   | 10   | 9    | 12   | 9    |
| Continental | 1    | 3    | 2    | 8    |
| All others  | 6    | 19   | 13   | 8    |

Utah Pie's strategy for penetrating the market was to set its prices below those of its competitors. Due to its immediate success, it built a new plant in 1958. Its local plants gave Utah Pie a locational advantage over its competitors. For most of the time in question, Utah Pie's prices were the lowest in the Salt Lake City market. The incumbent firms, of course, responded to Utah Pie's entry and lower prices by reducing their own prices. As a result, all the larger firms sold frozen pies in Salt Lake City at prices lower than those charged for pies of like grade and quality in other geographic markets considerably closer to their California plants.

Utah Pie sued these three firms, claiming price discrimination. Ultimately, the case was reviewed by the Supreme Court [in 1967], which took a dim view of such pricing behavior: "Sellers may not sell like goods to different purchasers at different prices if the result may be to injure competition in either the sellers' or the buyers' market unless such discriminations are justified as permitted by the Act." Consequently, the Supreme Court found the defendants guilty of price discrimination. Inasmuch as no competitors had been forced from the market, it appears that price discrimination does not have to have an obviously predatory impact to be ruled illegal. All the Court saw in this case was a pattern of falling prices. It feared that such a pattern could result in a lessening of competition if one or more competitors dropped out of the market.

### ANALYZE THE ISSUE

Utah Pie sued its three outside competitors under the Robinson-Patman Act. Some have criticized this case because it is an example of the type of bizarre result that can be produced by antitrust policy. Do you agree? Explain.

*Source: David L. Kaserman and John W. Mayo,* Government and Business: The Economics of Antitrust and Regulation *(Fort Worth: Dryden Press, 1995), p. 282.*

base to home plate, rather than from third base to home plate. Similarly, the Sherman Act forbids monopolization through predatory pricing by businesses. This brings us to the role of the umpire. After a game, a Little League player asked the first base umpire, "What do you call when the runner and the ball reach first base at exactly the same time?" The umpire replied, "There's no such thing as a tie. It's always the way I call it." That's how it is with court decisions on antitrust laws, and, just like many of the umpire's calls, all the courts' decisions are not "crowd pleasers." With this point in mind, let's look at some important "calls" of courts on antitrust cases.

## THE STANDARD OIL CASE (1911)

President Theodore Roosevelt's administration took action to break up Standard Oil under the Sherman Act. After 10 years of litigation, the Supreme Court ruled in 1911 that Standard Oil had achieved its monopoly position in the oil refining industry through illegal business practices. John D. Rockefeller's trust had used railroad rebates, discounts, espionage, control of supplies to rivals, and predatory pricing to gain a monopoly. The remedy was for the Standard Oil Trust to be broken into competing companies: Standard Oil of New York became Mobil, Standard Oil of California became Chevron, Standard Oil of Indiana became Amoco, and Standard Oil of New Jersey became Exxon.

The Standard Oil Trust case established a standard for antitrust rulings. The Supreme Court ruled that (1) Standard Oil was a monopoly with a 90 percent share of the refined-oil market and (2) Standard Oil achieved its monopoly through illegal business behavior intended to exclude rivals. The Court stated that point (2) was critical to its decision and not point (1). This doctrine became known as the **rule of reason**. The rule of reason is the antitrust doctrine that the existence of monopoly alone is not illegal unless the monopoly engages in illegal business practices. Stated differently, monopoly per se is not illegal. Thus, "big is not necessarily bad." Standard Oil and other dominant firms would be broken up not merely because of their dominance, but also because of their abusive behavior.

**Rule of reason**
The antitrust doctrine that the existence of monopoly alone is not illegal unless the monopoly engages in illegal business practices.

Between 1911 and 1920, the courts applied the rule of reason in breaking up the American Tobacco Trust and other trusts. In 1920, the Supreme Court also applied the rule of reason when it decided that U.S. Steel was not guilty under the Sherman Act. Although U.S. Steel controlled almost 75 percent of the domestic iron and steel industry, the Supreme Court ruled that it is not *size* that violates the law. Since there was no evidence of unfair pricing practices, U.S. Steel was a "good citizen" not in violation of the Sherman Act.

## THE ALCOA CASE (1945)

Thirty-four years after the Standard Oil case, the courts did a "flip flop" on the rule of reason. In 1940, the Aluminum Company of America (Alcoa) was the only producer of aluminum in the United States. Alcoa's monopoly was primarily the result of its patents and its ownership of a unique resource, bauxite. Moreover, Alcoa kept its prices low to avoid competition and prosecution, behaving as a "good citizen" despite its size. A federal appeals court ruled that Alcoa had violated the Sherman Act and declared:

> *Having proved that Alcoa had a monopoly of the domestic ingot market the government had gone far enough. . . . Congress did not condone "good trusts" and condemn "bad" ones; it forbade all.*[3]

With the Alcoa decision, the courts turned from "big is not necessarily bad" to "big is bad." The rule of reason was transformed into the **per se rule**. The per se rule is the antitrust doctrine that the existence of monopoly alone is illegal regardless of whether or not the monopoly engages in illegal business practices.

**Per se rule**
The antitrust doctrine that the existence of monopoly alone is illegal, regardless of whether or not the monopoly engages in illegal business practices.

[3]U.S. v. Aluminum Co. of America, 148 F.2d 416 (2d Cir. 1945).

Instead of judgments based on the performance of a monopoly, antitrust policy in the United States was switched by the court's interpretation to judgments based solely on the market structure. Interestingly, the court's solution was not to break up Alcoa. Instead, the federal government subsidized its competitors. War plants were sold at bargain prices to Reynolds Aluminum and Kaiser Aluminum, and later more rivals entered the aluminum industry.

## THE IBM CASE (1982)

In 1969, the U.S. Department of Justice brought antitrust action against IBM because of its dominance in the mainframe computer market. The government argued that IBM had a 72 percent share of the electronic digital computing industry. IBM argued that the relevant market was broader and included programmable calculators and other information-processing products. After 13 years of litigation, IBM had spent over $100 million on its defense and had constructed an entire building to store case documents. Finally, in 1982, the government dropped the case. One reason was that Digital Equipment, Apple Computer, and Japanese companies were competing with IBM. Another reason illustrates the mix of politics and antitrust policy. In 1982, Ronald Reagan was president, and he believed in a much less restrictive interpretation of antitrust laws. In any event, the IBM case represented a shift in the general sentiment among those enforcing the antitrust laws from the per se rule back to the rule of reason.

## THE AT&T CASE (1982)

In 1978, the U.S. Department of Justice brought an antitrust suit against AT&T and the Bell System. The issue was complicated. At this time, AT&T was a *natural monopoly* regulated by the government. (Regulation of a natural monopoly will be explained later in this chapter; see Exhibit 5.) The government allowed AT&T to have a monopoly in long-distance and local telephone service and in the production of telephones. The Federal Communications Commission (FCC) regulated long-distance rates, and state utility commissioners regulated local rates. What was the objective of giving one company the exclusive right to provide telephone services in the United States? In order to provide everyone with low-cost local services, the regulatory commissions set AT&T's local charges low and its long-distance rates high to cover the lower local rates.

In the 1970s, advances in technology changed the nature of the long-distance telephone industry. Telephone service was no longer a natural monopoly because fiber optics and satellites made cable connections obsolete. Competitors developed, and the government alleged that these rivals were being charged unfairly high fees for access to AT&T's local telephone lines.

On the same day the IBM case ended in 1982, AT&T and the Department of Justice announced this case was settled. AT&T ("Ma Bell") divested itself of 22 local companies ("Baby Bells"), but retained its long-distance telephone service, its research facilities (Bell Laboratories), and its manufacturing facilities (Western Electric Company). As a result, local companies became regulated monopolies in their areas, and local phone rates rose sharply. In nationwide long-distance telephone service, AT&T's competition with MCI and Sprint lowered the price of long-distance telephone service. Moreover, individual customers became responsible for buying their own phones, rather than using only AT&T phones. The result

## CHECKPOINT

### Does Price-Fixing Improve Your Education?

Price-fixing agreements are among the monopolistic restraint-of-trade practices prohibited by Section 1 of the Sherman Act. The Supreme Court has concluded that a formal agreement is not necessary to prove conspiracy. Instead, conspiracy may be inferred from the acts of the accused even if the consequences might be considered socially desirable. The presidents of the universities charged with price-fixing in the MIT case defended their business practices with the argument that they openly met to fix prices in order to improve education. With tuition and the amount of financial aid fixed, students and parents will choose their university on the basis of academic quality alone. Consider the discussion of pricing strategies for an oligopoly discussed in Chapter 10. Can you give the presidents a better argument for their defense?

has been a highly competitive market, offering a wide range of phone prices and a wide variety of phones.

## THE MIT CASE (1992)

For many years, the presidents of many of the nation's top universities—Cornell, Harvard, Yale, Columbia, Brown, Princeton, the University of Pennsylvania, Dartmouth, and MIT—attended annual meetings to discuss tuition, faculty salaries, and financial aid packages. After such meetings, these schools often adjusted tuition charges, salary increases, and even fees for room and board. For example, one year Dartmouth planned to raise faculty salaries by 8.5 percent. The other schools wanted to hold the line at 6.5 percent, so Dartmouth was persuaded to cave in. At other meetings, the group's goal was to make sure each student who applied to more than one of the schools would be offered the same financial aid. At another meeting, Harvard and Yale accused Princeton of offering excessively generous scholarships to top students.

The U.S. Justice Department investigated and charged the eight Ivy League universities and MIT with an illegal conspiracy to fix prices. The Ivy League schools settled the case with a consent decree. This agreement required these schools to cease colluding on tuition, salaries, and financial aid in the future, and, in return, none of the schools admitted guilt for a price conspiracy. MIT refused to sign the consent order and pursued the case all the way to the Supreme Court. In 1992, the Court ruled that MIT had violated antitrust laws and concluded that students and parents have the right to compare prices when choosing a university.

## THE MICROSOFT CASE (2001)

Microsoft Corporation dominated the personal computer (PC) software industry with about a 90 percent share of the PC operating system software and Internet browser markets. And Microsoft had tied its Windows operating systems at zero price (predatory pricing) to its Internet Explorer browser in order to eliminate competition and establish a monopoly in the browser market. The remedies discussed included both conduct and structural remedies. A conduct remedy was a judicial instruction against engaging in specific behavior. For example, Microsoft could be required to include major rival browsers with its browser. Bill Gates likened this proposal to "requiring Coca-Cola to include three cans of Pepsi in every six-pack it sells." Moreover, Microsoft claimed that by integrating Internet Explorer with Windows it was creating one product and not tying two products. In short, no one using the Windows operating system needed a separate browser.

A structural remedy is a "surgical fix" aimed at permanently altering a company so substantially that further violations are not possible. For example, Microsoft could be split into three companies. One company would have operating systems, such as Windows. A second company could have applications, such as Word, Excel, and PowerPoint. The third company would get Internet Explorer and related Internet business. A major concern with this remedy was that a three-headed monopoly monster might destroy innovation and a seamless transition between Windows and other software applications. Another fear was that prices might rise and software would become much more complicated.

In 2001, a federal appeals court ruled that Microsoft did violate antitrust law to protect a monopoly for its Windows operating system. However, the court ruled the government had failed to prove Microsoft illegally attempted to monopolize the Internet browser market. In response, Microsoft announced that it would allow PC manufacturers to continue adding icons of other technology companies to Microsoft's operating system. In 2002, a federal judge approved most of the provisions of the antitrust settlement reached the previous year with Microsoft.

Finally, the major antitrust cases are summarized in Exhibit 2.

| EXHIBIT 2 | SUMMARY OF MAJOR ANTITRUST CASES |
|---|---|
| **Case (date)** | **Key provision** |
| Standard Oil (1911) | ■ This case established the rule of reason, allowing a monopoly unless it engages in illegal practices. |
| Alcoa (1945) | ■ This case overturned the rule of reason and established the per se rule, under which all monopolies are illegal. |
| IBM (1982) | ■ The government dropped its case after 13 years and shifted antitrust policy back to the rule of reason. |
| AT&T (1982) | ■ Technology made this government-regulated natural monopoly obsolete, and AT&T was found guilty of anticompetitive pricing. |
| MIT (1992) | ■ Eight Ivy League schools agreed to stop colluding to fix prices, and MIT was found guilty of price-fixing while attending open meetings. |
| Microsoft (2001) | ■ Microsoft and the government reached a settlement after an appeals court held that the firm illegally protected its Windows monopoly. |

# Mergers and International Antitrust Policy

The decades of the 1980s and 1990s were characterized by a wave of mergers. Mergers are a concern to antitrust regulators because firms can avoid charges of price-fixing by merging into one firm. The antitrust policy toward mergers depends on the type of merger and its likely effect on the relevant market.

## TYPES OF MERGERS

A **horizontal merger** is a merger of firms that compete in the same market. The mergers of Coca-Cola and PepsiCo, Ford Motor Company and General Motors, and Anheuser Bush and Coors would be hypothetical examples of horizontal mergers. Horizontal mergers raise a "red flag" because they decrease competition in a market. For example, in 1986, the government blocked the proposed merger between Coca-Cola and Seven-Up.

A **vertical merger** is a merger of a firm with its suppliers. This type of merger occurs between companies at different stages of a production process. Hypothetical examples of vertical mergers would be General Motors merging with a major tire company and Ford Motor Company merging with a large number of car dealerships. Although the government often challenges vertical mergers, international competition has reduced antitrust scrutiny of vertical mergers. If this type of merger lowers costs by eliminating unnecessary supplier charges, U.S. firms will be more competitive in world markets.

A **conglomerate merger** is a merger between firms in unrelated markets. Suppose an insurance company buys a computer software company or a cigarette company merges with a hotel chain. Actual examples are Phillip Morris merging with Miller Brewing Company and General Motors merging with Electronic Data Systems Corporation. No antitrust action was taken to prevent these mergers because the products of the two firms were considered to be unrelated. Conglomerate mergers are generally allowed because they do not significantly decrease competition.

**Horizontal merger**
A merger of firms that compete in the same market.

**Vertical merger**
A vertical merger is a merger of a firm with its suppliers.

**Conglomerate merger**
A merger between firms in unrelated markets.

## ANTITRUST POLICIES IN OTHER COUNTRIES

Early antitrust laws were aimed at the domestic economy with little concern for international competitiveness. Because of the internationalization of competition in recent decades, some economists call for a relaxation of antitrust laws to allow firms to merge and compete more effectively in the world economy. Other economists disagree and argue that strong antitrust laws are necessary because small firms create most jobs and innovations.

One reason firms in other countries are so competitive with U.S. firms is that other countries' antitrust laws are weak in comparison to U.S. antitrust laws. For example, no other country breaks up companies for antitrust violations. There are two basic explanations. First, most other countries have smaller populations than the United States. Because other countries have fewer potential customers, they view the international market as the target and design weak antitrust laws accordingly. Stated differently, other countries must sell their products internationally in order to achieve economies of scale and be competitive.

Second, other countries have weak antitrust laws based on their culture and history. In the United States, there is a strong belief in Adam Smith's individualistic competition among small firms. This "big is bad" ideology is the foundation of U.S. antitrust laws, but this belief is not prevalent in other countries. In other countries, "big is better," and in countries such as Japan and Germany, government and business work together to compete internationally. In contrast, there is a general mistrust of big government working directly with big businesses in the United States.

# Regulation

The same distrust of big business that is the basis of antitrust laws also led to the evolution of regulation and federal regulatory agencies in the United States. The regulatory process in the United States has gone through several phases. In the first phase, from 1887 to the Great Depression, the railroads were the primary target. During the 1930s, the Great Depression created a favorable environment in which regulation spread to the communications, financial, and other industries. After 1970, regulation increased steadily in the areas of health, safety, and the environment until the 1980s, when a deregulation movement began and it continued to have momentum in the early 2000s.

## HISTORICAL ORIGINS OF REGULATION

**The Early Years**  The railroads came under regulation in the late 19th century as a result of their unfair pricing practices. At that time in history, railroads faced little competition from other carriers, so there was little to prevent railroads from overcharging. Railroads also practiced price discrimination against isolated rural customers by charging them higher rates for short hauls than they charged city customers for long hauls. In 1887, the Interstate Commerce Commission (ICC) was established to regulate rail prices and to cut the costs of rail transportation by reducing duplicate trains, depots, and tracks.

**The Great Depression Era**  During the 1930s, regulation was extended to other industries. The Food and Drug Administration (FDA) was established in 1931 to oversee the safety of food and drugs. All surface transportation, including trucks, barges, and oil pipelines, came to be regulated by the ICC. The Civil Aeronautics Board (CAB) was created in 1938 to regulate air travel, and the Federal Communications Commission (FCC) was established in 1934 to regulate telephones, telegraphs, and broadcasting industries. In 1934, as a result of the stock market crash of 1929, the Securities and Exchange Commission (SEC) was created to combat fraud and malpractice in the securities industry.

**Health, Safety, and Environment Era**  The Occupational Safety and Health Administration (OSHA) was created in 1970 to reduce the incidence of injury and death in the workplace. This agency cites and fines employers who violate safety and health rules. In the same year, the Environmental Protection Agency (EPA) was established to set and enforce pollution standards. In 1972, the Consumer Product Safety Commission (CPSC) was established to protect the public against injury from unsafe products. The CPSC has the power to ban the sale of hazardous products.

## THE DEREGULATION TREND

In the 1970s, the higher production costs resulting from regulation generated widespread dissatisfaction with government regulation. The result was a movement toward **deregulation** in the late 1970s and 1980s. Deregulation is the elimination or phasing out of government restrictions on economic activity. Initially, the major thrust of deregulation was in the transportation and telecommunications industries. The Airline Deregulation Act of 1978 removed regulated airfares and restrictions against competition in air travel markets. The Staggers Rail Act of 1980 deregulated the railroads, the Motor Carrier Act of 1980 deregulated trucking, and the Bus Regulatory Reform Act of 1982 deregulated bus transportation. The Civil Aeronautics Board (CAB), established in 1938 to regulate airline fares and air routes, was abolished in 1984. The You're the Economist at the end of the chapter examines the effects on the airline industry.

In telecommunications, the most important case was the deregulation and dismantling of AT&T. As explained above, technological innovations made competition in telecommunications possible, and, as a result of an antitrust lawsuit, AT&T was broken up and forced to compete with MCI, Sprint, and other companies for long-distance service. In 1996, Congress passed a telecommunications bill that made additional changes in U.S. telecommunications. This bill deregulated cable television rates, while allowing local and long-distance telephone companies and cable companies to compete. This bill also required television manufacturers to equip new sets with a computer chip to block shows parents do not wish their children to watch.

For nearly 100 years electricity was a regulated industry in the United States. Privately held utility companies obtained the right to operate a monopoly in exchange for government regulations that set rates and capped profits. In 1992, Congress started the deregulation movement for power companies when it approved the Energy Policy Act, which opened competition at the wholesale level. By 2001, 24 states and the District of Columbia had approved deregulation plans, but the California power shortage created a deregulation backlash (see You're the Economist on California electricity deregulation).

The principal functions of the federal regulatory agencies discussed above are summarized in Exhibit 3.

**Deregulation**
The elimination or phasing out of government restrictions on economic activity.

# Three Cases for Government Regulation

Government regulation involves political, social, and economic factors, and the general justification for regulation is to protect the public. In this section, we examine three basic situations in which regulation is often imposed: (1) natural monopoly, (2) externalities, and (3) imperfect information. In each of these cases, the argument in favor of regulation is *market failure*. Recall from Chapter 4 that market failure is a situation in which the market operating on its own fails to lead to an efficient allocation of resources.

| EXHIBIT 3 | FEDERAL REGULATORY AGENCIES | |
|---|---|---|
| **Agency** | **Year created** | **Function** |
| Interstate Commerce Commission (ICC) | 1887* | Regulated interstate ground transportation, including the railroad, trucking, bus, and water carrier industries. |
| Food and Drug Administration (FDA) | 1931 | Protects the health of the nation against impure and unsafe foods, drugs, and cosmetics. Develops policy regarding labeling of all drugs. |
| Securities and Exchange Commission (SEC) | 1934 | Provides for complete financial disclosure and protects investors in stock and other securities against fraud. |
| Federal Communications Commission (FCC) | 1934 | Regulates television, radio, telephone, and telegraph services; satellite transmissions; and cable TV. |
| Civil Aeronautics Board (CAB) | 1938† | Regulated airline fares and routes. |
| Occupational Safety and Health Administration (OSHA) | 1970 | Enforces rules in cases involving safety and health violations in the workplace. |
| Environmental Protection Agency (EPA) | 1970 | Regulates pollution in the areas of air, water, waste, noise, radiation, and toxic substances. |
| Consumer Product Safety Commission (CPSC) | 1972 | Protects the public against unreasonable risks of injury from consumer products. |

*Abolished in 1995.
†Abolished in 1984.

## NATURAL MONOPOLY

The objective of antitrust policy is to create a level playing field for competing firms. Depending on the case, antitrust policy can result in breaking up a monopoly, preventing formation of a monopoly, and/or punishing anticompetitive business practices of a monopoly. But, what happens when it is inefficient for more than one company to operate in a particular market? Stated another way, creation of a level playing field for competitors may not be in the best interest of economic efficiency. This situation exists in a *natural monopoly*. As explained earlier in Exhibit 1 in Chapter 9 on monopoly, a natural monopoly is an industry in which long-run average cost is minimized when only one firm serves the market. Recall that the services of such public utilities as local telephone, gas, electric, cable TV, and water companies are natural monopolies subject to government regulation. To avoid abuse of this type of monopoly, the prices or rates these public utilities can charge are determined by a federal, state, or local regulatory commission or board.

Exhibit 4 illustrates the demand curve, long-run marginal cost curve (*LRMC*), and long-run average cost curve (*LRAC*) for a natural monopoly in the cable TV market—say, a company called Vision Cable. Because of *economies of scale*, the *LRAC* curve is negatively sloped. Following the *marginal-average rule* explained

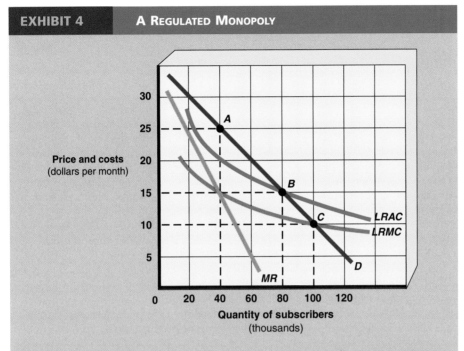

**EXHIBIT 4    A REGULATED MONOPOLY**

If an unregulated monopolist serves the cable TV market, it will set $MR = LRMC$, charge a price of $25 per month, and provide service to only 40,000 customers (point A). To improve the efficiency of the market by taking advantage of the lower costs of a natural monopoly, government regulators could set the price at $10, which equals long-run marginal cost (point C). This policy is efficient, but losses require public subsidies. The typical solution is to set a "fair-return" price of $15, which allows the monopolist to earn zero economic profit and serve 80,000 customers at point B. This condition does not fully correct the underallocation of resources caused by an unregulated natural monopoly.

in Chapter 7, the $LRMC$ curve is below the falling $LRAC$ curve. Given this condition, the firm's demand curve intersects the $LRAC$ curve at a quantity of 80,000 subscribers and a cost of $15 per month equal to the price (point B). Suppose this output is divided equally between Vision Cable and another cable company. As discussed earlier in Exhibit 1 of Chapter 9, the result of competition between cable TV companies is that the cost per subscriber is much higher—and even higher if output is divided among more than two cable companies.

To take advantage of the lower cost, the policy prescription is to create a cable TV market served by only one producer—Vision Cable. The policy problem now is how to keep this unregulated natural monopoly from enjoying a substantial monopoly profit. Instead of providing services for 80,000 customers, Vision Cable will service only 40,000 customers by following the $MR = MC$ rule to maximize profits. The price that corresponds to this output is $25 per month at point A. Because the profit-maximizing price exceeds the $LRAC$ curve, monopoly pricing creates too high a price and too small an output. Stated differently, the result is an

**You're the Economist**

# Who Turned Out the Lights in California?
*Applicable Concept: price ceiling regulation*

In order to keep electricity cheap for its state, the California legislature in 1996 set a retail ceiling price of 10 cents per kilowatt-hour. Moreover, no new power-generating plants were built during the 1990s. The plan was to require utilities to sell their power plants and import electricity as needed from the "spot market" through high-speed transmission lines from other states. In the deregulated wholesale electricity market, a spot market is one in which the price of electricity is determined by supply and demand conditions each hour.

The stage was set for the forces of supply and demand to "turn out the lights." First, demand soared during a heat wave in the summer of 2000 as consumers turned on their air conditioners. Second, there was a leftward shift in supply. High natural gas prices increased the cost of producing electricity in all states. Also, low snowpacks and a drought in the Pacific Northwest reduced the capacity of hydroelectric dams in this region.

Facing shortages from both increased demand and decreased supply, California utilities had no choice but to buy electricity on the spot market as prices soared tenfold over their normal levels. Since customer rates were capped, the price paid by consumers did not cover what the utilities were paying for electricity. The utilities quickly found themselves facing bankruptcy, and this threat caused additional spot

rate increases. Duke Power Company of North Carolina, for example, stated that 8 percent of its spot price was a premium to cover the risk of selling to California utilities that might not pay their bills. A subsequent investigation by the Federal Energy Regulatory Commission (FERC) reported evidence that power companies, such as Enron, developed strategies to drive up prices.

Faced with this crisis, Governor Gray Davis, who was governor of California at the time, called for more price caps. He convinced the FERC to cap wholesale prices in the West during hours of highest demand, combined with a daily regime of rolling blackouts, and calls for conservation. In April 2001, Davis abandoned the 1996 price ceiling by sharply increasing the retail electricity price.

### ANALYZE THE ISSUE

Draw a graph illustrating California's electricity crisis. Put the label "Price of electricity (cents per kilowatt-hour)" on the vertical axis and "Quantity of electricity (megawatts per hour)" on the horizontal axis. As explained in Chapter 4, draw the changes in demand and supply for electricity in California described above. (Hint: Begin the graph in equilibrium below the price ceiling.)

---

**Marginal cost pricing**
A system of pricing in which the price charged equals the marginal cost of the last unit produced.

inefficient cable TV market, in which there is an underallocation of resources to produce cable TV service.

For the cable television market to be efficient, regulators must set a price ceiling at $10 per month, which is equal to long-run marginal cost at point C on the demand curve. This pricing strategy follows the competitive principle of **marginal cost pricing**. Marginal cost pricing is a system of pricing in which the price charged equals the marginal cost of the last unit produced. At a price of $10, Vision Cable suffers a loss because although the price covers long-run marginal cost, the price is not high enough to cover long-run average cost. This means the firm can survive in the long run only if the government subsidizes the loss.

What to do? Is there an option that does not require taxpayers' money? Yes! In practice, regulatory commissions have relaxed the objective of efficiency and have focused on establishing a "fair-return" price to be charged by the monopolist. In Exhibit 4, the commission would establish the fair-return price at $15 per

**CHECKPOINT**

## Why Doesn't the Water Company Compete?

The local water company is considered to be a natural monopoly, and the government prohibits other firms from competing with it. If a natural monopoly can produce water at a lower price than other firms, then why would the government protect the water company from competitors?

month at point *B*, where the demand curve intersects the *LRAC* curve. Because the price ceiling equals long-run average cost, Vision Cable earns zero economic profit and serves 80,000 customers in the long run. However, remember from the chapter on production costs that in economics cost includes a normal profit, which is just enough to keep the firm in the cable industry.

> **CONCLUSION** *Government regulators can achieve efficiency for a natural monopoly by setting a price ceiling equal to the intersection of the demand and the marginal cost curves, but this policy results in losses. An alternative is to set a price ceiling, called the fair-return price, that yields a normal profit but is somewhat inefficient.*

## EXTERNALITIES

The case of pollution was treated in detail in Exhibit 8(a) in Chapter 4. To refresh your memory, recall that the individual firm in a competitive market has no incentive to eliminate pollution voluntarily. Pollution is an *external cost* imposed on *third parties* who neither produce nor consume a good. Pollution causes polluting firms to overproduce while causing firms that pay the cost of cleaning up the pollution to underproduce. Therefore, expenditures on pollution control would place firms at a competitive disadvantage with respect to firms that do not pay the cost of controlling pollution. If society wants less pollution, this type of market failure justifies government regulation from, say, the EPA. The exact nature of the regulation, however, may take a variety of forms, ranging from direct controls requiring specific pollution-control equipment to taxation.

Without repeating the explanation given in Exhibit 8(b) in Chapter 4, note that the *external benefits* of a good, such as a vaccination, can lead to underproduction of the good. Again, regulation is necessary if society is to respond to externalities. In this case, the government solution can take various forms, including requiring consumption or providing special subsidies.

## IMPERFECT INFORMATION

In some cases, consumers lack important information about a product, and they cannot make rational decisions. Without complete and reliable information, consumers may be unaware of the dangers of unsafe drugs, hazardous chemicals, and defective products. The source of imperfect information about products may be

You're the Economist

# Does Airline Deregulation Mean Friendlier Skies?
*Applicable Concept: regulation versus deregulation*

A much-publicized case of deregulation is the airline industry. Under regulation by the Civil Aeronautics Board (CAB), airfare competition and the incentive to control costs were reduced or eliminated. The CAB set both fares and routes for carriers. Unable to compete with price, the carriers could compete only with costly nonprice competition, such as advertising. Once the CAB authorized a carrier to provide service between two cities, the frequency of service remained unregulated. When carriers purchased fleets of planes and provided too many flights for their protected routes, profits were squeezed because the percentage of seats filled with passengers (load factor) fell, and the average cost rose. Carriers would then attempt to boost profits by lobbying the CAB for higher fares. In addition to eliminating price competition between established carriers, the CAB restricted entrants into the industry. From 1938 until 1977, the CAB never awarded a major route to any new airline.

Successful deregulation of an industry would be expected to provide the following three results:

- The average price of the service falls.
- The volume and variety of services rise.
- New firms enter the industry, and other firms fail and exit the industry.

The Airline Deregulation Act of 1978 provided these results by changing the structure and business behavior of the airline industry. Although the Federal Aviation Administration (FAA) would still regulate the safety of air service, the CAB was eliminated under this act in 1984, and price competition produced the expected results of lower fares and greater quantity of service. Revenue per passenger mile of airline travel declined from 1978 to 1990 on an inflation-adjusted basis, saving consumers billions of dollars in lower fares. Over this same period, the fall in fares contributed to a doubling of passenger miles flown per year. Since 1990, fares adjusted for inflation have continued to fall, and passenger miles flown rose from 458 billion to 732 billion in 2004. After the barrier to entry was removed, the number of carriers increased sharply between 1978 and 1980 from 37 to 214. Since 1980, many carriers, such as the "few frills" People Express and mainline carriers such as Trans World Airlines, have exited the industry, and by 2004, the number of carriers dropped to 74.[1]

The airline deregulatory movement is not without criticism. One concern is that lots of airlines went "belly up," and these exits from the industry increased the percentage of all domestic air travel controlled by the industry's largest carriers. Moreover, under the pressure of competition, carriers searched for ways to cut costs, and they created the hub-and-spoke delivery system. This system allows carriers to gather passengers from the spoke routes by using smaller, less efficient planes and fly them from the hub in fully occupied, bigger planes at lower cost. Many carriers have gained near monopoly power in hub airports. These dominant hub carriers can control access to terminal gates, takeoff time slots, and baggage service, and they can charge smaller lines high rates for using these airport rights.

Today, deregulation continues to exert downward pressure on fares, and old-guard carriers scramble to compete with low-cost carriers such as Southwest and Jet Blue. Low-fare tickets, cyberfares, and frequent flyer miles are popular. Quality of service is higher, measured by fewer consumer complaints today than in the regulation era.[2] Should the airlines remain deregulated or return to a government-enforced cartel? Defenders of deregulation argue that growth of market concentration and its abuses can be controlled by enforcing antitrust laws and allowing international competition.

## ANALYZE THE ISSUE

Prior to deregulation, critics argued that airline safety would suffer. Instead, although the Federal Aviation Administration's budget was cut following deregulation, the accident rate involving fatalities has fallen. Give a rationale for why the critics' prediction did not come to pass.

[1]*Statistical Abstract of the United States*, 2006, http://www.census.gov/prod/ www/statistical-abstract.html, Table 1052, p. 697, and Table 1061, p. 701.

[2]Ibid. Table 1060, p. 706.

company errors. Much worse, companies may be able to boost sales by withholding valuable information about a problem with their products.

Let's consider a hypothetical case in which an unsafe Tucker Motors (TM) truck is sold. Suppose the safety defect is a gas tank that is located too close to the side of the truck. As a result, another vehicle can crash into the side of the TM truck and hit the gas tank. Such an accident can cause a deadly explosion. Assume further that TM is aware of this safety problem, but the cost of recalling and fixing the trucks exceeds the estimated cost of lawsuits caused by the defective gas tanks. The market incentive is therefore for TM to withhold knowledge of this defect from uninformed consumers.

Exhibit 5 illustrates this case. With consumers unaware of the defect, the interaction of the supply and demand curves for TM trucks yields an equilibrium at

**EXHIBIT 5** — **THE IMPACT OF IMPERFECT INFORMATION ON THE MARKET FOR TM TRUCKS**

**CAUSATION CHAIN**

Consumers informed of defect ⇒ Decrease in demand ⇒ Decrease in the quantity supplied

An initial equilibrium is established at point $E_1$, with 100,000 TM trucks purchased each year for $15,000 per truck. This equilibrium is reached without consumers having knowledge of a safety defect. Once consumers are informed of the safety defect, the demand curve shifts leftward from $D_1$ to $D_2$. At the new equilibrium point of $E_2$, 75,000 TM trucks are purchased each year for $10,000 per truck. Thus, imperfect information has resulted in a waste of the resources used to produce 25,000 TM trucks.

$E_1$, with 100,000 trucks being sold per year at a price of $15,000 per truck. Next, suppose the Consumer Product Safety Commission (CPSC) exposes the problem, and the media report stories about crash victims who have been severely burned or even killed by the flames from the exploding gas tanks in TM trucks. Once the consuming public is aware of the defect, consumers' preferences for TM trucks change, and the demand curve decreases from $D_1$ to $D_2$. The result is a new equilibrium at $E_2$, with 75,000 TM trucks being sold per year at a price of $10,000 per truck. In other words, this case is an application of market supply and demand analysis as presented in Chapter 4.

> **CONCLUSION** *Deficient information on unsafe products can cause consumers to overconsume a product.*

In the TM truck example, resources were used to produce 25,000 trucks that consumers would not purchase when given complete information. These resources were misallocated because they could have been used to produce other goods and services. The solution is for government to prevent companies from making false or deceptive claims by gathering and disseminating accurate information to consumers. This is the rationale for the safety testing of cars, EPA mileage ratings on cars, and warning labels on cigarettes. In extreme cases, a product may be deemed too unsafe, and it is outlawed from sale. Others disagree with this view and argue that the government should only provide information. Once consumers have sufficient information, they should be free to choose.

## Key Concepts

Trust
Predatory pricing
Sherman Act of 1890
Clayton Act of 1914
Federal Trade Commission Act
     of 1914

Robinson-Patman Act of 1936
Celler-Kefauver Act of 1950
Rule of reason
Per se rule
Horizontal merger
Vertical merger

Conglomerate merger
Deregulation
Marginal cost pricing

## Summary

- A **trust** is a cartel that places the assets of competing companies in the custody of a board of trustees. During the last decades of the nineteenth century, trusts engaged in anticompetitive strategies, such as *predatory pricing*, to eliminate competition and raise prices.

- The **Sherman Act of 1890** and the **Clayton Act of 1914** are the two most important antitrust laws. The Sherman Act marked the first attempt of the U.S. government to outlaw monopolizing behavior. Because this act was vague, the Clayton Act was passed to define anticompetitive behavior more precisely. The Clayton Act prohibited (1) price discrimination, (2) exclusive dealing, (3) tying contracts, (4) stock acquisition of competing companies, and (5) interlocking directorates.

- The **Federal Trade Commission Act of 1914** estab-lished the Federal Trade Commission (FTC) to inves-tigate unfair competitive practices of firms.

- The **Robinson-Patman Act of 1936** strengthened the Clayton Act by prohibiting certain forms of price discrimination. This law is called the "Chain Store Act" because it was aimed at large retail chain stores that were obtaining volume discounts.

- The **Celler-Kefauver Act of 1950** strengthened the Clayton Act by declaring illegal the acquisition of the assets of one firm by another firm if the effect is to lessen competition.

- The **rule of reason** and the **per se rule** are the two main doctrines the courts have used in interpreting antitrust law. Under the rule of reason, monopolists were not subject to prosecution unless they acted in an anticompetitive manner. The court decision in the Alcoa case of 1945 replaced the rule of reason with the per se rule, which states that the mere existence of monopoly is illegal. Today, the trend is in favor of dominant firms because of international competition.

- A **horizontal merger** is a merger of two competing firms. A **vertical merger** is a merger of two firms in which one produces an input used by the other firm. A **conglomerate merger** is a merger of two firms pro-ducing unrelated products.

- **Deregulation** is a movement that began in the late 1970s and 1980s to eliminate regulations, primarily in the transportation and telecommunications indus-tries. Today, the movement to further deregulate electric utilities is being questioned.

- **Marginal cost pricing** is a competitive pricing strat-egy for a regulated natural monopoly. Using this approach, regulators set the monopolist's price equal to its marginal cost. Another method is for regula-tors to establish a fair-return price equal to long-run average cost, and the monopolist earns zero eco-nomic profit. Regulation of a natural monopoly is justified on the basis of market failure. Two other cases based on market failure include externalities and imperfect information.

### MARGINAL COST PRICING

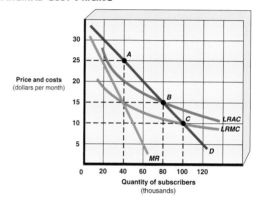

## Summary of Conclusion Statements

- Government regulators can achieve efficiency for a natural monopoly by setting a price ceiling equal to the intersection of the demand and the marginal cost curves, but this policy results in losses. An alter-native is to set a price ceiling, called the fair-return price, yields a normal profit, but is somewhat inefficient.

- Deficient information on unsafe products can cause consumers to overconsume a product.

## Study Questions and Problems

1. Describe the major provisions of the Sherman Act and the Clayton Act. Who is responsible for enforcing these laws?

2. Two business practices outlawed by the Clayton Act are tying contracts and interlocking directorates. Explain the condition required for these two practices to be a violation of this antitrust law.

3. Distinguish between the Robinson-Patman Act of 1936 and the Celler-Kefauver Act of 1950.

4. Using cases presented in the text, explain the issue in the courts' interpretation of "monopoly versus monopolizing."

5. A controversy in many antitrust court cases involves the definition of the relevant market for a firm's product. How would you argue in the Alcoa case that the government's claim of the firm's high market share was in error?

6. In the MIT case, which students are harmed by the Ivy League schools' coordination of scholarship policy? Professional baseball is exempt from antitrust laws. Should colleges and universities also be exempt from antitrust laws?

7. Based on the antitrust laws, how would you expect the federal government to react to the following situations?
   a. A college bookstore deliberately reduces prices until its only rival is driven out of business. The bookstore then raises its prices.
   b. Real estate firms meet in an open meeting and agree to charge 6 percent commission on sales.
   c. Microsoft merges with WordPerfect by a stock acquisition.
   d. A small tax preparation company merges with a regional grocery store chain.

8. Based on the cases discussed in the chapter, is the following statement correct? "The antitrust laws in reality deal less with monopolies than with oligopolies."

9. Assume a regulatory agency is given authority over prices and entry conditions for a given industry. Also assume the agency decides to allow new entry, as the CAB actually did before deregulation, only when it is proven to be "necessary." Would this condition be expected to favor (a) existing regulated firms, (b) new entrants, or (c) consumers? Explain.

10. Exhibit 6 represents a natural monopolist.

**Exhibit 6**

a. If the monopolist is not regulated, what price will it charge, and what quantity will it produce?
b. If the monopolist is required to use marginal cost pricing, what price will it charge, and what quantity will it produce? Why will the monopolist stay in business?
c. Assume regulators set a fair-return price at $P_b$. Why would the monopolist stay in business?

11. Assume a natural monopolist is required to use marginal cost pricing and a government subsidy covers the loss. What problems might be associated with a public subsidy?

12. Do you agree that "cost does not really matter" as a principle for safety regulation, or do you believe that the cost of a safety device must be justified on the basis of the value of human life protected from a hazard?

## Study Guide Questions

1. The antitrust doctrine that the existence of monopoly alone is not illegal unless the monopoly engages in illegal business practices is called the _____.

2. Suppose a firm offers quantity discounts or special promotional allowances only to favored distributors and the effect is to substantially lessen competition. This firm would be in violation of the
   a. Celler-Kefauver Act.
   b. Sherman Antitrust Act.
   c. Federal Trade Commission Act.
   d. Clayton Act.
   e. Robinson-Patman Act.

3. Which antitrust act prohibits price fixing and other conspiracies and combinations that restrain trade and attempts to monopolize?
   a. Sherman Act of 1890
   b. Clayton Act of 1914

   c. Federal Trade Commission Act of 1914
   d. Robinson-Patman Act of 1936
   e. Celler-Kefauver Act of 1950

4. Which of the following statements is *true*?
   a. A vertical merger is a merger of firms that compete in the same market.
   b. The rule of reason doctrine declares that the existence of monopoly alone is illegal.
   c. Government regulation of a natural monopoly is economically justifiable.
   d. Deficient information on unsafe products causes underconsumption.

5. T  F  The Robinson-Patman Act strengthened the merger provisions of the Clayton Act.

**Answers to these questions are in the complete Study Guide at www.thomsonedu.com/thomsonnow.**

**For Online Exercises, go to the text Web site at www.thomsonedu.com/economics/tucker.**

## Checkpoint Answers

### Does Price-Fixing Improve Your Education?

Accepting the schools' argument that they improve quality by price-fixing makes no more sense than allowing General Motors, Ford, DaimlerChrysler, and Japanese automakers to fix prices in order to improve quality. However, there is often a thin line between price-fixing and price leadership. Price leadership is not illegal as long as the price followers are not coerced. If you said price leadership is defendable and price fixing is not, **YOU ARE CORRECT.**

### Why Doesn't the Water Company Compete?

Suppose new firms are allowed to compete with the water company, which is a natural monopolist. The concern is that the rivals will be outcompeted. New water companies must build plants, dig up the streets, and lay new water pipes and duplicate other resources in the same neighborhood. Because the competitors cannot produce water at a lower cost, they will leave the industry, and the resources used to compete with the natural monopolist will be wasted. If you said the government is not protecting the natural monopolist from competition so much as it is protecting against inefficient competitors wasting resources, **YOU ARE CORRECT.**

## Practice Quiz

For an explanation of the correct answers, please visit the tutorial at www.thomsonedu.com/economics/tucker.

1. Which of the following is illegal under the Sherman Act?
   a. Attempts to monopolize
   b. Price-fixing
   c. Formation of cartels
   d. All of the above are illegal.

2. Officers of five large building-materials companies meet and agree that none of them will submit bids on government contracts lower than an agreed-upon level. This is an example of
   a. price-fixing.
   b. vertical restriction.
   c. a tying contract.
   d. an interlocking directorate.

3. A fabric shop cannot sell Singer sewing machines if it also sells other brands of sewing machines. This is an example of
   a. resale price maintenance.
   b. territorial restrictions.
   c. a tying agreement.
   d. exclusive dealing.

4. Under the Clayton Act, horizontal mergers by stock acquisition were
   a. not considered.
   b. illegal if they could be shown to lessen competition.
   c. illegal under any circumstances.
   d. legal if they could be shown to lessen competition.

5. Under the Clayton Act, which of the following was illegal even if it was *not* shown to lessen competition substantially?
   a. Price discrimination
   b. Tying contracts
   c. Horizontal mergers by stock acquisition
   d. Interlocking directorates

6. The importance of the Federal Trade Commission Act of 1914 is that it
   a. set up an independent antitrust agency with the power to investigate complaints.
   b. strengthened the law against mergers.
   c. strengthened the law against price discrimination.
   d. did none of the above.

7. Which of the following is concerned primarily with price discrimination?
   a. Sherman Act
   b. Clayton Act
   c. Robinson-Patman Act
   d. Celler-Kefauver Act

8. Which of the following is concerned primarily with mergers?
   a. Sherman Act
   b. Clayton Act
   c. Robinson-Patman Act
   d. Celler-Kefauver Act

9. The Utah Pie case was brought under which of the following laws?
   a. Sherman Act
   b. Federal Trade Commission Act
   c. Robinson-Patman Act
   d. Celler-Kefauver Act

10. Although U.S. Steel controlled nearly 75 percent of the domestic iron and steel industry, in 1920 the Supreme Court ruled that the firm was *not* in violation of the Sherman Act because there was no evidence of abusive behavior. What antitrust doctrine was the Court applying in this case?
    a. The rule of reason
    b. The per se rule
    c. The marginal cost pricing rule
    d. The natural monopoly rule

11. In which antitrust case did the courts first apply the per se rule to determine whether a firm was in violation of the Sherman Act?
    a. Standard Oil case
    b. Alcoa case
    c. IBM case
    d. MIT case

12. The Interstate Commerce Commission (ICC) was established in
    a. 1887.
    b. 1890.
    c. 1929.
    d. 1933.

13. Today, the Civil Aeronautics Board (CAB) regulates
    a. airline ticket prices.
    b. airline routes.
    c. airline safety.
    d. all of the above.
    e. none of the above; the CAB was abolished in 1984.

14. Which of the following provides the basis for regulation?
    a. Natural monopoly
    b. Externalities
    c. Imperfect information
    d. All of the above

15. Consider a regulated natural monopoly. If the regulatory commission wants to establish a fair-return price, then it should set a price ceiling where the demand curve crosses the monopoly's long-run
    a. marginal revenue curve.
    b. average revenue curve.
    c. marginal cost curve.
    d. average cost curve.

# Environmental Economics

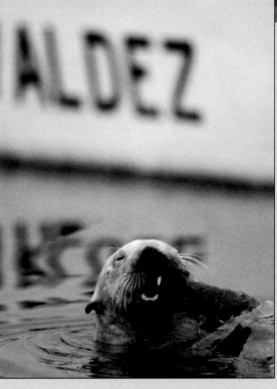

© Photodisc/Getty Images

The United States is the envy of many of the world's citizens for its quality of life. Americans can choose from an almost unlimited number of goods and services. When it comes to transportation, for example, the typical family may own two or three cars. This same family may own touring bikes, mountain bikes, and hybrids that incorporate features of each. Some U.S. citizens own boats, and others own jet skis. Those in colder climates may get around on snow skis, snowshoes, or snowmobiles. Some families even own their own planes. The choice of what to buy in the United States is a private decision. I will choose a snowmobile over snowshoes if I want to travel fast and am willing to spend the money. I will choose a jet ski over a kayak if I find high-speed travel more exciting than paddling along quietly. While my choice is private, my decision has consequences for others.

My jet ski may create waves that threaten to tip your kayak. The noise I make may spoil your desire for peace and quiet. It may also scare wildlife. And the fuel I use to power the jet ski not only adds to fuel consumption, but can contribute to water pollution. Engine exhaust may even make a small contribution to carbon emissions, which may contribute to climate change. Within the next 50 years, some fear that global warming could cause melting of the polar ice caps, resulting in rising ocean levels and massive flooding of coastal areas

throughout the world, as well as climate shifts that could render today's farms tomorrow's deserts.

Up to this point, the competitive market has been shown to be the best engine to generate what consumers want at the lowest possible price. Yet the unbridled use of many of these goods, from jet skis and snowmobiles to Coke cans and cigarettes, may not be the best choice for society or the planet. Competitive markets work well when producers and consumers consider all costs in their decisions. But for some goods and services, decision makers fail to include the cost to others of their decision, such as revving the jet ski or snowmobile to the detriment of others, or throwing the Coke can or cigarette butt out the car window. Although these are local problems, other problems are global in scale, such as carbon emissions from gasoline-burning engines that many believe cause global warming. This chapter will begin by showing why competitive markets may fail to sufficiently protect the environment. First, we will see that

competitive markets result in market failure by producing "too much pollution." Then we will see how we might correct the market failure. Finally, we will consider the pros and cons of government intervention to improve our environment.

**In this chapter, you will learn to solve these economics puzzles:**

- Why do competitive markets produce too many hogs and charge too low a price for those hogs?
- How can government legislation, taxes, and permits help society achieve its environmental goals?
- Can government intervention actually reduce environmental quality?

# Competitive Markets and Environmental Efficiency

While society values goods and services produced in markets, it also values air, water, and other environmental amenities. Air and water are shared resources that generally are not priced in the marketplace. The result is that markets often treat these resources as if they were free, resulting in their overuse. Competitive markets, which are the ideal in efficiently allocating many goods and services, fail to achieve preferred levels of output when they treat valuable resources such as air and water as if they were free.

The competitive market has been shown in earlier chapters to achieve *economic efficiency*. This efficiency exists when the price to consumers, reflecting marginal benefit, equals marginal cost. Consumers, such as jet ski buyers, consider purchase price, styling, and performance features, such as speed, when comparing models. Producers choose what type of jet ski to make based on profit maximization. Assuming perfect competition, profit maximization occurs where price equals marginal cost.

Buyers and sellers consider only their personal or **private benefits and costs.** Private benefits and costs are benefits and costs to the decision maker, ignoring benefits and costs to third parties. Third parties are people outside the market transaction who are affected by the product. As explained in Chapter 4, benefits and costs to third parties are known by a variety of names, including third-party effects, spillovers, and most commonly *external benefits and costs*, or *externalities*. Recall that externalities are benefits or costs that are not considered by market buyers and sellers. Noise pollution is an externality that affects third parties not powering jet skis.

Other externalities that degrade the environment include sulfur emissions from coal-burning electric power plants and the emission of chlorofluorocarbons (CFCs), associated with aerosol sprays and air conditioners. Sulfur emissions are widely thought to contribute to acid rain, resulting in tree deaths and fish kills. CFCs may be linked to a hole in the atmosphere's ozone layer, which increases the chance of skin cancer from the sun's ultraviolet rays.

Everyday externalities include the secondhand effects of cigarette smoke on the health of nonsmokers, as well as cigarette butts tossed out of car windows, farmers' use of pesticides that wash into soil and water with detrimental health effects, and even noise from your next-door neighbor who is having a loud party while you are trying to study for an economics exam. Externalities can be positive as well as negative. You benefit from your classmate's decision to get a flu vaccine.

When externalities are present, competitive markets are not likely to achieve economic efficiency. In competitive markets, price, which reflects marginal private benefit, equals marginal private cost. Efficiency for society requires consideration of both private and **social benefits and costs.** Social benefits are the sum of benefits to everyone in society, including both private benefits and external benefits. Social costs are the sum of costs to everyone in society, including both private costs and external costs. The condition for economic efficiency occurs when each unit of a good that is produced creates at least as much benefit to society as it does social cost. As a society, we do not want to produce any units of a good that creates more in additional social cost than it creates in extra social benefit. In other words, we do not want our scarce resources used up on items that will not enhance

**Private benefits and costs**
Benefits and costs to the decision maker, ignoring benefits and costs to third parties. Third parties are people outside the market transaction who are affected by the product.

**Social benefits and costs**
The sum of benefits to everyone in society, including both private benefits and external benefits. Social costs are the sum of costs to everyone in society, including both private costs and external costs.

our collective well-being. A succinct way of stating this condition for maximizing social welfare is to produce units of any good up to the point where

**Marginal social benefit = marginal social cost**

Environmental regulations force market participants to include externalities in their decision making. For example, United States regulations prohibit the use of CFCs in air conditioners, aerosol cans, and other products. Although regulations like the ban on CFCs reduce emissions, they are not necessarily the most efficient approach to achieving less pollution.

Alternatively, instead of mandating the technology to achieve the goal, the government can specify the goal, but leave the method to achieve the goal up to the firm. Suppose businesses wish to expand in areas with high levels of pollution. As an alternative to reducing their own emissions, they can pay another party to reduce its emissions to meet the regulation. For example, a steel company wishing to expand can buy up old cars and retire them as a way of reducing emissions. It may be cheaper for the company to pay someone else to reduce emissions than to achieve an in-house reduction. We discuss this approach in more detail later in the chapter in the section on emissions trading.

## PRIVATE AND SOCIAL COSTS

When a producer of jet skis or any other product chooses a production method, the producer is motivated by profit maximization. To maximize profit, the firm must choose the most efficient, least costly production method. Production costs include the costs of capital, labor, natural resources (such as land or energy), and entrepreneurship. External costs to others, such as pollution, are not included in production costs because the firm considers only its private costs. Social costs include private costs and external costs.

## COMPETITION AND EXTERNAL COSTS

Suppose considerable amounts of carbon emissions are produced by gasoline powered lawn mowers. To reduce pollution, the manufacturer must redesign the engine. Also, suppose there is a lawn mower manufacturer, GreenAcres, that considers social costs. It will choose a different production method for lower emissions lawn mowers. This production method for lower emissions lawn mowers must have a higher cost than the method used by other, more polluting lawn mowers produced by other firms. If this were not the case, other companies would already be using this method.

In a perfectly competitive market, consumers perceive all products as identical. While there may be exceptions, the typical consumer will pay no more for an environmentally friendly GreenAcres mower than for other lawn mowers. In the short run, GreenAcres will earn less than other firms because its costs are higher. In the long run, GreenAcres will lose money and eventually go out of business. Only the lowest-cost firms will survive in the long run. Since price exactly equals minimum private average (and marginal) cost in the long run, average cost for the environmentally conscious company will lie above price, resulting in losses and eventual exit from the industry.

Exhibit 1(a) compares the typical and the "green" lawn mower companies in the short run. Exhibit 1(b) compares the two companies in the long run. The

| EXHIBIT 1 | A COMPARISON OF COSTS FOR TYPICAL AND "GREEN" FIRMS |

A "green" firm has higher costs in both the short run and the long run. The typical firm considers only private costs, as shown by *MPC* (marginal private cost) in Part (a) and *APC* (average private cost) in Part (b). The "green" firm includes both private and external costs, as shown by *MSC* (marginal social cost) in Part (a) and *ASC* (average social cost) in Part (b). These curves reflect social costs. In the short run, price in a competitive industry equals marginal private cost. The "green" firm produces a smaller quantity than the competitive firm. In the long run, price equals minimum long-run average private cost in a competitive industry. Minimum cost for the "green" firm is above price, so the "green" firm loses money and eventually leaves the industry.

typical company chooses the lowest-cost method of production, considering *private cost* only. Its marginal private cost and average private cost are shown as *MPC* and *APC*, respectively. The green company chooses the production method that has the lowest marginal and average *social cost*, shown as *MSC* and *ASC*, respectively. In the short run, *MSC* lies above *MPC*, so that the green company produces less. In the long run, *ASC* lies above *APC*, so the "green" company loses money and eventually exits the industry.

## COMPETITIVE MARKET INEFFICIENCY WHEN EXTERNALITIES EXIST

In competition, only firms that choose the lowest-cost method of production will survive. Firms that choose higher-cost methods will lose money and eventually exit the industry. There is no room for GreenAcres or any firm that does not minimize cost.

Rewarding firms that ignore externalities while punishing firms that recognize externalities is not socially efficient. Efficiency requires that price reflect marginal social benefit and equal marginal social cost. Competition results in a price that reflects marginal private benefit and equals marginal private cost. Efficiency

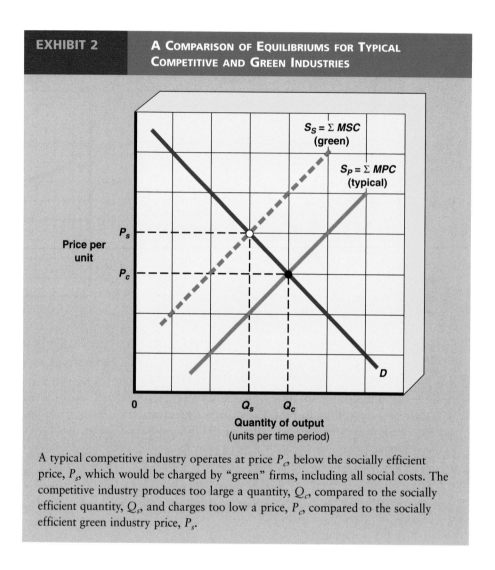

**EXHIBIT 2**          A COMPARISON OF EQUILIBRIUMS FOR TYPICAL COMPETITIVE AND GREEN INDUSTRIES

$S_S = \Sigma MSC$ (green)

$S_P = \Sigma MPC$ (typical)

$P_s$

Price per unit

$P_c$

D

0          $Q_s$    $Q_c$

**Quantity of output**
(units per time period)

A typical competitive industry operates at price $P_c$, below the socially efficient price, $P_s$, which would be charged by "green" firms, including all social costs. The competitive industry produces too large a quantity, $Q_c$, compared to the socially efficient quantity, $Q_s$, and charges too low a price, $P_c$, compared to the socially efficient green industry price, $P_s$.

requires that all relevant opportunity costs be included in marginal social cost, while competition forces firms to consider only private costs if they are to survive. If they are allowed to, competitive firms will ignore harmful by-products of their products, such as pollution, climate change, and congestion.

Exhibit 2 shows lawn mower market equilibrium in a competitive market of traditional firms compared to a market of environmentally sensitive green firms. Competitive industry supply, $S_P$, sums the *marginal private costs* of typical individual firms that ignore externalities, while green industry supply, $S_S$, sums the *marginal social costs* of GreenAcres and other firms that recognize external costs in their engine design.

When externalities are present, competition leads to a lower price and a larger quantity than the socially efficient point (also see Exhibit 8(a) in Chapter 4). By ignoring external costs, competitive firms produce "too much," and the market equilibrium price is "too low," compared to a socially efficient industry.

Competition leads to too many lawn mowers bought and sold because neither the buyers nor the sellers take into account the external cost of lawn mower engines that release emissions when used for mowing. When there are external costs, the efficient point is at the intersection of the demand curve and the social supply curve, $S_S$.

From society's point of view, the efficient outcome is an equilibrium quantity of $Q_s$ lawn mowers sold at price $P_s$. Associated with this outcome is a smaller quantity of pollution than the quantity at the competitive equilibrium. The quantity of pollution associated with quantity $Q_s$ of lawn mowers is the efficient quantity of pollution.

If left to the competitive market, profit-maximizing producers would have no reason to reduce emissions. Emissions reductions, if they occurred at all, would be only an unintended by-product of technological change. For example, if manufacturers substitute a smaller engine so as to reduce lawn mower fuel use, the smaller engine would emit fewer pollutants. The emissions reduction is a by-product of the market reward for a more fuel-efficient mower, which consumers want and are willing to pay for. For emissions reduction to be worthwhile in its own right in a competitive market, it is necessary that consumers be willing to pay for a lower emissions mower.

Why won't consumers offer more for a cleaner mower, just as they might for a more fuel-efficient one? First, consider choosing between two mowers that are identical except that one mower uses one gallon of gas per acre, while the other uses two gallons per acre. You will be willing to pay more for the first mower because you will get to keep the full monetary benefit of reduced fuel purchases.

Now suppose you must choose between two identical mowers except that the green mower emits only half as much pollution as the other one. The typical consumer will not be willing to pay more for the "green" mower because individually he or she will get only a negligible benefit. Benefits will extend to everyone, in the form of cleaner air and reduced global warming. Furthermore, if others buy "green" mowers, you will get the benefits whether or not you purchase a low-emission machine. You are better off being a **free rider**. Recall from the definition of a public good in Chapter 4 that a free rider is someone who enjoys benefits without paying the cost. You will get the same benefit of cleaner air whether or not you buy the clean mower. So you will choose to be a free rider and pay nothing for cleaner air rather than paying extra to get a low-emission machine and still breathing the same cleaner air.

The end result is that no one buys a low-emission mower. Each individual chooses to free-ride, hoping to benefit from others who choose the "green" model. Once again, competitive markets are unlikely to be efficient.

**Free rider**
An individual who enjoys benefits without paying the costs.

> **CONCLUSION** *Unregulated competitive markets will over-supply and under-price products that pollute.*

## EFFICIENT QUANTITY OF POLLUTION

The efficient production level for society is where marginal social benefit equals marginal social cost. The efficient amount of pollution is the amount generated at the socially efficient output level. It is of utmost importance to recognize that the efficient quantity of pollution is not zero. Zero pollution would require zero lawn mowers. Unless society is willing to abandon the American ideal of a neatly trimmed, emerald green lawn, there will continue to be lawn mowers. Nor is it likely that many Americans will return to manual push mowers that do not require fuel, but are slower and take more effort to use than gasoline-engine mowers.

Other alternatives to consider are reduced-emission or emission-free lawn mowers, such as electric mowers. For a parallel situation, consider alternatives to conventional gasoline-engine automobiles. Alternatives include solar and electric vehicles, as well as other transport modes, such as bus, rail, and bicycle. Solar cars, powered by photovoltaic cells, and hydrogen-powered cars are among the virtually emission-free alternatives. But a fundamental concept in economics is that there are tradeoffs. Currently, the cost of solar and hydrogen cars is too high given society's willingness to pay for reduced emissions. Performance may suffer as well; solar cars, for example, are slower and less able to climb mountainous terrain than gasoline-powered cars.

# Achieving Environmental Efficiency

**Market failure**
A situation in which market equilibrium results in too few or too many resources used in the production of a good or service.

Competitive markets fail to produce the socially efficient quantity when there are externalities. Externalities are a cause of **market failure**. As explained in Chapter 4, market failure occurs when the private market fails to produce society's preferred outcome.

When there is market failure, we must consider alternatives to the market to achieve efficiency. Government has a potential role when market failure occurs. Just as government can apply antitrust laws when an industry is not competitive, government can apply environmental laws when an industry ignores external costs. Not only are cars required to have catalytic converters, but many states also require annual inspections to make sure the converters are working properly (and also to check that consumers have not removed the converters in order to improve gas mileage!).

**Government failure**
Government intervention or lack of intervention that fails to correct market failure.

In the environmental arena, as in other areas of government intervention, there is always the possibility of **government failure**. Government failure occurs when the government fails to correct market failure. Government officials may fail to achieve an efficient outcome either by doing too little about pollution or by doing too much.

**Incentive-based regulations**
Government regulations that set an environmental goal but are flexible as to how buyers and sellers achieve the goal.

Government officials motivated to keep their jobs may be influenced by large campaign contributors as well as by voter desires. A Michigan legislator is likely to be sympathetic to the concerns of the auto industry and will also be aware of the autoworker layoffs and unemployment that accompany reduced car production. The official may be less motivated by externalities that are borne by third parties who do not vote in Michigan. On the other hand, a New York legislator may support an overly strict emissions standard for automobiles. New York voters benefit from cleaner air and are less concerned about auto-industry job losses.

**Command-and-control regulations**
Government regulations that set an environmental goal and dictate how the goal will be achieved.

Much of the effort of environmental economists has gone toward improving the odds that government will help, rather than hinder, attempts to reach environmental goals. Economists generally favor **incentive-based regulations** over **command-and-control regulations**. Incentive-based (IB) regulations set an environmental goal, but are flexible as to how buyers and sellers achieve the goal.

Incentive-based regulations can make it profitable for firms to reduce emissions. Command-and-control (CAC) regulations set an environmental goal and also dictate how the goal will be achieved. Firms unable to meet the goal are penalized, and those that exceed it are not rewarded.

The advantage of IB over CAC regulations is comparable to the advantages of a market system over those of a command system. Market systems are more efficient because they allow gains from comparative advantage. Businesses can pursue activities with low opportunity costs. Similarly, allowing firms to choose how to achieve environmental goals encourages firms that can improve at low cost to reduce emissions more than firms less able to achieve lower emissions.

More efficiency gains are obtainable from IB regulations than from CAC regulations in both the short run and long run. In the short run, allowing firms to choose how they will reduce emissions is more efficient than prescribing a single approach because firms incur different opportunity costs to lower emissions. In the long run, firms have an incentive to further reduce emissions by improving their technology. It is possible, though unlikely, that CAC regulations will be as efficient as IB regulations in the short run, just as it is possible, though unlikely, that a command system will happen to choose the lowest-cost method of production. In the long run, however, command systems do not encourage innovative technology. There is no reward for improving, only a penalty for not meeting the standard. Let's consider how CAC and IB regulations reduce auto emissions.

## COMMAND-AND-CONTROL REGULATIONS

In the 1970s, the U.S. government mandated the use of catalytic converters to reduce auto pollutants. The converter results in reduced hydrocarbon emissions associated with the burning of gasoline. While the catalytic converter undoubtedly reduces pollution, it suffers from several inefficiencies.

First, the requirement that cars have catalytic converters is uniform throughout the country. The marginal car in a high-pollution region, such as Los Angeles, has a much higher external cost than the same car driven across the prairies of Kansas. Efficiency calls for stricter regulations in automobile-intensive regions, such as Los Angeles. Second, there may be other technologies that can achieve the same reduced emissions at a lower cost. Finally, automakers have little incentive to invest in better future technology because the regulations require the firm to meet, but not beat, the standard.

A more subtle inefficiency is that CAC regulations may act as a barrier to entry to other firms, both domestic and international. The U.S. auto industry initially resisted environmental controls, knowing that controls would drive up costs. Foreign manufacturers, such as the Japanese automakers, already met the proposed U.S. standards, but achieved their goal with a different technology. Catalytic converters put the Japanese at a temporary cost disadvantage. Japanese cars were required to have catalytic converters even though they already met the air quality standard.

Another example of CAC regulations is the use of Corporate Average Fuel Economy (CAFE) standards. These oft-discussed standards require each automaker to achieve a minimum number of miles per gallon (mpg) for its fleet. For example, Ford's cars might be required to achieve at least 27 mpg. When this standard was imposed, Ford and other manufacturers invented minivans and sport utility vehicles (SUVs), which were classified as trucks and therefore not subject to the standard. Since then, consumers have shifted to minivans and SUVs despite their lower fuel efficiency. In the end, Ford met the higher fuel standard, while the average mpg of vehicles actually on the road decreased!

## INCENTIVE-BASED REGULATIONS

**Effluent tax**
A tax on the pollutant.

**Effluent Taxes**  The simplest type of incentive-based (IB) regulation is an **effluent tax**. An effluent tax is a tax on the pollutant. If car manufacturers face a tax that depends on emissions, they can no longer ignore externalities. They must consider the tax based on emissions in addition to private resource costs. Exhibit 3 shows how an effluent tax can achieve efficiency.

A less direct way of reducing pollutants is a gasoline tax. By increasing the price of gasoline to car owners, the tax results in a smaller quantity demanded of gasoline and lower gasoline emissions. Over time, consumers faced with high gas prices seek more fuel-efficient cars, lowering emissions even more.

Taxes can achieve efficiency directly or indirectly and can be placed on buyers or sellers. Although the tax approach may appear simple in theory, some important practical difficulties limit the use of pollution taxes. First, how do we measure external cost? There is no market that buys and sells air pollution or climate change. So the tax is at best an approximation of external cost. Second, studies that have attempted to measure external cost find it to be quite large, requiring a substantial tax. It is widely thought that the price of a gallon of gasoline would have to increase by $1 to approximate the external costs of auto emissions. Such a $1 tax, added to the approximately 40 cents in gasoline taxes that are already imposed to pay for roads, would be unpopular with voters and as a consequence are unattractive to politicians.

**Emissions trading**
Firms buying and selling the right to pollute.

**Emissions Trading**  What if there were a market in which air pollution or climate change could be traded? As a result of the 1990 amendments to the Clean Air Act, there are markets for **emissions trading**. Emissions trading allows firms to buy and sell the right to pollute. The most active market so far is for sulfur emissions. Sulfur dioxide causes increased rain acidity. Acid rain can cause damage to lakes, trees, and even cars.

**Offset**
Reduction in an existing pollution source to counteract pollution from a new source.

There are markets for air pollution rights. A firm that wishes to build new factories that would add to pollution in an already polluted area may have to find *offsets* before it can relocate. An **offset** is a reduction in an existing pollution source that offsets a new pollution source. For example, U.S. Generating Company, an independent power producer, offered in 1992 to buy up automobile "clunkers" in return for permission to expand a coal-fired generating facility that would use the Deleward River and pollute the air. Under this program, the company offered to pay $500 to owners of cars that are at least 16 years old. The factory scraps the old clunkers, thereby offsetting its new source of pollution. The clunker approach makes use of the fact that a small percentage of cars are responsible for a disproportionate share of pollution.

To set up trading for lawn mower or car emissions, the government could require manufacturers to buy permits for each unit of emissions. In the short run, firms would include the cost of permits along with private costs as a component of price. The price would increase most for the dirtiest machines. In the long run, firms would have an incentive to build cleaner products. Firms with the cleanest

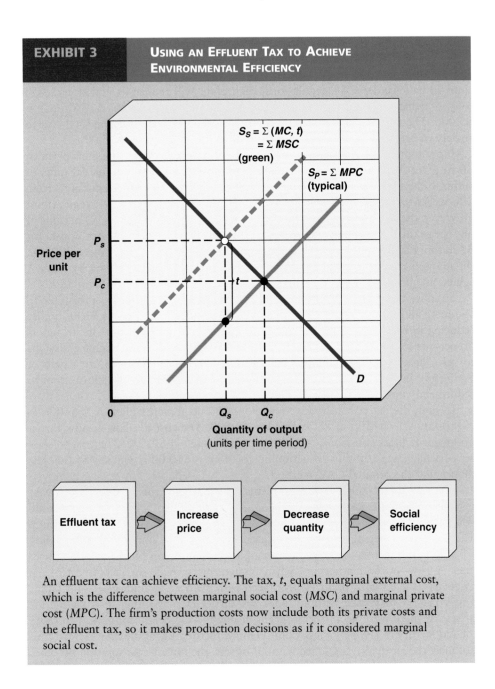

**EXHIBIT 3**   **USING AN EFFLUENT TAX TO ACHIEVE ENVIRONMENTAL EFFICIENCY**

An effluent tax can achieve efficiency. The tax, *t*, equals marginal external cost, which is the difference between marginal social cost (*MSC*) and marginal private cost (*MPC*). The firm's production costs now include both its private costs and the effluent tax, so it makes production decisions as if it considered marginal social cost.

products would need the fewest permits and might even profit by selling permits to companies that cannot improve as quickly. Whereas GreenAcres lawn mowers would go out of business in an unfettered competitive lawn mower industry, the company would now be in position to succeed.

A simple example can demonstrate the cost savings of an IB approach, such as emissions trading, compared to a CAC approach. Suppose two coal-fired electric plants each emit 100 tons of sulfur into the air. Plant A can reduce sulfur at a constant cost of $100/ton, while plant B can do so at a cost of $200/ton. The Environmental Protection Agency (EPA) announces that it wishes to cut sulfur emissions in half. Under CAC regulations, each plant will reduce its emissions to 50 tons, a reduction of 100 tons. The cost to plant A is $100/ton × (50 tons) = $5,000. The cost to plant B is $200/ton × (50 tons) = $10,000. The total cost to society of achieving a 100-unit reduction in sulfur emissions is $15,000.

Now suppose the EPA announces that it will give away 100 emissions permits, 50 to plant A and 50 to plant B. Each plant now is allowed to emit 50 units of sulfur. If the two plants do nothing more, each will have to reduce emissions from 100 to 50 tons, and each will do so at the same cost as with CAC regulations. However, there is a lower cost solution. Plant A is willing to sell its 50 permits at any price above $100/ton because it can reduce its emissions in-house for $100/ton. Plant B is willing to buy emissions permits at any price below $200/ton, the marginal cost of reducing its own emissions. Both plants can gain by plant A selling an additional 50 permits to plant B at a price between $100 and $200.

Suppose they agree to a price of $150/ton. Plant A now finds it profitable to eliminate all its emissions. Its marginal cost of reducing emissions is $100/ton. By reducing its emissions to zero, Plant A no longer needs any permits. It can sell its 50 permits for $150/ton, making a profit of $50 per ton by reducing its emissions to zero (at a cost of $100/ton) and selling its permits to Plant B (at a gain of $150/ton). In turn, plant B finds it cheaper to buy permits for $150/ton than to reduce emissions, at a cost of $200/ton.

In sum, the net cost to reduce emissions by 100 tons for Plant A is $100/ton × (100 tons) − $150/ton × (50 tons) = $2,500. The cost to plant B, now that it no longer reduces emissions, is $150/ton × (50 tons) = $7,500. The cost to society of achieving a 100-unit reduction in emissions is $10,000, which is $5,000 less than under the original CAC method.

The real world helps us see problems that textbook theory does not always reveal. Emissions trading has the theoretical potential to achieve environmental goals at the lowest cost, but, so far, real-world trading has fallen short of efficiency. There are a number of obstacles to efficient trading, some minor and some major.

**New-source bias**
Bias that occurs when regulations provide an incentive to keep assets past the efficient point.

Taking the factory and clunker example, one minor problem is a **new-source bias**. A new-source bias occurs when regulations provide an incentive to keep assets past the efficient point. A firm faced with the need to find offsets if it builds a new factory may stick with an older and dirtier factory rather than paying for offsets. If there were no offset program, it might have been economical to retire the old factory in favor of a less-polluting new factory. But if the new factory cannot meet the air quality standard without offsets, the lowest-cost solution becomes extending the life of the old plant. Electric utilities are also finding it worthwhile to continue to operate old coal-fired plants that are exempt from stringent regulations known as New Source Performance Standards that can only be met by newer technology. There also may be a type of free-rider problem. Car owners about to junk their 15-year-old clunkers for $25 may keep them another year if a firm might be willing to pay $500 for them. These minor problems are just growing pains of emissions trading, and future emissions markets will find ways to reduce these undesirable outcomes.

Other growing pains include small numbers of buyers or sellers, imperfect information about the value of a permit, and concerns about permit value in the future. Firms will trade actively only if trading is a better alternative than other alternatives. Some firms may shut down or perhaps relocate in other countries where permits are not needed. Also, emissions may be higher in regions where electric utilities buy permits rather than reduce emissions. The Tennessee Valley Authority has been a buyer of permits. Not only does Tennessee's air qualify suffer, but North Carolina believes its air quality is also compromised as pollution drifts east.

Nevertheless, emissions trading is probably here to stay. The government may initiate emissions trading by distributing permits according to production or pollution over a designated period, or it may sell permits through an auction to the highest bidders. Buyers may be electric utilities, or they may be environmentalists. Environmentalists can achieve pollution reduction by outbidding utilities for permits and then refusing to sell them to utilities, thereby forcing the utilities to reduce pollution.

The Chicago Board of Trade, or "Smog" Exchange, allows trading in pollution permits much like trading on the New York Stock Exchange. Companies are required to own a permit for each unit of emissions. Clean companies need fewer permits and offer to sell their extra permits on the exchange. Dirty companies need additional permits and are buyers on the exchange. They will only buy if the permit price is less than what it would cost them to reduce pollution by one more unit. Sellers of permits will charge at least what it costs them to reduce pollution by one more unit.

Exhibit 4 shows the permit price of sulfur dioxide allowances since trading began in 1994. Over the years, the permit price has fluctuated widely before reaching the current level of about $175. For example, the peak price of over $200 in February 1999 was in anticipation of the greater demand for allowances beginning in the year 2000 when a second phase of the emissions trading program began. In the second phase, additional utilities that were not included in Phase I had to meet emissions requirements. One explanation of the subsequent drop in price was an announcement by the EPA that they were interested in phasing out the use of high-sulfur coal for electric power generation in the Midwest.

There is concern that the benefits of emissions trading will be diminished by lack of trading and opposition to the idea of creating a market for pollution rights. There is even a revival of interest in command-and-control regulation. If the government happens to pick the right approach and rewards cleaner technology, some economists favor CAC over the imperfect emissions trading to date. For example, there are supporters of California's approach to reducing auto emissions. California considered a requirement that 10 percent of the cars sold within California must be emissions free. They anticipated that the mandate would be met with electric vehicles (EVs).

Critics of the California approach point out that EVs are not emissions free if they require electricity from a power plant. Certainly, power plants also pollute, although there may be an advantage to transferring pollution away from the most densely populated areas. EVs powered by photovoltaic cells (PVCs) that use solar energy are closer to being emissions free, but there is still pollution in the PVC production process. Perhaps the greatest drawback to EVs is their poor performance to date. They suffer from poor acceleration, limited range, and limited ability to climb hills. Critics maintain that inferior products continue to be the legacy of CAC approaches. In response to rising gas prices, Toyota and other

EXHIBIT 4        **MONTHLY AVERAGE PRICE OF SULFUR DIOXIDE ALLOWANCES UNDER THE ACID RAIN PROGRAM**

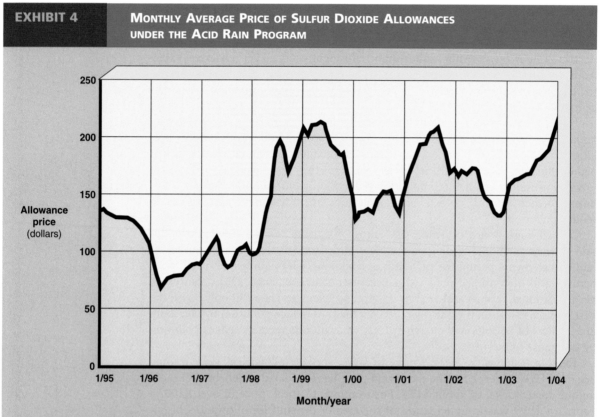

The Chicago Board of Trade allows trading in pollution permits much like trading on the New York Stock Exchange. This figure shows the sulfur dioxide allowance prices reported by brokerage firms and Fieldston Publications' market survey.

*Source: Environmental Protection Agency, http://www.epa.gov/airmarkts/trading/so2market/alprices.jpg.*

car manufacturers responded with gas-electric hybrid vehicles. Critics suggest that the market has a superior ability to innovate, such as a hybrid vehicle with low emissions, as compared to CAC requiring zero emissions that could not be met by a gas-electric hybrid.

**CONCLUSION** *Economists generally believe that incentive-based regulations are more efficient than command-and-control regulations.*

Still, much of the public seems more comfortable with controls and rules than with prices and trading. There are a number of possible explanations for the public's view. First, people have difficulty accepting that any pollution is efficient. Nobody wants to think about a higher risk of cancer due to a leak from a nuclear power plant.

Another possible reason for the public's view is a mistrust of experts. People were told by experts that nuclear power would be safe, that hazardous waste

## You're the Economist

# Does Emissions Trading Work?
*Applicable Concepts: emissions trading, command-and-control regulation*

The New York State Legislature in 1894 created the Adirondack Forest Preserve as the first wild land preserve to gain constitutional protection in the United States. Today the Adirondack Park and Forest Preserve is the largest park in the nation outside of Alaska. When the Adirondacks began serving the public, each of its many lakes, rivers, and streams offered an abundant supply of fish and plants.

Now imagine your surprise if you were to approach the water and discover a sign saying "Toxic Water." The threat is real, and it is from the influx of acid rain due to weather patterns blowing in pollution from Southern and Midwestern factories. Attempts have been made to combat the ill effects to the lakes, but the acid rain keeps coming.

Acid rain occurs when coal-fired power plants emit sulfur and nitrogen into the atmosphere because the burning of fossil fuels reacts with moisture in the atmosphere to create nitric and sulfuric acid. The acid then falls to earth in the form of acid rain, snow, or fog.

A major provision in the 1990 Clean Air Act advocated by economists set up a marketplace in which companies can trade the right to pollute in the form of credits, as a commodity. The most active market has been for sulfur dioxide emissions that increase rain acidity. However, electric power plants and automobiles also release nitrogen, which has not been targeted by emissions trading.

A General Accounting Office study in 2000 found that sulfur levels had decreased substantially in 92 percent of the 48 of 52 Adirondack lakes examined, and nitrogen levels were dramatically higher in these tested lakes. The issue for New Yorkers is that a New York State law forced their utilities to cut emissions in the 1980s below federal law requirements. As a result, the good news was a windfall of pollution credits under the 1990 Clean Air Act to sell to companies outside New York that failed to meet the federal pollution standards. But the bad news is that this sale gives companies in other states the right to allow their pollution to blow through the air into New York.

© Photodisc/Getty Images

### ANALYZE THE ISSUE

1. What has been the primary benefit of emissions trading?

2. Why do investigators believe nitrogen levels have risen?

3. How could emissions trading be expanded to further reduce sulfur emissions and at the same time reduce nitrogen levels?

*Source: Based on Raymond Hernandez, "Albany Battles Acid Rain Fed by Other States," May 2, 2000, http://www.nytimes.com.*

disposal sites would not leak, and that people living near oil tanks would not have higher risks of cancer. When outcomes differ from what experts promise, the public favors safety over efficiency. No one wants to take a chance on illness or death if the experts are wrong again. And yet would you give up your car or favor a law that set the speed limit at 20 miles per hour? These laws might increase safety, but they would certainly be inefficient.

## GOVERNMENT AND ENVIRONMENTAL EFFICIENCY

Market failure is likely for products with external costs. To achieve efficiency, buyers and sellers must consider external costs. Government has the power to establish laws, taxes, or permit systems so that market participants pay for external costs.

Although government policy can potentially improve efficiency, there is no guarantee. The countries that emerged from the Soviet Union, where government played a far more dominant role than in the United States, have environmental problems that dwarf those in the United States. In these countries, air and water quality borders on ecocide, with high rates of illness due to environmental degradation. The Chernobyl disaster, in which a nuclear plant malfunctioned and released radioactivity, has caused thousands of premature deaths. In China, another nation where the government plays a major role in the economy, the Beijing weather report frequently calls for "smoky" skies.

In the United States, large numbers of U.S. Department of Defense sites are among the biggest environmental challenges. Hazardous wastes from the production of weapons are now leaking in burial sites, including Oak Ridge, Tennessee, and Richland, Washington. The U.S. Forest Service frequently permits lumber companies to harvest trees from national forests at subsidized prices. Government environmental officials have even gone to prison for illegally meeting with industry representatives to weaken environmental regulations. And government has tended to ignore the cost to firms of complying with hundreds of thousands of pages of environmental legislation, a set of regulations more voluminous than the U.S. Tax Code. For all these reasons, as well as the widespread dissatisfaction with government in general, there is concern about the effectiveness of government policy in achieving environmental goals. Government officials may pursue self-interest, which could favor polluting industries over societal interests as a whole, especially if industry executives are major campaign contributors.

**The Coase Theorem** Ronald Coase, an economist at the University of Chicago and the winner of the 1991 Nobel Prize in economics, was among the first to caution against the assumption that government intervention in the environmental arena would improve upon private-sector environmental performance. In his famous 1960 paper, "The Problem of Social Cost," he even questioned the fundamental assumption of market failure. According to the **Coase Theorem**, the private sector could achieve social efficiency with minimal government intervention. The role of the government should be limited to the legal establishment of property rights, with environmental disputes resolved in court. The Coase Theorem is the proposition that private market negotiations can achieve social efficiency regardless of the initial definition of property rights.

As an example of how the Coase Theorem works, consider a train that throws off sparks and occasionally burns a farmer's crops. Exhibit 5 shows railroad profits increasing and farm profits decreasing as more trains run.

Each train has an external cost. Emitted sparks can cause fires, which reduce the farmer's crops. If the railroad ignores external cost, it appears that the railroad would choose to run five trains so as to maximize profit, leaving the farmer with no crops. It also appears that to protect the farmer, there should be a law requiring the railroad to find a spark-free technology.

**Coase Theorem**
The proposition that private market negotiations can achieve social efficiency regardless of the initial definition of property rights.

| EXHIBIT 5 | CHOOSING THE EFFICIENT AMOUNTS OF SPARK-EMITTING TRAINS AND FARM CROPS | | | | |
|---|---|---|---|---|---|
| Number of trains | Total railroad profit | Marginal railroad profit | Number of crops | Total farm profit | Marginal farm profit |
| 0 | $0 | | 10.5 | $105 | |
| | | $20 | | | $ −5 |
| 1 | 20 | | 10 | 100 | |
| | | 20 | | | −10 |
| 2 | 40 | | 9 | 90 | |
| | | 20 | | | −20 |
| 3 | 60 | | 7 | 70 | |
| | | 20 | | | −30 |
| 4 | 80 | | 4 | 40 | |
| | | 20 | | | −40 |
| 5 | 100 | | 0 | 0 | |

Suppose the courts establish a law that farmers have the right to spark-free trains. How could the railroad meet this tougher environmental standard? The railroad could change to a new, higher-cost technology. The cost must be higher, or the railroad would have chosen this environmentally friendly technology in the first place. If the cost is too high, the railroad might go out of business or relocate its tracks away from farms. Alternatively, it may be less expensive to offer the farmer money for any burned crops.

If the trains continue to throw off sparks, the first train will reduce the farmer's profits by $5 and will add $20 to the railroad's profits. The two parties will be able to negotiate a deal, with the farmer receiving a payment of between $5 and $20 from the railroad. What about a second train? This train will add another $20 to railroad profits, but will reduce farm profits by $10. Again, the farmer will permit the railroad to run a second train as long as the railroad pays the farmer at least $10. If a third train runs, marginal social benefit will equal marginal social cost. Society will benefit from more train service, but will lose from fewer crops. The third train will be marginally worthwhile, but additional trains will not run. The fourth train will add $20 to railroad profits but will reduce farm profit by $30. Thus, the railroad will lose money if it runs the fourth train. By clearly establishing the farmer's right to spark-free trains, the number of trains will be decreased from five to three trains.

Notice that the farmer will be better off if he or she allows sparks as long as the railroad compensates the farmer for damage than if the government requires a spark-free technology. The farmer earns $105 when there are no sparks. With sparks, the farmer will earn at least $105, receiving between $5 and $20 for permitting the first train, at least $10 (and possibly as much as $20) for permitting the second train, and another $20 for the third train. With three trains, the farmer will still earn $70 from crops, in addition to a minimum of $35 for allowing trains, for a total of at least $105.

## International Economics

# European Trading in Carbon-Emission Permits Begins
*Applicable Concepts: externalities, free-rider problem*

Most power stations are surrounded by coal tips or pipes carrying gas. But round the plant that powers the Swedish town of Enkoping, some 70 kilometers west of Stockholm, there is willow coppice stretching as far as the eye can see. Enkoping is probably the only town in Europe that is powered by biofuels.

The plant's director, Eddie Johansson, says willow is as economic as coal or gas because Sweden levies a tax on carbon emissions from most power plants. Under the government's rules, he does not have to pay the tax because for every ton of carbon dioxide that disappears up the stack, the plant's willow trees soak up a ton from the air as they grow. Hundreds of willow-powered plants could operate across Europe, he says, if power companies had similar incentives to cut carbon emissions.

On 1 January, the European Union introduced a system that, if the optimists are right, could make that happen. Rather than imposing a carbon tax, the EU has launched the world's first carbon trading scheme. Its aim is to force down industrial emissions of greenhouse gases and so moderate global warming, while preserving the competitiveness of European companies.

Under the scheme, companies are issued pieces of paper that grant them permission to emit a certain quantity of $CO_2$ into the atmosphere in a particular year. Companies that do not have enough permits to cover their emissions will have to buy them from someone who does.

**Trading Nations**
While the system was initially designed only for industrial installations in Europe, the US-based corporation DuPont says it believes the EU's trading system could become the hub of a global carbon trading market. Countries outside the EU, such as Norway, have already said they would like to join and issue their companies with emissions allocations that could, in future, be traded on the EU market.

So far the scheme covers emissions until 2007, but the EU hopes it will pave the way for governments to force down their national emissions through 2008, as they are required to do under the Kyoto protocol. The current permits also only cover around half of the carbon emitted by the EU. Most of the rest is produced by vehicles, which are outside the scheme.

But amid the euphoria at the launch of the scheme, there is concern. Three EU countries, Italy, Poland and the Czech

This outcome is similar to the government solutions examined earlier. Efficiency leads to the efficient amount of pollution, which is typically not zero. No sparks may mean no trains. But Coase asks, Why assume that society is best served by assuming the railroad is the polluter and the farmer the victim? In the 1800s, sparking engines may have been the best available technology, and an occasional fire may have been a natural consequence.

So consider the outcome if property rights to produce sparks are given to the railroads so that trains are allowed to throw off sparks. If the farmer does nothing, the railroad will run five trains, and the farmer will end up with no crops and no profit. The farmer will increase profit by $40 if only four trains run. Since the fifth train will add only $20 to railroad profit, the farmer can afford to pay as much as $40 (or as little as $20) to stop the fifth train. Similarly, the farmer will gain $30 by stopping the fourth train—more than enough to pay the railroad for forgoing $20 in profit. Once again, negotiations will stop at three trains, the efficient number.

Republic, cannot yet trade in carbon as they failed to submit their allocations in time. Greece has yet to submit any allocations at all.

More worrisome, some analysts fear that overcautious governments may have wrecked the market before it starts by being too generous with the permits they have issued. If everyone has a generous allocation, no one will have any incentive to cut down the quantities of greenhouses gases they pump into the atmosphere.

**Future Measures**
But if governments seriously want to use industry trading to meet their Kyoto targets, then the industries covered by the scheme have to widen. Emissions permits for other greenhouse gases, such as methane, will also have to be issued and traded. And in future, governments might up the ante by auctioning allocations of emissions permits,

rather than simply handing them out.

One area of confusion will be the relationship between this commercial market in carbon and the various trading systems included in the Kyoto protocol itself. There are in essence two separate markets: for companies, which have to meet targets imposed by governments; and the other for governments themselves, which have internationally agreed targets for national emissions.

This will mean that there could be two different prices for carbon. Analysts agree this will be confusing, but say that if governments could buy or sell their national entitlements to emit $CO_2$ there would be chaos.

So will the system lead to willow coppice plantations, across the industrial heartlands of Europe, and reduced emissions? It looks as if the market will decide.

**ANALYZE THE ISSUE**

1. How does the electrical plant in Enkoping, Sweden avoid the Swedish tax on carbon emissions?

2. Why is there a concern that the new European carbon-trading system may not reduce carbon emissions?

3. What changes will eventually be needed to improve the European carbon emissions trading program?

Source: Fred Pearce, "European trading in carbon-emission permits begins," NewScientist.com, http://www.newscientist.com/article.ns?id=dn6846&print=true. Reprinted by permission.

This example demonstrates the Coase Theorem: As long as the courts clearly establish property rights, markets may achieve social efficiency *regardless of the initial assignment of property rights*. Coase's great contribution was to focus attention on property rights, a focus that foreshadowed the emissions-trading approach that allows firms to negotiate by buying and selling the right to pollute. But Coase argues for an even more limited role for government. In his view, the government should establish courts and then let markets negotiate.

**Some Limitations on the Coase Theorem**   Coase was instrumental in raising concern about government solutions. It might then seem a simple step to accept his claim that private markets would efficiently resolve environmental problems. In actuality, only a small number of environmental problems readily qualify for Coase Theorem solutions.

First, there are no **transactions costs** in the Coase Theorem. Transactions costs are the costs of negotiating and enforcing a contract. Turning to the courts is a

**Transactions costs**
The costs of negotiating and enforcing a contract.

## CHECKPOINT

### Is It Efficient to Buy Odor-Reducing Technology if You Live Next to a Hog Farm?

You live next door to a hog farm. It is estimated that the smell from the hog farm reduces the value of your home by $7,000. For $5,000, you can purchase technology that reduces the hog smell by half, so your house value would decrease by only $3,500. Assuming the hog farm has the property right to locate next door and that it is not required to reduce the hog smell, what will you do? Will you do nothing or buy the new technology?

costly process, in terms of both time and money. And dealing with the source of the externality has its own costs. Have you ever tried to negotiate with a noisy neighbor at 2 a.m.? However, there are also transactions costs associated with government solutions. So Coasean negotiations may be preferable to government intervention even when there are substantial private transactions costs.

Second, there are no differences in willingness to pay (WTP) and willingness to accept (WTA) in the Coase Theorem. Many studies have found that people's willingness to pay to acquire a property right, such as an improvement in air quality, is less than the compensation they require to give up a property right, such as accepting lower air quality. If the farmer has the right to spark-free air, he/she may require $50 to allow sparks. Alternatively, if the farmer has to buy that right, he/she may only be willing to pay $20. In other words, people may not view giving up an environmental right you already own as equivalent to buying a right you do not currently own.

Third, Coase assumes there are only two parties in the negotiation. Externalities are typically third-party problems, and there may be many third parties. Do all the farmers get together to negotiate with the railroad, and do all the neighbors get together to reduce noise from the party? With many parties, there is once again a **free-rider problem**. If noise levels decrease, I get the benefit whether or not I contribute to the negotiations. So why contribute? Stated as a concept, if some individuals benefit while others pay, the free-rider problem is that few will be willing to pay for improvement of the environment or other public goods. As a result, these goods are underproduced.

**Free-rider problem** The problem that if some individuals benefit while others pay, few will be willing to pay for improvement of the environment or other public goods. As a result, these goods are underproduced.

**CONCLUSION** *Neither government nor the markets can be asserted to be the best solution to environmental problems. On balance, though, the effort to work toward improved government solutions seems worthwhile, given the outcome for the environment of purely self-interested markets.*

## Key Concepts

| | | |
|---|---|---|
| Private benefits and costs | Incentive-based regulations | New-source bias |
| Social benefits and costs | Command-and-control regulations | Coase Theorem |
| Free rider | Effluent tax | Transaction costs |
| Market failure | Emissions trading | Free-rider problem |
| Government failure | Offset | |

## Summary

- **Externalities** are benefits or costs that fall on third parties who are neither buyers nor sellers. Pollution is a negative externality or an external cost that is a by-product of many industrial production processes.

- **Market failure** is present when the market produces a socially inefficient outcome—for example, when there are externalities. All firms, including competitive firms, consider private costs but disregard external costs in making decisions.

- **Government failure** occurs when public-sector actions or lack of actions move us away from desired outcomes, such as efficiency. Government officials seeking campaign contributions and votes may choose environmental measures that favor wealthy contributors over society's best interests.

- **Command-and-control regulations** occur when the government dictates the approach to achieving an environmental goal. Command-and-control regulations are generally inefficient on three grounds: they do not distinguish between high- and low-pollution areas, they do not allow firms to choose lower-cost technologies that could achieve the environmental standard, and they do not encourage investment in improved technology to lower future emissions.

- **Incentive-based regulations** build on markets to achieve environmental efficiency. Effluent taxes are taxes that reflect external costs. Emissions trading allows firms to buy and sell the "right to pollute."

- The **Coase Theorem** maintains that markets can be efficient in the presence of externalities with minimal government intervention. Even in the presence of externalities, markets may produce efficient outcomes so long as property rights are clearly established.

- **Transactions costs, income effects, and free-rider problems** are obstacles to achieving environmental efficiency through markets. Transactions costs are the costs of negotiating an agreement, income effects are present when limited income prevents one party from being able to afford the efficient solution, and free-rider problems are present when participants are better off hiding than revealing their willingness to pay for an environmental improvement.

## Summary of Conclusion Statements

- Unregulated competitive markets will over-supply and under-price products that pollute.

- Economists generally believe that incentive-based regulations are more efficient than command-and-control regulations.

- Neither government nor the markets can be asserted to be the best solution to environmental problems. On balance, though, the effort to work toward improved government solutions seems worthwhile, given the outcome for the environment of purely self-interested markets.

1. Compare price and quantity in a competitive industry to those of a "green" industry for a product that generates pollution.

2. Suppose a car sells for $20,000 in a market with no pollution restrictions. Will the car sell for more than $20,000, less than $20,000, or $20,000 when there are pollution restrictions? Explain.

3. You are considering whether to buy one house for $100,000 or another, identical house located near high-voltage electric power lines for $90,000. Assume that it has been established that living near high-voltage lines increases the risk of cancer due to electromagnetic fields (EMFs). If you choose the $90,000 house, is the radiation from EMFs an externality? Explain.

4. Restaurants have observed that large parties (eight or more) leave a lower average tip than smaller parties. Identify the effect, which also makes it more difficult to reach global environmental agreements, responsible for this phenomenon.

5. Suppose your instructor gives eight homework assignments during the semester. She indicates that anyone who does not turn in all eight assignments will automatically fail the course. Is this an example of a command-and-control or an incentive-based regulation? Explain any inefficiencies of your instructor's approach.

6. Environmentalists in Tennessee brought suit against the Champion Paper Company of North Carolina for polluting the Pigeon River, which flows from North Carolina into eastern Tennessee. Tennessee claimed that the coffee-colored water smelled bad and would not support fishing or swimming. Environmentalists requested that the river be restored to its pristine state, whereby water quality is restored to the level before the coming of industry. The Environmental Protection Agency heard the suit and applied an efficiency standard. Is pristine water an efficiency standard? Explain.

7. Draw a graph to demonstrate your answer to question 6.

8. California once proposed legislation that would have required 10 percent of its car fleet to be nearly emissions free by the year 2005. This mandate spurred electric vehicle research. Such vehicles could be powered by photovoltaic cells or by batteries that are recharged using an electrical outlet. Would you agree that it is correct to conclude that electric vehicles that use electrical outlets are emissions free? What about electric vehicles powered by photovoltaic cells?

9. Explain why consumers would not be willing to pay the full costs of a less-polluting car in the absence of government regulations.

10. Evaluate the following statement: "When products pollute, government solutions are more efficient than market solutions."

11. Provide an example of a market where you think the Coase Theorem applies. Explain why you think the market satisfies assumptions regarding transactions costs, income effects, and free riders.

12. In a study of ranching laws in the 1800s, an economic researcher found that as these laws restricted the ability of cattle to roam freely, agricultural output increased. Do this researcher's results support the Coase Theorem? Explain.

13. If we are to take action against global warming, we must reduce carbon emissions. Explain how to reduce carbon emissions by using
   a. command-and-control regulation.
   b. an effluent tax.
   c. emissions trading.

14. A global agreement known as the Montreal Protocol led to the phase-out of chlorofluorocarbons (CFCs), chemical compounds found in aerosol cans and refrigerants. CFCs may have contributed to the growing hole in the ozone layer. With a diminished ozone layer, there is an increased chance of skin cancer. Explain the effect of this agreement on the price of deodorants and air-conditioning. Also, is a ban on CFCs an efficient approach to the ozone hole problem?

## Study Guide Questions

1. _____ is the proposition that private market negotiations will achieve social efficiency, regardless of the initial definition of property rights.

2. Compared to incentive-based regulation, command-and-control legislation
   a. discourages the use of comparative advantage in the short run, but encourages the development of new technology in the long run.
   b. encourages the use of comparative advantage in the short run, but discourages the development of new technology in the long run.
   c. encourages the use of comparative advantage in the short run, and the development of new technology in the long run.
   d. none of the above.

3. Which of the following offers the best economic justification for subsidizing vaccinations for infectious disease on the basis of efficiency?
   a. Vaccinations create a positive externality for society because they reduce the chances and the scope of epidemics.

   b. Vaccinations are a type of pollution that increase the chances and the scope of epidemics.
   c. A politician offering subsidized vaccinations may be able to get more votes from lower-income people and get elected.
   d. All of the above.

4. Which of the following statements is *true*?
   a. Competitive markets result in the socially efficient price and quantity when externalities exist.
   b. Command-and-control regulations set an environmental goal and dictate how the goal will be achieved.
   c. Economists prefer command-and-control regulations to incentive-based pollution programs.
   d. An effluent tax is a tax imposed on rich people.

5. T F The Coase Theorem states that the public sector can achieve environmental efficiency, as long as property rights are clearly assigned.

**Answers to these questions are in the complete Study Guide at www.thomsonedu.com/thomsonnow.**

 **For Online Exercises, go to the text Web site at www.thomsonedu.com/economics/tucker.**

 ## Checkpoint Answers

### Is It Efficient to Buy Odor-Reducing Technology if You Live Next to a Hog Farm?

It is not efficient to purchase the new odor-reducing technology. It would cost $5,000 but would increase your house value by only $3,500. It is not efficient to cut the odor by half if the market will not compensate you sufficiently for reduced hog odors. If your only options are to do nothing or to buy the new technology, and you said do nothing, **YOU ARE CORRECT.** (A third option is to pay the hog farm to locate elsewhere. You would be willing to pay up to $7,000 to avoid the $7,000 lost due to the smell of the nearby farm.)

## Practice Quiz

For an explanation of the correct answers, please visit the tutorial at www.thomsonedu.com/economics/tucker.

1. Recently, the city of New Orleans discovered chemical compounds in its drinking water that may cause cancer. Since New Orleans's drinking water comes from the Mississippi River, the source of these chemicals is the waste discharges of industrial plants upstream from New Orleans. This is an example of
   a. an external cost imposed on the citizens of New Orleans by the industrial plants upstream.
   b. a market failure where the market price of the output of these industrial plants does not fully reflect the social cost of producing these goods.
   c. an externality where the marginal social costs of producing these industrial goods differ from the marginal private costs.
   d. all of the above.

2. A government policy that charges steel firms a fee per ton of steel produced (an "effluent charge") where the fee is determined by the amount of pollutants discharged into the air or water will lead to
   a. a decrease in the market equilibrium quantity of steel produced.
   b. a decrease in the market equilibrium price of steel.
   c. an increase in the market equilibrium price of steel.
   d. the results in (a) and (b).
   e. the results in (a) and (c).

3. Social costs are
   a. the full resource costs of an economic activity.
   b. usually less than private costs.
   c. the costs of an economic activity borne by the producer.
   d. all of the above.

4. As a general rule, if pollution costs are external, firms will produce
   a. too much of a polluting good.
   b. too little of a polluting good.
   c. an optimal amount of a polluting good.
   d. an amount that cannot be determined without additional information.

5. Many economists would argue that
   a. the optimal amount of pollution is greater than zero.
   b. all pollution should be eliminated.
   c. the market mechanism can handle pollution without any government intervention.

   d. central planning is the most efficient way to eliminate pollution.

6. Which of the following used marketable pollution permits as an incentive for reducing pollution?
   a. The Clean Air Act of 1970
   b. The Comprehensive Environmental Response, Compensation, and Liability Act of 1980
   c. The Clean Air Act amendments of 1990
   d. The Water Quality and Improvement Act of 1970

7. The disposable diaper industry is perfectly competitive. Which of the following is *true*?
   a. Since the industry is perfectly competitive, price and quantity are at the socially efficient levels.
   b. Competitive price is higher and competitive quantity lower than the socially efficient point.
   c. Competitive price is higher and competitive quantity higher than the socially efficient point.
   d. Competitive price is lower and competitive quantity higher than the socially efficient point.

8. An example of the command-and-control approach to environmental policy is
   a. placing a tax on high-sulfur coal to reduce its use and the corresponding sulfur emissions (which contribute to acid rain).
   b. requiring electric utilities to install scrubbers to reduce sulfur dioxide emissions (which contribute to acid rain).
   c. allowing coal producers to buy and sell permits to allow sulfur emissions.
   d. allowing individuals to sue coal producers if sulfur emissions exceed a government-set standard.

**EXHIBIT 6**

9. The profit-maximizing firm in Exhibit 6 creates water and air pollution as a consequence of producing its output of beef cattle. If pollution costs are borne by third parties, the firm will maximize economic profit by choosing to
   a. voluntarily incur costs to reduce its pollution.
   b. produce at output rate $Q_3$.
   c. produce at output rate $Q_2$.
   d. produce at output rate $Q_4$.

10. To maximize social welfare, the firm in Exhibit 6 should produce at output rate
    a. $Q_1$.
    b. $Q_2$.
    c. $Q_3$.
    d. $Q_4$.

**EXHIBIT 7  IMPACT OF FLIGHTS ON HOUSE VALUE**

| Number of flights | Total profits | Marginal profits | Value of Wilbur's house |
|---|---|---|---|
| 1 | $10,000 | $10,000 | $100,000 |
| 2 | 18,000 | 8,000 | 95,000 |
| 3 | 24,000 | 6,000 | 90,000 |
| 4 | 28,000 | 4,000 | 85,000 |
| 5 | 30,000 | 2,000 | 80,000 |

11. As shown in Exhibit 7, if Orville has the property right to fly over Wilbur's house, but Wilbur is allowed to negotiate with Orville on the number of flights, what will be the number of flights?
    a. 2
    b. 3
    c. 4
    d. 5

12. As shown in Exhibit 7, if Wilbur has the property right to have no planes flying over his house, but Orville is allowed to negotiate with Wilbur, what will be the number of fights?
    a. 2
    b. 3
    c. 4
    d. 5

13. As shown in Exhibit 7, at the socially efficient number of flights, what will be the market value of Orville's house?
    a. $100,000
    b. $95,000
    c. $90,000
    d. $85,000
    e. $80,000

The following currency table appears as part of the image:

| | Kenyan Schilling | 0.01271 | 78.67 |
| 0.665 | Korean Won | 0.00079 | 1,264 |
| 1.498 | Kuwaiti Dinar | 3.2787 | 0.305 |
| 569.2 | Luxembourg Franc | 0.02352 | 42.61 |
| 8.267 | Moroccan Dihram | 0.09557 | 10.463 |
| 2.165 | Malaysian Ringgit | 0.26319 | 3.799 |
| 5.79 | Mexico Peso | 0.10277 | 9.73 |
| 791 | Norwegian Krone | 0.11562 | 8.649 |
| 905 | Oman Riyal | 2.5994 | 0.385 |
| 75 | Peruvian Nuevo Sol | 0.29326 | 3.41 |
| 47 | Pakistan Rupee | 0.017 | 58.82 |
| 3 | Portuguese Escudo | 0.00476 | 210.1 |
| 3 | Saudi Arabia Riyal | 0.26664 | |
| | Singapore Dollar | 0.57887 | |
| | South African Rand | 0.13347 | |
| | Spanish Peseta | 0.00575 | |

| 0.00049 | 2,029 | Tunisian Dinar | 0.73126 | 1.367 |
| 0.00859 | 116.5 | UAE Dirham | 0.27237 | 3.6 |
| | | Venezuela Bolivar | 0.00143 | |

# part

# 5

# The International Economy

© Photodisc/Getty Images

The final part of this text is devoted to global topics. The first chapter explains the importance of free trade and the mechanics of trade bookkeeping and exchange rates. Here you will find a feature on the birth of the euro. The second chapter takes a historical look at the theoretical debate over capitalism and the transition of Cuba, Russia, and China toward this system. The final chapter provides comparisons of advanced and developing countries. The chapter concludes with the fascinating economic success story of Hong Kong.

# International Trade and Finance

© Photodisc/Getty Images

Just imagine your life without world trade. For openers, you could not eat bananas from Honduras or chocolate from Nigerian cocoa beans. Nor could you sip French wine, Colombian coffee, or Indian tea. Also forget about driving a Japanese motorcycle or automobile. In addition, you could not buy Italian shoes and most DVDs, televisions, fax machines, and personal computers because they are foreign made. Taking your vacation in London would also be ruled out if there were no world trade. And the list goes on and on, so the point is clear. World trade is important because it gives consumers more power by expanding their choices. Today, the speed of transportation and communication means producers must compete on a global basis for the favor of consumers. Trade has become highly controversial. Regardless of whether it was a World Trade Organization (WTO) meeting in Hong Kong, or a G-8 summit meeting in Scotland, global trade talks in 2005 faced turmoil in the streets as thousands of demonstrators protested "new world order" trading rules, while police were

forced to break up the demonstrations. And outsourcing jobs to lower paid workers overseas continues to be a debated issue in the United States.

The first part of this chapter explains the theoretical reason for why countries should specialize in producing certain goods and then trade them for imports. Also, you will study arguments for and against the United States protecting itself from "unfair" trade practices by other countries. In the second part of the chapter, you will learn how nations pay each other for world trade. Here you will explore interna-

tional bookkeeping and discover how supply and demand forces determine that, for example, 1 dollar is worth 100 yen.

**In this chapter, you will learn to solve these economics puzzles:**

- How does Babe Ruth's decision not to remain a pitcher illustrate an important principle in international trade?
- Is there a valid argument for trade protectionism?
- Should the United States return to the gold standard?

# Why Nations Need Trade

Exhibit 1 reveals which regions are our major trading partners. Leading the list of nations are Canada, our largest trading partner, Mexico, China, and Japan. Leading U.S. exports are chemicals, machinery, airplanes, and computers. Major imports include cars, trucks, petroleum, electronics, and clothing. Why does a

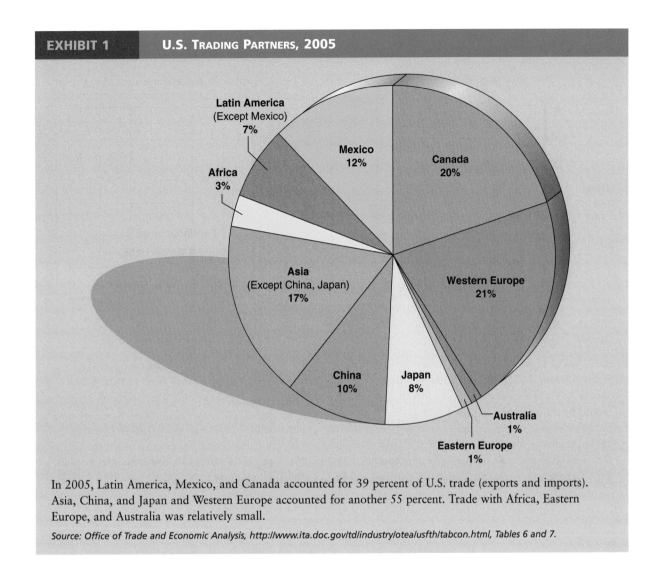

**EXHIBIT 1**     **U.S. Trading Partners, 2005**

In 2005, Latin America, Mexico, and Canada accounted for 39 percent of U.S. trade (exports and imports). Asia, China, and Japan and Western Europe accounted for another 55 percent. Trade with Africa, Eastern Europe, and Australia was relatively small.

*Source: Office of Trade and Economic Analysis, http://www.ita.doc.gov/td/industry/otea/usfth/tabcon.html, Tables 6 and 7.*

nation even bother to trade with the rest of the world? Does it seem strange for the United States to import goods it could produce for itself? Indeed, why doesn't the United States become self-sufficient by growing all its own food, including bananas, sugar, and coffee, making all its own cars, and prohibiting sales of all foreign goods? This section explains why specialization and trade are a nation's keys to a higher standard of living.

## THE PRODUCTION POSSIBILITIES CURVE REVISITED

Consider a world with only two countries—the United States and Japan. To keep the illustration simple, also assume *both* countries produce only two goods—grain and steel. Accordingly, we can construct in Exhibit 2 a *production possibilities curve* for each country. We will also set aside the *law of increasing opportunity*

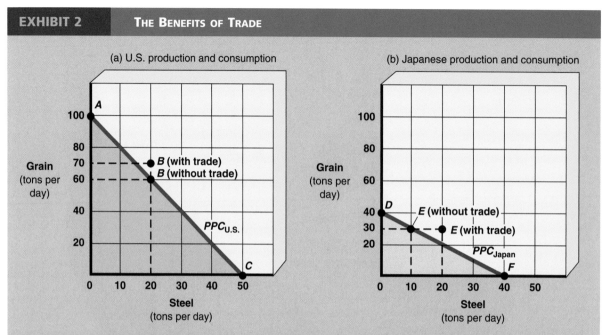

**EXHIBIT 2         THE BENEFITS OF TRADE**

As shown in Part (a), assume the United States chooses point *B* on its production possibilities curve, *PPC*$_{U.S.}$. Without trade, the United States produces and consumes 60 tons of grain and 20 tons of steel. In Part (b), assume Japan also operates along its production possibilities curve, *PPC*$_{Japan}$, at point *E*. Without trade, Japan produces and consumes 30 tons of grain and 10 tons of steel.

Now assume the United States specializes in producing grain at point *A* and imports 20 tons of Japanese steel in exchange for 30 tons of grain. Through specialization and trade, the United States moves to consumption possibility point *B'*, outside its production possibilities curve. Japan also moves to a higher standard of living at consumption possibility point *E'*, outside its production possibilities curve.

*costs*, explained in Chapter 2, and assume workers are equally suited to producing grain or steel. This assumption transforms the bowed-out shape of the production possibilities curve into a straight line.

Comparing Parts (a) and (b) of Exhibit 2 shows that the United States can produce more grain than Japan. If the United States devotes all its resources to this purpose, 100 tons of grain are produced per day, represented by point *A* in Exhibit 2(a). The maximum grain production of Japan, on the other hand, is only 40 tons per day because Japan has less labor, land, and other factors of production than the United States. This capability is represented by point *D* in Exhibit 2(b).

Now consider the capacities of the two countries for producing steel. If all their respective resources are devoted to this output, the United States produces 50 tons per day (point *C*), and Japan produces only 40 tons per day (point *F*). Again, the greater potential maximum steel output of the United States reflects its greater resources. Both countries are also capable of producing other combinations of grain and steel along their respective production possibilities curves, such as point *B* for the United States and point *E* for Japan.

## SPECIALIZATION WITHOUT TRADE

Assuming no world trade, the production possibilities curve for each country also defines its *consumption possibilities*. Stated another way, we assume that both countries are *self-sufficient* because without imports they must consume only the combination chosen along their production possibilities curve. Under the assumption of self-sufficiency, suppose the United States prefers to produce and consume 60 tons of grain and 20 tons of steel per day (point *B*). Also assume Japan chooses to produce and consume 30 tons of grain and 10 tons of steel (point *E*). Exhibit 3 lists data corresponding to points *B* and *E* and shows that the total world output is 90 tons of grain and 30 tons of steel.

Now suppose the United States specializes by producing and consuming at point *A* rather than point *B*. Suppose also that Japan specializes by producing and consuming at point *F* rather than point *E*. As shown in Exhibit 3, specialization in each country increases total world output per day by 10 tons of grain and 10 tons of steel. Because this extra world output has the potential for making both countries better off, why wouldn't the United States and Japan specialize and produce at points *A* and *F*, respectively? The reason is that although production at these points is clearly possible, neither country wants to consume these combinations of output. The United States prefers to consume less grain and more steel at point *B* compared to point *A*. Japan, on the other hand, prefers to consume more grain and less steel at point *E* rather than point *F*.

> **CONCLUSION** *When countries specialize, total world output increases, and, therefore, the potential for greater total world consumption also increases.*

## SPECIALIZATION WITH TRADE

Now let's return to Exhibit 2 and demonstrate how world trade benefits countries. Suppose the United States agrees to specialize in grain production at point

| EXHIBIT 3 | EFFECT OF SPECIALIZATION ON WORLD OUTPUT | |
|---|---|---|
| | Grain production (tons per day) | Steel production (tons per day) |
| *Before specialization* | | |
| United States (at point *B*) | 60 | 20 |
| Japan (at point *E*) | 30 | 10 |
| Total world output | 90 | 30 |
| *After specialization* | | |
| United States (at point *A*) | 100 | 0 |
| Japan (at point *F*) | 0 | 40 |
| Total world output | 100 | 40 |

*A* and to import 20 tons of Japanese steel in exchange for 30 tons of its grain output. Does the United States gain from trade? The answer is Yes. At point *A*, the United States produces 100 tons of grain per day. Subtracting the 30 tons of grain traded to Japan leaves the United States with 70 tons of its own grain production to consume. In return for grain, Japan unloads 20 tons of steel on U.S. shores. Hence, specialization and trade allow the United States to move from point *A* to point *B′*, which is a consumption possibility *outside* its production possibilities curve in Exhibit 2(a). At point *B′*, the United States consumes the same amount of steel and 10 more tons of grain compared to point *B* (without trade).

Japan also has an incentive to specialize by moving its production mix from point *E* to point *F*. With trade, Japan's consumption will be at point *E′*. At point *E′*, Japan has as much grain to consume as it had at point *E*, plus 10 more tons of steel. After trading 20 tons of the 40 tons of steel produced at point *F* for grain, Japan can still consume 20 tons of steel from its production, rather than only 10 tons of steel at point *E*. Thus, point *E′* is a consumption possibility that lies *outside* Japan's production possibilities curve.

> **CONCLUSION** *International trade allows a country to consume a combination of goods that exceeds its production possibilities curve.*

# Comparative and Absolute Advantage

Why did the United States decide to produce and export grain instead of steel? Why did Japan choose to produce steel, rather than grain? Here you study the economic principle that determines specialization and trade.

## COMPARATIVE ADVANTAGE

**Comparative advantage**
The ability of a country to produce a good at a lower opportunity cost than another country.

Engaging in world trade permits countries to escape the prison of their own production possibilities curves by producing bread, cars, or whatever goods they make best. The decision of the United States to specialize in and export grain and the decision of Japan to specialize in and export steel are based on **comparative advantage**. Comparative advantage is the ability of a country to produce a good at a lower opportunity cost than another country. Continuing our earlier example, we can calculate opportunity costs for the two countries and use comparative advantage to determine which country should specialize in grain and which in steel. For the United States, the opportunity cost of producing 50 tons of steel is 100 tons of grain not produced, so 1 ton of steel costs 2 tons of grain. For Japan, the opportunity cost of producing 40 tons of steel is 40 tons of grain, so 1 ton of steel costs 1 ton of grain. Japan's steel is therefore cheaper in terms of grain forgone. This means Japan has a comparative advantage in steel production because it must give up less grain to produce steel than the United States. Stated differently, the opportunity cost of steel production is lower in Japan than in the United States.

The other side of the coin is to measure the cost of grain in terms of steel. For the United States, 1 ton of grain costs 1/2 ton of steel. For Japan, 1 ton of grain costs 1 ton of steel. The United States has a comparative advantage in grain because its opportunity cost in terms of steel forgone is lower. Thus, the United

States should specialize in grain because it is more efficient in grain production. Japan, on the other hand, is relatively more efficient at producing steel and should specialize in this product.

> **CONCLUSION** *Comparative advantage refers to the relative opportunity costs between different countries producing the same goods. World output and consumption are maximized when each country specializes in producing and trading goods for which it has a comparative advantage.*

## ABSOLUTE ADVANTAGE

So far, a country's production and international trade decisions depend on comparing what a country gives up to produce more of a good. It is important to note that comparative advantage is based on opportunity costs, regardless of the absolute costs of resources used in production. We have not considered how much labor, land, or capital either the United States or Japan uses to produce a ton of grain or steel. For example, Japan might have an **absolute advantage** in producing *both* grain and steel. Absolute advantage is the ability of a country to produce a good using fewer resources than another country. In our example, Japan might use fewer resources per ton to produce grain and steel than the United States. Maybe the Japanese work harder or are more skilled. In short, the Japanese may be more productive producers, but their absolute advantage does not matter in specialization and world trade decisions. If the United States has a comparative advantage in grain, it should specialize in grain even if Japan can produce both grain and steel with fewer resources.

**Absolute advantage**
The ability of a country to produce a good using fewer resources than another country.

Perhaps another example will clarify the difference between absolute advantage and comparative advantage. When Babe Ruth played for the New York Yankees, he was the best hitter and the best pitcher, not only on the team, but in all of major league baseball. In fact, before Ruth was traded to the Yankees and switched to the outfield, he was the best left-handed pitcher in the American League for a few seasons with the Boston Red Sox. His final record was 99–46. In other words, he had an *absolute advantage* in both hitting and throwing the baseball. Stated differently, Babe Ruth could produce the same home runs as any

## CHECKPOINT

### Do Nations with an Advantage Always Trade?

Comparing labor productivity, suppose the United States has an absolute advantage over China in the production of calculators and towels. In the United States, a worker can produce 4 calculators or 400 towels in 10 hours. In China, a worker can produce 1 calculator or 100 towels in the same time. Under these conditions, are specialization and trade advantageous?

other teammate with fewer times at bat. The problem was that if he pitched, he would bat fewer times because pitchers need rest after pitching. The coaches decided that the Babe had a *comparative advantage* in hitting. A few pitchers on the team could pitch almost as well as the Babe, but no one could touch his hitting. In terms of opportunity costs, the Yankees would lose fewer games if the Babe specialized in hitting.

# Free Trade versus Protectionism

**Free trade**
The flow of goods between countries without restrictions or special taxes.

**Protectionism**
The government's use of embargoes, tariffs, quotas, and other restrictions to protect domestic producers from foreign competition.

**Embargo**
A law that bars trade with another country.

**Tariff**
A tax on an import.

In theory, international trade should be based on comparative advantage and **free trade**. Free trade is the flow of goods between countries without restrictions or special taxes. In practice, despite the advice of economists, every nation protects its own domestic producers to some degree from foreign competition. Behind these barriers to trade are special-interest groups whose jobs and incomes are threatened, so they clamor to the government for **protectionism**. Protectionism is the government's use of embargoes, tariffs, quotas, and other restrictions to protect domestic producers from foreign competition.

## EMBARGO

**Embargoes** are the strongest limit on trade. An embargo is a law that bars trade with another country. For example, the United States and other nations in the world imposed an arms embargo on Iraq in response to its invasion of Kuwait in 1990. The United States also maintains embargoes against Cuba and North Korea.

## TARIFF

**Tariffs** are the most popular and visible measures used to discourage trade. A tariff is a tax on an import. Tariffs are also called customs duties. Suppose the United States imposes a tariff of 2.9 percent on autos. If a foreign car costs $40,000, the amount of the tariff equals $1,160 ($40,000 × 0.029), and the U.S. price, including the tariff, is $41,160. The current U.S. tariff code specifies tariffs on nearly 70 percent of U.S. imports. A tariff can be based on weight, volume, or number of units, or it can be *ad valorem* (figured as a percentage of the price). The average U.S. tariff is less than 5 percent, but individual tariffs vary widely. Tariffs are imposed to reduce imports by raising import prices and to generate revenues for the U.S. Treasury. Exhibit 4 shows the trend of the average tariff rate since 1930.

During the worldwide depression of the 1930s, when one nation raised its tariffs to protect its industries, other nations retaliated by raising their tariffs. Under the Smoot-Hawley tariffs of the 1930s, the average tariff in the United States reached a peak of 20 percent. (One third of imports was subject to an unbelievable tariff rate of 60 percent). In 1947, most of the world's industrialized nations mutually agreed to end the tariff wars by signing the *General Agreement on Tariffs and Trade (GATT)*. Since then, GATT nations have met periodically to negotiate lower tariff rates. GATT agreements have significantly reduced tariffs over the years among member nations. In the 1994 *Uruguay round*, member nations signed a GATT agreement that decreased tariffs and reduced other trade barriers. The most divisive element of this agreement was the creation in 1995 of the

| EXHIBIT 4 | THE UNITED STATES AVERAGE TARIFF RATE, 1930–2005 |
|---|---|

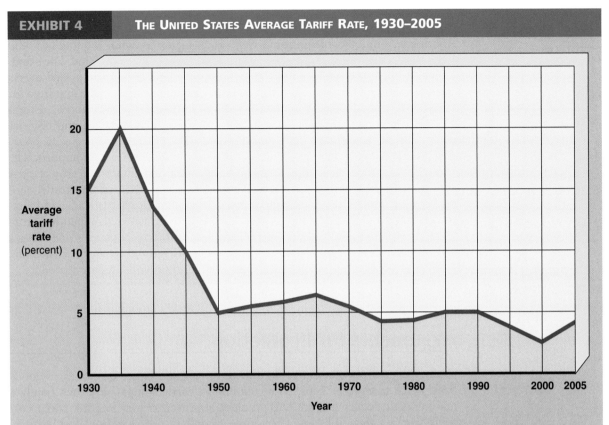

Under the Smoot-Hawley Act of 1930, the average tariff rate peaked at 20 percent. Since the GATT in 1947 and other trade agreements, tariffs have declined to less than 5 percent.

*Sources:* Economic Report of the President, *1989, http://www.gpo.access.gov/eop/, p. 152, and United States International Trade Commission,* The Economic Effect of Significant U.S. Import Restraints, *June 2002, p. 146, and Trade Profiles, http://stat.wto.org/CountryProfiles/US_e.htm.*

Geneva-based **World Trade Organization (WTO)** to enforce rulings in global trade disputes. The WTO has more than 149 members and a standing appellate body to render final decisions regarding disputes between WTO members. Critics fear that the WTO might be far more likely to rule in favor of other countries in their trade disputes with the United States. Some people argue that the WTO is unaccountable, and these critics reject free trade and globalization.

To illustrate a recent interesting case, the United States imposed tariffs in 2002 on steel imports to protect jobs in the struggling U.S. steel industry against foreign competition. The WTO ruled these tariffs were illegal, and countries in Europe and Asia prepared a list of retaliatory tariffs. These levies targeted products such as citrus fruit grown in Florida and apparel produced in southern states crucial to President Bush's reelection. Meanwhile, U.S. automakers and other steel-consuming industries complained because the tariffs increased their costs. Facing these threats, the United States removed the tariffs on steel imports in 2003. It is interesting to compare this case to the You're the Economist titled World Trade Slips on Banana Peel.

**World Trade Organization (WTO)**
An international organization of member countries that oversees international trade agreements and rules on trade disputes.

## QUOTA

**Quota**
A limit on the quantity of a good that may be imported in a given time period.

Another way to limit foreign competition is to impose a **quota**. A quota is a limit on the quantity of a good that may be imported in a given time period. For example, the United States may allow 10 million tons of sugar to be imported over a one-year period. Once this quantity is reached, no more sugar can be imported for the year. About 12 percent of U.S. imports are subject to import quotas. Examples include import quotas on sugar, dairy products, textiles, steel, and even ice cream. Quotas can limit imports from all foreign suppliers or from specific countries. In 2005, for example, global quotas were lifted from Chinese imports. The United States and other European countries demanded quotas to protect their countries from Chinese textiles. Critics argue that, like all barriers to trade, quotas invite nations to retaliate with their own measures to restrict trade, and consumers are harmed by higher prices because of the lack of competition from lower-priced imports. In addition to embargoes, tariffs, and quotas, some nations use subtler measures to discourage trade, such as setting up an overwhelming number of bureaucratic steps that must be taken in order to import a product.

# Arguments for Protection

Free trade provides consumers with lower prices and larger quantities of goods from which to choose. Thus, removing import barriers might save each family a few hundred dollars a year. The problem, however, is that imports could cost some workers their jobs and thousands of dollars per year from lost income. Thus, it is no wonder that, in spite of the greater total benefits from free trade to consumers, trade barriers exist. The reason is primarily because workers and owners from import-competing firms have more at stake than consumers, so they go to Washington and lobby for protection. The following are some of the most popular arguments for protection. These arguments have strong political or emotional appeal, but weak support from economists.

## INFANT INDUSTRY ARGUMENT

As the name suggests, the *infant industry argument* is that a new domestic industry needs protection because it is not yet ready to compete with established foreign competitors. An infant industry is in a formative stage and must bear high start-up costs to train an entire workforce, develop new technology, establish marketing channels, and reach economies of scale. With time to grow and protection, an infant industry can reduce costs and "catch up" with established foreign firms.

Economists ask where one draws the arbitrary line between an "infant" and a "grown-up" industry. It is also difficult to make a convincing case for protecting an infant industry in a developed country, such as the United States, where industries are well established. The infant industry argument, however, may have some validity for less-developed countries. Yet, even for these countries, there is a danger. Once protection is granted, the new industry will not experience the competitive pressures necessary to encourage reasonably quick growth and participation in world trade. Also, once an industry is given protection, it is difficult to take it away.

## NATIONAL SECURITY ARGUMENT

Another common argument is that defense-related industries must be protected with embargoes, tariffs, and quotas to ensure national security. By protecting critical defense industries, a nation will not be dependent on foreign countries for the essential defense-related goods it needs to defend itself in wartime. The *national defense argument* has been used to protect a long list of industries, including petrochemicals, munitions, steel, and rubber.

This argument gained validity during the War of 1812. Great Britain, the main trading partner of the United States, became an enemy that blockaded our coast. Today, this argument makes less sense for the United States. The government stockpiles missiles, sophisticated electronics, petroleum, and most goods needed in wartime.

## EMPLOYMENT ARGUMENT

The *employment argument* suggests that restricting imports increases domestic jobs in protected industries. According to this protectionist argument, the sale of an imported good comes at the expense of its domestically produced counterpart. Lower domestic output therefore leads to higher domestic unemployment than would otherwise be the case.

It is true that protectionism can increase output and save jobs in some industries at home. Ignored, however, are the higher prices paid by consumers because protectionism reduces competition between domestic goods and imported goods. In addition, there are employment reduction effects to consider. For example, suppose a strict quota is imposed on steel imported into our nation. Reduced foreign competition allows U.S. steelmakers to charge higher prices for their steel. As a result, prices rise and sales fall for cars and other products using steel, causing production and employment to fall in these industries. Thus, the import quota on steel may save jobs in the steel industry but at the expense of more jobs lost in the steel-consuming industries. Also, by selling U.S. imports foreigners earn dollars that they can use to buy U.S. exports. Import quotas cause foreigners to have fewer dollars to spend on U.S. exports, resulting in a decrease in employment in U.S. export industries. In short, protectionism may cause a net reduction in the nation's total employment.

## CHEAP FOREIGN LABOR ARGUMENT

Another often heard popular claim is the *cheap labor argument*. It goes something like this: "How can we compete with such unfair competition? Labor costs $10 an hour in the United States, and firms in many developing countries pay only $1 an hour. Without protection against outsourcing our jobs, U.S. wages will be driven down, and our standard of living will fall."

A major flaw in this argument is that it neglects the reason for the difference in the wage rates between countries. A U.S. worker has more education, training, capital, and access to advanced technology. Therefore, if U.S. workers produce more output per hour than workers in another country, U.S. workers will earn higher wages without a competitive disadvantage. Suppose textile workers in the United States are paid $10 per hour. If a U.S. worker takes 1 hour to produce a rug, the labor cost per rug is $10. Now suppose a worker in India earns $1 per

## You're the Economist

# World Trade Slips on Banana Peel
*Applicable Concept: protectionism*

Growing bananas for European markets was a multibillion-dollar bright spot for Latin America's struggling economies. In fact, about half of this region's banana exports traditionally were sold to Europe. Then, in 1993, the European Union (EU) adopted a package of quotas and tariffs aimed at cutting Europe's banana imports from Latin America. The purpose of these restrictions was to give trade preference to 66 banana-growing former colonies of European nations in Africa, the Caribbean, and the Pacific. Ignored was the fact that growers in Latin America grow higher-quality bananas at half the cost of EU-favored growers because of their low labor costs and flat tropical land near port cities.[1]

In 1999, the World Trade Organization (WTO) ruled that the EU was discriminating in favor of European companies importing the fruit and the WTO imposed $191.4 million per year in punitive tariffs on European goods. This was the first time in the four years the WTO had been in existence that such retaliation had been approved, and only the second time going back to its predecessor, the General Agreement on Tariffs and Trade. When the EU failed to comply with the WTO findings, the United States enforced its WTO rights by imposing increased duties on EU imports including goods ranging from cashmere sweaters and Italian handbags to sheep's milk cheese, British biscuits, and German coffeemakers. The effect of the U.S. sanctions was to double the wholesale prices of these items. Denmark and the Netherlands were exempt from the U.S. tariffs because they were the only nations that voted against the EU banana rules.

Critics charged that the United States was pushing the case for political reasons. American companies, including Chiquita Brands International and Dole Food Company, grow most of their bananas in Latin America. With America's trade deficit running at a record level, U.S. trade experts also argued that the United States had little choice but to act against the EU for failing to abide by the WTO's ruling. Moreover, with increasing voices in the United States questioning the wisdom of international trade and globalization, it was important that the WTO prove that it can arbitrate these disputes.

In 2001, it appeared that the banana dispute might be resolved. The EU agreed to increase market access for U.S. banana distributors, and the United States lifted its retaliatory duties on EU products. The agreement also provided that the United States could reimpose the duties if the EU did not complete its phased-in reductions in restrictions on banana imports.[2]

And the banana story just keeps "slipping along."

*European Union anti-fraud officials say that illegal banana trafficking is proving more lucrative than that in cocaine. A recently exposed scheme saw Italian banana importers use false licenses to pay greatly reduced customs duties on non-quota fruit. The fraud netted smugglers hundreds of millions of euros over a two-year period. Italian public prosecutor, Fabio Scavone, says more is being made from simple customs fraud than from serious crimes such as narcotics trafficking.[3]*

And in 2004, Latin American growers again complained that the EU was discriminating against their bananas in favor of producers from African and Caribbean countries. Under the 2001 WTO ruling, the EU was compelled to replace its complex quota and tariff system on bananas with a tariff-only regime. So the EU placed a 75 Euro tariff on Latin American suppliers to get into the EU market, while bananas from African and Caribbean countries are duty-free. An EU report, supported by large EU members such as France and the United Kingdom, proposed a 230 Euro tariff on all banana imports. A memorandum issued by the Swedish government attacked the "considerable overprice" European consumers pay for banana protection.[4]

### ANALYZE THE ISSUE

Make an argument in favor of the European import restrictions. Make an argument against this plan.

[1]James Brooke, "Forbidden Fruit in Europe: Latin Bananas Face Hurdles," *The New York Times*, April 5, 1993, p. A1.
[2]"U.S. Lifts Sanctions in Banana War," *The Food Institute Report*, July 9, 2001, p. 9.
[3]"Banana Scam Beats Cocaine," *Australian Business Intelligence*, July 24, 2002.
[4]"Bananas: Commission Proposes New Import Tariff at Euro 230 a Ton," *European Report*, Oct. 30, 2004, p. 506.

hour, but requires 20 hours to produce a rug on a handloom. In this case, the labor cost per rug is $20. Although the wage rate is 10 times higher in the United States, U.S. productivity is 20 times higher because a U.S. worker can produce 20 rugs in 20 hours, while the worker in India produces only 1 rug in the same amount of time.

Sometimes U.S. companies move their operations to foreign countries where labor is cheaper. Such moves are not always successful because the savings from paying foreign workers a lower wage rate are offset by lower productivity. Other disadvantages of foreign operations include greater transportation costs to U.S. markets and political instability.

# Free Trade Agreements

The trend in recent years has been for nations to negotiate a reduction in trade barriers. In 1993, Congress approved the *North American Free Trade Agreement (NAFTA)*, which linked the United States to its first- and third-largest trading partners, Canada and Mexico. Under NAFTA, which became effective January 1, 1994, tariffs will be phased out over 15 years, and other impediments to trade and investment are being eliminated among the three nations. For example, elimination of trade restrictions allows the United States to supply Mexico with more U.S. goods and to boost U.S. jobs. On the other hand, NAFTA was expected to raise Mexico's wages and standard of living by increasing Mexican exports to the United States. Note that NAFTA made no changes in restrictions on labor movement and workers must enter the United States under a limited immigration quota or illegally. The success of NAFTA remains controversial. At the conclusion of this chapter, we will use data to examine its impact.

The United States and other countries are considering other free trade agreements. In Europe, 25 nations have joined the *European Union (EU)*, which is dedicated to removing all trade barriers within Europe and thereby creating a single European economy almost as large as the U.S. economy. See the Birth of the Euro box insert in this chapter.

The *Asian-Pacific Economic Cooperation (APEC)* was formed in 1989 and today has 21 member nations, including China, Hong Kong, Russia, Taiwan, and Mexico. This organization is based on a nonbinding agreement to reduce trade barriers between member nations.

In 2003, trade ministers from 34 nations met in Miami to create a plan for the world's largest free-trade area that would tear down trade barriers from Alaska to Argentina. The Free Trade Area of the Americas (FTAA) would span the Western Hemisphere except Cuba. In 2005, the Central American Free Trade Agreement (CAFTA) extended the free trade zone to six Central American countries that signed, including Costa Rica, Guatemala, El Salvador, Honduras, Nicaragua, and Dominican Republic. The success or failure of CAFTA will have an impact on future negotiation for FTAA.

Critics are concerned that regional free trade accords will make global agreements increasingly difficult to achieve. Some fear that trading blocs may erect new barriers, creating "Fortress North America," "Fortress Europe," and similar impediments to the worldwide reduction of trade barriers.

# Birth of the Euro

In 1958, several European nations formed a Common Market to eliminate trade restrictions among member countries. The Common Market called for gradual removal of tariffs and import quotas on goods traded among member nations. Later the name was changed to the European Economic Community (EEC), and it is now called the European Union (EU). This organization established a common system of tariffs for imports from non-member nations and created common policies for economic matters of joint concern, such as agriculture and transportation. The EU now comprises 25 nations listed in the table.

In 1999, 11 European countries, joined later by Greece, followed the United States as an example and united in the *European Monetary Union (EMU)*, also shown in the table. In the United States, 50 states are linked with a common currency, and the Federal Reserve serves as the central bank by conducting monetary policy for the nation. Among the states, trade, labor, and investment enjoy freedom of movement. In 2002, the EMU members replaced their national currencies with a single currency, the euro. The objective is to remove exchange rate fluctuations that impede cross-border transactions. This is why the U.S. Congress created a national currency in 1863 to replace state and private bank currencies.

The EMU faces many unanswered questions. Unlike the states of the United States, the EMU's 12 member nations do not share a common language or governments. This makes maintaining common macro policies difficult. France, for example, might seek to control inflation, while Germany has reducing unemployment as its highest priority.

Coordinating monetary policy among EMU nations is also difficult. Although the EMU has established the *European Central Bank* with sole authority over the supply of euros, the central banks of member nations still function. But these national central banks operate similar to the district banks of the Federal Reserve System in the United States. Only time will tell whether EMU nations will perform better with a single currency than with separate national currencies. It is possible that the euro could become a strong alternative to the U.S. dollar as a key currency for the global financial systems.

© Image 100/Jupiterimages

| European Union (EU) Members | | European Monetary Union (EMU) Members |
|---|---|---|
| Austria | Latvia | Austria |
| Belgium | Lithuania | Belgium |
| Cyprus | Luxembourg | Finland |
| Czech Republic | Malta | France |
| Denmark | Netherlands | Germany |
| Estonia | Poland | Greece |
| Finland | Portugal | Ireland |
| France | Slovakia | Italy |
| Germany | Slovenia | Luxembourg |
| Greece | Spain | Netherlands |
| Hungary | Sweden | Portugal |
| Ireland | United Kingdom | Spain |
| Italy | | |

# The Balance of Payments

When trade occurs between the United States and other nations, many types of financial transactions are recorded in a summary called the **balance of payments**. The balance of payments is a bookkeeping record of all the international transactions between a country and other countries during a given period of time. This summary is the best way to understand interactions between economies because it records the value of a nation's spending inflows and outflows made by individuals, firms, and governments. Exhibit 5 presents a simplified U.S. balance of payments for 2005.

Note the pluses and minuses in the table. A transaction that is a payment to the United States is entered as a positive amount. A payment by the United States to another country is entered with a minus sign. As our discussion unfolds, you will learn that the balance of payments provides much useful information.

**Balance of payments**
A bookkeeping record of all the international transactions between a country and other countries during a given period of time.

## CURRENT ACCOUNT

The first section of the balance of payments is the *current account*, which includes, as the name implies, trade in currently produced goods and services. The most widely reported and largest part of the current account is the **balance of trade**, also called the trade balance. The balance of trade is the value of a nation's goods imports subtracted from its goods exports. As shown in Exhibit 4, the United States had a *balance of trade deficit* of −$781 billion in 2005. A trade deficit

**Balance of trade**
The value of a nation's goods imports subtracted from its goods exports.

| EXHIBIT 5 | U.S. BALANCE OF PAYMENTS, 2005 (BILLIONS OF DOLLARS) | |
|---|---|---|
| **Type of transaction** | | |
| *Current account* | | |
| 1. | Goods exports | $ +893 |
| 2. | Goods imports | −1,674 |
| | Trade balance (lines 1–2) | −781 |
| 3. | Service exports | +380 |
| 4. | Service imports | −322 |
| 5. | Investment income (net) | +2 |
| 6. | Unilateral transfers (net) | −83 |
| | Current account balance (lines 1–6) | −804 |
| *Capital account* | | |
| 7. | U.S. capital inflow | +1,293 |
| 8. | U.S. capital outflow | −491 |
| | Capital account balance (lines 7–8) | +802 |
| 9. | Statistical discrepancy | +2 |
| | Net balance (lines 1–9) | 0 |

Source: Bureau of Economic Analysis, U.S. International Transactions Accounts Data, http://www.bea.doc.gov/, Table 1.

occurs when the value of a country's imports of goods (not services) exceeds the value of its exports of goods. When a nation has a trade deficit, it is called an *unfavorable balance of trade* because more is spent for imports than is earned from exports. Recall that net exports can have a positive (favorable) or negative (unfavorable) effect on GDP = $C + I + G + (X - M)$.

Exhibit 6 charts the annual balance of trade for the United States from 1975 through 2005. Observe that the United States experienced a *balance of trade surplus* in 1975. A trade surplus arises when the value of a country's merchandise exports is greater than the value of its merchandise imports. This is called a *favorable balance of trade* because the United States earned more from exports than it spent for imports. Since 1975, however, sizable trade deficits have occurred. These trade deficits have attracted much attention because in part they reflect the popularity of foreign goods and the lack of competitiveness of goods "Made in U.S.A."

| EXHIBIT 6 | U.S. BALANCE OF TRADE, 1975–2005 |
|---|---|

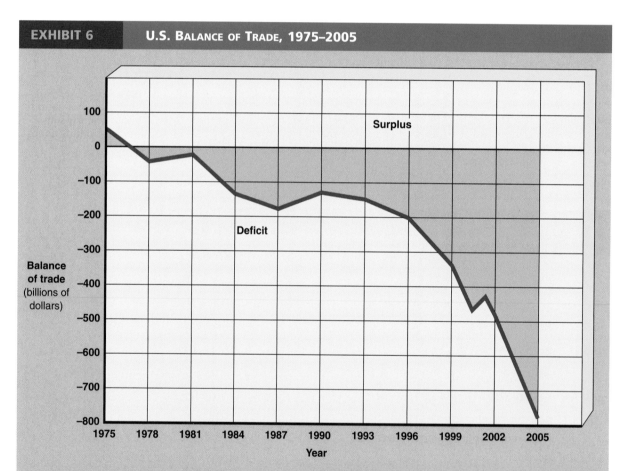

Since 1975, the United States has experienced trade deficits, in which the value of goods imports has exceeded the value of exports. These goods trade deficits attract much attention because in part they reflect the popularity of foreign goods in the United States. During the recession in 2001, the U.S. trade deficit narrowed as spending for imports fell relative to exports. As the U.S. economy recovered, the deficit continued to grow to an all-time high of about $800 billion in 2005.

*Source: Bureau of Economic Analysis,* International Transactions Accounts Data, *http://www.bea.gov/, Table 1.*

In 2001, the U.S. trade deficit narrowed slightly due to the recession. Because of this weakness in the economy, spending for imports fell slightly relative to exports and the gap was reduced. By the end of 2005, the U.S. trade deficit reached an all-time high of almost $800 billion due in part to the recovery of the U.S. economy, which boosted U.S. demand foreign-made goods. Conversely, foreign countries were not growing fast enough to sufficiently stimulate U.S. exports. The trade deficit also reflected record oil purchases as the price of oil increased sharply.

Lines 3–6 of the current account in Exhibit 5 list ways other than goods to move dollars back and forth between the United States and other countries. For example, a Japanese tourist who pays a hotel bill in Hawaii buys an export of services, which is a plus or credit to our current account (line 3). Similarly, an American visitor to foreign lands buys an import of services, which is a minus or debit to our services and therefore a minus to our current account (line 4). Income flowing back from U.S. investments abroad, such as plants, real estate, and securities, is a payment for use of the services of U.S. capital. Foreign countries also receive income flowing from the services of their capital owned in the United States. In 2005, line 5 of the table reports a net flow of $2 billion to the United States.

Finally, we consider line 6, unilateral transfers. This category includes gifts made by our government, charitable organizations, or private individuals to other governments or private parties elsewhere in the world. For example, this item includes U.S. foreign aid to other nations. Similar unilateral transfers into the United States must be subtracted to determine the *net* unilateral transfers. Net unilateral transfers for the United States were −$83 billion in 2005.

Adding lines 1–6 gives the current account balance deficit of −$804 billion in 2005. This deficit means that foreigners sent us more goods and services than we sent to them. Because the current account balance includes *both* goods and services, it is a broader measure than the trade balance. Since 1982, the trend in the current account balance has followed the swing into the red shown by the trade balance in Exhibit 6.

## CAPITAL ACCOUNT

The second section of the balance of payments is the *capital account*, which records payment flows for financial capital, such as real estate, corporate stocks, bonds, government securities, and other debt instruments. For example, when Japanese investors buy U.S. Treasury bills, Rockefeller Center, or farmland in Hawaii, there is an inflow of dollars into the United States. As Exhibit 5 shows, foreigners made payments of $1,293 billion to our capital account (line 7). This exceeded the −$491 billion outflow (line 8) from the United States to purchase foreign-owned financial capital.

An important feature of the capital account is that the United States finances any deficit in its current account through this account. The capital account balance in 2005 was $802 billion. This surplus indicates that there was more foreign investment in U.S. assets than U.S. investment in foreign assets during this year.

> **CONCLUSION** *A current account deficit is financed by a capital account surplus.*

The current account deficit should equal the capital account surplus, but line 9 in the exhibit reveals that the balance of payments is not perfect. The capital account balance does not exactly offset the current account balance. Hence, a credit amount is simply recorded as a statistical discrepancy; therefore, the balance of payments always balances, or equals zero.

## THE INTERNATIONAL DEBT OF THE UNITED STATES

If each nation's balance of payments is always zero, why is there so much talk about a U.S. balance of payments problem? The problem is with the *composition* of the balance of payments. Suppose the United States runs a $500 billion deficit in its current account. This means that the current account deficit must be financed by a net annual capital inflow in the capital account of $500 billion. That is, foreign lenders, such as banks and businesses, must purchase U.S. assets and grant loans to the United States that on balance equal $500 billion. For example, a Japanese bank could buy U.S. Treasury bonds. Recall from Exhibit 7 in the chapter on federal deficits and the national debt that the portion of the national debt owed to lenders outside the United States is called *external debt*.

In 1984, the United States became a net debtor for the first time in about 70 years. This means that investments in the United States accumulated by foreigners—stocks, bonds, real estate, and so forth—exceeded the stock of foreign assets owned by the United States. In fact, during the decade of the 1980s, the United States moved from being the world's largest creditor nation to being the largest debtor nation.

Exhibit 7 shows that the United States has its largest trade deficits with China, Japan, and Canada. The concern over continuing trade deficits and the rising international debt that accompanies them is that the United States is artificially enjoying a higher standard of living. When the United States continues to purchase more goods and services abroad than it exports, it might find itself "enjoying now and paying later." Suppose the Japanese and other foreigners decide not to make new U.S. investments and loans. In this case, the United States will be forced to eliminate its trade deficit by bringing exports and imports into balance. In fact, if other countries not only refuse to provide new capital inflows, but also decide to liquidate their investments, the United States would be forced to run a trade surplus. Stated differently, we would be forced to tighten our belts and accept a lower standard of living. How a change in foreign willingness to purchase U.S. assets also affects the international value of the dollar is the topic to which we now turn.

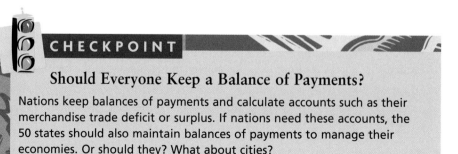

## CHECKPOINT

### Should Everyone Keep a Balance of Payments?

Nations keep balances of payments and calculate accounts such as their merchandise trade deficit or surplus. If nations need these accounts, the 50 states should also maintain balances of payments to manage their economies. Or should they? What about cities?

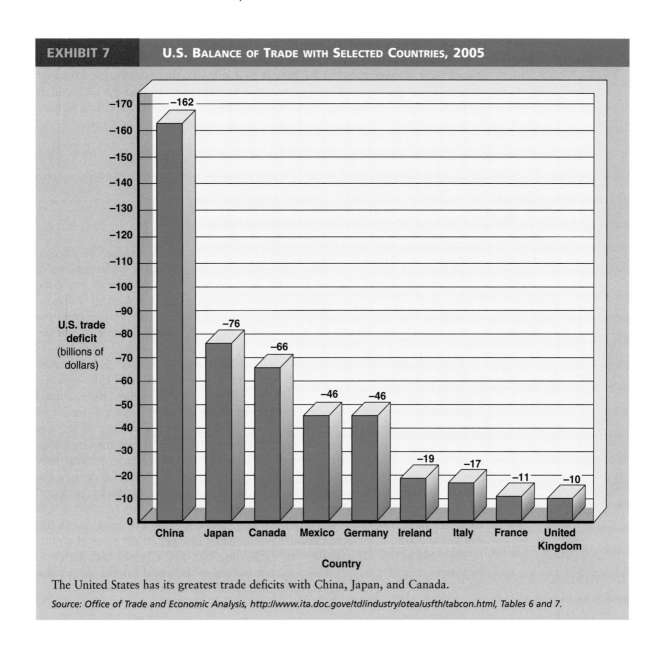

**EXHIBIT 7** — **U.S. BALANCE OF TRADE WITH SELECTED COUNTRIES, 2005**

The United States has its greatest trade deficits with China, Japan, and Canada.

Source: Office of Trade and Economic Analysis, http://www.ita.doc.gov/td/industry/otea/usfth/tabcon.html, Tables 6 and 7.

# Exchange Rates

Each transaction recorded in the balance of payments requires an exchange of one country's currency for that of another. Suppose you buy a Japanese car made in Japan, say, a Mazda. Mazda wants to be paid in yen and not dollars, so dollars must be traded for yen. On the other hand, suppose Pink Panther Airline Company in France purchases an airplane from Boeing in the United States. Pink Panther has euros to pay the bill, but Boeing wants dollars. Consequently, euros must be exchanged for dollars.

The critical question for Mazda, Pink Panther, Boeing, and everyone involved in world trade is, "What is the **exchange rate**?" The exchange rate is the number

**Exchange rate**
The number of units of one nation's currency that equals one unit of another nation's currency.

of units of one nation's currency that equals one unit of another nation's currency. For example, assume 1.81 dollars can be exchanged for 1 British pound. This means the exchange rate is 1.81 dollars = 1 pound. Alternatively, the exchange rate can be expressed as a reciprocal. Dividing 1 British pound by 1.81 dollars gives 0.552 pound per dollar. Now suppose you are visiting England and want to buy a T-shirt with a price tag of 10 pounds. Knowing the exchange rate tells you the T-shirt costs $18.10 (10 pounds × $1.81/pound).

> **CONCLUSION**  *An exchange rate can be expressed as a reciprocal.*

## SUPPLY AND DEMAND FOR FOREIGN EXCHANGE

The exchange rate for dollars, or any nation's currency, is determined by international forces of supply and demand. For example, consider the exchange rate of yen to dollars, shown in Exhibit 8. Like the price and the quantity of any good traded in markets, the quantity of dollars exchanged is measured on the horizontal axis, and the price per unit is measured on the vertical axis. In this case, the price per unit is the value of the U.S. dollar expressed as the number of yen per dollar.

The demand for dollars in the world currency market comes from Japanese individuals, corporations, and governments that want to buy U.S. exports. Because the Japanese buyers must pay for U.S. exports with dollars, they *demand* to exchange their yen for dollars. As expected, the demand curve for dollars or any foreign currency is downward sloping. A decline in the number of yen per dollar means that one yen buys a larger portion of a dollar. This means U.S. goods and investment opportunities are less expensive to Japanese buyers because they must pay fewer yen for each dollar. Thus, as the yen price of dollars decreases, the quantity of dollars demanded by the Japanese to purchase Fords, stocks, land, and other U.S. products and investments increases. For example, suppose a CD recording of the hottest rock group has a $20 price tag. If the exchange rate is 200 yen to the dollar, a Japanese importer would pay 4,000 yen. If the price of dollars to Japanese buyers falls to 100 yen each, the same $20 CD will cost Japanese importers only 2,000 yen. This lower price causes Japanese buyers to increase their orders, which, in turn, increases the quantity of dollars demanded.

The supply curve of dollars is upward sloping. This curve shows the amount of dollars offered for exchange at various yen prices per dollar in the world currency exchange market. Similar to the demand for dollars, the supply of dollars in this market flows from individuals, corporations, and governments in the United States that want to buy Mazdas, stocks, land, and other products and investments from Japan. Because U.S. citizens must pay for the Japanese goods and services in yen, they must exchange dollars for yen. An example will illustrate why the supply curve of dollars slopes upward. Suppose a Nikon camera sells for 100,000 yen in Tokyo and the exchange rate is 100 yen per dollar or .01 dollar per yen ($1/100 yen). This means the camera costs an American tourist $1,000. Now assume the exchange rate rises to 250 yen per dollar or .004 dollar per yen ($1/250 yen). The camera will now cost the American buyer only $400. Because the prices of the Nikon camera and other Japanese products fall when the number of yen per dollar rises, Americans respond by purchasing more Japanese imports, which, in turn, increases the quantity of dollars supplied.

| EXHIBIT 8 | THE SUPPLY OF AND DEMAND FOR DOLLARS |

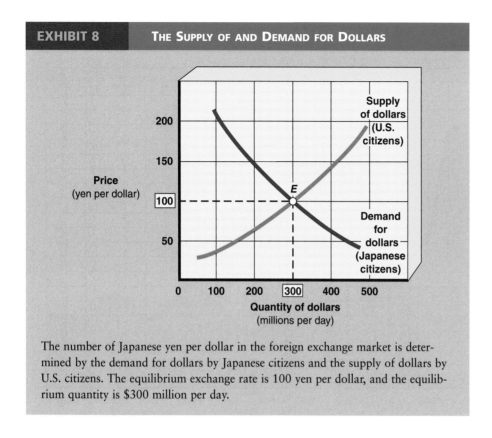

The number of Japanese yen per dollar in the foreign exchange market is determined by the demand for dollars by Japanese citizens and the supply of dollars by U.S. citizens. The equilibrium exchange rate is 100 yen per dollar, and the equilibrium quantity is $300 million per day.

The foreign exchange market in Exhibit 8 is in equilibrium at an exchange rate of 100 yen for $1. As you learned in Chapter 3, if the exchange rate is above equilibrium, there will be a surplus of dollars in the world currency market. Citizens of the United States are supplying more dollars than the Japanese demand, and the exchange rate falls. On the other hand, below equilibrium, there will be a shortage of dollars in the world currency market. In this case, the Japanese are demanding more dollars than Americans supply, and the exchange rate rises.

## SHIFTS IN SUPPLY AND DEMAND FOR FOREIGN EXCHANGE

For most of the years between World War II and 1971, currency exchange rates were *fixed*. Exchange rates were based primarily on gold. For example, the German mark was fixed at about 25 cents. The dollar was worth 1/35 of an ounce of gold, and 4 German marks were worth 1/35 of an ounce of gold. Therefore, 1 dollar equaled 4 marks, or 25 cents equaled 1 mark. In 1971, Western nations agreed to stop fixing their exchange rates and to allow their currencies to *float* according to the forces of supply and demand. Exhibit 9 illustrates that these rates can fluctuate widely. For example, in 1980, 1 dollar was worth about 230 Japanese yen. After gyrating up and down over the years, the exchange rate hit a postwar low of 94 yen per dollar in 1995. In 2005, the exchange rate was about 110 yen per dollar.

| EXHIBIT 9 | CHANGES IN THE YEN-PER-DOLLAR EXCHANGE RATE, 1980–2005 |

Today, most economies are on a system of flexible exchange rates. As the demand and supply curves for currencies change, exchange rates change. In 1980, 1 dollar was worth about 230 Japanese yen. By 1995, the
exchange rate had dropped to 94 yen per dollar. In 2005, a dollar was worth 110 Japanese yen.

*Source: Economic Report of the President, 2006, http://www.gpoaccess.gov/eopl, Table B-110.*

Recall from Chapter 3 that the equilibrium price for products changes in
response to shifts in the supply and demand curves. The same supply and demand
analysis applies to equilibrium exchange rates for foreign currency. There are four
important sources of shifts in the supply and demand curves for foreign exchange.
Let's consider each in turn.

**Tastes and Preferences**  Exhibit 10(a) illustrates one important factor that
causes the demand for foreign currencies to shift. Suppose the Japanese lose their
"taste" for tobacco, U.S. government bonds, and other U.S. products and investment opportunities. This decline in the popularity of U.S. products in Japan
decreases the demand for dollars at each possible exchange rate, and the demand
curve shifts leftward from $D_1$ to $D_2$. This change causes the equilibrium exchange
rate to fall from 150 yen to the dollar at $E_1$ to 100 yen to the dollar at $E_2$. Because
the number of yen to the dollar declines, the dollar is said to *depreciate* or become
*weaker*. **Depreciation of currency** is a fall in the price of one currency relative to
another.

**Depreciation
of currency**
A fall in the price of
one currency relative
to another.

**EXHIBIT 10**          **CHANGES IN THE SUPPLY AND DEMAND CURVES FOR DOLLARS**

CAUSATION CHAIN

| U.S. exports less popular | ⇨ | Decrease in the demand for dollars | ⇨ | Value of the dollar falls (dollar depreciates) |

CAUSATION CHAIN

| Japanese imports less popular | ⇨ | Decrease in the supply of dollars | ⇨ | Value of the dollar rises (dollar appreciates) |

In Part (a), U.S. exports become less popular in Japan. This change in tastes for U.S. products and investments decreases the demand for dollars, and the demand curve shifts leftward from $D_1$ to $D_2$. As a result, the equilibrium exchange rate falls from 150 yen to the dollar at $E_1$ to 100 yen to the dollar at $E_2$.

Part (b) assumes U.S. citizens are influenced by the "Buy American" idea. In this case, our demand for Japanese imports decreases, and U.S. citizens supply fewer dollars to the foreign currency market. The result is that the supply curve shifts leftward from $S_1$ to $S_2$, and the equilibrium exchange rate rises from 100 yen per dollar at $E_1$ to 150 yen per dollar at $E_2$.

What happens to the exchange rate if the "Buy American" idea changes our tastes and the demand for Japanese imports decreases? In this case, U.S. citizens supply fewer dollars at any possible exchange rate, and the supply curve in Exhibit 10(b) shifts leftward from $S_1$ to $S_2$. As a result, the equilibrium exchange rate rises from 100 yen to the dollar at $E_1$ to 150 yen to the dollar at $E_2$. Because the number of yen per dollar rises, the dollar is said to *appreciate* or become *stronger*. **Appreciation of currency** is a rise in the price of one currency relative to another.

**Relative Incomes**   Assume income in the United States rises, while income in Japan remains unchanged. As a result, U.S. citizens buy more domestic products and more Japanese imports. The results are a rightward shift in the supply curve for dollars and a decrease in the equilibrium exchange rate. Paradoxically, growth of U.S. income leads to the dollar depreciating, or becoming weaker, against the Japanese yen.

**Appreciation of currency**
A rise in the price of one currency relative to another.

> **CONCLUSION** *An expansion in relative U.S. income causes a deprecia-tion of the dollar.*

**Relative Price Levels**   Now we consider a more complex case, in which a change in a factor causes a change in both the supply and the demand curves for dollars. Assume the foreign exchange rate begins in equilibrium at 100 yen per dollar, as shown at point $E_1$ in Exhibit 11. Now assume the price level increases in Japan, but remains constant in the United States. The Japanese therefore want to buy more U.S. exports because they have become cheaper relative to Japanese prod-ucts. This willingness of the Japanese to buy U.S. goods and services shifts the demand curve for dollars rightward from $D_1$ to $D_2$. In addition, U.S. products are cheaper for U.S. citizens compared to Japanese imports. As a result, the willing-ness to import from Japan is reduced at each exchange rate, which means the sup-ply curve of dollars decreases from $S_1$ to $S_2$. The result of the shifts in both the demand and the supply curves for dollars is to establish a new equilibrium at point $E_2$, and the exchange rate reaches 200 yen per dollar.

> **CONCLUSION** *A rise in a trading partner's relative price level causes the dollar to appreciate.*

**Relative Real Interest Rates**   Changes in relative real (inflation-adjusted) inter-est rates can have an important effect on the exchange rate. Suppose real interest rates in the United States rise, while those in Japan remain constant. To take advantage of more attractive yields, Japanese investors buy an increased amount of bonds and other interest-bearing securities issued by private and government borrowers in the United States. This change increases the demand for dollars, which increases the equilibrium exchange rate of yen to the dollar, causing the dollar to appreciate (or the yen to depreciate).

There can also be an effect on the supply of dollars. When real interest rates rise in the United States, our citizens purchase fewer Japanese securities. Hence, they offer fewer dollars at each possible exchange rate, and the supply curve for dollars shifts leftward. As a result, the equilibrium exchange rate increases, and the dollar appreciates from changes in both the demand for and the supply of dollars.

## THE IMPACT OF EXCHANGE RATE FLUCTUATIONS

Now it is time to stop for a minute, take a breath, and draw some important con-clusions. As you have just learned, exchange rates between most major currencies are flexible. Instead of being pegged to gold or another fixed standard, their value is determined by the laws of supply and demand. Consequently, shifts in supply and demand create a weaker or a stronger dollar. But it should be noted that exchange rates do not fluctuate with total freedom. Governments often buy and sell currencies to prevent wide swings in exchange rates. In summary, the strength or weakness of any nation's currency has a profound impact on its economy.

A weak dollar is a "mixed blessing." Ironically, a weak dollar makes U.S. pro-ducers happy because they can sell their less expensive exports to foreign buyers.

## EXHIBIT 11 — THE IMPACT OF RELATIVE PRICE LEVEL CHANGES ON EXCHANGE RATES

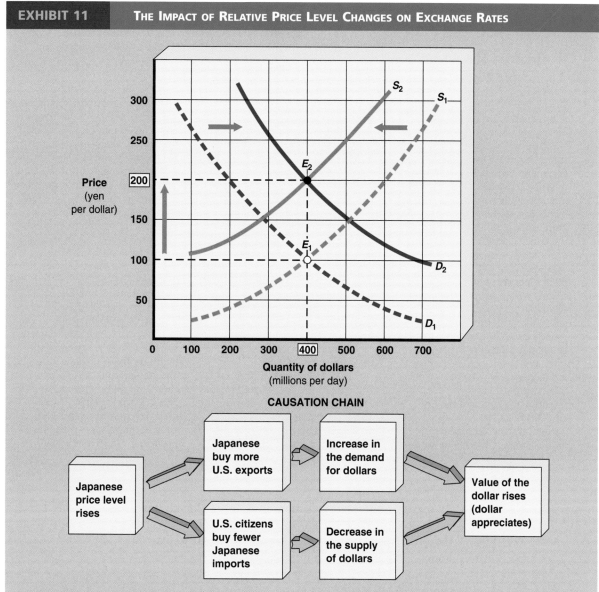

CAUSATION CHAIN

Begin at $E_1$, with the exchange rate equal to 100 yen per dollar. Assume prices in Japan rise relative to those in the United States. As a result, the demand for dollars increases, and the supply of dollars decreases. The new equilibrium is at $E_2$ when the dollar appreciates (rises in value) to 200 yen per dollar.

## International Economics

### Return to the Gold Standard?
*Applicable Concept: exchange rates*

From the 1870s until the 1930s, most industrial countries were on the gold standard. The gold standard served as an international monetary system in which currencies were defined in terms of gold. Under the gold standard, a nation with a balance of payments deficit was required to ship gold to other nations to finance the deficit. Hence, a large excess of imports over exports meant a corresponding outflow of gold from a nation. As a result, that nation's money supply decreased, which, in turn, reduced the aggregate demand for goods and services. Lower domestic demand led to falling prices, lower production, and fewer jobs. In contrast, a nation with a balance of payments surplus would experience an inflow of gold and the opposite effects. In this case, the nation's money supply increased, and its aggregate demand for

goods and services rose. Higher aggregate spending, in turn, boosted employment and the price level. In short, the gold standard meant that governments could not control their money supplies and thereby conduct monetary policy.

The gold standard worked fairly well as a fixed exchange rate system so long as nations did not face sudden or severe swings in flows from their stocks of gold. The Great Depression marked the beginning of the end of the gold standard. Nations faced with trade deficits and high unemployment began going off the gold standard, rather than contracting their money supplies by following the gold standard.

In 1933, President Franklin D. Roosevelt took the United States off the gold standard and ordered all 1933 gold double eagle coins already manufactured to be melted down and not circulated.

Through a long twisted story worthy of a Sherlock Holmes mystery novel involving the Smithsonian Institution, the former king of Egypt, the Treasury Department, the Justice Department, the U.S. Mint, and a long list of intriguing supporting characters, one 1933 double eagle surfaced and was sold for $7.59 million in 2002. This was double the previous record for a coin.[1]

Once the Allies felt certain they would win World War II, the finance ministers of Western nations met in 1944 at Bretton Woods, New Hampshire, to establish a new international monetary system. The new system was based on fixed exchange rates and an international central bank called the International Monetary Fund (IMF). The IMF makes loans to countries faced with short-term balance of payments problems. Under this system,

As export sales rise, jobs are created in the United States. On the other hand, a weak dollar makes foreign producers and domestic consumers unhappy because the prices of Japanese cars, French wine, and Italian shoes are higher. As U.S. imports fall, jobs are lost in foreign countries.

> **CONCLUSION** *When the dollar is weak or depreciates, U.S. goods and services cost foreign consumers less, so they buy more U.S. exports. At the same time, a weak dollar means foreign goods and services cost U.S. consumers more, so they buy fewer imports.*

A strong dollar is also a "mixed blessing." A strong dollar makes our major trading partners happy because the prices of Japanese cars, French wine, and Italian shoes are lower. A strong dollar, contrary to the implication of the term, makes U.S. producers unhappy because their exports are more expensive and related jobs decline. Conversely, a strong dollar makes foreign producers happy because the prices of their goods and services are lower, causing U.S. imports to rise.

nations were expected to maintain fixed exchange rates within a narrow range. In the 1960s and early 1970s, the Bretton Woods system became strained as conditions changed. In the 1960s, inflation rates in the United States rose relative to those in other countries, causing U.S. exports to become more expensive and U.S. imports to become less expensive. This situation increased the supply of dollars abroad and caused an increasing surplus of dollars, thus putting downward pressure on the exchange rate. Monetary authorities in the United States worried that central banks would demand gold for their dollars, the U.S. gold stock would diminish sharply, and the declining money supply would adversely affect the economy.

Something had to give, and it did. In August 1971, President Richard Nixon announced that the United States would no longer honor its obligation to sell gold at $35 an ounce. By 1973, the gold standard was dead, and most of our trading partners were letting the forces of supply and demand determine exchange rates.

Today, some people advocate returning to the gold standard. These gold buffs do not trust the government to control the money supply without the discipline of a gold standard. They argue that if governments have the freedom to print money, political pressures will sooner or later cause them to increase the money supply too much and let inflation rage.

One argument against the gold standard is that no one can control the supply of gold. Big gold discoveries can cause inflation and have done so in the past. On the other hand, slow growth in the stock of mined gold can lead to slow economic growth and a loss of jobs. Governments therefore are unlikely to return to the gold standard because it would mean turning monetary policy over to uncontrollable swings in the stock of gold.

**ANALYZE THE ISSUE**

Return to Exhibit 8, and assume the equilibrium exchange rate is 150 yen per dollar and the equilibrium quantity is $300 million. Redraw this figure, and place a horizontal line through the equilibrium exchange rate to represent a fixed exchange rate. Now use this figure to explain why a country would abandon the gold standard.

[1]Brooks Barnes, "Rare Gold Coin Sells at Sotheby's for $7.6 Million, Setting Record," *The Wall Street Journal*, July 31, 2002.

---

**CONCLUSION** *When the dollar is strong or appreciates, U.S. goods and services cost foreign consumers more, so they buy fewer U.S. exports. At the same time, a strong dollar means foreign goods and services cost U.S. consumers less, so they buy more foreign imports.*

---

Finally, as promised earlier in this chapter, we return to the discussion of NAFTA in order to illustrate the impact of this free trade agreement and the effect of a strong dollar. Recall that in January 1994, NAFTA began a 15-year gradual phase-out of tariffs and other trade barriers. Exhibit 12 provides trade data for the United States and Mexico for the years surrounding NAFTA. As the exhibit shows, both exports and imports of goods increased sharply after NAFTA. On the other hand, a small U.S. trade surplus of $2 billion with Mexico in 1993 turned into a huge trade deficit of $51 billion in 2005.

Before blaming this trade deficit entirely on NAFTA, you must note that the exchange rate rose from 3.12 to 10.89 pesos per dollar in 2005. Since 1995, the

| EXHIBIT 12 | U.S. TRADE BALANCES WITH MEXICO, 1993–2005 | | | |
|---|---|---|---|---|
| Year | U.S. exports to Mexico (billions of dollars) | U.S. imports from Mexico (billions of dollars) | Exchange rate (pesos per dollar) | U.S. trade surplus (+) or deficit (−) (billions of dollars) |
| 1993 | $ 42 | $ 40 | 3.12 | $ +2 |
| 1995 | 46 | 63 | 6.45 | −17 |
| 1997 | 71 | 87 | 7.92 | −16 |
| 1999 | 87 | 111 | 9.55 | −24 |
| 2001 | 101 | 132 | 9.34 | −31 |
| 2003 | 97 | 139 | 10.79 | −42 |
| 2005 | 120 | 171 | 10.89 | −51 |

*Sources: Bureau of Economic Analysis,* International Transactions Accounts Data, *http://www.bea.doc.gov/, Table 11;* Federal Reserve Statistical Release, *http://www.federalreserve.gov/releases/G5A/current/.*

peso was devalued and the stronger dollar has put the price of U.S. goods out of reach for many Mexican consumers. This is one reason U.S. exports to Mexico have been lower than they have been otherwise. At the same time, Mexican goods became less expensive for U.S. consumers, so U.S. imports from Mexico have risen.

## Key Concepts

| | | |
|---|---|---|
| Comparative advantage | Tariff | Exchange rate |
| Absolute advantage | World Trade Organization (WTO) | Depreciation of currency |
| Free trade | Quota | Appreciation of currency |
| Protectionism | Balance of payments | |
| Embargo | Balance of trade | |

## Summary

- **Comparative advantage** is a principle that allows nations to gain from trade. Comparative advantage means that each nation *specializes* in a product for which its opportunity cost is lower in terms of the production of another product, and then nations trade. When nations follow this principle, they gain. The reason is that world output increases, and each nation ends up with a higher standard of living by consuming more goods and services than would be possible without specialization and trade.

### COMPARATIVE ADVANTAGE

(a) U.S. production and consumption

(b) Japanese production and consumption

- **Free trade** benefits a nation as a whole, but individuals may lose jobs and incomes from the competition from foreign goods and services.

- **Protectionism** is a government's use of embargoes, tariffs, quotas, and other methods to impose barriers intended to both reduce imports and protect particular domestic industries. *Embargoes* prohibit the import or export of particular goods. *Tariffs* discourage imports by making them more expensive. *Quotas* limit the quantity of imports or exports of certain goods. These trade barriers often result primarily from domestic groups that exert political pressure on government in order to gain from these barriers.

- The **balance of payments** is a summary bookkeeping record of all the international transactions a country makes during a year. It is divided into different accounts, including the *current account*, the *capital account*, and the *statistical discrepancy*. The current account summarizes all transactions in currently produced goods and services. The overall balance of payments is always zero after an adjustment for the statistical discrepancy.

- The **balance of trade** measures only goods (not services) that a nation exports and imports. A balance of trade can be in deficit or in surplus. The balance of trade is the most widely reported and largest part of the current account. Since 1975, the United States has experienced balance of trade deficits.

### BALANCE OF TRADE

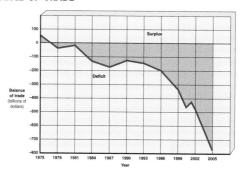

- An **exchange rate** is the price of one nation's currency in terms of another nation's currency. Foreigners who wish to purchase U.S. goods, services, and financial assets demand dollars. The supply of dollars reflects the desire of U.S. citizens to purchase foreign goods, services, and financial assets. The intersection of the supply and demand curves for dollars determines the number of units of a foreign currency per dollar.

### EXCHANGE RATE

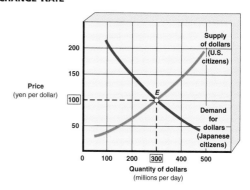

- **Shifts in supply and demand for foreign exchange** result from changes in such factors as tastes, relative price levels, relative real interest rates, and relative income levels.

- **Depreciation of currency** occurs when one currency becomes worth fewer units of another currency. If a currency depreciates, it becomes weaker. Deprecia-

tion of a nation's currency increases its exports and decreases its imports.

- **Appreciation of currency** occurs when one currency becomes worth more units of another currency. If a currency appreciates, it becomes stronger. Apprecia-tion of a nation's currency decreases its exports and increases its imports.

## Summary of Conclusion Statements

- When countries specialize, total world output increases, and, therefore, the potential for greater total world consumption also increases.

- International trade allows a country to consume a combination of goods that exceeds its production possibilities curve.

- Comparative advantage refers to the relative oppor-tunity costs between countries of producing the same goods. World output and consumption are maxi-mized when each country specializes in producing and trading goods for which it has a comparative advantage.

- A current account deficit is financed by a capital account surplus.

- An exchange rate can be expressed as a reciprocal.

- An expansion in relative U.S. income causes a depre-ciation of the dollar.

- A rise in a trading partner's relative price level causes the dollar to appreciate.

- When the dollar is weak or depreciates, U.S. goods and services cost foreign consumers less, so they buy more U.S. exports. At the same time, a weak dollar means foreign goods and services cost U.S. con-sumers more, so they buy fewer imports.

- When the dollar is strong or appreciates, U.S. goods and services cost foreign consumers more, so they buy fewer U.S. exports. At the same time, a strong dollar means foreign goods and services cost U.S. consumers less, so they buy more foreign imports.

## Study Questions and Problems

1. The countries of Alpha and Beta produce diamonds and pearls. The production possibilities schedule below describes their potential output in tons per year:

| Points on production possibilities curve | Alpha | | Beta | |
|---|---|---|---|---|
| | Diamonds | Pearls | Diamonds | Pearls |
| A | 150 | 0 | 90 | 0 |
| B | 100 | 25 | 60 | 60 |
| C | 50 | 50 | 30 | 120 |
| D | 0 | 75 | 0 | 180 |

Using the data in the table, answer the following questions:

a. What is the opportunity cost of diamonds for each country?

b. What is the opportunity cost of pearls for each country?
c. In which good does Alpha have a comparative advantage?
d. In which good does Beta have a comparative advantage?
e. Suppose Alpha is producing and consuming at point B on its production possibilities curve and Beta is producing and consuming at point C on its production possibilities curve. Use a table such as Exhibit 3 to explain why both nations would benefit if they specialize.
f. Draw a graph, and use it to explain how Alpha and Beta benefit if they specialize and Alpha agrees to trade 50 tons of diamonds to Beta and Alpha receives 50 tons of pearls in exchange.

2. Bill can paint either two walls or one window frame in one hour. In the same time, Frank can paint either three walls or two window frames. To minimize the time spent painting, who should specialize in painting walls, and who should specialize in painting window frames?

3. Consider this statement: "The principles of specialization and trade according to comparative advantage among nations also apply to states in the United States." Do you agree or disagree? Explain.

4. Would the U.S. government gain any advantage from using tariffs or quotas to restrict imports?

5. Suppose the United States passed a law stating that we would not purchase imports from any country that imposed any trade restrictions on our exports. Who would benefit and who would lose from such retaliation?

6. Now consider question 5 in terms of the law's impact on domestic producers that export goods. Does this policy adversely affect domestic producers that export goods?

7. Consider this statement: "Unrestricted foreign trade costs domestic jobs." Do you agree or disagree? Explain.

8. Do you support a constitutional amendment to prohibit the federal government from imposing any trade barriers, such as tariffs and quotas, except in case of war or national emergency? Why or why not?

9. Discuss this statement: "Because each nation's balance of payments equals zero, it follows that there is actually no significance to a balance of payments deficit or surplus."

10. For each of the following situations, indicate the direction of the shift in the supply curve or the demand curve for dollars, the factor causing the change, and the resulting movement of the equilibrium exchange rate for the dollar in terms of foreign currency:
   a. American-made cars become more popular overseas.
   b. The United States experiences a recession, while other nations enjoy economic growth.
   c. Inflation rates accelerate in the United States, while inflation rates remain constant in other nations.
   d. Real interest rates in the United States rise, while real interest rates abroad remain constant.
   e. The Japanese put quotas and high tariffs on all imports from the United States.
   f. Tourism from the United States increases sharply because of a fare war between airlines.

11. The following table summarizes the supply and the demand for euros:

| | U.S. dollars per euro | | | | |
| | $.05 | $.10 | $.15 | $.20 | $.25 |
|---|---|---|---|---|---|
| Quantity demanded (per day) | 500 | 400 | 300 | 200 | 100 |
| Quantity supplied (per day) | 100 | 200 | 300 | 400 | 500 |

Using the above table:
a. Graph the supply and demand curves for euros.
b. Determine the equilibrium exchange rate.
c. Determine what the effect of a fixed exchange rate at $.10 per euro would be.

## Study Guide Questions

1. A (an) prohibits the import or export of particular goods and a (an) _____ discourages imports by making them more expensive. These trade barriers often result primarily from domestic groups that exert political pressure to gain from these barriers.

2. Which of the following statements is true?
   a. Specialization and trade along the lines of comparative advantage allows nations to consume more than if they were to produce just for themselves.
   b. Free trade theory suggests that when trade takes place any gains made by one nation comes at the expense of another.
   c. According to the theory of comparative advantage, a nation should specialize in the production of those goods for which it has an absolute advantage.
   d. All of the above.

3. If the dollar appreciates (becomes stronger) this causes
   a. the relative price of U.S. goods to increase for foreigners.
   b. the relative price of foreign goods to decrease for Americans.
   c. U.S. exports to fall and U.S. imports to rise.
   d. a balance of trade deficit for the U.S.
   e. all of the above.

4. The value of the U.S. dollar in terms of Japanese yen has declined substantially since the mid-1980s. Which of the following would be consistent with that fact?
   a. The supply of yen generated by Japanese buying U.S. goods is low, while the demand for yen generated by U.S. consumers buying Japanese goods is high.
   b. The supply of yen generated by Japanese buying U.S. goods is high, while the demand for yen generated by U.S. consumers buying Japanese goods is low.
   c. Both the supply of yen and the demand for yen are low because there is relatively little trade between Japan and the U.S.
   d. None of the above.

5. T  F  Other things being equal, an increase in U.S. interest rates would be likely to cause an increase in the capital account surplus or a decrease in the capital account deficit.

**Answers to these questions are in the complete Study Guide at www.thomsonedu.com/thomsonnow.**

 **For Online Exercises, go to the text Web site at www.thomsonedu.com/economics/tucker.**

 Checkpoint Answers

## Do Nations with an Advantage Always Trade?

In the United States, the opportunity cost of producing 1 calculator is 100 towels. In China, opportunity cost of producing 1 calculator is 100 towels. If you said, because the opportunity cost is the same for each nation, specialization and trade would not boost total output, and therefore China would not trade these products, **YOU ARE CORRECT.**

## Should Everyone Keep a Balance of Payments?

The principal purpose of the balance of payments is to keep track of payments of national currencies. Because states and cities within the same nation use the same national currency, payments for goods and services traded between these parties do not represent a loss (outflow) or gain (inflow). If you said only nations need to use the balance of payments to account for flows of foreign currency across national boundaries, **YOU ARE CORRECT.**

## Practice Quiz

For an explanation of the correct answers, please visit the tutorial at www.thomsonedu.com/economics/tucker.

1. With trade, the production possibilities for two nations lie
   a. outside their consumption possibilities.
   b. inside their consumption possibilities.
   c. at a point equal to the world production possibilities curve.
   d. none of the above.

2. Free trade theory suggests that when trade takes place
   a. both nations will be worse off.
   b. one nation must gain at the other nation's expense.
   c. both nations will be better off.
   d. one nation will gain and the other nation will be neither better nor worse off.

3. Which of the following is *true* when two countries specialize according to their comparative advantage?
   a. It is possible to increase their total output of all goods.
   b. It is possible to increase their total output of some goods only if both countries are industrialized.
   c. One country is likely to gain from trade, while the other loses.
   d. None of the above is true.

4. According to the theory of comparative advantage, a country should produce and
   a. import goods in which it has an absolute advantage.
   b. export goods in which it has an absolute advantage.
   c. import goods in which it has a comparative advantage.
   d. export goods in which it has a comparative advantage.

### EXHIBIT 13 POTATOES AND WHEAT OUTPUT (TONS PER HOUR)

| Country | Potatoes | Wheat |
|---|---|---|
| United States | 1 | 3 |
| Ireland | 1 | 2 |

5. In Exhibit 13, which country has the comparative advantage in the production of potatoes?
   a. The United States because it requires fewer resources to produce potatoes
   b. The United States because it has the lower opportunity cost of potatoes
   c. Ireland because it requires fewer resources to produce potatoes
   d. Ireland because it has the lower opportunity cost of potatoes

6. In Exhibit 13, the opportunity cost of wheat is
   a. 1/3 ton of potatoes in the United States and 1/2 ton of potatoes in Ireland.
   b. 2 tons of potatoes in the United States and 1 1/2 tons of potatoes in Ireland.
   c. 8 tons of potatoes in the United States and 4 tons of potatoes in Ireland.
   d. 1/2 ton of potatoes in the United States and 2/3 ton of potatoes in Ireland.

7. In Exhibit 13, the opportunity cost of potatoes is
   a. 1/2 ton of wheat in the United States and 2/3 ton of wheat in Ireland.
   b. 2 tons of wheat in the United States and 1 1/2 tons of wheat in Ireland.
   c. 16 tons of wheat in the United States and 6 tons of wheat in Ireland.
   d. 3 tons of wheat in the United States and 2 tons of wheat in Ireland.

8. If the countries in Exhibit 13 follow the principle of comparative advantage, the United States should
   a. buy all of its potatoes from Ireland.
   b. buy all of its wheat from Ireland.
   c. buy all of its potatoes and wheat from Ireland.
   d. produce both potatoes and wheat and not trade with Ireland.

9. A tariff increases
   a. the quantity of imports.
   b. the ability of foreign goods to compete with domestic goods.
   c. the prices of imports to domestic buyers.
   d. all of the above.

10. The infant industry argument for protectionism is based on which of the following views?
   a. Foreign buyers will absorb all of the output of domestic producers in a new industry.

b. The growth of an industry that is new to a nation will be too rapid unless trade restrictions are imposed.

c. Firms in a newly developing domestic industry will have difficulty growing if they face strong competition from established foreign firms.

d. It is based on none of the above.

11. The figure that results when goods imports are subtracted from goods exports is
a. the capital account balance.
b. the balance of trade.
c. the current account balance.
d. always less than zero.

12. Which of the following international accounts records payments for exports and imports of goods, military transactions, foreign travel, investment income, and foreign gifts?
a. The capital account
b. The merchandise account
c. The current account
d. The official reserve account

13. Which of the following international accounts records the purchase and sale of financial assets and real estate between the United States and other nations?
a. The balance of trade account
b. The current account
c. The capital account
d. The balance of payments account

14. If a Japanese radio priced at 2,000 yen can be purchased for $10, the exchange rate is
a. 200 yen per dollar.
b. 20 yen per dollar.
c. 20 dollars per yen.
d. none of the above.

15. The United States
a. was on a fixed exchange rate system prior to late 1971, but now is on a flexible exchange rate system.
b. has been on a fixed exchange rate system since 1945.

c. has been on a flexible exchange rate system since 1945.
d. was on a flexible exchange rate system prior to late 1983, but now is on a fixed exchange rate system.

16. Suppose the exchange rate changes so that fewer Japanese yen are required to buy a dollar. We would conclude that
a. the Japanese yen has depreciated in value.
b. U.S. citizens will buy fewer Japanese imports.
c. Japanese will demand fewer U.S. exports.
d. none of the above will occur.

17. Which of the following would cause a decrease in the demand for euros by those holding U.S. dollars?
a. Inflation in France, but not in the United States
b. Inflation in the United States but not in France
c. An increase in the real rate of interest on investments in France above the real rate of interest on investments in the United States
d. None of the above

18. An increase in the equilibrium price of a nation's money could be caused by a (an)
a. decrease in the supply of the money.
b. decrease in the demand for the money.
c. increase in the supply of the money.
d. increase in the quantity of money demanded.

19. If the dollar appreciates (becomes stronger), this causes
a. the relative price of U.S. goods to increase for foreigners.
b. the relative price of foreign goods to decrease for Americans.
c. U.S. exports to fall and U.S. imports to rise.
d. a balance of trade deficit for the United States.
e. all of the above to occur.

20. Which of the following would cause the U.S. dollar to depreciate against the Japanese yen?
a. Greater popularity of U.S. exports in Japan
b. A higher price level in Japan
c. Higher real interest rates in the United States
d. Higher incomes in the United States.

# Economies in Transition

*The inherent vice of capitalism is the unequal sharing of blessings. The inherent virtue of communism is the equal sharing of miseries.*

**—Winston Churchill**

The rapid emergence of the market system in Russia, China, and other countries continues to fascinate us. Newspapers and periodicals report the astonishing news that leaders of countries that used to be devoted followers of Marxist ideology now say they believe that capitalism, private property, and profit are ideas superior to the communist system. The failure of communism and the transformation toward a market system is personified by the success of McDonald's in Russia and Wal-Mart in China. Today, Russia and other countries continue to experience economic problems during their restructuring, but the commitment to free-market reforms remains. What caused this astonishing turn of events?

To understand how the pieces of the global economic puzzle fit together, this chapter begins with a discussion of the three basic types of economies. Then you will examine the pros and cons of the "isms"—capitalism, socialism, and communism. Here you will explore the worldwide clash between the ideas of Adam Smith and Karl Marx and study their current influence on economic systems. Finally, you will examine economic reforms in Cuba, Russia, and China.

**In this chapter, you will learn to solve these economics puzzles:**

- Why did drivers in the former Soviet Union remove the windshield wipers and side mirrors whenever they parked their cars?
- What did Adam Smith mean when he said that an "invisible hand" promotes the public interest?
- If the Soviet Union was foolish to run its economy on five-year plans, why do universities, businesses, and governments in a capitalistic economy plan?

## Basic Types of Economic Systems

An **economic system** consists of the organizations and methods used to determine what goods and services are produced, how they are produced, and for whom they are produced. As explained earlier in Chapter 2, scarcity forces each economic system to decide what combination of goods to produce, how to produce

**Economic system**
The organizations and methods used to determine what goods and services are produced, how they are produced, and for whom they are produced.

such goods, and who gets the output once produced. The decision-making process involves interaction among many aspects of a nation's culture, such as its laws, form of government, ethics, religions, and customs. Economist Robert L. Heilbroner established a simple way to look at the basic methods society can employ. Each economic system can be classified into one of three basic types: (1) *traditional*, (2) *command*, and (3) *market*.

## THE TRADITIONAL ECONOMY

**Traditional economy**
A system that answers the *What*, *How*, and *For Whom* questions the way they always have been answered.

Why does England have a king or queen? Tradition is the answer. Historically, the **traditional economy** has been a common system for making economic decisions. The traditional economy is a system that answers the *What*, *How*, and *For Whom* questions the way they have always been answered. People in this type of society learn that copying the previous generation allows them to feel accepted. Anyone who changes ways of doing things asks for trouble from others. This is because people in such a society believe that what was good yesterday, and years ago, must still be a good idea today.

Traditional systems are used by primitive tribes, the Ainu of Japan, the native people of Brazil's rain forest, and the Amish of Pennsylvania. In these societies, the way past generations decided what crops are planted, how they are harvested, and to whom they are distributed remains unchanged today. People perform their jobs in the manner established by their ancestors. The Amish are well known for rejecting tractors and using horse-drawn plows. Interestingly, the Amish reject Social Security because their society voluntarily redistributes wealth to members who are needy.

## THE TRADITIONAL ECONOMY'S STRENGTHS AND WEAKNESSES

The benefit of the traditional approach is that it minimizes friction among members because relatively little is disputed. Consequently, people in this system may cooperate more freely with one another. In today's industrial world, the Amish and other traditional economies appear very satisfied with their relatively uncomplicated systems. However, critics argue that the traditional system restricts individual initiative and therefore does not lead to the production of advanced goods, new technology, and economic growth.

## THE COMMAND ECONOMY

**Command economy**
A system that answers the *What*, *How*, and *For Whom* questions by central authority.

In a **command economy**, a dictator or group of central planners makes economic decisions for society. In this system, the *What*, *How*, and *For Whom* questions are answered by central authority. The former Soviet Union in the past and Cuba today are examples of nations with command economies using national economic plans implemented through powerful government committees. Politically selected committees decide on everything, including the number, color, size, quality, and price of autos, brooms, sweaters, and tanks. The state owns the factors of production and dictates answers to the three basic economic questions. The authorities might decide to produce modern weapons instead of schools, or they might decide to devote resources to building huge monuments, like the pyramids, built by the rulers of ancient Egypt to honor their dead kings and queens.

In the old Soviet economy, for example, the three basic economic questions were answered by a central planning agency called the *Gosplan*. Following the policies of the political authority (the Politburo), the Gosplan set production quotas and prices for farms, factories, mines, housing construction, medical care, and other producing units. What should the cows be fed? If it is hay, how much land can be used to grow it? How much milk should the cows give? How many people will be dairy farmers? What wages should a dairy farmer earn? Should milk be given to everyone, to a few, or to any persons chosen by the leaders? The Gosplan tried to make all these decisions. Today, in Russia and the other former Soviet republics, the Gosplan is a distant memory of the discarded Soviet command system.

We can represent the command economy by the pyramid shown in Exhibit 1. At the top of the pyramid is a supremely powerful group of central planners, such as the old Soviet Gosplan. That agency established production targets and prices for goods and services. Then the Gosplan transmitted this information to a second layer of specialized state planning agencies. One of these specialized government bureaucracies purchased raw materials, another agency established fashion trends, another set prices, and another government bureaucracy made decisions based on employment and wages.

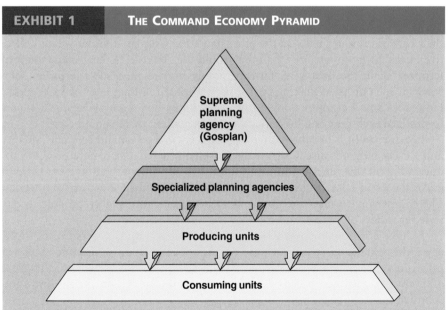

**EXHIBIT 1** **THE COMMAND ECONOMY PYRAMID**

The principal feature of a command economy is the central planning board at the top, which transmits economic decisions down to the various producing and consuming units below. This process begins with an overall plan from a supreme planning board, such as the old Soviet Gosplan. The Gosplan established production targets and was the ultimate authority over a layer of specialized planning agencies, which authorized capital expansion, raw material purchases, prices, wages, and all other production decisions for individual producing units. Finally, the factories, farms, mines, and other producers distributed the specified output to consumers according to the approved master plan.

Production objectives were transmitted from the upper authority layers to the individual producing units, represented by the third layer of the pyramid in Exhibit 1. These producers supplied goods and services to the consumers, as commanded by the central authorities. The bottom portion of the pyramid illustrates the distribution, according to the master plan, of output to consuming units of individuals and households.

## THE COMMAND ECONOMY'S STRENGTHS AND WEAKNESSES

Believe it or not, the command system can be defended. Proponents argue that economic change occurs much faster than in a traditional economy. This is one reason those dissatisfied with a traditional society might advocate establishment of a command system. The central authorities can ignore custom and order new ways of doing things. Another reason for adopting a command economy is the controversial belief that the government will provide economic security and equity. It is alleged that central authorities ensure that everyone is provided food, clothing, shelter, and medical care regardless of their ability to contribute to society.

The absolute power of central authorities to make right decisions is also the power to be absolutely wrong. Often the planners do not set production goals accurately, and either shortages or surpluses of goods and services are the result. For example, at one point the planners miscalculated and produced too few windshield wipers and side mirrors for Soviet cars. Faced with shortages of these parts, Soviet drivers removed windshield wipers and side mirrors whenever they parked their cars to prevent theft. On the other hand, the Gosplan allocated some collective farms far more fertilizer than they could use. To receive the same amount of fertilizer again the next year, farmers simply burned the excess fertilizer. As a result of such decision-making errors, people waited in long lines or stole goods. How does any decision-making group really know how many windshield wipers to produce each year and how much workers making them should earn?

Because profit is not the motive of producers in a command economy, quality and variety of goods also suffer. If the Gosplan ordered a state enterprise to produce 400,000 side mirrors for cars, for example, producers had little incentive to make the extra effort required to create a quality product in a variety of styles. The easiest way to meet the goal was to produce a low-quality product in one style regardless of consumer demand.

Exhibit 2 illustrates how the pricing policy of central planners causes shortages. The demand curve for side mirrors conforms to the law of demand. At lower prices in rubles, the quantity demanded increases. The supply curve is fixed at 400,000 side mirrors because it is set by the central planners and is therefore unresponsive to price variations.

Suppose one of the principal goals of the command economy is to keep the price low. To reach this goal, the central planners set the price of side mirrors at 20 rubles, which is below the equilibrium price of 40 rubles. At 20 rubles, more people can afford a side mirror than at the equilibrium price set by an uncontrolled marketplace. The consequence of this lower price set by the planners is a shortage. The quantity demanded at 20 rubles is 800,000 side mirrors, and the quantity supplied is only 400,000 mirrors. Thus, the model explains why side mirrors disappeared from stores long before many who were willing to buy them could do so.

The same graphical analysis applies to centrally planned rental prices for apartments. The central planners in the former Soviet Union set rents below the

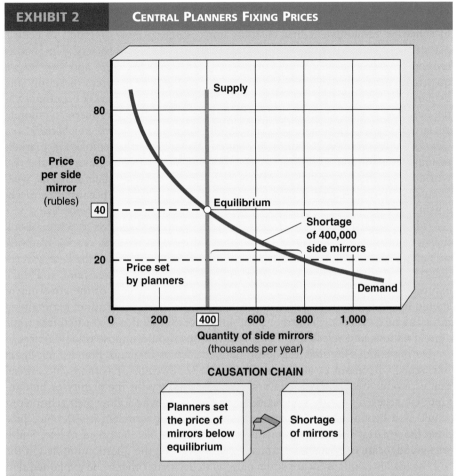

**EXHIBIT 2    CENTRAL PLANNERS FIXING PRICES**

**CAUSATION CHAIN**

Planners set the price of mirrors below equilibrium ⟹ Shortage of mirrors

The central planners' goal is to keep prices low, so they set the price of a side mirror for a car at 20 rubles, which is below the market-determined equilibrium price of 40 rubles. At the set price, however, the quantity demanded is 800,000 side mirrors per year. Also set by the planners, the quantity supplied is 400,000 per year. Thus, the shortage at the government-established price is 400,000 side mirrors per year. As a result, long lines form to buy side mirrors, and black markets appear.

equilibrium rental prices for apartments. As the model predicts, low rents resulted in a shortage of housing. Meanwhile, the planners promised that improvements in housing would come in time.

**CONCLUSION** *When central planners set prices below equilibrium for goods and services, they create shortages, which mean long lines, empty shelves, and black markets.*[1]

---

[1]Recall from Exhibit 5 of Chapter 4 that a black market is an illegal market that emerges when a price ceiling is imposed in a free market.

## THE MARKET ECONOMY AND THE IDEAS OF ADAM SMITH

**Market economy**
An economic system that answers the *What, How,* and *For Whom* questions using prices determined by the interaction of the forces of supply and demand.

In a **market economy**, neither customs nor a single person or group of central planners answers the three basic economic questions facing society. The market economy is an economic system that answers the *What, How,* and *For Whom* questions using prices determined by the interaction of the forces of supply and demand. One of the first people to explain the power of a market economy was the Scottish economist Adam Smith. In the same year that the American colonies declared their political independence, Smith's *An Inquiry into the Nature and Causes of the Wealth of Nations* presented the blueprint for employing markets to improve economic performance. Smith spent over 10 years observing the real world and writing about how nations could best improve their material well-being. He concluded that the answer was to use free markets because this mechanism provides the incentive for everyone to follow his or her *self-interest.*

Adam Smith is the *father of modern economics.* He intended to write a book that would influence popular opinion, and unlike many famous works, his book was an immediate success. The basic philosophy of his book is "the best government is the least government." This belief is known as *laissez faire,* a French expression meaning "allow to act." As Smith stated, the role of the government should be limited to providing national defense, providing education, maintaining infrastructure, enforcing contracts, and little else. Smith also advocated free trade among nations and rejected the idea that nations should impose trade barriers.

**Adam Smith** (1723–1790) The father of modern economics who wrote *The Wealth of Nations* published in 1776.

During Smith's lifetime, European nations such as England, France, and Spain intervened to control economic activities. In *The Wealth of Nations,* he argued that economic freedoms are "natural rights" necessary for the dignity of humankind. He believed that free competition among people who follow their self-interest would best benefit society because markets free of government interference produce the greatest output of goods and services possible. As noted above, Smith was an advocate of free international trade and asked the question implied in the full title of his book: Why are some nations richer than others? He explained that the source of any nation's wealth is not really the amount of gold or silver it owns. This was an idea popular during Smith's time called *mercantilism.* Instead, he argued that it is the ability of people to produce products and trade in free markets that creates a nation's wealth.

**Invisible hand**
A phrase that expresses the belief that the best interests of a society are served when individual consumers and producers compete to achieve their own private interests.

The importance of markets is that they harness the power of self-interest to answer the *What, How,* and *For Whom* questions. Without central planning, markets coordinate the actions of millions of consumers and producers. Smith said that the market economy seemed to be controlled by an **invisible hand**. The invisible hand is a phrase that expresses the belief that the best interests of a society are served when individual consumers and producers compete to achieve their own private interests. Guided by an invisible hand, producers must compete with one another to win consumers' money. The *profit motive* in a competitive marketplace provides profits as a reward for efficient producers, while losses punish inefficient producers. Smith saw profit as the necessary driving force in an individualistic market system. The profit motive leads the butcher, the baker, and other producers to answer the *What, How,* and *For Whom* questions at the lowest prices. Consumers also compete with one another to purchase the best goods at the lowest price. Competition automatically regulates the economy and provides more goods and services than a system in which government attempts to accomplish the same task in the *public interest.* In Smith's own words:

*Every individual necessarily labours to render the annual revenue of the society as great as he can. He generally, indeed, neither intends to promote the public interest, nor knows how much he is promoting it. By . . . directing that industry in such a manner as its produce may be of the greatest value, he intends only his own gain, and he is in this, as in many other cases, led by an* invisible hand *to promote an end which was no part of his intention. Nor is it always the worse for the society that it was no part of it. By pursuing his own interest he frequently promotes that of the society more effectually than when he really intends to promote it.*[2]

## THE MARKET ECONOMY'S STRENGTHS AND WEAKNESSES

In a market system, if consumers want Beanie Babies, they can buy them because sellers seek to profit from the sale of Beanie Babies. No single person or central planning board makes a formal decision to shift resources and tell firms how to produce what many might view as a frivolous product. Because no central body or set of customs interferes, the market system provides a wide variety of goods and services that buyers and sellers exchange at the lowest prices.

**CONCLUSION** *A market economy answers the* What to produce *and* How to produce *questions very effectively.*

Those who attack the market economy point out the market failure problems of lack of competition, externalities, public goods, and income inequality, discussed in Chapter 4. For example, critics contend that competition among buyers and sellers results in people who are very wealthy and people who are very poor. In a market economy, output is divided in favor of people who earn higher incomes and own property. Some people will dine on caviar in a fine restaurant, while others will wander the street and beg for food and shelter. Supporters of the market system argue that this inequality of income must exist to give people incentives or rewards for the value of their contributions to others.

## THE MIXED ECONOMY

In the real world, no nation is a pure traditional, command, or market economy. Even primitive tribes employ a few markets in their system. For example, members of a tribe may exchange shells for animal skins. In China, the government allows many private shops and farms to operate in free markets. Although the United States is best described as a market economy, it is also a blend of the other two systems. As mentioned earlier, the Amish operate a well-known traditional economy in our nation. The draft during wartime is an example of a command economy in which the government obtains involuntary labor. In addition, taxes "commanded" from taxpayers fund government programs, such as national defense and Social Security. If the economic systems of most nations do not perfectly fit one of the basic definitions, what term best describes their economies? A more appropriate description is that most countries employ a blend of the basic

[2]Adam Smith, *An Inquiry into the Nature and Causes of the Wealth of Nations* (1776; reprint, New York: Random House, 1937), p. 423.

## International Economics

## Choosing an Economic System on Another Planet
*Applicable Concept: basic types of economic systems*

Suppose we discover life on a new planet and the chief of their society learns of the successful economy of the United States and summons an economic advisor to learn the secret.

Sitting at the head of a huge oval table, the chief addresses the advisor seated at the other end saying, "Our economic system depends on tradition and command. It works, but not nearly so well as the U.S. economy. Our men and women lead a highly tradition-bound way of life. Men farm and hunt like their forefathers. Women work only in the home and care for children following the role approved by their elders. There is no confusion over how things are done, and there is no chaos over what work, or what output will be produced. People are simply assigned jobs by their leaders and told how much to produce. Likewise, people are told to work on community projects for our planet's benefit. If anyone refuses to follow instructions, they are shunned or banished. Tell me, how could there possibly be a better way to organize our economy?"

The advisor confidently responds, "Yes, there is definitely a better way. Replace tradition and command systems with the 'invisi-ble hand' of the market system. This idea was explained long ago by a scholar named Adam Smith, the father of modern economics."

The chief is puzzled. "I have never heard of Adam Smith or the market economy. In a nutshell, explain to me how it differs from our system."

"Very well," says the advisor. "In a market economy, each person is allowed to decide for himself or herself what to do based on price signals."

The chief is horrified and takes umbrage. "But what happens when they do not choose correctly? Let's talk about something specific, like computer production. Unless we designate people to make computers, how do we know the right number will select this job? What if women want to work in this industry? Who decides how much these workers should be paid and how many computers should be produced to satisfy the demand for them?"

"You may rest assured," says the advisor. "Using prices determined in markets free from intervention will answer all your questions better than if leaders try to control everything."

The chief interrupts triumphantly. "Do you really expect me to believe that without instructions from the leaders, too few or too many products will not be bought and sold?"

"Ah, exactly!" the advisor quickly answers. "The market will automatically do all these wonderful things. People will be more motivated by their own rational self-interest than by tradition or central authority. In short, the system runs itself."

"The economy runs without my leaders' directions!" says the chief. "That's absurd and you have wasted my time. I thought you had a meaningful proposal. Good day!"

### ANALYZE THE ISSUE

1. Describe how a traditional or a command system would make employment and production decisions compared to a market system.

2. Why might the leader find a market system inconceivable? Is it possible for economic activities not based on self-interest to take place in a market economy?

*Source: Adapted from Robert L. Heil-broner, The Making of Economic Society, 5th ed. (Englewood Cliffs, N.J.: Prentice-Hall, 1993), pp. 12–13.*

**Mixed economy**
An economic system that answers the *What, How,* and *For Whom* questions through a mixture of traditional, command, and market systems.

types of economic systems, broadly called a **mixed economy**. A mixed economy is a system that answers the *What, How,* and *For Whom* questions through a mixture of traditional, command, and market systems.

The traditional, command, and market economies can exist in a wide variety of political situations. For instance, the United States and Japan are politically "free" societies in which the market system flourishes. But China uses the market system to a limited degree in spite of its lack of political freedom. Moreover, some of the Western democracies engage in central economic planning. French officials representing government, business, and labor meet annually to discuss economic goals for industry for the next five-year period, but compliance is voluntary. In Japan, a government agency called the *Ministry of Economy, Trade and Industry (METI)* engages in long-term planning. One of the goals of the METI is to encourage exports so that Japan can earn the foreign currencies it needs to pay for oil and other resources.

# The "Isms"

What type of economic system will a society choose to answer the *What, How,* and *For Whom* questions? We could call most economies "mixed," but this would be too imprecise. In the real world, economic systems are labeled with various forms of the popular "isms"—capitalism, socialism, and communism—which are based on the basic types of systems.

## CAPITALISM

The popular term for the market economy discussed previously is *capitalism*. **Capitalism** is an economic system characterized by private ownership of resources and markets. *Capitalism* is also called the *free enterprise system*. Regardless of its political system, a capitalist economic system must possess two characteristics: (1) private ownership of resources and (2) decentralized decision-making using markets.

**Private Ownership** Ownership of resources determines to a great degree who makes the *What, How,* and *For Whom* decisions. In a capitalist system, resources are primarily *privately* owned and controlled by individuals and firms, rather than having property rights be *publicly* held by government on behalf of society. In the United States, most capital resources are privately owned, but the term *capitalism* is somewhat confusing because it stresses private ownership of factories, raw materials, farms, and other forms of *capital* even though public ownership of land exists as well.

**Decentralized Decision Making** This characteristic of capitalism allows buyers and sellers to exchange goods in markets without government involvement. A capitalist system operates on the principle of **consumer sovereignty**. Consumer sovereignty is the freedom of consumers to cast their dollar votes to buy, or not to buy, at prices determined in competitive markets. As a result, consumer spending determines what goods and services firms produce. In a capitalist system, most allocative decisions are coordinated by consumers and producers interacting through markets and making their own decisions guided by Adam Smith's invisible hand. Friedrick von Hayek, an Austrian economist who was a 1974 recipient of the Nobel Prize and author of *The Road to Serfdom*, argued that political and economic freedoms are inseparable.

In the real world, many U.S. markets are not perfectly open or free markets with the consumer as sovereign. For example, consumers cannot buy illegal drugs or body organs. In Chapter 4, you learned that the U.S. government sets minimum prices (support prices) for wheat, milk, cheese, and other products. These markets

**Capitalism**
An economic system characterized by private ownership of resources and markets.

**Consumer sovereignty**
The freedom of consumers to cast their dollar votes to buy, or not to buy, at prices determined in competitive markets.

are free only if the market price is above the support price. Similarly, the minimum wage law forces employers to pay a wage above some dollar amount per hour regardless of market conditions.

> **CONCLUSION** *No nation in the world precisely fits the two criteria for capitalism; however, the United States comes close.*

## CAPITALISM'S STRENGTHS AND WEAKNESSES

One of the major strengths of capitalism is its capacity to achieve *economic efficiency* because competition and the profit motive force production at the lowest cost. Another strength of pure capitalism is *economic freedom* because economic power is widely dispersed. Individual consumers, producers, and workers are free to make decisions based on their own self-interest. Economist Milton Friedman makes a related point: Private ownership limits the power of government to deny goods, services, or jobs to political adversaries.

Critics of capitalism cite several shortcomings. First, capitalism tends toward an unequal distribution of income. This inequality of income among citizens results for several reasons. Private ownership of capital and the other factors of production can cause these factors to become concentrated in the hands of a few individuals or firms. Also, people do not have equal labor skills, and the marketplace rewards those with greater skills. These inequalities may be perpetuated because the rich can provide better education, legal aid, political platforms, and wealth to their heirs. Second, pure capitalism is criticized for its failure to protect the environment. The pursuit of profit and self-interest can take precedence over damage or pollution to the air, rivers, lakes, and streams. Recall the graphical model used in Chapter 4 to illustrate the socially unacceptable impact of producers who pollute the environment.

## SOCIALISM

**Socialism**
An economic system characterized by government ownership of resources and centralized decision making.

The idea of socialism has existed for thousands of years. Its basis is the command system. **Socialism** is an economic system characterized by government ownership of resources and centralized decision making. Socialism is also called *command socialism*. Under a socialist economy, a command system owns and controls in the *public interest* the major industries, such as steel, electricity, and agriculture. However, some free markets can exist in farming, retail trade, and certain service areas. Just as no pure capitalist system exists in the real world, none of the socialist countries in the world today practices pure socialism. In fact, there are as many variants of socialism as there are countries called socialist.

Before discussing socialism further, you must realize that socialism is an economic system, and politics should not be confused with economics. Great Britain, France, and Italy have representative democracies, but many of their major industries are or have been nationalized. In the United States, the federal government owns and operates the Tennessee Valley Authority (TVA), the National Aeronautics and Space Administration (NASA), and the U.S. Postal Service, while at the same time allowing private utilities and mail service firms to operate.

## THE IDEAS OF KARL MARX

In spite of the transition to capitalism in Russia and eastern Europe, socialism still prevails in China, Cuba, and many less-developed countries. The theory for socialism and *communism* can be traced to Karl Marx. Marx was a nineteenth-century German philosopher, revolutionary, and economist. Unlike other economists of the time who followed Adam Smith, Marx rejected the concept of a society operating through private interest and profit.

Karl Marx was born in Germany, the son of a lawyer. He was an outstanding student at Berlin University. In 1841, after receiving a doctorate in philosophy, he turned to journalism. In 1843, Marx married the daughter of a wealthy family and moved to Paris, but his political activities forced him to leave Paris for England. From the age of 31, he lived and wrote his books in London. In London, Marx lived an impoverished life while he and his lifelong friend Friedrich Engels wrote the *Communist Manifesto*, published in 1848. A massive work followed, titled *Das Kapital*, which was published in three volumes in 1867, 1884, and 1885.

These two works made Karl Marx the most influential economist in the history of socialism. In fact, he devoted his entire life to a revolt against capitalism. As Marx read *The Wealth of Nations*, he saw profits as unjust payments to owners of firms—the capitalists. Marx predicted that the market system would destroy itself because wealthy owners would go too far and exploit workers because unrelenting greed for profits would lead the owners to pay starvation wages. Moreover, the owners would force laborers to work in unsafe conditions, and many would not have a job at all.

Marx believed that private ownership and exploitation would produce a nation driven by a class struggle between a few "haves" and many "have-nots." As he stated in the *Communist Manifesto*, "The history of all existing society is the history of class struggle. Freeman and slave, patrician and plebeian, lord and serf, guildmaster and journeyman, in a word, oppressor and oppressed."[3] In Marx's vision, capitalists were the modern-day oppressors, and the workers were the oppressed proletariat. Someday, Marx predicted, the workers would rise up in a spontaneous bloody revolution against a system benefiting only the owners of capital. Marx believed **communism** to be the ideal system, which would evolve in stages from capitalism through socialism. Communism is a stateless, classless economic system in which all the factors of production are owned by the workers and people share in production according to their needs. This is the highest form of socialism, toward which the revolution should strive.

Under communism, no private property exists to encourage self-interest. There is no struggle between classes of people, and everyone cooperates. In fact, there is no reason to commit crime, and police, lawyers, and courts are unnecessary. Strangely, Marx surpassed Adam Smith in advocating a system with little central government. Marx believed that those who work hard, or are more skilled, will be public spirited. Any "haves" will give voluntarily to "have-nots" until everyone has exactly the same material well-being. In Marx's own words, people would be motivated by the principle "from each according to his ability, to each according to his need." World peace would evolve as nation after nation accepted cooperation and rejected profits and competition. Under the idealized society of commu-

**Communism**
A stateless, classless economic system in which all the factors of production are owned by the workers, and people share in production according to their needs. In Marx's view, this is the highest form of socialism toward which the revolution should strive.

[3]Karl Marx and Friedrich Engels, *The Communist Manifesto* (New York: International Press, 1848), p. 31.

**Karl Marx** (1818–1883)
His criticism of capitalism
advanced communism.
He wrote *Communist
Manifesto* and *Das
Kapital.*

nism, there would be no state. No central authority would be necessary to pursue the interests of the people.

Today, we call the economic systems that existed in the former Soviet Union and Eastern Europe, and still exist in China, Cuba, and other countries *communist*. However, the definition for *socialism* given in this chapter more accurately describes their real-world economic systems. Actually, no nation has achieved the ideal communist society described by Marx, nor has capitalism self-destructed as he predicted. The 1917 communist revolution in Russia did not fit Marx's theory. At that time, Russia was an underdeveloped country, rather than an industrial country filled with greedy capitalists who exploited workers.

## CHARACTERISTICS OF SOCIALISM

Regardless of a society's political system, a socialist economy has two basic characteristics: (1) public ownership and (2) centralized decision making.

**Public Ownership**   Under socialism, the government owns most of the factors of production, including factories, farms, mines, and natural resources. Agriculture in the old Soviet Union illustrates how even this real-world socialist country deviated from total public ownership. In the Soviet Union, there were three rather distinct forms of agriculture: state farms, collective farms, and private plots. In both the state-farm and the collective-farm sectors, central planning authorities determined prices and outputs. In contrast, the government allowed those holding small private plots on peasant farms to operate primarily in free markets that determined price and output levels. Reforms now allow farmers to buy land, tractors, trucks, and other resources from the state. If these reforms continue, they will dramatically end the collectivization of agriculture begun under Josef Stalin.

**Centralized Decision Making**   Instead of the pursuit of *private interest*, the motivation of pure socialism is the *public interest* of the whole society. For instance, a factory manager cannot decide to raise or lower prices to obtain maximum profits for the factory. Regardless of inventory levels or the opportunity to raise prices, the planners will not permit this action. Instead of exploiting the ups and downs of the market, the goal of the socialist system is to make centralized decisions that protect workers and consumers from decentralized market decisions. Critics argue that the main objective of this centralization is to perpetuate the personal dictatorships of leaders such as Stalin in the old Soviet Union and Fidel Castro in Cuba.

Before the open market reforms, Soviet planners altered earnings to attract workers into certain occupations and achieve planned goals. For example, if space projects needed more engineers, then the state raised the earnings of engineers until the target number of people entered the engineering profession.

As shown earlier in Exhibit 2, central planners in the Soviet Union also manipulated consumer prices. If consumers desired more cars than were available, the authorities increased the price of cars. If people wished to purchase less of an item than was available, planners lowered prices. The problem was that this decision process took time. And while the market awaited its orders from the Soviet planners, excess inventories of some items accumulated, and consumers stood in line for cheap products that never seemed to be available. There was an old Soviet saying, "If you see a line, get in it. Whatever it is, it's scarce, and you will not see it tomorrow."

**CHECKPOINT**

### To Plan or Not to Plan—That Is the Question

You make plans. You planned to go to college. You plan which career to follow. You plan to get married, and so on. Businesses plan. They plan to hire employees, expand their plants, increase profits, and so forth. Because individuals and businesses plan in a market economy, there is really no difference between our system and a command economy. Or is there?

The Soviet factory system did not adhere completely to the command system. The government rewarded successful managers with bonuses that could be substantial. Better apartments, nice vacations, and medals were incentives for outstanding performance. Under economic reforms, plant managers now make decisions based on profitability instead of centralized controls.

## Socialism's Strengths and Weaknesses

Proponents of the socialism model argue that this system is superior in achieving an equitable distribution of income. This is because government ownership of capital and other resources prevents a few individuals or groups from acquiring a disproportionate share of the nation's wealth. Also, supporters argue that rapid economic growth is achieved when planners have the power to direct more resources to producing capital goods and fewer resources to producing consumer goods (see Exhibit 5 of Chapter 2).

National goals may seem to be easily formulated and pursued under state directives, but there are problems. For example, proponents of such an economy can claim there is no unemployment because the government assigns all workers a job and allocates resources to complete their production goals. However, economic inefficiency results because the government often uses many workers to perform work requiring only one or two workers. Critics also point out that the absence of the profit motive discourages entrepreneurship and innovation and thus suppresses economic growth.

Socialism is particularly vulnerable to the charge that it ignores the goal of economic freedom and instead creates a privileged class of government bureaucrats who assume the role of "capitalists." Central planners are the key translators of information about consumer preferences and production capabilities flowing to millions of economic units. This complex and cumbersome process is subject to errors and unresponsiveness to the wants of the majority of the population. Critics also question whether the distribution of income under socialism is more equitable than under capitalism. In the socialist system, "perks" for government officials, nepotism, and the illegal use of markets create disparities in income.

# Comparing Economic Systems

In reality, all nations operate economic systems that blend capitalism and socialism. Exhibit 3 presents a continuum that attempts to place countries between the

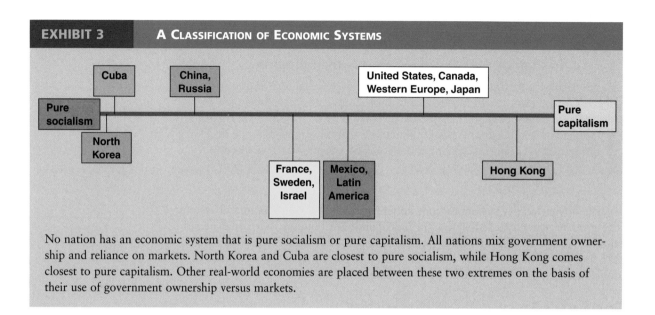

| EXHIBIT 3 | A CLASSIFICATION OF ECONOMIC SYSTEMS |

No nation has an economic system that is pure socialism or pure capitalism. All nations mix government owner-ship and reliance on markets. North Korea and Cuba are closest to pure socialism, while Hong Kong comes closest to pure capitalism. Other real-world economies are placed between these two extremes on the basis of their use of government ownership versus markets.

two extremes of pure socialism on the left and pure capitalism on the right. Economies characterized by a high degree of both private ownership and market allocation are closest to pure capitalism. Hong Kong (now part of China), Japan, the United States, and Canada fall at the capitalism end of the line. Conversely, economies characterized by much government ownership of resources and central planning are closest to pure socialism. North Korea and Cuba fall close to the pure socialism end of the spectrum, with China and Russia further away from pure socialism.

# Economies in Transition

By the early 1990s, the centrally planned economies in the old Soviet Union and Eastern Europe had collapsed. After more than 70 years in the Soviet Union and over 40 years in Eastern Europe and China, the failed communist economies made a startling switch to embrace capitalism. Faced with severe shortages of food, housing, cars, and other consumer goods, communism could no longer claim bet-ter living standards for its citizens. The following is a brief discussion of reforms aimed at introducing market power into the economic systems of Cuba, Russia, and China. This section concludes with a discussion of Japan's financial crisis.

## CUBA

Today, Cuba experiences daily power blackouts, fuel shortages, and other eco-nomic hardships. But regardless of its economics woes, Cuba remains wedded to the communist system. Nevertheless, the collapse of Soviet bloc aid coupled with the effects of the U.S. trade embargo have forced Fidel Castro, a die-hard Marx-ist, to reluctantly adopt limited free market reforms. To earn foreign exchange, the dollar has been legalized, and the Cuban government has poured capital into tourism by building several new state-owned hotels and restoring historic sections of Havana. Cuba has also set up quasi-state enterprises that accept only hard currency. Since few Cubans have dollars or other hard currency, many are earning it by turning to illegal schemes, such as driving gypsy cabs, engaging in prostitution, or selling Cuba's famous cigars and coffee on the black market. Other Cubans have abandoned state jobs and opened small businesses under these new rules. However, these small-scale businesses cannot employ anyone beyond the family of the owner. Also, spare rooms in houses can be rented, and artisans can sell their work to tourists. In addition, state farm enterprises have been broken into worker-owned units, and the government allows farmers to sell produce left over after they have met the state's quota. As a result, more food and a greater variety of food are becoming available.

In spite of the private enterprise reforms, Cuba remains essentially a communist system. Workers receive free education, housing, health care, low state salaries in pesos, and rations of staples. Profits from hotels and shops go directly into the central bank and help finance Castro's government. The state also discourages private enterprises by taxing them heavily on expected earnings rather than on actual sales. In addition, there are highly restrictive regulations. For example, restaurants in Havana are limited to 12 seats and cannot expand regardless of demand. And in 2004, Cuba halted new licenses for some types of self-employment, including jewelers, mousetrap makers, and magicians or clowns.

## RUSSIA

In 1991, communist rule ended in Russia. To function efficiently, markets must offer incentives, so workers, the public, and even foreign investors were permitted to buy state property. This meant individuals could own the factors of production and earn profits. Such market incentives are a dagger thrust into the heart of a system previously devoted to rejecting capitalism.

A key reform for Russia was to allow supply and demand to set higher prices for basic consumer goods. As shown earlier in Exhibit 2, without central planners, when prices rise to their equilibrium level, the quantity supplied increases and the quantity demanded decreases. At the beginning of 1992, the Russian government removed direct government price controls on most market goods. As the model predicts, average prices rose, leaping 1,735 percent in 1992, and a greater variety of goods started appearing on the shelves. Although workers had to pay more for basic consumer goods, they could at least find goods to buy.

Since 1992, Russia has established an independent central bank and implemented anti-inflationary monetary policies. As a result, the inflation rate fell to 15 percent in 1997. Nevertheless, Russia continued to face financial crises. In the late spring of 1998, its stock market crashed, payment on its foreign debt was suspended, and the ruble was devalued. In 1999, Russia proposed that its commercial bank creditors agree to a significant reduction in the $31 billion debt owed to them as part of a restructuring agreement. In 2000, the inflation rate was 21 percent, and many companies were not paying their bills, wages, or taxes. By 2005, the inflation rate had fallen to 9 percent. Russian entrepreneurial spirit is in an embryonic stage, and corruption is a frequent way of life. Although Russia is far from a successful market economy, the nation is struggling to achieve an amazing economic transition. Russian privatization plans are being implemented and steps are continuing to create a dynamic economy embracing capitalism. And *Forbes* magazine reports that there are now several billionaires who reside in Russia.

## International Economics

# China Seeks Free Market Revolution
*Applicable Concept: comparative economic systems*

For more than 2,000 years, China had a "self reliance" policy that caused its economy to lag far behind advanced economies. In 1978, China adopted new economic reforms that are continuing to transform one of the poorest economies in the world into one of the fastest growing. Under this reform system, households operate in a mixed world of state controls and free markets. A two-track pricing system still exists for some key goods and services, such as coal, petroleum, steel, transportation, and agriculture. The rural economy is central to China's economic reforms. In the past, farmers worked collectively in people's communes. The government told the farmers what to produce and how much to produce. They could sell their products only to the state at a price fixed by the government, rather than in markets.

© Photodisc/Getty Images

A so-called household contract responsibility system was created as a reform to assign land owned by the state to farmers. The farmers must pay an annual share of their profits to the government, and the state does not cover losses. Farmers, however, have the authority to decide what to produce and the price at which to sell in open markets. As a result, both farmers and consumers are noticeably better off because everyone can find and afford more food.

As farming productivity rose sharply, fewer farmers were needed to work on the land, and this surplus labor moved into emerging township and village nonstate enterprises. These enterprises were mostly in light industry and owned collectively by townships or villages. As a result, the composition of rural output has changed. When the reforms began in the late 1970s, farming accounted for 70 percent of the total rural output and industry for 20 percent. Overall, the structure of the economy has changed. In 1976, agriculture accounted for 33 percent of GDP and by 2005, its share had fallen to 13 percent.[1]

A 1993 article in the *Boston Globe* provides an interesting observation on China's economic transformation:

> *Stuffing the genie back into the bottle might prove diffi-*

## THE PEOPLE'S REPUBLIC OF CHINA

Unlike Russia, China has sought economic reform under the direction of its Communist Party. Fundamental economic reforms began in China after the death of Mao Tse-Tung in 1976. Much of this reform was due to the leadership of Deng Xiaoping. Mao was devoted to the egalitarian ideal of communist ideology. Under his rule, thoughts of self-interest were counterrevolutionary, and photographs of Marx, Lenin, and Mao hung on every street corner and in every office and factory. Deng shifted priorities by increasing production of consumer goods and steering China toward becoming a global economic power. And the results have been dramatic. International trade expanded from less than 1 percent of U.S. trade in 1975 to 10 percent in 2005. China joined the WTO in 2001 and agreed to open some markets closed to foreigners. China's real GDP growth rate averaged 8.4 percent between 1995 and 2005, making it the world's fastest growing economy.

To make China an industrial power in the twenty-first century, Chinese planners introduced a two-tier system for industry and agriculture in 1978. Each farm *cult. The flood of money has created a bubble, particularly in stocks and property, making some people in China very rich, very fast. The* China Daily, *China's official English-language newspaper, recently heralded the existence of 1 million millionaires.... These millionaires, many of whom just five years ago were still wearing Mao outfits and following the party's socialist dictates, now sport stylish Western-style suits with the label ostentatiously left on the cuff.*[2]

A 2001 *Time* article described China's controversial womb police, who have spent two decades attempting to control the nation's population by fining citizens with more than one child. They have succeeded remarkably well. Today, the average Chinese woman has two children, compared with six 30

years ago. "For all the bad press, China has achieved the impossible," says Sven Burmester, the U.N. Population Fund representative in Beijing. "The country has solved its population problem." In fact, China's population will actually start declining in 2042, according to U.N. projections.[3]

At the sixteenth Communist Party Congress in 2003, President Hu Jintao and Communist Party leaders announced "another turning point and a new starting point in China's reform process." A key debate concerned reforms that would move China closer to capitalism, including the first-ever guarantee of private property under communist rule.[4] However, a 2004 Congressional report noted that corrupt land requisitions and unfair compensation schemes were fueling a wave of protests across China. The report stated, "Farmers end up landless and, once they have

exhausted their small subsidies, unemployed and without a course of income."[5]

## ANALYZE THE ISSUE

1. Why would China abandon the goal of income equality and shift from a centrally planned system to a more market-oriented economy?

2. Which groups in China are likely to resist the reforms?

[1]World Bank, *Key Development Data & Statistics*, http://www.worldbank.org/.
[2]Maggie Farley, "China's Economic Boom Energizing Inflation," *Boston Globe*, Aug. 13, 1993, p. 1A.
[3]"China's Lifestyle Choice: Changes to the Famous One-Child Policy Miss the Point," *Time*, Aug. 6, 2001, p. 32.
[4]Joe McDonald, "China Debates Private Property," *Sun News*, Oct. 12, 2003, p. 14A.
[5]Tim Johnson, "Local Protests Increase in China," *Charlotte Observer*, Oct. 26, 2004, p. 12A.

and state enterprise was given a contract to produce a quota. Any amount produced over the quota could be sold in an open market. The Chinese government also encouraged the formation of nonstate enterprises owned jointly by managers and their workforces and special economic zones open to foreign investment. In other words, a blend of capitalism and socialism would provide the incentives needed to increase output. As Deng Xiaoping explained, "It doesn't matter whether the cat is black or white as long as it catches mice." These reforms worked, leading to huge increases in farm and industrial output in the 1980s. In fact, some peasant farmers became the wealthiest people in China. After Deng's death in the mid-1990s, leadership of China passed to leaders who continued the policy of free market reforms. Today, forests of glossy skyscrapers, expressways, upscale apartments, and shopping malls in Beijing, Shanghai, and other cities attest to the market-oriented reforms begun years ago. (See International Economics: China Seeks Free Market Revolution.)

Today, China is a huge nation transforming itself swiftly into a powerful player in the global economy. U.S. exporters are overjoyed at the prospect of selling products to over a billion Chinese consumers. For example, swarms of bicyclists once synonymous with urban China are being pushed off the road by consumers who now can afford cars and trucks. In 2005, Rolls-Royce and Bentley, the ultra-luxury cars, expanded into China. And more Chinese are traveling by air. Consequently, the Chinese are buying more Boeing airplanes and American-made cars. The other side of the coin is the threat of what goods the industrious Chinese workers, with increasing training and foreign investment, might produce and sell abroad. For example, China manufactures most of the world's copiers, microwave ovens, DVD players, and shoes. A ballooning U.S. trade deficit with China is often cited as evidence that China is not playing fair, and the political rhetoric has intensified on both sides of the issue. Other countries fear that China will eliminate their export business with the United States. Moreover, there is concern that lowering trade barriers under free-trade agreements will increase Chinese imports into domestic markets and eliminate jobs. Currently, China's leaders are dealing with an economy that is experiencing overheating. Factories suffer electricity shortages, while ports and railways cannot handle all the cargo flowing in and out of the country. China is consuming huge quantities of crude oil, copper, steel, and aluminum, and consumer prices have risen from 0.4 percent in 2000 to 3.0 percent in 2005. Moreover, there is discontent over labor issues, pollution, and income inequality. While some dig through trash bins, there are now wealthy private business owners. Despite the growing unease, China remains a market of great profit and promise as it continues its transition from a communist command economy to capitalism. And the debate continues over whether China, a socialist economy, is a strategic trading partner or an emerging rival that will dominate the world economy.

## Key Concepts

Economic system
Traditional economy
Command economy
Market economy

Invisible hand
Mixed economy
Capitalism
Consumer sovereignty

Socialism
Communism

## Summary

■ An **economic system** is the set of established procedures by which a society answers the *What, How,* and *For Whom to produce* questions.

■ **Three basic types of economic systems** are the traditional, command, and market systems. The **traditional system** makes decisions according to custom, and the **command system,** shown in the figure to the right, answers the three economic questions through some powerful central authority. In contrast, the **market system** uses the impersonal mechanism of the interaction of buyers and sellers in markets to answer the *What, How,* and *For Whom* questions.

**COMMAND ECONOMY**

- **Capitalism** is an economic system in which the factors of production are privately owned and economic choices are made by consumers and firms in markets. As prescribed by Adam Smith, government plays an extremely limited role, and self-interest is the driving force—held in check, or regulated, by competition.

- **Consumer sovereignty** is the freedom of consumers to determine the types and quantities of products that are produced in an economy by choosing to buy or not to buy.

- **Socialism** is an economic system in which the government owns the factors of production. The central authorities make the myriad of society's economic decisions according to a national plan. The collective good, or public interest, is the intended guiding force behind the central planners' decisions.

- **Communism** is an economic system envisioned by Karl Marx to be an ideal society in which the workers own all the factors of production. Marx believed that workers who work hard will be public spirited and voluntarily redistribute income to those who are less productive. Such a communist nation described by Marx does not exist.

## Summary of Conclusion Statements

- When central planners set prices below equilibrium for goods and services, they create shortages, which mean long lines, empty shelves, and black markets.

- A market economy answers the *What to produce* and *How to produce* questions very effectively.

- No nation in the world precisely fits the two criteria for capitalism; however, the United States comes close.

## Study Questions and Problems

1. Give an example of how a nation's culture affects its economic system.

2. Explain the advantages and the disadvantages of any two of the three basic types of economic systems.

3. Suppose a national program of free housing for the elderly is paid for by a sizable increase in income taxes. Explain a tradeoff that might occur between economic security and efficiency.

4. "The schools are not in the business of pleasing parents and students, and they cannot be allowed to set their own agendas. Their agendas are set by politicians, administrators, and various constituencies that hold the keys to political power. The public system is built to see to it that the schools do what their government wants them to do—that they conform to the higher-order values their governors seek to impose."[4] Relate this statement to Exhibit 1.

5. Suppose you are a farmer. Explain why you would be motivated to work in traditional, command, and market economies.

6. Karl Marx believed the market system was doomed. Why do you think he was right or wrong?

7. If all real-world economies are mixed economies, why is the U.S. economy described as capitalist, while the Cuban economy is described as communist?

8. Suppose you are a factory manager. Describe how you might reach production goals under a system of pure capitalism and under a system of pure socialism.

[4]John Chubb and Terry More, *Politics, Markets, and the Nation's Public Schools* (Washington, D.C.: Brookings Institution, 1990), p. 38.

## Study Guide Questions

1. Three basic types of economic systems are the _____, based on decisions made according to customs, and the _____, which answers the three economic questions through some powerful central authority. In contrast, the _____ uses the impersonal mechanism of the interaction of buyers and sellers through markets to answer the *What*, *How*, and *For Whom* questions.

2. Which of the following statements is *true*?
   a. The doctrine of laissez-faire advocates an economic system with extensive government intervention and little individual decision making.
   b. In capitalism income is distributed on the basis of need.
   c. Adam Smith was the father of socialism.
   d. Most real-world economies are mixed economic systems.
   e. The "invisible hand" refers to government economic control.

3. Which of the following statements is *true*?
   a. The United States today comes closer to the socialist form of economic organization than it does capitalism.
   b. When central planners set prices above equilibrium for goods and services they create shortages.
   c. According to Karl Marx, under capitalism, workers would be exploited and would revolt against the owners of capital.
   d. Adam Smith argued that government's role in society would be to do absolutely nothing.

4. In Adam Smith's competitive market economy, the question of what goods to produce is determined by
   a. the "invisible hand" of the price system.
   b. businesses.
   c. unions.
   d. the government, through laws and regulations.

5. T  F  When the official price for goods and services is below the equilibrium price in a market, prices no longer perform their rationing function efficiently.

**Answers to these questions are in the complete Study Guide at www.thomsonedu.com/thomsonnow.**

**For Online Exercises, go to the text Web site at www.thomsonedu.com/economics/tucker.**

## Checkpoint Answer

### To Plan or Not to Plan—That Is the Question

When an individual or a business plans in a market economy, other individuals are free to make and follow their own plans. Suppose Hewlett-Packard decides to produce *X* number of laser printers and sell them at a certain price. The decision does not prohibit IBM from producing *Y* number of laser printers and selling them for less than Hewlett-Packard's printers. If either firm makes a mistake, only that firm suffers, and other industries are for the most part unaffected. Under a command system, a central economic plan would be made for all laser printer manufacturers. If the central planners order the wrong quantity or quality, there could be major harm to other industries and society. If you said there is a major difference between individual planning and central planning for all society, **YOU ARE CORRECT.**

## Practice Quiz

For an explanation of the correct answers, please visit the tutorial at www.thomsonedu.com/economics/tucker.

1. The economic system in which all of the basic decisions are made through a centralized authority, such as a government agency, is termed a
   a. market economy.
   b. capitalistic economy.
   c. command economy.
   d. traditional economy.

2. Command economies typically suffer from
   a. unemployment, but not underemployment.
   b. neither unemployment nor underemployment.
   c. both unemployment and underemployment.
   d. underemployment, but not unemployment.

3. Adam Smith stated that the role of government in society should be to
   a. provide defense.
   b. enforce contracts.
   c. do absolutely nothing.
   d. do both (a) and (b).

4. When making economic decisions, Adam Smith urged society to
   a. follow the principle of self interest.
   b. follow the principle of public interest.
   c. transfer wealth according to need.
   d. provide equal income for all citizens.

5. The doctrine of laissez faire
   a. advocates an economic system with extensive government intervention and little individual decision making.
   b. was advocated by Adam Smith in his book *The Wealth of Nations*.
   c. was advocated by Karl Marx in his book *Das Kapital*.
   d. is described by none of the above.

6. In Adam Smith's competitive market economy, the question of what goods to produce is determined by the
   a. "invisible hand" of the price system.
   b. "invisible hand" of government.
   c. "visible hand" of public interest.
   d. "visible hand" of laws and regulations.

7. Adam Smith wrote that the
   a. economic problems of eighteenth-century England were caused by free markets.
   b. government should control the economy with an "invisible hand."
   c. pursuit of private self interest promotes the public interest in a market economy.
   d. public or collective interest is not promoted by people pursuing their self interest.

8. Adam Smith, in his book *The Wealth of Nations*, advocated
   a. socialism.
   b. an economy guided by an "invisible hand."
   c. government control of the "invisible hand."
   d. the adoption of mercantilism.

9. The economic system in which private individuals own the factors of production is
   a. a planned economy.
   b. capitalism.
   c. collectivism.
   d. socialism.

10. Which of the following is *not* a basic characteristic of capitalism?
    a. Economic decisions occur in markets.
    b. Factors of production are privately owned.
    c. Income is distributed on the basis of need.
    d. Businesses make their own product and price decisions.

11. According to Karl Marx, under capitalism,
    a. profits would be shared fairly.
    b. incomes would be distributed equally.
    c. workers would be exploited and revolt against owners of capital.
    d. workers would actually own the factors of production.

12. Karl Marx predicted which of the following?
    a. The market system would self-destruct.
    b. The "haves" would revolt against the "have-nots."
    c. The wealthy were entitled to profits as their reward for risk taking.
    d. None of the above.

13. How many nations in the world today operate totally according to Karl Marx's theory of communism?
    a. None
    b. Several
    c. Only the United States
    d. Many

14. In Marx's ideal communist society, the state
    a. actively promotes income equality.
    b. follows the doctrine of laissez faire.
    c. owns resources and conducts planning.
    d. does not exist.

15. Karl Marx was a (an)
    a. nineteenth-century German philosopher.
    b. eighteenth-century Russian economist.
    c. fourteenth-century Polish banker.
    d. nineteenth-century Russian journalist.

# Growth and the Less-Developed Countries

© Photodisc/Getty Images

How would your life be different if you lived in Rwanda, Vietnam, or Haiti instead of the United States? It is unlikely that anyone in your family would have a telephone or a car. You surely would not own a personal computer or a compact disc player. You would not have new clothes and be enrolled in a college or university studying economics. You would not be going out to restaurants or movies. You would be fortunate to have shoes and one full meal each day. You would receive little or no medical care and live in unsanitary surroundings. Hunger, disease, and squalor would engulf you. In fact, the World Bank estimates that over 20 percent of people in developing countries survive on less than $1 per day.

It is exceedingly difficult for Americans to grasp that one-fifth of the world's population lives at such a meager subsistence level. This brings us to this chapter's important task of unraveling the secrets of economic growth and development. Why do some countries prosper while others decline?

At different times in history, Egypt, China, Italy, and Greece were highly developed by the standards of their time. On the other hand, at one time the United States was a struggling, relatively poor country on the path to becoming a rich country. Its growth came in three stages: First was the agricultural stage. Then came the manufacturing stage when industries such as railroads, steel, and automobiles were driving forces toward economic growth. And, finally, there has been a shift toward service industries. This is the U.S. success story, but it is not the only road countries can follow to lift themselves from the misery of poverty.

**In this chapter, you will learn to solve these economics puzzles:**

- Is there a difference between economic growth and economic development?
- Why are some countries rich and others poor?
- Is trade a better "engine of growth" than foreign aid and loans?

## Comparing Developed and Less-Developed Countries

Income disparity exists not only among families within the United States but also among nations. In this section, the great inequality of income between the families of nations will be used to classify nations as rich or poor.

425

## CLASSIFYING COUNTRIES BY GDP PER CAPITA

**GDP per capita**
The value of final goods produced (GDP) divided by the total population.

**Industrially advanced countries (IACs)**
High-income nations that have market economies based on large stocks of technologically advanced capital and well-educated labor. The United States, Canada, Australia, New Zealand, Japan, and most of the countries of Western Europe are IACs.

**Less-developed countries (LDCs)**
Nations without large stocks of technologically advanced capital and well-educated labor. LDCs are economies based on agriculture, such as most countries of Africa, Asia, and Latin America.

There are more than 180 countries in the world. Exhibit 1 shows a ranking of selected countries from high to low **GDP per capita**. GDP per capita is the value of final goods produced (GDP) divided by the total population. Although any system of defining rich versus poor countries is arbitrary, GDP per capita or average GDP is a fundamental measure of a country's economic well-being. At the top of the income ladder are 27 developed countries called the **industrially advanced countries (IACs)**. Industrially advanced countries are high-income nations that have market economies based on large stocks of technologically advanced capital and well-educated labor. The United States, Canada, Australia, New Zealand, Japan, and most of the countries of western Europe are IACs. Excluded from the IACs are countries with high incomes whose economies are based on oil under the sand, and not on widespread industrial development. The United Arab Emirates is an example of such a country.

Countries of the world other than IACs are classified as underdeveloped or **less-developed countries (LDCs)**. Less-developed countries are nations without large stocks of technologically advanced capital and well-educated labor. Their economies are based on agriculture, as in most countries of Africa, Asia, and Latin America. Over three-fourths of the world's population, consisting of about 150 countries, live in LDCs and share widespread poverty.

A closer examination of Exhibit 1 reveals that the differences in living standards between the IACs and LDCs are enormous. For example, the GDP per capita in the United States was $41,849 greater than the average income in Ethiopia. Stated differently, the 2005 average income in the United States was about 330 times larger than the average income in Ethiopia ($41,976/$127). What a difference! Imagine trying to live on only $127 for a year in the United States. You probably would not survive.

Exhibit 2 compares GDP per capita for IACs to LDCs by regions of the world for 2005. The average citizen in the IACs enjoyed an income of $34,799, which was 55 times that of the average citizen in South Asia ($34,799/$629). The exhibit also reveals that the greatest concentrations of world poverty are located in the rural areas of South Asia and Sub-Saharan Africa. The East Asia and Pacific region has many countries characterized by bleak and pervasive poverty, but there are notable exceptions, nicknamed the "Four Tigers" of East Asia—Hong Kong, Singapore, South Korea, and Taiwan. These Pacific Rim countries are newly industrialized economies, which we discuss at the end of this chapter.

## PROBLEMS WITH GDP PER CAPITA COMPARISONS

Several problems are associated with using GDP per capita to compare rich versus poor countries. First, there is a measurement problem because countries tabulate GDP with differing degrees of accuracy. LDCs in general do not use sophisticated methods of gathering and processing GDP and population data. For example, in countries whose economies are based largely on agriculture, a family is more likely to produce goods and services outside the price system. In LDCs, families often grow their own food, make their own clothes, and build their own homes. Estimating the value of this output at market prices is difficult.

| EXHIBIT 1 | ANNUAL GDP PER CAPITA FOR SELECTED COUNTRIES, 2005 | | |
|---|---|---|---|
| Country | GDP per capita | Country | GDP per capita |
| **Industrially Advanced Countries (IACs)** | | | |
| Luxembourg | $73,147 | France | $33,854 |
| Norway | 63,795 | Germany | 33,785 |
| Switzerland | 50,158 | Australia | 33,526 |
| Ireland | 48,753 | Italy | 29,635 |
| Denmark | 46,691 | Spain | 27,175 |
| United States | 41,976 | Singapore | 26,253 |
| Sweden | 39,101 | New Zealand | 26,233 |
| Netherlands | 38,180 | Hong Kong | 24,715 |
| Austria | 37,688 | Greece | 20,006 |
| Japan | 36,599 | Israel | 18,464 |
| Finland | 36,522 | Portugal | 16,525 |
| United Kingdom | 36,429 | South Korea | 16,493 |
| Belgium | 35,068 | Taiwan | 14,447 |
| Canada | 34,375 | | |
| | | | |
| **Less-Developed Countries (LDCs)** | | | |
| Mexico | 7,183 | China | 1,461 |
| Chile | 6,224 | Egypt | 1,283 |
| Russia | 5,459 | Indonesia | 1,233 |
| South Africa | 4,993 | Bolivia | 1,024 |
| Turkey | 4,925 | Georgia | 1,000 |
| Panama | 4,513 | Pakistan | 777 |
| Brazil | 4,297 | India | 687 |
| Romania | 3,603 | Vietnam | 568 |
| Iran | 2,926 | Haiti | 517 |
| Thailand | 2,563 | Bangladesh | 401 |
| Jordan | 2,163 | Mozambique | 363 |
| Ukraine | 1,739 | Rwanda | 233 |
| Morroco | 1,712 | Ethiopia | 127 |

*Source: International Monetary Fund, World Economic Outlook Database, http://www.imf.org/external/pubs/ft/weo/2005/02/data/dbginim.cfm.*

**CONCLUSION** *LDCs' GDP per capita is subject to greater measurement errors than data for IACs.*

Second, GDP per capita comparisons among countries can be misleading because they ignore the relative income distribution. Some countries have very high per capita incomes, yet most of the income goes to just a few wealthy families.

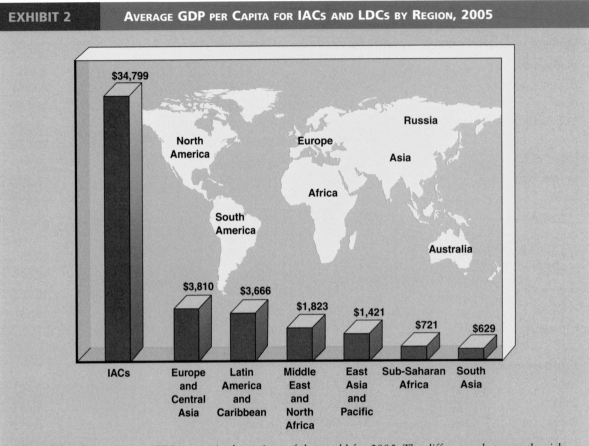

**EXHIBIT 2        AVERAGE GDP PER CAPITA FOR IACs AND LDCs BY REGION, 2005**

This exhibit shows average GDP per capita by regions of the world for 2005. The differences between the rich, industrially advanced countries (IACs) and the poor less-developed countries (LDCs) in the various regions of the world are enormous. For example, the average citizen in the IACs had an income 55 times that of the average citizen in the LDCs of South Asia.

*Source: World Bank Group,* Key Development Data & Statistics, *http://www.worldbank.org/.*

The United Arab Emirates' GDP per capita is higher than that of several IACs. However, the United Arab Emirates earns its income from oil exports, and its income is actually distributed disproportionately to a relatively small number of wealthy families.

**CONCLUSION** *GDP per capita comparisons among nations can be misleading because GDP per capita does not measure income distribution.*

Third, GDP per capita comparisons between nations are subject to conversion problems. Making these data comparisons requires converting one nation's currency—say, Japan's yen—into a common currency, the U.S. dollar. Because, as explained in the chapter on international trade and finance, the value of a country's currency can rise or fall for many reasons, the true value of a nation's output can be distorted. For example, during a given year, one government might maintain an artificially high exchange rate and another government might not.

> **CONCLUSION** *A conversion problem may widen or narrow the GDP per capita gap between nations because the fluctuations in exchange rates do not reflect actual differences in the value of goods and services produced.*

## QUALITY-OF-LIFE MEASURES OF DEVELOPMENT

GDP per capita measures market transactions, but this measure does not give a complete picture of differences in living standards among nations. Exhibit 3 presents other selected socioeconomic indicators of the quality of life. These are variables such as life expectancy at birth, infant mortality rate, illiteracy rate, per capita energy consumption and economic freedom ranking. Take a close look at the statistics in Exhibit 3. These data reflect the dimensions of poverty in many of the LDCs. For example, a person born in the United States has a life expectancy that is much longer than a person born in Mozambique, and the infant mortality rate is dramatically higher in Mozambique. Per capita energy consumption measures the use of nonhuman energy to perform work. In IACs, most work is done by machines, and in LDCs, virtually all work is done by people. For example, the average American uses 7,843 kilograms of (oil-equivalent) energy per year, while the average person in Mozambique uses only 430 kilograms. Finally, it is interesting to note that GDP per capita and ranking in economic freedom are related.

| EXHIBIT 3 | QUALITY-OF-LIFE INDICATORS FOR SELECTED COUNTRIES, 2005 | | | | | |
|---|---|---|---|---|---|---|
| **Country** | **(1)**<br>**GDP**<br>**per capita** | **(2)**<br>**Life expectancy at birth (years)** | **(3)**<br>**Infant mortality rate[1]** | **(4)**<br>**Illiteracy rate[2]** | **(5)**<br>**Per capita energy consumption[3]** | **(6)**<br>**Economic freedom rank[4]** |
| United States | $41,976 | 77 | 7% | 3% | 7,843 | 4 |
| Japan | 36,599 | 82 | 4 | 1 | 4,053 | 30 |
| China | 1,462 | 72 | 26 | 9 | 1,094 | 87 |
| Egypt | 1,283 | 70 | 26 | 42 | 735 | 80 |
| India | 687 | 63 | 62 | 39 | 520 | 68 |
| Bangladesh | 401 | 63 | 56 | 57 | 159 | 96 |
| Mozambique | 363 | 42 | 104 | 52 | 430 | 106 |

[1]Per 1,000 live births.
[2]Percentage age 15 and over who cannot read and write.
[3]Kilograms of oil equivalent.
[4]The Fraser Institute

*Sources: World Bank Group,* Key Development Data & Statistics, *http://www.worldbank.org/; The Fraser Institute, http://www.freetheworld .com and The CIA World Factbook, http://www.odci.gov/cia/publications/factbook/index.html.*

How good an indicator of the quality of life is GDP per capita? Exhibit 3 reflects the principle that lower GDP per capita is directly correlated with measures of the quality of life.

> **CONCLUSION** *In general, GDP per capita is highly correlated with alternative measures of quality of life.*

# Economic Growth and Development around the World

Economic growth and development are major goals of IACs and LDCs. People all over the world strive for a higher quality of life for their generation and future generations. However, growth is closer to a life-or-death situation for many LDCs, such as Bangladesh and Mozambique.

Economic growth and economic development are somewhat different, but related, concepts. As shown in Exhibit 4, recall from Chapter 2 that economic growth is the ability of an economy to produce greater levels of output, represented by an outward shift of its production possibilities curve (*PPC*). Thus, economic growth is defined on a *quantitative* basis using the percentage change in GDP per capita. When a nation's GDP rises more rapidly than its population, GDP per capita rises, and the nation experiences economic growth. Conversely, if GDP expands less than the population of a nation, GDP per capita falls, and the nation experiences negative economic growth.

Economic development is a broader concept that is more *qualitative* in nature. Economic development encompasses improvement in the quality of life, including economic growth in the production of goods and services. In short, continuous economic growth is necessary for economic development, but economic growth is not the only consideration. For example, as explained earlier, GDP per capita does not measure the distribution of income or the political environment that provides the legal, monetary, education, and transportation structures necessary for economic growth.

Economic growth and development involve a complex process that is determined by several interrelated factors. Like the performance of an NBA basketball team, success depends on the joint effort of team players, and one or two weak players can greatly reduce overall performance. However, there is no precise formula for winning. If your team has a player like Michael Jordan, it can win even with a few weak players. The remainder of this section examines the key factors, or players, that operate together to produce a nation's economic well-being.

## ENDOWMENT OF NATURAL RESOURCES

Most of the LDCs have comparatively limited bases of natural resources, including mineral deposits and arable land resources. In these countries, most of the available land is used for agricultural production, and clearing tropical forests to obtain more land can cause soil erosion. Also, tropical climates prevail in Central and South America, Africa, the Indian subcontinent, and Southeast Asia. The hot,

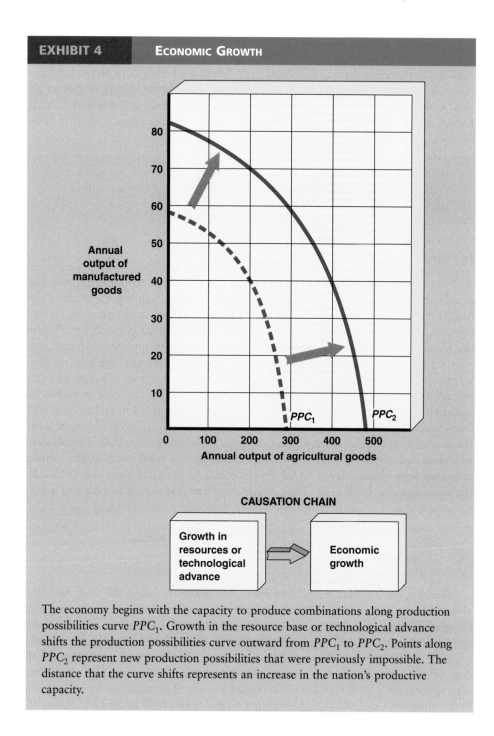

**EXHIBIT 4**  **ECONOMIC GROWTH**

**CAUSATION CHAIN**

Growth in resources or technological advance → Economic growth

The economy begins with the capacity to produce combinations along production possibilities curve $PPC_1$. Growth in the resource base or technological advance shifts the production possibilities curve outward from $PPC_1$ to $PPC_2$. Points along $PPC_2$ represent new production possibilities that were previously impossible. The distance that the curve shifts represents an increase in the nation's productive capacity.

humid climate in these regions is conducive to weed and insect infestations that plague agriculture.

Although a narrow base of resources does pose a barrier to economic growth and development, no single conclusion can be drawn. For example, how have Hong Kong, Japan, and Israel achieved high standards of living in spite of limited natural resource bases? Each has practically no minerals, little fertile land, and no domestic sources of energy. Nonetheless, these economies have become prosperous. In contrast, Argentina, Venezuela, and Brazil have abundant fertile land and minerals. Yet these and other countries have been growing slowly or not at all. Venezuela, for example, is one of the most oil-rich countries in the world. Ghana, Kenya, and Bolivia are also resource-rich countries that are poor, with little or no economic growth.

> **CONCLUSION** *Natural resource endowment can promote economic growth, but a country can develop without a large natural resource base.*

## INVESTMENT IN HUMAN RESOURCES

A low level of human capital can also present a barrier to economic growth and development. Recall that human capital is the education, training, experience, and health that improve the knowledge and skills of workers to produce goods and services. In most of the LDCs, investment in human capital is much less than in the IACs. Look back at column 4 in Exhibit 3. Consider how the illiteracy rate rises for the poorer countries. A country with a higher illiteracy rate has less ability to educate its labor force and create a basic foundation for economic growth. In fact, often the skills of workers in the poor countries are suited primarily to agriculture, rather than being appropriate for a wide range of industries and economic growth. Further complicating matters is a "brain drain" problem because the best educated and trained workers of poor countries pursue their education in wealthier countries. Column 2 of Exhibit 3 also gives a measure of health among countries with varying levels of GDP per capita. As the GDP per capita falls, the life expectancy at birth falls. Thus, richer countries have the advantage of a better educated and healthier workforce.

> **CONCLUSION** *Investment in human capital generally results in increases in GDP per capita.*

Thus far, the discussion has been about the quality of labor. We must also talk about the quantity of labor because productivity is related to both the quality and the quantity of labor. Overpopulation is a problem for LDCs. In a nutshell, here is why: Other factors held constant, population (labor force) growth can increase a country's GDP. Yet rapid population growth can convert an expanding GDP into a GDP per capita that is stagnant, slow growing, or negative. Stated another way, there is no gain if an increase in output is more than matched by an increase in the number of mouths that must be fed. Suppose the GDP of an LDC grows at, say, 3 percent per year. If there is no growth in population, GDP per capita also grows at 3 percent per year. But what if the population also grows at 3 percent per year? The result is that GDP per capita remains unchanged. If the population growth is instead only 1 percent per year, GDP per capita rises 2 percent per year. Obstacles to population control are great and include strong religious and sociocultural arguments against birth control programs.

## CHECKPOINT

### Does Rapid Growth Mean a Country Is Catching Up?

Suppose country Alpha has a production possibilities curve closer to the origin than the curve for country Beta. Now assume Alpha experiences a 3 percent growth rate in GDP for 10 years and Beta experiences a 6 percent growth rate in GDP for 10 years. At the end of five years, which of the following is the best prediction for the standard of living? (1) Alpha's residents are better off. (2) Beta's residents are better off. (3) Which country's residents are better off cannot be determined.

**CONCLUSION** *Rapid population growth combined with low human capital investment explains why many countries are LDCs.*

## ACCUMULATION OF CAPITAL

It did not take long for Robinson Crusoe on a deserted island to invest in a net in order to catch more fish than he could catch with his hands. Similarly, farmers working with modern tractors can cultivate more acres than farmers working with horse-drawn plows. Recall from Chapter 1 that capital in economics means factories, tractors, trucks, roads, computers, irrigation systems, electricity-generating facilities, and other human-made goods used to produce goods and services.

LDCs suffer from a critical shortage of capital. A family in Somalia owns little in the way of tools except a wooden plow. To make matters worse, roads are terrible, there are few plants generating electricity, and telephone lines are scarce. As shown in Exhibit 5, recall from Chapter 2 that a high-investment country can shift its production possibilities curve outward, but investment in capital goods is not a "free lunch." When more resources are used to produce more factories and machines, there is an opportunity cost of fewer resources available for the production of current consumer goods. This means that LDCs are often caught in a **vicious circle of poverty**. A vicious circle of poverty is the trap in which countries are poor and cannot afford to save. And low savings translate into low investment. Low investment results in low productivity, which, in turn, keeps incomes low. Any savings that do exist among higher-income persons in poor LDCs are often invested in IACs. This phenomenon is often called "capital flight." These wealthy individuals are afraid to save in their own countries because they fear that their governments may be overthrown and their savings could be lost.

The United States and other nations have attempted to provide LDCs with foreign aid so that they might grow. These countries desperately need more factories and **infrastructure**. Infrastructure is capital goods usually provided by the government, including highways, bridges, waste and water systems, and airports. Unfortunately, the amount of capital given to the LDCs is relatively small, and, as

**Vicious circle of poverty**
The trap in which countries are poor because they cannot afford to save and invest, but they cannot save and invest because they are poor.

**Infrastructure**
Capital goods usually provided by the government, including highways, bridges, waste and water systems, and airports.

**EXHIBIT 5**          **ALPHA'S AND BETA'S PRESENT AND FUTURE PRODUCTION POSSIBILITIES CURVES**

In Part (a), each year Alpha produces only enough capital ($K_a$) to replace existing capital that is worn out. Without greater capital, and assuming other resources remain fixed, Alpha is unable to shift its production possibilities curve outward. In Part (b), each year Beta produces $K_b$ capital, which is more than the amount required to replenish its depreciated capital. In 2010, this expanded capital provides Beta with the extra production capacity to shift its production possibilities curve to the right. If Beta chooses point $B$ on its curve, it has the production capacity to increase the amount of consumer goods from $C_b$ to $C_c$ without producing fewer capital goods.

explained above, workers in the LDCs lack the skills necessary to use the most modern forms of capital. More specifically, LDCs face a major obstacle to capital accumulation because of the lack of entrepreneurs to assume the risks of capital formation.

**CONCLUSION**  *There is a significant positive relationship between investment and economic growth and development.*

## TECHNOLOGICAL PROGRESS

As explained earlier in Chapter 2, holding natural resources, labor, and capital constant, advancing the body of knowledge applied to production shifts the production possibilities curve of a country. In fact, technological advances have been at the heart of economic growth and development in recent history. During the last 250 years, brainpower has discovered new power-driven machines, advanced communication devices, new energy sources, and countless ways to produce more output with the same resources. How have innovative products improved your productivity? Consider, to name just a few products, the impact of CD-ROMs, fax machines, DVDs, personal computers, word-processing software, cell phone photography, and the Internet. In contrast, in many poor countries, waterwheels still bring water to the surface, cloth is woven on handlooms, and oxcarts are the major means of transportation. Consequently, large inputs of human effort are used relative to capital resources.

The United States and other IACs have provided the world with an abundant accumulation of technological knowledge that might be adopted by those LDCs without the resources to undertake the required cost of research and development. However, the results of this transfer process have been mixed. For example, China, Hong Kong, Singapore, Taiwan, South Korea, and Japan have surely achieved rapid growth in part from the benefit of technological borrowing. Currently, Russia and other Eastern European nations are attempting to apply existing technological knowledge to boost their rates of growth.

The other side of the coin is that much available technology is not suited to LDCs. The old saying "You need to learn to walk before you can run" often applies to the LDCs. For example, small farms of most LDCs are not suited for much of the agricultural technology developed for IACs' large farms. And how many factories in the LDCs are ready to use the most modern robotics in the production process? Stated differently, LDCs need appropriate technology, rather than necessarily the latest technology.

> **CONCLUSION** *Many LDCs continue to experience low growth rates even though IACs have developed advanced technologies that the world can utilize.*

## POLITICAL ENVIRONMENT

The discussion above leads to the generalization that in order for LDCs to achieve economic growth and development, they must wisely use natural resources, invest in human and physical capital, and adopt advanced technology. This list of policies is not complete. LDC governments must also create a political environment favorable to economic growth. All too often a large part of the problem in poor countries is that resources are wasted as a result of war and political instability. Political leaders must not be corrupt and/or incompetent. Instead of following policies that favor a small elite ruling class, LDC governments must adopt appropriate domestic and international economic policies, discussed under the following three headings of law and order, infrastructure, and international trade.

**Law and Order** A basic governmental function is to establish domestic law and order. This function includes many areas, such as a stable legal system, stable money and prices, competitive markets, and private ownership of property. In particular, expropriation of private property rights among LDCs is a barrier to growth. Well-defined private property rights have fostered economic growth in the IACs because this institutional policy has encouraged an entrepreneurial class. Private ownership provides individuals with the incentive to save money and invest in businesses. A stable political environment that ensures private ownership of profits also provides an incentive for individuals in other countries to invest in developing poor countries.

**Infrastructure**   Assuming an LDC government maintains law and order and the price system is used to allocate goods and services, it is vital that wise decisions be made concerning infrastructure. Indeed, inadequate infrastructure is one of the greatest problems of LDCs' concern. Without such public goods as roads, schools, bridges, and public health and sanitation services, poor countries are unable to generate the substantial external benefits that are an important ingredient in economic growth and development. From the viewpoint of individual firms, government must provide infrastructure because these public goods projects are too costly for a firm to undertake.

**International Trade**   In general, LDCs can benefit from an expanding volume of trade. This is the theory behind the North American Free Trade Agreement (NAFTA), the General Agreement on Tariffs and Trade (GATT), and the World Trade Organization (WTO) discussed in the chapter on international trade and finance. As explained earlier in this chapter, policies such as tariffs and quotas restrain international trade and thereby inhibit economic growth and development. These trade policies are antigrowth because they restrict the ability of people in one country to trade with people in other countries. Similarly, a country that fixes the exchange rate of its own currency above the market-determined exchange rate makes that country's exports less attractive to foreigners. This means, in turn, that domestic citizens sell less of their goods to foreigners and earn less foreign currency with which to buy imports.

> **CONCLUSION** *Exchange rate controls artificially set by government above the market exchange rates reduce the volume of both exports and imports (international trade).*

Exhibit 6 summarizes the key factors explained above that determine the economic growth and development of countries. Analysis of this exhibit reveals that economic growth and development are the result of a multidimensional process. This means that it is difficult for countries to break the poverty barrier because they must follow various avenues and improve many factors in order to increase their economic well-being. But it is important to remember that lack of one or more key factors, such as natural resources, does not necessarily keep an LDC in the trap of underdevelopment.

> **CONCLUSION** *There is no single strategy for economic growth and development.*

# The Helping Hand of Advanced Countries

How can poor countries escape the vicious circle of poverty? Low GDP per capita leads to low savings and investment, which lead, in turn, to low growth. Although there is no easy way for poor countries to become richer, the United States and other advanced countries can be an instrument of growth. The necessary funds

**EXHIBIT 6**    KEY CATEGORIES THAT DETERMINE ECONOMIC GROWTH AND DEVELOPMENT

There are five basic categories that interact to determine the economic growth and development of countries: natural resources, human resources, capital, technological progress, and the political environment. The exhibit also indicates important factors that influence investment in human resources, capital, technological advances, and the political environment. LDCs are faced with a formidable task. Since economic growth and development are multidimensional, LDCs must improve many factors in order to achieve economic progress.

can come from the LDCs' own domestic savings, or it can come from external sources that include foreign private investment, foreign aid, and foreign loans.

Exhibit 7 illustrates how external funds can shift a country's production possibilities curve outward. Here you should look back and review Exhibit 5. Suppose country Alpha is trapped in poverty and produces only enough capital $(K_a)$ to replace the existing capital being worn out. Alpha's consumption level is at $C_a$, corresponding to point $A$ on production possibilities curve $PPC_1$. Because $C_a$ is at the subsistence level, Alpha cannot save and invest by substituting capital for current consumption and move upward along $PPC_1$. This inability to increase capital means Alpha cannot use internal sources of funds to increase its production possibilities curve in the future. There is a way out of the trap using external sources. Now assume Alpha receives an inflow of funds from abroad and buys capital goods that increase its rate of investment from $K_a$ to $K_b$. At $K_b$, the rate of capital formation exceeds the value of capital depreciated, and Alpha's production possibilities curve shifts rightward to $PPC_2$. Economic growth made possible by external investment means Alpha can achieve economic growth without reducing its consumption level $(C_a)$ at point $B$ on $PPC_2$.

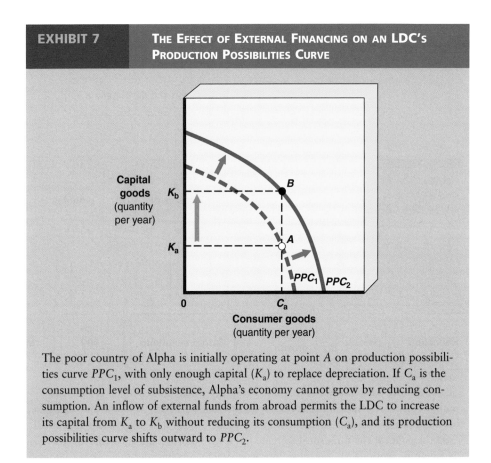

**EXHIBIT 7**       **THE EFFECT OF EXTERNAL FINANCING ON AN LDC'S PRODUCTION POSSIBILITIES CURVE**

The poor country of Alpha is initially operating at point $A$ on production possibilities curve $PPC_1$, with only enough capital ($K_a$) to replace depreciation. If $C_a$ is the consumption level of subsistence, Alpha's economy cannot grow by reducing consumption. An inflow of external funds from abroad permits the LDC to increase its capital from $K_a$ to $K_b$ without reducing its consumption ($C_a$), and its production possibilities curve shifts outward to $PPC_2$.

## FOREIGN PRIVATE INVESTMENT

Many countries' development benefits from private-sector foreign investment from private investors. For example, Microsoft might finance construction of a plant in the Philippines to manufacture software, or Bank of America may make loans to the government of Haiti. These large multinational corporations and commercial banks supply scarce capital to the LDCs. A multinational corporation is a firm with headquarters in one country and one or more branch plants in other countries. Multinational firms often seek new investment opportunities in LDCs because these poor countries offer abundant supplies of low-wage labor and raw materials. But the political environment in the LDCs must be conducive to investment. Multinational corporations often become the largest employers, largest taxpayers, and largest exporters in the LDCs.

## FOREIGN AID

**Foreign aid**
The transfer of money or resources from one government to another for which no repayment is required.

About 1 percent of the U.S. federal budget is spent on **foreign aid**. Foreign aid is the transfer of money or resources from one government to another with no repayment required. These transfers may be made as outright grants, technical assistance, or food supplies. Foreign aid flows from country to country through governments and voluntary agencies, such as the Red Cross, CARE, and Church World Relief. The United States distributes most of its official development assistance through the **Agency for International Development (AID)**, established in 1961. The AID is the agency of the U.S. State Department that is in charge of U.S. aid to foreign countries.

One reason that countries like the United States provide foreign aid to LDCs is the belief that it is a moral responsibility of richer countries to share their wealth with poorer countries. A second reason is that it is in the best economic interest of the IACs to help the LDCs. When these countries become more prosperous, the IACs have more markets for their exports, and thereby all countries benefit from trade.

The LDCs often complain that foreign aid comes with too many economic and political strings attached. Loans are often offered on a "take it or leave it" basis, tied to policies other than basic trade policies, such as human rights, politics, or the military. Consequently, many LDCs argue for "trade, not aid." If the IACs would simply buy more goods from the LDCs, the LDCs could use their gains in export earnings to purchase more capital and other resources needed for growth. Many people in the United States feel that most foreign aid is a waste of money because it is misused by the recipient countries. This belief has caused Congress to grow increasingly reluctant to send taxpayers' money abroad except in the clearest cases of need or for reasons of national security.

## FOREIGN LOANS

A third source of external funds that can be used to finance LDCs' domestic investment is loans from abroad. Governments, international organizations, and private banks all make loans to LDCs. Like foreign private investment and foreign aid, loans give LDCs the opportunity to shift their production possibilities curves outward. There are various types of loan sources for LDCs. Bilateral loans are made directly from one country to another. The principal agent for official U.S. bilateral loans is the U.S. Agency for International Development, introduced earlier.

One prominent multilateral lending agency is the **World Bank**. The 184-member World Bank is the lending agency affiliated with the United Nations that makes long-term, low-interest loans and provides technical assistance to LDCs. Loans are made only after a planning period lasting a year or more. The World Bank was established in 1944 by major nations meeting in Bretton Woods, New Hampshire. Its first charge was to assist with reconstruction after World War II. Today, the World Bank is located in Washington, D.C., and its main purpose is to channel funds from rich countries to poor countries. Voting shares are in proportion to the money provided by the members. The World Bank makes "last resort" loans to LDCs that are limited to financing basic infrastructure projects, such as schools, health centers, dams, irrigation systems, and transportation facilities, for which private financing is not available. In addition, the World Bank helps LDCs get loans from private lenders by insuring the loans. Thus, the poor countries are able to complete projects and use the economic returns to pay off the lender with interest.

The World Bank is not the only multilateral lending agency making loans to LDCs. The World Bank's partner institution is the **International Monetary Fund (IMF)**. The International Monetary Fund is the lending agency that makes short-term conditional low-interest loans to developing countries. The IMF was also

**Agency for International Development (AID)**
The agency of the U.S. State Department that is in charge of U.S. aid to foreign countries.

**World Bank**
The lending agency that makes long-term low-interest loans and provides technical assistance to less-developed countries.

**International Monetary Fund (IMF)**
The lending agency that makes short-term conditional low-interest loans to developing countries.

## International Economics

## Hong Kong: A Leaping Pacific Rim Tiger
*Applicable Concept: newly industrialized economies*

As the map shows, the Pacific Rim economies are located along an arc extending from Japan and South Korea in the north to New Zealand in the south. The Four Tigers of East Asia are Hong Kong, Singapore, South Korea, and Taiwan. These "miracle economies" have often experienced higher economic growth rates, lower inflation rates, and lower unemployment rates than many long-established advanced countries.

Hong Kong is a great success story. When Adam Smith published his famous book, *The Wealth of Nations*, in 1776, Hong Kong was little more than a small barren rock island almost void of natural resources except fish. Today, Hong Kong is a bustling model of free enterprise in spite of the fact that seven million inhabitants are crowded into only about 400 square miles-one of the highest population densities in the world.

What is the reason for Hong Kong's success? Following the doctrine of Adam Smith, this economy is a paragon of laissez faire. Hong Kong has among the lowest individual and corporate income tax rates in the world and

almost no legal restrictions on business. It has no capital gains tax, no interest tax, no sales tax, and no withholding tax. Hong Kong has become the largest banking center in the Pacific region after Tokyo. International trade is also largely unrestricted, and Hong Kong depends to a large extent on trade through its magnificent harbor for its economic success. Tariffs on imported goods are low, and Hong Kong is known as a safe-haven warehouse and trading center, with little or no interference from the government.

Hong Kong has proved that industrious people and entrepreneurs working hard on a crowded island with minimum regulations and open trade can improve their living standard without natural resources. Nevertheless, Hong Kong faces economic and political uncertainty. Under a 99-year lease

signed in 1898, the United Kingdom transferred Hong Kong to the People's Republic of China in 1997. Will China allow Hong Kong to continue to follow Adam Smith's laissez-faire philosophy, resulting in high growth rates, or will Hong Kong change direction? It is anyone's guess. After a 10.2 percent growth rate in 2000, the falloff in global demand triggered by the recession in the United States slowed Hong Kong's real GDP growth rate to only 0.5 percent in 2001. In 2004, however, Hong Kong's growth rate jumped to 8.1 percent and it was 6.3 percent in 2005. So, as this text is written in 2006, it appears that this East Asian tiger is leaping forward and roaring again. And in 2005 Hong Kong Disneyland opened months ahead of schedule.

### ANALYZE THE ISSUE

One of the keys to Hong Kong's success is its free trade policy. Why is this so important for a developing country? What would be the effect of Hong Kong attempting to protect its domestic industries by raising tariffs and following other protectionist trade policies?

established at Bretton Woods in 1944. Its purpose is to help countries overcome short-run financial difficulties. Typically, the IMF makes conditional loans that require the debtor countries to implement fiscal and monetary policies that will alleviate balance-of-payments deficit problems and promote noninflationary economic growth. The 184-member IMF is not a charitable institution. It operates like a credit union with funding quotas that earn interest on the loans. The United States is the IMF's largest shareholder and thus has effective veto power over IMF decisions.

In recent years, the IMF has performed a major role in providing short-term loans to developing countries and to economies making the transition to capital-

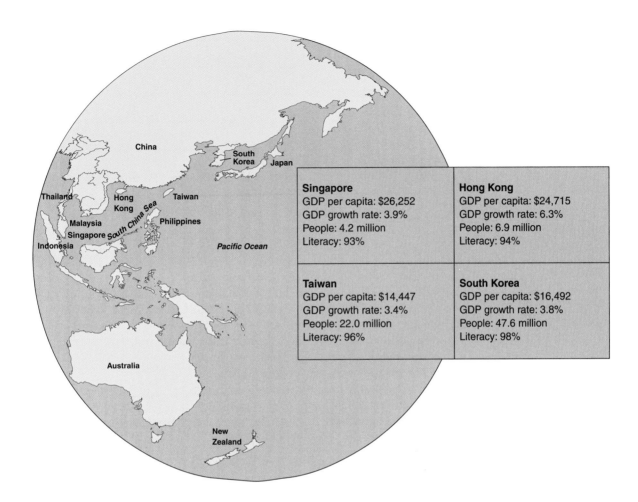

Singapore
GDP per capita: $26,252
GDP growth rate: 3.9%
People: 4.2 million
Literacy: 93%

Hong Kong
GDP per capita: $24,715
GDP growth rate: 6.3%
People: 6.9 million
Literacy: 94%

Taiwan
GDP per capita: $14,447
GDP growth rate: 3.4%
People: 22.0 million
Literacy: 96%

South Korea
GDP per capita: $16,492
GDP growth rate: 3.8%
People: 47.6 million
Literacy: 98%

ism. In the late 1990s, the IMF provided multibillion-dollar bailouts to Russia, several Asian countries, Brazil, and other countries experiencing economic turmoil. Critics argue that as long as governments believe the IMF will bail them out, they will fail to correct their own problems. IMF supporters counter that if the IMF does not intervene, troubled economies will default on outstanding loans and cause a worldwide ripple effect. Critics respond that a flood of low-cost short-term loans from the IMF encourages bad government policies and excessive risk taking by banks. Consequently, a bailout in a crisis generates new financial crises and reduces world economic growth.

Finally, private banks also engage in lending to LDCs. Until the 1970s, LDCs borrowed primarily from the World Bank and foreign governments. In the 1970s, private banks began to lend to both governments and private firms in LDCs. During the 1980s, the news was full of stories that some U.S. banks had made so many risky loans to LDCs that default on these loans would lead to the failure of one major U.S. bank after another. As the story goes, "If you can't repay the bank for your car loan, you're in trouble. If a government can't repay the bank a billion dollars, the bank's in trouble."

## CHECKPOINT

### Is the Minimum Wage an Antipoverty Solution for Poor Countries?

Imagine you are an economic advisor to the president of a poor LDC. The president is seeking policies to promote economic growth and a higher standard of living for citizens of this country. You are asked whether adopting a minimum wage equal to the average of the IACs' average hourly wages would achieve these goals. Recall the discussion of the minimum wage from Chapter 4 and evaluate this policy.

In the late 1980s, the debt crisis was avoided by (1) writing off some of the loans, (2) lowering the interest rate of remaining loans, and (3) lending LDCs more money to pay interest on their debt. The U.S. government, other Western governments, and the IMF were active in these solutions. Was this a case of "throwing good money after bad" because many loans would never be repaid? The answer is no. Easing the debt burden salvaged some payments and was in the best interest of both rich and poor countries because a fresh start encouraged trade. Nevertheless, the huge outstanding debts of some LDCs make another debt crisis a lingering possibility. In 2005, the wealthiest countries (G-8) reached a groundbreaking agreement to eliminate the debt of some of the world's most impoverished countries.

## Key Concepts

GDP per capita
Industrially advanced countries (IACs)
Less-developed countries (LDCs)

Vicious circle of poverty
Infrastructure
Foreign aid

Agency for International Development (AID)
World Bank
International Monetary Fund (IMF)

## Summary

- **GDP per capita** provides a general index of a country's standard of living. Countries with low GDP per capita and slow growth in GDP per capita are less able to satisfy basic needs for food, shelter, clothing, education, and health.

- **Industrially advanced countries (IACs)** are countries with high GDP per capita and output is produced by technologically advanced capital. Countries that have high incomes without widespread industrial develop-

ment, such as the oil-rich Arab countries, are not included in the IAC list.

- **Less-developed countries (LDCs)** are countries with low production per person. In these countries, output is produced without large amounts of technologically advanced capital and well-educated labor. The LDCs account for about three-fourths of the world's population.

- The **Four Tigers of the Pacific Rim** are Hong Kong, Singapore, South Korea, and Taiwan. These newly industrialized countries have achieved high growth rates and standards of living.

- **GDP per capita comparisons** are subject to four problems: (1) the accuracy of LDC data is questionable, (2) GDP per capita ignores income distribution, (3) fluctuations in exchange rates affect GDP per capita gaps between countries, and (4) there is no adjustment for cost-of-living differences between countries.

- **Economic growth** and **economic development** are related, but somewhat different concepts. Economic growth is measured quantitatively by GDP per capita, while economic development is a broader concept. In addition to GDP per capita, economic development includes quality-of-life measures, such as life expectancy at birth, adult literacy rate, and per capita energy consumption. Economic growth and development are the result of a complex process that is determined by five major factors: (1) natural resources, (2) human resources, (3) capital, (4) technological progress, and (5) the political environment. There is no single correct strategy for economic development, and a lack of strength in one or more of the five areas does not prevent growth.

- The **vicious circle of poverty** is a trap in which an LDC is too poor to save and therefore it cannot invest and shift its production possibilities curve outward. As a result, the LDC remains poor. One way for a poor country to gain savings, invest, and grow is to use funds from external sources such as foreign private investment, foreign aid, and foreign loans. Borrowing by many LDCs led to the debt crisis of the 1980s, which was resolved by writing off and restructuring the loans.

## Summary of Conclusion Statements

- LDCs' GDP per capita is subject to greater measurement errors than data for IACs.

- GDP per capita comparisons among nations can be misleading because GDP per capita does not measure income distribution.

- A conversion problem may widen or narrow the GDP per capita gap between nations because the fluctuations in exchange rates do not reflect actual differences in the value of goods and services produced.

- Differences in purchasing power that affect living standards can alter the interpretation of international comparisons of GDP per capita.

- In general, GDP per capita is highly correlated with alternative measures of quality of life.

- Natural resource endowment can promote economic growth, but a country can develop without a large natural resource base.

- Investment in human capital generally results in increases in GDP per capita.

- Rapid population growth combined with low human capital investment explains why many countries are LDCs.

- Nations that grow slowly or experience declines in GDP per capita will fail to catch up with the IACs' standard of living.

- There is a significant positive relationship between investment and economic growth and development.

- Many LDCs continue to experience low growth rates even though IACs have developed advanced technologies that the world can utilize.

- Exchange rate controls artificially set by government above the market exchange rates reduce the volume of both exports and imports (international trade).

- There is no single strategy for economic growth and development.

## Study Questions and Problems

1. What is the difference between industrially advanced countries (IACs) and less-developed countries (LDCs)? List five IACs and five LDCs.

2. Explain why GDP per capita comparisons among nations are not a perfect measure of differences in economic well-being.

3. Assume you are given the following data for country Alpha and country Beta:

| Country | GDP per capita |
|---------|----------------|
| Alpha   | $25,000        |
| Beta    | 15,000         |

   a. Based on GDP per capita data given above, in which country would you prefer to live?

   b. Now assume you are given the following additional quality-of-life data. In which country would you prefer to reside?

| Country | Life expectancy at birth (years) | Daily per capita calorie supply | Per capita energy consumption* |
|---------|----------------------------------|----------------------------------|--------------------------------|
| Alpha   | 65                               | 2,500                            | 3,000                          |
| Beta    | 70                               | 3,000                            | 4,000                          |

*Kilograms of oil equivalent.

4. What is the difference between economic development and economic growth? Give examples of how each of these concepts can be measured.

5. Do you agree with the argument that the rich nations are getting richer and the poor nations are getting poorer? Is this an oversimplification? Explain.

6. Explain why it is so difficult for poor LDCs to generate investment in capital in order to increase productivity and growth and therefore improve their standard of living.

7. Why is the quest for economic growth and development complicated?

8. Indicate whether each of the following is associated with a high or low level of economic growth and development:

|                                        | High | Low |
|----------------------------------------|------|-----|
| a. Overpopulation                      | ____ | ____ |
| b. Highly skilled labor                | ____ | ____ |
| c. High savings rate                   | ____ | ____ |
| d. Political stability                 | ____ | ____ |
| e. Low capital accumulation            | ____ | ____ |
| f. Advanced technology                 | ____ | ____ |
| g. Highly developed infrastructure     | ____ | ____ |
| h. High proportion of agriculture      | ____ | ____ |
| i. High degree of income inequality    | ____ | ____ |

9. Without external financing from foreign private investment, foreign aid, and foreign loans, poor countries are caught in the vicious circle of poverty. Explain. How does external financing help poor countries achieve economic growth and development?

10. What are some of the problems for LDCs of accepting foreign aid?

11. Why would an LDC argue for "trade, not aid"?

12. Explain the differences between the Agency for International Development (AID), the World Bank, and the International Monetary Fund (IMF).

## Study Guide Questions

1. The _____ is a trap in which countries are poor because they cannot afford to save and invest, but they cannot save and invest because they are poor.

2. Which of the following statements is *true*?

   a. A less developed country (LDC) is a country with a low GDP per capita, low levels of capital, and uneducated workers.

   b. The vicious circle of poverty exists because GDP must rise before people can save and invest.

   c. LDCs are characterized by rapid population growth and low levels of investment in human capital.

   d. All of the above.

3. Which of the following is *true* concerning GDP per capita comparisons?
   a. The accuracy of LDC GDP per capita data is questionable.
   b. GDP per capita ignores the degree of income distribution.
   c. GDP per capita is affected by exchange rate changes.
   d. GDP per capita does not account for the difference in the cost of living among nations.
   e. All of the above are true.

4. Which of the following is an example of a multilateral lending agency that makes loans, rather than gifts of foreign aid, to less-developed countries?
   a. The Agency for International Development
   b. The International Red Cross
   c. The World Bank
   d. Church World Relief

5. T  F  In general, GDP per capita is not highly correlated with alternative measures of quality of life.

**Answers to these questions are in the complete Study Guide at www.thomsonedu.com/thomsonnow.**

**For Online Exercises, go to the text Web site at www.thomsonedu.com/economics/tucker.**

## Checkpoint Answers

### Does Rapid Growth Mean a Country Is Catching Up?

GDP growth alone does not measure the standard of living. You must also consider population. Even though Beta experienced a greater GDP growth rate, its GDP per capita might be less than Alpha's because its population growth rate is greater. Of course, the reverse is also possible, but without population data, we cannot say. If you said which country's people are better off cannot be determined because the GDP must be divided by the population to measure the average standard of living, **YOU ARE CORRECT.**

### Is the Minimum Wage an Antipoverty Solution for Poor Countries?

An important source of foreign investment for LDCs is multinational corporations that locate plants and other facilities in these countries. LDCs compete with each other for the economic growth and development benefits that these multinational corporations can provide. For an LDC to win the competition, it must offer political stability, adequate infrastructure, a favorable business climate, and a cheap labor force. If you said you would not support the president's proposal to raise the minimum wage because it would place the LDC at a competitive disadvantage in the labor market, thereby reducing foreign private investment and growth, **YOU ARE CORRECT.**

## Practice Quiz

For an explanation of the correct answers, please visit the tutorial at www.thomsonedu.com/economics/tucker.

1. An LDC is defined as a country
   a. without large stocks of advanced capital.
   b. without well-educated labor.
   c. with low GDP per capita.
   d. that is described by all of the above.

2. According to the definition given in the text, which of the following is *not* an LDC?
   a. India
   b. Egypt
   c. China
   d. Ireland

3. Which of the following is *true* when making GDP per capita comparisons among nations?
   a. The GDP per capita is subject to greater measurement errors for LDCs compared to IACs.
   b. The GDP per capita does not measure income distribution.
   c. The GDP per capita is subject to fluctuations from changes in exchange rates.
   d. All of the above are true.

4. LDCs are characterized by
   a. high life expectancy.
   b. high adult literacy.
   c. high infant mortality.
   d. all of the above.
   e. none of the above.

5. According to the classification in the text, which of the following is *not* an IAC?
   a. United Arab Emirates
   b. Israel
   c. Hong Kong
   d. Greece

6. When the government fixes the exchange rate above market exchange rates,
   a. international trade falls.
   b. the infrastructure improves.
   c. real GDP per capita rises.
   d. the vicious circle of poverty is broken.

7. Which of the following statements is *true*?
   a. An LDC is a country with a low GDP per capita, low levels of capital, and uneducated workers.
   b. The vicious circle of poverty exists because GDP must rise before people can save and invest.

   c. LDCs are characterized by rapid population growth and low levels of investment in human capital.
   d. All of the above are true.

8. An outward shift of the production possibilities curve represents
   a. economic growth.
   b. a decline in economic development.
   c. a decrease in human capital.
   d. a decrease in resources.

9. Which of the following problems do LDCs face?
   a. Low per capita income and high GDP growth rate
   b. Low population growth and low per capita income
   c. Rapid population growth and low human capital
   d. Low per capita income and high saving rate

10. Which of the following *best* defines the vicious circle of poverty?
    a. The GDP per capita must rise before people can save and invest.
    b. People cannot save while capital accumulates.
    c. Increased GDP per capita relates to lower population growth.
    d. Poverty, saving, and investment are related like a circle.

11. Which of the following is infrastructure?
    a. International Harvester tractor plant
    b. Waste and water system provided by government
    c. US Airways airplane
    d. Service of postal workers

12. Economic growth and development in LDCs are low because many of them lack
    a. capital investment.
    b. technological progress.
    c. a favorable political environment.
    d. all of the above.
    e. none of the above.

13. Which of the following makes short-term conditional low-interest loans to developing countries?
    a. Agency for International Development (AID)
    b. World Bank
    c. International Monetary Fund (IMF)
    d. New International Economic Order (NIEO)

14. Which of the following groups makes long-term low-interest loans to less-developed countries (LDCs)?
    a. Agency for International Development (AID)
    b. New International Economic Order (NIEO)
    c. International Monetary Fund (IMF)
    d. World Bank

15. In order for Ethiopia to increase its future economic growth, it must choose a point that is
    a. below its production possibilities curve.
    b. further along on its production possibilities curve toward the capital goods axis.
    c. further along on its production possibilities curve toward the consumption goods axis.
    d. further along on its production possibilities curve away from the population axis.
    e. above its production possibilities curve.

# Answers to Odd-Numbered Study Questions and Problems*

## CHAPTER 1 INTRODUCING THE ECONOMIC WAY OF THINKING

1. A poor nation with many people who lack food, clothing, and shelter certainly experiences wants beyond the availability of goods and services to satisfy these unfulfilled wants. On the other hand, no wealthy nation has all the resources necessary to produce everything everyone in the nation wishes to have. Even if you had $1 million and were completely satisfied with your share of goods and services, other desires would be unfulfilled. There is never enough time to accomplish all the things that you can imagine would be worthwhile.

3. a. capital.

5. a. microeconomic issue
   b. macroeconomic issue
   c. microeconomic issue
   d. macroeconomic issue

7. The real world is full of complexities that make it difficult to understand and predict the relationships between variables. For example, the relationship between changes in the price of gasoline and changes in consumption of gasoline requires abstraction from the reality that such variables as the fuel economy of cars and weather conditions often change at the same time as the price of gasoline.

9. The two events are associated, and the first event (cut in military spending) is the cause of the second event (higher unemployment in the defense industry). The point is that association does not necessarily mean causation, but it might.

11. d. statement of normative economics.

## APPENDIX TO CHAPTER 1 APPLYING GRAPHS TO ECONOMICS

1. a. The probability of living is *inversely* related to age. This model could be affected by improvements in diet, better health care, reductions in hazards to health in the workplace, or changes in the speed limit.

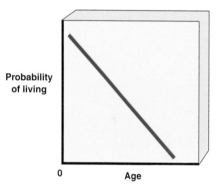

b. Annual income and years of formal education are *directly* related. This relationship might be influenced by changes in such human characteristics as intelligence, motivation, ability, and family background. An example of an institutional change that could affect this relationship over a number of years is the draft.

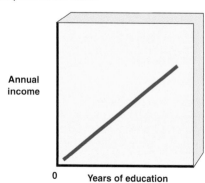

*Note: Answers to even-numbered questions and problems are in the Instructor's Manual.

c. Inches of snow and sales of bathing suits are *inversely* related. The weather forecast and the price of travel to sunny vacation spots can affect this relationship.

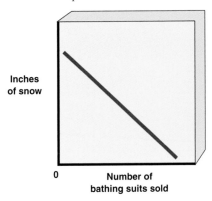

Inches of snow

0     Number of bathing suits sold

d. Most alumni and students will argue that the number of football games won is *directly* related to the athletic budget. They reason that winning football games is great advertising and results in increased attendance, contributions, and enrollment that, in turn, increase the athletic budget. Success in football can also be related to other factors, such as school size, age and type of institution, number and income of alumni, and quality of the faculty and administrators.

Number of football games won

0     Athletic budget (dollars)

## CHAPTER 2  PRODUCTION POSSIBILITIES, OPPORTUNITY COST, AND ECONOMIC GROWTH

1. Because the wants of individuals and society exceed the goods and services available to satisfy these desires, choices must be made. The consumption possibilities of an individual with a fixed income are limited, and as a result, additional consumption of one item necessarily precludes an expenditure on another next-best choice. The forgone alternative is called the opportunity cost, and this concept also applies to societal decisions. If society allocates resources to the production of guns, then those same resources cannot be used at the same time to make butter.

3. Regardless of the price of a lunch, economic resources—land, labor, and capital—are used to produce the lunch. These scarce resources are no longer available to produce other goods and services.

5. Using marginal analysis, students weigh the benefits of attending college against the costs. There is an incentive to attend college when the benefits (improved job opportunities, income, intellectual improvement, social life, and so on) outweigh the opportunity costs.

7.

| Flower boxes | Opportunity cost (pies forgone) |
|---|---|
| 0 | |
| 1 | 4 (30−26) |
| 2 | 5 (26−21) |
| 3 | 6 (21−15) |
| 4 | 7 (15−8) |
| 5 | 8 (8−0) |

9. Movements along the curve are efficient points and conform to the well-known "free lunch" statement. However, inefficient points are exceptions because it is possible to produce more of one output without producing less of another output.

11.

Capital goods

A

0          A   B′
Consumer goods

B′

Capital goods

A

0          A
Consumer goods

## CHAPTER 3  MARKET DEMAND AND SUPPLY

1. If people buy a good or service because they associate higher quality with higher price, this is a violation of the ceteris paribus assumption. An increase in the quantity demanded results only from a decrease in price. Quality and other nonprice determinants of demand, such as tastes and preferences and the price of related goods, are held constant in the model.

3. a. Demand for cars decreases; oil and cars are *complements*.
   b. Demand for insulation increases; oil and home insulation are *substitutes*.
   c. Demand for coal increases; oil and coal are *substitutes*.
   d. Demand for tires decreases; oil and tires are *complements*.

5. One reason that the demand curve for word processing software shifted to the right might be that people desire new, higher-quality output features. The supply curve can shift to the right when new technology makes it possible to offer more software for sale at different prices.

7. a. Demand shifts to the right.
   b. Supply shifts to the left.
   c. Supply shifts to the right.
   d. Demand shifts to the right.
   e. Demand shifts to the right.
   f. Supply of corn shifts to the left.

9. a. The supply of CD players shifts rightward.
   b. The demand for CD players is unaffected.
   c. The equilibrium price falls, and the equilibrium quantity increases.
   d. The demand for CDs increases because of the fall in the price of CD players (a complementary good).

11. The number of seats (quantity supplied) remains constant, but the demand curve shifts because tastes and preferences change according to the importance of each game. Although demand changes, the price is a fixed amount, and to manage a shortage, colleges and universities use amount of contributions, number of years as a contributor, or some other rationing device.

## APPENDIX TO CHAPTER 3  CONSUMER SURPLUS, PRODUCER SURPLUS, AND MARKET EFFICIENCY

1. $80

3.

| Price | $30 | $15 |
|---|---|---|
| Consumer surplus | $80 | $105 |
| Producer surplus | 25 | 5 |
| Total surplus | $105 | $110 |

The lower price results in higher total surplus because in this case the rise in consumer surplus exceeds the fall in producer surplus.

## CHAPTER 4  MARKETS IN ACTION

1.

a. The equilibrium price is $1.50 per gallon, and the equilibrium quantity is 300 million gallons per month. The price system will restore the market's $1.50 per gallon price because either a surplus will drive prices down or a shortage will drive prices up.

b. The support price results in a persistent surplus of 200 million gallons of milk per month, which the government purchases with taxpayers' money. Consequently, taxpayers who do not drink milk are still paying for milk. The purpose of the support price is to bolster the incomes of dairy farmers.

c. The ceiling price will result in a persistent shortage of 200 million gallons of milk per month, but 200 million gallons are purchased by consumers at the low price of $1.00 per gallon. The shortage places a burden on the government to ration milk in order to be fair and to prevent black markets. The government's goal is to keep the price of milk below the equilibrium price of $1.50 per gallon, which would be set by a free market.

3. The labor market can be divided into two separate markets, one for skilled union workers and one for unskilled workers. If the minimum wage is above the equilibrium wage rate and is raised, the effect will be to increase the demand for, and the wage of, skilled union workers because the two groups are substitutes.

5. The equilibrium price rises.

7. The government can reduce emissions by (a) regulations that require smoke-abatement equipment or (b) imposing pollution taxes that shift supply leftward.

9. Pure public goods are not produced in sufficient quantities by private markets because there is no feasible method to exclude free riders.

## CHAPTER 5  PRICE ELASTICITY OF DEMAND AND SUPPLY

1. Demand is elastic because the percentage change in quantity is greater than the percentage change in price.

3. If the price of used cars is raised 1 percent, the quantity demanded will fall 3 percent. If the price is raised 10 percent, the quantity demanded will fall 30 percent.

5.
$$E_d = \frac{\%\Delta Q}{\%\Delta P} = \frac{\dfrac{4{,}500 - 5{,}000}{5{,}000 + 4{,}500}}{\dfrac{3{,}500 - 3{,}000}{3{,}000 + 3{,}500}} = \frac{\dfrac{1}{19}}{\dfrac{1}{13}} = 0.68$$

The price elasticity of demand for the university is inelastic.

7. Demand for popcorn is perfectly inelastic, and total revenue will increase.

9. a. Sunkist oranges
   b. Cars
   c. Foreign travel in the long run

11. Furniture sales fall by 30 percent and physician services by only 3 percent. Thus, the demand for physician services is much less responsive to a reduction in income than the demand for furniture.

13. The negative number tells you car tires are complements. If the price of cars rises by 10 percent, the quantity demanded of car tires falls by 20 percent.

15. As the demand for a product becomes more inelastic, the greater the amount of a tax on this product that sellers can pass on to consumers by raising the product's price.

## CHAPTER 6  CONSUMER CHOICE THEORY

1. Utility is a subjective concept, and, therefore, this statement may or may not be true.

3. Marginal utility is 10 utils. When you attend the fourth party, total utility will increase, but marginal utility will be less than 10 utils.

5. In consumer equilibrium, the marginal utility ratio is 3/4, which is equal to the price ratio.

7. As people consume more of any product, eventually the satisfaction per unit decreases. Since the marginal utility from additional units falls, people will not buy a greater quantity unless the price falls.

9. The initial consumer equilibrium is as follows:

$$\frac{MU \text{ of steak meal}}{\text{Price of steak meal}} = \frac{MU \text{ of hamburger meal}}{\text{Price of hamburger meal}}$$

$$\frac{12 \text{ utils}}{\$10} = \frac{6 \text{ utils}}{\$5}$$

The marginal utility per dollar for each good equals 1.2. If the price of a hamburger meal falls to $2, this equality no longer holds. Now the marginal utility per dollar for a hamburger meal becomes higher at 3 (6 utils/$2). James can now increase his total utility by purchasing more hamburger meals per month. Given the law of diminishing returns, the marginal utility of hamburger meals falls until consumer equilibrium is restored.

## APPENDIX TO CHAPTER 6 INDIFFERENCE CURVE ANALYSIS

1. *MRS* = 3 (3 slices of pizza per Coke), but the ratio of prices is 1/2 ($1.00 per Coke/$2.00 per slice of pizza). Since *MRS* > slope (the ratio of prices), the consumer is not maximizing total utility. Therefore, the consumer should consume less pizza and more Coke in order to maximize total utility by moving downward along the consumer's indifference curve until consumer equilibrium is achieved where *MRS* = price ratio = 1/2.

3. a. and b.

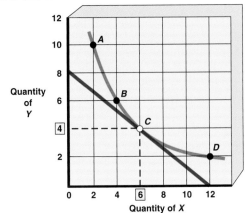

c. Consumer equilibrium occurs at point $C$ with 6 units of $X$ and 4 units of $Y$ purchased.

d. $MRS = P_x/P_y = \dfrac{\$1}{\$1.50} = \dfrac{2}{3}$

e. Hold the price of $Y$ constant at $1.50 and decrease the price of $X$ from $1.00 to $0.50. The new budget line will shift northeastward from the $Y$ axis intercept point of 8 units. Now draw a new indifference curve and determine the new equilibrium point. Finally, draw a graph with various prices of $X$ on the vertical axis and the quantity of $X$ on the horizontal axis. Connecting the two consumer equilibrium points will allow you to draw a downward-sloping demand curve.

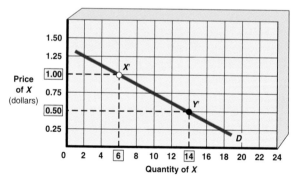

3. a.

| Labor | Marginal product |
| --- | --- |
| 1 | 8 |
| 2 | 10 |
| 3 | 12 |
| 4 | 13 |
| 5 | 12 |
| 6 | 10 |
| 7 | 8 |
| 8 | 6 |
| 9 | 3 |
| 10 | −2 |

b.

## CHAPTER 7 PRODUCTION COSTS

1. a. explicit cost
   b. explicit cost
   c. implicit cost
   d. implicit cost
   e. explicit cost
   f. implicit cost

5. None. The position of a firm's short-run average total cost curve is not related to the demand curve.

7. The $ATC$ and $AVC$ curves converge as output expands because $ATC = AVC + AFC$. As output increases, $AFC$ declines, so most of $ATC$ is therefore $AVC$.

9. The average total cost–marginal cost rule states that when the marginal cost is below the average total cost, the addition to total cost is below the average total cost, and the average total cost falls. When the marginal cost is greater than the average total cost, the average total cost rises. In this case, the average total cost is at a minimum because it is equal to the marginal cost.

11. The marginal product for any number of workers is the slope of the total output curve. The marginal product is the derivative of the total output curve $dTO/dQ$, where $TO$ is the total output and $Q$ is the number of workers.

    This condition occurs when input prices do not increase or decrease as firms expand output. This means that the long-run supply curve is a horizontal line and the industry is a constant-cost industry. If input prices increase as firms expand output, the long-run supply curve is upward sloping, and the industry is an increasing-cost industry.

## CHAPTER 8  PERFECT COMPETITION

1. A perfectly competitive firm will not advertise. Because all firms in the industry sell the same product, there is no reason for customers to be influenced by ads into buying one firm's product rather than another firm's product.

3.

(a) Wheat market supply and demand

(b) Wheat farmer's demand

A single wheat farmer is a price taker facing a perfectly elastic demand curve because in perfect competition one seller has no control over its price. The reason is that each wheat farmer is one among many, sells a homogeneous product, and must compete with any new farmer entering the wheat market.

5. At a price of $150, the firm produces 4 units and earns an economic profit of $70 ($TR - TC = \$600 - \$530$). The firm breaks even at an output of 2 units.

7. This statement is incorrect. A firm can earn maximum profit (or minimum loss) when marginal revenue equals marginal cost. The confusion is between the "marginal" and the "total" concepts. Marginal cost is the change in total cost from one additional unit of output, and marginal revenue is the change in total revenue from one additional unit of output.

9. The statement is incorrect. The perfectly competitive firm must consider both its marginal revenue and its marginal cost. Instead of trying to sell all the quantity of output possible, the firm will sell the quantity where $MR = MC$ because beyond this level of output the firm earns less profit.

11. Advise the residential contractor to shut down because the market price exceeds the average variable cost and the firm cannot cover its operating costs.

# CHAPTER 9 MONOPOLY

1. Each market is served by a single firm providing a unique product. There are no close substitutes for local telephone service, professional football in San Francisco, and first-class mail service. A government franchise imposes a legal barrier to potential competitors in the telephone and first-class mail services. An NFL franchise grants monopoly power to its members in most geographic areas.

3. The reason may be that the hospital has monopoly power because it is the only hospital in the area and patients have no choice. On the other hand, there may be many drugstores competing to sell drugs, and this keeps prices lower than those charged by the hospital.

5. In a natural monopoly, a single seller can produce electricity at a lower cost because the $LRAC$ curve declines. One firm can therefore sell electricity at a cheaper price and drive its competitor out of business over time. Another possibility would be for two competing firms to merge and earn greater profit by lowering cost further.

7. In this special case, sales maximization and profit maximization are the same. The monopolist should charge $2.50 per unit, produce 5 units of output, and earn $12.50 in profit. When the marginal cost curve is not equal to zero, the monopolist's $MR = MC$ output is less than 5 units, the price is higher than $2.50 per unit, and profit is below $12.50.

9. a. increase output
   b. decrease output

11. a. not price discrimination
    b. price discrimination
    c. not price discrimination if justified by a transportation cost difference
    d. price discrimination

# CHAPTER 10 MONOPOLISTIC COMPETITION AND OLIGOPOLY

1. The monopolistically competitive firm's demand curve is less elastic (steeper) than a perfectly competitive firm's demand curve, but more elastic (flatter) than a monopolist's demand curve.

3. a. $P_1$
   b. $Q_1$
   c. $Q_3$
   d. greater than the marginal cost ($B > A$)

5.

Because $P_{mc} > MC$, the monopolistically competitive firm fails to achieve allocative efficiency. The monopolistically competitive firm is also inefficient because it charges a higher price and produces less output than under perfect competition. The perfectly competitive firm sets $P_{pc}$ equal to $MC$ and produces a level of output corresponding to the minimum point on the $LRAC$ curve.

7. Answers might include automobiles, airline travel, personal computers, and cigarettes. An oligopoly differs from monopolistic competition by having few sellers, rather than many sellers; either a homogeneous or a differentiated product, rather than all differentiated products; and difficult entry rather than easy entry.

9. Any maverick jeans firm that raises or lowers its price will earn less profits. Therefore, firms in the jeans industry face a kinked demand curve, and prices remain rigid. Although firms do not engage in price competition, they can engage in nonprice competition. Each firm can use advertising and style to market its brand-name product.

11. The pricing behavior follows the price leadership model. The price leader is Hewlett-Packard, which is the largest and most dominant firm in the computer printer industry. After a price war, IBM followed each of Hewlett-Packard's price hikes.

13. If both firms spend no money advertising, they each earn a profit of $8 billion in cell A. If either firm does not advertise and the other firm does in cell B or cell C, then the advertising firm attracts more customers and earns $10 billion compared to a −$2 billion loss for the rival without ads. This outcome forces both firms to advertise and reduce mutual profits at cell D. As a result of both firms spending large budgets on advertising, their mutual profits are reduced to $5 billion. If the government bans all cigarette advertising, the result is that both firms will move to the mutually high profit cell A.

## CHAPTER 11  LABOR MARKETS

1. This statement is incorrect. Workers supply their labor to employers. Demand refers to the quantity of labor employers hire at various wage rates based on the marginal revenue product of labor.

3. The *MRP* of the second worker is this person's contribution to total revenue, which is $50 ($150 − $100). Because $MRP = P \times MP$ and $MP = MRP/P$, the second worker's marginal product (*MP*) is 10 ($50/$5).

5. The firm in a perfectly competitive labor market is a price taker. Because a single firm buys the labor of a relatively small portion of workers in an industry, it can hire additional workers and not drive up the wage rate. For the industry, however, all firms must offer higher wages to attract workers from other industries.

7. Students investing in education are increasing their human capital. A student with greater human capital increases his or her marginal product. At a given product price, the *MRP* is higher, and firms find it profitable to hire the better educated worker and pay higher wages.

9. At a wage rate of $90 per day, Zippy Paper Company hires 3 workers because each worker's *MRP* exceeds or equals the wage rate. Setting the wage rate at $100 per day causes Zippy Paper Company to cut employment from 3 to 2 workers because the third worker's *MRP* is $10 below the union-caused wage rate of $100 per day.

11. As shown in the exhibit below, for a monopsony, the optimum quantity of labor is 3 quarterbacks, determined at point *A*, where the *MFC* curve intersects the *MRP* curve. However, the team can attract and hire 3 quarterbacks for an annual salary of $300,000 each at point *B* on the supply of labor curve, rather than paying a quarterback's contribution to the team's revenues (*MRP*), which is $500,000 per year at point *A*. In a competitive labor market, the Jacksonville Jaguars hire 4 quarterbacks and pay each $400,000 per year.

## CHAPTER 12  INCOME DISTRIBUTION, POVERTY, AND DISCRIMINATION

1.  a.

|  | Alpha | | Beta | |
|---|---|---|---|---|
| Percentage of families | Percentage share | Cumulative share | Percentage share | Cumulative share |
| Lowest fifth | 17.7% | 17.7% | 9.0% | 9.0% |
| Second-lowest fifth | 19.9 | 37.6 | 14.2 | 23.2 |
| Middle fifth | 20.4 | 58.0 | 17.5 | 40.7 |
| Second-highest fifth | 20.7 | 78.7 | 21.9 | 62.6 |
| Highest fifth | 21.3 | 100.0 | 37.4 | 100.0 |

b.

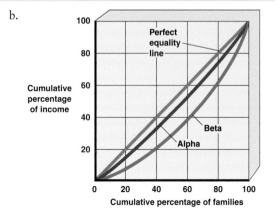

c. Because the Lorenz curve for Alpha is closest to the perfect equality line, Alpha's distribution of income is more equal compared to Beta.

3. Absolute poverty is defined as a dollar figure that represents some level of income per year required to purchase some minimum amount of goods and services essential to meeting a person's or a family's basic needs. Relative poverty is defined as a level of income required to place a person or family in, say, the lowest 20 percent among all persons or families receiving incomes. The poverty line is based on the absolute definition.

5. In-kind transfers are payments in the form of goods and services rather than cash. Examples include such government programs as food stamps, Medicaid, and housing. Noncash income is not counted in a family's income to determine whether the family's income is below the poverty line.

7. The percentage of families in the United States classified as poor was about 12 percent. Poor families are more likely to live in the South. The age, race, and education of the head of the family are also important characteristics of poor families.

9. The three major criticisms are that welfare: (1) reduces the work incentive, (2) is inefficient because the programs cost too much to administer, and (3) treats poor persons with the same needs unequally because the states pay different benefits.

11. This is an opinion question. To agree, you assume that markets are perfectly competitive and discrimination is therefore unprofitable. To disagree, you can argue that in reality labor markets will never be perfectly competitive and the government must therefore address the institutional causes of poverty.

## CHAPTER 13 ANTITRUST AND REGULATION

1. The Sherman Act outlaws price-fixing or anticompetitive practices designed to eliminate rivals. The Clayton Act clarifies the Sherman Act by outlawing specific business practices, including price discrimination, exclusive dealing, tying contracts, stock acquisition, and interlocking directorates. The U.S. Department of Justice and Federal Trade Commission (FTC) are responsible for enforcing these laws. Private firms can also bring suit against other firms under these laws.

3. Both the Robinson-Patman Act and the Celler-Kefauver Act were amendments to close loopholes in the Clayton Act. The Robinson-Patman Act expanded the list of illegal price discrimination practices to include quantity discounting, free advertising, and promotional allowances offered that "substantially lessen competition or tend to create a monopoly." The Celler-Kefauver Act closed the loophole in the Clayton Act whereby competing firms could merge by asset acquisition (not outlawed in the Clayton Act), rather than by acquiring stock (outlawed in the Clayton Act).

5. In fact, Alcoa argued that metals such as copper and steel are substitutes for aluminum. Therefore, the relevant industry to compute market share was the metals industry and not the aluminum industry. If the court had chosen the U.S. metals industry as the relevant industry, Alcoa would not have a monopoly.

7. a. The federal government will charge the bookstore with predatory pricing in order to monopolize its college market for books, which is a violation of the Sherman Act.
b. The federal government will charge the real estate firms with collusion to fix prices, which is a violation of the Sherman Act.
c. The federal government will charge a violation of the Clayton Act because the combined market share of this horizontal merger would substantially lessen competition in the word processing market.
d. The federal government will not charge a violation because this is a conglomerate merger between firms in unrelated industries.

9. The "necessary" condition would be expected to favor existing regulated firms by eliminating or greatly restricting competition and raising prices. The existing regulated firms are better organized politically than either new competitors or consumers. While consumers favor competition and lower prices, regulators would be expected to interpret "necessary" to mean that the service provided by existing firms is sufficient without new firms.

11. Although a public subsidy achieves efficiency, marginal-cost pricing is usually unpopular with voters, who must provide the monopolist with public funds. Moreover, a public subsidy gives the monopolist a disincentive to minimize costs.

## CHAPTER 14 ENVIRONMENTAL ECONOMICS

1. A competitive industry selling a pollution-generating product will charge a lower price and sell a larger quantity than would be the case for a "green" industry. The competitive industry has lower costs because it fails to include external costs. Lower costs allow a lower price. A lower price leads to a larger quantity demanded and sold.

3. If you choose the $90,000 house, the EMF radiation is *not* an externality. An externality is a third-party effect, whereby buyers and sellers of a product ignore the spillover effects of their transaction. In this case, the market reflects the risk of cancer, with the seller accepting a lower price and the buyer saving $10,000 to reflect the cancer risk.

  Houses have many characteristics that influence their price, including number of rooms, location, nearby schools, and environmental amenities. If you are willing to buy a house near a nuclear plant, or near EMFs, you, the buyer, bear the consequences, not a third party.

5. An instructor who automatically flunks students who do not turn in all homework assignments is exhibiting command-and-control regulation. She is dictating the production process for achieving knowledge. The inefficiencies are that students may turn in poorly done assignments or may copy assignments and that some students may understand the material without doing the homework or may have an alternative production method, such as the use of computer software, to achieve knowledge. The instructor's method is particularly inefficient if her assignments are busywork and do not really help the students to achieve knowledge.

7.

At $Q_p$, pollution from paper production leads to coffee-colored rivers. At socially efficient $Q_s$, there is less pollution, and rivers are less polluted. The rivers are unlikely to be pristine, which requires no production at all.

9. Consumers will share in the benefits of cleaner air if any individual buys a less polluting car. Since they enjoy the same benefit whether they pay extra or their neighbor pays extra for a cleaner car, they will let the neighbor buy the cleaner car. Of course, since their neighbor uses the same reasoning, no one ends up paying extra to buy a cleaner car.

11. Convincing examples should be sent to the author of the text. It is very difficult to find markets where the transactions costs of reaching an agreement are near zero. It is also difficult to find two-party situations, since most pollution spills over to many individuals. With many individuals involved, the free-rider problem arises, as a given individual wants to benefit from pollution agreements, but let others bear the cost. There can often be income effects, as fighting pollution may take a large amount of one's income. Candidates for markets where the Coase Theorem might apply include convincing your neighbor to leash her dog (you might help finance invisible fencing), enforcing laws concerning the fencing of cattle (see question 12 for a further discussion), and settling disputes when one builder interferes with the views of existing homes.

13. a. Command-and-control regulation would dictate the use of an alternative technology with lower carbon emissions.

  b. An effluent tax would place a tax on carbon emissions so that firms could no longer ignore these costs. In turn, prices of carbon-emitting products would increase, and quantities would decrease.

  c. Permits would be issued giving the right to emit carbon. The number of permits would equal the socially efficient emissions level. Firms would be allowed to buy or sell these permits. Firms with higher marginal costs of emissions abatement would buy permits, while firms that could reduce emissions at a lower cost would profit from selling permits.

# CHAPTER 15  INTERNATIONAL TRADE AND FINANCE

1. a. In Alpha, the opportunity cost of producing 1 ton of diamonds is 1/2 ton of pearls. In Beta, the opportunity cost of producing 1 ton of diamonds is 2 tons of pearls.

  b. In Alpha, the opportunity cost of producing 1 ton of pearls is 2 tons of diamonds. In Beta, the opportunity cost of producing 1 ton of pearls is 1/2 ton of diamonds.

  c. Because Alpha can produce diamonds at a lower opportunity cost than Beta can, Alpha has a comparative advantage in the production of diamonds.

  d. Because Beta can produce pearls at a lower opportunity cost than Alpha can, Beta has a comparative advantage in the production of pearls.

e.

|  | Diamonds (tons per year) | Pearls (tons per year) |
|---|---|---|
| *Before specialization* |  |  |
| Alpha (at point *B*) | 100 | 25 |
| Beta (at point *C*) | 30 | 120 |
| Total output | 130 | 145 |
| *After specialization* |  |  |
| Alpha (at point *A*) | 150 | 0 |
| Beta (at point *D*) | 0 | 180 |
| Total output | 150 | 180 |

As shown in the above table, specialization in each country increases total world output per year by 20 tons of diamonds and 35 tons of pearls.

f.

(a) Alpha

Without trade, Alpha produces and consumes 100 tons of diamonds and 25 tons of pearls at point *B* on its production possibilities curve. Without trade, Beta produces and consumes

30 tons of diamonds and 120 tons of pearls (point *C*). Now assume Alpha specializes in producing diamonds at point *A* and imports 50 tons of pearls in exchange for 50 tons of diamonds. Through specialization and trade, Alpha moves its consumption possibility to point *B'*, outside its production possibilities curve.

3. The principle of specialization and trade according to comparative advantage applies to both nations and states in the United States. For example, Florida grows oranges, and Idaho grows potatoes. Trade between these states, just like trade between nations, increases the consumption possibilities.

5. U.S. industries (and their workers) that compete with restricted imports would benefit. Consumers would lose from the reduced supply of imported goods from which to choose and from higher prices for domestic products, resulting from lack of competition from imports.

7. Although some domestic jobs may be lost, new ones are created by international trade. Stated differently, the economy as a whole gains when nations specialize and trade according to the law of comparative advantage, but imports will cost jobs in some specific industries.

9. Although each nation's balance of payments equals zero, its current and capital account balances usually do not equal zero. For example, a current account deficit means a nation purchased more in imports than it sold in exports. On the other hand, this nation's capital account must have a surplus to offset the current account deficit. This means that foreigners are buying more domestic capital (capital inflow) than domestic citizens are buying foreign capital (capital outflow). Thus, net ownership of domestic capital stock is in favor of foreigners.

11. a.

b. $0.15 per euro
c. An excess quantity of 200 million euros would be demanded.

## CHAPTER 16  ECONOMIES IN TRANSITION

1. Americans prefer large cars and canned soup. Europeans predominantly buy small cars and dry soup. The role of women and minorities in the workplace is an excellent example of how culture relates to the labor factor of production.

3. Such a program would provide additional economic security for the elderly, but higher taxes could reduce the incentive to work, and economic efficiency might be reduced.

5. In a traditional agricultural system, a benefit would be that members of society would cooperate by helping to build barns, harvest, and so on. Under the command system, worrying about errors and crop failures would be minimized because the state makes the decisions and everyone in society has a basic income. In a market economy, a bumper crop would mean large profits and the capacity to improve one's standard of living.

7. Because most economies are *mixed* systems, this term is too broad to be very descriptive. The terms *capitalism* and *communism* are more definitive concerning the roles of private ownership, market allocations, and decentralized decision making. Embracing a market-oriented system means a transfer of power from the command bureaucracy to consumers. Markets are incompatible with the principle that socialist citizens are supposed to be concerned with the collective interest.

## CHAPTER 17  GROWTH AND THE LESS-DEVELOPED COUNTRIES

1. The difference between IACs and LDCs is based on GDP per capita. This classification is somewhat arbitrary. A country with a high GDP per capita and narrow industrial development based on oil, such as the United Arab Emirates, is excluded from the IAC list. There are 27 economies listed in the text as

IACs, including Switzerland, Japan, the United States, Singapore, and Hong Kong. The following countries are considered to be LDCs: Argentina, Mexico, South Africa, Jordan, and Bangladesh.

3. a. Based only on GDP per capita, you would conclude that Alpha is a better place to live because this country produces a greater output of goods and services per person.
   b. Based on the additional evidence, you would change your mind and prefer to live in Beta because the quality-of-life data indicate a higher standard of living in this country.

5. The average growth rate of GDP per capita for IACs exceeds the GDP per capita growth rate for LDCs. This evidence is consistent with the argument. The argument is oversimplified because there is considerable diversity among the LDCs. In a given year, a LDC may have a GDP per capita growth rate greater than many IACs.

7. Economic growth and development are complicated because there is no single prescription that a country can follow. The text presents a multidimensional model with five basic categories: natural resources, human resources, capital, technological progress, and political environment. Because an LDC is weak in one or more of the key factors, such as natural resources, does not necessarily mean that the LDC cannot achieve economic success.

9. Because they are poor countries with low GDP per capita, they lack domestic savings to invest in capital; and lacking investment, they remain poor. The rich in these poor countries often put their savings abroad because of the fear of political instability. An inflow of external funds from abroad permits the LDC to increase its capital without reducing its consumption and to shift its production possibilities curve outward.

11. Poor countries are too poor to save enough to finance domestic capital formation. International trade is a way LDCs can generate savings from abroad. Exports provide the LDCs with foreign exchange to pay for imports of capital stock that is necessary for economic growth and development.

# Answers to Practice Quizzes

## CHAPTER 1  INTRODUCING THE ECONOMIC WAY OF THINKING

1. c  2. d  3. c  4. c  5. a  6. a
7. a  8. a  9. a  10. c  11. a  12. b
13. c  14. d  15. d

## APPENDIX TO CHAPTER 1  APPLYING GRAPHS TO ECONOMICS

1. d  2. d  3. a  4. d  5. d  6. c
7. c  8. c  9. d  10. d  11. d  12. b

## CHAPTER 2  PRODUCTION POSSIBILITIES, OPPORTUNITY COST, AND ECONOMIC GROWTH

1. c  2. a  3. c  4. c  5. b  6. c
7. c  8. e  9. a  10. c  11. b  12. d
13. e  14. c  15. a

## CHAPTER 3  MARKET DEMAND AND SUPPLY

1. e  2. a  3. b  4. b  5. a  6. b
7. c  8. b  9. c  10. b  11. c  12. c
13. d  14. d  15. c  16. d  17. d
18. c  19. d  20. d

## APPENDIX TO CHAPTER 3  CONSUMER SURPLUS, PRODUCER SURPLUS, AND MARKET EFFICIENCY

1. c  2. b  3. d  4. e  5. d

## CHAPTER 4  MARKETS IN ACTION

1. a  2. a  3. c  4. d  5. d  6. d
7. c  8. b  9. a  10. b  11. c  12. a
13. c  14. d  15. d

## CHAPTER 5  PRICE ELASTICITY OF DEMAND AND SUPPLY

1. a  2. b  3. a  4. a  5. a  6. d
7. a  8. a  9. d  10. c  11. c  12. c
13. c  14. b  15. b

## CHAPTER 6  CONSUMER CHOICE THEORY

1. c  2. d  3. a  4. a  5. d  6. d
7. c  8. b  9. a  10. a  11. b  12. a
13. d  14. a  15. d

## APPENDIX TO CHAPTER 6  INDIFFERENCE CURVE ANALYSIS

1. d  2. d  3. c  4. d  5. b  6. d
7. a  8. c  9. b  10. a

## CHAPTER 7  PRODUCTION COSTS

1. d  2. b  3. c  4. c  5. d  6. d
7. c  8. d  9. d  10. c  11. c  12. b
13. c  14. b  15. d  16. c  17. d
18. e  19. c  20. d

## CHAPTER 8  PERFECT COMPETITION

1. b  2. b  3. b  4. b  5. c  6. d
7. b  8. d  9. b  10. b  11. a  12. d
13. b  14. d  15. d  16. a  17. d
18. d  19. b  20. a

## CHAPTER 9  MONOPOLY

1. d  2. d  3. d  4. d  5. b  6. d
7. b  8. d  9. b  10. d  11. e  12. b
13. b  14. d  15. e

## CHAPTER 10  MONOPOLISTIC COMPETITION AND OLIGOPOLY

1. b   2. b   3. d   4.d   5. d   6. d
7. a   8. a   9. b   10. d   11. d   12. a
13. c   14. b   15. a   16. a   17. d
18. a   19. a   20. d

## CHAPTER 11  LABOR MARKETS

1. d   2. a   3. c   4. a   5. c   6. b
7. d   8. b   9. c   10. c   11. b   12. c
13. c   14. a   15. b

## CHAPTER 12  INCOME DISTRIBUTION, POVERTY, AND DISCRIMINATION

1. a   2. c   3. c   4. a   5. b   6. d
7. d   8. a   9. d   10. c   11. a   12. d
13. d   14. d   15. c

## CHAPTER 13  ANTITRUST AND REGULATION

1. d   2. a   3. d   4. b   5. d   6. a
7. c   8. d   9. c   10. a   11. b   12. a
13. e   14. d   15. d

## CHAPTER 14  ENVIRONMENTAL ECONOMICS

1. d   2. e   3. a   4. a   5. a   6. c
7. d   8. b   9. d   10. b   11. b   12. b
13. c

## CHAPTER 15  INTERNATIONAL TRADE AND FINANCE

1. b   2. c   3. a   4. d   5. d   6. a
7. d   8. a   9. c   10. c   11. b   12. c
13. c   14. a   15. a   16. b   17. a
18. a   19. e   20. d

## CHAPTER 16  ECONOMIES IN TRANSITION

1. c   2. d   3. d   4. a   5. b   6. a
7. c   8. b   9. b   10. c   11. c   12. a
13. a   14. d   15. a

## CHAPTER 17  GROWTH AND THE LESS-DEVELOPED COUNTRIES

1. d   2. d   3. d   4. c   5. a   6. a
7. d   8. a   9. c   10. a   11. b   12. d
13. c   14. d   15. b

# Glossary

## A

**Absolute advantage** The ability of a country to produce a good using fewer resources than another country.

**Agency for International Development (AID)** The agency of the U.S. State Department that is in charge of U.S. aid to foreign countries.

**Appreciation of currency** A rise in the price of one currency relative to another.

**Arbitrage** The practice of earning a profit by buying a good at a low price and reselling the good at a higher price.

**Average fixed cost (*AFC*)** Total fixed cost divided by the quantity of output produced.

**Average total cost (*ATC*)** Total cost divided by the quantity of output produced.

**Average variable cost (*AVC*)** Total variable cost divided by the quantity of output produced.

## B

**Balance of payments** A bookkeeping record of all the international transactions between a country and other countries during a given period of time.

**Balance of trade** The value of a nation's goods imports subtracted from its goods exports.

**Budget line** A line that represents all combinations of two goods that a consumer can purchase with a fixed amount of money given the price of each good.

## C

**Capital** The physical plants, machinery, and equipment used to produce other goods. Capital goods are human-made goods that do not directly satisfy human wants.

**Capitalism** An economic system characterized by private ownership of resources and markets.

**Cartel** A group of firms that formally agree to control the price and the output of a product.

**Celler-Kefauver Act** A 1950 amendment to the Clayton Act that prohibits one firm from merging with a competitor by purchasing its physical assets if the effect is to substantially lessen competition.

**Ceteris paribus** A Latin phrase that means while certain variables change, "all other things remain unchanged."

**Change in demand** An increase or a decrease in the quantity demanded at each possible price. An increase in demand is a rightward shift in the entire demand curve. A decrease in demand is a leftward shift in the entire demand curve.

**Change in quantity demanded** A movement between points along a stationary demand curve, ceteris paribus.

**Change in quantity supplied** A movement between points along a stationary supply curve, ceteris paribus.

**Change in supply** An increase or a decrease in the quantity supplied at each possible price. An increase in supply is a rightward shift in the entire supply curve. A decrease in supply is a leftward shift in the entire supply curve.

**Clayton Act** A 1914 amendment that strengthens the Sherman Act by making it illegal for firms to engage in certain anticompetitive business practices.

**Coase Theorem** The proposition that private market negotiations can achieve social efficiency regardless of the initial definition of property rights.

**Collective bargaining** The process of negotiating labor contracts between the union and management concerning wages and working conditions.

**Command economy** A system that answers the *What*, *How*, and *For Whom* questions by central authority.

**Command-and-control regulations** Government regulations that set an environmental goal and dictate how the goal will be achieved.

**Communism** A stateless, classless economic system in which all the factors of production are owned by the workers, and people share in production according to their needs. In Marx's view, this is the highest form of socialism toward which the revolution should strive.

**Comparable worth** The principle that employees who work for the same employer must be paid the same wage when their jobs, even if different, require similar levels of education, training, experience, and responsibility. A nonmarket wage-setting process is used to evaluate and compensate jobs according to point scores assigned to different jobs.

**Comparative advantage** The ability of a country to produce a good at a lower opportunity cost than another country.

**Complementary good** A good that is jointly consumed with another good. As a result, there is an inverse relationship between a price change for one good and the demand for its "go together" good.

**Conglomerate merger** A merger between firms in unrelated markets.

**Constant-cost industry** An industry in which the expansion of industry output by the entry of new firms has no effect on the individual firm's cost curve.

**Constant returns to scale** A situation in which the long-run average cost curve does not change as the firm increases output.

**Consumer equilibrium** A condition in which total utility cannot increase by spending more of a given budget on one good and spending less on another good.

**Consumer sovereignty** The freedom of consumers to cast their dollar votes to buy, or not to buy, at prices determined in competitive markets.

**Consumer surplus** The value of the difference between the price consumers are willing to pay for a product on the demand curve and the actual price paid for it.

**Cross-elasticity of demand** The ratio of the percentage change in quantity demanded of a good or service to a given percentage change in the price of another good or service.

## D

**Deadweight loss** The net loss of consumer and producer surplus for underproduction or over-production of a product.

**Decreasing-cost industry** An industry in which the expansion of industry output by the entry of new firms decreases the individual firm's cost curves (cost curve shifts downward).

**Demand** A curve or schedule showing the various quantities of a product consumers are willing to purchase at possible prices during a specified period of time, ceteris paribus.

**Demand curve for labor** A curve showing the different quantities of labor employers are willing to hire at different wage rates in a given time period, ceteris paribus. It is equal to the marginal revenue product of labor.

**Depreciation of currency** A fall in the price of one currency relative to another.

**Deregulation** The elimination or phasing out of government restrictions on economic activity.

**Derived demand** The demand for labor and other factors of production that depends on the consumer demand for the final goods and services the factors produce.

**Direct relationship** A positive association between two variables. When one variable increases, the other variable increases, and when one variable decreases, the other variable decreases.

**Diseconomies of scale** A situation in which the long-run average cost curve rises as the firm increases output.

## E

**Economic growth** The ability of an economy to produce greater levels of output, represented by an outward shift of its production possibilities curve. Also, an expansion in national output measured by the annual percentage increase in a nation's GDP.

**Economic profit** Total revenue minus explicit and implicit costs.

**Economic system** The organizations and methods used to determine what goods and services are produced, how they are produced, and for whom they are produced.

**Economics** The study of how society chooses to allocate its scarce resources to the production of goods and services in order to satisfy unlimited wants.

**Economies of scale** A situation in which the long-run average cost curve declines as the firm increases output.

**Effluent tax** A tax on a pollutant.

**Elastic demand** A condition in which the percentage change in quantity demanded is greater than the percentage change in price.

**Emissions trading** Firms buying and selling the right to pollute.

**Entrepreneurship** The creative ability of individuals to seek profits by taking risks and combining resources to produce innovative products.

**Equilibrium** A market condition that occurs at any price and quantity where the quantity demanded and the quantity supplied are equal.

**Exchange rate** The number of units of one nation's currency that equals one unit of another nation's currency.

**Explicit costs** Payments to nonowners of a firm for their resources.

**Externality** A cost or benefit imposed on people other than the consumers and producers of a good or service.

## F

**Federal Trade Commission Act** The federal act that in 1914 established the Federal Trade Commission (FTC) to investigate unfair competitive practices of firms.

**Fixed input** Any resource for which the quantity cannot change during the period of time under consideration.

**Foreign aid** The transfer of money or resources from one government to another for which no repayment is required.

**Free trade** The flow of goods between countries without restrictions or special taxes.

**Free rider** An individual who enjoys benefits without paying the costs.

**Free-rider problem** The problem that if some individuals benefit while others pay, few will be willing to pay for improvement of the environment or other public goods. As a result, these goods are under produced.

## G

**GDP per capita** The value of final goods produced (GDP) divided by the total population.

**Game theory** A model of the strategic moves and countermoves of rivals.

**Government failure** Government intervention or lack of intervention that fails to correct market failure.

## H

**Horizontal merger** A merger of firms that compete in the same market.

**Human capital** The accumulation of education, training, experience, and health that enables a worker to enter an occupation and be productive.

## I

**Implicit costs** The opportunity costs of using resources owned by the firm.

**Incentive-based regulations** Government regulations that set an environmental goal but are flexible as to how buyers and sellers achieve the goal.

**Income effect** The change in quantity demanded of a good or service caused by a change in real income (purchasing power).

**Income elasticity of demand** The ratio of the percentage change in quantity demanded for a good or service to a given percentage change in income.

**Increasing-cost industry** An industry in which the expansion of industry output by the entry of new firms increases the individual firm's cost curves (cost curve shifts upward).

**Independent relationship** A zero association between two variables. When one variable changes, the other variable remains unchanged.

**Indifference curve** A curve showing the different combinations of two goods that provide the same satisfaction or total utility to a consumer.

**Indifference map** A selection of indifference curves with each curve representing a different level of satisfaction or total utility.

**Industrially advanced countries (IACs)** High-income nations that have market economies based on large stocks of technologically advanced capital and well-educated labor. The United States, Canada, Australia, New Zealand, Japan, and most of the countries of Western Europe are IACs.

**Inelastic demand** A condition in which the percentage change in quantity demanded is less than the percentage change in price.

**Inferior good** Any good for which there is an inverse relationship between changes in income and its demand curve.

**Infrastructure** Capital goods usually provided by the government, including highways, bridges, waste and water systems, and airports.

**In-kind transfers** Government payments in the form of goods and services, rather than cash, including such government programs as food stamps, Medicaid, and housing.

**International Monetary Fund (IMF)** The lending agency that makes short-term conditional low-interest loans to developing countries.

**Inverse relationship** A negative association between two variables. When one variable increases, the other variable decreases, and when one variable decreases, the other variable increases.

**Investment** The accumulation of capital, such as factories, machines, and inventories, that is used to produce goods and services.

**Invisible hand** A phrase that expresses the belief that the best interests of a society are served when individual consumers and producers compete to achieve their own private interests.

# K

**Kinked demand curve** A demand curve facing an oligopolist that assumes rivals will match a price decrease, but ignore a price increase.

# L

**Labor** The mental and physical capacity of workers to produce goods and services.

**Land** A shorthand expression for any natural resource provided by nature.

**Law of demand** The principle that there is an inverse relationship between the price of a good and the quantity buyers are willing to purchase in a defined time period, ceteris paribus.

**Law of diminishing marginal utility** The principle that the extra satisfaction of a good or service declines as people consume more in a given period.

**Law of diminishing returns** The principle that beyond some point the marginal product decreases as additional units of a variable factor are added to a fixed factor.

**Law of increasing opportunity costs** The principle that the opportunity cost increases as production of one output expands.

**Law of supply** The principle that there is a direct relationship between the price of a good and the quantity sellers are willing to offer for sale in a defined time period, ceteris paribus.

**Less-developed countries (LDCs)** Nations without large stocks of technologically advanced capital and well-educated labor. LDCs are economies based on agriculture, such as most countries of Africa, Asia, and Latin America.

**Long run** A period of time so long that all inputs are variable.

**Long-run average cost curve (*LRAC*)** The curve that traces the lowest cost per unit at which a firm can produce any level of output when the firm can build any desired plant size.

**Lorenz curve** A graph of the actual cumulative distribution of income compared to a perfectly equal cumulative distribution of income.

# M

**Macroeconomics** The branch of economics that studies decision making for the economy as a whole.

**Marginal analysis** An examination of the effects of additions to or subtractions from a current situation.

**Marginal-average rule** The rule states when marginal cost is below average cost, average cost falls. When marginal cost is above average cost, average cost rises. When marginal cost equals average cost, average cost is at its minimum point.

**Marginal cost** The change in total cost when one additional unit of output is produced.

**Marginal cost pricing** A system of pricing in which the price charged equals the marginal cost of the last unit produced.

**Marginal factor cost (*MFC*)** The additional total cost resulting from a one-unit increase in the quantity of a factor.

**Marginal product** The change in total output produced by adding one unit of a variable input, with all other inputs used being held constant.

**Marginal rate of substitution (*MRS*)** The rate at which a consumer is willing to substitute one good for another good without a change in total utility. The MRS equals the slope of an indifference curve at any point on the curve.

**Marginal revenue (*MR*)** The change in total revenue from the sale of one additional unit of output.

**Marginal revenue product (*MRP*)** The increase in firm's total revenue resulting from hiring an additional unit of labor or other variable resource.

**Marginal utility** The change in total utility from one additional unit of a good or service.

**Market** Any arrangement in which buyers and sellers interact to determine the price and quantity of goods and services exchanged.

**Market economy** An economic system that answers the *What*, *How*, and *For Whom* questions using prices determined by the interaction of the forces of supply and demand.

**Market failure** A situation in which market equilibrium results in too few or too many resources used in the production of a good or service. This inefficiency may justify government intervention.

**Market structure** A classification system for the key traits of a market, including the number of firms, the similarity of the products they sell, and the ease of entry into and exit from the market.

**Means test** A requirement that a family's income not exceed a certain level to be eligible for public assistance.

**Microeconomics** The branch of economics that studies decision making by a single individual, household, firm, industry, or level of government.

**Mixed economy** An economic system than answers the *What*, *How*, and *For Whom* questions through a mixture of traditional, command, and market systems.

**Model** A simplified description of reality used to understand and predict the relationship between variables.

**Monopolistic competition** A market structure characterized by (1) many small sellers, (2) a differentiated product, and (3) easy market entry and exit.

**Monopoly** A market structure characterized by (1) a single seller, (2) a unique product, and (3) impossible entry into the market.

**Monopsony** A labor market in which a single firm hires labor.

**Mutual interdependence** A condition in which an action by one firm may cause a reaction from other firms.

# N

**Natural monopoly** An industry in which the long-run average cost of production declines throughout the entire market. As a result, a single firm can supply the entire market demand at a lower cost than two or more smaller firms.

**Negative income tax (NIT)** A plan under which families below a certain break-even level of income would receive cash payments that decrease as their incomes increase.

**New-source bias** Bias that occurs when regulations provide an incentive to keep assets past the efficient point.

**Nonprice competition** The situation in which a firm competes using advertising, packaging, product development, better quality, and better service, rather than lower prices.

**Normal good** Any good for which there is a direct relationship between changes in income and its demand curve.

**Normal profit** The minimum profit necessary to keep a firm in operation. A firm that earns normal profit earns total revenue equal to its total opportunity cost.

**Normative economics** An analysis based on value judgment.

# O

**Offset** Reduction in an existing pollution source to counteract pollution from a new source.

**Oligopoly** A market structure characterized by (1) few sellers, (2) either a homogeneous or a differentiated product, and (3) difficult market entry.

**Opportunity cost** The best alternative sacrificed for a chosen alternative.

# P

**Per se rule** The antitrust doctrine that the existence of monopoly alone is illegal, regardless of whether or not the monopoly engages in illegal business practices.

**Perfect competition** A market structure characterized by (1) a large number of small firms, (2) a homogeneous product, and (3) very easy entry into or exit from the market. Perfect competition is also referred to as *pure competition*.

**Perfectly competitive firm's short-run supply curve** The firm's marginal cost curve above the minimum point on its average variable cost curve.

**Perfectly competitive industry's long-run supply curve** The curve that shows the quantities supplied by the industry at different equilibrium prices after firms complete their entry and exit.

**Perfectly competitive industry's short-run supply curve** The supply curve derived from horizontal summation of the marginal cost curves of all firms in the industry above the minimum point of each firm's average variable cost curve.

**Perfectly elastic demand** A condition in which a small percentage change in price brings about an infinite percentage change in quantity demanded.

**Perfectly inelastic demand** A condition in which the quantity demanded does not change as the price changes.

**Positive economics** An analysis limited to statements that are verifiable.

**Poverty line** The level of income below which a person or a family is to be considered poor.

**Predatory pricing** The practice of one or more firms temporarily reducing prices in order to eliminate competition and then raising prices.

**Price ceiling** A legally established maximum price a seller can charge.

**Price discrimination** The practice of a seller charging different prices for the same product that are not justified by cost differences.

**Price elasticity of demand** The ratio of the percentage change in the quantity demanded of a product to a percentage change in its price.

**Price elasticity of supply** The ratio of the percentage change in the quantity supplied of a product to the percentage change in its price.

**Price floor** A legally established minimum price a seller can be paid.

**Price leadership** A pricing strategy in which a dominant firm sets the price for an industry and the other firms follow.

**Price maker** A firm that faces a downward-sloping demand curve and therefore it can choose among price and output combinations along the demand curve.

**Price system** A mechanism that uses the forces of supply and demand to create an equilibrium through rising and falling prices.

**Price taker** A seller that has no control over the price of the product it sells.

**Private benefits and costs** Benefits and costs to the decision maker, ignoring benefits and costs to third parties. Third parties are people outside the market transaction who are affected by the product.

**Producer surplus** The value of the difference between the actual selling price of a product and the price producers are willing to sell it for on the supply curve.

**Product differentiation** The process of creating real or apparent differences between goods and services.

**Production function** The relationship between the maximum amounts of output that a firm can produce and various quantities of inputs.

**Production possibilities curve** A curve that shows the maximum combinations of two outputs an economy can produce in a given period of time with its available resources and technology.

**Protectionism** The government's use of embargoes, tariffs, quotas, and other restrictions to protect domestic producers from foreign competition.

**Public good** A good or service with two properties: (1) users collectively consume benefits, and (2) there is no way to bar people who do not pay (free riders) from consuming the good or service.

# Q

**Quota** A limit on the quantity of a good that may be imported in a given time period.

# R

**Resources** The basic categories of inputs used to produce goods and services. Resources are also called *factors of production*. Economists divide resources into three categories: land, labor, and capital.

**Robinson-Patman Act** A 1936 amendment to the Clayton Act that strengthens the Clayton Act against price discrimination.

**Rule of reason** The antitrust doctrine that the existence of monopoly alone is not illegal unless the monopoly engages in illegal business practices.

# S

**Scarcity** The condition in which human wants are forever greater than the available supply of time, goods, and resources.

**Sherman Act** The federal antitrust law enacted in 1890 that prohibits monopolization and conspiracies to restrain trade.

**Short run** A period of time so short that there is at least one fixed input.

**Shortage** A market condition existing at any price where the quantity supplied is less than the quantity demanded.

**Slope** The ratio of the change in the variable on the vertical axis (the rise or fall) to the change in the variable on the horizontal axis (the run).

**Social benefits and costs** The sum of benefits to everyone in society, including both private benefits and external benefits. Social costs are the sum of costs to everyone in society, including both private costs and external costs.

**Substitute good** A good that competes with another good for consumer purchases. As a result, there is a direct relationship between a price change for one good and the demand for its "competitor" good.

**Substitution effect** The change in quantity demanded of a good or service caused by a change in its price relative to substitutes.

**Supply** A curve or schedule showing the various quantities of a product sellers are willing to produce and offer for sale at possible prices during a specified period of time, ceteris paribus.

**Supply curve of labor** A curve showing the different quantities of labor workers are willing to offer employers at different wage rates in a given time period, ceteris paribus.

**Surplus** A market condition existing at any price where the quantity supplied is greater than the quantity demanded.

# T

**Tariff** A tax on an import.

**Tax incidence** The share of a tax ultimately paid by consumers and sellers.

**Technology** The body of knowledge applied to how goods are produced.

**Total cost (*TC*)** The sum of total fixed cost and total variable cost at each level of output.

**Total fixed cost (*TFC*)** Costs that do not vary as output varies and that must be paid even if output is zero. These are payments that the firm must make in the short run, regardless of the level of output.

**Total revenue** The total number of dollars a firm earns from the sale of a good or service, which is equal to its price multiplied by the quantity demanded.

**Total utility** The amount of satisfaction received from all the units of a good or service consumed.

**Total variable cost (*TVC*)** Costs that are zero when output is zero and vary as output varies.

**Traditional economy** A system that answers the *What*, *How*, and *For Whom* questions the way they always have been answered.

**Transaction costs** The costs of negotiating and enforcing a contract.

**Trust** A combination or cartel consisting of firms that place their assets in the custody of a board of trustees.

# U

**Unemployment compensation** The government insurance program that pays income for a short time period to unemployed workers.

**Unitary elastic demand** A condition in which the percentage change in quantity demanded is equal to the percentage change in price.

**Utility** The satisfaction, or pleasure, that people receive from consuming a good or service.

## V

**Variable input** Any resource for which the quantity can change during the period of time under consideration.

**Vertical merger** A merger of a firm with its suppliers.

**Vicious circle of poverty** The trap in which countries are poor because they cannot afford to save and invest, but they cannot save and invest because they are poor.

## W

**World Bank** The lending agency that makes long-term low-interest loans and provides technical assistance to less-developed countries.

**World Trade Organization (*WTO*)** An international organization of member countries that oversees international trade agreements and rules on trade disputes.

# Index

## A

Absolute advantage, 375–376
Absolute poverty, 300
Accounting profit, 163–164
Acid rain, 357
Advertising
  advantages/disadvantages, 245–248
  economies of scale, 247
  market entry/exit, 247
  monopolistic competition, 245–248
  oligopoly, 254
Agency for International Development
  (AID), 439
Agricultural price supports
  as price floor, 96, 97
Agriculture. *See* Farming
AIDS vaccination
  government regulation and, 101
  government subsidies, 101
Airline Deregulation Act, 331, 336
Airline industry
  cartel, 256
  deregulation, 336
  deregulation of, 331
  hub-and-spoke delivery system, 336
  price elasticity of demand, 123
Air pollution. *See* Externalities; Pollution
Alcoa, 219
  antitrust case against, 325–326, 328
  as price leader, 257
  Sherman Act, 325–326
Alligator farming, 211
AMD, 67
American Federation of Government
    Employees, 274
American Greetings, 11
American Medical Association (AMA), 112
American Tobacco, 321
  as price leader, 257
  rule of reason, 325
Amish, 404
Amoco, 325
Antimerger Act, 323
Antipoverty programs, 302–309. *See also*
    Welfare
  cash transfer programs, 303–304
  as entitlement programs, 302
  in-kind transfers, 300
  means test for, 302
  Sherman Act, 320–321
  welfare criticism, 304–305
Antitrust policy/regulation. *See also*
    Monopoly; Trusts
  Alcoa case, 325–326
  AT&T, 326–327
  big is bad ideology, 325, 330
  Celler-Kefauver Act, 323

Clayton Act, 321–322
  conduct remedy, 328
  Federal Trade Commission Act, 322
  historical view of trusts, 320
  IBM, 326
  mergers, 329–330
  Microsoft case, 327–328
  MIT case, 327
  policies in other countries, 329–330
  predatory pricing, 320
  Robinson-Patman Act, 322–323
  rule of reason, 325
  Standard Oil case, 325
  structural remedy, 328
  summary of major antitrust cases, 328
  summary of major laws of, 323
Apple Computer, 180, 326
Appreciation of currency, 391
Arbitrage, 231
Archer Daniels Midland Company, 321
Argentina
  resources and economic growth in, 432
Asian-Pacific Economic Cooperation
  (APEC), 382
Association
  vs. causation, 9–10
AT&T
  antitrust case against, 326–327, 328
  dismantling of, 331
  as natural monopoly, 326–327
Automobile industry
  command-and-control regulations,
    351–352
  electric vehicles, 355–356
  income elasticity of demand, 126
  price elasticity of demand, 122–123
Average cost curve
  long run, 175–177
  short-run, 169–172
Average fixed cost, 170
Average total cost, 171
Average variable cost, 171

## B

Balance of payments, 383–387
  balance of trade, 383–385
  capital account, 385–386
  current account, 383–385
  defined, 383
  international debt of U.S., 386–387
Balance of trade, 383–385. *See also* Trade
  defined, 383
  historical record of, in U.S., 384
  with selected countries, 387
Bangladesh
  quality-of-life measures of development,
    429

Banking system. *See also* Money
  foreign loans and banking crisis of
    1980s, 442
Bank One Investment, 11
Black market
  price ceiling, 92
Blacks
  discrimination and wages for, 309–310
  poverty rate for, 301
Bolivia
  resources and economic growth in, 432
Boston Snow Index (BSI), 11
Brain drain, 432
Brazil
  economic bailout of, by IMF, 441
  income distribution in, 298–299
  resources and economic growth in, 432
Bretton Woods, 394–395, 440
British East India Company, 222
Brown, 327
Budget line, 153–156
Bus Regulatory Reform Act, 331
Buyers. *See* Consumers

## C

Canada
  on capitalism/socialism continuum, 416
  GDP per capita, 427
  labor membership in, 280
  North American Free Trade Agreement
    (NAFTA), 381
  U.S. balance of trade with, 387
Capital
  accumulation of, and economic growth
    in countries, 433–434
  defined, 5
  economic vs. financial, 5
  efficiency of, and economies of scale,
    180
  as resource, 5
Capital account of balance of payments,
  385–386
Capital flight, 433
Capital formation, 44
Capitalism, 411–412
  capitalism/socialism continuum, 416
  characteristics of, 411
  consumer sovereignty, 411
  decentralized decision making, 411–412
  defined, 411
  economic efficiency, 412
  economic freedom, 412
  Marx on, 413
  private ownership in, 411
  strengths/weaknesses of, 412
Carbon dioxide
  carbon trading, 360–361